*collecting*

# COSTUME JEWELRY

# 202

*the basics of*
## Dating Jewelry
### 1935 – 1980

IDENTIFICATION
AND
VALUE GUIDE

## Julia C. Carroll

**Front Cover:** Top left: 1966 Trifari Modern Mosaics leaf pin and earrings shown with 1966 Trifari advertisement, $95.00 – 135.00. Top Right: 1955 – 1960 B.S.K. enameled fish pin, $45.00 – 65.00. Second row left: 1948 Corocraft Sterling bird pin, design patent number 148546 (patent not shown), $200.00 – 275.00. Second row middle: 1976 – 1979 ART Egyptian-style necklace (earrings shown inside), $65.00 – 95.00 set. Third row left: 1953 Trifari flower basket pin shown with design patent 170208, $35.00 – 45.00. Fourth row left: 1948 Coro hand brooch shown with design patent number 149186, $65.00 – 100.00. Bottom left: 1951 Coro female dancer pin shown with design patent number 162420, $75.00 – 120.00. Bottom center: 1962 Laguna Crown Jewels bracelet shown with 1962 Laguna Crown Jewels advertisement, $85.00 – 100.00 for full parure (other pieces shown inside). Bottom center: 1960s DeNicola Aquarius pin, $100.00 – 200.00. Bottom right: 1951 Trifari double sunflower necklace shown with design patent number 162747, $50.00 – 65.00.

**Back Cover:** Top left: 1952 Trifari Promenade necklace and earrings shown with design patent number 167652 for the necklace and the 1962 Trifari advertisement featuring the set. Bottom center: Matching Trifari Promenade bracelet and design patent number 167654. Total value for all of the Trifari Promenade jewelry shown on the back cover, $75.00 – 125.00. Top center: 1956 Coro Lovebirds bracelet shown with the 1956 Coro advertisement featuring the Coro Lovebirds jewelry, $35.00 – 50.00. Right from top to bottom: 1953 Trifari fish pin shown with design patent number 169172, $65.00 – 85.00. 1953 Trifari elephant pin shown with design patent number 169171, $75:00 – 90.00. 1941 Trifari sterling key pin shown with design patent number 125158, $120.00 – 150.00. 1945 Coro jelly belly swan pin shown with design patent number 140945, $175.00 – 275.00. 1953 Trifari flower basket pin shown with design patent number 170208, $35.00 – 45.00. Center: 1962 Whiting & Davis Limoges portrait bracelet and earrings set, $75.00 – 100.00. Bottom left: 1960s Hollycraft Christmas tree pin, $60.00 – 90.00. Below: 1960s Boucher griffin pin, $75.00 – 125.00.

Cover design by Beth Summers
Book design by Christen Byrd

COLLECTOR BOOKS
P.O. Box 3009
Paducah, Kentucky 42002-3009

www.collectorbooks.com

Copyright © 2007 Julia C. Carroll

The current values in this book should be used only as a guide. They are not intended to set prices, which vary from one section of the country to another. Auction prices as well as dealer prices vary greatly and are affected by condition as well as demand. Neither the author nor the publisher assumes responsibility for any losses that might be incurred as a result of consulting this guide.

*Searching for a Publisher?*
We are always looking for people knowledgeable within their fields.
If you feel that there is a real need for a book on your collectible subject
and have a large comprehensive collection, contact Collector Books.

*Proudly printed and bound in the*
**United States of America**

# CONTENTS

# DEDICATION

I vividly recall standing in the doorway of the church on my wedding day, linked arm in arm with my father and looking toward the altar, searching for the face of my soon-to-be husband. When my eyes found him standing there in his blue tuxedo, all handsome and sweet, I felt love, joy, and a sense of astonishment. I could not believe my good fortune. Thirty years later I still feel that way about my husband, Dan. I look at his handsome face in the morning and I feel love, joy, and astonishment that I have this amazing man as my life mate. This book is dedicated to Dan. I am endlessly grateful for him and his devoted presence in my life.

# ACKNOWLEDGMENTS

*"You don't choose your family. They are God's gift*
*to you, as you are to them." ~Desmond Tutu*

I wish to express my love and gratitude to the following special members of my family:

…my husband, Dan, for taking on the role of photographer again and for doing so with good humor and patience. Thank you, darling!

…my daughter, Karen, for making time in her busy life to proofread the manuscript and for helping me redecorate my office. I also want to thank my new son-in-law, Paul, for sacrificing his free time to assemble furniture and hang window treatments. Thank you, sweeties!

…my son, Dan, for figuring out how to find and print the patent information from the U.S. Patent office website, and his sweet wife, Kate, for generously loaning us her camera. Thank you, cuties!

…my mother, for "lending" me jewelry for the book and then refusing to take it back! Thank you, Mom!

*"The best antiques are old friends."*
*~Unknown*

In addition, I wish to express my love and gratitude to:

…my good friend and best jewelry buddy, Debi Reece, for all of her generous support. Debi and I consumed many cell phone minutes discussing various aspects of this book. I value her advice almost as much as I do her friendship. She generously permitted me to photograph and feature a portion of her excellent jewelry collection for this book. Thank you, Debi; you are deeply prized and respected more than any possession I could ever acquire.

…my friend Carol Dike, who generously spent many hours sitting at my kitchen table carefully proofreading the manuscript. She also loaned me vintage treasures for the book. Thank you, Carol!

…my friend David Mayer, owner of the Millsboro Bazaar antique store, who shared his collection of jewelry books, catalogs, and advertisements for this book. Thank you, Dave!

…my friends from Spences Bazaar who sweetly loaned me jewelry for this book. Thank you Marty Morganstern, Esta Pratt, Barbara Magee, and Julia Tingle! Thanks you Robert Cote, for donating vintage ads from your magazine collection.

…a sweet lady, Marian Dietrich, for generously lending me jewelry for the book. Thank you!

I also wish to express my appreciation and gratitude to:

Researching Costume Jewelry authors Dotty Stringfield and Pat Seal. This Internet page is housed on Dotty's Illusion Jewels Vintage Jewelry website, www.illustionjewels.com. Thank you, ladies, for this well-researched website and for graciously granting me permission to use it for this book!

# About the Author

In the course of a year, I receive many different greeting cards. In a special way, these cards define my life and represent a pictorial biography of who I am. Several times a year I receive "For My Wife" cards from my loving husband of 30 years. My relationship with my husband is by far the most important connection in my life. He has sustained me through huge life obstacles with love and friendship.

In the same calendar year I also receive "For Mom" cards from my son and daughter. It is especially wonderful to be remembered by two people I love so much. Given with humor and (I hope) affection, are "For My Mother-in-Law" cards from my other son and daughter, which is how I think of these special people added to my life.

I'm fortunate to be the daughter of a mother who gives me love and moral support. I have a beautiful sister who can still tease me until I dissolve in laughter. From them I receive "For My Daughter" and "To My Sister" cards.

The "My Friend" cards I receive are especially precious to me. I was once told that in a lifetime a person can count his or her true friends on one hand. I feel blessed to be able to do that.

When I was teaching I received many "To My Teacher" cards from some of the sweetest people on earth. For over 12 years, I taught computer science to children from ages 5 to 14. Each child and each age group presented different challenges, and I loved them all.

I don't think I have ever received a "To a Collector" card, but such a card would be appropriate for me. I began collecting costume jewelry 15 years ago as a hobby. This is my second book on the subject, which testifies to the extent my hobby has astoundingly expanded to make me eligible for yet another card, a "To a Writer" card.

# INTRODUCTION

One of the most frequently asked questions I receive from beginning and intermediate collectors is "How old is this piece?" *Collecting Costume Jewelry 202: The Basics of Dating Jewelry, 1935 – 1980* is intended to help collectors answer this question. This text explores, with clear instructions and colorful illustrations, the following six methods for dating costume jewelry:

- Method one: Dating jewelry from the maker's signature.
- Method two: Dating jewelry using patent information.
- Method three: Dating jewelry by reviewing vintage advertisements.
- Method four: Dating jewelry by the style or design of the piece.
- Method five: Dating jewelry using books and the internet.
- Method six: Dating jewelry by provenance.

I love research, so this book is packed full of information. I also love the charm, glamour, and artistic design of costume jewelry; therefore *Collecting Costume Jewelry 202* includes over 600 clear and colorful photographs of vintage jewelry. These photographs exquisitely illustrate the ideas presented in the book about dating jewelry, while illuminating the beauty of these vintage treasures. Since the focus of this volume is to date jewelry, the picture captions provide dating information for each piece. Amazingly, using design patents, signatures, and vintage advertisements, many of these vintage "jewels" can be dated to a specific year. For others, detective work regarding style trends provides a range of years when the pieces could have been produced.

A large reference section features design patent number charts for each maker. These informative and well-researched charts catalog over 4,000 design patent numbers issued from 1935 to 1954. Each chart records the design patent number, date issued, designer's name, maker, and jewelry type, and provides a brief description of the piece. Over 550 carefully selected illustrations, showing original patent drawings, are incorporated with these charts. These fascinating illustrations proffer a peak into the minds of the designers. By viewing one of these drawings, the collector can appreciate the designer's original artistic vision for a piece.

In addition, sprinkled throughout this volume are over 160 vintage advertisements from 1943 through 1982, complete with photographs of example jewelry featured in many of the ads. These ads establish dates of manufacture for the featured jewelry. Furthermore, these advertisements chronicle the fashions of the time, providing precious clues regarding changing style trends over time.

Chapter 1 clearly defines each of the six methods for dating costume jewelry, including examples and illustrations demonstrating each technique. At heart I am a teacher. This is the teaching chapter. Chapter 1 trains the reader in the techniques for dating jewelry with interesting examples, colorful and instructive photographs, and easy-to-follow jewelry-dating guidelines.

Most of the design patents from 1935 through 1954 were issued for designs manufactured by Coro and Trifari. Therefore, chapters 2 and 3 are dedicated to Coro and Trifari jewelry. These chapters present the collector with a snapshot of how jewelry designs produced by these giants of the industry progressed and changed over time. By studying these chapters, a collector begins to recognize jewelry trends particular to a specific time in history. A collector can then apply this knowledge to help identify the probable date of manufacture for unpatented jewelry designs from Trifari and Coro, as well as jewelry designed by other makers.

Chapter 4 provides a large reference section for collectors that includes patents, advertisements, and photos of jewelry for over 125 different makers (including over 40 makers that were not part of my first book, *Collecting Costume Jewelry 101*).

Informative appendixes supply the collector with three easy-to-use reference charts:

1. Appendix A: Manufacturer and Marks Chart lists the dates of operation and the most commonly found signatures for over 125 different makers. For example, the following information about Avon is easily accessed using this chart.
   - Avon jewelry was produced 1971 – present.

- The signature "K.J.L for Avon" was used 1986 – 1995 for designs created by Kenneth J. Lane and manufactured by Avon.
2. Appendix B: Designer Chart lists the dates when specific designers worked for manufacturers. For example, Alfred Philippe designed for Trifari from 1930 through 1968.
3. Appendix C: View Patents Online supplies step-by-step instructions on how to view original patents online. Over 4,000 patent numbers are included in this volume illustrated with over 500 patent drawings. However, serious collectors must have the ability to view the drawings for other patent numbers online. This section provides clear instructions on how to easily accomplish this important task.

## VALUES OF JEWELRY IN THIS BOOK

Depending on the location of the shops, prices in antique stores can vary widely across the country. Therefore, the values of the jewelry in this book are based on an average selling price of like or similar pieces on eBay. An average is used because the values of jewelry on eBay rise and fall due to many factors. For example, at the time of the writing of this book, vintage rhinestone brooches are hugely popular. The increasing prices for brooches on eBay reflect this fashion trend. In determining the market value for the jewelry in this book, these trends are filtered out. Note. Unless otherwise indicated in the captions, the values given are for the complete sets as shown in the photographs.

# CHAPTER 1

# SIX METHODS FOR DATING
## *Costume Jewelry*

Six methods for dating costume jewelry are defined in this chapter. Examples, complete with illustrations, interpret each of these methods.

1. Method one provides three effective techniques to help date jewelry using the manufacturer's dates of operation and the maker's mark.
2. Method two clearly delineates the difference between utility and design patents and clarifies how to use these patents, especially design patents, to date jewelry. In addition, a utility patent chart is provided which lists a smattering of interesting utility patents.
3. Method three discusses three easy-to-find sources to locate vintage jewelry advertisements and defines two interesting techniques to date jewelry using these ads.
4. Method four, dating jewelry by the style or design of the piece, is one of the most challenging methods presented in this book. To assist the collector with this method, a style chart for 1935 – 1980 that lists the style trends for those years is included.
5. Method five explores the world of jewelry books with specific recommendations of beneficial books for dating costume jewelry.
6. Method six, dating jewelry by provenance, is one of the most fun techniques for dating jewelry. An amazing anecdote recounts how this pleasant method helps to date jewelry.

It is my belief that by understanding all six methods defined in this chapter, a collector can establish a reasonably accurate range of years when a specific piece of costume jewelry was produced. For me, investigating the dates of manufacture for costume jewelry is fun. I hope that by the end of this chapter, my readers think so too.

## METHOD ONE: *Signatures*

The signature on a vintage costume jewelry piece offers the collector valuable clues to help determine the age of the piece. The following four techniques detail how to use the maker's mark to date jewelry designs.

### TECHNIQUE ONE: DATING JEWELRY USING THE DATES OF OPERATION

The dates of operation are the years a maker was in the business of selling costume jewelry. This range of dates helps a collector to define a span of time when jewelry could have been produced. For example, Louis Kramer founded Kramer Jewelry Creations, Inc., in 1943. Kramer Jewelry Creations, Inc., ceased operations in 1979 or early 1980. Therefore, the Kramer pin and earrings set in Figure 1 must have been produced between 1943 and 1980. To help with this consult Appendix A: Manufacturer and Marks Chart. This chart provides the dates of operation for most collectible makers of costume jewelry.

**Figure 1.** 1955 – 1980 Kramer amber colored rhinestone and "black diamond" colored rhinestone brooch and earrings. The sparkly 2" Kramer brooch and matching 1" clip earrings are signed "Kramer" with the copyright symbol, indicating they were produced after 1955. Kramer Jewelry Creations, Inc., produced jewelry from 1943 to 1980. This information narrows the range of years when this Kramer set was produced to between 1955 and 1980. $60.00 – 80.00.

## TECHNIQUE TWO: IMPORTANCE OF THE COPYRIGHT SYMBOL

Jewelry manufacturers and designers protected original jewelry designs from design pirates by either applying for patents or by copyrighting the designs. In the 1930s and 1940s, many makers patented the designs. (In 1947 the copyright law was first available for jewelry designs; however, the law was not widely used by makers at this time. The law was untested and did not provide enough protection.) A design patent was in effect for three and a half years but could be extended to seven years. The process of patenting designs was expensive and time consuming. Many manufacturers did not wait several months for patents to be issued before producing and marketing jewelry. Therefore, many patented designs from this time period are signed "Des. Pat. Pend." or only signed with the makers' signatures.

This practice changed in 1955 when Trifari won a lawsuit against Charel Jewelry Co. after Charel had pirated one of Trifari's copyrighted designs. The ruling in this lawsuit helped to define costume jewelry designs as unique "works of art" deserving of copyright protection. This ruling strengthened the copyright laws so that after 1955 most manufacturers ceased applying for design patents in favor of copyrighting designs. (Note: Interestingly, Coro continued to patent jewelry designs until the end of 1956.) A copyright lasted for 20 years and was less expensive to obtain than a design patent.

The beautiful Kramer pin and earrings set in Figure 1 is signed "Kramer," with the copyright symbol indicating it was produced after 1955. Remember the dates of operation for Kramer Jewelry Creations, Inc., were 1943 to 1980. The presence of the copyright symbol narrows the range of years when this set could have been produced from 1943 through 1980 to 1955 through 1980.

## TECHNIQUE THREE: SIGNIFICANCE OF SIGNATURE VARIATIONS

Throughout the years, a manufacturer sometimes changed the look of its signature. This change can be a simple variation of the original signature or a completely new signature. For example, "KTF" (no crown over the "T") is an early Trifari signature used from 1935 through 1938, when it was gradually discontinued. However, in 1954 Trifari reused the "KTF" signature but added a variation. A crown was placed over the "T." This variation in the "KTF" signature helps to distinguish "KTF" jewelry produced in 1954 from older 1930s jewelry. Variations in signatures can be valuable tools for dating costume jewelry.

Some makers, especially makers like Eisenberg who have been in business for decades, have many different signatures. The company did not abruptly cease using one signature in favor of another. The changes were more gradual. Even after a new signature was established by the company, hardware with an old signature was not discarded. Nothing was wasted. Hardware with an old signature was used until it was gone.

Therefore, it is only possible to estimate the dates when specific Eisenberg signatures were used. The following is a partial list of several, but not all, Eisenberg signatures with estimated dates when a signature was in use. This partial list is taken from Appendix A: Manufacturer and Marks Chart.

- "Eisenberg Original" (1935 – 1945)
- The letter "E" in block or script without the copyright symbol (1942 – 1945)
- "Eisenberg Original Sterling" (1941 – 1945)
- "Eisenberg Sterling" (1943 – 1948)
- "Eisenberg" or "Eisenberg Ice" in block letters (1945 – 1958)
- "Eisenberg" or the letter "E" in block letters with the copyright symbol (1972 for enamels)
- "Eisenberg Ice" in block letters with the copyright symbol (1970's – 1985)
- "Eisenberg Ice" in script with the copyright symbol (1985 – present)
- "Eisenberg Ice" in script with the copyright symbol and the date "1994"

(Please note that the above dates are approximate. The company did not strictly adhere to these markings in the manufacturing process.)

Using the above information about Eisenberg signatures it is possible to approximate the dates of manufacture for the Eisenberg jewelry shown in Figures 2 and 3. The rare pink Eisenberg clip in Figure 2 is signed "Eisenberg Original." The above information on Eisenberg signatures indicates a brooch with this signature dates to 1935 – 1945.

Two different Eisenberg signatures are found on the adorable Eisenberg green and blue enamel turtle pendant and earrings set shown in Figure 3. The pendant is signed "Eisenberg" in block letters with the copyright symbol. The earrings are signed with the block letter "E" and the copyright symbol. (It is not unusual for pieces in a set to have different signatures.) The above signature information for Eisenberg jewelry indicates these two Eisenberg pieces date to 1972.

*Fig. 1.*

**Figure 2.** 1935 – 1945 Eisenberg Original pink rhinestone brooch. There are several shades of pink decorating this brooch. The subtle differences in shades of the pink color are part of the allure of Eisenberg jewelry. The clip measures 4½" x 2¼" and is signed "Eisenberg Original" with "6" in a circle. The Eisenberg Original signature dates this clip to between 1935 and 1945, when this signature was most often used. The "6" refers to the craftsperson who worked on the piece. The mark of the craftsperson on jewelry is an indication the piece dates to the 1930s or early 1940s. $400.00 – 600.00.

**Figure 3.** 1972 Eisenberg enamel turtle pendant and matching earrings. This adorable Eisenberg enameled turtle pendant measures 3¼" x 2¼" and is suspended from a long gold-tone snake chain. The matching clip earrings are ¾" in diameter. The pendant is signed "Eisenberg" in block letters with the copyright symbol. The earrings are signed "E" in block print with the copyright symbol. In 1972, Eisenberg commissioned famous artists of the time to create jewelry designs like this creative turtle pendant and earrings set. Some of the important contributing artists include Braque, Calder, Chagall, Miro, and Picasso. Amazingly, there are eight different colors of enamel on this set! $50.00 – 70.00.

For more information on jewelry marks or signatures, consult Appendix A: Manufacturer and Marks Chart. This chart provides not only the dates of operation for the most collectible costume jewelry makers, but also a list of the most commonly found signatures for these makers and the approximate dates when these signatures were in use. Variations in signatures and unusual signatures are also listed.

### TECHNIQUE FOUR: UNDERSTANDING SUPPLEMENTARY MARKS

Occasionally vintage costume jewelry signatures include supplementary marks in addition to the manufacturers' signatures. Four of the most commonly found supplemental marks are described below.

*Supplementary Mark One: Year of Manufacture*

Some makers add the actual year of manufacture to the signature. For example, Hollycraft jewelry from the 1950s is sometimes signed "Hollycraft Corp." followed by the date of manufacture. The beautiful pink and lavender brooch in Figure 4 is signed "Hollycraft Corp. 1954," firmly establishing the date of manufacture to 1954.

**Figure 4.** 1954 Hollycraft pink, purple, and green rhinestone brooch. This lovely lavender and olivine green 1¾" five-sided brooch is easy to date because it is signed "Hollycraft Corp. 1954." $60.00 – 80.00.

Hobé is another example of a maker that occasionally both signed and dated jewelry. Hobé jewelry produced from 1957 to 1966 sometimes includes the date of manufacture. For example, the bright red Christmas wreath in Figure 5 is signed "Hobé" with the copyright symbol and the year "1965."

**Figure 5.** 1965 Hobé red wreath pin. This rare Hobé 1½" red Christmas wreath is signed "Hobé 1965." The bright red beads are all hand wired to a gold-tone filigree frame and then attached to a solid gold-tone frame. $45.00 – 65.00.

Other makers who occasionally date jewelry designs include, but are not limited to, Trifari, Coro, and Mimi di N.

*Supplementary Mark Two: Inventory Numbers*

Marcel Boucher jewelry produced after 1945 includes both the "Boucher" signature and a three- or four-digit company inventory number. For example, the beautiful bow brooch in Figure 6 is signed "Boucher" with the inventory number 3309. This inventory number is assigned to the design by Boucher. There are no known records definitively establishing dates of manufacture for Boucher designs based on these inventory numbers. However, an excellent reference titled *A Tribute to America* by Carla Ginelli Brunialti and Roberto Brunialti provides some insight into dating Boucher jewelry by using the inventory number. The following passage is from page 25 of this must-have reference:

From 1945 onwards a progressive number appeared on the items, obviously an internal company catalogue number which, by checking the patent number of other items allows us to know with certainty the exact date of manufacture of the not patented but numbered items. In 1945 the numbers are from 2300 to 2350 circa, in 1946 from 2351 to 2450 circa, in 1947 from 2450 to 2550 circa, in 1948 the numbers are from 2550 to 2750 circa, in 1949 from 2750 to circa 3000, in 1950 from 3000 to 3500 circa.

The Boucher bow brooch in Figure 6 is signed "Boucher" with the inventory number 3309. Utilizing the above progression, the Boucher bow brooch was produced in 1950.

**Figure 6.** 1950 Boucher gold-tone and rhinestone bow pin. Measuring 2¼", this lovely bow brooch is signed "Boucher" without a copyright symbol and with inventory number 3309. The rhinestones are set in silver-tone metal, but the willowy, four-strand ribbon is gold tone. Based on the information about Boucher inventory numbers found in the book *A Tribute to America* by Carla Ginelli Brunialti and Roberto Brunialti, the inventory number indicates this bow dates to 1950. $70.00 – 90.00.

*Supplementary Mark Three: The Importance of "Sterling" as Part of the Signature*

In the 1930s, jewelry was often produced using pot metal or white metal. This is a hard metal that is an alloy of antimony, cadmium, tin, lead, and bismuth. During World War II, these metals were needed for the war effort. Beginning in approximately 1943, some large jewelry makers including Trifari, Coro, Eisenberg, Mazer, Pennino, and Boucher (to name just a few) manufactured costume jewelry in sterling silver. Some of these designs were made in Mexico. The sterling silver was often coated with a gold wash to simulate the look of gold (vermeil). In approximately 1948 these makers returned to producing most jewelry designs in white metal. The sterling designs produced from 1943 to 1948 are signed with the maker's mark and "Sterling."

For example, the Pennino brooch shown in Figure 7 is signed "Pennino Sterling," indicating it was produced from approximately 1943 to 1948.

*Supplementary Mark Four: the Craftsperson's Mark*

The fourth technique to use the signature to date costume jewelry is to look for the mark of the craftsperson who worked on the piece.

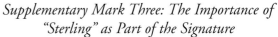

*Fig. 1.*

**Figure 7.** 1943 – 1948 Pennino sterling silver brooch. Measuring 2", this rare stylized flower brooch signed "Pennino Sterling" is encrusted with tiny clear rhinestones graduating in size as they cover the swirling surface of the brooch. Since this brooch is signed by a costume jewelry maker active in the 1940s and is signed "Sterling," this brooch was produced from 1943 to 1948, when major makers utilized sterling silver for jewelry designs in place of the harder metals needed for the war. $100.00 – 130.00.

Early jewelry produced before World War II sometimes includes a mark separate from the maker's signature, which is believed to be the identifying mark of the craftsperson who worked on the piece. The supplemental mark can be one or two letters of the alphabet, such as the letter "L" or the initials "MB." Sometimes this identifying mark is a one-digit or a two-digit number. For example, the pink Eisenberg brooch shown earlier in this chapter (Figure 2) is signed "Eisenberg Original" and "6." The presence of the craftsperson mark indicates the jewelry was produced before World War II. (Note: Little Nemo Jewelry is signed "LN/25" or some version of this signature. This mark is not a craftsperson mark. It is the signature of Little Nemo Jewelry.)

## METHOD TWO: *Patents*

Original patents are endlessly fascinating to collectors interested in dating vintage costume jewelry designs. These pieces of history are first-source records unchanged from the day they were issued. There are two types of patents that apply to costume jewelry.

### DEFINITIONS OF DESIGN AND UTILITY PATENTS

The first type of jewelry patent is a utility patent. A utility patent is issued for a practical, mechanical invention. It is not for the beauty or the look of the item. It is for the hardware or mechanism. Figure 8 shows utility patent number 1798867 issued March 31, 1931, to Gaston Candas for the design of the Coro Duette mechanism.

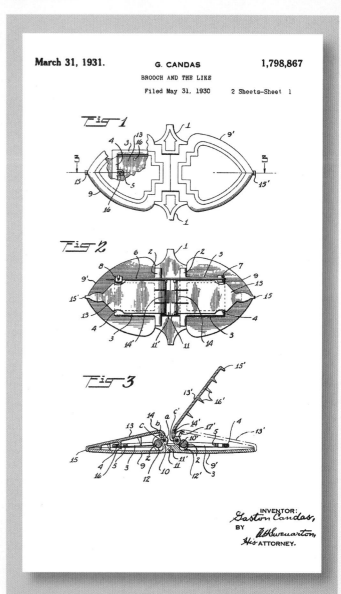

**Figure 8.** 1931 utility patent for the famous Coro Duette mechanism. This patent is utility patent number 1798867 issued March 31, 1931, to Gaston Candas for Coro. It protects the design of the famous Coro Duette mechanism that uniquely attaches two clips together using a specially designed frame. Once attached to the frame, the two clips can be worn together as one brooch. Coro marked the Coro Duette frames with patent number 1798867 for more than 17 years. This number indicates the earliest a piece could have been made, but does not identify when a specific Duette design was produced.

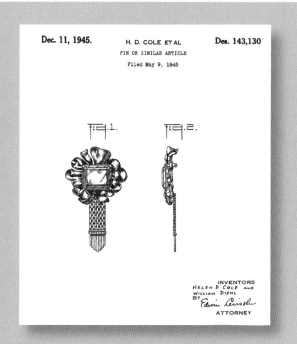

Dec. 11, 1945.                H. D. COLE ET AL        Des. 143,130
                        PIN OR SIMILAR ARTICLE
                           Filed May 9, 1945

                                                    INVENTORS
                                                  HELEN D COLE AND
                                                  WILLIAM DIEHL
                                                BY
                                                  Edwin Lewisohn
                                                      ATTORNEY

**Figure 9.** Design patent number 143130 issued December 11, 1945, to Helen D. Cole and William Diehl for the design of a military ribbon–style brooch.

The second type of jewelry patent is a design patent, which is issued to protect the artistic design of the jewelry. Design patents protect the artist's rendering or vision of how the finished jewelry will look. Figure 9 shows design patent number 143130 issued

December 11, 1945, to H. D. Cole for the unique look of a military-style brooch.

Original patents, both utility and design patents, contain the following useful information:

- Both utility and design patents feature one or more detailed illustrations showing the jewelry design from different views. From these illustrations, a collector can see the designer's original vision for the jewelry.
- Each type of patent is numbered and dated. The issue date is in the left corner. The patent number is in the right corner.
- The jewelry type is listed. For example, the jewelry type may be listed as a brooch, a clip, a necklace, earrings, a bracelet, a chatelaine, or a separable brooch (Duette).
- The name of the artist or designer is listed at both the top and the bottom of the patent.
- Often, on a separate page, the name of the manufacturer is also included. For example, Figure 10 shows the front page of the H. D. Cole design patent. Notice that the front page of this patent assigns the design to "Jacques Kreisler Manufacturing Corporation." This page of the design patent clearly defines the maker of the brooch. It is wonderful for a collector when this information is part of the patent. Unfortunately, this is not always the case.

Patented Dec. 11, 1945                              Des. 143,130

# UNITED STATES PATENT OFFICE

143,130

**DESIGN FOR A PIN OR SIMILAR ARTICLE**

Helen D. Cole, New York, N. Y., and William Diehl, Summit, N. J., assignors to Jacques Kreisler Manufacturing Corporation, North Bergen, N. J.

Application May 9, 1945, Serial No. 119,454

Term of patent 7 years

(Cl. D45—19)

*To all whom it may concern:*
 Be it known that we, Helen D. Cole and William Diehl, citizens of the United States of America, residing at 106 East 65th Street, New York, New York, and 22 Division Avenue, Summit, New Jersey, respectively, have invented a new, original, and ornamental Design for a Pin or Similar Article, of which the following is a specification, reference being had to the accompanying drawing, forming a part thereof.

Fig. 1 is a front elevational view of a pin showing my new design; and
 Fig. 2 is a side elevational view thereof.
 We claim:
 The ornamental design for a pin or similar article, substantially as shown.

                                    HELEN D. COLE.
                                    WILLIAM DIEHL.

**Figure 10.** Front page of design patent number 143130 issued December 11, 1945, to Helen D. Cole and William Diehl. This cover page states that this design is assigned to Jacques Kreisler Manufacturing Corporation, establishing Kreisler as the maker of this design.

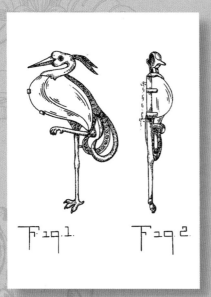

**Figure 11.** Design patent number 135175 issued March 2, 1943, to Alfred Philippe.

Fig. 1.

## UNITED STATES PATENT OFFICE

### 135,175

#### DESIGN FOR A BROOCH OR SIMILAR ARTICLE

**Alfred Philippe, Cranston, R. I.**

Application February 3, 1943, Serial No. 109,430

**Term of patent 3½ years**

To all whom it may concern:

Be it known that I, Alfred Philippe, a citizen of the United States of America, residing in Cranston, county of Providence, and State of Rhode Island, have invented a new, original, and ornamental Design for a Brooch or Similar Article, of which the following is a specification, reference being had to the accompanying drawing, forming part thereof.

Fig. 1 is a plan view of a brooch or similar article showing my new design.

Fig. 2 is an edge view thereof.

I claim:

The ornamental design for a brooch or similar article, substantially as shown.

ALFRED PHILIPPE.

**Figure 12.** Front page of design patent number 135175 issued March 2, 1943, to Alfred Philippe. This is the cover page for the famous Trifari heron Jelly Belly pin. Even though the cover page does not specifically assign this design to Trifari, it is known that Philippe worked for Trifari from 1930 to 1968. (See Appendix B: Designers Chart.) This information plus the Trifari signature on the actual jewelry firmly establishes Trifari as the maker of this design.

## DESIGN PATENTS

Design patents are used to protect the artist's depiction of the piece. These patents are for the style of the jewelry. For example, design patent number 135175 issued March 2, 1943, to Alfred Philippe is shown in Figure 11. This patent is for a large heron Jelly Belly brooch. The design patent protects the unique appearance of this bird. Other heron pins may have patents, but design patent 135175 is for the distinctive appearance of this brooch.

Notice that the design patent lists the date the patent was issued, the designer, and the design patent number, and has one or more illustrations of the unique design.

Figure 12 shows the front page of this patent. This page lists Alfred Philippe as the designer, but does not list a maker or manufacturer. Most collectors know that Alfred Philippe designed for Trifari in 1943, but in many cases, this information is unknown. When this happens, the maker can often be determined by one of the following methods:

1. The easiest way to determine the maker is to find the maker's mark on jewelry matching the patent. Figure 13 shows a picture of a heron pin matching this patent. This pin is signed "Trifari Des. Pat. No. 135175" and "Sterling," clearly indicating that Trifari was the maker. Of course, this method is only effective if a sample of the jewelry is available and if the jewelry is marked with the design patent number.

**Figure 13.** 1943 Trifari heron Jelly Belly. This noble, 3½" giant heron brooch is signed "Trifari," "Sterling," and "Des. Pat. No. 135175." The patent for this design was issued to Alfred Philippe on March 2, 1943. Notice the large clear Lucite belly that is the centerpiece of the design. Philippe is credited with creating Jelly Belly jewelry during World War II as a way of creatively utilizing Lucite and sterling silver in jewelry designs. During the war years, rhinestones could not be imported from Europe. In addition, the harder metals were needed for the war effort. Authentic Trifari Jelly Belly jewelry from the 1940s is extremely rare. Hard-to-find examples can be valued at well over $1,000.00. However, please be aware that many of these designs have been reproduced. If authentic, the value of this brooch is $900.00 – 1,200.00.

2. The second method is to refer to Appendix B: Designers Chart for a list of well-known jewelry makers and the designers known to have created designs for them. The dates when each designer worked are included. This chart indicates that Alfred Philippe worked for Trifari from 1930 to 1968. Even if the heron pin had not been signed, the information in Appendix B establishes that in 1943, at the time design patent 135175 was issued, Philippe designed for Trifari.

## HOW TO LOCATE UNKNOWN DESIGN PATENT NUMBERS

Some pieces of patented jewelry are signed "Des. Pat. Pend." (design patent pending), indicating that a patent was applied for but not yet issued. It was a common practice to produce and market jewelry without waiting for the patent to be officially issued. For example, Figure 14 is a Coro medieval axe pin signed "Coro," without the copyright symbol, and "Des. Pat. Pend." No patent was found for this piece. There may or may not be a patent for this design. However, Coro clearly produced this piece before the patent number was issued.

Figure 14. 1948 – 1955 Coro medieval axe pin. Heraldic jewelry (including crown pins, shield pins, knight pins, and king and queen pins) was popular in the 1940s and 1950s. This interesting Coro 2¾" x ¾" medieval axe pin is signed "Coro Des. Pat. Pend." I was unable to locate the patent for this piece. It is decorated with jewel-tone red, green, and sapphire rhinestones. The design, nonuse of sterling, and Coro signature without the copyright symbol indicate this pin dates to 1948 – 1955. $45.00 – 65.00.

Often, the signatures on many patented jewelry designs do not indicate that the piece is patented even if a patent exists for the piece. For example, the fabulous fish pin in Figure 15 is signed "BB Sterling." There is no indication in the signature that the piece is patented. Yet it is an exact match for design patent number 141282 (see Figure 16) issued May 29, 1945, to Oscar F. Placco.

The following three techniques are useful in locating unknown design patent numbers utilizing the reference materials included in this book.

Figure 15. 1945 BB Sterling fish pin. Absolutely splendid, this 2" sterling silver fish pin exactly matches design patent 141382 issued May 29, 1945, to Oscar F. Placco. It is believed that Placco designed for Coro from 1938 to 1945; however, this pin is not signed Coro. It is signed "BB Sterling," which is the mark of E.A. Bennett, which later became Bennett & Bradford. Placco must have been working as a freelance designer for both companies at the time this patent was issued. Notice the expressive face, detailed markings, and red cabochon eyes. This is a top-notch figural fish pin dating to 1945. $200.00 – 400.00.

Figure 16. Design patent number 141382 issued May 29, 1945, to Oscar F. Placco.

### Technique One: Find the Correct Design Patent Chart

If a piece of jewelry is signed by the maker and "Des. Pat. Pend.," then it is possible a design patent exists for the piece. The first step in locating a patent for this jewelry is to turn to the correct chapter in the book. Chapter 2 in this book contains the patent numbers for Coro jewelry. Chapter 3 contains the Trifari patents. Patents from the other makers are listed alphabetically in chapter 4.

*Fig. 1.*

*Technique Two: Narrow the Range of Dates*

The design patent number charts in this book span the years 1935 through 1954. There are 16 different design patent charts for Coro jewelry. These charts all provide brief descriptions of each patented piece; however, searching through all of the charts (and accompanying illustrations) is time consuming. It is better to narrow the range of years a piece could have been produced, to reduce the number of charts that need to be reviewed. There are two ways to accomplish this:

1.  First, check the signature to establish the dates of operation for the maker. (Remember, if there is a copyright symbol, then the piece is usually not patented.) Use Appendix A: Manufacturer and Marks Chart to find this information. For example, the Coro signature in thick script was not used until 1940. If a piece has this style of Coro mark, then the design patent will be found in the design patent charts from 1940 to 1954. There is no reason to search for the piece in the earlier charts.
2.  Next, check to see if the piece is signed "Sterling." Remember, during the war years and for several years after the war, jewelry makers produced jewelry in sterling silver. If the piece is signed "Sterling," then the piece was likely produced from 1943 to 1948.

For example, the medieval axe pin shown earlier in Figure 14 is signed "Coro" in script at an angle and "Des. Pat. Pend." This style of this signature was first used in 1945, so there is no reason to check for the axe design patent earlier than that date. The lack of a copyright symbol indicates it was produced before 1955. It is not sterling. Therefore, a logical range of years when this piece could have been produced is from 1948, when Coro ceased using sterling silver, and before 1955, when the copyright symbol was added. The range of dates where the patent for this piece is most likely to be found is 1948 – 1954.

*Technique Three: Locate the Piece
in a Vintage Advertisement*

Generally, costume jewelry featured in vintage advertisements was produced and patented in the same year as the advertisement. Reviewing the jewelry featured in vintage advertisements helps to establish a starting date to begin looking for the patents. (See Method Three: Vintage Advertisements for more

details on using vintage advertisements for this purpose.)

*Technique Four: Identify Style Traits*

Over 500 design patent drawings are shown in this book. These have been carefully selected to represent jewelry trends. For example, the Trifari necklace in Figure 17 was advertised in 1952 as "Twinkle." Figure 18 shows the original design patent for this necklace. Notice the two five-point rhinestone stars decorating this necklace. These five-point rhinestone stars are a characteristic trait of Twinkle jewelry. Other pieces from the Twinkle line can be identified by these stars. Design patent number 167229 in Figure 19 illustrates this idea. The brooch in this patent features seven of these five-point rhinestone stars. This brooch is clearly an example of the Trifari Twinkle jewelry. A logical conclusion is that most Trifari jewelry, with this characteristic five-point rhinestone star motif, also dates to 1952.

When reviewing the patent charts and illustrations in this book, please keep this idea in mind. Many of the illustrations reflect a characteristic trait or trend commonly found on jewelry designs produced in a particular year.

**Figure 17.** 1952 Twinkle two-flower rhinestone star necklace. In 1952, Trifari advertised two variations of the Twinkle necklace, one with two stars and one with five stars. (See the 1952 "The Most Enchanted Gift of All" advertisement on page 197.) This gold-tone 15" necklace is an example of the two-star design. It is design patent number 167421 issued August 5, 1952, to Alfred Philippe for Trifari, and it originally sold for $7.50. $35.00 – 50.00.

**Figure 18.** Design patent number 167421 issued August 5, 1952, to Alfred Philippe for Trifari. Notice the two five-point rhinestone stars decorating the center of this necklace.

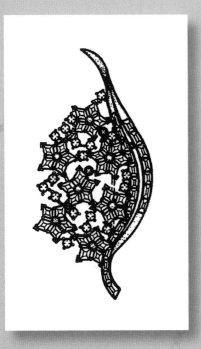

**Figure 19.** Design patent number 167229 issued July 8, 1952, to Alfred Philippe for Trifari. Notice the seven five-point rhinestone stars decorating this brooch.

## UTILITY PATENTS

Utility patents are issued for the unique design of a mechanism associated with jewelry, including types of ear clips, clasps, plating processes, and devices such as the Coro Duette mechanism shown earlier in this chapter (see Figure 8). Even in the 1930s, utility patents numbered over a million, so the utility patents on jewelry at that time were already seven digits long.

Design patents are usually more useful than utility patents for dating costume jewelry, so it is important for a collector to be able to distinguish between them. There are four distinct differences between design patents and utility patents.

### Differences between Utility and Design Patents

- First, design patents are issued for the look, the beauty, the aesthetic style of the jewelry. Utility patents are issued for a practical functional invention.
- Next, there are fewer design patents than utility patents. Utility patents have seven-digit patent numbers. Design patents have only six digits. Counting the number of digits is by far the easiest way to distinguish a design from a utility patent number.
- In addition, utility patents are issued for 17 years. Design patents are only good for three and a half years. After that a design patent may be renewed, though doing so requires time and money.
- Finally, and most importantly for this book, design patent numbers are useful for dating costume jewelry. Design patents indicate the year when the design was produced. Generally, utility patents do not accurately indicate the date jewelry was produced. They are only useful to indicate the earliest date a mechanism could have been used. The mechanism could have been in continuous use for 17 or more years.

### Utility Patent Chart

Since there are so many utility patents, and since they are limited in their usefulness for dating costume jewelry, very few utility patents are included in this volume. The following is a short list of utility patents. Please note that this is an incomplete list. These patents are interesting and provide a peek into the types of mechanisms protected by utility patents. Appendix C: View Patents Online provides step-by-step instructions for how to view these patents or any utility patents online.

SIX METHODS FOR DATING COSTUME JEWELRY

## UTILITY PATENT CHART

| Patent Number | Date Issued | Designer | Maker (if known) | Brief Description of Function |
|---|---|---|---|---|
| 1798867 | 3/31/1931 | Gaston Candas | Coro | Duette mechanism. |
| 1801128 | 4/14/1931 | Anthony E. Waller | | Finding for clasps. |
| 1852188 | 4/5/1932 | Elisha A. Phinney | Geo. H. Fuller & Son Company | Brooch or clasp with an ornamental design. |
| 1878028 | 9/20/1932 | Gustavo Trifari | Trifari | Separable clip mechanism to attach two clips together. |
| 1967965 | 7/24/1934 | Eugene Morehouse & Melvin W. Moore | B.A. Ballou & Co., Inc. | Earring clip. |
| 1970041 | 8/14/1934 | Sylvester A. Johnson | Sammartino & Sanchirico Company | A mechanism for enlarging a bracelet without separating the ends. |
| 2045385 | 6/23/1936 | Wilhelm Goetz | C. & G. Manufacturing Company, Inc. | Separable clip mechanism to attach two clips together. |
| 2050804 | 8/11/1936 | Alfred Philippe | Trifari | Famous Trifari "Clip-mate" mechanism for attaching two brooches together. |
| 2066969 | 1/5/1937 | Frank E. Farnham | | Safety catch for pins. |
| 2119178 | 5/31/1938 | Oreste Pennino | Pennino | Combination clip and brooch structure for attaching two clips together. |
| 2143538 | 1/10/1939 | Marcel Boucher | Boucher | A brooch assemblage to attach two brooches together. |
| 2145716 | 1/31/1939 | John Fielding | Joseph P. Whitaker | Separable clip mechanism to attach two clips together. |
| 2161668 | 6/6/1939 | John Fielding | Joseph P. Whitaker | Clip assembly to attach two brooches together. |
| 2400513 | 5/21/1946 | Markus Jellinek | | Earring clip with adjustable screw mechanism. |
| 2583988 | 1/29/1952 | Frederick A. Ballou Jr. and Rogers T. Stafford | B. A. Ballou and Co. | Clip earring with mechanism for attaching a drop. (See Kramer lavender earrings in chapter 4 with this utility patent number.) |
| 2668341 | 2/9/1954 | Emanuel L. Artz | | Adjustable stop for the spring clips of earrings. |
| 2752764 | 7/3/1956 | H. B. Lederer | | Use of magnets for interchangeable earrings. |
| 3176475 | 4/6/1965 | Nazareno J. Saccoccio | Aro-Sac Inc. | Adjustable clip for earrings having a single tooth thread. |
| 3427691 | 2/18/1969 | James R. Johnson | | Clasp. |

# METHOD THREE: *Vintage Advertisements*

A wonderful and fun way to date vintage costume jewelry is to review vintage jewelry advertisements. Included in this volume are over 160 advertisements for dozens of makers and spanning the years 1943 – 1982. These often colorful records of fashion history not only provide pictures of the jewelry, but these beautiful historical records also reveal how the jewelry was worn, the original names assigned to the designs, and in most cases, the original selling prices. The captions for the advertisements in this book spell out this information.

**Figure 20.** 1954 Star-Art advertisement from the 1954 *Jewelers' Buyers Guide*. This advertisement showcases jewelry called Jewels by Helene in original, period presentation boxes. The advertisement reads, "…Here are just two selections from a complete line of lovely gold filled and sterling jewelry…beautiful…unusual designs, expertly crafted and finished to an everlasting luster." This advertisement was intended to encourage retailers to carry the Star-Art line of jewelry.

## THREE SOURCES FOR VINTAGE ADVERTISEMENTS
### *First Source: Books*

Look for vintage advertisements in costume jewelry and reference books. Almost every costume jewelry book includes several vintage advertisements. Other, jewelry-related books have interesting advertisements, too. For example, every year a new *Jewelers' Buyers Guide* was published. These guides listed the names of most of the makers of costume jewelry for any given year. (This book also included the makers of fine jewelry and the makers of jewelry hardware.) Many makers advertised in this guide to encourage retailers to carry their jewelry. Since these guides are out-of-print, the best way to search for them online is with a search engine or on eBay. Figure 20 is a vintage advertisement from the 1954 *Jewelers' Buyers Guide*, advertising Star-Art Jewels by Helene.

### *Second Source: Magazines and Catalogs*

Another excellent source for vintage advertisements is vintage magazines and catalogues. Some useful sources for these advertisements include the following publications: *Women's Wear Daily*, *Vogue*, *Life*, *Harper's Bazaar*, *McCalls*, *Jewelers' Circular-Keystone*, *Mademoiselle*, *Glamour*, *The New York Times Magazine*, and *The New Yorker*.

Vintage catalogs including those for Sears and Montgomery Ward are also useful sources for vintage costume jewelry advertisements.

Some of the rarest but best sources for information about vintage costume jewelry are original maker catalogs. These catalogs were sent to retailers. The retailers reviewed the jewelry in the catalogs and then placed orders for selected designs to be sold in the stores. Figures 21 and 22 are two pages from the *Monet…Fall 1963* catalog (see next page). Figure 21 is a page from this catalog showcasing the Monet Bolero lariat-style necklace. This page features two different ways of wearing this style of necklace. Figure 22 showcases an array of Monet pins, including the Spinnerets line and a selection of leaf-style filigree pins.

### *Third Source: View and/or Purchase Online*

Vintage advertisements can be purchased online at eBay auctions for approximately $10.00 each. (Some rare advertisements sell for as much as $50.00.) Be sure that the advertisement purchased this way includes the date. If the date is not mentioned in the listing, ask the seller for the date before bidding. Sometimes the

Fig. 1.

**Figure 21.** Page 24 of the *Monet...Fall 1963* catalog and mat book. This beautiful mat page features Monet's Bolero necklace. The advertisement reads, "Bolero in the golden manner of Monet. Monet captivates the newest necklines with this great golden lariat. Worn to the back or to the front, Bolero adds elegance to every look from day to evening. A versatile spinning of golden links and satiny beads holding filigree encased teardrops. The earring carries out the necklace motif...in the important drop shape. Each piece bears the Monet signature. The lariat $7.50, drop earring $5. Prices plus tax." From the collection of David Mayer.

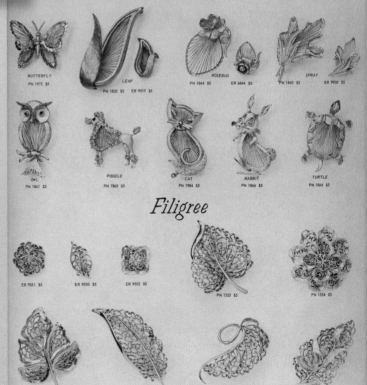

**Figure 22.** Page 31 of the *Monet...Fall 1963* catalog and mat book. This page features an interesting array of pins. The first two rows are pins called Spinnerets. Each of these wire designs originally sold for $5.00. The bottom two rows feature leaf-style filigree pins and earrings that each originally sold for $5.00. From the collection of David Mayer.

seller does not know the date, which is why it is not mentioned in the description.

Several websites feature vintage advertisements as a resource for potential customers. These sites give the collector a free look at vintage advertisements. For dating purposes, these sites are wonderful resources. Do an internet search on "vintage jewelry advertisement" and an array of sites will appear. It is fun to look through them and bookmark the sites featuring interesting advertisements.

Unfortunately, most of the advertisements online, and in some jewelry books, are so small that it is difficult to read the advertising information. The jewelry can be viewed for dating purposes, but the smaller print listing the original jewelry names and prices for the jewelry is obscured. For this reason, the captions for the vintage advertisements in this book provide this interesting information to the reader. In addition, the original selling prices and original jewelry names are clearly listed in each caption.

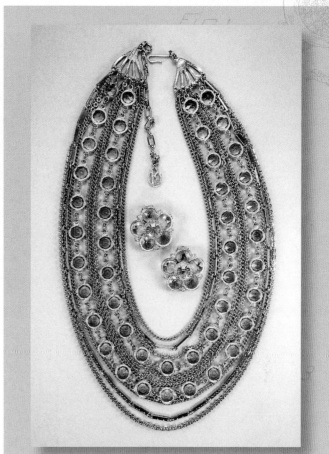

**Figure 24.** This spectacular Kramer set in mint condition is featured in a 1961 Kramer "Mi-Lady, The Fluid Beauty of Fall" advertisement. The necklace originally sold for $20.00 and measures 17½" inches. The 1" clip earrings sold for $4.00 a pair. Today's value, $45.00 – 60.00.

## USING VINTAGE ADVERTISEMENTS TO DATE JEWELRY

There are two important methods to use vintage advertisements to date jewelry designs.

### Method One: Locate the Actual Piece in the Advertisement

First, the easiest way to use a vintage advertisement to date jewelry is to see the actual jewelry piece illustrated in the advertisement. For example, Figure 23 is a 1961 advertisement for Kramer jewelry. A beautiful model is peeking over a Kramer 16-strand necklace. The advertisement is titled "Mi-Lady: The Fluid Beauty of Fall." The jewelry shown in the black and white advertisement was available in "crystal, topaz, ruby, emerald or sapphire with gold; or a rajah's multi-mix of them all." Figure 24 shows a photograph of the emerald version of this necklace and earrings set. This emerald set is an exact match to the necklace in the advertisement, firmly dating the gorgeous green Kramer necklace and earrings set to 1961.

**Figure 23.** 1961 Kramer "Mi-Lady: The Fluid Beauty of Fall" advertisement. This advertisement features a multistrand necklace, earrings, and bracelet. It reads, "A stream of daringly realistic brilliants and golden chains. Crystal, topaz, ruby, emerald or sapphire with gold; or a rajah's multi-mix of them all. Will you be the first to wear them? Necklace, as shown $20. Flexible Bracelet, $5. Cluster Button Earrings, $4. Other necklaces, $8, $10. Drop or Contour Earrings, $4."

Sparkling rhinestones gracefully draped around your ear by the comfortable

EARRITE* (no screws, no clips). Pair, $17
plus tax

Styled by

*Marcel Boucher*

*Boucher Jewelry available at better stores in United States and Canada*

Marcel Boucher et Cie, 347 Fifth Ave., New York

Avon Jewelry Ltd., Belleville, Ontario, Canada

*Design Pat. Pending. U. S. Pat. Office.

**Figure 25.** 1950 Marcel Boucher Earrite advertisement. This interesting advertisement features a unique over-the-ear earring invented by Marcel Boucher and called the Earrite. The advertisement reads, "Sparkling rhinestones gracefully draped around your ear by the comfortable EARRITE (no screws, no clips). Pair, $17."

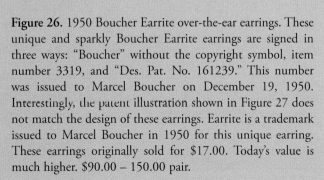

**Figure 26.** 1950 Boucher Earrite over-the-ear earrings. These unique and sparkly Boucher Earrite earrings are signed in three ways: "Boucher" without the copyright symbol, item number 3319, and "Des. Pat. No. 161239." This number was issued to Marcel Boucher on December 19, 1950. Interestingly, the patent illustration shown in Figure 27 does not match the design of these earrings. Earrite is a trademark issued to Marcel Boucher in 1950 for this unique earring. These earrings originally sold for $17.00. Today's value is much higher. $90.00 – 150.00 pair.

**Figure 27.** Design patent number 161289 issued December 19, 1950, to Raymonde Semensohn of Boucher. This patent protects the unique design of Boucher's Earrite over-the-ear earrings.

*Method Two: Locate Similar or Coordinating Pieces not Shown in the Advertisement*

It is possible to use vintage advertisements to date jewelry that is only similar to the jewelry featured in the advertisement. Sometimes, the advertisement does not show all of the pieces in a group. For example, the advertisement description for the emerald Kramer necklace set shown in Figure 23 lists "Other Necklaces, $8, $10. Drop or Contour Earrings, $4." From this information, a collector knows there were other pieces to this group not shown in the advertisement. Therefore, this advertisement helps to date similarly styled Kramer necklaces or earrings not specifically pictured in the advertisement.

It is also not necessary for the jewelry to exactly match the pieces featured in an advertisement for the advertisement to be useful in dating the jewelry. The 1950 Marcel Boucher earring advertisement shown in Figure 25 illustrates this idea. The advertisement is for a style of over-the-ear earring called an Earrite. "Earrite" is a trademark assigned to Boucher, who invented and patented this style of earring. The earrings in the

advertisement originally sold for $17.00. Figure 26 is a photograph of a similarly styled pair of Boucher Earrite earrings. The earrings in Figure 26 do not exactly match the earrings in the advertisement, but likely date to the same time period.

A general rule to follow when dating jewelry from vintage advertisements is as follows: *Jewelry similar in style to an advertised design likely dates to the same era.*

This rule can be proven by the markings on these Boucher earrings. The earrings in the photograph are signed "Boucher" and have the inventory number 3319 and the design patent number 161239. This inventory number indicates these earrings were produced in 1950. The year 1950 corresponds with the date of the advertisement. In addition, these earrings are marked with the 1950 design patent number 161239 (see Figure 27 for the original design patent). This information also corresponds with the date of the advertisement. Although not an exact match for the advertised Earrite earrings, the Boucher over-the-ear earrings in the photograph date from 1950.

Vintage advertisements are a fun and efficient source for dating costume jewelry designs. Another side benefit to these advertisements is their beauty. Collectors enjoy framing and displaying these advertisements (especially if the collectors own the jewelry featured in the advertisements).

## METHOD FOUR: *Dating Jewelry by Style*

If a piece of jewelry cannot be dated by the signature, a patent, or a vintage advertisement, the next method for establishing an approximate date of manufacture is to examine the style of the jewelry. This method is less efficient than the other three methods. Styles throughout the years are repeated and vary greatly from one company to another. The following guidelines (not rules, just guidelines) provide some assistance in dating jewelry by style.

To begin, use the following chart to narrow the range of dates when jewelry could have been produced by matching the style and materials found on the piece to one of the following eras. Please remember the dates assigned to the traits described in the Style Chart 1935 – 1980 are suppositions and guidelines only. Jewelry makers did not abruptly change styles and materials with the start of a new year. These changes were gradual.

*1935 – 1940*

- Often jewelry from this era is covered with clear rhinestones called pavé rhinestones. See Figure 28 for an example of a bird brooch from this era coated with pavé rhinestones. (Today is it normal for these stones to sometimes be darkened by age.)
- Designs from this era are often flat and two dimensional. The bird brooch in Figure 28 is flat. (Figure 29 shows the 1941 patented version of this brooch.)
- Much of the jewelry from this era is made in pot metal. The metal is heavy and dull. It is not vermeil or coated with rhodium.

- Often black or red enameling is used to highlight designs. See Figure 30 for a horse brooch from this era with black enamel highlights. Note: this enameling continues into the early 1940s.
- In 1936 the King of England, Edward VIII, abdicates his throne and marries Mrs. Simpson.
- At this time crown pins and other royal designs are popular motifs and remain popular throughout the 1940s. Many are produced in sterling silver.

**Figure 28.** 1937 – 1940 unmarked bird brooch. The overall design of the brooch strongly resembles design patent number 129843 issued October 7, 1941, to Marcel Boucher. (See Figure 29 to view a copy of this 1941 patent.) However, the materials and the workmanship in this piece are vastly different from what is normally seen in 1941 Boucher designs. This brooch is made of pot metal and covered with rhinestones. The 1941 Boucher pin is brightly enameled along the body, head, and tailfeathers. It is possible that this brooch is an early version of the patented 1941 Boucher bird. Before 1937 Boucher designed for Mazer. This brooch is possibly an unsigned Boucher design dating to 1937, when Boucher started his own company. As an early, unmarked Boucher brooch the value is $400.00 – 600.00. From the collection of Debi Reece.

**Figure 30.** Late 1930s or early 1940s Coro horse-racing brooch. Unfortunately, I was unable to locate a patent to match this magnificent Coro 2¾" x 1¼" horse-racing brooch. This brooch features pavé rhinestones and black enamel highlights. Both of these traits are characteristic of 1930s and early 1940s jewelry and help to date this wonderful brooch to that era. $175.00 – 300.00.

**Figure 29.** Design patent number 129843 issued October 7, 1941, to Marcel Boucher for Boucher. The original of this brooch is decorated with metallic red and green enamel.

SIX METHODS FOR DATING COSTUME JEWELRY

24

**Figure 31.** 1937 marked "MB" basket pin. This 1¾" basket pin is most likely a Mazer piece. The light pink plastic leaves decorating this basket are reminiscent of the leaves shown in an early Boucher design, patent number 103385 issued March 2, 1937. (See Figure 31 for the original patent drawing.) Before starting his own business, Boucher designed for Mazer Bros. In my opinion, this rare and intriguing basket pin was made in 1937 for Mazer Bros. based on a Marcel Boucher design. $100.00 – 150.00.

**Figure 33.** 1930s pot metal treble clef brooch. This colorful brooch measures 3" x 1¾" and features bright red, green, and clear rhinestones. Colorful rhinestones encrusting a flat pot metal brooch is typical of jewelry from this era. $35.00 – 50.00.

**Figure 32.** Design patent number 103385 issued March 2, 1937, to Marcel Boucher for Mazer.

- Some designs include colorful plastic inserts. The pastel pink leaves in the early basket pin shown in Figure 31 are similar in style to the design of the leaves in the patent shown in Figure 32. This is design patent number 103385 issued March 2, 1937, to Marcel Boucher for Mazer. (Boucher worked for Mazer at this time.)
- Much of the jewelry from this time is unmarked or only marked with an alphabetical letter or a number. For example, the unmarked basket brooch in Figure 31 is signed "MB." It is probably a coincidence that these are the initials of Marcel Boucher and more likely the mark of the craftsperson who worked on the piece. Early designs frequently include the craftsperson's mark.
- Sometimes jewelry from this era features brightly colored rhinestones. The flat, pot-metal treble clef brooch in Figure 33 is typical of 1930s costume jewelry decorated with colorful rhinestones.
- Many of the brooches are clips. If a brooch has a pin back, the pin is soldered to the piece in two places. (Later pin backs are V-shaped and attached by one central rivet.)
- In 1937, Lucite is patented by DuPont. This material is the inspiration for the famous Trifari and Coro jelly belly jewelry designs produced in the early 1940s.

Fig. 1.

*1940 – 1945*

- At this time, long-stemmed flower brooches are popular. Figure 34 is an example of a colorful long-stemmed flower brooch made in pot metal and decorated with colorful enamel.
- Brooches from this era can be very large. The brooch in Figure 35 measures 3½" x 2½".
- Beautifully crafted whimsical clips with both pavé rhinestones and enameling are popular. These clips are usually sold and worn in pairs. Figure 36 is an example of a beautiful bird clip. Notice that by this time the designs are three dimensional.
- In 1940 Trifari launches a series of jewelry designs with irregularly shaped pearls as the central design element, referred to by collectors today as "pearl belly" jewelry.
- Patriotic designs like the wonderful enameled eagle brooch in Figure 37 are popular.

**Figure 34.** 1930s unmarked long-stemmed flower clip. This colorful 3" x 2" clip resembles an early Trifari brooch. Note the way the tips of the enameled leaves are turned and decorated with rhinestones. This is a design trait of Trifari jewelry. This brooch features yellow translucent cabochons stones, prevalent in 1930s jewelry, and typical enameling of the time. As an unsigned 1930s clip, the value of the piece is $55.00 – 75.00.

**Figure 35.** Unmarked early 1940s red and pavé rhinestone brooch. This ravishing red 3½" x 2½" brooch is made in pot metal. Large brooches like this were common in the 1940s, either with pin backs, like this example, or clip backs. Notice the pavé rhinestones, also typical of this time, decorating the beautifully sculpted leaves. $65.00 – 85.00. *From the collection of Debi Reece.*

**Figure 36.** Unmarked early 1940s 1¾" x 1¼" bird clip. This clip is likely half of a pair. The style of the clip and the presence of old enameling indicate this piece dates to the early 1940s. $35.00 – 45.00.

- Combined brooches and watches, like the wonderful brooch in Figure 38, are produced at this time.
- In 1942, white metal use is limited because of the war.
- Jewelry designs coordinate with the movie industry.
- At this time, as the United States fully enters World War II, the harder metals are needed for the war effort. By 1943, costume jewelry makers produce jewelry designs in sterling silver. This continues until 1948. Imported rhinestones are also unavailable, so jewelry designs from this time limit the use of rhinestones. For example, the Coro sterling silver brooches shown in Figure 39, with one central rhinestone each, date from this era.
- In 1942 Alfred Philippe for Trifari designs the Ming series. (See chapter 3 for design patents showcasing jewelry from this famous and valuable series.)

**Figure 37.** Unmarked 1940s enameled eagle pin. Dating to the 1940s, this beautifully enameled patriotic bird pin is, unfortunately, unmarked. Well crafted and a good example of 1940s enamel jewelry, this pin measures 3¾" x 1¼". $25.00 – 35.00.

**Figure 38.** 1940s Gotham brooch and watch combination. Brooches with watches, like the 3½" x 1½" Gotham brooch/watch above were popular in the 1940s. Other than the Gotham name, there are no other markings on this brooch. The style of this long-stemmed floral decorated with blue rhinestones suggests this piece dates from the early 1940s. The watch is high quality, and amazingly, it still works. This brooch is designed to be worn on a lapel, so that when the lapel is raised, the watch face is easily read. $150.00 – 225.00.

**Figure 39.** Two 1943 – 1948 Coro sterling brooches. Each of these sterling silver brooches features one large, single rhinestone decoration. Beginning in approximately 1943, due to the war, Coro limited the use of hard-to-obtain rhinestones and created many different sterling silver designs each utilizing only one central rhinestone. Coro continued to produce sterling silver designs similar to these two brooches until approximately 1948, helping to date these brooches to between 1943 and 1948. Left: Measuring 2¾" and featuring one large amber center rhinestone, this brooch is signed "Sterling Craft" and "Coro." Right: Slightly smaller, this 2¼" brooch features one emerald green central rhinestone. It is signed "Coro Sterling." $30.00 – 45.00 each. From the collection of Debi Reece.

- In 1942 and 1943, to combat the shortage of materials, Alfred Philippe of Trifari designs the famous Jelly Belly series utilizing clear Lucite (the same Lucite used for airplane windshields) as the main element of the design. (See Figure 13 earlier in this chapter for a photograph of the Trifari heron.) Additional examples of jelly belly jewelry are featured in chapters 2 and 3. Trifari will become most famous for this kind of jewelry, but other makers, especially Coro, produce jewelry with the same Lucite motif.
- Figure 40 is an amazing wood and Lucite African mask produced at this time. The war necessitated this creative use of materials, resulting in some of the most unusual and wonderful costume jewelry produced.
- In 1943 Elzac produced ceramic jewelry with Lucite enhancements. Elzac jewelry is increasingly popular with collectors. See chapter 4 for several examples of Elzac designs.

**Figure 40.** Unmarked 1943-era Lucite and wood African mask brooch. This unmarked brooch is a spectacular example of the Lucite and wooden jewelry produced in the early 1940s. Jewelry makers including Elzac (see Elzac designs in chapter 4) produced wonderful, creative jewelry designs using unconventional materials. This African mask pin measures 3" x 2½". The face is wooden and has inlaid strips of metal to define the cheekbones. The headdress is a large bonnet of carved Lucite. $75.00 – 125.00.

### 1945 – 1950

- From 1945 to 1948, jewelry trends remain constant. However, by 1948, when the country is once again at peace and the factories and materials are available, costume jewelry production changes.
- Many new makers enter the marketplace. The demand for affordable costume jewelry and the mass production techniques implemented during the war result in mass-produced costume jewelry.
- Immediately after the war, much of the costume jewelry is still made in sterling silver. By 1948, this practice diminishes.
- Rhodium plating was available before the war, but not widely used. Now, with the war years over, some high-quality costume jewelry designs feature this type of highly reflective plating, giving the designs a quality "finished" appearance very different from the earlier pot metal or sterling silver jewelry.
- In 1947 Coro creates the wire works jewelry. These are whimsical figural pieces made of twisted wire, each with one central rhinestone body. (See chapter 2 for examples of Coro wire works designs.)
- At this time, Coro also produces many figural pieces depicting everyday household items such as bookshelves and coffeepots.
- Duette brooches, always popular, are produced in great numbers at this time.

- In mid-1947, Trifari invents Trifanium, a new plating process simulating the look of gold or silver. This plating is used by Trifari throughout the 1950s. Interestingly, it was never applied over sterling.
- The use of the copyright symbol becomes law in 1947. It is possible that jewelry with the copyright symbol dates to this time; however, most makers do not routinely mark jewelry with this symbol until 1955.
- Matching sets are increasing popular. Before this time many, but not all, patented designs were for single brooches or brooches with earrings. At this time, makers offer customers matching necklaces, bracelets, earrings, brooches, and Duettes.
- In 1950, Alfred Philippe designs jewelry with Claire de Lune stones. (See chapter 3 for examples of Trifari Claire de Lune jewelry.)
- Choker necklaces are popular. Some of these necklaces are designed with adjustable lengths rather than the fixed lengths of the early and mid-1940s. The trend toward adjustable-length necklaces continues to grow until, by the mid-1950s, most necklaces are made this way.

### *1950 – 1955*

- Jewelry from these years is mass produced. While much of it is still decorated with rhinestones, the use of plastic is increasing.
- Necklaces are often adjustable rather than fixed length.
- Jewelry is advertised in matching sets.
- In 1955, the aurora borealis coating for rhinestones is invented.
- Trifari almost completely ceases patenting jewelry designs by 1955. By 1955, most makers are marking jewelry designs with the copyright symbol.
- Many new makers enter the marketplace. The 1954 *Jewelers' Buyers Guide* lists over 8,000 (fine and costume jewelry) company names in the index.
- Many more companies advertise in national magazines. (View the many different advertisements in this volume.)
- Ballet dancer pins are popularized by Boucher at this time. (See examples of Boucher ballet dancer pins in chapter 4.) Figure 41 is an unmarked dancer pin from this time similar in style to the famous Boucher jewelry.

**Figure 41.** Unmarked 1954 ballet dancer pin. Measuring 2" x 2", this graceful ballet dancer pin features silver-tone metal and mother-of-pearl disks. The dancer pin is unsigned, but resembles dancer pins designed in the early 1950s by Marcel Boucher. (See page 272 for examples of Boucher ballet dancer pins.) The 1954 Boucher Nautic jewelry advertisement shown in chapter 4 features jewelry decorated with mother-of-pearl disks similar to those on this pin. These clues help to establish the date of manufacture for this unmarked ballerina to approximately 1954. $30.00 – 40.00.

- Har produces magnificent Oriental-theme designs. Figure 42 features a wonderful unmarked Oriental-theme set dating to the early 1950s.
- DeLizza and Elster (Juliana) begin to manufacture jewelry for many different makers, including Coro and Kramer.

**Figure 42.** 1950s unmarked Oriental-theme necklace, bracelet, and earrings set. Unmarked jewelry such as this wonderful parure can be dated by comparing the design to other like pieces when the date of manufacture is known. Hobé patented many brooches in 1948 featuring plastic Oriental figures similar to the figures in this set. Few adjustable necklaces were made before 1950, so I believe this set dates to the 1950s. The necklace measures 16½", the bracelet is 7¾", and the clip earrings are 1¼". $95.00 – 150.00 set. From the collection of Debi Reece.

*1955 – 1960*
- Most jewelry signatures include the copyright symbol.
- Elaborate chunky bracelets like the colorful confetti Lucite bracelet in Figure 43 are popular.
- Unlike jewelry from the 1940s, when the designers tried to match the look of fine jewelry designs, many jewelry styles from this era are flagrantly fake. Colorful plastic and enameled jewelry abounds.
- The Weiss black diamonds jewelry is produced. See Figure 44 for an example of Weiss black diamonds jewelry advertised for sale in 1958.

**Figure 43.** Unmarked 1950s colorful confetti Lucite chunky-style bracelet. Heavy and well made, this 7½" x 1½" unmarked bracelet dates to the 1950s, when chunky bracelets of this style were popular. This especially nice example features red, green, and gold flecks of confetti embedded in oval Lucite inserts. The metal is antiqued gold-tone highlighted with green rhinestones and pearls. $50.00 – 70.00.

**Figure 44.** 1958 Weiss Black Diamonds bracelet and brooch. Advertised in 1958 as "Black Diamond Imperial Pretenders" (ad not shown), this 2½" brooch and 7" bracelet represent top-of-the-line Weiss jewelry. The rhinestones are dark to simulate the look of black diamonds. Notice the decorative bands of pavé rhinestones, called "icing" by collectors. This icing is a design trait for Eisenberg jewelry and some high-end Weiss designs from this era. The bracelet originally sold for $10.00 and the pin for $7.50. Today's value for this glorious set is $150.00 – 225.00.

## 1960 – 1965

- Highly imaginative designs in realistic gemstone colors are produced by fashion kings like Kenneth J. Lane, Boucher, Schreiner, Schiaparelli, and Eisenberg.
- The movie *Cleopatra*, with Elizabeth Taylor, is released, sparking a resurgence of interest in Egyptian-theme and Middle Eastern jewelry.
- Thin navette-shaped rhinestones are incorporated in many designs.
- Weiss and other makers produce jewelry with jet black rhinestones to coordinate with the pastel fashions of the time. Japanned (black enamel) jewelry is also popular at this time. Figure 45 is a 1962 Weiss advertisement featuring six pieces of black rhinestone jewelry set in japanned metal and selling for between $5.00 and $10.00 each.
- Glitzy rhinestone jewelry is highly fashionable in the 1960s. Weiss and other makers produce huge amounts of rhinestone jewelry for evening and daytime wear.
- Several different jewelry motifs are popular at this time, including bib necklaces, Maltese crosses (also popular in the 1950s) and snake motif jewelry. The Florenza Maltese cross pin shown in Figure 46 dates from this era.
- Ring watches, bracelet watches, and pendant watches are fashionable.
- Long crystal necklaces and pearl necklaces are popular. Shorter multistrand crystal necklaces and chokers are also plentiful.
- Long tassel necklaces are popular. Figure 47 shows a page from a Monet store catalog advertising the Fatima tassel jewelry set.
- Adjustable screw-back clip earrings, patented in the 1950s, are the clips of choice at this time. Coro's Vendôme jewelry line focuses on the use of crystal beads for necklaces, brooches, and earrings. (See the Vendôme advertisements in chapter 2 for examples of 1960s designs.)

Fig. 1.

**Figure 45.** 1962 Weiss black rhinestone jewelry advertisement. This rare advertisement is from the 1962 *New York Times Magazine* and features six brooches and one pair of earrings, all designed with black rhinestones set in japanned metal. Original prices: top left, round brooch, $7.50; bottom left, triple flower brooch, $5.00; top right, open-design brooch, $6.00; right middle, Dangle earrings, $10.00, and brooch, $5.00; bottom right, brooch, $5.00. The advertisement reads, "Pastels look pastellier when worn with jet by Albert Weiss."

**Figure 47.** 1963 Monet fall catalog page 32. This page features a tassel motif necklace, brace-let, and earrings set called Fatima by Monet. The advertisement reads "Tasseled to tempt... *Fatima* is a glittering expression of Monet's fashion instinct. Delicate chains, finely textured links and filigreed motifs are tastefully combined in the golden manner. The tasseled sautoir $7.50, matching fluid bracelet $6, drop earrings $7.50." From the collection of David Mayer.

**Figure 46.** Early 1960s Florenza Maltese cross pin. This 2½" Florenza Maltese cross pin features ribbed gold-tone metal decorated with molded glass stones and sparkling rhinestones. The interesting glass fruit salad-style stones have both red and blue highlights. Maltese cross jewelry was popular in the 1960s. $60.00 – 75.00.

## 1965 – 1970

- Multichain necklaces are in vogue. Earth tones are popular.
- Large enameled flower pins are in keeping with the hippie movement of the time.
- Plastic bangle bracelets are worn in bundles.
- Many long beaded necklaces are produced at this time.
- Pierced ears are gaining in popularity.
- At the end of the 1960s, William de Lillo jewelry is fashionable, with dog-collar necklaces and other jewelry designs utilizing creative materials like mirrors and Lucite.
- In 1970, Diane Love designs a line of jewelry for Trifari. (See chapter 3 for an example of Diane Love 1970s jewelry.)

## 1970 – 1980

- Jewelry is smaller and more conservative. Simple chain necklaces, unadorned with rhinestones, are popular.
- Cord and string necklaces with natural elements like wooden beads or seashells are produced.
- Simple gold hoop earrings are fashionable.
- Initial jewelry and astrological jewelry personalized to the wearer is in fashion. See Figure 48 for a 1973 Sarah Coventry advertisement featuring zodiac symbol necklaces.

**Figure 48.** 1973 Sarah Coventry zodiac symbol jewelry advertisement. This advertisement is for Sarah Coventry zodiac symbol jewelry that can be worn as necklace, bracelet, or belt. The advertisement reads, "Sarah Coventry's new quick-change jewelry. Necklace, bracelet, belt…all three in one! You wear the 31" goldtone necklace and matching bracelet as you see them here. Or link the two together to form a 38" chain that becomes a longer necklace…or a belt. The pendant is a disc of clear Lucite with your own zodiac symbol…or that of a gift recipient." The set originally sold for $16.00. Interestingly, at the time, Sarah Coventry jewelry was sold in the United States, Canada, the United Kingdom, Australia, and Belgium.

- The King Tut exhibit touring the U.S. sparks the creation of Egyptian-style jewelry. Many colorful types of enamel are produced at this time. Some of the enamels, especially the Eisenberg enamels, are gaining in popularity with collectors today.
- The bicentennial in 1976 is celebrated by jewelry makers with many different red, white, and blue jewelry designs.
- Fewer and fewer companies produce rhinestone jewelry with prong-set stones.
- Modern lobster-claw clasps are popular.
- In the 1980s, Monet manufactures designs for Yves Saint Laurent (YSL). The YSL four-leaf clover brooch in Figure 49 dates to this era.
- Sadly, many great jewelry companies go out of business, including but not limited to such giants as Weiss, Schiaparelli (jewelry), Hollycraft, Carnegie, Boucher, and Bogoff.

**Figure 49.** 1980s YSL four-leaf clover pin. This wonderful 2¾" x 2¼" Yves Saint Laurent four-leaf clover pin is part of a limited edition series. It is number 262 of 500. Yves Saint Laurent originally worked with Christian Dior, until he began his own fashion line in 1961. Jewelry was added to the fashion line in the 1970s. YSL jewelry was manufactured by Monet in the 1980s which is when this pin was most likely, produced. $60.00 – 95.00.

# METHOD FIVE: *Books and the Internet*

Establishing the manufacture dates for costume jewelry requires effort. Method one requires researching the signatures and dates of manufacture for jewelry makers. Method two requires researching patent numbers. Method three requires reviewing vintage advertisements for like or similar jewelry. Method four, probably the most challenging method of all, requires researching the sometimes subtle changes in jewelry styles and trends over the years. Method five, which concerns dating jewelry using books and the Internet, also requires effort. It requires obtaining a useful library of reference books and developing the skills to do research online. Hopefully the following sections will help with this task.

## REFERENCE BOOKS

Serious jewelry collectors must acquire a library of reference books. Some costume jewelry books are beautiful coffee-table-style books with colorful pictures of vintage jewelry but are not particularly useful when trying to date a specific piece of costume jewelry. The following costume jewelry books contain wonderful photographs of jewelry but are much more than pretty books. Each volume contains well-researched information about jewelry makers and the history of costume jewelry. I recommend these treasures to anyone interested in this subject. Shamelessly, of course, I'm including my first book, *Collecting Costume Jewelry 101: The Basics of Starting, Building & Upgrading*, in this list. This is a partial list designed to provide information on dating jewelry. There are many, many other wonderful costume jewelry reference books available.

*American Costume Jewelry 1935 – 1950* by Carla Ginelli Brunialti and Roberto Brunialti. Edizioni Gabriele Mazzotta, Foro Buonaparte 52-201121 Milano, 1997. This book is written in Italian; however, the patent information and photographs of the patented jewelry are easy to decipher. This book is not available in bookstores, but can be ordered online for a cost of $80.00 to $85.00. (Do a search online to find a dealer.)

*A Tribute to American Costume Jewelry 1935 – 1950* by Carla Ginelli Brunialti and Roberto Brunialti. Publishing project by EDITA Milan, January 2002. This is an English language version of the above Italian Brunialti book, with different pictures and patents. A serious collector must own both of these volumes. This book is not available in bookstores, but can be ordered online for a cost of $80.00 to $85.00.

*Answers to Questions about Old Jewelry 1840 – 1950*, 3rd edition, by Jeanenne Bell. Florence, AL: Books Americana, Inc., 1992.

*Collecting Costume Jewelry 101: The Basics of Starting, Building & Upgrading* by Julia C. Carroll. Paducah, KY: Collector Books, 2004.

*How to Be a Jewelry Detective* by Jeannenne Bell. Shawnee, KS: A.D. Publishing, 2000.

*Inside the Jewelry Box* by Ann Mitchell Pitman. Paducah, KY: Collector Books, 2004.

*Miriam Haskell Jewelry* by Cathy Gordon and Sheila Pamfiloff. Atglen, PA: Schiffer Publishing, Ltd., 2004.

*Popular Jewelry 1840 – 1940* by Roseann Ettinger. Atglen, PA: Schiffer Publishing Ltd., 1997.

*Popular Jewelry of the '60s, '70s & '80s* by Roseann Ettinger. Atglen, PA: Schiffer Publishing, Ltd., 1997.

*Warman's Jewelry* (any edition) by Christie Romero. Iola, WI: Krause Publications, 1998.

Volume 1 and volume 2 of *Signed Beauties of Costume Jewelry* by Marcia "Sparkles" Brown. Paducah, KY: Collector Books, 2002 (vol. 1) and 2004 (vol. 2).

## ONLINE RESEARCH

The Internet provides a plentitude of information about costume jewelry. Some of this information is accurate and useful. Some of it is not. My recommendation is to enjoy the Internet, do research on the Internet, but double or triple check the accuracy of any information.

For example, when I was researching information about Napier jewelry, several Internet sites stated with certainty that Napier was no longer in business. This idea didn't make sense to me, because stores in my local mall were actively selling Napier products. Since I doubted the veracity of this information, I decided to try to verify the information from a reliable source. Ironically, I used the Internet to locate a phone number for the distributor of Napier jewelry. One phone call settled the matter. Napier jewelry is alive and well.

With these words of caution in mind, use the Internet to establish dates for costume jewelry in three ways:

1. Look for vintage advertisements. The best way to find ads is to do a search on a specific maker. For

example, search for "Trifari vintage advertisement" or "Trifari vintage ad."

2. Locate reliable websites with information that is well researched and accurate. The book *Inside the Jewelry Box* by Anne Mitchell Pitman describes many interesting and reliable websites.

3. If you are trying to date a specific piece of jewelry, search eBay auctions or online malls for similar items. Read the descriptions. Some sellers are knowledgeable and provide accurate information about items, including patent information. Verify any questionable information obtained in this way.

## METHOD SIX: *Provenance*

Provenance is defined as "origin or source." Dating jewelry by provenance is to date jewelry from information about the jewelry obtained from the original owner. Many women who were adults in the 1940s and 1950s are still living. These ladies are wonderful sources of information about costume jewelry, including information about when a specific piece was purchased,

**Figure 51.** Mid-1950s Opalite earrings. These fiery 1¼" earrings, in their original Opalite box, are set in ½₀-12 kt. gold fill. $75.00 – 100.00. Courtesy of Esta Pratt.

**Figure 50.** Mid-1950s Iris Floating Opals necklace and earrings in original box. This Iris Floating Opals necklace and earrings set is sterling silver. The screw-back-style earrings measure 1", and the pendant is approximately 20" in length. In the right light, the opal chips swimming in oil exhibit an interesting pink-opal inner fire. $150.00 – 175.00 set. Courtesy of Esta Pratt.

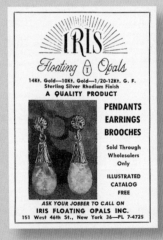

**Figure 52.** 1954 Iris Floating Opal advertisement. This interesting advertisement is from the 1954 *Jewelers' Buyers Guide*. The advertisement reads, "Iris Floating Opals 14Kt. Gold — 10Kt. Gold — ½₀-12Kt. G. F. Sterling Silver Rhodium Finish. A Quality Product. Pendants. Earrings. Brooches. Sold Through Wholesalers Only." This advertisement is intended to encourage retailers to stock Iris Floating Opals jewelry in retail stores.

what styles were popular at a given time, and how the different styles of jewelry were worn. To help illustrate this idea, I want to share with you a true story.

I regularly attend a local flea market and talk to many different people about jewelry. Over time, I met a wonderful lady who remembers purchasing and wearing jewelry in the 1950s. One day she asked me if I knew where she could get her floating opal necklace repaired. I had no advice since, until that moment, I had never heard of "floating" opal jewelry.

Later that summer, she permitted me to photograph her floating opal jewelry. Figures 50 and 51 are photographs of this interesting jewelry. Popular in the 1950s, floating opal jewelry consists of bits of real opals suspended in oil and encased in clear glass. Often teardrop shaped, these clear glass containers were then incorporated into attractive jewelry designs done in 14 kt. gold, 10 kt. gold, ⅟₂₀-12 kt. gold fill, sterling silver, or a rhodium finish. Iris Floating Opals Inc. was one of the largest producers of this unique jewelry. The advertisement in Figure 52 from the *1954 Jewelers' Buyers Guide* illustrates the popularity of this style of jewelry.

Floating opal jewelry straddles the line between fine jewelry and costume jewelry. The opal chips are real opals, but the jewelry is often made with non-precious metals, keeping it within the realm of costume jewelry. No matter how it is classified, the jewelry is interesting, and the popularity of "floating" opal jewelry in the mid-1950s is firmly established from the provenance provided to me by this wonderful lady. Interestingly, the floating opal jewelry is reminiscent of the confetti Lucite costume jewelry also popular in the 1950s. Instead of bits of opal stones in oil, confetti Lucite jewelry consists of tiny flakes of color, resembling confetti, embedded in clear Lucite. Earlier in this chapter, Figure 43 showed an example of a colorful confetti Lucite bracelet.

Some of the information in the captions of the jewelry shown in the following chapters comes from provenance. Dating costume jewelry in this way is fun. The right conversation is like a little time machine taking me back to an era when the vintage jewelry I treasure was considered to be contemporary, modern, trendy, and popular.

# A FEW WORDS ABOUT THIS BOOK AND ITS CHARTS

## ABOUT THIS BOOK

The tenets set forth in this book for dating costume jewelry are guidelines only. In many cases, the dating information is based on suppositions about the dating process. For example, after 1955, many makers opted to copyright rather than patent jewelry designs. This is a supposition, based on the low number of design patents issued for costume jewelry designs after this date. This supposition is certainly not always true. The copyright symbol was used before 1955, and costume jewelry designs (especially Coro designs) were patented after that date. However, this supposition is true often enough to be a useful tool when dating costume jewelry. It is a guideline proposed to help the sometimes subjective process of dating costume jewelry. The process of dating jewelry presented in this book is accurate only to the extent that these suppositions are true. In other words, these guidelines are as accurate as possible based on the information about costume jewelry available at the time of the writing.

## ABOUT THE DESIGN PATENT NUMBER CHARTS IN THIS BOOK

The design patent number charts in this book reflect many of the designs patented by each maker, but certainly not all. For example, to preserve book space, many earring patents have been eliminated. However, it is estimated that over 80 percent of the design patent numbers issued from 1935 to 1954 are included in this volume.

The jewelry types listed in the design patent number charts have sometimes been modified from the original patents. For example, the original patents may describe a brooch as a "pin," "clip," "brooch," "brooch clip," "separable brooch," and so forth. To simplify and standardize the charts in this book, the jewelry types shown on the original patents have been adjusted to one of the following types: brooch, necklace, bracelet, earring, Duette, clipmate, or chatelaine.

Sometimes the correct jewelry type for a piece is not accurately listed on the patent. For example, Duette-style brooches are often listed on the original patents as "separable brooches," but not always. Occasionally, the patent drawing clearly indicates a Duette-style design, but the jewelry type listed on the patent describes the piece as a brooch or clip. The design patent number charts in this book reflect the jewelry type shown in the illustration and, in this case, list the piece as a Duette.

Third, the design patent number charts in this book list both the designer and the maker of the piece. Sometimes the original patent provides this information. Often the patent only lists the designer. For organizational purposes, design patents issued to designers known to have worked for a particular maker are listed in the charts with that maker. For example, David Mir is a freelance designer known to have worked for Trifari from 1941 to 1942. In 1941, he also created designs for Leo Glass. Sometimes the David Mir patents indicate the correct maker and sometimes the patents do not. When known, the David Mir designs are assigned to Leo Glass. However, in this book, since David Mir is most famous for his Trifari designs, the designs not specifically assigned to any maker are assigned to Trifari.

Brief descriptions are provided for each patent on the design patent number chart. When possible, these descriptions provide enough information to identify a piece. For example, a brief description for a brooch might be "key." This description is sufficient for the reader to know the corresponding patent number is for a brooch in the shape of a key.

Sometimes, the brief description delineates a specific design feature. For example, a brief description for

a brooch might be "floral with five-pointed rhinestone flower stones." This description defines a specific design trait of the brooch — the five-pointed flower-shaped rhinestones.

When appropriate, the brief description will lead the reader to other items from the same jewelry group. For example, the description for the "floral with five-pointed rhinestone flower stones" brooch might be "Floral with five-pointed rhinestone flower stones (See 153026 for another rhinestone flower piece)." The design patent number listed in the description will lead the reader to another piece with the same "five-pointed rhinestone flower stones" trait. Jewelry was often designed in groups. By following this process, the reader can find many of the patented jewelry designs with the same design elements. When the patent drawing itself is shown, its listing is highlighted.

Note: When the description simply states "abstract," then no definable trait could be identified to clearly differentiate the design from other like pieces. There is no alternative but to view the original patent illustrations for these items.

Finally, the design patent number charts in this book are limited to the years 1935 through 1954. Design patents continued to be issued, mostly for Coro, until 1956 and in a limited way after that. While useful for dating 1955 and 1956 Coro jewelry, these patents have been eliminated from this book. To meet the overall goal of dating costume jewelry designs through 1980, it was more important to include as many vintage advertisements as possible.

# CHAPTER 2

# CORO AND VENDÔME
## *Jewelry*

### CORO
#### (1901 – 1979 in the U.S.A, 1998 in Canada)

"Corocraft" (also "Coro Craft") and "Vendôme" are commonly found Coro signatures. The Corocraft designs are included in the Coro gallery. The Vendôme jewelry is grouped together at the end.

Most makers began to copyright rather than patent designs by 1955. This is a general rule for dating jewelry that I follow when assigning dates to the jewelry in this book. However, Coro continued to patent designs through 1956 and sporadically after that. Coro seemed to go through a transitional period in 1955 and 1956. Some designs are patented. Some are copyrighted. The jewelry in this book is dated assuming that the copyright symbol was added to the signature by 1955. Note: One set featured in this section is signed "Coro" with the copyright symbol and "Pat. Pend." When I am aware of this kind of aberration to the general rule, it is mentioned in the caption.

CORO AND VENDÔME JEWELRY

101368

107111

107115

110141

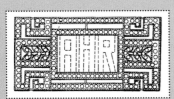

108468

| Design Patent Number | Date Issued | Designer | Jewelry Type | Brief Description |
|---|---|---|---|---|
| 101368 | 9/29/1936 | Adolph Katz | Brooch | Movie camera |
| 104925 | 6/15/1937 | Adolph Katz | Brooch | Peacock |
| 105112 | 6/29/1937 | Adolph Katz | Brooch | Bows |
| 107110 | 11/23/1937 | Adolph Katz | Brooch | Geometric |
| 107111 | 11/23/1937 | Adolph Katz | Brooch | Geometric floral |
| 107112 | 11/23/1937 | Adolph Katz | Brooch | Geometric |
| 107113 | 11/23/1937 | Adolph Katz | Brooch | Geometric |
| 107114 | 11/23/1937 | Adolph Katz | Brooch | Geometric |
| 107115 | 11/23/1937 | Adolph Katz | Brooch | Geometric floral |
| 107116 | 11/23/1937 | Adolph Katz | Brooch | Geometric |
| 107117 | 11/23/1937 | Adolph Katz | Brooch | Geometric |
| 107118 | 11/23/1937 | Adolph Katz | Brooch | Geometric |
| 107119 | 11/23/1937 | Adolph Katz | Brooch | Geometric |
| 107120 | 11/23/1937 | Adolph Katz | Brooch | Geometric |
| 107121 | 11/23/1937 | Adolph Katz | Brooch | Geometric |
| 107648 | 12/28/1937 | Adolph Katz | Brooch | Spider |
| 107776 | 1/4/1938 | Adolph Katz | Brooch | Geometric |
| 108461 | 2/15/1938 | Gene Verrecchio | Brooch | Initials |
| 108462 | 2/15/1938 | Gene Verrecchio | Brooch | Initials |
| 108463 | 2/15/1938 | Gene Verrecchio | Brooch | Initials |
| 108464 | 2/15/1938 | Gene Verrecchio | Brooch | Initials |
| 108465 | 2/15/1938 | Gene Verrecchio | Brooch | Initials |
| 108466 | 2/15/1938 | Gene Verrecchio | Brooch | Initials |
| 108467 | 2/15/1938 | Gene Verrecchio | Brooch | Initials |
| 108468 | 2/15/1938 | Gene Verrecchio | Brooch | Initials |
| 108469 | 2/15/1938 | Gene Verrecchio | Brooch | Initials |
| 108470 | 2/15/1938 | Gene Verrecchio | Brooch | Initials |
| 108471 | 2/15/1938 | Gene Verrecchio | Brooch | Initials |
| 110141 | 6/21/1938 | Robert Geissmann | Brooch | Owl |
| 110142 | 6/21/1938 | Robert Geissmann | Brooch | Flying goose |
| 110143 | 6/21/1938 | Robert Geissmann | Brooch | Parrot on a branch |

**1938 Coro sterling initial brooch.** Much of the late 1930s jewelry is made in pot metal; however, sterling initial brooches, like this example, were popular in the late 1930s. This 2" x 1" initial brooch is signed "Coro Sterling." It is design patent number 108468 issued February 15, 1938, to Gene Verrecchio for Coro. The initials of the customer, in this case MFH, were added at the time of purchase. $50.00 – 70.00.

| | | | | |
|---|---|---|---|---|
| 110296 | 6/28/1938 | Gene Verrecchio | Brooch | Quivering Camellias |
| 110469 | 7/12/1938 | Gene Verrecchio | Brooch | Vase of flowers in frame |
| 111087 | 8/30/1938 | Oscar Placco | Duette | Geometric |
| 112148 | 11/15/1938 | Adolph Katz | Brooch | Floral decoration on double picture locket |
| 112153 | 11/15/1938 | Gene Verrecchio | Brooch | Frame |
| 112154 | 11/15/1938 | Gene Verrecchio | Brooch | Frame |
| 112155 | 11/15/1938 | Gene Verrecchio | Brooch | Frame |
| 112156 | 11/15/1938 | Gene Verrecchio | Brooch | Frame |
| 112157 | 11/15/1938 | Gene Verrecchio | Brooch | Frame |
| 112158 | 11/15/1938 | Gene Verrecchio | Brooch | Frame |
| 112159 | 11/15/1938 | Gene Verrecchio | Brooch | Frame |
| 112160 | 11/15/1938 | Gene Verrecchio | Brooch | Frame |
| 112161 | 11/15/1938 | Gene Verrecchio | Brooch | Frame |
| 112162 | 11/15/1938 | Gene Verrecchio | Brooch | Frame |
| 112163 | 11/15/1938 | Gene Verrecchio | Brooch | Frame |
| 113766 | 3/14/1939 | Henry Rosenblatt | Brooch | Cat |
| 114219 | 4/11/1939 | Adolph Katz | Brooch | Cowboy (See 114220 for cowgirl.) |
| 114220 | 4/11/1939 | Adolph Katz | Brooch | Cowgirl (See 114219 for cowboy.) |
| 114221 | 4/11/1939 | Adolph Katz | Brooch | Frog |
| 114282 | 4/11/1939 | Adolph Katz | Brooch | Prince (See 114283 for princess.) |
| 114283 | 4/11/1939 | Adolph Katz | Brooch | Princess (See 114282 for prince.) |
| 114483 | 4/25/1939 | Adolph Katz | Brooch | Storybook character holding a bell |
| 114484 | 4/25/1939 | Adolph Katz | Brooch | Juliet on a balcony (See 114485 for Romeo brooch.) |
| 114485 | 4/25/1939 | Adolph Katz | Brooch | Romeo kneeling (See 114484 for Juliet brooch.) |
| 114486 | 4/25/1939 | Adolph Katz | Brooch | Storybook character in pointed hat |
| 115043 | 5/30/1939 | Adolph Katz | Brooch | Tulips |
| 115266 | 6/13/1939 | Adolph Katz | Brooch | Bell flowers |
| 115852 | 7/25/1939 | Adolph Katz | Brooch | Double flower |
| 116095 | 8/8/1939 | Adolph Katz | Brooch | Floral with enameled leaves and berries (See 116096 for similar brooch.) |
| 116233 | 8/22/1939 | Adolph Katz | Brooch | Floral with five rhine-stone dangles |
| 116288 | 8/22/1939 | Adolph Katz | Bracelet | Camellia bracelet |
| 116289 | 8/22/1939 | Adolph Katz | Brooch | Floral |

110296

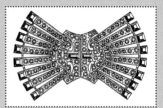

111087

114219

114282

114484

115043

CORO AND VENDÔME JEWELRY

116095

118121

116478

117802

118129

| 116476 | 9/5/1939 | Adolph Katz | Bracelet | Floral |
|--------|----------|-------------|----------|--------|
| 116477 | 9/5/1939 | Adolph Katz | Brooch | Double flower |
| 116478 | 9/5/1939 | Adolph Katz | Brooch | Camellias |
| 116607 | 9/12/1939 | Adolph Katz | Brooch | Double flower |
| 116711 | 9/19/1939 | Adolph Katz | Brooch | LS floral |
| 116712 | 9/19/1939 | Adolph Katz | Brooch | Floral |
| 117802 | 11/28/1939 | Gene Verrecchio | Brooch | Floral |
| 118121 | 12/19/1939 | Adolph Katz | Brooch | Flower and bud (See 118122 for matching pendant.) |
| 118122 | 12/19/1939 | Adolph Katz | Necklace | Flower and bud (See 118121 for matching brooch.) |
| 118129 | 12/19/1939 | Charles E. Pauzat | Brooch | Flower with sliced pie pavé center (See 118130 for double flower version.) |
| 118130 | 12/19/1939 | Charles E. Pauzat | Brooch | Double flower with sliced pie pavé center (See 118129 for single flower version.) |

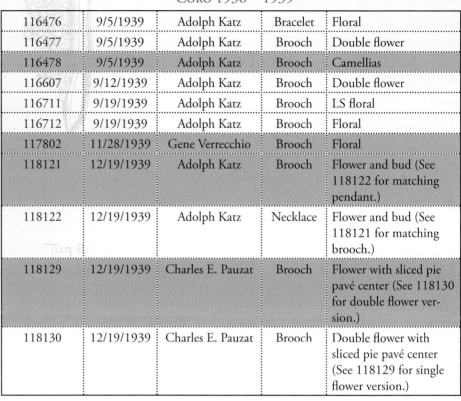

**1939 Quivering Camellias Duette.** One of the most famous Duettes designed by Adolph Katz of Coro is the Quivering Camellias Duette. It is design patent number 116478 issued September 5, 1939, to Adolph Katz for Coro. This Duette features bell-shaped flowers with a rhinestone flower center mounted on a spring, so it quivers when worn. The photograph shows half of this Duette separated from the frame. Each clip measures 1½". In good condition, this Duette is worth $300.00 – 350.00.

**1939 Coro red enameled clip.** This ravishing red clip is only 2¼" long, but it is packed with style and mystery. First, although unsigned, this clip is a match for patent number 117802 issued November 28, 1939, to Adolph Katz of Coro. Next, the center of the flower is on a little spring, so that it trembles when worn. In addition, the petals are decorated with red enamel, a typical trait of the late 1930s and early 1940s. Finally, each petal features invisibly set square-cut rhinestones. Despite all of the above 1939 traits, the condition of the above brooch is too good, indicating this may be a newer piece made from the old 1939 mold, or an old brooch that has been beautifully restored. As found, the value is $45.00 – 60.00. If proven to be an authentic 1939 clip, in mint condition, the value is much higher: $85.00 – 125.00. From the collection of Debi Reece.

# Coro 1940

| Design Patent Number | Date Issued | Designer | Jewelry Type | Brief Description |
|---|---|---|---|---|
| 118565 | 1/16/1940 | Oscar Placco | Brooch | Floral |
| 119306 | 3/5/1940 | Adolph Katz | Brooch | Dutch woman |
| 119307 | 3/5/1940 | Adolph Katz | Brooch | Dutch man |
| 119308 | 3/5/1940 | Adolph Katz | Brooch | Floral |
| 119309 | 3/5/1940 | Adolph Katz | Brooch | Floral |
| 119756 | 4/2/1940 | Adolph Katz | Chatelaine | Cat and bird |
| 119830 | 4/2/1940 | Carol McDonald | Brooch | Man with balloons |
| 120124 | 4/23/1940 | Adolph Katz | Brooch | Peacock |
| 120381 | 5/7/1940 | Adolph Katz | Brooch | Hand holding flowers |
| 120925 | 6/4/1940 | Marion Weeber | Brooch | Band hat |
| 120942 | 6/4/1940 | Charles E. Pauzat | Brooch | Floral |
| 120979 | 6/11/1940 | Gene Verrecchio | Brooch | Double flower trembler |
| 121109 | 6/18/1940 | Gene Verrecchio | Brooch | Marcasite initial brooch |
| 121208 | 6/25/1940 | Adolph Katz | Bracelet | Flower and leaf charm |
| 121209 | 6/25/1940 | Adolph Katz | Brooch | Dragonfly |
| 121349 | 7/2/1940 | Adolph Katz | Brooch | Cameo |
| 121487 | 7/16/1940 | Gene Verrecchio | Brooch | Marcasite initial brooch |
| 121735 | 7/30/1940 | Gene Verrecchio | Brooch | Floral |
| 121840 | 8/6/1940 | Adolph Katz | Brooch | Floral |
| 122195 | 8/27/1940 | Adolph Katz | Brooch | Flowerpot with ribbon |
| 122196 | 8/27/1940 | Adolph Katz | Brooch | Floral |
| 122197 | 8/27/1940 | Adolph Katz | Brooch | Floral |
| 122198 | 8/27/1940 | Adolph Katz | Brooch | Floral |
| 122199 | 8/27/1940 | Adolph Katz | Brooch | Floral |
| 122436 | 9/3/1940 | Adolph Katz | Brooch | Double flower |
| 122437 | 9/10/1940 | Adolph Katz | Brooch | Rose |
| 122438 | 9/10/1940 | Adolph Katz | Brooch | Double floral |
| 122439 | 9/10/1940 | Adolph Katz | Brooch | Floral |
| 122440 | 9/10/1940 | Adolph Katz | Brooch | Floral |
| 122441 | 9/10/1940 | Adolph Katz | Brooch | Floral |
| 122442 | 9/10/1940 | Adolph Katz | Brooch | Floral |
| 122443 | 9/10/1940 | Adolph Katz | Brooch | Patriotic ribbons |
| 122485 | 9/10/1940 | Adolph Katz | Duette | Floral |
| 122550 | 9/10/1940 | Adolph Katz | Brooch | Floral |
| 122601 | 9/17/1940 | Adolph Katz | Bracelet | Geometric decorations on strap bracelet |
| 122602 | 9/17/1940 | Adolph Katz | Brooch | Floral, possibly a trembler |
| 122603 | 9/17/1940 | Adolph Katz | Duette | Floral, possibly a trembler |
| 122604 | 9/17/1940 | Adolph Katz | Duette | Floral, possibly a trembler |
| 122605 | 9/17/1940 | Adolph Katz | Brooch | Floral |

118565

120979

122199

122441

122604

123165

123166     123280

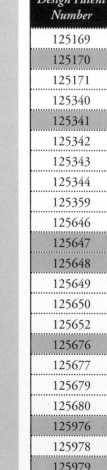

123655

| 122614 | 9/17/1940 | Adolph Katz | Brooch | Floral |
|---|---|---|---|---|
| 123165 | 10/22/1940 | Adolph Katz | Duette | Floral |
| 123166 | 10/22/1940 | Adolph Katz | Brooch | Floral with round cabochon stones (See 123210 for matching necklace.) |
| 123210 | 10/22/1940 | Adolph Katz | Necklace | Floral |
| 123280 | 10/29/1940 | Gene Verrecchio | Duette | Trembling floral |
| 123655 | 11/19/1940 | Adolph Katz | Brooch | Floral |
| 124125 | 12/17/1940 | Marion Weeber | Brooch | Airplane and parachute |

# Coro 1941

125170

125341

125647

| Design Patent Number | Date Issued | Designer | Jewelry Type | Brief Description |
|---|---|---|---|---|
| 125169 | 2/11/1941 | Gene Verrecchio | Brooch | Floral |
| 125170 | 2/11/1941 | Gene Verrecchio | Brooch | Basket |
| 125171 | 2/11/1941 | Gene Verrecchio | Brooch | Double floral |
| 125340 | 2/18/1941 | Adolph Katz | Brooch | Floral |
| 125341 | 2/18/1941 | Adolph Katz | Brooch | Floral |
| 125342 | 2/18/1941 | Adolph Katz | Brooch | Floral |
| 125343 | 2/18/1941 | Adolph Katz | Brooch | Floral |
| 125344 | 2/18/1941 | Adolph Katz | Brooch | Floral |
| 125359 | 2/18/1941 | Gene Verrecchio | Necklace | Bows and cabochons |
| 125646 | 3/4/1941 | Gene Verrecchio | Brooch | Floral |
| 125647 | 3/4/1941 | Gene Verrecchio | Brooch | Floral |
| 125648 | 3/4/1941 | Gene Verrecchio | Brooch | Floral |
| 125649 | 3/4/1941 | Gene Verrecchio | Brooch | Floral |
| 125650 | 3/4/1941 | Gene Verrecchio | Brooch | Bird |
| 125652 | 3/4/1941 | Gene Verrecchio | Brooch | Flying duck |
| 125676 | 3/4/1941 | Gene Verrecchio | Brooch | Floral |
| 125677 | 3/4/1941 | Gene Verrecchio | Brooch | Floral |
| 125679 | 3/4/1941 | Gene Verrecchio | Brooch | Floral |
| 125680 | 3/4/1941 | Gene Verrecchio | Brooch | Floral |
| 125976 | 3/18/1941 | Gene Verrecchio | Chatelaine | Male and female birds |
| 125978 | 3/18/1941 | Gene Verrecchio | Necklace | Stylized floral |
| 125979 | 3/18/1941 | Gene Verrecchio | Brooch | Basket |

| 125980 | 3/18/1941 | Gene Verrecchio | Brooch | Floral |
|--------|-----------|-----------------|--------|--------|
| 125981 | 3/18/1941 | Gene Verrecchio | Brooch | Floral |
| 125982 | 3/18/1941 | Gene Verrecchio | Brooch | Floral |
| 125983 | 3/18/1941 | Gene Verrecchio | Brooch | Floral |
| 125984 | 3/18/1941 | Gene Verrecchio | Brooch | Floral |
| 125985 | 3/18/1941 | Gene Verrecchio | Brooch | Floral |
| 125986 | 3/18/1941 | Gene Verrecchio | Brooch | Floral |
| 125987 | 3/18/1941 | Gene Verrecchio | Brooch | Floral |
| 126490 | 4/8/1941 | Adolph Katz | Duette | Birds |

125648

125676

125976

**1941 unmarked Coro Mr. and Mrs. Bird chatelaine.** Although unmarked, this cute chatelaine matches patent number 125976 issued March 18, 1941, to Gene Verrecchio for Coro. Each bird measures 2" x 1" and features a sapphire blue cabochon belly. $90.00 – 120.00. From the collection of Debi Reece.

125979

**1941 Coro bird clips.** These two 3½" x 2" unsigned clips are part of a Coro Duette that would only have been signed on the Duette frame. The design of these clips is similar to design patent number 126490 issued April 8, 1941, to Adolph Katz for Coro. The wear on the metal, the size of the clips, and the colorful enamel are all consistent with clips from this era. Without the frame, $75.00 – 100.00. With the frame, $150.00 – 200.00.

125984

**1941 Coro unsigned bird brooches.** All three of these bird brooches strongly resemble design patent number 126490 issued April 8, 1941, to Adolph Katz of Coro. This design patent is for a Duette, but once issued, Coro could have produced both pins and clips in various sizes using the same patented design. The first bird is a pin, not a clip, and measures 3½" long. The middle bird is also a pin, and measures 3¼". The last, 3⅛" bird is a clip, and it is half of a Duette. Produced in the early 1940s, these bird brooches are plentiful in the collectible market today. $25.00 – 35.00 each. From the collection of Debi Reece.

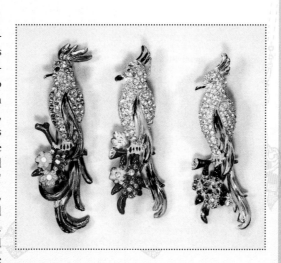

126490

126630

127648

129437

127909

129433

CORO AND VENDÔME JEWELRY

| 126630 | 4/15/1941 | Sidney Pearl | Brooch | Floral |
|---|---|---|---|---|
| 126922 | 4/29/1941 | Gene Verrecchio | Brooch | Female duck with cane and hat |
| 126923 | 4/29/1941 | Gene Verrecchio | Brooch | Family of trucks chatelaine |
| 127445 | 5/27/1941 | Charles E. Pauzat | Brooch | Double sea horses |
| 127446 | 5/27/1941 | Gene Verrecchio | Chatelaine | Bagpipe player and dancer |
| 127648 | 6/3/1941 | Gene Verrecchio | Brooch | Birdhouse locket dangling from bird's mouth |
| 127746 | 6/10/1941 | Adolph Katz | Brooch | Bird in rectangular frame |
| 127747 | 6/10/1941 | Adolph Katz | Brooch | Bird in oval frame |
| 127909 | 6/24/1941 | Adolph Katz | Brooch | Two songbirds |
| 128822 | 8/12/1941 | Adolph Katz | Brooch | Large enameled parrot |
| 128823 | 8/12/1941 | Adolph Katz | Duette | Pheasants |
| 128824 | 8/12/1941 | Adolph Katz | Brooch | Barrel with flowers |
| 129427 | 9/9/1941 | Adolph Katz | Duette | Floral |
| 129428 | 9/9/1941 | Adolph Katz | Duette | Floral |
| 129429 | 9/9/1941 | Adolph Katz | Duette | Floral |
| 129430 | 9/9/1941 | Adolph Katz | Brooch | Floral |
| 129431 | 9/9/1941 | Adolph Katz | Brooch | Floral |
| 129432 | 9/9/1941 | Adolph Katz | Brooch | Floral |
| 129433 | 9/9/1941 | Adolph Katz | Brooch | Bird of paradise |
| 129434 | 9/9/1941 | Adolph Katz | Brooch | Floral |
| 129435 | 9/9/1941 | Adolph Katz | Brooch | Floral lily |
| 129436 | 9/9/1941 | Adolph Katz | Brooch | Floral |
| 129437 | 9/9/1941 | Adolph Katz | Duette | Owls |
| 129438 | 9/9/1941 | Adolph Katz | Brooch | Door knocker in form of a face or mask |
| 129560 | 9/16/1941 | Gene Verrecchio | Brooch | Floral |
| 129611 | 9/23/1941 | Gene Verrecchio | Brooch | Art Deco abstract |
| 130144 | 10/28/1941 | Gene Verrecchio | Duette | Love birds in a heart |
| 130726 | 12/9/1941 | Adolph Katz | Brooch | Stylized bow |
| 130727 | 12/9/1941 | Adolph Katz | Brooch | Stylized bow |
| 130728 | 12/9/1941 | Adolph Katz | Brooch | Bird |
| 130836 | 12/23/1941 | Lester Gaba | Brooch | "Emblem of the Americas" |
| 133479 | 8/18/1941 | Adolph Katz | Duette | Birds, blue jay |

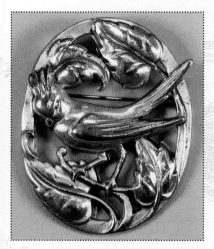

127747

**1941 Coro Norseland sterling brooch.** This highly detailed 2¼" x 2" sterling silver brooch is design patent number 127747 issued June 10, 1941, to Adolph Katz for Coro. At this time, Coro produced several similar brooches. This example is signed "Norseland by Coro Sterling Reg. U.S. Pat. Off." $75.00 – 125.00.

128822

**1941 Coro (reissue?) bird clip.** Wow, this big bird measures 5" x 1¾"! While the design is similar to design patent number 128822 issued August 12, 1941, to Adolph Katz for Coro, there are some differences. The patent shows the crown feathers, two tail feathers, and the tree branch all decorated with rhinestones. In addition, the leaves in the patent picture are surrounded by rhinestones. The bird in the photograph does not have any of these elements. Adding to the mystery, the bird in the photograph is in *mint* condition. It is rare to find a 1941 piece in totally unused condition. In my opinion, this bird clip is too good to be true and is a later version of the 1941 patented bird. It is difficult to date this Coro mystery piece. Value as a recent piece (within the last 10 years), $55.00 – 65.00. If established as an original 1941 Coro clip, the value is $175.00 – 300.00.

129438

130144

130728

**1941 Coro Emblem of the Americas brooch.** This 2½" x 2¼" brooch is called the Emblem of the Americas. It is design patent number 130836 issued December 23, 1941, to Lester Gaba for Coro. The 21 flags represent the 21 Republics in the Western Hemisphere. The words *Amigos Siempre* on the brooch mean "Friends Forever." $75.00 – 150.00.

130836

CORO AND VENDÔME JEWELRY

131519      131523

131525

131561

131754

131759      131770

CORO AND VENDÔME JEWELRY

| Design Patent Number | Date Issued | Designer | Jewelry Type | Brief Description |
|---|---|---|---|---|
| 131105 | 1/13/1942 | Adolph Katz | Brooch | Turtle |
| 131106 | 1/13/1942 | Adolph Katz | Brooch | Floral |
| 131107 | 1/13/1942 | Adolph Katz | Brooch | Floral |
| 131108 | 1/13/1942 | Adolph Katz | Brooch | Floral |
| 131110 | 1/13/1942 | Gene Verrecchio | Brooch | Floral |
| 131262 | 1/27/1942 | Adolph Katz | Brooch | Stylized floral |
| 131515 | 3/10/1942 | Adolph Katz | Brooch | Floral |
| 131516 | 3/10/1942 | Adolph Katz | Brooch | Floral |
| 131517 | 3/10/1942 | Adolph Katz | Brooch | Floral |
| 131518 | 3/10/1942 | Adolph Katz | Brooch | Floral |
| 131519 | 3/10/1942 | Adolph Katz | Brooch | Floral |
| 131520 | 3/10/1942 | Adolph Katz | Brooch | Leaf |
| 131521 | 3/10/1942 | Adolph Katz | Brooch | Floral |
| 131522 | 3/10/1942 | Adolph Katz | Brooch | Floral |
| 131523 | 3/10/1942 | Adolph Katz | Brooch | Floral tulip |
| 131524 | 3/10/1942 | Adolph Katz | Duette | Floral |
| 131525 | 3/10/1942 | Adolph Katz | Brooch | Male dog with hat, "Mr. Dog" (See 131526 for female.) |
| 131526 | 3/10/1942 | Adolph Katz | Brooch | Female dog with hat, "Mrs. Dog" (See 131525 for male.) |
| 131558 | 3/10/1942 | Adolph Katz | Brooch | Floral |
| 131559 | 3/10/1942 | Adolph Katz | Brooch | Thistle |
| 131560 | 3/10/1942 | Adolph Katz | Brooch | Floral |
| 131561 | 3/10/1942 | Adolph Katz | Brooch | Floral |
| 131732 | 3/24/1942 | Adolph Katz | Brooch | Grasshopper |
| 131733 | 3/24/1942 | Adolph Katz | Brooch | Grasshopper |
| 131734 | 3/24/1942 | Adolph Katz | Brooch | Floral |
| 131735 | 3/24/1942 | Adolph Katz | Brooch | Smoking man |
| 131736 | 3/24/1942 | Adolph Katz | Brooch | Oriental man |
| 131737 | 3/24/1942 | Adolph Katz | Brooch | Floral |
| 131739 | 3/24/1942 | Adolph Katz | Necklace | Lilies (See 131812 for similar brooch.) |
| 131741 | 3/24/1942 | Adolph Katz | Necklace | Cluster of flowers (See 131770 for similar brooch.) |
| 131744 | 3/24/1942 | Adolph Katz | Necklace | Floral |
| 131752 | 3/24/1942 | Adolph Katz | Brooch | Floral |
| 131753 | 3/24/1942 | Adolph Katz | Brooch | Floral |
| 131754 | 3/24/1942 | Adolph Katz | Brooch | Bow |
| 131755 | 3/24/1942 | Adolph Katz | Brooch | Female Apache dancer |
| 131756 | 3/24/1942 | Adolph Katz | Brooch | Flower basket |
| 131757 | 3/24/1942 | Adolph Katz | Brooch | Spider |
| 131758 | 3/24/1942 | Adolph Katz | Brooch | Rooster |

| 131759 | 3/24/1942 | Adolph Katz | Brooch | Indian (See 131760 for another Indian.) |
| 131759 | 3/24/1942 | Adolph Katz | Brooch | Female Indian head (See 131760 for male Indian.) |
| 131760 | 3/24/1942 | Adolph Katz | Brooch | Indian (See 131759 for another Indian.) |
| 131760 | 3/24/1942 | Adolph Katz | Brooch | Male Indian head (See 131759 for female Indian.) |
| 131761 | 3/24/1942 | Adolph Katz | Brooch | Bird |
| 131762 | 3/24/1942 | Adolph Katz | Brooch | Floral |
| 131763 | 3/24/1942 | Adolph Katz | Brooch | Long stemmed lilies (See 131739 for matching necklace.) |
| 131764 | 3/24/1942 | Adolph Katz | Brooch | Floral |
| 131765 | 3/24/1942 | Adolph Katz | Brooch | Bird |
| 131766 | 3/24/1942 | Adolph Katz | Brooch | Bird |
| 131767 | 3/24/1942 | Adolph Katz | Brooch | African man |
| 131768 | 3/24/1942 | Adolph Katz | Brooch | African woman |
| 131769 | 3/24/1942 | Adolph Katz | Brooch | Battleship |
| 131770 | 3/24/1942 | Adolph Katz | Brooch | Long-stemmed cluster of flowers (See 131771 for similar brooch.) |
| 131771 | 3/24/1942 | Adolph Katz | Brooch | Circular cluster of flowers (See 131741 for similar necklace.) |
| 131772 | 3/24/1942 | Adolph Katz | Brooch | Bird |
| 131773 | 3/24/1942 | Adolph Katz | Brooch | Monkey playing the piano |
| 131774 | 3/24/1942 | Adolph Katz | Brooch | Dog playing cello |
| 131775 | 3/24/1942 | Adolph Katz | Brooch | Bird |
| 131776 | 3/24/1942 | Adolph Katz | Brooch | Floral |
| 131779 | 3/24/1942 | Adolph Katz | Necklace | Pansy (See 131877 for matching brooch.) |
| 131811 | 3/31/1942 | Adolph Katz | Brooch | Clock hanging from bow |
| 131812 | 3/31/1942 | Adolph Katz | Brooch | Lilies in oval frame (See 131763 for similar brooch.) |

131772

131779

131859

131959

131812

**Early 1940s Coro sterling lily brooch.** This simple yet elegant 3" x 1½" lily brooch is signed "Sterling Craft by Coro." It features green enameled leaves, vermeil, and rounded Lucite flowers with yellow stamen. Stylistically this piece is similar to design patent number 131812 issued March 31, 1942, to Adolph Katz for Coro, and it dates from the same time. $40.00 – 70.00.

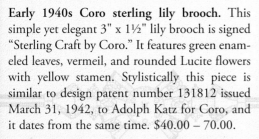

CORO AND VENDÔME JEWELRY

131969

131970

131976

132069

132077

132334

CORO AND VENDÔME JEWELRY

| 131813 | 3/31/1942 | Adolph Katz | Brooch | Flower |
| 131859 | 3/31/1942 | Adolph Katz | Brooch | Long-stemmed blooming flowers (See 131861 for similar brooch.) |
| 131860 | 3/31/1942 | Adolph Katz | Duette | Floral |
| 131861 | 3/31/1942 | Adolph Katz | Brooch | Blooming flowers in vase (See 131859 for similar brooch.) |
| 131862 | 3/31/1942 | Adolph Katz | Brooch | Female with headdress |
| 131877 | 3/31/1942 | Adolph Katz | Brooch | Long-stemmed pansy flowers (See 131779 for matching necklace.) |
| 131878 | 3/31/1942 | Adolph Katz | Brooch | Abstract |
| 131959 | 4/7/1942 | Adolph Katz | Brooch | Asian woman in hat |
| 131960 | 4/7/1942 | Adolph Katz | Brooch | Rooster |
| 131969 | 4/7/1942 | Adolph Katz | Brooch | Flowers in pot |
| 131970 | 4/7/1942 | Adolph Katz | Brooch | Bird |
| 131972 | 4/7/1942 | Adolph Katz | Brooch | Peacock on branch |
| 131973 | 4/7/1942 | Adolph Katz | Brooch | Floral |
| 131976 | 4/7/1942 | Gene Verrecchio | Duette | Floral |
| 132067 | 4/14/1942 | Adolph Katz | Brooch | Floral in oval frame |
| 132068 | 4/14/1942 | Adolph Katz | Brooch | Floral in oval frame |
| 132069 | 4/14/1942 | Adolph Katz | Brooch | Swan in rectangular frame |
| 132077 | 4/14/1942 | Adolph Katz | Brooch | Bird in circular frame |
| 132078 | 4/14/1942 | Adolph Katz | Brooch | Bird in circular frame |
| 132079 | 4/14/1942 | Adolph Katz | Brooch | Floral |
| 132080 | 4/14/1942 | Adolph Katz | Brooch | Floral |
| 132331 | 5/5/1942 | Adolph Katz | Brooch | Floral in oval frame |
| 132332 | 5/5/1942 | Adolph Katz | Brooch | Floral |
| 132333 | 5/5/1942 | Adolph Katz | Brooch | Long-stemmed double flower with round stone centers (See 132527 for similar brooch.) |
| 132334 | 5/5/1942 | Adolph Katz | Brooch | Long-stemmed flower with round stone center (See 132333 for similar brooch.) |
| 132335 | 5/5/1942 | Adolph Katz | Brooch | Birds in heart-shaped frame |
| 132336 | 5/5/1942 | Adolph Katz | Brooch | Mother baby birds in square frame |
| 132337 | 5/5/1942 | Adolph Katz | Brooch | Roosters in square frame |
| 132338 | 5/5/1942 | Adolph Katz | Brooch | Floral |
| 132524 | 5/26/1942 | Adolph Katz | Brooch | Abstract |
| 132527 | 5/26/1942 | Adolph Katz | Brooch | Long-stemmed floral with large round stone center (See 132334 for similar brooch.) |

| 133467 | 8/18/1942 | Adolph Katz | Brooch | Winking owl |
| 133468 | 8/18/1942 | Adolph Katz | Duette | Floral |
| 133469 | 8/18/1942 | Adolph Katz | Brooch | Lizard eating egg |
| 133470 | 8/18/1942 | Adolph Katz | Brooch | Jelly belly fish |
| 133471 | 8/18/1942 | Adolph Katz | Brooch | Floral |
| 133472 | 8/18/1942 | Adolph Katz | Duette | Birds |
| 133473 | 8/18/1942 | Adolph Katz | Brooch | Mexican woman and boy |
| 133474 | 8/18/1942 | Adolph Katz | Brooch | Butterfly |
| 133475 | 8/18/1942 | Adolph Katz | Brooch | Sparrow |
| 133476 | 8/18/1942 | Adolph Katz | Brooch | Bird |
| 133477 | 8/18/1942 | Adolph Katz | Duette | Bees |
| 133478 | 8/18/1942 | Adolph Katz | Brooch | Bird |
| 133668 | 9/1/1942 | Adolph Katz | Brooch | Bird |
| 133728 | 9/8/1942 | Adolph Katz | Brooch | Floral |
| 133729 | 9/8/1942 | Adolph Katz | Brooch | Horse head |
| 133730 | 9/8/1942 | Adolph Katz | Brooch | Bird |
| 133731 | 9/8/1942 | Adolph Katz | Brooch | Ribbons |
| 133732 | 9/8/1942 | Adolph Katz | Brooch | Scorpion |
| 133734 | 9/8/1942 | Adolph Katz | Brooch | Bug |
| 133735 | 9/8/1942 | Adolph Katz | Brooch | Bird |
| 133737 | 9/8/1942 | Adolph Katz | Brooch | Woman with flower basket balanced on head |
| 133738 | 9/8/1942 | Adolph Katz | Brooch | Leaf |
| 133739 | 9/8/1942 | Adolph Katz | Brooch | Butterfly profile |
| 133740 | 9/8/1942 | Adolph Katz | Brooch | Woman playing harp |
| 133741 | 9/8/1942 | Adolph Katz | Brooch | Josephine Baker profile |
| 133742 | 9/8/1942 | Adolph Katz | Brooch | Crane |
| 133743 | 9/8/1942 | Adolph Katz | Brooch | Bug |
| 133744 | 9/8/1942 | Adolph Katz | Brooch | Swan |
| 133745 | 9/8/1942 | Adolph Katz | Duette | Ribbons |
| 133746 | 9/8/1942 | Adolph Katz | Chatelaine | Two owls |
| 133936 | 9/8/1942 | Adolph Katz | Brooch | Bird |

132335

133470

133471

133472

133477

138612

133668

133729

133740

CORO AND VENDÔME JEWELRY

134981

134982

134984

135970

136311

136868

| Design Patent Number | Date Issued | Designer | Jewelry Type | Brief Description |
|---|---|---|---|---|
| 134981 | 2/9/1943 | Adolph Katz | Duette | Sparrows |
| 134982 | 2/9/1943 | Adolph Katz | Brooch | Birds |
| 134983 | 2/9/1943 | Adolph Katz | Brooch | Poodle |
| 134984 | 2/9/1943 | Adolph Katz | Brooch | Floral |
| 135969 | 7/13/1943 | Adolph Katz | Brooch | Bird |
| 135970 | 7/13/1943 | Adolph Katz | Duette | Horses heads |
| 135971 | 7/13/1943 | Adolph Katz | Brooch | Bird Toucan |
| 135972 | 7/13/1943 | Adolph Katz | Brooch | Floral |
| 135973 | 7/13/1943 | Adolph Katz | Brooch | Abstract |
| 136309 | 9/7/1943 | Adolph Katz | Brooch | Floral |
| 136310 | 9/7/1943 | Adolph Katz | Brooch | Bird |
| 136311 | 9/7/1943 | Adolph Katz | Brooch | African woman with headdress |
| 136312 | 9/7/1943 | Adolph Katz | Brooch | Fish |
| 136313 | 9/7/1943 | Adolph Katz | Brooch | Rooster |
| 136505 | 10/12/1943 | Adolph Katz | Brooch | Floral |
| 136506 | 10/12/1943 | Adolph Katz | Brooch | Floral |
| 136507 | 10/12/1943 | Adolph Katz | Brooch | Floral |
| 136832 | 12/14/1943 | Adolph Katz | Brooch | Floral |
| 136833 | 12/14/1943 | Adolph Katz | Brooch | Squirrel |
| 136868 | 12/21/1943 | Adolph Katz | Brooch | LS floral |

**1943 Coro Craft horse heads Duette.** Made in sterling silver, this Duette measures 2" x 2¼". One clip is signed "Sterling" and the other is signed "Coro Craft Sterling." The Duette mechanism is signed "Coro Duette" with the utility patent number 1798867. (Note: the Duette mechanism was patented in 1931; however, Coro continued to produce Duettes marked with the same utility patent number for over 20 years.) These horse head clips feature red rhinestone ears and clear baguette rhinestones outlining the manes and necklines. Black enamel highlights the centers of the foreheads, outlines the eyes, and darkens the nostrils. Red and black enamel decorate the mouths. This is design patent number 135970 issued July 13, 1943, to Adolph Katz for Coro. $125.00 – 200.00. From the collection of Debi Reece.

**1943 Coro horse head pins.** These 2⅛" x ¾" horse pins are only signed "Sterling"; however, they were produced by Coro as variations on the Coro horse heads Duette, design patent number 135970 issued July 13, 1943, to Adolph Katz for Coro. Note the black enamel on the ears and the red enamel on the mouth. This type of enameling is commonly found on jewelry from this time. Interestingly, these pins have green rhinestones instead of traditional clear rhinestones outlining the mane. $30.00 – 50.00 pair. From the collection of Debi Reece.

# CORO 1944

| Design Patent Number | Date Issued | Designer | Jewelry Type | Brief Description |
|---|---|---|---|---|
| 136998 | 1/11/1944 | Adolph Katz | Brooch | Floral |
| 136999 | 1/11/1944 | Adolph Katz | Brooch | Abstract |
| 137000 | 1/11/1944 | Adolph Katz | Brooch | Floral |
| 137001 | 1/11/1944 | Adolph Katz | Brooch | Floral |
| 137002 | 1/11/1944 | Adolph Katz | Brooch | Owl |
| 137003 | 1/11/1944 | Adolph Katz | Brooch | Gazelle |
| 137004 | 1/11/1944 | Adolph Katz | Brooch | Stylized bow |
| 137153 | 1/25/1944 | Adolph Katz | Brooch | Man on horse |
| 137154 | 1/25/1944 | Adolph Katz | Brooch | Floral |
| 137333 | 2/22/1944 | Adolph Katz | Brooch | Cowgirl |
| 137349 | 2/22/1944 | Adolph Katz | Brooch | Stylized bird |
| 137350 | 2/22/1944 | Adolph Katz | Brooch | Jelly belly bird |
| 137351 | 2/22/1944 | Adolph Katz | Brooch | Floral |
| 13/352 | 2/22/1944 | Adolph Katz | Brooch | Bird |
| 137353 | 2/22/1944 | Adolph Katz | Brooch | Bird |
| 137354 | 2/22/1944 | Adolph Katz | Brooch | Bird |
| 137355 | 2/22/1944 | Adolph Katz | Brooch | Floral |
| 137356 | 2/22/1944 | Adolph Katz | Brooch | Jelly belly bird |
| 137461 | 3/14/1944 | Adolph Katz | Brooch | Floral |
| 137511 | 3/21/1944 | Adolph Katz | Brooch | Jelly belly beetle |
| 137681 | 4/18/1944 | Adolph Katz | Brooch | Floral |
| 137682 | 4/18/1944 | Adolph Katz | Brooch | Birds |
| 137683 | 4/18/1944 | Adolph Katz | Brooch | Abstract |
| 137780 | 4/25/1944 | Adolph Katz | Brooch | Bird Willet |
| 137781 | 4/25/1944 | Adolph Katz | Brooch | Stylized bouquet |
| 138605 | 8/22/1944 | Adolph Katz | Brooch | Floral |
| 138612 | 8/22/1944 | Adolph Katz | Brooch Triplet | Three owls that can be worn together or individually |
| 138694 | 9/5/1944 | Adolph Katz | Duette | Floral sunflowers |
| 138958 | 10/3/1944 | Adolph Katz | Duette | Frogs |
| 138959 | 10/3/1944 | Adolph Katz | Brooch | Ribbon |
| 138960 | 10/3/1944 | Adolph Katz | Duette | Owls |
| 138961 | 10/3/1944 | Adolph Katz | Brooch Triplet | Three swallows graduating in size |
| 139072 | 10/10/1944 | Adolph Katz | Brooch | Jelly belly Pegasus horse |
| 139073 | 10/10/1944 | Adolph Katz | Brooch | Jelly belly gazelle |
| 139074 | 10/10/1944 | Adolph Katz | Brooch | Abstract floral |
| 139075 | 10/10/1944 | Adolph Katz | Brooch | Hand |
| 139096 | 10/10/1944 | Adolph Katz | Duette | Floral |
| 139100 | 10/10/1944 | Adolph Katz | Brooch | Crown |
| 139101 | 10/10/1944 | Adolph Katz | Duette | Fish |
| 139102 | 10/10/1944 | Adolph Katz | Duette | Shells |
| 139250 | 10/24/1944 | Adolph Katz | Brooch | Abstract floral |

137001

137004

137153

137356

137682

138612

CORO AND VENDÔME JEWELRY

| 139251 | 10/24/1944 | Adolph Katz | Brooch | Abstract floral |
|---|---|---|---|---|
| 139405 | 11/14/1944 | Adolph Katz | Duette | Angel fish jelly belly |
| 139406 | 11/14/1944 | Adolph Katz | Duette | Floral |
| 139407 | 11/14/1944 | Adolph Katz | Brooch | Floral |
| 139408 | 11/14/1944 | Adolph Katz | Brooch | Floral |
| 139409 | 11/14/1944 | Adolph Katz | Brooch | Floral |
| 139688 | 12/12/1944 | Adolph Katz | Brooch | Abstract floral |
| 139689 | 12/12/1944 | Adolph Katz | Brooch | Ribbon floral |
| 139690 | 12/12/1944 | Adolph Katz | Brooch | Stylized floral |
| 139691 | 12/12/1944 | Adolph Katz | Duette | Stylized floral |
| 139692 | 12/12/1944 | Adolph Katz | Duette | Stylized floral |

138960

139072

139100

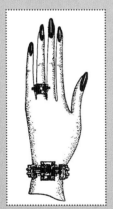

139075

139405

**1944 Corocraft sterling crown pin.** This 1¾" x 1½" imperial crown brooch is signed "Corocraft Sterling." It is design patent number 139100 issued October 10, 1944, to Adolph Katz for Coro. $75.00 – 100.00.

**1944 Coro jelly belly fish clip.** This fish clip is half of a Coro Duette. It matches design patent number 139405 issued November 14, 1944, to Adolph Katz for Coro. The clip measures 1¼" x 1¾" and is only signed "Sterling." (It is not unusual for individual Duette clips, separated from the Coro Duette frame, to be unsigned.) This authentic Coro jelly belly fish clip features a Lucite belly studded with clear rhinestones and has a red rhinestone eye and a blue rhinestone mouth. The Duette, complete with both angel fish clips and the Duette mechanism, is valued at $300.00 – 400.00. The individual clip as shown is valued at $80.00 – 150.00.

CORO AND VENDÔME JEWELRY

# Coro 1945

| Design Patent Number | Date Issued | Designer | Jewelry Type | Brief Description |
|---|---|---|---|---|
| 140014 | 1/16/1945 | Adolph Katz | Duette | Birds |
| 140015 | 1/16/1945 | Adolph Katz | Brooch | Heart |
| 140016 | 1/16/1945 | Adolph Katz | Brooch | Floral |
| 140017 | 1/16/1945 | Adolph Katz | Brooch | Bow with floral center |
| 140018 | 1/16/1945 | Adolph Katz | Brooch | Geometric floral |
| 140019 | 1/16/1945 | Adolph Katz | Brooch | Floral |
| 140020 | 1/16/1945 | Adolph Katz | Brooch | Floral |
| 140143 | 1/30/1945 | Adolph Katz | Brooch | Leaves |
| 140326 | 2/13/1945 | Adolph Katz | Duette | Fighting hens |
| 140602 | 3/20/1945 | Adolph Katz | Duette | Floral |
| 140604 | 3/20/1945 | Adolph Katz | Brooch | Sword |
| 140605 | 3/20/1945 | Adolph Katz | Brooch | Frog |
| 140606 | 3/20/1945 | Adolph Katz | Brooch | Bird |
| 140607 | 3/20/1945 | Adolph Katz | Brooch | Genie with crystal ball |
| 140608 | 3/20/1945 | Adolph Katz | Brooch | Cat jelly belly |
| 140940 | 4/24/1945 | Adolph Katz | Brooch | Floral |
| 140941 | 4/24/1945 | Adolph Katz | Brooch | Floral bow |
| 140942 | 4/24/1945 | Adolph Katz | Brooch | Floral |
| 140943 | 4/24/1945 | Adolph Katz | Brooch | Helmet and axe |
| 140944 | 4/24/1945 | Adolph Katz | Brooch | Sword |
| 140945 | 4/24/1945 | Adolph Katz | Brooch | Jelly belly swan |
| 140946 | 4/24/1945 | Adolph Katz | Brooch | Figural knight with sword and shield |
| 140947 | 4/24/1945 | Adolph Katz | Brooch | Butterfly |
| 140949 | 4/24/1945 | Adolph Katz | Brooch | Leaf hanging from bow |
| 140950 | 4/24/1945 | Adolph Katz | Brooch | Floral leaves |
| 140951 | 4/24/1945 | Adolph Katz | Brooch | Stylized floral |
| 140952 | 4/24/1945 | Adolph Katz | Brooch | Stylized floral |
| 140999 | 4/24/1945 | Adolph Katz | Brooch | Crown (See 142564 for matching bracelet.) |

140607

140608

140941

140945

140999

**1945 Coro jelly belly swan pin.** Swan pins are symbols of everlasting love and devotion, because swans mate for life. Usually swan pins are worn in pairs to celebrate and symbolize this lifelong unity. This beautiful and authentic Coro jelly belly swan pin measures 1½" x 1" and features a clear Lucite belly. It is design patent number 140945 issued April 24, 1945, to Adolph Katz for Coro. $175.00 – 275.00.

CORO AND VENDÔME JEWELRY

141045

141073

141468

141469

141470

141637

| 141045 | 4/24/1945 | Adolph Katz | Brooch | Sword |
| 141073 | 5/1/1945 | Adolph Katz | Duette | Jelly belly turtles |
| 141116 | 5/8/1945 | Adolph Katz | Duette | Birds |
| 141117 | 5/8/1945 | Adolph Katz | Brooch | Lucky wishbone |
| 141118 | 5/8/1945 | Adolph Katz | Duette | Floral |
| 141119 | 5/8/1945 | Adolph Katz | Brooch | Jelly belly rabbit |
| 141120 | 5/8/1945 | Adolph Katz | Duette | Jelly belly birds |
| 141121 | 5/8/1945 | Adolph Katz | Duette | Bow |
| 141180 | 5/8/1945 | Adolph Katz | Duette | Jelly belly birds |
| 141345 | 5/22/1945 | Adolph Katz | Duette | Floral |
| 141346 | 5/22/1945 | Adolph Katz | Duette | Female dancers |
| 141347 | 5/22/1945 | Adolph Katz | Duette | Floral |
| 141348 | 5/22/1945 | Adolph Katz | Duette | Abstract |
| 141383 | 5/29/1945 | Oscar F. Placco | Brooch | Beetle |
| 141384 | 5/29/1945 | Oscar F. Placco | Brooch | Bird |
| 141457 | 6/5/1945 | Adolph Katz | Brooch | Mouse |
| 141467 | 6/5/1945 | Adolph Katz | Brooch | Jelly belly fish |
| 141468 | 6/5/1945 | Adolph Katz | Brooch | Jelly belly fox |
| 141469 | 6/5/1945 | Adolph Katz | Brooch | Bird |
| 141470 | 6/5/1945 | Adolph Katz | Brooch | Swordfish |
| 141637 | 6/19/1945 | Adolph Katz | Brooch | Insect |
| 141687 | 6/26/1945 | Adolph Katz | Brooch | Gem belly monkey (Also found as a Duette.) |
| 141961 | 8/7/1945 | Adolph Katz | Brooch | Leaf |
| 142183 | 8/14/1945 | Adolph Katz | Brooch | Donkey called "Dancing Monkey" |
| 142184 | 8/14/1945 | Adolph Katz | Brooch | Man sitting on moon |
| 142185 | 8/14/1945 | Adolph Katz | Brooch | Bug |
| 142186 | 8/14/1945 | Adolph Katz | Brooch | Bug |
| 142187 | 8/14/1945 | Adolph Katz | Brooch | Rooster, crown, dagger |
| 142188 | 8/14/1945 | Adolph Katz | Brooch | Bug |
| 142189 | 8/14/1945 | Adolph Katz | Brooch | Aladdin's lamp |
| 142190 | 8/14/1945 | Adolph Katz | Brooch | Bug |
| 142191 | 8/14/1945 | Adolph Katz | Brooch | Poodle |
| 142192 | 8/14/1945 | Adolph Katz | Brooch | Floral |
| 142200 | 8/14/1945 | Adolph Katz | Brooch | Man in turban |

**1945 – 1948 Coro sterling sword pin.** This 3¼" x 1¼" gold-tone, jeweled sword pin is signed "Coro Sterling." I was unable to locate a patent for this design; however, in 1945 Coro patented several similar sword pins. Sterling silver metal was routinely utilized by Coro during the war years, and its use continued through 1948. The 1945 style and the use of sterling date this brooch to 1945 – 1948. $75.00 – 125.00.

| 142201 | 8/14/1945 | Adolph Katz | Brooch | Bird with flag |
| 142214 | 8/21/1945 | Adolph Katz | Brooch | Key |
| 142420 | 8/25/1945 | Adolph Katz | Brooch | Pinwheel |
| 142421 | 8/25/1945 | Adolph Katz | Brooch | Alligator with pearl in mouth |
| 142422 | 8/25/1945 | Adolph Katz | Brooch | Pony cart (chariot style) |
| 142423 | 8/25/1945 | Adolph Katz | Brooch | Floral |
| 142483 | 10/2/1945 | Adolph Katz | Duette | Rabbits |
| 142564 | 10/16/1945 | Adolph Katz | Bracelet | Center crown decoration (See 140999 for matching brooch.) |
| 142567 | 10/16/1945 | Adolph Katz | Brooch | Open-mouth fish |
| 142568 | 10/16/1945 | Adolph Katz | Brooch | Bird |
| 142569 | 10/16/1945 | Adolph Katz | Brooch | Heart and key |
| 142570 | 10/16/1945 | Adolph Katz | Brooch | Saber, crescent moon, flower |
| 142642 | 10/23/1945 | Adolph Katz | Brooch | Male figural (See 142643 for matching female.) |
| 142643 | 10/23/1945 | Adolph Katz | Brooch | Female figural (See 142642 for matching male.) |
| 142644 | 10/23/1945 | Adolph Katz | Brooch | Female face called "Siren" |
| 142645 | 10/23/1945 | Adolph Katz | Brooch | Liberty bell |
| 142646 | 10/23/1945 | Adolph Katz | Brooch | Bow |
| 142921 | 11/13/1945 | Gene Verrecchio | Brooch | Abstract with crown |
| 143211 | 12/18/1945 | Adolph Katz | Brooch | Rag doll man (See 143212 for rag doll woman.) |
| 143212 | 12/18/1945 | Adolph Katz | Brooch | Rag doll woman (See 143211 for rag doll man.) |
| 143213 | 12/18/1945 | Adolph Katz | Brooch | Floral |
| 143214 | 12/18/1945 | Adolph Katz | Brooch | Floral |
| 143215 | 12/18/1945 | Adolph Katz | Brooch | Giraffe |
| 143216 | 12/18/1945 | Adolph Katz | Brooch | Ink well with feather pen |
| 143217 | 12/18/1945 | Adolph Katz | Brooch | Bird |
| 143218 | 12/18/1945 | Adolph Katz | Brooch | Siam dancer |
| 143219 | 12/18/1945 | Adolph Katz | Brooch | Elizabethan man with heart on his chest and holding a sword |
| 143220 | 12/18/1945 | Adolph Katz | Brooch | Floral |
| 143221 | 12/18/1945 | Adolph Katz | Brooch | Bow and arrows |
| 143222 | 12/18/1945 | Adolph Katz | Brooch | Ballerina with flowers |
| 143223 | 12/18/1945 | Adolph Katz | Duette | Floral |
| 143224 | 12/18/1945 | Adolph Katz | Duette | Abstract floral |
| 145253 | 7/23/1945 | Adolph Katz | Brooch | Floral |

141687

142183

142643

143211

143219

CORO AND VENDÔME JEWELRY

144950

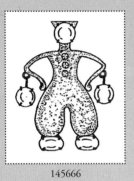

145666

CORO AND VENDÔME JEWELRY

146045

| Design Patent Number | Date Issued | Designer | Jewelry Type | Brief Description |
|---|---|---|---|---|
| 143974 | 2/26/1946 | Adolph Katz | Brooch | Spider in web |
| 143975 | 2/26/1946 | Adolph Katz | Brooch | Lion |
| 143976 | 2/26/1946 | Adolph Katz | Brooch | Asian man |
| 144116 | 3/12/1946 | Adolph Katz | Duette | Abstract floral |
| 144117 | 3/12/1946 | Adolph Katz | Brooch | Floral |
| 144118 | 3/12/1946 | Adolph Katz | Brooch | Sailboat |
| 144194 | 3/19/1946 | Adolph Katz | Chatelaine | Matador and bull |
| 144195 | 3/19/1946 | Adolph Katz | Duette | King and queen |
| 144196 | 3/19/1946 | Adolph Katz | Duette | Bird heads |
| 144197 | 3/19/1946 | Adolph Katz | Duette | Floral |
| 144198 | 3/19/1946 | Adolph Katz | Chatelaine (also found as a Duette) | Comedy and tragedy masks |
| 144926 | 6/4/1946 | Adolph Katz | Brooch | Starburst |
| 144927 | 6/4/1946 | Adolph Katz | Brooch | Bird |
| 144950 | 6/4/1946 | Gene Verrecchio | Brooch | Crown |
| 144972 | 6/11/1946 | Adolph Katz | Brooch | Ballerina |
| 145250 | 7/23/1946 | Adolph Katz | Brooch | Flying insect |
| 145251 | 7/23/1946 | Adolph Katz | Brooch | Abstract horn of plenty style |
| 145252 | 7/23/1946 | Adolph Katz | Brooch | Abstract floral |
| 145301 | 7/30/1946 | Adolph Katz | Brooch | Floral with ribbon |
| 145302 | 7/30/1946 | Adolph Katz | Brooch | Floral |
| 145525 | 9/3/1946 | Adolph Katz | Brooch | Abstract floral |
| 145526 | 9/3/1946 | Adolph Katz | Brooch | Abstract floral |
| 145628 | 9/24/1946 | Adolph Katz | Brooch | Abstract floral |
| 145629 | 9/24/1946 | Adolph Katz | Brooch | Abstract floral |
| 145630 | 9/24/1946 | Adolph Katz | Brooch | Abstract floral |
| 145631 | 9/24/1946 | Adolph Katz | Brooch | Ribbon |
| 145632 | 9/24/1946 | Adolph Katz | Brooch | Abstract floral |
| 145633 | 9/24/1946 | Adolph Katz | Brooch | Floral |
| 145665 | 10/1/1946 | Adolph Katz | Brooch | Bird |
| 145666 | 10/1/1946 | Adolph Katz | Brooch | Male carrying water (See 145667 for female.) |
| 145667 | 10/1/1946 | Adolph Katz | Brooch | Female carrying water (See 145666 for male.) |
| 145733 | 10/15/1946 | Adolph Katz | Brooch | Sword |
| 145847 | 10/29/1946 | Adolph Katz | Brooch | Starburst with lightening bolts (See 146111 for similar brooch.) |
| 146031 | 12/10/1946 | Adolph Katz | Duette | Abstract fan shape |
| 146032 | 12/10/1946 | Adolph Katz | Duette | Female masks |
| 146033 | 12/10/1946 | Adolph Katz | Duette | Deer heads |
| 146034 | 12/10/1946 | Adolph Katz | Duette | Abstract |

*Sun Goddess by Coro*

Inspired by David O. Selznick's
**DUEL** in the **SUN**

Flawlessly beautiful jewels, sparkling with simulated,
gem colored stones. Gold finished sterling.
At leading stores everywhere.

*Coro*
CRAFT

MASTERPIECES OF FASHION JEWELRY

*Coro* INC. NEW YORK · CHICAGO · LOS ANGELES · SAN FRANCISCO · MIAMI · TORONTO · LONDON

1946 "Sun Goddess by Coro" ad. The line was inspired by the movie *Duel in the Sun.*

*Extravaganza by Coro*

Old world grandeur eloquently portrayed in a lavish fob . . . embellished with turquoise and other jewel color stones. Real watch case, delicately engraved, holds two photographs. Gold finished metal.

About $8.00 plus federal tax at your favorite store.

*Coro* JEWELRY

*Coro* INC. NEW YORK · CHICAGO · LOS ANGELES · SAN FRANCISCO · TORONTO · LONDON

1946 "Extravaganza by Coro" ad. This fob pin originally sold for $8.00 and features a real watch case designed to hold two photographs.

146141

146140

| 146035 | 12/10/1946 | Adolph Katz | Duette | Abstract |
|---|---|---|---|---|
| 146036 | 12/10/1946 | Adolph Katz | Duette | Peacocks |
| 146037 | 12/10/1946 | Adolph Katz | Duette | Abstract |
| 146038 | 12/10/1946 | Adolph Katz | Duette | Floral |
| 146039 | 12/10/1946 | Adolph Katz | Duette | Abstract |
| 146040 | 12/10/1946 | Adolph Katz | Duette | Lamppost |
| 146045 | 12/10/1946 | Adolph Katz | Bracelet | Abstract starburst (See 146052 for similar brooch.) |
| 146046 | 12/10/1946 | Adolph Katz | Brooch | Angel with violin wearing a crown |
| 146047 | 12/10/1946 | Adolph Katz | Brooch | Abstract floral |
| 146048 | 12/10/1946 | Adolph Katz | Duette | Abstract |
| 146049 | 12/10/1946 | Adolph Katz | Brooch | Hands holding bird |
| 146050 | 12/10/1946 | Adolph Katz | Brooch | Abstract floral |
| 146051 | 12/10/1946 | Adolph Katz | Duette | Abstract floral |
| 146052 | 12/10/1946 | Adolph Katz | Brooch | Pinwheel starburst (See 145847 for similar brooch.) |
| 146053 | 12/10/1946 | Adolph Katz | Bracelet | Abstract starburst |
| 146111 | 12/24/1946 | Adolph Katz | Brooch | Abstract starburst (See 146045 for similar bracelet.) |
| 146112 | 12/24/1946 | Adolph Katz | Bracelet | Abstract floral |
| 146140 | 12/31/1946 | Adolph Katz | Brooch | Floral |
| 146141 | 12/31/1946 | Adolph Katz | Duette | Birds |

**1946 Corocraft red and green enameled sterling clip.** Some of the best jewelry ever produced was designed and manufactured by Coro in the 1940s. This 1¼" red and green long-stemmed flower clip certainly qualifies as one of Coro's great designs. Signed "Corocraft Sterling," this clip is design patent number 146140 issued December 3, 1946, to Adolph Katz for Coro. Note the tiny rhinestones on the stem and at the tips of each sweeping flower petal. $95.00 – 135.00.

| Design Patent Number | Date Issued | Designer | Jewelry Type | Brief Description |
|---|---|---|---|---|
| 146281 | 1/28/1947 | Adolph Katz | Brooch | Sword |
| 146312 | 2/4/1947 | Adolph Katz | Brooch | Hands holding flaming heart |
| 146503 | 3/25/1947 | Adolph Katz | Brooch | Leaf |
| 146575 | 4/8/1947 | Adolph Katz | Brooch | Stand-up child's toy horse |
| 146576 | 4/8/1947 | Adolph Katz | Brooch | Hobby horse |
| 146769 | 5/13/1947 | Adolph Katz | Brooch | Feather-style leaf |
| 146859 | 6/3/1947 | Adolph Katz | Bracelet | Flat band with three raised floral decorations. |
| 146919 | 6/10/1947 | Adolph Katz | Brooch | Lobster |
| 146958 | 6/24/1947 | Adolph Katz | Brooch | Bow |
| 146959 | 6/24/1947 | Adolph Katz | Brooch | Floral |
| 146961 | 6/24/1947 | Adolph Katz | Brooch | Stylized bow |
| 146962 | 6/24/1947 | Adolph Katz | Brooch | Starburst |
| 146963 | 6/24/1947 | Adolph Katz | Brooch | Abstract |
| 146964 | 6/24/1947 | Adolph Katz | Brooch | Crown |
| 146965 | 6/24/1947 | Adolph Katz | Brooch | Bow with dangles |
| 146966 | 6/24/1947 | Adolph Katz | Brooch | Floral |
| 147012 | 7/1/1947 | Adolph Katz | Brooch | Floral |
| 147047 | 7/8/1947 | Adolph Katz | Brooch | Weather station (See 147048 and 147049 for matching earrings.) |
| 147048 | 7/8/1947 | Adolph Katz | Earring | Rhinestone belly female figural |
| 147049 | 7/8/1947 | Adolph Katz | Earring | Rhinestone belly male figural |
| 147129 | 7/15/1947 | Adolph Katz | Brooch | Jeweled lizard |
| 147130 | 7/15/1947 | Adolph Katz | Brooch | Bird |
| 147179 | 7/22/1947 | Adolph Katz | Duette | Eye-shaped abstract |

147047

1947 "Forecast by Coro." The two jeweled figures represent fair and foul weather. Amazingly, the figures rotate so that the fair weather figure can be worn in the weather station on good days and the foul weather figure can be moved forward on rainy days. The pin originally sold for $6.00 and the matching earrings for $2.00.

FORECAST *by Coro*

You'll be showered with compliments when you wear this fair and sunny show of be-jeweled glamour.

Pin about $6.00
Matching earrings about $2.00
plus federal tax.
At leading stores everywhere.

*Coro* JEWELRY

design patented

Coro, Inc. New York 1, N.Y.

**AMERICA'S BEST DRESSED WOMEN WEAR CORO JEWELRY**

147245

**1947 Coro "wire works" bird pin.**
In 1947 Coro designed a line of figural pieces sometimes referred to by collectors as "wire work" jewelry. Wires were creatively bent to form the image of each piece. This delightful design trait was an imaginative way to produce jewelry using very little metal, which was in short supply during the war years. This 2¾" x 1¼" bird brooch is one of the easier-to-find examples of this design motif. Notice the sparse use of metal and, at the time, hard-to-get rhinestones. Design patent number 147245 was issued August 5, 1947, to Adolph Katz for this design. Other "wire works" design patents include 147244, 147246, 147273, 147275, 147276, 147284, and 147285. The asking price for "wire works" jewelry varies greatly depending on rarity and the acumen of the seller. $45.00 – 100.00.

| 147180 | 7/22/1947 | Adolph Katz | Brooch | Abstract |
|---|---|---|---|---|
| 147181 | 7/22/1947 | Adolph Katz | Brooch | Floral |
| 147182 | 7/22/1947 | Adolph Katz | Brooch | Floral |
| 147183 | 7/22/1947 | Adolph Katz | Brooch | Lyre |
| 147184 | 7/22/1947 | Adolph Katz | Brooch | Abstract floral |
| 147185 | 7/22/1947 | Adolph Katz | Brooch | Floral |
| 147186 | 7/22/1947 | Adolph Katz | Brooch | Floral |
| 147187 | 7/22/1947 | Adolph Katz | Brooch | Floral bouquet |
| 147188 | 7/22/1947 | Adolph Katz | Brooch | Floral |
| 147189 | 7/22/1947 | Adolph Katz | Brooch | Female Dutch |
| 147190 | 7/22/1947 | Adolph Katz | Brooch | Abstract floral |
| 147191 | 7/22/1947 | Adolph Katz | Brooch | Bird at water fountain |
| 147192 | 7/22/1947 | Adolph Katz | Brooch | Key with lock |
| 147193 | 7/22/1947 | Adolph Katz | Brooch | Abstract |
| 147194 | 7/22/1947 | Adolph Katz | Brooch | Floral |
| 147195 | 7/22/1947 | Adolph Katz | Brooch | Floral |
| 147196 | 7/22/1947 | Adolph Katz | Brooch | Floral |
| 147197 | 7/22/1947 | Adolph Katz | Brooch | Bug |
| 147241 | 8/5/1947 | Adolph Katz | Brooch | Stylized floral |
| 147242 | 8/5/1947 | Adolph Katz | Brooch | Floral |
| 147243 | 8/5/1947 | Adolph Katz | Brooch | Male Dutch |
| 147244 | 8/5/1947 | Adolph Katz | Brooch | Wire bird (See 147285 for wire bird.) |
| 147245 | 8/5/1947 | Adolph Katz | Brooch | Wire bird (See 147246 for wire monkey.) |
| 147246 | 8/5/1947 | Adolph Katz | Brooch | Wire monkey (See 147284 for wire bird on perch.) |
| 147271 | 8/12/1947 | Adolph Katz | Brooch | Floral |
| 147272 | 8/12/1947 | Adolph Katz | Brooch | Floral leaves |
| 147273 | 8/12/1947 | Adolph Katz | Brooch | Wire cat (See 147275 for wire horse.) |
| 147274 | 8/12/1947 | Adolph Katz | Brooch | Violin |
| 147275 | 8/12/1947 | Adolph Katz | Brooch | Wired horse (See 147276 for wire woman walking wire dog chatelaine.) |
| 147276 | 8/12/1947 | Adolph Katz | Chatelaine | Wire woman walking wire dog (See 147244 for wire bird.) |

**1947 Coro "wire works" swan.** Unfortunately, I can not locate a design patent for this "wire works" swan; however, the style dates this piece to 1947. This lovely 1¾" x 1" bird pin features sapphire blue rhinestones on the tail, green rhinestone feathers, and a large red rhinestone head. $30.00 – 45.00.

| | | | | |
|---|---|---|---|---|
| 147277 | 8/12/1947 | Adolph Katz | Brooch | Insect |
| 147282 | 8/12/1947 | Adolph Katz | Brooch | Bow |
| 147283 | 8/12/1947 | Adolph Katz | Brooch | Bird |
| 147284 | 8/12/1947 | Adolph Katz | Brooch | Wire bird on perch (See 147273 for wire cat.) |
| 147285 | 8/12/1947 | Adolph Katz | Brooch | Wire bird (See 147245 for another wire bird.) |
| 147286 | 8/12/1947 | Adolph Katz | Brooch | Bug |
| 147290 | 8/12/1947 | Adolph Katz | Brooch | Floral |
| 147409 | 9/2/1947 | Adolph Katz | Brooch | Crown |
| 147410 | 9/2/1947 | Adolph Katz | Duette | Floral |
| 147441 | 9/2/1947 | Adolph Katz | Duette | Butterflies |
| 147442 | 9/9/1947 | Adolph Katz | Brooch | Floral |
| 147443 | 9/9/1947 | Adolph Katz | Brooch | Floral |
| 147444 | 9/9/1947 | Adolph Katz | Necklace | Floral |
| 147448 | 9/9/1947 | Adolph Katz | Brooch | Abstract |
| 147449 | 9/9/1947 | Adolph Katz | Brooch | Crown |
| 147451 | 9/9/1947 | Adolph Katz | Brooch | Floral |
| 147452 | 9/9/1947 | Adolph Katz | Duette | Abstract |
| 147454 | 9/9/1947 | Adolph Katz | Necklace | Abstract bow |
| 147455 | 9/9/1947 | Adolph Katz | Brooch | Bow with dangles |

147410

147455

1947 Coro advertisement featuring Mrs. Bertrand L. Taylor III, one of "America's best dressed women." Interestingly, the Coro jewelry in this advertisement is small and difficult to see. The ad seems to be promoting Coro jewelry in general as being lovely enough for socially prominent women.

147620

147661

| 147456 | 9/9/1947 | Adolph Katz | Brooch | Windmill |
|--------|----------|-------------|--------|----------|
| 147457 | 9/9/1947 | Adolph Katz | Brooch | Bowl of fruit |
| 147620 | 10/7/1947 | Adolph Katz | Necklace | Slide with stars and bow (See 148170 for earring.) |
| 147655 | 10/14/1947 | Adolph Katz | Brooch | Stylized floral |
| 147656 | 10/14/1947 | Adolph Katz | Brooch | Looking glass |
| 147657 | 10/14/1947 | Adolph Katz | Brooch | Locket |
| 147659 | 10/14/1947 | Adolph Katz | Bracelet | Bank with abstract center decoration |
| 147661 | 10/14/1947 | Adolph Katz | Duette | Deco-style |
| 147664 | 10/14/1947 | Adolph Katz | Duette | Abstract |
| 147665 | 10/14/1947 | Adolph Katz | Duette | Abstract |
| 147666 | 10/14/1947 | Adolph Katz | Duette | Abstract |
| 147667 | 10/14/1947 | Adolph Katz | Duette | Abstract bows |
| 147669 | 10/14/1947 | Adolph Katz | Duette | Floral |
| 147670 | 10/14/1947 | Adolph Katz | Necklace | Slide with stars and center band of stones |
| 147792 | 11/4/1947 | Adolph Katz | Brooch | Bow |
| 147908 | 11/18/1947 | Adolph Katz | Bracelet | Floral |
| 148169 | 12/23/1947 | Adolph Katz | Brooch | Asian water man |
| 148170 | 12/23/1947 | Adolph Katz | Earring | Bow (See 147620 for matching slide necklace.) |
| 148171 | 12/23/1947 | Adolph Katz | Brooch | Arrow |
| 148172 | 12/23/1947 | Adolph Katz | Brooch | Stylized double circle |
| 148174 | 12/23/1947 | Adolph Katz | Duette | Abstract |
| 148246 | 12/30/1947 | Adolph Katz | Duette | Abstract leaves |

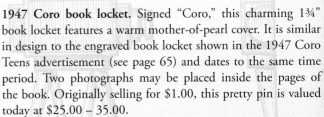

**1947 Coro book locket.** Signed "Coro," this charming 1¾" book locket features a warm mother-of-pearl cover. It is similar in design to the engraved book locket shown in the 1947 Coro Teens advertisement (see page 65) and dates to the same time period. Two photographs may be placed inside the pages of the book. Originally selling for $1.00, this pretty pin is valued today at $25.00 – 35.00.

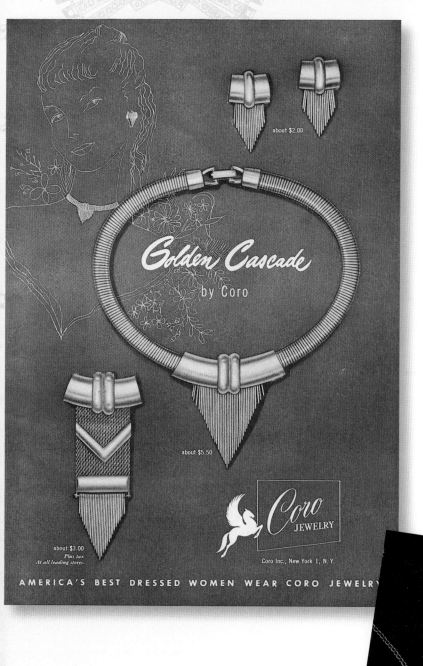

1947 "Golden Cascade by Coro." Coro produced many different versions of this snake chain collar necklace, some plain like this example, and some adorned with rhinestones. The necklace in the ad originally sold for $5.50, the pin for $3.00, and the earrings for $2.00.

Coro Teens 1947 Book Locket. Marketed to teens, both the necklace and the book locket pin originally sold for $1.00.

148362

148792

148868

148546

| Design Patent Number | Date Issued | Designer | Jewelry Type | Brief Description |
|---|---|---|---|---|
| 148305 | 1/6/1948 | Adolph Katz | Brooch | Musicians on stage |
| 148306 | 1/6/1948 | Adolph Katz | Brooch | Dancers on stage |
| 148362 | 1/13/1948 | Adolph Katz | Brooch | Wishing well |
| 148363 | 1/13/1948 | Adolph Katz | Brooch | Stylized bow over double circle |
| 148364 | 1/13/1948 | Adolph Katz | Brooch | Stylized bow |
| 148423 | 1/20/1948 | Adolph Katz | Brooch | Stylized leaf |
| 148428 | 1/20/1948 | Adolph Katz | Brooch | Floral |
| 148471 | 1/27/1948 | Adolph Katz | Brooch | Floral |
| 148545 | 2/3/1948 | Adolph Katz | Brooch | Flying insect |
| 148546 | 2/3/1948 | Adolph Katz | Brooch | Bird |
| 148547 | 2/3/1948 | Adolph Katz | Brooch | Scepter |
| 148548 | 2/3/1948 | Adolph Katz | Brooch | Key |
| 148792 | 2/24/1948 | Adolph Katz | Brooch | Spoon |
| 148793 | 2/24/1948 | Adolph Katz | Brooch | Butterfly |
| 148863 | 3/2/1948 | Adolph Katz | Necklace | Floral |
| 148864 | 3/2/1948 | Adolph Katz | Brooch | Floral |
| 148865 | 3/2/1948 | Adolph Katz | Bracelet | Band with stars and stylized center decoration |
| 148866 | 3/2/1948 | Adolph Katz | Brooch | Symmetrical abstract |
| 148867 | 3/2/1948 | Adolph Katz | Bracelet | Deco-style geometric design |
| 148868 | 3/2/1948 | Adolph Katz | Brooch | Center flower with six surrounding leaves (See 149128 for matching bracelet.) |
| 148872 | 3/2/1948 | Adolph Katz | Brooch | Floral |
| 148873 | 3/2/1948 | Adolph Katz | Earring | Center flower with six surrounding leaves (See 148878 for matching necklace.) |
| 148875 | 3/2/1948 | Adolph Katz | Duette | Stylized floral |
| 148876 | 3/2/1948 | Adolph Katz | Duette | Floral |
| 148877 | 3/2/1948 | Adolph Katz | Duette | Floral |

**1948 Corocraft sterling jeweled bird pin.** This magnificent 2¾" x 1" bird brooch is signed "Corocraft Sterling." It is design patent number 148546 issued February 3, 1948, to Adolph Katz for Coro. $150.00 – 225.00.

| 148878 | 3/2/1948 | Adolph Katz | Necklace | Center flower with six surrounding leaves (See 148868 for matching brooch.) |
|---|---|---|---|---|
| 148994 | 3/16/1948 | Adolph Katz | Brooch | Scarf or shawl |
| 148995 | 3/16/1948 | Adolph Katz | Brooch | Horseshoe with floral decoration |
| 148996 | 3/16/1948 | Adolph Katz | Necklace | Abstract deco-style |
| 148997 | 3/16/1948 | Adolph Katz | Brooch | Donkey pulling cart |
| 148998 | 3/16/1948 | Adolph Katz | Duette | Stylized floral |
| 148999 | 3/16/1948 | Adolph Katz | Brooch | Abstract |
| 149128 | 3/30/1948 | Adolph Katz | Bracelet | Center flower with six surrounding leaves (See 148873 for matching earring.) |
| 149186 | 4/6/1948 | Adolph Katz | Brooch | Hand holding flowers (See 149358 for another rose inspired piece.) |
| 149187 | 4/6/1948 | Adolph Katz | Duette | Turtles |
| 149188 | 4/6/1948 | Adolph Katz | Necklace | Slide with embedded flowers |
| 149189 | 4/6/1948 | Adolph Katz | Duette | Jelly belly fish |
| 149270 | 4/13/1948 | Adolph Katz | Chatelaine | Pirate and ship |
| 149357 | 4/20/1948 | Adolph Katz | Necklace | Abstract |
| 149358 | 4/20/1948 | Adolph Katz | Brooch | Heart with rose (See 149359 for another rose inspired piece.) |
| 149359 | 4/20/1948 | Adolph Katz | Brooch | Wishbone with rose (See 149360 for another rose inspired piece.) |
| 149360 | 4/20/1948 | Adolph Katz | Brooch | Key with rose (See 149361 for rose inspired necklace.) |
| 149361 | 4/20/1948 | Adolph Katz | Necklace | Rose inspired necklace (See 150874 for another rose inspired necklace.) |
| 149362 | 4/20/1948 | Adolph Katz | Necklace | Floral |
| 149363 | 4/20/1948 | Adolph Katz | Duette | Floral trembler |

149761

149820

149186

**1948 Coro hand brooch.** Coro created numerous lovely variations of hand brooches like this 3¼" x 1¼" example. The poised gold-tone hand is gently grasping a bouquet of colorful rhinestone flowers. It is design patent number 149186 issued April 6, 1948, to Adolph Katz for Coro. Hand brooches, especially those wearing rings (see design patent number 139075 issued October 10, 1944, to Adolph Katz for Coro) were sometimes lovingly given as pre-engagement presents. $55.00 – 95.00.

149948

**Coro 1948 Owlet pin and matching earrings.** This easy-to-find vintage set was featured in the 1948 "Coro Originals" advertisement as the "Owlet." (See page 69.) Each piece originally sold for $2.00. The 1½" owl pin matches design patent number 149948 issued June 15, 1948, to Adolph Katz for Coro and is signed "Coro des. pat. pend." The matching ½" earrings are unmarked except for utility patent number 1967965. This utility patent number refers to a 1934 utility patent issued to Eugene Morehouse and Melvin W. Moore for the clip mechanism. Note: this utility patent is not useful for dating these earrings other than indicating they could not have been made before 1934. $50.00 – 70.00.

149880

| Number | Date | Designer | Type | Description |
|---|---|---|---|---|
| 149558 | 5/11/1948 | Adolph Katz | Necklace | Abstract with dangles |
| 149760 | 5/25/1948 | Adolph Katz | Chatelaine | Floral |
| 149761 | 5/25/1948 | Adolph Katz | Brooch | Fan with tassel (See 149762 for matching earrings.) |
| 149762 | 5/25/1948 | Adolph Katz | Brooch | Fan with tassel (See 149761 for matching brooch.) |
| 149820 | 6/1/1948 | Adolph Katz | Chatelaine | Woman walking dog |
| 149881 | 6/8/1948 | Adolph Katz | Brooch | Floral |
| 149880 | 6/8/1948 | Adolph Katz | Brooch | Key |
| 149882 | 6/8/1948 | Adolph Katz | Brooch | Plain key |
| 149884 | 6/8/1948 | Adolph Katz | Brooch | Abstract |
| 149948 | 6/15/1948 | Adolph Katz | Brooch | Owl sitting on branch; called the "Owlet," originally selling for $2.00. |
| 150234 | 7/13/1948 | Adolph Katz | Brooch | Decorative pot |
| 150235 | 7/13/1948 | Adolph Katz | Brooch | Pump and bucket |
| 150301 | 7/20/1948 | Adolph Katz | Necklace | Nine rhinestone drops |
| 150302 | 7/20/1948 | Adolph Katz | Brooch | Portrait with mermaids and tassel (See 150620 for another tassel piece.) |

**1948 Coro decorated key pin.** This 2¾" x 1" stylized key brooch is design patent number 149880 issued June 8, 1948, to Adolph Katz for Coro. While attractive, this Coro key pin is lightweight compared to the gorgeous key pins produced by Trifari at the same time. A Trifari key pin from this era sells for $85.00 – 125.00, while the value of this Coro example is $35.00 – 50.00.

**1948 – 1955 Coro key pin.** This decorative Coro key pin measures 3" x 1". It is signed "Coro" without the copyright symbol and is similar in style to design patent number 149880 issued June 8, 1948, to Adolph Katz for Coro. The style and the lack of a copyright symbol date this pin to 1948 – 1955. $20.00 – 35.00.

1948 "Coro Originals." Several popular Coro styles are featured in this advertisement. Original prices: top center, Harlequin Duette, $6.00; top left, Spring Flowers basket pin, $5.50; second row center, the Owlet pin and earrings, $2.00 each; bottom left, the Victor horse pin and earrings, $2.00 each; bottom center, Bill and Coo jewel belly birds pin and earrings, $2.00 each; bottom right, the Lark pin and earrings, $3.00 each.

**1948 Coro Victor horse head pin and earrings set.** This 2" golden horse pin with bright pink rhinestone ears was named the "Victor" in the 1948 "Coro Originals" advertisement. It originally sold for $2.00. The 1" screw-back earrings sold for $2.00. All three pieces are signed "Coro" in script and "Des. Pat. Pend." Unfortunately, I was unable to locate the patents for these pieces. $50.00 – 70.00.

### • CORO 1948 •

| 150303 | 7/20/1948 | Adolph Katz | Necklace | Golden cascade slide |
|---|---|---|---|---|
| 150418 | 8/3/1948 | Adolph Katz | Brooch | Abstract floral with Lariat Style dangles |
| 150419 | 8/3/1948 | Adolph Katz | Brooch | Lantern |
| 150420 | 8/3/1948 | Adolph Katz | Brooch | Candelabra |
| 150421 | 8/3/1948 | Adolph Katz | Brooch | Coffee pot |
| 150422 | 8/3/1948 | Adolph Katz | Brooch | Winged lion with tassel (See 150429 for another tassel piece.) |
| 150423 | 8/3/1948 | Adolph Katz | Brooch | Arrow with rose (See 149186 for another rose inspired piece.) |
| 150424 | 8/3/1948 | Adolph Katz | Brooch | Scissors |
| 150425 | 8/3/1948 | Adolph Katz | Brooch | Spinning wheel |
| 150426 | 8/3/1948 | Adolph Katz | Brooch | Woman carrying basket |
| 150427 | 8/3/1948 | Adolph Katz | Brooch | Four armed goddess |
| 150428 | 8/3/1948 | Adolph Katz | Brooch | Oriental-theme tree (See 151834 for another Oriental piece.) |

150583

**1948 Coro cameo brooch.** Three heavy gold-tone drops dangle from this lovely 3" x 1½" cameo brooch signed "Coro." It is design patent number 150583 issued August 17, 1948, to Adolph Katz for Coro. $55.00 – 80.00.

150598

| 150429 | 8/3/1948 | Adolph Katz | Brooch | Elaborate key with tassel (See 150302 for another tassel piece.) |
|---|---|---|---|---|
| 150501 | 8/10/1948 | Adolph Katz | Locket | Four-picture locket |
| 150502 | 8/10/1948 | Adolph Katz | Necklace | Advertised as "Enchantment" originally selling for $11.00 (See 150617 for matching earring.) |
| 150503 | 8/10/1948 | Adolph Katz | Necklace | Abstract |
| 150513 | 8/10/1948 | Adolph Katz | Necklace | Abstract |
| 150515 | 8/10/1948 | Adolph Katz | Brooch | Advertised (not shown) as "Floral Leaf" |
| 150579 | 8/17/1948 | Adolph Katz | Brooch | Shoe |
| 150582 | 8/17/1948 | Adolph Katz | Brooch | Portrait with tassel (See 150602 for another tassel piece.) |
| 150583 | 8/17/1948 | Adolph Katz | Brooch | Portrait with three drops connected by chain (See 150584 for matching earrings.) |
| 150584 | 8/17/1948 | Adolph Katz | Earring | Portrait with three drops (See 150583 for matching brooch.) |
| 150587 | 8/17/1948 | Adolph Katz | Necklace | Three diamond shapes with drops |
| 150591 | 8/17/1948 | Adolph Katz | Bracelet | Shell style bracelet with pearls (See 150592 for matching necklace.) |
| 150592 | 8/17/1948 | Adolph Katz | Necklace | Shell style abstract with pearl drops (See 150591 for matching bracelet.) |
| 150593 | 8/17/1948 | Adolph Katz | Brooch | Shell style abstract with pearl decorations (See 150594 for matching earring.) |
| 150594 | 8/17/1948 | Adolph Katz | Earring | Shell style abstract with pearl decorations (See 150593 for matching brooch.) |
| 150596 | 8/17/1948 | Adolph Katz | Necklace | Abstract |
| 150598 | 8/17/1948 | Adolph Katz | Brooch | Archer |

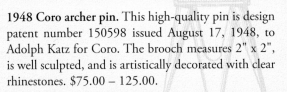

**1948 Coro archer pin.** This high-quality pin is design patent number 150598 issued August 17, 1948, to Adolph Katz for Coro. The brooch measures 2" x 2", is well sculpted, and is artistically decorated with clear rhinestones. $75.00 – 125.00.

CORO AND VENDÔME JEWELRY

| 150599 | 8/17/1948 | Adolph Katz | Brooch | Carousel horse |
|---|---|---|---|---|
| 150600 | 8/17/1948 | Adolph Katz | Brooch | Woman balancing basket on head |
| 150601 | 8/17/1948 | Adolph Katz | Brooch | Planter with flowers |
| 150602 | 8/17/1948 | Adolph Katz | Brooch | Portrait on cross with tassel (See 150611 for another tassel piece.) |
| 150603 | 8/17/1948 | Adolph Katz | Necklace | Rose decorated slide (See 150708 for another rose inspired piece.) |
| 150604 | 8/17/1948 | Adolph Katz | Brooch | Circle with bow at top |
| 150606 | 8/17/1948 | Adolph Katz | Necklace | Abstract bow |
| 150609 | 8/17/1948 | Adolph Katz | Necklace | Abstract slide |
| 150611 | 8/17/1948 | Adolph Katz | Brooch | Aladdin style lamp with tassel |
| 150612 | 8/17/1948 | Adolph Katz | Brooch | Wreath with portrait and three pearl drops |
| 150613 | 8/17/1948 | Adolph Katz | Necklace | Floral slide |
| 150615 | 8/17/1948 | Adolph Katz | Brooch | Abstract floral |
| 150616 | 8/17/1948 | Adolph Katz | Duette | Advertised as "Enchantment" originally selling for $15.00 (See 150502 for matching necklace.) |

150604

**Late 1940s Coro double-circle brooch.** This commonly found but lovely Coro 1¾" brooch is similar in style to design patent number 150604 issued August 17, 1948, to Adolph Katz for Coro and dates to the same era. It is signed "Coro" in script without the copyright symbol. This pretty Coro double-circle brooch features an Art Deco design decorated with dark red rhinestones. $25.00 – 45.00.

150616

1947 "Enchantment by Coro" advertisement. The complete Enchantment set and the original prices for the pieces: slide necklace, $11.00; earrings, $10.00; Duette, $15.00; pin, $11.00; bracelet, $11.00. The total cost for all of the pieces in 1948 was $58.00! Note: Interestingly, the patents for the Enchantment group were issued in 1948.

CORO AND VENDÔME JEWELRY

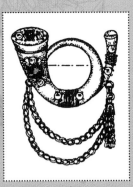

150620

**1948 Coro jeweled horn tassel pin.** Coro designed many pins with tassels in 1948 including this red and green jeweled 1¾" horn. It is design patent number 150620 issued August 17, 1948, to Adolph Katz for Coro. Other tassel jewelry design patents issued in 1948 include 150302, 150422, 150429, 150582, 150602, 150611, 150621, and 150624. $55.00 – 80.00.

150781

| 150617 | 8/17/1948 | Adolph Katz | Earring | "Enchantment" originally selling for $10.00 (See 150616 for matching Duette.) |
|---|---|---|---|---|
| 150618 | 8/17/1948 | Adolph Katz | Necklace | Star burst style floral (See 150619 for matching necklace.) |
| 150619 | 8/17/1948 | Adolph Katz | Necklace | Star burst style floral (See 150618 for matching necklace.) |
| 150620 | 8/17/1948 | Adolph Katz | Brooch | Horn with tassel (See 150624 for another tassel piece.) |
| 150621 | 8/17/1948 | Adolph Katz | Brooch | Axe with tassel (See 150621 for another tassel piece.) |
| 150622 | 8/17/1948 | Adolph Katz | Brooch | Abstract floral |
| 150623 | 8/17/1948 | Adolph Katz | Brooch | Circle with bow |
| 150624 | 8/17/1948 | Adolph Katz | Brooch | Pipe with tassel (See 150582 for another tassel piece.) |
| 150625 | 8/17/1948 | Adolph Katz | Brooch | Leaf |
| 150648 | 8/17/1948 | Adolph Katz | Brooch | Scarf-style pin (See149214 for another scarf-style pin.) |
| 150698 | 8/24/1948 | Adolph Katz | Necklace | Seven rhinestone decorations dangling from rhinestone chain |
| 150706 | 8/24/1948 | Adolph Katz | Brooch | Potted plant |
| 150708 | 8/24/1948 | Adolph Katz | Brooch | Double arrows double hearts rose center (See 150423 for another rose brooch.) |
| 150709 | 8/24/1948 | Adolph Katz | Brooch | Plain shell-shaped bow |
| 150711 | 8/24/1948 | Adolph Katz | Brooch | Comma shape |
| 150714 | 8/24/1948 | Adolph Katz | Necklace | Abstract with three dangles |
| 150777 | 8/31/1948 | Adolph Katz | Brooch | Abstract |
| 150778 | 8/31/1948 | Adolph Katz | Necklace | Slide with three abstract decorations |
| 150781 | 8/31/1948 | Adolph Katz | Brooch | Bird called the "Lark"; originally sold for $3.00. |
| 150782 | 8/31/1948 | Adolph Katz | Brooch | Fleur-de-lis |
| 150783 | 8/31/1948 | Adolph Katz | Brooch | Lamp |
| 150784 | 8/31/1948 | Adolph Katz | Brooch | Woman with tray (Possibly cigarette seller) |
| 150785 | 8/31/1948 | Adolph Katz | Brooch | Bird house on tall post |
| 150787 | 8/31/1948 | Adolph Katz | Brooch | Abstract floral |
| 150788 | 8/31/1948 | Adolph Katz | Necklace | Slide with deco-style center decoration |

| 150789 | 8/31/1948 | Adolph Katz | Brooch | Tall vase of flowers |
|---|---|---|---|---|
| 150791 | 8/31/1948 | Adolph Katz | Brooch | Garden gate |
| 150792 | 8/31/1948 | Adolph Katz | Necklace | Five dangling rhinestones from arch-style center |
| 150793 | 8/31/1948 | Adolph Katz | Bracelet | Deco-style rhinestone (See 150872 for matching necklace.) |
| 150794 | 8/31/1948 | Adolph Katz | Necklace | Deco-style center decoration with flower |
| 150795 | 8/31/1948 | Adolph Katz | Necklace | Slide with deco-style center decoration with flower |
| 150808 | 8/31/1948 | Adolph Katz | Necklace | "Trifari" link with scroll-style decoration |
| 150865 | 9/7/1948 | Adolph Katz | Brooch | Floral |
| 150866 | 9/7/1948 | Adolph Katz | Brooch | Floral |
| 150867 | 9/7/1948 | Adolph Katz | Necklace | Snake advertised as "Serpentine" (Ad not shown.) |
| 150868 | 9/7/1948 | Adolph Katz | Brooch | Floral |
| 150870 | 9/7/1948 | Adolph Katz | Necklace | Slide with abstract decoration |
| 150871 | 9/7/1948 | Adolph Katz | Necklace | Elaborate bell shaped dangles |
| 150872 | 9/7/1948 | Adolph Katz | Necklace | Déco style rhinestones (See 150793 for matching bracelet.) |
| 150873 | 9/7/1948 | Adolph Katz | Necklace | Slide with tie-shaped decoration |
| 150874 | 9/7/1948 | Adolph Katz | Necklace | Slide with open-work rose decoration |
| 150896 | 9/14/1948 | Adolph Katz | Earring | Abstract (See 150985 for matching brooch.) |
| 150959 | 9/14/1948 | Adolph Katz | Bracelet | Abstract floral |
| 150960 | 9/14/1948 | Adolph Katz | Brooch | Bow with five dangles |
| 150961 | 9/14/1948 | Adolph Katz | Necklace | Slide with Deco center decoration |

150961

**1948 Coro slide necklace.** This 14" gold-tone slide necklace measuring 14" is design patent number 150961 issued September 14, 1948, to Adolph Katz for Coro. The slide is enhanced with colorful emerald rhinestones and sparkling clear rhinestones. In the mid-to-late 1940s, Coro produced many versions of slide necklaces. $45.00 – 60.00.

CORO AND VENDÔME JEWELRY

73

CORO AND VENDÔME JEWELRY

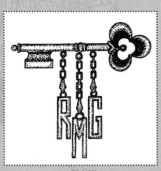

150967

151147

151151

| | | | | |
|---|---|---|---|---|
| 150962 | 9/14/1948 | Adolph Katz | Brooch | Bow with floral center |
| 150963 | 9/14/1948 | Adolph Katz | Brooch | Abstract, no rhinestones |
| 150964 | 9/14/1948 | Adolph Katz | Brooch | Abstract, no rhinestones |
| 150965 | 9/14/1948 | Adolph Katz | Brooch | Abstract bow |
| 150966 | 9/14/1948 | Adolph Katz | Brooch | Arrow with initials NTN dangling (See 150968 for another initial piece.) |
| 150967 | 9/14/1948 | Adolph Katz | Brooch | Key with initials RMG dangling (See 150966 for another initial piece.) |
| 150968 | 9/14/1948 | Adolph Katz | Brooch | Abstract with initials GKB dangling (See 150969 for another initial piece.) |
| 150969 | 9/14/1948 | Adolph Katz | Brooch | Abstract with initials MHE dangling (See 150967 for another initial piece.) |
| 150970 | 9/14/1948 | Adolph Katz | Brooch | Floral |
| 150971 | 9/14/1948 | Adolph Katz | Brooch | Book shelf |
| 150972 | 9/14/1948 | Adolph Katz | Brooch | Man on horse |
| 150973 | 9/14/1948 | Adolph Katz | Brooch | Street lighter |
| 150974 | 9/14/1948 | Adolph Katz | Brooch | Castle |
| 150975 | 9/14/1948 | Adolph Katz | Brooch | Rattle |
| 150977 | 9/14/1948 | Adolph Katz | Brooch | Purse |
| 150978 | 9/14/1948 | Adolph Katz | Brooch | Maypole dancers |
| 150981 | 9/14/1948 | Adolph Katz | Brooch | Coffee pot |
| 150985 | 9/14/1948 | Adolph Katz | Brooch | Abstract circle (See 150986 for matching earring.) |
| 151133 | 9/28/1948 | Adolph Katz | Brooch | Bow with two dangles |
| 151137 | 9/28/1948 | Adolph Katz | Brooch | Abstract |
| 151140 | 9/28/1948 | Adolph Katz | Brooch | Floral |
| 151142 | 9/28/1948 | Adolph Katz | Brooch | Feather |
| 151144 | 9/28/1948 | Adolph Katz | Brooch | Abstract |

**1948 Coro Lovebirds Duette.** Coro Duette brooches, like this 1½" x 2½" Coro Lovebirds Duette, are treats for collectors. One of the easiest Coro Duettes to find, this popular Duette is design patent number 151151 issued September 28, 1948, to Adolph Katz for Coro. It is featured in the 1948 "Coro 'Duettes'" advertisement (see page 75) and originally sold for $4.00. Each bird clip measures 2" x ¾" and is signed "Coro Des. Pat. Pend." The Duette frame is signed with utility patent number 1798867 and "Coro Duette" in script. This utility patent was issued March 31, 1931, to Gaston Candas for Coro. It does not help to date Coro Duettes. Most Coro Duettes, no matter when they were produced, have this utility patent number. $125.00 – 175.00.

| 151147 | 9/28/1948 | Adolph Katz | Brooch | Two Birds on branch called "Bill and Coo" in 1948 advertisement (See 151148 for matching earring.) |
| 151148 | 9/28/1948 | Adolph Katz | Earring | One bird on branch, matches Bill and Coo advertised in 1948 (See 151147 for matching brooch.) |
| 151151 | 9/28/1948 | Adolph Katz | Duette | Advertised as "Lovebirds"; originally sold for $4.00. |

1948 "Coro 'Duettes'" advertisement. Six different Duette pins and matching earrings are featured in this advertisement. Original prices: top right, Lovebirds Duette, $4.00, and earrings, $2.00; second row right, Apple Blossom Duette, $5.50, and earrings, $2.00; third row right, Daily Double Duette, $4.50, and earrings, $2.00; bottom left, Gay Swirl Duette, $5.50, and earrings, $2.00; fourth row right, Jeweled Comet Duette, $9.00, and earrings, $3.00; bottom center, Merry Whirl Duette, $6.00, and earrings, $3.00.

151258

151259

| | | | | |
|---|---|---|---|---|
| 151245 | 10/5/1948 | Adolph Katz | Brooch | Abstract floral |
| 151246 | 10/5/1948 | Adolph Katz | Necklace | Abstract with two drops |
| 151247 | 10/5/1948 | Adolph Katz | Necklace | Abstract |
| 151249 | 10/5/1948 | Adolph Katz | Necklace | Abstract with three rhinestone drops |
| 151250 | 10/5/1948 | Adolph Katz | Necklace | Abstract with two rhine-stone drops |
| 151251 | 10/5/1948 | Adolph Katz | Necklace | Abstract with three drops |
| 151256 | 10/5/1948 | Adolph Katz | Necklace | Abstract with five drops |
| 151258 | 10/5/1948 | Adolph Katz | Duette | Called "Jeweled Comet"; originally sold for $9.00. |
| 151259 | 10/5/1948 | Adolph Katz | Duette | Advertised as "Harle-quin"; originally sold for $6.00. |
| 151260 | 10/5/1948 | Adolph Katz | Brooch | Abstract broken circle |
| 151261 | 10/5/1948 | Adolph Katz | Brooch | Abstract floral starburst |
| 151262 | 10/5/1948 | Adolph Katz | Duette | Abstract |
| 151264 | 10/5/1948 | Adolph Katz | Duette | Abstract |
| 151265 | 10/5/1948 | Adolph Katz | Duette | Advertised as "Gay Swirl"; originally sold for $5.50. |
| 151266 | 10/5/1948 | Adolph Katz | Duette | Abstract |
| 151267 | 10/5/1948 | Adolph Katz | Brooch | Caged pearls with bow |

**1948 Coro Jeweled Comet Duette.** Originally selling for $9.00, this 2½" x 1½" lovely rhinestone Duette was called "Jeweled Comet" in the 1948 "Coro 'Duettes'" advertisement (see page 75). The Duette frame is signed "Coro Duette" in script and "Pat. No. 1798867." Each clip is marked "Coro Pat. Pend." This sparkling Duette matches design patent number 151258 issued October 5, 1948, to Adolph Katz for Coro. $75.00 – 150.00.

**1948 Coro Harlequin Duette.** Complete with matching ¾" screw-back earrings, this well-crafted, aqua rhinestone Duette brooch was advertised by Coro in 1948 as "Harlequin." The 2" x 1" Duette (shown in the 1948 "Coro 'Duettes'" advertisement, see page 75) originally sold for $6.00. The Duette is design patent number 151259 issued October 5, 1948, to Adolph Katz for Coro. It is signed "Coro Duette" and "Pat. No. 1798867" on the Duette frame. $125.00 – 200.00. From the collection of Debi Reece.

| | | | | |
|---|---|---|---|---|
| 151269 | 10/5/1948 | Adolph Katz | Necklace | Navette rhinestone center (See 151367 for matching bracelet.) |
| 151353 | 10/12/1948 | Adolph Katz | Necklace | Abstract with pearls and three drops |
| 151357 | 10/12/1948 | Adolph Katz | Necklace | Abstract broken circle style |
| 151358 | 10/12/1948 | Adolph Katz | Brooch | Male angel/cherub on phone |
| 151359 | 10/12/1948 | Adolph Katz | Brooch | Female angel/cherub on phone |
| 151360 | 10/12/1948 | Adolph Katz | Brooch | Floral |
| 151364 | 10/12/1948 | Adolph Katz | Duette | Long-stemmed flowers advertised as "Apple Blossom"; originally sold for $5.50. |
| 151365 | 10/12/1948 | Adolph Katz | Brooch | Heart with flowers |
| 151366 | 10/12/1948 | Adolph Katz | Brooch | Bow and arrow with flowers |
| 151367 | 10/12/1948 | Adolph Katz | Bracelet | Navette rhinestone center (See 151694 for matching brooch.) |
| 151368 | 10/12/1948 | Adolph Katz | Necklace | Floral |
| 151369 | 10/12/1948 | Adolph Katz | Necklace | Abstract with drops |
| 151370 | 10/12/1948 | Adolph Katz | Necklace | Faux lariat-style with three drops |
| 151452 | 10/19/1948 | Adolph Katz | Necklace | Lacy open-work slide |
| 151453 | 10/19/1948 | Adolph Katz | Necklace | Abstract slide |
| 151694 | 11/9/1948 | Adolph Katz | Brooch | Navette rhinestone center (See 151269 for matching necklace.) |
| 151763 | 11/16/1948 | Adolph Katz | Brooch | Stylized leaf |
| 151764 | 11/16/1948 | Adolph Katz | Brooch | Bird |
| 151765 | 11/16/1948 | Adolph Katz | Brooch | Crane or powered shovel |
| 151767 | 11/16/1948 | Adolph Katz | Brooch | Bow with flowers |
| 151768 | 11/16/1948 | Adolph Katz | Brooch | Rectangle with abstract decoration |
| 151769 | 11/16/1948 | Adolph Katz | Brooch | Asian woman by tree (See 152095 for another Oriental-theme piece.) |
| 151770 | 11/16/1948 | Adolph Katz | Necklace | Faux lariat-style with cascade of rhinestones |
| 151824 | 11/23/1948 | Adolph Katz | Brooch | Floral |
| 151825 | 11/23/1948 | Adolph Katz | Brooch | Asian men carrying woman in elaborate chaise |
| 151826 | 11/23/1948 | Adolph Katz | Brooch | Floral |
| 151827 | 11/23/1948 | Adolph Katz | Brooch | Bird |
| 151828 | 11/23/1948 | Adolph Katz | Brooch | Floral bow |

151364

151694

151834

151840

152096

152102

| 151829 | 11/23/1948 | Adolph Katz | Brooch | Floral |
|---|---|---|---|---|
| 151831 | 11/23/1948 | Adolph Katz | Brooch | Scepter |
| 151832 | 11/23/1948 | Adolph Katz | Brooch | Floral |
| 151833 | 11/23/1948 | Adolph Katz | Brooch | Elaborate bow |
| 151834 | 11/23/1948 | Adolph Katz | Brooch | Asian man carrying branch with cage (See 151769 for another oriental theme piece.) |
| 151835 | 11/23/1948 | Adolph Katz | Necklace | Rhinestone "U" shaped center decoration |
| 151837 | 11/23/1948 | Adolph Katz | Necklace | Rhinestone center floral with three dangles (See151840 for matching bracelet.) |
| 151838 | 11/23/1948 | Adolph Katz | Necklace | Abstract bib-shape |
| 151839 | 11/23/1948 | Adolph Katz | Necklace | Floral |
| 151840 | 11/23/1948 | Adolph Katz | Bracelet | Rhinestone flower center (See 151898 for matching brooch.) |
| 151841 | 11/23/1948 | Adolph Katz | Necklace | Abstract |
| 151842 | 11/23/1948 | Adolph Katz | Necklace | Geometric abstract "U" shaped center |
| 151844 | 11/23/1948 | Adolph Katz | Necklace | Rhinestone "U" shaped center decoration |
| 151846 | 11/23/1948 | Adolph Katz | Necklace | Plain with small rhinestone center decoration |
| 151847 | 11/23/1948 | Adolph Katz | Necklace | Curling petal flowers (See 151851 for matching bracelet.) |
| 151851 | 11/23/1948 | Adolph Katz | Bracelet | Curling flowers cuff (See 152096 for matching brooch.) |
| 151888 | 11/30/1948 | Adolph Katz | Brooch | Floral grapes |
| 151889 | 11/30/1948 | Adolph Katz | Brooch | Floral |
| 151890 | 11/30/1948 | Adolph Katz | Brooch | Floral leaf |
| 151891 | 11/30/1948 | Adolph Katz | Brooch | Floral |
| 151892 | 11/30/1948 | Adolph Katz | Brooch | Abstract floral |
| 151893 | 11/30/1948 | Adolph Katz | Brooch | Ribbon |
| 151894 | 11/30/1948 | Adolph Katz | Brooch | Floral |
| 151895 | 11/30/1948 | Adolph Katz | Brooch | Floral |
| 151896 | 11/30/1948 | Adolph Katz | Brooch | Abstract floral |

**Late 1940s Coro picture locket.** Locket pins must have been best sellers for Coro, because the company produced and patented many variations on this idea. This four-picture locket measures 2¼" x 1" and is signed "Coro" without the copyright symbol. The clasp at the top opens to release the spring-loaded picture frames. The original instructions for closing the locket read, "To press frame into shell after inserting your pictures use 1¢ coin. Press coin on frame at all sides until frame clicks into shell." The design of this locket closely resembles design patent number 152102 issued December 14, 1948, to Adolph Katz for Coro and dates to the same era. Selling for $5.00 – 10.00 in 1948, this locket is a bargain today at under $35.00.

| 151897 | 11/30/1948 | Adolph Katz | Brooch | Floral |
|---|---|---|---|---|
| 151898 | 11/30/1948 | Adolph Katz | Brooch | Rhinestone floral center (See 151899 for matching brooch.) |
| 151899 | 11/30/1948 | Adolph Katz | Brooch | Rhinestone center floral with three dangles (See 151837 for matching necklace.) |
| 151902 | 11/30/1948 | Adolph Katz | Duette | Deco style |
| 151914 | 11/30/1948 | Adolph Katz | Brooch | Floral circle |
| 151995 | 12/7/1948 | Adolph Katz | Brooch | Portrait with tassel |
| 151996 | 12/7/1948 | Adolph Katz | Duette | Abstract |
| 151997 | 12/7/1948 | Adolph Katz | Duette | Leaves |
| 151998 | 12/7/1948 | Adolph Katz | Duette | Abstract |
| 151999 | 12/7/1948 | Adolph Katz | Duette | Abstract |
| 152092 | 12/14/1948 | Adolph Katz | Brooch | Heart |
| 152093 | 12/14/1948 | Adolph Katz | Brooch | Floral |
| 152094 | 12/14/1948 | Adolph Katz | Brooch | Floral |
| 152095 | 12/14/1948 | Adolph Katz | Brooch | Sitting Asian man (See 150428 for another oriental theme piece.) |
| 152096 | 12/14/1948 | Adolph Katz | Brooch | Curling petal flowers (See 151847 for matching necklace.) |
| 152097 | 12/14/1948 | Adolph Katz | Brooch | Tree |
| 152100 | 12/14/1948 | Adolph Katz | Brooch | Floral |
| 152102 | 12/14/1948 | Adolph Katz | Brooch | "Family Album Locket"; originally sold for $5.00. (See 152106 for another locket.) |
| 152103 | 12/14/1948 | Adolph Katz | Brooch | Four-picture locket (See 152402 for another locket.) |
| 152104 | 12/14/1948 | Adolph Katz | Brooch | Four-picture locket (See 152403 for another locket.) |
| 152105 | 12/14/1948 | Adolph Katz | Brooch | Four-picture locket (See 152404 for another locket.) |
| 152106 | 12/14/1948 | Adolph Katz | Brooch | Four-picture locket (See 152105 for another locket.) |

1948 Coro "Family Album Locket" advertisement. Four different versions of these popular four-frame spring lockets are advertised as "Exquisitely engraved and bejeweled with all of the artistry of antique watch cases…these fob-lockets are real Heirlooms of Tomorrow!" Amazingly, this ad copy has come true. Coro fob-locket pins are heirlooms and highly collectible today. The lockets originally sold for $5.00 – 10.00 each.

CORO AND VENDÔME JEWELRY

1948 "For Graduation – give Coro pearls" advertisement. Available in jet black or white, the graduate-cap jewel case was advertised as "a permanent memory of the occasion" and sold with a single strand of simulated pearls for $5.00.

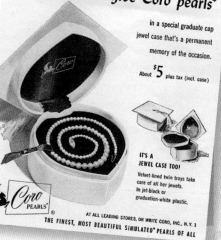

152481

153693

153696

| Design Patent Number | Date Issued | Designer | Jewelry Type | Brief Description |
|---|---|---|---|---|
| 152481 | 1/25/1949 | Adolph Katz | Duette | Abstract |
| 152694 | 2/15/1949 | Adolph Katz | Brooch | Floral |
| 152695 | 2/15/1949 | Adolph Katz | Brooch | Floral |
| 152696 | 2/15/1949 | Adolph Katz | Brooch | Floral |
| 152697 | 2/15/1949 | Adolph Katz | Brooch | Floral |
| 152698 | 2/15/1949 | Adolph Katz | Brooch | Abstract, no rhinestones |
| 152700 | 2/15/1949 | Adolph Katz | Brooch | Long-stemmed floral |
| 152790 | 2/22/1949 | Adolph Katz | Necklace | Geometric lariat |
| 152792 | 2/22/1949 | Adolph Katz | Necklace | Geometric lariat |
| 152793 | 2/22/1949 | Adolph Katz | Necklace | Geometric lariat |
| 152794 | 2/22/1949 | Adolph Katz | Necklace | Geometric |
| 152798 | 2/22/1949 | Adolph Katz | Necklace | Hands holding ring |
| 152800 | 2/22/1949 | Adolph Katz | Necklace | Belt buckle (See 152885 for matching earring.) |
| 152885 | 3/1/1949 | Adolph Katz | Earring | Belt buckle (See 152800 for matching necklace.) |
| 152975 | 3/8/1949 | Adolph Katz | Brooch | Abstract |
| 152976 | 3/8/1949 | Adolph Katz | Necklace | Lariat style |
| 152979 | 3/8/1949 | Adolph Katz | Necklace | Lariat style |
| 152980 | 3/8/1949 | Adolph Katz | Necklace | Lariat style |
| 153066 | 3/15/1949 | Adolph Katz | Brooch | Venetian gondolier |
| 153067 | 3/15/1949 | Adolph Katz | Brooch | Bird on branch |
| 153068 | 3/15/1949 | Adolph Katz | Duette | Abstract |
| 153077 | 3/15/1949 | Adolph Katz | Duette | Abstract |
| 153292 | 4/5/1949 | Adolph Katz | Necklace | Abstract floral |
| 153360 | 4/12/1949 | Adolph Katz | Necklace | Floral with enameled guilloche rose (See 154389 for matching brooch.) |
| 153361 | 4/12/1949 | Adolph Katz | Necklace | Lariat style |
| 153362 | 4/12/1949 | Adolph Katz | Necklace | Lariat style |
| 153435 | 4/19/1949 | Adolph Katz | Necklace | Abstract |
| 153527 | 4/26/1949 | Adolph Katz | Brooch | Double heart with arrow |
| 153528 | 4/26/1949 | Adolph Katz | Brooch | Dagger and heart |
| 153691 | 5/10/1949 | Adolph Katz | Brooch | Three leaf clover |
| 153692 | 5/10/1949 | Adolph Katz | Brooch | Floral |
| 153693 | 5/10/1949 | Adolph Katz | Brooch | Cameo |
| 153696 | 5/10/1949 | Adolph Katz | Brooch | Fish jelly belly advertised in 1949 as "Sea Imps" and originally selling for $5.00. |
| 153697 | 5/10/1949 | Adolph Katz | Pin Clip | Bird on branch |
| 153698 | 5/10/1949 | Adolph Katz | Brooch | Horse head |

| 153699 | 5/10/1949 | Adolph Katz | Brooch | Butterfly advertised in 1949 as "Glamorette" (ad not shown); originally sold for $2.00. (See 154398 for another Glamorette piece.) |
|---|---|---|---|---|
| 153700 | 5/10/1949 | Adolph Katz | Brooch | Wheelbarrow advertised in 1949 as "Glamorette" (ad not shown); originally sold for $2.00. (See 153699 for another Glamorette piece.) |
| 153701 | 5/10/1949 | Adolph Katz | Brooch | Crown |
| 153702 | 5/10/1949 | Adolph Katz | Brooch | Horse shoe |
| 153879 | 5/24/1949 | Adolph Katz | Bracelet | Floral enamel rose guilloche cuff (See 153360 for matching necklace.) |
| 154043 | 6/7/1949 | Adolph Katz | Necklace | Abstract |
| 154045 | 6/7/1949 | Adolph Katz | Necklace | Floral |
| 154046 | 6/7/1949 | Adolph Katz | Necklace | Seven hearts |
| 154279 | 6/28/1949 | Adolph Katz | Duette | Abstract |
| 154280 | 6/28/1949 | Adolph Katz | Brooch | Abstract |
| 154281 | 6/28/1949 | Adolph Katz | Brooch | Floral enameled rose |
| 154283 | 6/28/1949 | Adolph Katz | Brooch | Floral leaf |
| 154284 | 6/28/1949 | Adolph Katz | Brooch | Wreath |
| 154285 | 6/28/1949 | Adolph Katz | Brooch | Floral heart |
| 154389 | 7/5/1949 | Adolph Katz | Brooch | Floral enameled guilloche rose (See 154390 for matching earring.) |

153879

153702

**1949 Coro lucky horseshoe pin.** This seemingly insignificant 1" horseshoe-shaped pin is a wonderful find for a collector interested in dating costume jewelry. First, this pin is design patent number 153702 issued May 10, 1949, to Adolph Katz for Coro. Next, the pin is signed "Coro" with the copyright symbol. Coro continued to issue patents for jewelry designs through 1956; however, as a general rule, jewelry with the copyright symbol was produced after 1955. This modest pin is proof that the copyright symbol was definitely in use before that date. Finally, this sweet pin is also signed with the year, 1949. I wish I knew why Coro elected to date this piece, but I am grateful for the history lesson it provides. Despite its intellectual interest, the monetary value of this piece is small. $25.00 – 35.00.

CORO AND VENDÔME JEWELRY

81

CORO AND VENDÔME JEWELRY

154398

156423

156430

| 154390 | 7/5/1949 | Adolph Katz | Brooch | Floral enameled guilloche rose (See 153879 for matching bracelet.) |
|---|---|---|---|---|
| 154391 | 7/5/1949 | Adolph Katz | Brooch | Maltese cross |
| 154392 | 7/5/1949 | Adolph Katz | Brooch | Long-stemmed floral |
| 154393 | 7/5/1949 | Adolph Katz | Brooch | Floral |
| 154394 | 7/5/1949 | Adolph Katz | Brooch | Floral |
| 154396 | 7/5/1949 | Adolph Katz | Brooch | Floral trembler center |
| 154397 | 7/5/1949 | Adolph Katz | Brooch | Long-stemmed floral |
| 154398 | 7/5/1949 | Adolph Katz | Brooch | Basket advertised in 1949 ad "Glamorette" (ad not shown); originally sold for $2.00. (See 153700 for another "Glamorette" piece.) |
| 154399 | 7/5/1949 | Adolph Katz | Brooch | Floral |
| 154400 | 7/5/1949 | Adolph Katz | Brooch | Basket |
| 155163 | 9/13/1949 | Adolph Katz | Duette | Abstract |
| 155164 | 9/13/1949 | Adolph Katz | Duette | Abstract |
| 155165 | 9/13/1949 | Adolph Katz | Necklace | Five pearl drops |
| 155166 | 9/13/1949 | Adolph Katz | Necklace | Abstract heart shaped crown (See 156113 for matching brooch.) |
| 155901 | 11/8/1949 | Adolph Katz | Brooch | Abstract |
| 156111 | 11/22/1949 | Adolph Katz | Brooch | Abstract Bow |
| 156112 | 11/22/1949 | Adolph Katz | Brooch | Wreath with ribbon |
| 156113 | 11/22/1949 | Adolph Katz | Brooch | Abstract heart shaped crown (See 155166 for matching necklace.) |
| 156116 | 11/22/1949 | Adolph Katz | Brooch | Abstract |
| 156118 | 11/22/1949 | Adolph Katz | Brooch | Two birds two hearts |
| 156119 | 11/22/1949 | Adolph Katz | Brooch | Abstract |
| 156120 | 11/22/1949 | Adolph Katz | Brooch | Floral |
| 156121 | 11/22/1949 | Adolph Katz | Brooch | Floral |
| 156122 | 11/22/1949 | Adolph Katz | Brooch | Long-stemmed floral |
| 156123 | 11/22/1949 | Adolph Katz | Brooch | Four dangles |
| 156246 | 11/29/1949 | Adolph Katz | Brooch | Floral |
| 156249 | 11/29/1949 | Adolph Katz | Brooch | Floral |
| 156250 | 11/29/1949 | Adolph Katz | Brooch | Abstract |
| 156251 | 11/29/1949 | Adolph Katz | Brooch | Floral |
| 156252 | 11/29/1949 | Adolph Katz | Brooch | Abstract floral bow |
| 156253 | 11/29/1949 | Adolph Katz | Brooch | Floral |
| 156422 | 12/13/1949 | Adolph Katz | Brooch | Abstract shell shape |
| 156423 | 12/13/1949 | Adolph Katz | Brooch | Heart advertised in 1949 as "Jewels of the French Court" (ad not shown) (See 156425 for matching earring.) |

| 156424 | 12/13/1949 | Adolph Katz | Brooch | Heart dangle |
|---|---|---|---|---|
| 156425 | 12/13/1949 | Adolph Katz | Earring | Heart advertised in 1949 as "Jewels of the French Court" (ad not shown). (See 156431 for matching necklace.) |
| 156426 | 12/13/1949 | Adolph Katz | Brooch | Abstract bell-shape floral |
| 156427 | 12/13/1949 | Adolph Katz | Brooch | Fish with round belly (See 156428 for another round belly piece.) |
| 156428 | 12/13/1949 | Adolph Katz | Brooch | Rooster with round belly (See 156429 for another round belly piece.) |
| 156429 | 12/13/1949 | Adolph Katz | Brooch | Bird with round belly holding an umbrella (See 156430 for another round belly piece.) |
| 156430 | 12/13/1949 | Adolph Katz | Brooch | Rabbit with round belly (See 156427 for another round belly piece.) |
| 156431 | 12/13/1949 | Adolph Katz | Necklace | Heart advertised in 1949 ad "Jewels of the French Court" (ad not shown). (See 156423 for matching brooch.) |
| 156432 | 12/13/1949 | Adolph Katz | Necklace | Bib style with 25 dangles |
| 156433 | 12/13/1949 | Adolph Katz | Necklace | Bib style with 23 dangles |
| 156434 | 12/13/1949 | Adolph Katz | Necklace | Large rhinestone center with three dangles advertised in 1949 as "Versailles" (ad not shown); originally sold for $7.00. |
| 156514 | 12/20/1949 | Adolph Katz | Necklace | Bow with two dangles |
| 156522 | 12/20/1949 | Adolph Katz | Brooch | Leaf |
| 156523 | 12/20/1949 | Adolph Katz | Brooch | Crown shape with floral dangle |
| 156524 | 12/20/1949 | Adolph Katz | Brooch | Anchor |
| 156525 | 12/20/1949 | Adolph Katz | Brooch | Abstract |
| 156527 | 12/20/1949 | Adolph Katz | Brooch | Abstract double floral |
| 156528 | 12/20/1949 | Adolph Katz | Brooch | Abstract |
| 156529 | 12/20/1949 | Adolph Katz | Brooch | Abstract |
| 156530 | 12/20/1949 | Adolph Katz | Necklace | 21 emerald-cut rhinestone drops |
| 156531 | 12/20/1949 | Adolph Katz | Bracelet | Abstract |
| 156532 | 12/20/1949 | Adolph Katz | Necklace | Abstract three dangles |
| 156534 | 12/20/1949 | Adolph Katz | Necklace | Abstract |
| 156630 | 12/27/1949 | Adolph Katz | Brooch | Basket |

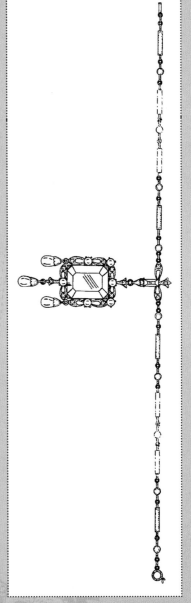

156434

156896

157964

157965

157967

157968

CORO AND VENDÔME JEWELRY

| Design Patent Number | Date Issued | Designer | Jewelry Type | Brief Description |
|---|---|---|---|---|
| 156887 | 1/17/1950 | Adolph Katz | Brooch | Abstract two dangles |
| 156888 | 1/17/1950 | Adolph Katz | Brooch | Double floral |
| 156891 | 1/17/1950 | Adolph Katz | Duette | Abstract |
| 156895 | 1/17/1950 | Adolph Katz | Duette | Double long-stemmed floral |
| 156896 | 1/17/1950 | Adolph Katz | Duette | Floral |
| 156898 | 1/17/1950 | Adolph Katz | Brooch | Floral |
| 156964 | 1/24/1950 | Adolph Katz | Brooch | Abstract |
| 156965 | 1/24/1950 | Adolph Katz | Duette | Abstract |
| 156967 | 1/24/1950 | Adolph Katz | Duette | Abstract |
| 156968 | 1/24/1950 | Adolph Katz | Duette | Abstract |
| 156969 | 1/24/1950 | Adolph Katz | Duette | Abstract |
| 156970 | 1/24/1950 | Adolph Katz | Duette | Abstract |
| 156971 | 1/24/1950 | Adolph Katz | Duette | Abstract |
| 157157 | 2/7/1950 | Adolph Katz | Duette | Abstract |
| 157158 | 2/7/1950 | Adolph Katz | Duette | Abstract |
| 157159 | 2/7/1950 | Adolph Katz | Duette | Abstract |
| 157160 | 2/7/1950 | Adolph Katz | Brooch | Large faceted rhinestone |
| 157164 | 2/7/1950 | Adolph Katz | Duette | Abstract floral |
| 157165 | 2/7/1950 | Adolph Katz | Duette | Abstract |
| 157166 | 2/7/1950 | Adolph Katz | Earring | Floral with four pearl drops (See 157264 for matching necklace.) |
| 157169 | 2/7/1950 | Adolph Katz | Brooch | Floral |
| 157264 | 2/14/1950 | Adolph Katz | Necklace | Double strand pearls with center decoration and four drops (See 157166 for matching earring.) |
| 157603 | 3/7/1950 | Adolph Katz | Brooch | Floral |
| 157962 | 4/4/1950 | Adolph Katz | Necklace | Abstract three dangles |
| 157963 | 4/4/1950 | Adolph Katz | Brooch | Abstract |
| 157964 | 4/4/1950 | Adolph Katz | Brooch | Dragonfly featured in "Lovely as Springtime" ad (not shown) |
| 157965 | 4/4/1950 | Adolph Katz | Brooch | Cuckoo clock featured in "Lovely as Springtime" ad (not shown) |
| 157966 | 4/4/1950 | Adolph Katz | Brooch | Swirling leaves floral featured in "Lovely as Springtime" ad (not shown) |
| 157967 | 4/4/1950 | Adolph Katz | Brooch | Floral with baguettes featured in "Lovely as Springtime" ad (not shown) |
| 157968 | 4/4/1950 | Adolph Katz | Brooch | Abstract floral |

| 157970 | 4/4/1950 | Adolph Katz | Brooch | Cage door opens |
| 157971 | 4/4/1950 | Adolph Katz | Brooch | Bird with heart dangling from beak |
| 157972 | 4/4/1950 | Adolph Katz | Brooch | Lyre |
| 157973 | 4/4/1950 | Adolph Katz | Brooch | Coat of arms with rhinestones |
| 157974 | 4/4/1950 | Adolph Katz | Brooch | Ballerina |
| 157975 | 4/4/1950 | Adolph Katz | Brooch | Man riding elephant |
| 157977 | 4/4/1950 | Adolph Katz | Necklace | Large faceted rhinestone three dangles |
| 158080 | 4/11/1950 | Adolph Katz | Brooch | Abstract |
| 158084 | 4/11/1950 | Adolph Katz | Brooch | Hat |
| 158085 | 4/11/1950 | Adolph Katz | Brooch | Leaf |
| 158086 | 4/11/1950 | Adolph Katz | Brooch | Floral |
| 158087 | 4/11/1950 | Adolph Katz | Brooch | Owl |
| 158088 | 4/11/1950 | Adolph Katz | Brooch | Double leaves |
| 158089 | 4/11/1950 | Adolph Katz | Brooch | Abstract |
| 158090 | 4/11/1950 | Adolph Katz | Brooch | Two birds over rhinestone mirror |
| 158091 | 4/11/1950 | Adolph Katz | Brooch | Crown |
| 158092 | 4/11/1950 | Adolph Katz | Brooch | Abstract |

157975

158080

**1950 Coro jelly belly elephant pin.** Although unmarked, this cute 1¼" x ¾" jelly belly elephant pin is by Coro. It is design patent number 157975 issued April 4, 1950, to Adolph Katz. Notice the elephant rider's sparkling blue rhinestone body and clear rhinestone face. The happy-looking elephant is designed with an upturned trunk for good luck. $95.00 – 125.00. From the collection of Debi Reece.

**Early 1950s Coro cameo pin.** This beautiful black and gold 1¼" Cameo pin is similar in style to the Coro pin shown in design patent number 158080 issued April 11, 1950, to Adolph Katz for Coro, and it dates to the same era. It is signed "Coro" in script without a copyright symbol. Small Coro pins like this one are easily found today. $20.00 – 30.00.

| 158093 | 4/11/1950 | Adolph Katz | Brooch | Abstract |
|---|---|---|---|---|
| 158094 | 4/11/1950 | Adolph Katz | Brooch | Abstract two dangles |
| 158387 | 5/2/1950 | Adolph Katz | Brooch | Abstract |
| 158559 | 5/16/1950 | Victor Di Mezza | Brooch | Abstract triangle |
| 158560 | 5/16/1950 | Victor Di Mezza | Brooch | Abstract parallelogram |
| 158561 | 5/16/1950 | Victor Di Mezza | Brooch | Abstract triangle circle |
| 158562 | 5/16/1950 | Victor Di Mezza | Brooch | Abstract triangle circle |
| 158583 | 5/16/1950 | Adolph Katz | Brooch | Long-stemmed floral |
| 158585 | 5/16/1950 | Adolph Katz | Necklace | Abstract three dangles |
| 158589 | 5/16/1950 | Adolph Katz | Necklace | Abstract |
| 158590 | 5/16/1950 | Adolph Katz | Brooch | Long-stemmed floral |
| 158592 | 5/16/1950 | Adolph Katz | Duette | Floral |
| 158594 | 5/16/1950 | Adolph Katz | Earring | No rhinestones lariat style (See 158861 for matching necklace.) |
| 158751 | 5/30/1950 | Adolph Katz | Necklace | Abstract double chain advertised as "Tailored Classics" |
| 158752 | 5/30/1950 | Adolph Katz | Bracelet | Cuff with gemstones (See 158863 for matching earring.) |
| 158753 | 5/30/1950 | Adolph Katz | Necklace | Abstract |
| 158754 | 5/30/1950 | Adolph Katz | Brooch | Floral |
| 158755 | 5/30/1950 | Adolph Katz | Brooch | Fish |
| 158757 | 5/30/1950 | Adolph Katz | Necklace | Abstract |
| 158758 | 5/30/1950 | Adolph Katz | Brooch | Long-stemmed floral |
| 158759 | 5/30/1950 | Adolph Katz | Bracelet | Abstract clamper, no rhinestones |

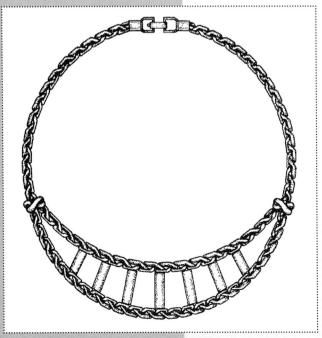

158751

| 158760 | 5/30/1950 | Adolph Katz | Bracelet | Stylized leaf clamper (See 158761 for matching earring.) |
| 158761 | 5/30/1950 | Adolph Katz | Earring | Stylized leaf (See 158760 for matching bracelet.) |
| 158762 | 5/30/1950 | Adolph Katz | Bracelet | Clamper with rhinestones |
| 158763 | 5/30/1950 | Adolph Katz | Bracelet | Abstract |
| 158764 | 5/30/1950 | Adolph Katz | Brooch | Abstract |
| 158861 | 6/6/1950 | Adolph Katz | Necklace | Lariat style no rhinestones (See 158594 for matching earring.) |
| 158863 | 6/6/1950 | Adolph Katz | Earring | Dangling gemstones (See 158752 for matching bracelet.) |
| 158864 | 6/6/1950 | Adolph Katz | Brooch | Floral one dangle |
| 158865 | 6/6/1950 | Adolph Katz | Brooch | Floral |
| 158866 | 6/6/1950 | Adolph Katz | Brooch | Long-stemmed floral |
| 158868 | 6/6/1950 | Adolph Katz | Brooch | Abstract |
| 159073 | 6/20/1950 | Adolph Katz | Necklace | Abstract |
| 159075 | 6/20/1950 | Adolph Katz | Necklace | Abstract slide with baguettes (See 159076 for matching clip.) |
| 159076 | 6/20/1950 | Adolph Katz | Brooch | Abstract with baguettes (See159075 for matching necklace) |
| 159077 | 6/20/1950 | Adolph Katz | Brooch | Safety pin featured in "the perfect jewel of a gift" 1950 ad; originally sold for $2.00. (See 159078 for another piece from this ad.) |
| 159078 | 6/20/1950 | Adolph Katz | Brooch | Floral large gemstone called "Charmian" in "perfect jewelry of a gift" 1950 ad (See 159629 for another piece from this ad.) |
| 159211 | 7/4/1950 | Adolph Katz | Brooch | Gramophone |
| 159267 | 7/11/1950 | Adolph Katz | Brooch | Leaves |
| 159269 | 7/11/1950 | Adolph Katz | Brooch | Bow |
| 159270 | 7/11/1950 | Adolph Katz | Brooch | Leaf |
| 159271 | 7/11/1950 | Adolph Katz | Brooch | Long-stemmed floral trembler center |
| 159272 | 7/11/1950 | Adolph Katz | Brooch | Long-stemmed floral |
| 159274 | 7/11/1950 | Adolph Katz | Brooch | Butterfly featured in "the perfect jewel of a gift" 1950 ad; originally sold for $5.00. (See 159077 for another piece from this ad.) |

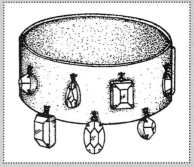
158752

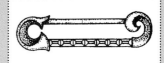
159077

159078

159274

159629

CORO AND VENDÔME JEWELRY

159633

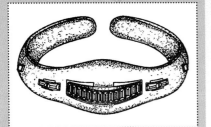

159636

159638

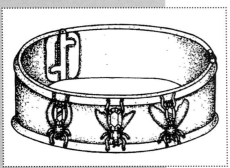

160613

| 159275 | 7/11/1950 | Adolph Katz | Brooch | Long-stemmed floral |
|---|---|---|---|---|
| 159626 | 8/8/1950 | Adolph Katz | Bracelet | Cuff large center rhinestone |
| 159627 | 8/8/1950 | Adolph Katz | Brooch | Bird birdhouse |
| 159628 | 8/8/1950 | Adolph Katz | Brooch | Steamboat |
| 159629 | 8/8/1950 | Adolph Katz | Brooch | Flower basket shown in 1950 "the perfect jewel of a gift" ad; originally sold for $6.00. (See 159633 for another piece from this ad.) |
| 159632 | 8/8/1950 | Adolph Katz | Duette | Abstract |

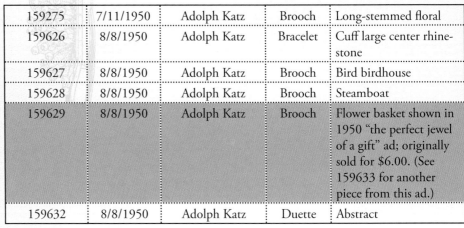

1950 Coro "the perfect jewel of a gift…" advertisement. Pieces surrounding the portrait, with original prices: Butterfly, $5.00; Bownot, $2.00; Flower Basket, $6.00. Other pieces, with original prices: top left, Trio Tricks, three bug pins, $3.50, and bracelet, $5.50; left middle, Family Album locket, $5.50; center, Charmain necklace, $4.00, and earrings, $2.00; right middle, Bug, $2.00, and Duette, $10.50; bottom center, Safety Pin, $2.00; bottom right, Spray Pin, $3.00.

**1950s Coro bug pin.** This well-made 1¼" Coro bug pin is similar in design to the trio of bug pins advertised in the 1950 Coro "Trio Tricks" advertisement and was made at the same time. It is signed "Coro" without the copyright symbol. $20.00 – 35.00. From the collection of Debi Reece.

| 159633 | 8/8/1950 | Adolph Katz | Brooch | Long-stemmed spray pin featured in 1950 "the perfect jewel of a gift" ad; originally sold for $3.00. (See 159638 for another piece from this ad.) |
|---|---|---|---|---|
| 159634 | 8/8/1950 | Adolph Katz | Brooch | Long-stemmed floral |
| 159636 | 8/8/1950 | Adolph Katz | Bracelet | Cuff baguette center decoration advertised as "Golden Gleams"; originally sold for $6.00. (See 159637 for matching necklace.) |
| 159637 | 8/8/1950 | Adolph Katz | Necklace | Baguette center decoration advertised as "Golden Gleams"; originally sold for $6.00. (See 159636 for matching bracelet.) |
| 159638 | 8/8/1950 | Adolph Katz | Brooch | bug advertised in "Trio of Tricks"; originally sold for $2.00. |
| 159642 | 8/8/1950 | Adolph Katz | Brooch | Flying insect advertised as "Trio of Tricks"; originally sold for $3.50. (See 160613 for matching bracelet.) |
| 160610 | 10/24/1950 | Adolph Katz | Brooch | Fountain with cherubs |
| 160611 | 10/24/1950 | Adolph Katz | Brooch | Castle with dangling key |
| 160613 | 10/24/1950 | Adolph Katz | Bracelet | Cuff with bugs advertised as "Trio of Tricks"; originally sold for $5.50. (See 159642 for matching brooch.) |
| 160615 | 10/24/1950 | Adolph Katz | Brooch | Long-stemmed floral with baguettes advertised as "White Fire" (See 160630 for "White Fire" necklace.) |
| 160616 | 10/24/1950 | Adolph Katz | Brooch | Abstract |
| 160617 | 10/24/1950 | Adolph Katz | Necklace | Abstract |
| 160618 | 10/24/1950 | Adolph Katz | Necklace | Abstract lariat style |
| 160619 | 10/24/1950 | Adolph Katz | Brooch | Leaf |
| 160620 | 10/24/1950 | Adolph Katz | Necklace | Abstract two dangles |
| 160621 | 10/24/1950 | Adolph Katz | Brooch | Abstract |
| 160622 | 10/24/1950 | Adolph Katz | Necklace | Lariat style with heart |
| 160623 | 10/24/1950 | Adolph Katz | Necklace | Abstract |
| 160624 | 10/2/1950 | Adolph Katz | Necklace | Floral grapes |
| 160625 | 10/24/1950 | Adolph Katz | Necklace | Abstract nine dangles |
| 160626 | 10/24/1950 | Adolph Katz | Necklace | Abstract three dangles |
| 160628 | 10/24/1950 | Adolph Katz | Necklace | Three leaves |

160630

CORO AND VENDÔME JEWELRY

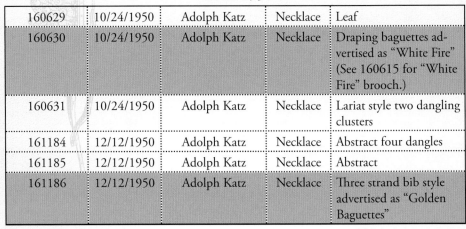

| 160629 | 10/24/1950 | Adolph Katz | Necklace | Leaf |
| 160630 | 10/24/1950 | Adolph Katz | Necklace | Draping baguettes advertised as "White Fire" (See 160615 for "White Fire" brooch.) |
| 160631 | 10/24/1950 | Adolph Katz | Necklace | Lariat style two dangling clusters |
| 161184 | 12/12/1950 | Adolph Katz | Necklace | Abstract four dangles |
| 161185 | 12/12/1950 | Adolph Katz | Necklace | Abstract |
| 161186 | 12/12/1950 | Adolph Katz | Necklace | Three strand bib style advertised as "Golden Baguettes" |

161186

# CORO 1951

161936

162418

| Design Patent Number | Date Issued | Designer | Jewelry Type | Brief Description |
| --- | --- | --- | --- | --- |
| 161464 | 1/2/1951 | Adolph Katz | Brooch | Bow with chandelier style drop |
| 161760 | 1/30/1951 | Adolph Katz | Necklace | Lariat style abstract |
| 161936 | 2/13/1951 | Adolph Katz | Brooch | Crown |
| 162416 | 3/13/1951 | Adolph Katz | Pin Clip | Butterfly |
| 162417 | 3/13/1951 | Adolph Katz | Brooch | Female dancer |
| 162418 | 3/13/1951 | Adolph Katz | Brooch | Vendor selling balloons |
| 162419 | 3/13/1951 | Adolph Katz | Brooch | Woman holding flowers |
| 162420 | 3/13/1951 | Adolph Katz | Brooch | Woman full rhinestone skirt |
| 162421 | 3/13/1951 | Adolph Katz | Brooch | Female dancer |
| 163186 | 5/8/1951 | Adolph Katz | Brooch | Seashell |
| 163187 | 5/8/1951 | Adolph Katz | Brooch | Asian woman sitting under a tree |

| 163188 | 5/8/1951 | Adolph Katz | Brooch | Abstract bird |
| 163189 | 5/8/1951 | Adolph Katz | Brooch | Bird on branch |
| 163190 | 5/8/1951 | Adolph Katz | Brooch | Two birds on branch with lantern |
| 163191 | 5/8/1951 | Adolph Katz | Brooch | Leaf |
| 163192 | 5/8/1951 | Adolph Katz | Brooch | Fawn drinking at waterfall |
| 163193 | 5/8/1951 | Adolph Katz | Brooch | Woman |
| 163194 | 5/8/1951 | Adolph Katz | Brooch | Man, woman buying beverages from cart |
| 163195 | 5/8/1951 | Adolph Katz | Brooch | Bird of paradise |
| 163196 | 5/8/1951 | Adolph Katz | Brooch | Abstract starburst |
| 163197 | 5/8/1951 | Adolph Katz | Brooch | Abstract bow |
| 163199 | 5/8/1951 | Adolph Katz | Brooch | Woman |
| 163200 | 5/8/1951 | Adolph Katz | Duette | Love birds Duette |
| 163201 | 5/8/1951 | Adolph Katz | Brooch | Heart |
| 163202 | 5/8/1951 | Adolph Katz | Brooch | Female dancer |

163192

163200

162420

**1951 Coro female dancer pin.** This 2½" x 1½" delightful dancing lady brooch is design patent number 162420 issued March 13, 1951, to Adolph Katz for Coro. It is one of many amazingly lovely figural brooches produced by Coro in that year. Her skirt brilliantly sparkles with clear rhinestones set in bright gold-tone metal. $75.00 – 120.00.

**1951 Coro soaring bird pin.** In the 1950s Coro continued to produce wonderful figural pieces, including this 2¾" x 1½" soaring bird brooch featuring gold-tone metal, red eyes, and sparkling golden topaz rhinestones. Heavy and well made, this brooch is design patent number 163188 issued May 8, 1951, to Adolph Katz for Coro. It is signed "Coro" without the copyright symbol. $60.00 – 85.00.

163188

**1951 Coro Craft Bird of Paradise pin.** This brightly decorated 2½" x 1½" bird brooch is signed "Coro Craft" without the copyright symbol. It was called "Bird of Paradise" in the Coro 1951 "South Season" advertisement (not shown). The advertisement for this brooch reads, "richly jeweled love-token of The Islands." The design was inspired by the movie *Bird of Paradise*, released by 20th Century Fox. The brooch originally sold for $12.00. Note the baguette-shaped rhinestones and clear rhinestones composing the bird's feathers. This brooch is design patent number 163195 issued May 8, 1951, to Adolph Katz for Coro. $90.00 – 125.00.

163195

CORO AND VENDÔME JEWELRY

91

165167

165334

**1951 Coro Craft owl Duette.**
This ½" x 1¾" clever owl
Duette matches design pat-
ent number 165334 issued
December 4, 1951, to Adolph
Katz for Coro. It is marked
"Coro Craft Duette Pat. No.
1798867." Interestingly, the
design of this 1951 Duette is
similar to the 1944 Katz owl
Duette design patent number
138960. $160.00 – 200.00.
From the collection of Debi Reece.

CORO AND VENDÔME JEWELRY

| 163203 | 5/8/1951 | Adolph Katz | Brooch | Profile of a man in turban |
|---|---|---|---|---|
| 163204 | 5/8/1951 | Adolph Katz | Brooch | Basket of flowers |
| 163205 | 5/8/1951 | Adolph Katz | Brooch | Bird |
| 163289 | 5/15/1951 | Adolph Katz | Necklace | Abstract chandelier style |
| 164995 | 10/30/1951 | Adolph Katz | Necklace | Abstract two dangles |
| 164996 | 10/30/1951 | Adolph Katz | Necklace | Floral |
| 164998 | 10/30/1951 | Adolph Katz | Necklace | Abstract |
| 164999 | 10/30/1951 | Adolph Katz | Necklace | Abstract |
| 165000 | 10/30/1951 | Adolph Katz | Necklace | Abstract |
| 165005 | 10/30/1951 | Adolph Katz | Brooch | Bug |
| 165006 | 10/30/1951 | Adolph Katz | Brooch | Female dancer |
| 165007 | 10/30/1951 | Adolph Katz | Brooch | Floral |
| 165008 | 10/30/1951 | Adolph Katz | Brooch | Abstract single dangle |
| 165009 | 10/30/1951 | Adolph Katz | Brooch | Abstract single dangle |
| 165158 | 11/13/1951 | Adolph Katz | Brooch | Floral |
| 165159 | 11/13/1951 | Adolph Katz | Brooch | Abstract single dangle |
| 165160 | 11/13/1951 | Adolph Katz | Brooch | Floral |
| 165161 | 11/13/1951 | Adolph Katz | Brooch | Bird |
| 165162 | 11/13/1951 | Adolph Katz | Brooch | Tree |
| 165163 | 11/13/1951 | Adolph Katz | Brooch | Long-stemmed floral |
| 165164 | 11/13/1951 | Adolph Katz | Brooch | Long-stemmed floral |
| 165165 | 11/13/1951 | Adolph Katz | Brooch | Abstract single dangle |
| 165166 | 11/13/1951 | Adolph Katz | Brooch | Abstract single dangle |
| 165167 | 11/13/1951 | Adolph Katz | Brooch | Thai or Siamese dancer |
| 165168 | 11/13/1951 | Adolph Katz | Brooch | Abstract |
| 165169 | 11/13/1951 | Adolph Katz | Brooch | Leaf |
| 165170 | 11/13/1951 | Adolph Katz | Brooch | Floral |
| 165171 | 11/13/1951 | Adolph Katz | Brooch | Floral |
| 165286 | 11/27/1951 | Adolph Katz | Brooch | Abstract |
| 165287 | 11/27/1951 | Adolph Katz | Duette | Calla lily Duette |
| 165288 | 11/27/1951 | Adolph Katz | Duette | Floral leaves |
| 165289 | 11/27/1951 | Adolph Katz | Duette | Rhinestone Duette |
| 165290 | 11/27/1951 | Adolph Katz | Duette | Leaf-style Duette |
| 165334 | 12/4/1951 | Adolph Katz | Duette | Owls |
| 165460 | 12/18/1951 | Adolph Katz | Brooch | Floral |
| 165461 | 12/18/1951 | Adolph Katz | Brooch | Floral leaves |
| 165462 | 12/18/1951 | Adolph Katz | Brooch | Abstract floral |
| 165463 | 12/18/1951 | Adolph Katz | Brooch | Floral |
| 165464 | 12/18/1951 | Adolph Katz | Brooch | Floral |
| 165465 | 12/18/1951 | Adolph Katz | Brooch | Abstract floral |
| 165466 | 12/18/1951 | Adolph Katz | Brooch | Leaf |
| 165467 | 12/18/1951 | Adolph Katz | Brooch | Floral |
| 165468 | 12/18/1951 | Adolph Katz | Brooch | Heart |
| 165527 | 12/25/1951 | Adolph Katz | Brooch | Floral |
| 165528 | 12/25/1951 | Adolph Katz | Brooch | Heart |
| 165541 | 12/25/1951 | Adolph Katz | Stick Pin | Abstract |

# CORO 1952

| Design Patent Number | Date Issued | Designer | Jewelry Type | Brief Description |
|---|---|---|---|---|
| 165586 | 1/1/1952 | Adolph Katz | Brooch | Bow |
| 166318 | 4/1/1952 | Adolph Katz | Necklace | Floral |
| 166319 | 4/1/1952 | Adolph Katz | Duette | Abstract |
| 166551 | 4/22/1952 | Adolph Katz | Necklace | Advertised in 1952 ad as "Eugenic" and most likely signed "Corocraft" |
| 166606 | 4/29/1952 | Adolph Katz | Brooch | Abstract |
| 166607 | 4/29/1952 | Adolph Katz | Necklace | Seven leaves separated by navette rhinestones (See 166969 for matching brooch.) |
| 166608 | 4/29/1952 | Adolph Katz | Bracelet | Cuff Rose (See patent number 166755 for another rose bracelet.) |
| 166609 | 4/29/1952 | Adolph Katz | Pin Clip | Tubes with pear shaped stones (See 166681 for matching necklace.) |
| 166674 | 5/6/1952 | Adolph Katz | Bracelet | Floral beaded center (See 166686 for matching necklace.) |
| 166675 | 5/6/1952 | Adolph Katz | Brooch | Rose (See 166608 for matching bracelet.) |
| 166676 | 6/5/1952 | Adolph Katz | Necklace | Abstract one dangle |
| 166677 | 5/6/1952 | Adolph Katz | Necklace | Broken circle abstract |
| 166680 | 5/6/1952 | Adolph Katz | Necklace | Rose (See 167036 for matching earring.) |
| 166681 | 5/6/1952 | Adolph Katz | Necklace | Tubes with pear shaped stones (See 166609 for matching brooch.) |
| 166682 | 5/6/1952 | Adolph Katz | Necklace | Floral leaves |
| 166683 | 5/6/1952 | Adolph Katz | Necklace | Necklace with invisibly set stones (See 166976 for matching bracelet.) |
| 166684 | 5/6/1952 | Adolph Katz | Necklace | Abstract two dangles |
| 166685 | 5/6/1952 | Adolph Katz | Necklace | Abstract |
| 166686 | 5/6/1952 | Adolph Katz | Necklace | Floral beaded center (See 166691 for matching brooch.) |
| 166687 | 5/6/1952 | Adolph Katz | Earring | Rose (See 166680 for matching necklace.) |
| 166690 | 5/6/1952 | Adolph Katz | Necklace | Floral leaves abstract |
| 166691 | 5/6/1952 | Adolph Katz | Brooch | Floral beaded center (See166674 for matching bracelet.) |
| 166755 | 5/13/1952 | Adolph Katz | Bracelet | Rose cuff (See 166687 for matching earring.) |

166319

166551

166608

166691

167037

167084

168042

168047

CORO AND VENDÔME JEWELRY

| 166969 | 6/10/1952 | Adolph Katz | Brooch | Seven leaves separated by navette rhinestones (See 166607 for matching necklace.) |
|---|---|---|---|---|
| 166970 | 6/10/1952 | Adolph Katz | Brooch | Bird |
| 166971 | 6/10/1952 | Adolph Katz | Brooch | Three leaves |
| 166972 | 6/10/1952 | Adolph Katz | Brooch | Leaf beaded center |
| 166973 | 6/10/1952 | Adolph Katz | Brooch | Bow |
| 166974 | 6/10/1952 | Adolph Katz | Brooch | Abstract broken circle |
| 166975 | 6/10/1952 | Adolph Katz | Brooch | Three circles tied by bow |
| 166976 | 6/10/1952 | Adolph Katz | Bracelet | Cuff invisibly set stones (See 166683 for matching necklace.) |
| 166980 | 6/10/1952 | Adolph Katz | Brooch | Bow |
| 167036 | 6/17/1952 | Adolph Katz | Earring | Rose (See167038 for matching brooch.) |
| 167037 | 6/17/1952 | Adolph Katz | Duette | Abstract |
| 167038 | 6/17/1952 | Adolph Katz | Brooch | Roses (See 166675 for matching brooch.) |
| 167039 | 6/17/1952 | Adolph Katz | Brooch | Fruit |
| 167040 | 6/17/1952 | Adolph Katz | Brooch | Four leaf floral |
| 167041 | 6/17/1952 | Adolph Katz | Brooch | Long-stemmed floral |
| 167084 | 6/24/1952 | Adolph Katz | Duette | Abstract |
| 167675 | 5/6/1952 | Adolph Katz | Brooch | Rose on branch |
| 168039 | 10/28/1952 | Adolph Katz | Brooch | Abstract |
| 168040 | 10/28/1952 | Adolph Katz | Brooch | Abstract |
| 168041 | 10/28/1952 | Adolph Katz | Brooch | Abstract |
| 168042 | 10/28/1952 | Adolph Katz | Brooch | Tiny baguette flowers (See 168350 for matching bracelet.) |
| 168043 | 10/28/1952 | Adolph Katz | Brooch | Abstract |
| 168044 | 10/28/1952 | Adolph Katz | Brooch | Abstract two dangles |
| 168045 | 10/28/1952 | Adolph Katz | Brooch | Abstract |
| 168046 | 10/28/1952 | Adolph Katz | Brooch | Long-stemmed flower with rose center (See 168353 for matching bracelet.) |
| 168047 | 10/28/1952 | Adolph Katz | Brooch | Seven petal floral (See 168050 for matching necklace.) |
| 168048 | 10/28/1952 | Adolph Katz | Brooch | Long-stemmed floral |
| 168049 | 10/28/1952 | Adolph Katz | Brooch | Leaf or feather |

**1952 Corocraft flower pin.** Emerald-colored rhinestones enhance the beautiful floral drop dangling from this 2¼" pin signed "Corocraft" without the copyright symbol. It is design patent number 168047 issued October 28, 1952, to Adolph Katz for Coro. A matching necklace (not shown) is design patent number 168050. $35.00 – 45.00.

| | | | | |
|---|---|---|---|---|
| 168050 | 10/28/1952 | Adolph Katz | Necklace | Seven petal floral (See 168047 for matching brooch.) |
| 168350 | 12/9/1952 | Adolph Katz | Bracelet | Tiny baguette flowers cuff (See 168042 for matching brooch.) |
| 168351 | 12/9/1952 | Adolph Katz | Bracelet | Rhinestone stripes (See 168512 for matching necklace.) |
| 168353 | 12/9/1952 | Adolph Katz | Bracelet | Flower with rose center (See 168046 for matching brooch.) |
| 168354 | 12/9/1952 | Adolph Katz | Bracelet | Abstract |
| 168356 | 12/9/1952 | Adolph Katz | Bracelet | Abstract |
| 168357 | 12/9/1952 | Adolph Katz | Bracelet | Abstract rhinestone |
| 168359 | 12/9/1952 | Adolph Katz | Bracelet | Abstract rhinestone |
| 168404 | 12/16/1952 | Adolph Katz | Brooch | Floral leaf abstract |
| 168405 | 12/16/1952 | Adolph Katz | Necklace | Abstract three dangles |
| 168406 | 12/16/1952 | Adolph Katz | Duette | Floral |
| 168407 | 12/16/1952 | Adolph Katz | Brooch | Abstract starburst |
| 168408 | 12/16/1952 | Adolph Katz | Necklace | Fancy rhinestone necklace advertised in 1952 ad "Royal Galaxy" |
| 168456 | 12/23/1952 | Adolph Katz | Necklace | Abstract floral leaves |
| 168457 | 12/23/1952 | Adolph Katz | Necklace | Abstract twist |
| 168458 | 12/23/1952 | Adolph Katz | Necklace | Abstract one drop |
| 168512 | 12/30/1952 | Adolph Katz | Necklace | Rhinestone stripes (See 168351 for matching bracelet.) |

168350

168406

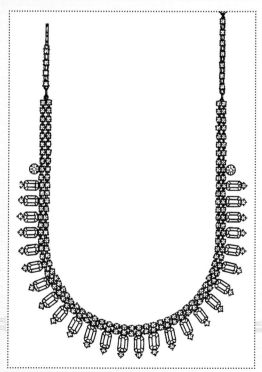
168512

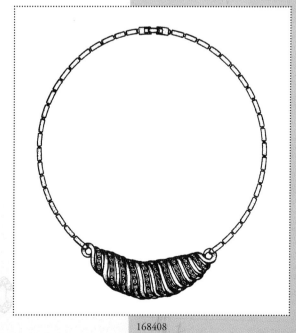
168408

CORO AND VENDÔME JEWELRY

169001

169002

169499

169503

CORO AND VENDÔME JEWELRY

| Design Patent Number | Date Issued | Designer | Jewelry Type | Brief Description |
|---|---|---|---|---|
| 168551 | 1/6/1953 | Adolph Katz | Necklace | Feathers or leaves |
| 168552 | 1/6/1953 | Adolph Katz | Necklace | Floral |
| 168553 | 1/6/1953 | Adolph Katz | Necklace | Abstract one dangle |
| 168554 | 1/6/1953 | Adolph Katz | Necklace | Abstract floral |
| 168555 | 1/6/1953 | Adolph Katz | Necklace | Floral double flower |
| 168556 | 1/6/1953 | Adolph Katz | Necklace | Abstract |
| 168557 | 1/6/1953 | Adolph Katz | Necklace | Floral with grapes |
| 168558 | 1/6/1953 | Adolph Katz | Necklace | Floral drop (168620 matching earring) |
| 168559 | 1/6/1953 | Adolph Katz | Necklace | Abstract five dangles |
| 168560 | 1/6/1953 | Adolph Katz | Necklace | Tiny rhinestone flowers and ribbon (168623 matching brooch) |
| 168561 | 1/6/1953 | Adolph Katz | Necklace | Rhinestones all around bib style (168572 matching earring) |
| 168562 | 1/6/1953 | Adolph Katz | Necklace | Locket |
| 168563 | 1/6/1953 | Adolph Katz | Brooch | Abstract |
| 168621 | 1/13/1953 | Adolph Katz | Brooch | Abstract one dangle |
| 168623 | 1/13/1953 | Adolph Katz | Brooch | Tiny rhinestone flowers and ribbon (168560 matching necklace) |
| 168938 | 3/3/1953 | Adolph Katz | Brooch | Floral |
| 168939 | 3/3/1953 | Adolph Katz | Brooch | Pinwheel style |
| 169001 | 3/10/1953 | Adolph Katz | Brooch | Female dancer holding fan |
| 169002 | 3/10/1953 | Adolph Katz | Duette | Male and female dancers |
| 169492 | 5/5/1953 | Adolph Katz | Brooch | Abstract floral |
| 169493 | 5/5/1953 | Adolph Katz | Brooch | Abstract interlocking loops |
| 169495 | 5/5/1953 | Adolph Katz | Earring | Rhinestone circle (See 169601 for matching bracelet.) |
| 169498 | 5/5/1953 | Adolph Katz | Brooch | Round baguette center (See 169598 for matching necklace.) |
| 169499 | 5/5/1953 | Adolph Katz | Brooch | Round baguette center (See 169597 for matching bracelet.) |
| 169500 | 5/5/1953 | Adolph Katz | Earring | Round baguette center (See 169499 for matching brooch.) |
| 169501 | 5/5/1953 | Adolph Katz | Brooch | Two leaves (169600 matching necklace) |
| 169503 | 5/5/1953 | Adolph Katz | Brooch | Cluster rhinestone flowers (See 169675 for matching bracelet.) |

| 169505 | 5/5/1953 | Adolph Katz | Brooch | Rhinestone circle (See 169495 for matching earring.) |
|---|---|---|---|---|
| 169506 | 5/5/1953 | Adolph Katz | Brooch | Abstract |
| 169593 | 5/19/1953 | Adolph Katz | Necklace | Interlocking ribbons (See 169595 for matching necklace.) |
| 169594 | 5/19/1953 | Adolph Katz | Bracelet | Interlocking ribbons (See 169493 for matching brooch.) |
| 169595 | 5/19/1953 | Adolph Katz | Necklace | Abstract interlocking loops |
| 169597 | 5/19/1953 | Adolph Katz | Bracelet | Round baguette center (See 169498 for matching brooch.) |
| 169598 | 5/19/1953 | Adolph Katz | Necklace | Round baguette center (See 169500 for matching earring.) |
| 169600 | 5/19/1953 | Adolph Katz | Necklace | Two leaves (169501 matching brooch) |
| 169601 | 5/19/1953 | Adolph Katz | Bracelet | Rhinestone circle (See 169677 for matching necklace.) |
| 169610 | 5/19/1953 | Adolph Katz | Brooch | Two leaves with rhinestone flowers (See 169849 for matching necklace.) |
| 169611 | 5/19/1953 | Adolph Katz | Brooch | Leaf |
| 169612 | 5/19/1953 | Adolph Katz | Brooch | Leaf |
| 169613 | 5/19/1953 | Adolph Katz | Brooch | Abstract |
| 169614 | 5/19/1953 | Adolph Katz | Brooch | Abstract wreath |
| 169615 | 5/19/1953 | Adolph Katz | Brooch | Two leaves |
| 169616 | 5/19/1953 | Adolph Katz | Brooch | Rhinestone drop (169762 matching necklace) |
| 169617 | 5/19/1953 | Adolph Katz | Brooch | Abstract |
| 169618 | 5/19/1953 | Adolph Katz | Brooch | Rose (See 170465 for matching bracelet.) |
| 169619 | 5/19/1953 | Adolph Katz | Brooch | Long-stemmed rose (169763 matching necklace) |
| 169620 | 5/19/1953 | Adolph Katz | Brooch | Abstract floral two dangles |
| 169621 | 5/19/1953 | Adolph Katz | Brooch | Abstract |
| 169622 | 5/19/1953 | Adolph Katz | Brooch | Curved leaves floral (169680 matching necklace) |
| 169675 | 6/26/1953 | Adolph Katz | Bracelet | Cluster rhinestone flowers (See 169676 for matching necklace.) |
| 169676 | 5/26/1953 | Adolph Katz | Necklace | Cluster rhinestone flowers (See 169503 for matching brooch.) |

169594

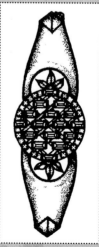

169601

CORO AND VENDÔME JEWELRY

97

CORO AND VENDÔME JEWELRY

169610

169618

169679

170261

| 169677 | 5/26/1953 | Adolph Katz | Necklace | Rhinestone circle (See 169505 for matching brooch.) |
|---|---|---|---|---|
| 169678 | 5/26/1953 | Adolph Katz | Brooch | Abstract floral, one dangle |
| 169679 | 5/26/1953 | Adolph Katz | Duette | Cancan dancers |
| 169680 | 5/26/1953 | Adolph Katz | Necklace | Curved leaves floral (169622 matching brooch) |
| 169681 | 5/26/1953 | Adolph Katz | Brooch | Abstract long-stemmed floral leaves |
| 169682 | 5/26/1953 | Adolph Katz | Brooch | Abstract |
| 169760 | 6/2/1953 | Adolph Katz | Bracelet | Abstract bell shapes probably plastic (169761 matching necklace) |
| 169761 | 6/2/1953 | Adolph Katz | Necklace | Abstract bell shapes probably plastic (169760 matching bracelet) |
| 169762 | 6/2/1953 | Adolph Katz | Necklace | Rhinestone drop (169616 matching brooch) |
| 169763 | 6/2/1953 | Adolph Katz | Necklace | Floral rose (169619 matching brooch) |
| 169764 | 6/2/1953 | Adolph Katz | Necklace | Abstract five dangles |
| 169765 | 6/2/1953 | Adolph Katz | Brooch | Long-stemmed floral |
| 169814 | 6/9/1953 | Adolph Katz | Necklace | Rose (See 169618 for matching brooch.) |
| 169849 | 6/16/1953 | Adolph Katz | Necklace | Two leaves with rhinestone flowers (See 170123 for matching bracelet.) |
| 169850 | 6/16/1953 | Adolph Katz | Necklace | Three row rhinestone center (170125 matching bracelet.) |
| 169852 | 6/16/1953 | Adolph Katz | Necklace | Floral |
| 169853 | 6/16/1953 | Adolph Katz | Necklace | Abstract |
| 169854 | 6/16/1953 | Adolph Katz | Necklace | Abstract |
| 170123 | 8/4/1953 | Adolph Katz | Bracelet | Two leaves with rhinestone flowers (See 169610 for matching brooch.) |
| 170124 | 8/4/1953 | Adolph Katz | Bracelet | Abstract rectangular rhinestone center |
| 170125 | 8/4/1953 | Adolph Katz | Bracelet | Three row rhinestone center (169850 matching necklace) |
| 170261 | 8/25/1953 | Adolph Katz | Brooch | Ornament drop (See 170582 for matching necklace.) |
| 170262 | 8/25/1953 | Adolph Katz | Earring | Ornament drop (See 170581 for matching bracelet.) |

| | | | | |
|---|---|---|---|---|
| 170263 | 8/25/1953 | Adolph Katz | Earring | Ornament drop (See 170262 for another earring style.) |
| 170264 | 8/25/1953 | Adolph Katz | Brooch | Wreath |
| 170266 | 8/25/1953 | Adolph Katz | Earring | Pearls rhinestone ribbon (See 170264 for matching brooch.) |
| 170465 | 9/22/1953 | Adolph Katz | Bracelet | Rose (See 169814 for matching necklace.) |
| 170579 | 10/13/1953 | Adolph Katz | Brooch | Rhinestone studded floral (170580, 170819 matching earrings) |
| 170581 | 10/13/1953 | Adolph Katz | Bracelet | Abstract |
| 170582 | 10/13/1953 | Adolph Katz | Necklace | Ornament drop (See 170263 for matching earring.) |
| 170583 | 10/13/1953 | Adolph Katz | Bracelet | Pearls rhinestone ribbon (See 170584 for matching necklace.) |
| 170584 | 10/13/1953 | Adolph Katz | Necklace | Pearls rhinestone ribbon (See 170266 for matching earring.) |
| 170587 | 10/13/1953 | Adolph Katz | Bracelet | Eye-shaped design (170588 matching necklace) |
| 170588 | 10/13/1953 | Adolph Katz | Necklace | Eye-shaped design (170587 matching bracelet) |
| 170589 | 10/13/1953 | Adolph Katz | Necklace | Heart (170808 matching brooch) |
| 170696 | 10/27/1953 | Adolph Katz | Necklace | Abstract loops advertised as "Chambord" (See 170697 for another necklace style.) |
| 170697 | 10/27/1953 | Adolph Katz | Necklace | Abstract loops advertised as "Chambord" (See 170867 for matching brooch.) |
| 170698 | 10/27/1953 | Adolph Katz | Bracelet | Figure eights (See 170699 for matching necklace.) |

170583

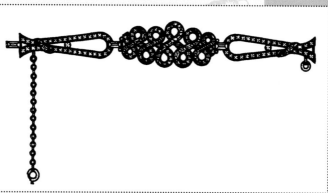

170698

170813

170818

CORO AND VENDÔME JEWELRY

| 170699 | 10/27/1953 | Adolph Katz | Necklace | Figure eights adjustable style (See 170870 for matching brooch.) |
|---|---|---|---|---|
| 170700 | 10/27/1953 | Adolph Katz | Bracelet | Basket weave (See 170701 for matching necklace.) |
| 170701 | 10/27/1953 | Adolph Katz | Necklace | Basket weave (See 171139 for matching earring.) |
| 170703 | 10/27/1953 | Adolph Katz | Necklace | Abstract center pendant |
| 170807 | 11/10/1953 | Adolph Katz | Brooch | Abstract |
| 170808 | 11/10/1953 | Adolph Katz | Brooch | Heart (170589 matching necklace) |
| 170811 | 11/10/1953 | Adolph Katz | Brooch | Abstract |
| 170813 | 11/10/1953 | Adolph Katz | Brooch | Abstract loops advertised as "Chambord" (See 170696 for matching necklace.) |
| 170814 | 11/10/1953 | Adolph Katz | Brooch | Abstract |
| 170816 | 11/10/1953 | Adolph Katz | Brooch | Overlapping wreath shapes (170817 matching earring) |
| 170818 | 11/10/1953 | Adolph Katz | Earring | Chandelier drop (See 170982 for matching necklace.) |
| 170820 | 11/10/1953 | Adolph Katz | Brooch | Abstract |
| 170867 | 11/17/1953 | Adolph Katz | Brooch | Abstract loops advertised as "Chambord" (See 170868 for matching brooch.) |
| 170868 | 11/17/1953 | Adolph Katz | Brooch | Abstract loops in heart shape advertised as "Chambord" (See 170813 for additional brooch.) |
| 170870 | 11/17/1953 | Adolph Katz | Brooch | Figure eights (See 170698 for matching bracelet.) |
| 170871 | 11/17/1953 | Adolph Katz | Brooch | Abstract |
| 170982 | 12/1/1953 | Adolph Katz | Necklace | Chandelier drop (See 171151 for matching bracelet.) |
| 170983 | 12/1/1953 | Adolph Katz | Necklace | Adjustable rhinestone abstract |
| 170984 | 12/1/1953 | Adolph Katz | Necklace | Adjustable rhinestone abstract |
| 170985 | 12/1/1953 | Adolph Katz | Necklace | Adjustable rhinestone abstract |
| 170986 | 12/1/1953 | Adolph Katz | Necklace | Adjustable rhinestone abstract |
| 170987 | 12/1/1953 | Adolph Katz | Necklace | Adjustable rhinestone abstract |

| | | | | |
|---|---|---|---|---|
| 170989 | 12/1/1953 | Adolph Katz | Necklace | Abstract |
| 170991 | 12/1/1953 | Adolph Katz | Bracelet | Abstract |
| 170993 | 12/1/1953 | Adolph Katz | Bracelet | Rows of rhinestones between abstract leaves (170994 matching necklace) |
| 170994 | 12/1/1953 | Adolph Katz | Necklace | Rows of rhinestones between abstract leaves (170993 matching bracelet) |
| 170995 | 12/1/1953 | Adolph Katz | Bracelet | Three abstract leaves (170996 matching necklace) |
| 170996 | 12/1/1953 | Adolph Katz | Necklace | Abstract leaves with two dangles (170995 matching bracelet) |
| 170997 | 12/1/1953 | Adolph Katz | Bracelet | Abstract |
| 170998 | 12/1/1953 | Adolph Katz | Necklace | Abstract |
| 171134 | 12/22/1953 | Adolph Katz | Brooch | Long-stemmed floral |
| 171138 | 12/22/1953 | Adolph Katz | Brooch | Basket weave (See 170700 for matching bracelet.) |
| 171139 | 12/22/1953 | Adolph Katz | Earring | Basket weave (See 1711398 for matching earring.) |
| 171140 | 12/22/1953 | Adolph Katz | Brooch | Abstract |
| 171142 | 12/22/1953 | Adolph Katz | Brooch | Abstract floral |
| 171143 | 12/22/1953 | Adolph Katz | Brooch | Abstract floral leaf |
| 171144 | 12/22/1953 | Adolph Katz | Brooch | Long-stemmed floral two oval flowers (171145 matching earring) |
| 171147 | 12/22/1953 | Adolph Katz | Brooch | Abstract |
| 171149 | 12/22/1953 | Adolph Katz | Brooch | Abstract floral |
| 171150 | 12/22/1953 | Adolph Katz | Brooch | Abstract floral |
| 171151 | 12/22/1953 | Adolph Katz | Bracelet | Chandelier drop (See 170818 for matching earring.) |
| 171152 | 12/22/1953 | Adolph Katz | Bracelet | Basket weave style |
| 171154 | 12/22/1953 | Adolph Katz | Bracelet | One center flower (171155 matching necklace) |
| 171155 | 12/22/1953 | Adolph Katz | Necklace | One center flower pendant (171154 matching bracelet) |
| 171157 | 12/22/1953 | Adolph Katz | Necklace | Seven abstract shell or fan shapes |
| 171158 | 12/22/1953 | Adolph Katz | Bracelet | Abstract |

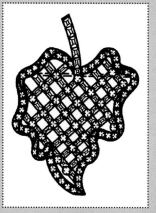

171138

171707

| Design Patent Number | Date Issued | Designer | Jewelry Type | Brief Description |
|---|---|---|---|---|
| 171333 | 1/26/1954 | Adolph Katz | Brooch | Abstract star shape |
| 171336 | 1/26/1954 | Adolph Katz | Brooch | Abstract round |
| 171338 | 1/26/1954 | Adolph Katz | Brooch | Abstract fern |
| 171339 | 1/26/1954 | Adolph Katz | Brooch | Abstract |
| 171340 | 1/26/1954 | Adolph Katz | Brooch | Abstract circle |
| 171341 | 1/26/1954 | Adolph Katz | Brooch | Round with pearls |
| 171344 | 1/26/1954 | Adolph Katz | Brooch | Abstract |
| 171346 | 1/26/1954 | Adolph Katz | Brooch | Circle rhinestone ribbons (See 171347 for matching earring.) |
| 171347 | 1/26/1954 | Adolph Katz | Earring | Circle rhinestone ribbons (See 171346 for matching brooch.) |
| 171352 | 1/26/1954 | Adolph Katz | Brooch | Abstract |
| 171353 | 1/26/1954 | Adolph Katz | Bracelet | Abstract |
| 171354 | 1/26/1954 | Adolph Katz | Necklace | Abstract |
| 171355 | 1/26/1954 | Adolph Katz | Bracelet | Center oval rhinestone (See 171407 for matching brooch.) |
| 171357 | 1/26/1954 | Adolph Katz | Necklace | Elaborate floral (See 171409 for matching brooch.) |
| 171358 | 1/26/1954 | Adolph Katz | Necklace | Heart (See 171410 for matching earring.) |
| 171403 | 2/2/1954 | Adolph Katz | Brooch | Abstract |
| 171406 | 2/2/1954 | Adolph Katz | Brooch | Abstract |
| 171407 | 2/2/1954 | Adolph Katz | Brooch | Center oval rhinestone (See 171355 for matching bracelet.) |
| 171409 | 2/2/1954 | Adolph Katz | Brooch | Elaborate floral (See171357 for matching necklace.) |
| 171410 | 2/2/1954 | Adolph Katz | Earring | Heart (See 171358 for matching necklace.) |
| 171500 | 2/16/1954 | Adolph Katz | Brooch | Abstract |
| 171501 | 2/16/1954 | Adolph Katz | Brooch | Abstract |
| 171502 | 2/16/1954 | Adolph Katz | Brooch | Abstract fan shape (See 171503 for matching earring.) |
| 171503 | 2/16/1954 | Adolph Katz | Earring | Abstract fan shape (See 171502 for matching brooch.) |
| 171649 | 3/9/1954 | Adolph Katz | Necklace | Adjustable rhinestone abstract |
| 171651 | 3/9/1954 | Adolph Katz | Necklace | Called "Laurel," plain and rhinestone leaves (See 171699 for matching brooch.) |

| 171699 | 3/16/1954 | Adolph Katz | Brooch | Called "Laurel," plain and rhinestone leaves (See 171651 for matching necklace.) |
|---|---|---|---|---|
| 171702 | 3/16/1954 | Adolph Katz | Brooch | Abstract |
| 171705 | 3/16/1954 | Adolph Katz | Brooch | Abstract pinwheel style |
| 171706 | 3/16/1954 | Adolph Katz | Brooch | Wreath |
| 171707 | 3/16/1954 | Adolph Katz | Brooch | Baroque pearl design (See 172616 for matching brooch.) |
| 171708 | 3/16/1954 | Adolph Katz | Earring | Leaves and beads (See 171771 for matching necklace.) |
| 171711 | 3/16/1954 | Adolph Katz | Brooch | Fish |
| 171712 | 3/16/1954 | Adolph Katz | Brooch | Abstract floral (See 171713 for matching earring.) |
| 171713 | 3/16/1954 | Adolph Katz | Earring | Abstract floral (See 171712 for matching brooch.) |
| 171722 | 3/23/1954 | Adolph Katz | Necklace | Adjustable baroque pearl |
| 171765 | 3/23/1954 | Adolph Katz | Bracelet | Chunky charm (See ad this chapter and 173740 for another version of this bracelet.) |
| 171766 | 3/23/1954 | Adolph Katz | Bracelet | Faux collar style (See 171767 for matching necklace.) |
| 171767 | 3/23/1954 | Adolph Katz | Necklace | Abstract faux collar (See 171766 for matching bracelet.) |
| 171769 | 3/23/1954 | Adolph Katz | Necklace | Leaves and beads (See 171708 for matching earrings.) |
| 171771 | 3/23/1954 | Adolph Katz | Necklace | Adjustable abstract floral |
| 171772 | 3/23/1954 | Adolph Katz | Necklace | Baroque pearl design (See 171707 for matching brooch.) |
| 171773 | 3/23/1954 | Adolph Katz | Necklace | Abstract |
| 171776 | 3/23/1954 | Adolph Katz | Brooch | Abstract wreath |
| 171779 | 3/23/1954 | Adolph Katz | Necklace | Abstract twist (See 171792 for matching brooch.) |
| 171780 | 3/23/1954 | Adolph Katz | Earring | Wreath twisted |
| 171781 | 3/23/1954 | Adolph Katz | Earring | Twisted style |
| 171782 | 3/23/1954 | Adolph Katz | Bracelet | Tiny flowers (See 171783 for matching necklace.) |
| 171783 | 3/23/1954 | Adolph Katz | Necklace | Tiny flowers (See 171787 for matching earring.) |

171708

171784

171789

171794

| 171784 | 3/23/1954 | Adolph Katz | Brooch | Heart tiny flowers (See 171785 for matching brooch.) |
| 171785 | 3/23/1954 | Adolph Katz | Brooch | Tiny flowers (See 171782 for matching bracelet.) |
| 171787 | 3/23/1954 | Adolph Katz | Earring | Tiny flowers (See 171784 for matching brooch.) |
| 171788 | 3/23/1954 | Adolph Katz | Brooch | Double birds (See 171981 for matching necklace.) |
| 171789 | 3/23/1954 | Adolph Katz | Brooch | Double birds in tree (See 171788 for matching brooch.) |
| 171790 | 3/23/1954 | Adolph Katz | Brooch | Double birds on branch |
| 171792 | 3/23/1954 | Adolph Katz | Brooch | Wreath twist-style (See 171779 for matching necklace.) |
| 171794 | 3/23/1954 | Adolph Katz | Duette | Owls |
| 171795 | 3/23/1954 | Adolph Katz | Brooch | Floral |
| 171796 | 3/23/1954 | Adolph Katz | Brooch | Fish |
| 171797 | 3/23/1954 | Adolph Katz | Brooch | Abstract floral |
| 171799 | 3/23/1954 | Adolph Katz | Brooch | Abstract |
| 171978 | 4/20/1954 | Adolph Katz | Necklace | Floral tiny flowers |
| 171979 | 4/20/1954 | Adolph Katz | Necklace | Floral |
| 171980 | 4/20/1954 | Adolph Katz | Necklace | Abstract |
| 171981 | 4/20/1954 | Adolph Katz | Necklace | Double birds (See 172097 for matching bracelet.) |
| 171982 | 4/20/1954 | Adolph Katz | Necklace | Abstract |
| 172032 | 4/27/1954 | Adolph Katz | Bracelet | Chunky charm (See ad this chapter and 171765 for similar bracelet.) |
| 172095 | 5/4/1954 | Adolph Katz | Necklace | Floral pendant |
| 172097 | 5/4/1954 | Adolph Katz | Bracelet | Double birds |
| 172149 | 5/11/1954 | Adolph Katz | Brooch | Knot style |
| 172152 | 5/11/1954 | Adolph Katz | Brooch | Long-stemmed floral (See 172154 for matching earring.) |
| 172154 | 5/11/1954 | Adolph Katz | Earring | Floral (See 171152 for matching long-stemmed floral brooch.) |
| 172158 | 5/11/1954 | Adolph Katz | Brooch | Abstract |
| 172161 | 5/11/1954 | Adolph Katz | Brooch | Floral wreath (See 172162 for matching earring.) |
| 172162 | 5/11/1954 | Adolph Katz | Earring | Floral (See 172161 for matching brooch.) |
| 172280 | 5/25/1954 | Adolph Katz | Brooch | Seahorse |

| | | | | |
|---|---|---|---|---|
| 172281 | 5/25/1954 | Adolph Katz | Brooch | Fruit drop (See 172283 for additional earring style.) |
| 172283 | 5/25/1954 | Adolph Katz | Earring | Fruit drop (See 172602 for matching bracelet.) |
| 172284 | 5/25/1954 | Adolph Katz | Brooch | Floral |
| 172286 | 5/25/1954 | Adolph Katz | Brooch | Floral |
| 172344 | 6/1/1954 | Adolph Katz | Bracelet | Crossing ribbons (See 172345 for matching necklace.) |
| 172345 | 6/1/1954 | Adolph Katz | Necklace | Crossing ribbons (See 172344 for matching bracelet.) |
| 172346 | 6/1/1954 | Adolph Katz | Necklace | Adjustable abstract |
| 172347 | 6/1/1954 | Adolph Katz | Necklace | Floral |
| 172348 | 6/1/1954 | Adolph Katz | Necklace | Adjustable abstract |
| 172349 | 6/1/1954 | Adolph Katz | Necklace | Adjustable floral small flowers |
| 172350 | 6/1/1954 | Adolph Katz | Necklace | Adjustable abstract |
| 172504 | 6/29/1954 | Adolph Katz | Necklace | Adjustable rhinestone floral |
| 172505 | 6/29/1954 | Adolph Katz | Locket | Book shape |
| 172599 | 7/13/1954 | Adolph Katz | Necklace | Abstract chandelier style |
| 172600 | 7/13/1954 | Adolph Katz | Necklace | Abstract |
| 172601 | 7/13/1954 | Adolph Katz | Necklace | Abstract |
| 172602 | 7/13/1954 | Adolph Katz | Bracelet | Fruit drop (See172603 for matching necklace.) |
| 172603 | 7/13/1954 | Adolph Katz | Necklace | Fruit drop (See 172281 for matching earring.) |
| 172605 | 7/13/1954 | Adolph Katz | Bracelet | Rose (See 172606 for matching necklace.) |
| 172606 | 7/13/1954 | Adolph Katz | Necklace | Adjustable rose (See 172605 for matching bracelet.) |
| 172607 | 7/13/1954 | Adolph Katz | Bracelet | Abstract |
| 172610 | 7/13/1954 | Adolph Katz | Necklace | Abstract |
| 172611 | 7/13/1954 | Adolph Katz | Necklace | Chain links with rhinestones |
| 172612 | 7/13/1954 | Adolph Katz | Earring | Chain link with rhinestone |
| 172613 | 7/13/1954 | Adolph Katz | Necklace | Rhinestone ribbon over beads (See172614 for matching brooch.) |
| 172614 | 7/13/1954 | Adolph Katz | Brooch | Rhinestone ribbon over beads (See 172613 for matching necklace.) |
| 172616 | 7/13/1954 | Adolph Katz | Brooch | Baroque pearl design (See 171772 for matching necklace.) |
| 172622 | 7/13/1954 | Adolph Katz | Brooch | Abstract |
| 172623 | 7/13/1954 | Adolph Katz | Earring | Fringe-style three stone dangles (See 172886 for matching necklace.) |

172281

173210

173358

173359

CORO AND VENDÔME JEWELRY

| 172794 | 8/10/1954 | Adolph Katz | Necklace | Adjustable floral with beads |
|---|---|---|---|---|
| 172883 | 8/24/1954 | Adolph Katz | Necklace | Double flower |
| 172886 | 8/24/1954 | Adolph Katz | Necklace | Fringe-style three stone dangles (See 172623 for matching earrings.) |
| 172889 | 8/24/1954 | Adolph Katz | Bracelet | Abstract |
| 173205 | 10/2/1954 | Adolph Katz | Brooch | Abstract |
| 173206 | 10/12/1954 | Adolph Katz | Brooch | Abstract (See 173348 for matching bracelet.) |
| 173207 | 10/12/1954 | Adolph Katz | Brooch | Leaf |
| 173208 | 10/12/1954 | Adolph Katz | Brooch | Double arrows with heart shaped tips (See 173209 for matching earring.) |
| 173209 | 10/12/1954 | Adolph Katz | Earring | Arrow with heart shaped tip (See 173208 for matching brooch.) |
| 173210 | 10/12/1954 | Adolph Katz | Brooch | Long-stemmed flowers and fruit (See 173211 for matching brooch.) |
| 173211 | 10/12/1954 | Adolph Katz | Brooch | Flowers and fruit (See 173213 for matching earring.) |
| 173213 | 10/12/1954 | Adolph Katz | Earring | Flowers and fruit (See 173352 for matching necklace.) |
| 173215 | 10/12/1954 | Adolph Katz | Brooch | Floral |
| 173216 | 10/12/1954 | Adolph Katz | Brooch | Abstract floral |
| 173217 | 10/12/1954 | Adolph Katz | Brooch | Abstract two dangles |
| 173218 | 10/12/1954 | Adolph Katz | Earring | Abstract two dangles |
| 173219 | 10/12/1954 | Adolph Katz | Brooch | Abstract |
| 173220 | 10/12/1954 | Adolph Katz | Earring | Abstract bow with large rectangular center stone (See 173359 for matching brooch.) |
| 173221 | 10/12/1954 | Adolph Katz | Brooch | Abstract broken circle |
| 173222 | 10/12/1954 | Adolph Katz | Brooch | Abstract |
| 173348 | 11/2/1954 | Adolph Katz | Bracelet | Abstract cuff (See 173206 for matching brooch.) |
| 173352 | 11/2/1954 | Adolph Katz | Necklace | Flowers and fruit (See 173353 for matching necklace.) |
| 173353 | 11/2/1954 | Adolph Katz | Necklace | Flowers and fruit (See 173210 for matching brooch.) |
| 173354 | 11/2/1954 | Adolph Katz | Brooch | Abstract floral |
| 173355 | 11/2/1954 | Adolph Katz | Brooch | Abstract |
| 173356 | 11/2/1954 | Adolph Katz | Earring | Coated with rhinestones (See 173492 for matching bracelet.) |

| | | | | |
|---|---|---|---|---|
| 173357 | 11/2/1954 | Adolph Katz | Brooch | Floral wreath |
| 173358 | 11/2/1954 | Adolph Katz | Brooch | Wreath coated with rhinestones (See173756 for matching earring.) |
| 173359 | 11/2/1954 | Adolph Katz | Brooch | Abstract bow with rectangular center stone (See 173576 for matching necklace.) |
| 173492 | 11/16/1954 | Adolph Katz | Bracelet | Cuff coated with rhinestones (See 173497 for matching necklace.) |
| 173493 | 11/16/1954 | Adolph Katz | Necklace | Abstract |
| 173494 | 11/16/1954 | Adolph Katz | Necklace | Bow |
| 173495 | 11/16/1954 | Adolph Katz | Bracelet | Interlocking floral branches called "Empire" (See photograph, ad, and 173496 for matching necklace.) |

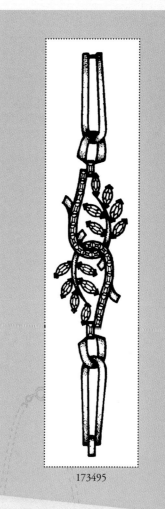

173495

**1954 Corocraft amber-colored rhinestone necklace and bracelet set.** Note the attractive intertwining vines design of the 7" amber and yellow rhinestone bracelet. The bracelet is signed "Corocraft" and is design patent 173495 issued November 16, 1954, to Adolph Katz for Coro. Note the double-band design of the gold-tone metal bracelet. Many bracelet design patents from 1954 show similar double-band designs. The 15" choker necklace is signed "Corocraft Pat. Pend.," but I was unable to locate the exact patent for this necklace. However, design patent number 173496 shows a similar intertwining vines necklace. $55.00 – 75.00.

1954 Coro "the gift that always wins her heart…Coro Jewelry" advertisement. Ten different sets are featured in this advertisement. Original prices, top row left to right: Nocturne necklace and bracelet, $2.00 each; Beatrice necklace, $5.00, and earrings, $3.00; Empire necklace, $5.00, and earrings, 5.00. Original prices, middle row left to right: Love Locket, $3.00, and earrings, $2.00; Sonata necklace, $3.00, and earrings, $2.00; Dazzler pin and earrings, $2.00 each; Belle Fleur necklace, $2.00, and earrings, $2.00. Original prices, bottom row left to right: Ultra bracelet, $10.00, and earrings, $5.00; Valois pin, $10.00, and earrings, $8.00; Corolite necklace, $10.00, and earrings, $2.00.

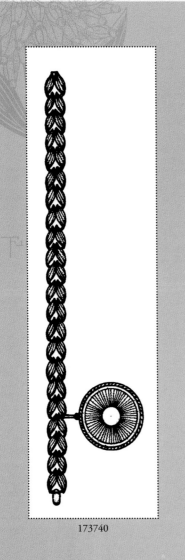

173740

173742

| 173496 | 11/16/1954 | Adolph Katz | Necklace | Interlocking floral branches called "Empire" (See photograph, ad and 173495 for matching bracelet.) |
|---|---|---|---|---|
| 173497 | 11/16/1954 | Adolph Katz | Necklace | Collar coated with rhinestones (See 173358 for matching wreath.) |
| 173498 | 11/16/1954 | Adolph Katz | Necklace | Abstract |
| 173499 | 11/16/1954 | Adolph Katz | Necklace | Abstract |
| 173576 | 11/30/1954 | Adolph Katz | Necklace | Abstract bow with large rectangular center stone (See 173220 for matching earring.) |
| 173577 | 11/30/1954 | Adolph Katz | Bracelet | Double trembling flower (See 173578 for matching necklace.) |
| 173578 | 11/30/1954 | Adolph Katz | Necklace | Double trembling flower (See 173577 for matching bracelet.) |
| 173734 | 12/28/1954 | Adolph Katz | Brooch | Abstract |
| 173735 | 12/28/1954 | Adolph Katz | Brooch | Leaf |
| 173736 | 12/28/1954 | Adolph Katz | Brooch | Leaf or feather |
| 173737 | 12/28/1954 | Adolph Katz | Bracelet | Chunky charm |
| 173740 | 12/28/1954 | Adolph Katz | Bracelet | Chunky charm (See ad this chapter for similar bracelet called "Nocturne" and 172032 for another version of this bracelet.) |
| 173742 | 12/28/1954 | Adolph Katz | Bracelet | "Ultra"; originally sold for $10.00. (See ad this chapter.) |
| 173745 | 12/28/1954 | Adolph Katz | Brooch | Abstract round |
| 173748 | 12/28/1954 | Adolph Katz | Brooch | Leaf |
| 173749 | 12/28/1954 | Adolph Katz | Brooch | Abstract |
| 173750 | 12/28/1954 | Adolph Katz | Brooch | Abstract floral |
| 173751 | 12/28/1954 | Adolph Katz | Brooch | Abstract bow |
| 173752 | 12/28/1954 | Adolph Katz | Brooch | Heart |
| 173754 | 12/28/1954 | Adolph Katz | Brooch | Floral |

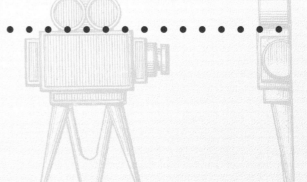

**1930s Coro book chain necklace.** The chain on this early 24" Coro pendant is in the style of turn of the century Victorian brass book chain necklaces, helping to date this fabulous Coro necklace to the 1930s, when Victorian revival jewelry was popular. The interesting button clasp is signed "Coro Pat. Pend." Unfortunately, I was unable to locate the patent for this piece. $65.00 – 85.00. From the collection of Debi Reece.

**1930s Coro green and clear rhinestone Duette.** Coro produced Duette-style brooches for over 20 years, so not all Duette brooches are from the 1930s. However, the Art Deco style of this 2" x ½" Coro Duette, the use of pavé rhinestones, and the nonuse of sterling dates this pretty green and clear rhinestone Duette to the late 1930s. It is signed "Coro Duette" in script and "Pat. No. 1798867," which refers to the Duette mechanism. $80.00 – 160.00.

121913

**Early 1940s Coro patriotic eagle brooch.** Many patriotic eagle brooches were produced in the early 1940s, including this regal 3½" x 2" eagle featuring spread wings. It is signed "Coro" without the copyright symbol and is similar in style to design patent number 121913 issued August 13, 1940, to L. C. Mark. As far as I can determine, L. C. Mark did not design for Coro. However, the similarity in style indicates the Coro eagle brooch dates to the same era. $45.00 – 70.00.

**Early 1940s Coro Oriental dragon clip.** This interesting Coro clip features a light green plastic insert designed to simulate the look of jade. The well-sculpted gold-tone dragon is prettily framed by bright red enamel. This piece is similar in style to the famous "Ming" series designed by Alfred Philippe in 1942. The Trifari Ming series utilized similar faux jade inserts and either red or black enameling. (See example design patent illustrations from this series in chapter 3.) The similarity to the Trifari Ming jewelry indicates the Coro clip also dates from the early 1940s. The above Coro clip is marked "Coro" without the copyright symbol and with utility patent number 1852188. This utility patent (shown below) was issued to Elisha A. Phinney on April 5, 1932, and refers to the clip hardware, not the design of the clip. While clips with this mechanism could have been used for many years, the early date of this utility patent supports the inference that this Coro Oriental dragon clip is an early 1940s Coro piece. $150.00 – 300.00.

CORO AND VENDÔME JEWELRY

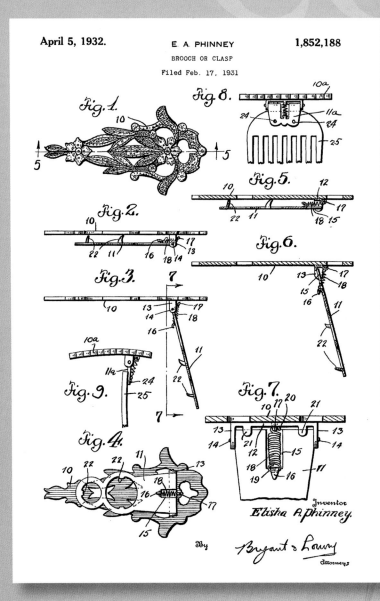

**1943 – 1948 Coro Glamour sterling brooch.** This lovely 3¾" x 1¼" brooch is signed "Glamour Sterling" without the copyright symbol. "Glamour" is one of the many trademarks assigned to Coro and was first used in 1940. This mark, the limited use of rhinestone decorations, and the use of sterling dates this brooch to 1943 – 1948. $65.00 – 80.00.

**1943 – 1948 Coro sterling faux moonstone parure.** All four pieces in this elegant set are marked "Coro Sterling." The faux opal stones are sometimes referred to as "moonstones." The large brooch measures 3¼" x 1¼", the bracelet is 7" x ½", and the clip earrings are ¾". Coro produced many long-stemmed sterling pieces in the years 1943 – 1948, dating this set to that era. $75.00 – 130.00.

**1943 – 1948 Coro sterling long-stemmed flower brooch.** This long 3" x 2¾" sterling brooch is signed "Coro Sterling." Coro long-stemmed sterling brooches are plentiful in the collectible market and are an affordable way to possess a great brooch from this era. $30.00 – 45.00.

**1943 – 1948 Coro sterling multi-color long-stemmed floral brooch.** This 3" long-stemmed sterling silver pin is typical of brooches produced by Coro during the war years and dates from 1943 to 1948. It is signed "Coro Sterling." At this time, Coro produced brooches in sterling silver because the harder metals were needed for the war. Designs from this era also limited the use of imported European rhinestones. Some brooches of this style are patented, but many, like this wonderful example, are not. $30.00 – 45.00. From the collection of Debi Reece.

**1943 – 1948 Coro sterling amber-colored rhinestone double-flower brooch.** This flowing 4" x 2" brooch is signed "Coro Sterling" and dates from 1943 to 1948, when most of these simple yet elegant Coro sterling brooches were produced. Note: Due to the large number of these sterling brooches in the marketplace today, collectors should only purchase mint-condition brooches that have pleasing designs. $30.00 – 45.00. From the collection of Debi Reece.

CORO AND VENDÔME JEWELRY

**1943 – 1948 Coro sterling bug pin.** Unfortunately, I could not locate a design patent for this exceptionally fine 2¼" Coro bug pin. It is signed "Coro Sterling." Notice the deep emerald colored rhinestones decorating the body and the creative enameling on the legs, wings, and antennae. The design and the use of sterling date this pin to 1943 – 1948. $100.00 – 150.00. From the collection of Debi Reece.

**1940s Coro purple enamel flower Duette.** Pretty purple enameling enhances the beauty of this 3" x 1" delightful Duette. It is in wonderful condition. Set in gold-tone metal, this lovely Duette also features green baguette and clear round rhinestones. It is signed "Coro Duette" in script and "Pat. No. 1798867" on the Duette frame. (This is the same utility patent number found on most Coro Duette mechanisms.) The clips are unmarked. Coro produced many Duettes in the 1930s and 1940s. $175.00 – 250.00.

**Late 1940s – 1955 Coro man-with-a-cane pin.** This sparkling 1½" dude with a cane is signed "Coro" without the copyright symbol. The use of wire to form the man's arms and legs is similar to the way Coro utilized wire to form the 1947 patented Coro "wire work" designs. (See page 62 for a 1947 wire work bird.) The nonuse of sterling, the design, and the lack of a copyright symbol date this piece to the late 1940s – 1955. $35.00 – 45.00.

**1949 Coro "glue-on" pins.** Provenance is one way of establishing the dates for costume jewelry. These fascinating pins belong to a friend of mine who remembers purchasing and wearing them in 1949. Notice the dried glue on the backs of the pins. Amazingly, these tiny 1" pins, signed "Coro" in script, were glued directly to the skin to compliment strapless or open-necked fashions. They were sold with a tube of special glue. The customer applied the glue to the back of the pin and then glued the pin, in a flattering position, to her skin. Can you imagine gluing jewelry to your skin? I do not know how to place a value on these great pins from the past. The story is priceless. From the collection of Marty Morganstern.

Back view of Coro "glue-on" pins showing the dried glue.

CORO AND VENDÔME JEWELRY

**1948 – 1955.** When I first purchased this amazingly vibrant raspberry colored enamel Coro 1¾" pin and 1¼" x ¾" clip earrings I assumed by the style the set was from the 1960s or 1970s. However, all pieces are signed "Coro" without the copyright symbol indicating the set was made before 1955. (Coro continued to issue patents for jewelry designs through 1956; however, as a general rule, jewelry with a copyright symbol was produced after 1955.) The nonuse of sterling and the signature date this set to 1948 – 1955. $35.00 – 50.00.

**1948 – 1955 Coro red and pink rhinestone earrings.** These 1" x ½" sparkling clip earrings are interesting because of the tall, three-dimensional design, and the rare combination of red and pink rhinestones. They are signed "Coro" without the copyright symbol. This signature and the non use of sterling date these earrings to 1948 – 1955. $8.00 – 12.00. From the collection of Debi Reece.

**Coro 1948 – 1955 antique-gold-tone and blue rhinestone necklace and pin.** This demi-parure features vibrant light blue rhinestones. It is signed "Coro" in script without the copyright symbol. The necklace measures 16" and the matching brooch measures 1¾". The signature, the style of necklace (an attractive center decoration attached to a plain chain), and the non use of sterling date this set to 1948 – 1955. $50.00 – 65.00. From the collection of Debi Reece.

**1950s Coro chunky charm bracelet.** Coro produced many versions of chunky charm bracelets in the 1950's and 1960's. This Coro example measures 7½" and features fifteen chunky charms. It is signed "Coro" without copyright symbol. This signature and the non use of sterling date this bracelet to 1948 – 1955. This chunky charm bracelet is especially collectible because the green and red balls are Bakelite! $60.00 – 80.00. From the collection of Debi Reece.

**1948 – 1955 Coro carousel pin.** This well-crafted 2" x 1¼" Coro carousel pin is signed "Coro" without the copyright symbol. Carousel jewelry is a popular motif with jewelry designers and has been produced since the early 1940s. The nonuse of sterling dates this fun figural pin to 1948 – 1955. $65.00 – 100.00. From the collection of Debi Reece.

**1948 – 1955 Coro crown pin.** Coro produced many lovely crown brooches including this 1¾" x 1" five-pointed crown featuring red tear-drop shaped rhinestones, aqua color baguette rhinestones, and tiny round clear rhinestones. Set in creamy gold-tone metal, this three dimensional crown sparkles with royal beauty. It is signed "Coro" without the copyright symbol. This signature and the non use of sterling date this piece to 1948 – 1955. $55.00 – 85.00.

**1955 – 1956 Corocraft rhinestone bow necklace and earrings set.** This lovely 16" choker and 1" clip earrings are an example of high-quality Coro jewelry. The necklace is signed "Corocraft Pat. Pend." Each earring is marked "Coro Pat. Pend." with the copyright symbol. Unfortunately, I was unable to find the design patents for this set. The signature on the earrings is confusing. As a general rule, jewelry that is copyrighted is not patented. I believe that this is a transitional set produced in 1955 or 1956, when Coro was starting to copyright rather than patent designs. $55.00 – 70.00.

**1948 – 1955 Coro multicolored rhinestone three-piece set.** Only the 1" clip earrings in this beautiful set are signed "Coro" without the copyright symbol. The 17½" choker and 18" pendant are clearly the same design but both are unmarked. This is a high quality set featuring light amber, dark amber, dark blue and clear prong-set rhinestones. The nonuse of sterling and the signature date this set to 1948 – 1955. $55.00 – 85.00. From the collection of Debi Reece.

**Coro 1955 red thermoset necklace and earrings set.** Called "Cambridge" in the "The Perfect Touch for Every Spring Fashion" advertisement (see page 116), this bright red 16" choker and matching 1" x ½" clip earrings originally sold for $2.00 each. Note that the set in the advertisement is shown in white. When using advertisements to date jewelry it is important to look at the design of the jewelry, not the color. Today's value, $30.00 – 40.00.

1955 "The Perfect Touch for Every
Spring Fashion/Coro Jewelry" advertisement. Eight different
spring jewelry sets are featured in this advertisement. Original prices, top row: Arbutus necklace,
bracelet, pin, and earrings, $2.00 each; Fragrance pin and earrings, $2.00 each; Empress large earrings,
$3.00, and smaller earrings, $2.00. Original prices, middle row: Cambridge necklace, $3.00, and ear-
rings, $2.00; Fanfare brooch and earrings, $5.00 each; 60-inch rope necklace, $3.00. Original prices,
bottom row: Monaco necklace, $3.00, with bracelet, $3.00, and earrings, $2.00; Lily of the Valley neck-
lace, $5.00, and earrings, $2.00; Jasmine necklace and earrings, $2.00 each.

**1955 Coro "Empress" earrings.** Originally selling for $2.00, these 1" clip
earrings feature clear rhinestones encircling a creamy white cabochon stone.
They were advertised as "Empress" in the 1955 Coro "The Perfect Touch
for Every Spring Fashion" advertisement. $8.00 – 12.00. From the collection
of Debi Reece.

**1955 Coro white flower bracelet.** Part of the Coro "Summer Garden" group advertised in 1955, this charming 7" bracelet originally sold for $3.00. The look of a "Summer Garden" is achieved by the pleasing arrangement of light-weight white plastic flowers enhanced by clear round and baguette shaped rhinestones. This bracelet is signed "Coro" without the copyright symbol. In 1955 and 1956 Coro was in the process of copyrighting rather than patenting designs. Many Coro designs produced through 1956 are still patented and do not have the copyright symbol in the signature. This bracelet is one of those transitional pieces. A patent may exist for this bracelet, but I was unable to locate it. $45.00 – 75.00.

**Mid-1950s Coro white plastic flower pin.** Measuring 2½" x 1½", this 2½" x 1½" pin is signed "Coro" without the copyright symbol. It is similar in style to Coro's "Summer Garden" suite advertised in 1955 which suggests this pretty summer flower pin dates to the same time period. $30.00 – 40.00.

1955 "Summer Garden by Coro" advertisement. The ad features a feminine flower set including a bracelet, brooch, necklace and earrings. Each piece originally sold for $3.00. The set in the advertisement features clear rhinestones; however, the set was also available with pink or multicolor rhinestones.

**1955 Coro "Honoré" clear rhinestone necklace and earrings set.** The 1955 Coro "fashionable gifts you know she will love!" advertisement (see page 119) showcases a multicolored version of this clear rhinestone Coro set. The beautiful 2" brooch and 15" choker are signed "Coro Des. Pat. Pend." The necklace is design patent number 175952 issued on November 1, 1955, to Adolph Katz for Coro. The brooch is design patent number 177253 issued March 27, 1956, to Adolph Katz for Coro. Originally selling in 1955 for $3.00 each piece, today's value for this set is $50.00 – 65.00.

Coro jewelry 1955 "fashionable gifts you know she will love!" advertisement. This advertisement features 12 Coro sets featured in four quadrants. Original prices, top left quadrant: Marseilles pin and earrings, $5.00 each; Daphne necklace, $7.50, and earrings, $3.00; Elegance necklace and pin, $5.00 each, and earrings, $3.00; La Rein bracelet, $3.00, and earrings, $2.00. Original prices, top right quadrant: Birch necklace, bracelet, and earrings, $2.00 each; Cultured Pearl Locket, $2.00; Fleur Royale necklace, bracelet, and earrings, $2.00 each. Original prices, bottom left quadrant: Honoré necklace, bracelet, and earrings, $3.00 each; Directoire necklace, $5.00, and earrings, $3.00. Original prices, bottom right quadrant: Sparklette pin, $2.00, and earrings, $2.00; Valencia necklace, $3.00, and earrings, $2.00; Picardy bracelet, $3.00, and earrings, $2.00.

**1956 Coro white enamel bracelet.** The design of this Coro 7" white enamel and white bead bracelet is stylistically similar to design patent number 177853 issued on May 29, 1956, to Adolph Katz for Coro. This design patent is for a brooch, not a bracelet, but the style is similar and indicates the bracelet dates to the same era. $35.00 – 45.00.

**Coro 1956 plastic pin, necklace, and earrings.** Named "Moonray" in the "created to flatter your spring-into-summer fashions" 1956 Coro advertisement (see page 121), this creamy pink necklace measures 16½" and has its original Coro Pegasus paper hang-tag. The 1" clip earrings, like the necklace, are in as-new condition. All pieces are marked "Coro" with the copyright symbol. Originally selling for $2.00 each, today this set is valued at $50.00 – 70.00.

**1956 Coro Love Birds bracelet.** Called the "Love Birds bracelet" in the "created to flatter your spring-into-summer fashions" 1956 advertisement (see page 121), this 7¼" charm bracelet originally sold for $3.00. The charm measures 1½" in diameter and features a pair of cuddling love birds perched over a pink rhinestone heart. It is signed "Coro" with the copyright symbol. $35.00 – 50.00.

**1956 Coro cherub charm bracelet.** This pretty pink and gold-tone 7¼" Coro charm bracelet is similar in design to the Love Birds bracelet shown in the 1956 Coro "created to flatter your spring-into-summer fashions" advertisement and dates to the same era. Instead of love birds, this bracelet features a cherub holding a tiny gold-tone heart engraved with "October." The cherub is sitting on a light pink rhinestone that simulates the look of pink tourmaline. (October has two accepted birthstones, opal and tourmaline.) The bracelet is signed "Coro" with the copyright symbol. $35.00 – 50.00. From the collection of Debi Reece.

Coro 1956 "created to flatter your spring-into-summer wardrobe." advertisement. This advertisement features one charm bracelet, six sets and one Duette. Original prices, top left: Love Birds bracelet, $3.00. Original prices, top right: Coquette necklace and pin, $3.00 each, and earrings, $2.00. Original prices, second row left to right: Ceres necklace and earrings, $2.00 each. Burma necklace, bracelet, and earrings, $2.00 each; Aloha necklace, $3.00, and earrings, $2.00; Chianti necklace, $6.00, and earrings, $4.00. Original prices, third row left to right: Miramar brooch, $5.00, and earrings, $3.00; Moonray necklace, bracelet, and earrings, $2.00 each. Original prices, bottom left: Blithe Blossoms necklace, $5.00, and earrings, $2.00. Original prices, bottom right: Cherubin Duette, $6.00.

1956 Coro "The 'Beautiful Lady' look by Coro" advertisement. Ten lovely Coro sets are featured in this advertisement. Original prices, top row: Thierry necklace, bracelet, and earrings, $3.00 each; Ardmore necklace and earrings, $2.00 each; Avondale necklace, $3.00, and earrings, $2.00; Amelia brooch and earrings, $3.00 each; Hidden Treasure locket, $2.00. Original prices, second row: Rosalinda necklace and earrings, $5.00 each. Original prices, third row: L'Opera necklace, $5.00, and earrings, $3.00; Beauvais necklace, $7.50, with bracelet, $5.00, and earrings, $3.00. Original prices, bottom row: My Fair Lady necklace, $10.00, and earrings, $4.00; Navarre necklace and earrings, $2.00 each.

**1956 Coro rhinestone flower pin.** This graceful 2¼" x 1½" gold-tone and hot pink rhinestone brooch is signed "Coro" with the copyright symbol. Jewelry featuring small rhinestone flowers was popular in the mid-1950s. The 1956 "The 'Beautiful Lady' Look" by Coro advertisement features two similar sets, the Beauvais and the Navarre, designed with rhinestone flowers. The signature and style indicate this pin dates to the same time. $25.00 – 35.00.

**Coro late 1950s travel charm bracelet.** In the late 1950s and 1960s Coro produced many charm bracelets, some with special themes or motifs. For example, the silver-tone charm bracelet advertised in the 1958 – 1959 Montgomery Ward catalog (see page 124) is described as a "Good Luck" charm bracelet featuring "lucky" charms. It originally sold for $3.29. This fun Coro gold-tone travel motif charm bracelet features eleven different travel related charms. It is signed "Coro" with the copyright symbol and dates from the same era. $35.00 – 65.00. From the collection of Debi Reece.

**Late 1950s Coro confetti Lucite parure.** Coro produced many pieces of lovely and inexpensive Lucite jewelry in the mid to late 1950's. The aqua colored confetti Lucite rectangular decorations pop with color on this 16" choker and matching 1" clip earrings. All pieces are signed "Coro" with the copyright symbol. Similar plastic jewelry is shown in the 1958/59 Montgomery Ward catalog (see page 124) helping to date this pretty set to the late 1950s. $25.00 – 35.00.

**Late 1950s Coro red plastic bracelet and earrings.** This pretty set is similar in design and materials to the red Luscious Moonmist set shown in row two of the 1958/59 Ward catalog (see page 124) and dates to the same era. All pieces are signed "Coro" with the copyright symbol. The gold-tone bracelet measures 7½" x ¾". The clip earrings are ¾". $35.00 – 55.00.

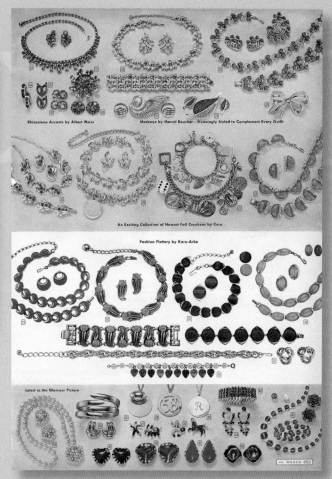

Late 1950s Coro blue thermoset necklace and bracelet set. Shades of blue plastic horse-shoe disks decorate this 16" choker and 7" Coro bracelet. All pieces are signed "Coro" with the copyright symbol. The design is similar to the plastic designs shown in the 1958 – 1959 Wards catalog, and the set dates to the same era. $45.00 – 60.00.

CORO AND VENDÔME JEWELRY

Montgomery Ward 1957/58 catalog page 653. This spectacular Wards catalogue page features jewelry by Albert Weiss, Marcel Boucher, Coro, and Karu-Arke. Top row: "Rhinestone Accents by Albert Weiss" (blue rhinestone jewelry originally ranging in price from $2.19 to $5.49), "Marboux by Marcel Boucher — Stunningly Styled to Complement Every Outfit" (five sets originally ranging in price from $2.19 to $5.49). Second row: "An Exciting Collection of Newest Fall Creations by Coro" (three sets and two charm bracelets originally ranging in price from $1.09 to $3.29). Third row: "Fashion Flattery by Karu-Arke" (five sets and one bracelet originally ranging in price from $1.09 to $2.19). Bottom row: Unmarked jewelry advertised as "Teen Tempters — big fashion at a little price" (a mix of jewelry originally ranging in price from 99¢ to $2.19). Interestingly, the Teen Temper blue expansion bracelet originally sold for $1.89. Today's value for the same bracelet is $30.00 – 45.00!

1956 Coro "Rosalinda" advertisement. The ad reads, "The Beautiful Lady Look captured for you in this exquisite fashion jewelry…created by Coro, to add importance to your loveliest costumes. $5 each, plus tax." Hand-wired Coro jewelry like the Rosalinda set in this ad is extraordinarily rare today. This Coro set today would sell for over $200.00.

**Late 1950s Coro multicolored rhinestone bracelet and earrings set.** This wonderful antique-gold-tone 7½" bracelet and matching 1¼" earrings date to the late 1950s. All pieces are signed "Coro" with the copyright symbol. The ear clip mechanism is design patent number 181904 issued January 14, 1958, to Hans J. Feibelman and assigned to Coro. Interestingly, this is a design patent and not a utility patent. It is for the "look" of the earring back, not the mechanical mechanism. (See utility patent 2400513 for an earlier version of an adjustable ear clip mechanism.) The signature and the utility patent indicate this set could not have been produced before 1958. The style places this set in the late 1950's. $50.00 – 65.00. From the collection of Debi Reece.

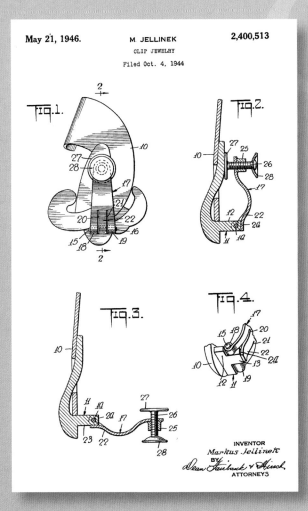

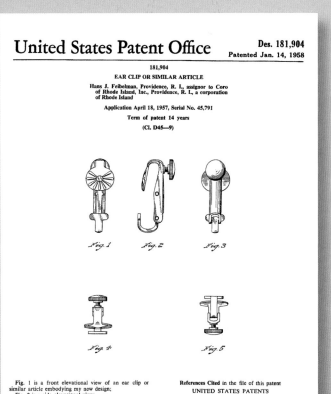

1958 Coro "brilliant jewelry in three beautiful colors for the most exciting fashion year of your life" advertisement. Top row states, "Light up everything — including your gift list with the iridescence of AURORA." Three sets featuring aurora borealis rhinestones are shown in this row. Original prices: Pendante necklace, $2.00; Empress necklace, bracelet, and earrings, $3.00 each; Valasquez necklace, $7.50, and earrings, $3.00. Middle row continues, "…or the rich red color of RUBY." Four sets and a locket are shown in this row. All feature ruby-colored rhinestones. Original prices: Gay Plumage pin, $3.00, and earrings, $2.00; Halcyon necklace and earrings, $2.00 each; Honoré pin and earrings, $2.00 each; Locarno necklace, $3.00, and earrings $2.00; Victoria locket, $2.00. Bottom row concludes, "…or the glowing blue tones of SAPPHIRE." Three sapphire rhinestone sets are shown in this row. Original prices: Desirée necklace and pin, $5.00, and earrings, $4.00; Lorelei necklace and earrings, $2.00 each; Lobelia pin, $5.00, and earrings, $4.00.

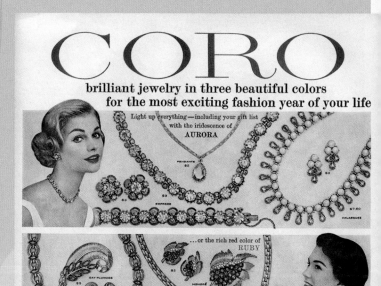

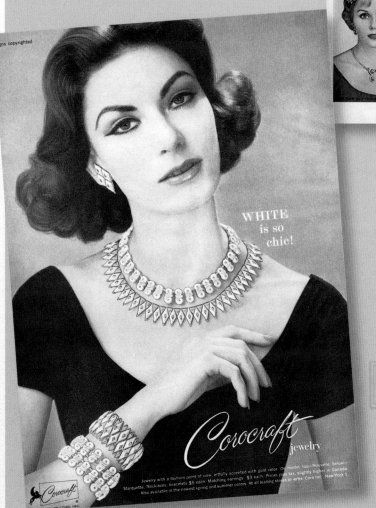

1958 Corocraft "White is so chic!" advertisement. The advertisement reads, "Jewelry with a fashion point of view, artfully accented with gold color. On model: top — Nouvelle, below — Marquette. necklaces, bracelets $5 each. Matching earrings $3 each."

**Coro late 1950s black enamel leaf necklace.** This classic black and white 16" choker necklace is signed "Coro" with the copyright symbol. It is similar in style to the Fragrance bracelet shown in the 1959 Coro "White 'n Hue" advertisement (see page 128) and dates from that time. $25.00 – 35.00. From the collection of Debi Reece.

**Coro late 1950s powder blue ribbed glass stone necklace.** This especially lovely 17" Coro necklace features molded glass stones similar to the stones shown in the 1959 Coro "White 'n Hue" advertisement (see page 128) and dates from the same time period. It is signed "Coro" with the copyright symbol. $65.00 – 95.00.

**Coro late 1950s pink cabochon and molded glass bracelet.** Glowing pink cabochon rhinestones and magnificent molded glass leaves decorate this silver-tone 7¼" bracelet signed "Coro" with the copyright symbol. Jewelry made with these wonderful molded glass leaves was popular from the second half of the 1950s through the 1960s. (See 1959 Coro "White 'n Hue," page 128, and 1960 "Coro in a Paris Garden," page 129, advertisements for more molded glass jewelry from this era.) $60.00 – 80.00. From the collection of Debi Reece.

CORO AND VENDÔME JEWELRY

**Late 1950s Coro ribbed stone brooch.** This beautiful 2¾" x 1¼" brooch features glowing aurora borealis ribbed glass stones arranged in a pleasing floral pattern. Two Coro advertisements in this book, the 1959 "White 'n Hue" ad and the 1960 "Coro in a Paris Garden" ad (see page 129), feature jewelry with interesting molded glass stones suggesting that this ribbed glass stone brooch also dates from the late 1950s or early 1960s. It is signed "Coro" with the copyright symbol. $50.00 – 70.00.

1959 Coro "White 'n Hue jewelry" advertisement. The advertisement reads "White 'n Hue jewelry…the dazzle of white with the drama of color…turns the Sun-Season into your loveliest time of the year!" Nine different jewelry sets are advertised. Original prices, top row: Radiance, $3.00 each piece; two sets of Corsage scatter pins, $2.00 a set; Arbutus necklace and earrings, $2.00 each. Original prices, middle row: Petal Rays bracelet, $3.00; Fragrance bracelet, $2.00; Woodbine pin and earrings, $3.00 each. Original prices, model: Allure pins in different styles, $2.00 each. Original prices, bottom row: Crystalia pin and earrings, $3.00 each; Berry Blossom necklace and earrings, $2.00 each.

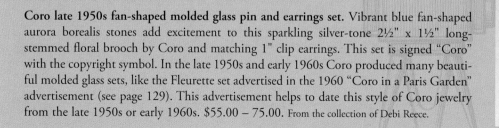

**Coro late 1950s fan-shaped molded glass pin and earrings set.** Vibrant blue fan-shaped aurora borealis stones add excitement to this sparkling silver-tone 2½" x 1½" long-stemmed floral brooch by Coro and matching 1" clip earrings. This set is signed "Coro" with the copyright symbol. In the late 1950s and early 1960s Coro produced many beautiful molded glass sets, like the Fleurette set advertised in the 1960 "Coro in a Paris Garden" advertisement (see page 129). This advertisement helps to date this style of Coro jewelry from the late 1950s or early 1960s. $55.00 – 75.00. From the collection of Debi Reece.

Late 1950s Coro gold-tone and emerald-cut clear rhinestone three-piece set. The 15½" choker is signed "Coro" with the copyright symbol. Interestingly, the 7½" bracelet and 1" clip earrings are unmarked. Coro produced many similar sets in the late 1950s into the 1960s; however, this set is particularly lovely because of the large rectangular rhinestones and high quality gold-tone metal. $45.00 – 70.00. From the collection of Debi Reece.

1960 "In a Paris Garden" advertisement. Three rhinestone sets are featured, two with molded glass stones. Original prices, top: Fleurette necklace and bracelet, $5.00 each, and earrings, $3.00. Original prices, middle: Paris Petals pin, necklace, and earrings, $3.00 each. Original prices, bottom: Mignon necklace, bracelet, and earrings, $3.00.

CORO AND VENDÔME JEWELRY

**Late 1950s Coro rhinestone and pearl parure.** Found in its original box (not shown), this lovely Coro set, including the original blue and silver Coro Pegasus hangtag, is in mint condition. The bracelet measures 7¼", the brooch 3" x 2", and the clip earrings 1¼". Each piece in this lovely parure is signed "Coro" with the copyright symbol. $65.00 – 80.00. From the collection of Debi Reece.

**Coro 1960s enamel and rhinestone owl pin.** Signed "Coro" with the copyright symbol, this sweet owl figural pin was produced in the mid-to-late 1960s. At that time the fashion trends temporarily moved away from glitzy rhinestones to long chain necklaces and nature-theme enameled jewelry, especially small enameled critter pins. This little critter measures 1½" x 1". The tiny cabochon eyes have black plastic pupils embedded in them so that they seem to follow you. In addition, the beautifully enameled and rhinestone encrusted head swivels from side to side. $45.00 – 65.00. From the collection of Debi Reece.

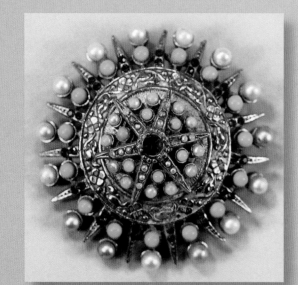

**Late 1950s or early 1960s Coro Byzantine-style brooch.** This wonderful Coro brooch is solidly made and decorated with seed pearls and deep red rhinestones. It has an Old World style that has been repeated many times over the years, making it difficult to date this pin by the style alone. The construction is excellent. It is made in two pieces that are riveted together. The large brooch is 2" in diameter and nearly 1" tall. It is marked "Coro" with the copyright symbol. This signature and the patina date this brooch to the late 1950s or the early 1960s. $40.00 – 65.00.

**Late 1950s or 1960s colorful glass fruit necklace.** The Coro Teens logo was first used in 1940; however, this yummy basket of glass fruit appears to be much newer. This piece is unmarked except for the Coro paper tag, which reads "Coro teens $1.00 plus tax." The glass fruit is glued into the 1" gold-tone basket. This necklace dates, in all probability, to the late 1950s or 1960s before inflation made it nearly impossible to purchase a pretty new necklace for only $1.00. $15.00 – 25.00.

**1960s Coro magnetic earrings.** The mark "Coro Magic" was first used in the 1960s for magnetic earrings. The magnets, one on the front and one on the back, hold the earrings tight to the ears. Measuring 1", these lovely five-star pearl earrings are signed "Coro Magic Pat. Pend." This signature refers to a utility patent, not a design patent. Unfortunately, I was unable to locate the utility patent for these interesting clips. $15.00 – 25.00.

Back view of "Coro Magic" magnetic earrings.

1962 Coro "Feline Beauty" advertisement. Amazingly, Coro was still producing jelly belly jewelry in the early 1960s. This advertisement shows a cat with an arching back (similar to patent number 140608 issued March 20, 1945, to Adolph Katz) described as "Sterling, gold finished, with Lucite body, rhinestones, unreal emeralds and rubies." This cat sold for $22.00 in 1962. The value today would be more than 10 times that amount.

**1960 Coro political charm bracelet.** It is easy to date this fascinating Coro 7½" charm bracelet to the 1960 Presidential election because the charm features a photograph of Richard M. Nixon on one side and his 1960 running mate, Henry Cabot Lodge, on the other. It is signed "Coro" with the copyright symbol. $30.00 – 45.00. From the collection of Debi Reece.

**1962 Coro long-stemmed gold-tone and rhinestone flower pin.** Described by Coro in a 1962 advertisement as part of a "…selection of pseudo-stone pins in six gem colors, enameled blossoms or gold-tone tailored beauties…" this 3½" x 1" long-stemmed flower originally sold for $2.00. It is signed "Coro" with the copyright symbol. $45.00 – 55.00.

1964 Coro "Glitterbirds don't fly. Glitterbirds don't sing." advertisement. This ad reads, "Glitterbirds are just the newest, gayest thing to pin on anything this spring. Exquisite gold-toned pins with multi gem-color accents, $3."

1962 Coro "Pin Fashions for a colorful spring" advertisement. Six lovely Coro pins ranging in value from $2.00 to $3.00 each are featured in this ad. The advertisement reads, "Spring dances in your heart…shines on your shoulder with gay pins in fruit or flower motifs. Coro offers you a delightful selection of pseudo-stone pins in six gem colors, enameled blossoms or gold-toned tailored beauties. Matching earrings available."

**1962 pink and white enameled François (Coro) flower pins.** François is a division of Coro. The trademark was first issued in 1937; however, most of the jewelry marked "François" was produced in the 1950s and 1960s. The most recognizable François designs are long- and short-stemmed enameled flower pins like the two pretty 4" x 2" examples pictured here. Each flower is decorated with black enameled stems and green enameled leaves. Note the high quality workmanship evident in these pretty pins. The flower petals are each outlined in black enamel and the large center rhinestones are prong set. Amazingly, the pink flower has its original François $3.00 price tag! The 1962 François "Paris Daisies" advertisement features four similar short-stemmed enameled flowers selling for $5.00 each. This advertisement helps to date these pins to that time period. Both pins are signed "François" in script with the copyright symbol. $25.00 – 35.00 each.

1962 "Les fleurs unique…Paris Daisies by François" advertisement. François is a division of Coro. This colorful advertisement features four enameled flower pins selling for $5.00 each. The caption reads, "Bright, bold and beautiful enameled daisies á la Paris…ready to be pinned on lapel, waist…wherever fashion calls for flair."

**Modern 1970s Coro black cat pin.** This perfect-for-Halloween cat pin measures 2" long. It is signed "Coro" with the copyright symbol. The simple flat design and clean lines indicate this is a newer piece dating to the 1970s. $20.00 – 30.00.

CORO AND VENDÔME JEWELRY

**1953 – 1955 Vendôme six-strand pearl bracelet.** This 7½" elegant six-strand pearl bracelet features a unique clasp that is beautifully encased within a decorative rhinestone cover. The clasp is signed "Vendôme Pat. Pend." No design patent for the style of the bracelet or utility patent for the design of the clasp was found. The lack of a copyright symbol dates this bracelet to between 1953, when the Vendôme name was first used, and 1955, when the copyright symbol was added. $50.00 – 70.00. From the collection of Debi Reece.

**1955 – 1960s Vendôme green and white floral brooch and earrings set.** This eye-catching flower set is signed "Vendôme" with the copyright symbol. Each large white flower is tipped in black enamel to give it depth. Speckled throughout the 2¼" brooch and 1½" earrings are tiny white plastic flowers with clear rhinestone centers. Underneath these bright white blooms are soft green plastic leaves resembling green gumdrops. $100.00 – 175.00.

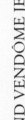

CORO AND VENDÔME JEWELRY

**1955 – 1960s Vendôme pink art glass necklace and earrings.** This 15½" necklace is signed "Vendôme" with the copyright symbol and features rare pink twisted-ribbon art glass beads interspersed with irregularly shaped creamy pink beads. Olivine green crystal beads enhance the delicious appeal of this set. Each 1" earring features all of the same elements as the necklace. $125.00 – 175.00.

**1953 – 1955 Vendôme triple-strand peach-colored necklace and earrings set.** This pretty set reminds me of peaches and raspberries because of the lightweight peach-colored plastic beads and the unusual raspberry-shaped plastic beads. The combination of colors and textures is eye-catching and unique. It is signed "Vendôme" without the copyright symbol, dating this set to 1953 – 1955. The triple-strand necklace measures approximately 15" – 18", the bracelet is 7½", and the clip earrings are 1". $65.00 – 85.00. From the collection of Debi Reece.

**1955 – 1960s Vendôme rivoli stone pin and bracelet.** Stunning, large ¾" sapphire and green rivoli stones decorate these bold pieces. The 2½" brooch and 6½" bracelet are heavy and well made. Both are signed "Vendôme" with the copyright symbol. $95.00 – 125.00 both.

**1955 – 1960s Vendôme Bakelite bubble fish necklace.** This amazing 16" bubble fish necklace is signed "Vendôme" with the copyright symbol. The amber-colored Bakelite beads, or "bubbles," add interest and value to this uniquely designed necklace. When worn, the gold-tone fish seems to be blowing bubbles around the wearer's neck! $95.00 – 145.00. From the collection of Debi Reece.

**1962 Vendôme triple-strand red crystal necklace and earrings set.** The photograph can not begin to capture the heart-stopping beauty of this triple-strand Siam red crystal necklace and matching earrings by Vendôme. The inside strand, including the extension chain, measures a comfortable 17". Each clip earring has the adjustable clip popular in the early 1960s and measures ¾" in diameter. Astoundingly, this glorious set has its original Vendôme paper tag and is signed "Vendôme" with the copyright symbol on the earrings and on the necklace hook. This is the necklace featured in the 1962 advertisement for Vendôme's "Cut-Glass." The collection pieces originally sold for between $5.00 (probably for the earrings) and $20.00 (for this exceptionally fine necklace). $175.00 – 225.00.

CORO AND VENDÔME JEWELRY

Cut here

to see how you look
in the great Cut-Glass look
by Vendôme.

Go ahead. Snip it out. And put it on. You'll get a glimmer of how exciting Vendôme's Cut-Glass Look really is…even on paper. Then, imagine the real thing on you! In many fashionable colors like Siam red, greige, peacock blue, topaz, crystal and simulated pearl or all crystal. The chic Cut-Glass Collection, exclusively Vendôme's, from $5 to $20. Available in choker and matinee lengths, matching pins, bracelets and earrings. At all fine stores or write Vendôme, N.Y.1.

PRICES PLUS TAX; SLIGHTLY HIGHER IN CANADA.

1962 Vendôme Cut-Glass advertisement. This advertisement features a life-size drawing of a red triple-strand crystal necklace designed to be cut-out and tried on by the reader. The advertisement reads, "Cut here to see how you look in the great Cut-Glass look by Vendôme. Go ahead. Snip it out. And put it on. You'll get a glimmer of how exciting Vendôme's Cut-Glass Look really is…even on paper. Then, imagine the real thing on you! In many fashionable colors like Siam red, greige [grayish beige], peacock blue, topaz, crystal and simulated pearl or all crystal. The chic Cut-Glass Collection, exclusively Vendôme's, from $5 to $20."

**1963-era Georges Braque–style Vendôme pin.** This interesting and rare brooch is one of six designs created by Helen Marion for Vendôme. Each design was inspired by the work of Georges Braque, who died in 1963. He was considered one of the founders of the Cubism art form. The six brooches in the series were most likely designed by Marion to honor his life and date from the time of his death. This wonderfully three dimensional 2¼" x 1¾" pin depicts the profile of a person sticking out his or her tongue. In the style of Cubism, the profile is "taken apart" and then reassembled abstractly so that various aspects of the object (in this case a person's head) can be seen at once. It is signed "Vendôme" with the copyright symbol. $200.00 – 300.00.

**1962 "Exquisite Perfection! The NEW Convertible Necklace Vendôme Simulated Pearls" advertisement.** This advertisement illustrates three ways to wear the simulated pearl necklace by rearranging the location of the clasp. The necklace originally sold for $12.50 and the earrings for $5.00.

**1964 Vendôme pink ruffle brooch and earrings set.** This Vendôme set, referred to by collectors as the "ruffle set," was produced in lavender, blue, clear, or pink crystals. It is signed "Vendôme" with the copyright symbol. Amazingly, the pink pastel crystal beads and creamy white pearls are hand wired to the filigree backs of the 2" brooch and 1" earrings. The lead designer for Vendôme in the 1960s was Helen Marion, whose innovative use of crystals was responsible for some of the most exciting jewelry designs of the time, including this ruffle set. $70.00 – 95.00.

**1964 Vendôme hand-strung lavender and pink beaded brooch and earrings set.** This 2½" brooch and 1" clip earrings set, signed "Vendôme" with the copyright symbol, is an especially lovely example of handmade jewelry produced by Vendôme in the early 1960s. Lovely lavender and bright pink beads are hand strung onto a gold-tone mesh frame. Light-green enameled leaves swirl sweetly around the lavender flower. The 1964 "Frankly, Vendome…" advertisement features a similar hand-strung pin, helping to date this set to 1964. $70.00 – 95.00. From the collection of Debi Reece.

CORO AND VENDÔME JEWELRY

Frankly, Vendome pins are not
for everybody.

Just for the woman who's a little more
fashion-conscious.

So many beautiful things go into Vendome
pins. Including continental craftsmanship and
fine hand work. Vendome takes more care.
Because Vendome pins are designed for you
who really care about the way you look.
See the complete collection, $7.50 to $17.50,
or write: Vendome, New York 1, N.Y.

DESIGN COPYRIGHTED. PRICES PLUS TAX. SLIGHTLY HIGHER IN CANADA.

1964 "Frankly, Vendome pins are not for everybody. Just for the woman who's a little more fashion-conscious." advertisement. This colorful advertisement features four creatively designed Vendôme pins selling for $7.50 – 17.50 each.

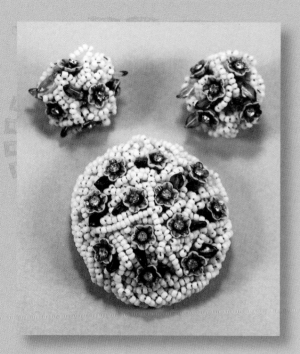

**1964 Vendôme white-beaded blue flower brooch and earrings set.** The 1964 "Frankly, Vendome…" advertisement (see page 138) features a hand-strung brooch similar in style to this signed 2" brooch and the 1" clip earrings, helping to date this pretty blue flower set to that time. All pieces are signed "Vendôme" with the copyright symbol. Note the tiny green glass leaves peeking out from the rows of white beads. $70.00 – 95.00.

**1964 Vendôme blue enamel flower brooch.** In 1964, Vendôme produced many large enameled brooches similar to this 3½" x 2¼" blue and green enameled brooch. Shades of blue enamel, tipped in black, decorate the blue metal flower petals. Notice the realistic-looking olivine green enamel leaves. It is signed "Vendôme" with the copyright symbol. The 1964 "Frankly, Vendome…" advertisement (see page 138) features a similar enameled brooch that originally sold for between $7.50 and $17.50. Today's value, $35.00 – 55.00.

**1964 Vendôme pearl and rhinestone brooch.** This delicate brooch is a departure from Vendôme's normally bold and sassy jewelry designs. The 2½" x 2" lightweight, feather-style brooch closely resembles the silver-tone pearl brooch shown in the 1964 "Frankly, Vendome…" advertisement (see page 138) and dates from the same time. It is signed "Vendôme" with the copyright symbol. $40.00 – 55.00.

CORO AND VENDÔME JEWELRY

**1968 Vendôme Ice Breakers necklace and earrings set.** In 1968, Vendôme launched a line of clear Lucite jewelry consisting of various geometric shapes. This line was called Ice Breakers. The 1968 Ice Breakers advertisement features a necklace, bracelet, and earrings set made of rectangular bars of clear Lucite surrounding silver-tone beads. The advertisement reads, "The Ice Age is over. The Ice Breakers are here with a breakthrough in jewelry design; clear lucite defrosting silver colored baubles in necklaces and bracelets and earrings." In 1968 the jewelry in the advertisement sold for between $5.00 and $15.00. This wonderful clear Lucite 16½" double-strand necklace and 1" clip earrings set exhibit the same clear Lucite design as the jewelry shown in the 1968 advertisement and dates from the same time. All pieces are signed "Vendôme" with the copyright symbol. $70.00 – 125.00.

1968 "Vendome clears the way with The Ice Breakers" advertisement. This advertisement features clear Lucite jewelry with silver color "baubles" originally selling for $5.00 to $15.00 each piece.

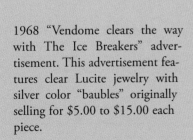

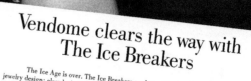

# Vendome clears the way with The Ice Breakers

The Ice Age is over. The Ice Breakers are here with a breakthrough in jewelry design; clear lucite defrosting silver colored baubles in necklaces and bracelets and earrings. Take in the whole collection. See your way clear on what you see here for just 5.00 to 15.00 at all the finest stores across the country.

VENDÔME, THE COUTURIER    DIVISION OF CORO, INC., 47 WEST 34TH ST., NEW YORK, N.Y. 10001

Droplets of new spring colors sparkle from
Vendome's exquisite "Cascade Collection." Necklace $20, and then
shown counter-clockwise, pin $17.50, earrings $12.50, pin $17.50, pin $15, pin $20, bracelet $30.
All with matching earrings. Prices plus tax, slightly higher in Canada. At fine stores or write: Vendome, 47 West 34th St., N. Y. 1.

VENDÔME • NEW YORK • PARIS • LONDON

*Designs Copyrighted*

New ways to look elegant this Spring

*Vendôme*
*Couturier Jewelry*

1959 "New ways to look elegant this Spring/Vendôme Couturier Jewelry" advertisement. The ad reads, "Droplets of new spring colors sparkle from Vendome's exquisite 'Cascade Collection.' Necklace $20, and then shown counterclockwise, pin $17.50, earrings $12.50, pin $17.50, pin $15, pin $20, bracelet $30. All with matching earrings."

Late 1970s yellow and black Vendôme necklace and stretch bracelet. Modern looking, this bright yellow and black 15½" Vendôme necklace and matching double-row elastic bracelet were made after 1970. The necklace is signed "Vendôme" with the copyright symbol. Although bright and attractive, this set lacks the quality of design and materials typically found on 1950s and 1960s Vendôme jewelry. For example, there are no rhinestones in this set. The shiny spacers are silver-tone plastic sandwiched between black plastic disks. The yellow beads are also plastic. $35.00 – 45.00. From the collection of Debi Reece.

# CHAPTER 3

# TRIFARI *Jewelry*

## TRIFARI
### (1918 – Present)

Note: In 1955, Trifari won an important lawsuit against the Charel Jewelry Co. for copying one of Trifari's copyrighted designs. Since this lawsuit concerned a copyrighted and not a patented piece, Trifari must have been copyrighting some designs before 1955. There are 1954 Trifari design patents in this section; however, I was unable to locate Trifari design patents from 1955 or later. It is clear that beginning in 1955, Trifari opted to copyright rather than patent most jewelry designs.

# TRIFARI 1937 – 1939

| Design Patent Number | Date Issued | Designer | Jewelry Type | Brief Description |
|---|---|---|---|---|
| 103595 | 3/16/1937 | Alfred Philippe | Brooch | LS six-petal flower |
| 103596 | 3/16/1937 | Alfred Philippe | Brooch | Pavé open rose |
| 103597 | 3/16/1937 | Alfred Philippe | Brooch | Pavé five-petal flower |
| 103598 | 3/16/1937 | Alfred Philippe | Brooch | Geometric |
| 103897 | 3/30/1937 | Alfred Philippe | Brooch | Geometric |
| 105136 | 6/29/1937 | Alfred Philippe | Brooch | Floral spray |
| 105402 | 7/27/1937 | Alfred Philippe | Brooch | Geometric floral |
| 105403 | 7/27/1937 | Alfred Philippe | Brooch | Geometric floral |
| 105404 | 7/27/1937 | Alfred Philippe | Brooch | Geometric floral |
| 105405 | 7/27/1937 | Alfred Philippe | Brooch | Floral wreath fruit salad |
| 105406 | 7/27/1937 | Alfred Philippe | Brooch | Floral spray |
| 105407 | 7/27/1937 | Alfred Philippe | Brooch | LS floral spray |
| 106120 | 9/21/1937 | Alfred Philippe | Brooch | Bird open wings on branch |
| 106121 | 9/21/1937 | Alfred Philippe | Brooch | Two love birds on branch |
| 106122 | 9/21/1937 | Alfred Philippe | Brooch | Circular floral fruit salad |
| 106123 | 9/21/1937 | Alfred Philippe | Brooch | Geometric |
| 106145 | 9/21/1937 | Alfred Philippe | Brooch | Bird holding twig |
| 106146 | 9/21/1937 | Alfred Philippe | Brooch | Bird on a branch with open wings |
| 107122 | 11/23/1937 | Alfred Philippe | Brooch | Geometric |
| 107123 | 11/23/1937 | Alfred Philippe | Brooch | Geometric |
| 107124 | 11/23/1937 | Alfred Philippe | Brooch | Geometric |
| 107125 | 11/23/1937 | Alfred Philippe | Brooch | Geometric floral |
| 107126 | 11/23/1937 | Alfred Philippe | Brooch | Geometric floral |

107124

**Late 1930s Trifari clip with five turquoise plastic inserts.** This clip is signed "KTF" and measures 1⅛" x 1". The style of the clip and the early KTF signature date this piece to the late 1930s. Notice the age-darkened rhinestones. This is a common flaw in jewelry of this age. Originally worn as part of a pair, this single clip is valued today at $45.00 – 75.00.

**Two late 1930s "KTF" Trifari clips with coral and light green plastic inserts.** The late 1930s pastel green and coral-colored plastic inserts add a plus quality to these clips. These ¾" clips are signed "KTF." Unfortunately, they have many age-darkened stones. $65.00 – 100.00.

**Late 1930s Trifari Clip-mates brooch.** The Trifari Clip-mates mechanism is utility patent number 2050804 issued August 11, 1936, to Alfred Philippe for Trifari. It consists of a thin metal bar that connects two clips together to form one brooch. The special clips are equipped with a groove that slides along the metal bar to form the brooch. This Clip-mates brooch measures 2¼" x 1". One clip is marked "KTF" and "Clip-mates." The other is marked "Pat. No. 2050804." "KTF" is an early Trifari signature that was in use from 1935 to the early 1940s. The clips are stylistically similar to design patent number 107124 issued November 23, 1937, to Alfred Philippe for Trifari. The early signature and the similar style to the patented 1937 clip date this Clip-mates brooch to the late 1930s. $200.00 – 300.00.

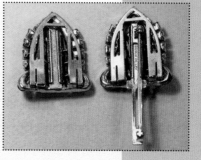

Back view of the Trifari Clip-mates brooch, showing the sliding mechanism.

107135

113523

113786

113788

113791

| 107127 | 11/23/1937 | Alfred Philippe | Brooch | Geometric floral |
|---|---|---|---|---|
| 107128 | 11/23/1937 | Alfred Philippe | Brooch | Geometric |
| 107129 | 11/23/1937 | Alfred Philippe | Brooch | Geometric floral |
| 107130 | 11/23/1937 | Alfred Philippe | Brooch | Geometric floral |
| 107131 | 11/23/1937 | Alfred Philippe | Brooch | Floral |
| 107132 | 11/23/1937 | Alfred Philippe | Brooch | LS floral |
| 107133 | 11/23/1937 | Alfred Philippe | Brooch | Basket |
| 107134 | 11/23/1937 | Alfred Philippe | Brooch | LS floral |
| 107135 | 11/23/1937 | Alfred Philippe | Clipmate | Double floral leaf, invisible setting (See 107136 for similar brooch.) |
| 107136 | 11/23/1937 | Alfred Philippe | Brooch | LS six leaves, invisible setting (See 107135 for clipmate.) |
| 107137 | 11/23/1937 | Alfred Philippe | Brooch | Pavé Leaves |
| 107138 | 11/23/1937 | Alfred Philippe | Brooch | Geometric floral |
| 107138 | 11/23/1937 | Alfred Philippe | Brooch | Geometric floral |
| 107139 | 11/23/1937 | Alfred Philippe | Brooch | Geometric floral |
| 107140 | 11/23/1937 | Alfred Philippe | Brooch | Geometric |
| 107141 | 11/23/1937 | Alfred Philippe | Brooch | Geometric |
| 107142 | 11/23/1937 | Alfred Philippe | Brooch | Geometric |
| 107143 | 11/23/1937 | Alfred Philippe | Brooch | Leaves and berries |
| 108797 | 3/15/1938 | Alfred Philippe | Brooch | Geometric |
| 108798 | 3/15/1938 | Alfred Philippe | Brooch | Geometric |
| 108799 | 3/15/1938 | Alfred Philippe | Brooch | Geometric |
| 108800 | 3/15/1938 | Alfred Philippe | Brooch | Geometric |
| 108801 | 3/15/1938 | Alfred Philippe | Brooch | Geometric floral |
| 108802 | 3/15/1938 | Alfred Philippe | Brooch | Floral leaf |
| 108803 | 3/15/1938 | Alfred Philippe | Brooch | Floral leaf |
| 108804 | 3/15/1938 | Alfred Philippe | Brooch | Two Leaves |
| 108805 | 3/15/1938 | Alfred Philippe | Brooch | Geometric |
| 108806 | 3/15/1938 | Alfred Philippe | Brooch | Geometric |
| 108807 | 3/15/1938 | Alfred Philippe | Brooch | Geometric |
| 108808 | 3/15/1938 | Alfred Philippe | Brooch | Floral |
| 108809 | 3/15/1938 | Alfred Philippe | Brooch | Horse head |
| 108810 | 3/15/1938 | Alfred Philippe | Brooch | Seashell |
| 109082 | 3/29/1938 | Alfred Philippe | Brooch | Arrow piercing heart |
| 110290 | 6/28/1938 | Alfred Philippe | Brooch | Grapes |
| 110291 | 6/28/1938 | Alfred Philippe | Brooch | Grapes |
| 110292 | 6/28/1938 | Alfred Philippe | Brooch | Grapes |
| 110293 | 6/28/1938 | Alfred Philippe | Brooch | Floral |
| 113523 | 2/28/1939 | Alfred Philippe | Pin | Woman, "Helen" (See 113524 for "Peter.") |
| 113524 | 2/28/1939 | Alfred Philippe | Pin | Man, "Peter" (See 113523 for "Helen.") |
| 113786 | 3/14/1939 | Alfred Philippe | Pin | Male monkey (See 113787 for female.) |

| | | | | |
|---|---|---|---|---|
| 113787 | 3/14/1939 | Alfred Philippe | Pin | Female monkey (See 113786 for male.) |
| 113788 | 3/14/1939 | Alfred Philippe | Pin | French woman's face (See 113789 for male.) |
| 113789 | 3/14/1939 | Alfred Philippe | Pin | French man's face (See 113788 for female.) |
| 113790 | 3/14/1939 | Alfred Philippe | Pin | Bird on branch |
| 113791 | 3/14/1939 | Alfred Philippe | Brooch | Female bronco rider (See 113792 for male.) |
| 113792 | 3/14/1939 | Alfred Philippe | Brooch | Male bronco rider (See 113791 for female.) |
| 113793 | 3/14/1939 | Alfred Philippe | Brooch | Male lion, "March Comes in Like a Lion" (See 114135 for "Out Like a Lamb.") |
| 113939 | 3/21/1939 | Alfred Philippe | Necklace | Floral with small five-rhinestone flowers (See 115422 for earring.) |
| 113946 | 3/21/1939 | Alfred Philippe | Pin | Floral spray small five-rhinestone flowers (See 113939 for matching necklace.) |
| 114135 | 4/4/1939 | Alfred Philippe | Pin | Lamb, "Out Like a Lamb" (See 113793 for March "In Like a Lion.") |
| 114136 | 4/4/1939 | Alfred Philippe | Brooch | Floral spray (See 114137 for matching necklace.) |
| 114137 | 4/4/1939 | Alfred Philippe | Necklace | Floral (See 114136 for matching pin.) |
| 114138 | 4/4/1939 | Alfred Philippe | Brooch | Floral spray double bell (See 114489 for similar pin.) |
| 114139 | 4/4/1939 | Alfred Philippe | Necklace | Floral triple bell (See 114138 for similar pin.) |
| 114140 | 4/4/1939 | Alfred Philippe | Brooch | Enameled floral spray with small rhinestone center (See 114141 for matching necklace.) |
| 114141 | 4/4/1939 | Alfred Philippe | Necklace | Enameled floral with small rhinestones center (See 114723 for matching bracelet.) |
| 114234 | 4/11/1939 | Alfred Philippe | Brooch | Floral |
| 114235 | 4/11/1939 | Alfred Philippe | Brooch | Monkey hanging from a branch |
| 114236 | 4/11/1939 | Alfred Philippe | Brooch | Female gypsy dancer (See 114237 for male.) |

113946

114136

114235

**1939 unsigned Trifari monkey brooch.** Even though it is unsigned, this marvelous monkey brooch stylistically matches Trifari design patent number 114235 issued April 11, 1939, to Alfred Philippe for Trifari. Unsigned gold-tone monkey, $150.00 – 250.00. With the Trifari signature, the value is much higher: $600.00 – 850.00.

TRIFARI JEWELRY

TRIFARI JEWELRY

114236

114296

114489

114723

| 114237 | 4/11/1939 | Alfred Philippe | Brooch | Male gypsy dancer (See 114236 for female) |
|---|---|---|---|---|
| 114238 | 4/11/1939 | Alfred Philippe | Brooch | Goat |
| 114296 | 4/11/1939 | Alfred Philippe | Brooch | Flowerpot |
| 114297 | 4/11/1939 | Alfred Philippe | Brooch | Laughing horse |
| 114488 | 4/25/1939 | Alfred Philippe | Brooch | Floral |
| 114489 | 4/25/1939 | Alfred Philippe | Brooch | Floral double bell (See 114722 for bracelet.) |
| 114490 | 4/25/1939 | Alfred Philippe | Brooch | Floral |
| 114491 | 4/25/1939 | Alfred Philippe | Brooch | LS floral |
| 114492 | 4/25/1939 | Alfred Philippe | Brooch | LS floral |
| 114493 | 4/25/1939 | Alfred Philippe | Brooch | Geometric floral |
| 114722 | 5/9/1939 | Alfred Philippe | Bracelet | Floral double bells (See 114139 for necklace.) |
| 114723 | 5/9/1939 | Alfred Philippe | Bracelet | Enameled floral with small rhinestones center (See 114140 for matching pin.) |
| 115127 | 6/6/1939 | Alfred Philippe | Brooch | LS floral |
| 115128 | 6/6/1939 | Alfred Philippe | Brooch | Floral |
| 115293 | 6/20/1939 | Alfred Philippe | Earring | Floral small five-rhinestone flowers (See 115294 for brooch.) |
| 115294 | 6/20/1939 | Alfred Philippe | Brooch | Floral small five-rhinestone flowers (See 115296 for brooch.) |
| 115295 | 6/20/1939 | Alfred Philippe | Brooch | Floral |
| 115296 | 6/20/1939 | Alfred Philippe | Brooch | Floral small five-rhinestone flowers (See 115297 for brooch.) |
| 115297 | 6/20/1939 | Alfred Philippe | Brooch | Floral small five-rhinestone flowers (See113946 for pin.) |
| 115422 | 6/27/1939 | Alfred Philippe | Earring | Floral with small five-rhinestone flowers (See 115293 for matching earring.) |
| 116081 | 8/8/1939 | Alfred Philippe | Pin | LS floral pavé floral with circle of rhinestones center (See 116100 for similar pin.) |
| 116082 | 8/8/1939 | Alfred Philippe | Pin | LS floral |
| 116083 | 8/8/1939 | Alfred Philippe | Pin | Pave floral with circle of rhinestones center (See 116575 for matching necklace.) |
| 116084 | 8/8/1939 | Alfred Philippe | Pin | Floral bow, two dangles |
| 116085 | 8/8/1939 | Alfred Philippe | Pin | Pavé floral with circle of rhinestone centers and four dangles (See 116081 for another brooch.) |

*Jewels by* **TRIFARI**

*The name that stands for leadership in distinguished designs for fashion effects, rendered with the craftsmanship of precious pieces. At all important stores.*

PHOTOGRAPH—HENRY WAXMAN

TRIFARI, KRUSSMAN & FISHEL · 377 FIFTH AVENUE · NEW YORK

1938 Trifari "The name that stands for leadership in distinguished designs…" advertisement. This beautiful advertisement features the profile of a lovely woman wearing Trifari jewelry in her hair, around her neck, and on both wrists. The ad reads, "The name that stands for leadership in distinguished designs for fashion effects, rendered with the craftsmanship of precious pieces. At all important stores."

### • TRIFARI 1937 – 1939 •

| | | | | |
|---|---|---|---|---|
| 116086 | 8/8/1939 | Alfred Philippe | Pin | Pavé floral with circle of rhinestone center (See 116085 for four-dangle version.) |
| 116087 | 8/8/1939 | Alfred Philippe | Pin | Pavé floral with circle of rhinestone centers (See 116086 for similar pin.) |
| 116088 | 8/8/1939 | Alfred Philippe | Pin | Pavé floral flower with circle of rhinestones center (See 116089 for double version.) |
| 116089 | 8/8/1939 | Alfred Philippe | Brooch | Pavé floral double flower with circle of rhinestones center (See 116090 for another version.) |

116088

TRIFARI JEWELRY

116105

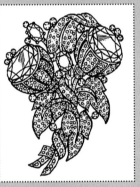

116292

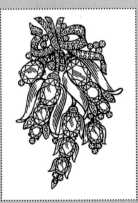

116295

| 116090 | 8/8/1939 | Alfred Philippe | Brooch | Pavé floral with circle of rhinestone centers and dangling flower (See 116087 for similar pin.) |
| 116099 | 8/8/1939 | Alfred Philippe | Pin | Floral with five dangles |
| 116100 | 8/8/1939 | Alfred Philippe | Pin | Pavé floral with circle of rhinestones center (See 116083 for similar pin.) |
| 116105 | 8/8/1939 | Alfred Philippe | Pin | LS floral with circle of rhinestone centers (See 116107 for similar pin.) |
| 116106 | 8/8/1939 | Alfred Philippe | Pin | Floral |
| 116107 | 8/8/1939 | Alfred Philippe | Pin | Floral with circle of rhinestone centers (See 116105 for similar pin.) |
| 116291 | 8/22/1939 | Alfred Philippe | Pin | Floral |
| 116292 | 8/22/1939 | Alfred Philippe | Pin | LS floral double flowers with large rhinestone centers (See 116297 for single-flower version.) |
| 116293 | 8/22/1939 | Alfred Philippe | Pin | LS floral with five flowers with large rhinestone centers (See 116292 for double-flower version.) |
| 116294 | 8/22/1939 | Alfred Philippe | Pin | LS floral triple flowers with large rhinestone centers (See 116293 for five-flower version.) |
| 116295 | 8/22/1939 | Alfred Philippe | Pin | Floral with stacked rhinestones (See 116296 for another version.) |
| 116296 | 8/22/1939 | Alfred Philippe | Pin | Floral with stacked rhinestones (See 116295 for another version.) |
| 116297 | 8/22/1939 | Alfred Philippe | Pin | LS floral with large rhinestone center (See 116294 for triple-flower version.) |
| 116378 | 8/29/1939 | Alfred Philippe | Necklace | Pavé floral with circle of rhinestone centers (See 116088 for similar brooch.) |
| 116575 | 9/12/1939 | Alfred Philippe | Necklace | Pavé floral with circle of rhinestone centers (See 116378 for another necklace.) |
| 118759 | 1/30/1939 | Alfred Philippe | Pin | Floral |

# TRIFARI 1940

| Design Patent Number | Date Issued | Designer | Jewelry Type | Brief Description |
|---|---|---|---|---|
| 118756 | 1/30/1940 | Alfred Philippe | Brooch | Rooster |
| 118757 | 1/30/1940 | Alfred Philippe | Brooch | Floral |
| 118758 | 1/30/1940 | Alfred Philippe | Brooch | Floral |
| 118875 | 2/6/1940 | Joseph Wuyts | Necklace | Metal beads |
| 119092 | 2/20/1940 | Alfred Philippe | Brooch | Floral |
| 119093 | 2/20/1940 | Alfred Philippe | Brooch | Fish pearl belly |
| 119094 | 2/20/1940 | Alfred Philippe | Brooch | Floral |
| 119095 | 2/20/1940 | Alfred Philippe | Brooch | Floral |
| 119096 | 2/20/1940 | Alfred Philippe | Brooch | Bird hummingbird |
| 119097 | 2/20/1940 | Alfred Philippe | Brooch | Floral |
| 119098 | 2/20/1940 | Alfred Philippe | Brooch | Fly |
| 119099 | 2/20/1940 | Alfred Philippe | Brooch | Bird |
| 119100 | 2/20/1940 | Alfred Philippe | Brooch | Floral |
| 119101 | 2/20/1940 | Alfred Philippe | Brooch | Floral |
| 119102 | 2/20/1940 | Alfred Philippe | Brooch | Love birds |
| 119103 | 2/20/1940 | Alfred Philippe | Brooch | Floral |
| 119104 | 2/20/1940 | Alfred Philippe | Brooch | Floral |
| 119105 | 2/20/1940 | Alfred Philippe | Brooch | Floral |
| 119107 | 2/20/1940 | Joseph Wuyts | Pin | Fish in tuxedo |
| 119108 | 2/20/1940 | Joseph Wuyts | Pin | Mermaid with fan |
| 119433 | 3/12/1940 | Alfred Philippe | Brooch | Floral |
| 119434 | 3/12/1940 | Alfred Philippe | Brooch | Flower basket |
| 119435 | 3/12/1940 | Alfred Philippe | Brooch | Diving bird pearl belly swallow |
| 119436 | 3/12/1940 | Alfred Philippe | Brooch | Bird pearl belly |
| 119437 | 3/12/1940 | Alfred Philippe | Brooch | Bird |
| 119438 | 3/12/1940 | Alfred Philippe | Brooch | Floral |
| 119445 | 3/12/1940 | Joseph Wuyts | Pin | Girl with goose |
| 119454 | 3/12/1940 | Alfred Philippe | Brooch | Floral |
| 119455 | 3/12/1940 | Alfred Philippe | Brooch | Floral |
| 119456 | 3/12/1940 | Alfred Philippe | Brooch | Bird |
| 119457 | 3/12/1940 | Alfred Philippe | Brooch | Flying duck pearl belly |
| 119466 | 3/12/1940 | Joseph Wuyts | Pin | Cupid heart |
| 119467 | 3/12/1940 | Joseph Wuyts | Pin | Mexican man pearl belly |
| 119525 | 3/19/1940 | Alfred Philippe | Brooch | Knight |
| 119529 | 3/19/1940 | Joseph Wuyts | Pin | Dutch woman with basket |
| 119530 | 3/19/1940 | Joseph Wuyts | Brooch | Drum major |
| 119531 | 3/19/1940 | Joseph Wuyts | Brooch | Woman |
| 119766 | 4/2/1940 | Alfred Philippe | Brooch | Floral |
| 119836 | 4/2/1940 | Joseph Wuyts | Brooch | Floral |
| 119837 | 4/2/1940 | Joseph Wuyts | Brooch | Floral |
| 119838 | 4/2/1940 | Joseph Wuyts | Brooch | Sailboat with girl |
| 120052 | 4/16/1940 | Joseph Wuyts | Brooch | Watering can |

119097

119457

120450

120475

120052

TRIFARI JEWELRY

119836

119837

120572

120573

120574

**Colorful 1940 Trifari flower brooch.** This beautifully enameled flower clip is design patent number 119836 issued April 2, 1940, to Joseph Wuyts for Trifari. Wuyts was a freelance designer who in 1940 created several notable designs for Trifari. (Wuyts also designed for Mazer at this time. See Mazer in chapter 4 for additional examples of Wuyts patents.) This colorful 2" x 1½" clip is typical of the well-crafted enameled flower clips produced by Trifari in the 1940s. Notice the sparkling rhinestones decorating the tips of the curling green enameled leaves. Curling leaves with rhinestone tips is a Trifari design trait found on many early 1940s designs. The brooch is signed "Trifari Des. Pat. No. 119836." $125.00 – 165.00.

**1940 Joseph Wuyts for Trifari large rhinestone flower clip.** This gloriously large and sparkling 3" x 2¼" Trifari clip is design patent number 119837 issued April 2, 1940, to Joseph Wuyts for Trifari. Notice the drooping flowers and the generous use of pavé rhinestones covering this magnificent clip. These are both design traits of jewelry produced in the early 1940s. The clip is signed "Trifari" without the copyright symbol. $200.00 – 300.00.

### • TRIFARI 1940 •

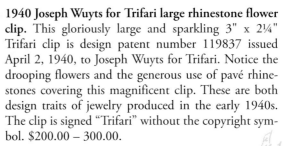

| | | | | |
|---|---|---|---|---|
| 120303 | 4/30/1940 | Alfred Philippe | Brooch | Fly pearl belly |
| 120448 | 5/7/1940 | Alfred Philippe | Brooch | Floral |
| 120449 | 5/7/1940 | Alfred Philippe | Brooch | Floral |
| 120450 | 5/7/1940 | Alfred Philippe | Brooch | Curling edges floral (See 120896 for matching bracelet.) |
| 120456 | 5/7/1940 | Joseph Wuyts | Pin | Bow (See 120457 for another bow.) |
| 120457 | 5/7/1940 | Joseph Wuyts | Pin | Bow (See 120458 for another bow.) |
| 120458 | 5/7/1940 | Joseph Wuyts | Pin | Bow (See 120475 for another bow.) |
| 120474 | 5/7/1940 | Joseph Wuyts | Pin | Floral |
| 120475 | 5/7/1940 | Joseph Wuyts | Brooch | Five-loop ribbon |
| 120560 | 5/14/1940 | Joseph Wuyts | Brooch | Bow (See 120456 for another bow.) |
| 120572 | 5/14/1940 | Alfred Philippe | Brooch | Floral multipetal (See 120589 for matching necklace.) |
| 120573 | 5/14/1940 | Alfred Philippe | Brooch | Floral five-petal flower (See 120591 for matching necklace.) |
| 120574 | 5/14/1940 | Alfred Philippe | Brooch | Floral pansy brooch (See 120592 for matching necklace.) |

| | | | | |
|---|---|---|---|---|
| 120575 | 5/14/1940 | Alfred Philippe | Brooch | Long-stemmed daisy-style flower (See 120594 for necklace.) |
| 120589 | 5/14/1940 | Alfred Philippe | Necklace | Floral multipetal (See 120572 from matching pin.) |
| 120590 | 5/14/1940 | Alfred Philippe | Bracelet | Floral |
| 120591 | 5/14/1940 | Alfred Philippe | Necklace | Floral five-petal flower (See 120573 from brooch.) |
| 120592 | 5/14/1940 | Alfred Philippe | Necklace | Floral pansy (See 120574 for matching brooch.) |
| 120593 | 5/14/1940 | Alfred Philippe | Bracelet | Floral |
| 120594 | 5/14/1940 | Alfred Philippe | Necklace | Daisy-style floral (See 120575 for matching brooch.) |
| 120896 | 6/4/1940 | Alfred Philippe | Bracelet | Curling edges floral (See 120450 for matching brooch.) |
| 120897 | 6/4/1940 | Alfred Philippe | Bracelet | Floral |
| 121222 | 6/25/1940 | Alfred Philippe | Brooch | Molded glass petal floral, no stem (See 121223 for matching necklace.) |
| 121223 | 6/25/1940 | Alfred Philippe | Necklace | Long-stemmed molded glass petal floral three blooms (See 121350 for matching pin.) |
| 121224 | 6/25/1940 | Alfred Philippe | Necklace | Molded glass petal long-stemmed floral (See 121252 for matching brooch.) |
| 121251 | 6/25/1940 | Alfred Philippe | Brooch | Long-stemmed molded glass petal floral (See 121222 for matching pin.) |
| 121252 | 6/25/1940 | Alfred Philippe | Brooch | Floral Lily of the Valley |
| 121253 | 6/25/1940 | Alfred Philippe | Brooch | Floral |
| 121254 | 6/25/1940 | Alfred Philippe | Brooch | Floral |
| 121255 | 6/25/1940 | Alfred Philippe | Brooch | Floral |
| 121350 | 7/2/1940 | Alfred Philippe | Brooch | Long-stemmed floral with molded glass petal, long stem, and six blooms (See 121224 for matching necklace.) |
| 121728 | 7/30/1940 | Alfred Philippe | Brooch | Floral |
| 121729 | 7/30/1940 | Alfred Philippe | Brooch | Leaf |
| 121730 | 7/30/1940 | Alfred Philippe | Brooch | Floral |

120575

121252

121350

**Substantial six-flower 1940 poured-glass Trifari clip.** Part of a series, this large 4" x 2" six-bloom flower clip is design patent number 121350 issued July 2, 1940, to Alfred Philippe for Trifari. (Interestingly, the following design patents all show different jewelry creations utilizing the same white glass flowers: 121222, 121223, 121224, 121251, and 121255.) The red enameling on the bow is typical of early 1940s Trifari jewelry designs. It is signed "Trifari" without the copyright symbol. $100.00 – 125.00.

TRIFARI JEWELRY

**TRIFARI JEWELRY**

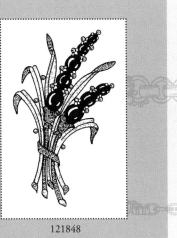

121848

122092

122204

122220

| 121731 | 7/30/1940 | Alfred Philippe | Brooch | Floral |
|---|---|---|---|---|
| 121821 | 8/6/1940 | Alfred Philippe | Brooch | Anchor, "Faith, Hope, Charity" |
| 121845 | 8/6/1940 | Alfred Philippe | Brooch | Floral |
| 121846 | 8/6/1940 | Alfred Philippe | Brooch | Floral |
| 121847 | 8/6/1940 | Alfred Philippe | Brooch | Floral |
| 121848 | 8/6/1940 | Alfred Philippe | Brooch | Floral |
| 121849 | 8/6/1940 | Alfred Philippe | Brooch | Floral |
| 121850 | 8/6/1940 | Alfred Philippe | Brooch | Floral |
| 121851 | 8/6/1940 | Alfred Philippe | Brooch | Floral |
| 121852 | 8/6/1940 | Alfred Philippe | Brooch | Floral leaf |
| 121859 | 8/6/1940 | Alfred Philippe | Bracelet | Floral |
| 121943 | 8/13/1940 | Alfred Philippe | Brooch | Floral leaf |
| 121944 | 8/13/1940 | Alfred Philippe | Brooch | Floral |
| 121945 | 8/13/1940 | Alfred Philippe | Brooch | Floral with dangles |
| 121964 | 8/13/1940 | Alfred Philippe | Brooch | Fleur-de-Lis |
| 122091 | 8/20/1940 | Alfred Philippe | Brooch | Floral |
| 122092 | 8/20/1940 | Alfred Philippe | Brooch | Long-stemmed floral with stacking rhinestone center (See 122219 for triple-bloom version.) |
| 122093 | 8/20/1940 | Alfred Philippe | Brooch | Floral |
| 122094 | 8/20/1940 | Alfred Philippe | Brooch | Floral |
| 122095 | 8/20/1940 | Alfred Philippe | Brooch | Floral |
| 122096 | 8/20/1940 | Alfred Philippe | Brooch | Floral |
| 122097 | 8/20/1940 | Alfred Philippe | Brooch | Floral |
| 122098 | 8/20/1940 | Alfred Philippe | Brooch | Floral |
| 122099 | 8/20/1940 | Alfred Philippe | Brooch | Floral |
| 122203 | 8/27/1940 | Alfred Philippe | Brooch | Patriotic bow |
| 122204 | 8/27/1940 | Alfred Philippe | Brooch | Long-stemmed tapering floral (See 122205 for three bloom version.) |
| 122205 | 8/27/1940 | Alfred Philippe | Brooch | Three bloom long-stem tapering floral (See 122204 for single bloom version) |
| 122206 | 8/27/1940 | Alfred Philippe | Brooch | Floral |
| 122219 | 8/27/1940 | Alfred Philippe | Brooch | Long-stemmed floral with stacking rhinestone-center triple bloom (See 122092 for single bloom version.) |
| 122220 | 8/27/1940 | Alfred Philippe | Brooch | Eagle |
| 122221 | 8/27/1940 | Alfred Philippe | Brooch | Bow |
| 122299 | 9/3/1940 | Alfred Philippe | Brooch | Sword |
| 122300 | 9/3/1940 | Alfred Philippe | Brooch | Sword |
| 122320 | 9/3/1940 | Alfred Philippe | Brooch | Floral |
| 122321 | 9/3/1940 | Alfred Philippe | Brooch | Sword |

| 122329 | 9/3/1940 | Alfred Philippe | Brooch | Floral |
|---|---|---|---|---|
| 122340 | 9/3/1940 | Alfred Philippe | Brooch | Floral |
| 122826 | 10/1/1940 | Alfred Philippe | Brooch | Sword |
| 123168 | 10/22/1940 | Alfred Philippe | Bracelet | Floral |
| 123169 | 10/22/1940 | Alfred Philippe | Brooch | Floral with cluster of eight navette-shaped stones (See123171 for similar piece.) |
| 123170 | 10/22/1940 | Alfred Philippe | Brooch | Long-stemmed floral cluster of eight navette-shaped stones (See 123169 for similar brooch.) |
| 123171 | 10/22/1940 | Alfred Philippe | Brooch | Floral with cluster of eight navette-shaped stones and ribbon (See 123172 for similar piece.) |
| 123172 | 10/22/1940 | Alfred Philippe | Brooch | Floral with cluster of eight navette-shaped stones (See 123173 for similar brooch.) |
| 123173 | 10/22/1940 | Alfred Philippe | Brooch | Floral with cluster of eight navette-shaped stones (See 123174 for similar piece.) |
| 123174 | 10/22/1940 | Alfred Philippe | Brooch | Floral with cluster of eight navette-shaped stones (See 123170 for similar brooch.) |
| 123175 | 10/22/1940 | Alfred Philippe | Brooch | Floral leaves with bow |
| 123176 | 10/22/1940 | Alfred Philippe | Brooch | Floral with pearl |
| 123177 | 10/22/1940 | Alfred Philippe | Brooch | Floral |
| 123178 | 10/22/1940 | Alfred Philippe | Brooch | Floral |
| 123179 | 10/22/1940 | Alfred Philippe | Brooch | Sword |
| 123272 | 10/29/1940 | Alfred Philippe | Brooch | Floral with pear, long stem |
| 123273 | 10/29/1940 | Alfred Philippe | Brooch | Circle with bows |
| 123300 | 10/29/1940 | Alfred Philippe | Brooch | Floral |
| 123301 | 10/29/1940 | Alfred Philippe | Brooch | Basket |

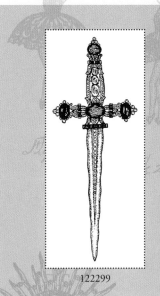

122299

123170

123176

123301

TRIFARI JEWELRY

153

125162

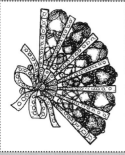

125164

125165

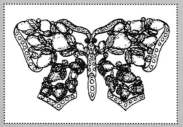

125166

125158

**TRIFARI JEWELRY**

| Design Patent Number | Date Issued | Designer | Jewelry Type | Brief Description |
|---|---|---|---|---|
| 125156 | 2/11/1941 | Alfred Philippe | Brooch | Flower basket with molded glass (See 125420 for another molded glass piece.) |
| 125157 | 2/11/1941 | Alfred Philippe | Brooch | Long-stemmed elaborate floral with molded glass (See 125156 for another molded glass piece.) |
| 125158 | 2/11/1941 | Alfred Philippe | Brooch | Key |
| 125159 | 2/11/1941 | Alfred Philippe | Brooch | Key |
| 125160 | 2/11/1941 | Alfred Philippe | Brooch | Key |
| 125161 | 2/11/1941 | Alfred Philippe | Brooch | Key |
| 125162 | 2/11/1941 | Alfred Philippe | Brooch | Flowerpot with cascading molded glass (See 125163 for another molded glass piece.) |
| 125163 | 2/11/1941 | Alfred Philippe | Brooch | Leaf with molded glass (See 125157 for another molded glass piece.) |
| 125164 | 2/11/1941 | Alfred Philippe | Brooch | Fan |
| 125165 | 2/11/1941 | Alfred Philippe | Brooch | Bird, fruit salad stones |
| 125166 | 2/11/1941 | Alfred Philippe | Brooch | Butterfly |
| 125167 | 2/11/1941 | Alfred Philippe | Brooch | Bird, fruit salad stones |
| 125184 | 2/11/1941 | Alfred Philippe | Brooch | Owl |
| 125185 | 2/11/1941 | Alfred Philippe | Brooch | Wheelbarrow, fruit salad stones |

**1941 Trifari key brooch.** The key brooch is a popular motif for Trifari. Over the years Trifari produced many variations of key brooches, including this regal 3" x ¾" key brooch signed "Trifari Pat. Pend." It is design patent number 125158 issued February 11, 1941, to Alfred Philippe. In addition to the red cabochons, clear rhinestones, and blue baguette rhinestone, this brooch features small stripes of black enameling. $120.00 – 150.00.

| 125186 | 2/11/1941 | Alfred Philippe | Brooch | Key |
|---|---|---|---|---|
| 125348 | 2/18/1941 | Alfred Philippe | Brooch | Floral |
| 125349 | 2/18/1941 | Alfred Philippe | Brooch | Bird |
| 125350 | 2/18/1941 | Alfred Philippe | Brooch | Rooster |
| 125351 | 2/18/1941 | Alfred Philippe | Brooch | Horseshoe |
| 125352 | 2/18/1941 | Alfred Philippe | Brooch | Anchor |
| 125353 | 2/18/1941 | Alfred Philippe | Brooch | Lyre |
| 125419 | 2/25/1941 | Alfred Philippe | Brooch | Floral |
| 125420 | 2/25/1941 | Alfred Philippe | Brooch | Flowerpot with molded glass (See 129538 for another molded glass piece.) |
| 125421 | 2/25/1941 | Alfred Philippe | Brooch | Floral |
| 125422 | 2/25/1941 | Alfred Philippe | Brooch | Floral |
| 125423 | 2/25/1941 | Alfred Philippe | Brooch | Floral |
| 125424 | 2/25/1941 | Alfred Philippe | Brooch | Flowerpot with cascading blooms |
| 125425 | 2/25/1941 | Alfred Philippe | Brooch | Floral |
| 125432 | 2/25/1941 | Alfred Philippe | Brooch | Floral |
| 125625 | 3/4/1941 | Alfred Philippe | Brooch | Long-stemmed floral with six-petal bloom (See 125626 for double-bloom version.) |
| 125626 | 3/4/1941 | Alfred Philippe | Brooch | Long-stemmed floral with two six-petal blooms (See 125625 for single-bloom brooch.) |
| 125627 | 3/4/1941 | Alfred Philippe | Brooch | Floral |
| 125816 | 3/11/1941 | Alfred Philippe | Brooch | Question mark |
| 125817 | 3/11/1941 | Alfred Philippe | Brooch | Fish |
| 125818 | 3/11/1941 | Alfred Philippe | Brooch | Bird |
| 125819 | 3/11/1941 | Alfred Philippe | Brooch | Bird in flight |
| 125820 | 3/11/1941 | Alfred Philippe | Brooch | Hyacinth |
| 125821 | 3/11/1941 | Alfred Philippe | Brooch | Jack-in-the-box |
| 125822 | 3/11/1941 | Alfred Philippe | Brooch | Fish |
| 125823 | 3/11/1941 | Alfred Philippe | Brooch | Bird with box |
| 125824 | 3/11/1941 | Alfred Philippe | Brooch | Treble clef |
| 125825 | 3/11/1941 | Alfred Philippe | Brooch | Axe |
| 125826 | 3/11/1941 | Alfred Philippe | Brooch | Figure with champagne glass sitting on gemstone |
| 125841 | 3/11/1941 | Alfred Philippe | Brooch | Floral |
| 125842 | 3/11/1941 | Alfred Philippe | Brooch | Floral |
| 125843 | 3/11/1941 | Alfred Philippe | Brooch | Bird |
| 125844 | 3/11/1941 | Alfred Philippe | Brooch | Heart |
| 125845 | 3/11/1941 | Alfred Philippe | Brooch | Bar tender |
| 125846 | 3/11/1941 | Alfred Philippe | Brooch | Vase of flowers |

125167

125185

125423

125626

125817

TRIFARI JEWELRY

TRIFARI JEWELRY

125820

125821

125849

126483

126633

| 125847 | 3/11/1941 | Alfred Philippe | Brooch | Bird by lake (large gemstone has been reproduced.) |
|---|---|---|---|---|
| 125848 | 3/11/1941 | Alfred Philippe | Brooch | Frog |
| 125849 | 3/11/1941 | Alfred Philippe | Brooch | Floral |
| 126246 | 4/1/1941 | Alfred Philippe | Brooch | Floral |
| 126247 | 4/1/1941 | Alfred Philippe | Brooch | Heron |
| 126248 | 4/1/1941 | Alfred Philippe | Brooch | Duck |
| 126271 | 4/1/1941 | Alfred Philippe | Bracelet | Floral |
| 126482 | 4/8/1941 | Alfred Philippe | Brooch | Long-stemmed floral four-petal single bloom Lucite (See 126483 for double bloom version) |
| 126483 | 4/8/1941 | Alfred Philippe | Brooch | Long-stemmed floral four-petal Lucite (See 126484 for triple-petal version.) |
| 126484 | 4/8/1941 | Alfred Philippe | Brooch | Long-stemmed floral four-petal triple blooms Lucite (See 126482 for single-bloom version.) |
| 126633 | 4/15/1941 | Alfred Philippe | Brooch | Floral |
| 126634 | 4/15/1941 | Alfred Philippe | Brooch | Bird |
| 126796 | 4/22/1941 | Alfred Philippe | Brooch | Floral |
| 126797 | 4/22/1941 | Alfred Philippe | Brooch | Floral |
| 126798 | 4/22/1941 | Alfred Philippe | Brooch | Floral |
| 126799 | 4/22/1941 | Alfred Philippe | Brooch | Soaring eagle |
| 126827 | 4/22/1941 | Alfred Philippe | Brooch | Floral |
| 127027 | 5/6/1941 | Alfred Philippe | Brooch | Floral |
| 127042 | 5/6/1941 | Alfred Philippe | Brooch | Floral fruit |
| 127043 | 5/6/1941 | Alfred Philippe | Brooch | Floral |
| 127327 | 5/20/1941 | Alfred Philippe | Brooch | Cherries |
| 127328 | 5/20/1941 | Alfred Philippe | Brooch | Floral |
| 127329 | 5/20/1941 | Alfred Philippe | Brooch | Bird |
| 129164 | 8/26/1941 | Norman Bel Geddes | Brooch | Jelly Belly swan |
| 129165 | 8/26/1941 | Norman Bel Geddes | Brooch | Jelly Belly fish |
| 129179 | 8/26/1941 | Alfred Philippe | Brooch | Floral |
| 129180 | 8/26/1941 | Alfred Philippe | Brooch | Floral with dangling rhinestone |
| 129181 | 8/26/1941 | Alfred Philippe | Brooch | Floral |
| 129182 | 8/26/1941 | Alfred Philippe | Brooch | Large basket weave bow (See 129853 for another basket weave bow.) |
| 129183 | 8/26/1941 | Alfred Philippe | Brooch | Floral |
| 129184 | 8/26/1941 | Alfred Philippe | Brooch | Floral |
| 129185 | 8/26/1941 | Alfred Philippe | Brooch | Five-pointed star |
| 129186 | 8/26/1941 | Alfred Philippe | Brooch | Circular floral |
| 129187 | 8/26/1941 | Alfred Philippe | Brooch | Floral |

| 129188 | 8/26/1941 | Alfred Philippe | Brooch | Flowers in basket weave bouquet |
|--------|-----------|-----------------|--------|--------------------------------|
| 129189 | 8/26/1941 | Alfred Philippe | Brooch | Rhinestone crescent |
| 129307 | 9/2/1941 | Alfred Philippe | Brooch | Floral |
| 129308 | 9/2/1941 | Alfred Philippe | Brooch | Floral |
| 129309 | 9/2/1941 | Alfred Philippe | Brooch | Heart |
| 129310 | 9/2/1941 | Alfred Philippe | Brooch | Floral |
| 129311 | 9/2/1941 | Alfred Philippe | Brooch | Large bow with rhine-stones |
| 129312 | 9/2/1941 | Alfred Philippe | Brooch | Stylized flower |
| 129313 | 9/2/1941 | Alfred Philippe | Brooch | Stylized flower |
| 129314 | 9/2/1941 | Alfred Philippe | Brooch | Eagle and Lion with both British and American flags |
| 129315 | 9/2/1941 | Alfred Philippe | Brooch | Floral |
| 129317 | 9/2/1941 | Alfred Philippe | Chatelaine | Hear-no-evil monkeys |
| 129318 | 9/2/1941 | Alfred Philippe | Brooch | Floral |
| 129319 | 9/2/1941 | Alfred Spaney | Brooch | Floral |
| 129320 | 9/2/1941 | Alfred Spaney | Brooch | Floral |
| 129321 | 9/2/1941 | Alfred Spaney | Brooch | Floral |
| 129439 | 99/1941 | David Mir | Brooch | Woman with turban |
| 129439 | 9/9/1941 | David Mir | Brooch | Asian face with turban |
| 129440 | 9/9/1941 | Alfred Philippe | Brooch | British lion and "V" |
| 129441 | 9/9/1941 | Adolph Katz | Brooch | Floral |
| 129442 | 9/9/1941 | Alfred Philippe | Brooch | Floral |

126634

129164

129165

129184

129320

**1941 Alfred Spaney for Trifari sweeping floral brooch.** This superb 4" x 2" brooch is design patent number 129320 issued September 2, 1941, to Alfred Spaney for Trifari. The flowing design and use of pavé rhinestones is typical of many Spaney designs from this era. It is signed "Trifari" and "Des. Pat. No. 129320." $100.00 – 150.00.

TRIFARI JEWELRY

129439

129535

129853

129854

| 129443 | 9/9/1941 | Alfred Philippe | Brooch | Floral |
|---|---|---|---|---|
| 129444 | 9/9/1941 | Alfred Philippe | Brooch | Floral |
| 129445 | 9/9/1941 | Alfred Philippe | Brooch | American eagle and "V" |
| 129516 | 9/16/1941 | Alfred Philippe | Brooch | Pineapple |
| 129535 | 9/16/1941 | David Mir | Brooch | Swan |
| 129538 | 9/16/1941 | Alfred Philippe | Brooch | Cascading bouquet with molded glass (See 129539 for another molded glass piece.) |
| 129539 | 9/16/1941 | Alfred Philippe | Brooch | Long-stemmed floral with molded glass (See 129542 for another molded glass piece.) |
| 129540 | 9/16/1941 | Alfred Philippe | Brooch | Floral |
| 129541 | 9/16/1941 | Alfred Philippe | Brooch | Floral |
| 129542 | 9/16/1941 | Alfred Philippe | Brooch | Floral with molded glass (See 129544 for another molded glass piece.) |
| 129543 | 9/16/1941 | Alfred Philippe | Brooch | Floral |
| 129544 | 9/16/1941 | Alfred Philippe | Brooch | Floral with molded glass (See 129545 for another molded glass piece.) |
| 129545 | 9/16/1941 | Alfred Philippe | Brooch | Floral with molded glass (See 125162 for another molded glass brooch.) |
| 129549 | 9/16/1941 | Alfred Spaney | Brooch | Floral leaves |
| 129550 | 9/16/1941 | Alfred Spaney | Brooch | Floral |
| 129551 | 9/16/1941 | Alfred Spaney | Brooch | Floral |
| 129552 | 9/16/1941 | Alfred Spaney | Brooch | Floral |
| 129553 | 9/16/1941 | Alfred Spaney | Brooch | Florals two flowers |
| 129659 | 9/23/1941 | Alfred Philippe | Brooch | Corn on the cob |
| 129849 | 10/7/1941 | Alfred Philippe | Brooch | Floral |
| 129850 | 10/7/1941 | Alfred Philippe | Brooch | Floral leaves |
| 129851 | 10/7/1941 | Alfred Philippe | Brooch | Folded-over ribbon with basket weave (See 130133 for another basket weave brooch.) |
| 129852 | 10/7/1941 | Alfred Philippe | Brooch | Ribbon with basket weave (See 129851 for another basket weave piece.) |
| 129853 | 10/7/1941 | Alfred Philippe | Brooch | Bow with basket weave (See 129852 for another basket weave piece.) |
| 129854 | 10/7/1941 | Alfred Spaney | Brooch | Floral |
| 129855 | 10/7/1941 | Alfred Spaney | Brooch | Floral |
| 129856 | 10/7/1941 | Alfred Spaney | Brooch | Floral |
| 129857 | 10/7/1941 | Alfred Spaney | Brooch | Floral |
| 130082 | 10/21/1941 | David Mir | Brooch | Floral |

| | | | | |
|---|---|---|---|---|
| 130086 | 10/21/1941 | Alfred Spaney | Brooch | Floral, one large flower |
| 130087 | 10/21/1941 | Alfred Spaney | Brooch | Floral |
| 130088 | 10/21/1941 | Alfred Spaney | Brooch | Floral, calla lily |
| 130089 | 10/21/1941 | Alfred Spaney | Brooch | Floral |
| 130096 | 10/21/1941 | David Mir | Brooch | Bird |
| 130133 | 10/28/1941 | Alfred Philippe | Brooch | Leaf with basket weave design (See 130134 for another basket weave pin.) |
| 130134 | 10/28/1941 | Alfred Philippe | Brooch | Curling basket weave ribbon (See 129182 for another basket weave piece.) |
| 130135 | 10/28/1941 | Alfred Philippe | Brooch | Three circles |
| 130136 | 10/28/1941 | Alfred Philippe | Brooch | Floral |
| 130137 | 10/28/1941 | Alfred Philippe | Brooch | Floral |
| 130154 | 10/28/1941 | David Mir | Brooch | Elephant |
| 130338 | 11/11/1941 | David Mir | Brooch | Horse |
| 130342 | 11/11/1941 | Alfred Philippe | Brooch | Floral |
| 130344 | 11/11/1941 | Alfred Spaney | Brooch | Floral |
| 130345 | 11/11/1941 | Alfred Spaney | Brooch | Floral |
| 130346 | 11/11/1941 | Alfred Spaney | Brooch | Floral |
| 130523 | 11/25/1941 | Alfred Philippe | Brooch | Stylized floral |
| 130524 | 11/25/1941 | Alfred Philippe | Brooch | Stylized floral |

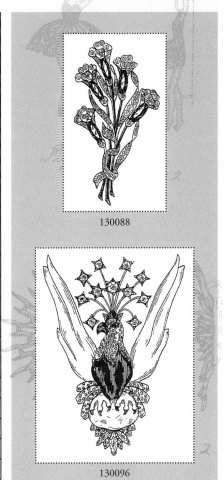

130088

130096

# TRIFARI 1942

| Design Patent Number | Date Issued | Designer | Jewelry Type | Brief Description |
|---|---|---|---|---|
| 131233 | 1/27/1942 | David Mir | Brooch | Russian dancing woman "Tania" (See 131233 for "Ivan.") |
| 131234 | 1/27/1942 | David Mir | Brooch | Male Russian dancer |
| 131234 | 1/27/1942 | David Mir | Brooch | Russian male dancer "Ivan" (See 131233 for "Tania.") |
| 131235 | 1/27/1942 | Alfred Philippe | Brooch | Two birds |
| 131236 | 1/27/1942 | Alfred Philippe | Brooch | Elephant |
| 131237 | 1/27/1942 | Alfred Philippe | Brooch | Female wearing a turban |
| 131238 | 1/27/1942 | Alfred Philippe | Brooch | Fly |
| 131239 | 1/27/1942 | Alfred Philippe | Brooch | Fly |
| 131240 | 1/27/1942 | Alfred Philippe | Brooch | Dog, greyhound |
| 131241 | 1/27/1942 | Alfred Philippe | Brooch | Beetle |
| 131242 | 1/27/1942 | Alfred Philippe | Brooch | Zebra |
| 131243 | 1/27/1942 | Alfred Philippe | Brooch | Mother bird, baby bird in birdhouse |

131234

131235

TRIFARI JEWELRY

131243

131248

131264

131266

131365

| 131245 | 1/27/1942 | Alfred Spaney | Brooch | Windmill |
|--------|-----------|---------------|--------|----------|
| 131246 | 1/27/1942 | Alfred Spaney | Brooch | Sailor carrying a globe |
| 131247 | 1/27/1942 | Alfred Spaney | Brooch | Riding crop and stirrups |
| 131248 | 1/27/1942 | Alfred Spaney | Brooch | Patriotic newspaper man |
| 131264 | 1/27/1942 | Alfred Philippe | Brooch | Floral |
| 131265 | 1/27/1942 | Alfred Philippe | Brooch | Snail |
| 131266 | 1/27/1942 | Alfred Philippe | Brooch | Bow |
| 131267 | 1/27/1942 | Alfred Philippe | Brooch | Bee |
| 131268 | 1/27/1942 | Alfred Philippe | Brooch | Bow |
| 131365 | 2/10/1942 | Alfred Philippe | Brooch | Birds in a tree |
| 131366 | 2/10/1942 | Alfred Philippe | Brooch | Tree |
| 131367 | 2/10/1942 | Alfred Philippe | Brooch | Palm tree |
| 131368 | 2/10/1942 | Alfred Philippe | Brooch | Horse |
| 131369 | 2/10/1942 | Alfred Philippe | Brooch | Tree with semicircle stones |
| 131370 | 2/10/1942 | Alfred Philippe | Brooch | Two flowers |
| 131371 | 2/10/1942 | Alfred Philippe | Brooch | Poodle jelly belly |
| 131378 | 2/10/1942 | Alfred Philippe | Brooch | Floral |
| 131379 | 2/10/1942 | Alfred Philippe | Brooch | Female ice skater |
| 131380 | 2/10/1942 | Alfred Philippe | Brooch | Female tennis player |
| 131381 | 2/10/1942 | Alfred Philippe | Brooch | Floral |
| 131425 | 2/17/1942 | David Mir | Brooch | Two flowers |
| 131426 | 2/17/1942 | Alfred Philippe | Brooch | Ming dragon |
| 131427 | 2/17/1942 | Alfred Philippe | Brooch | Butterfly |
| 131428 | 2/17/1942 | Alfred Philippe | Brooch | Ming horse |
| 131429 | 2/17/1942 | Alfred Philippe | Brooch | Ming camel |
| 131430 | 2/17/1942 | Alfred Philippe | Brooch | Ming bat |
| 131458 | 3/3/1942 | Alfred Spaney | Brooch | Top hat and riding crop |
| 131533 | 3/10/1942 | Alfred Philippe | Jewelry Finding | Bird, Ming duck |
| 131534 | 3/10/1942 | Alfred Philippe | Brooch | Ming elephant |
| 131535 | 3/10/1942 | Alfred Philippe | Brooch | Ming dragon |
| 131536 | 3/10/1942 | Alfred Philippe | Brooch | Ming turtle |
| 131537 | 3/10/1942 | Alfred Philippe | Brooch | Ming frog |

131371

131425

| 131538 | 3/10/1942 | Alfred Philippe | Brooch | Ming ape |
|--------|-----------|-----------------|--------|----------|
| 131539 | 3/10/1942 | Alfred Philippe | Brooch | Tree |
| 131563 | 3/10/1942 | Alfred Philippe | Brooch | Ming cow |
| 131564 | 3/10/1942 | Alfred Philippe | Brooch | Ming swan |
| 131565 | 3/10/1942 | Alfred Philippe | Brooch | Ming fish |
| 131566 | 3/10/1942 | Alfred Philippe | Jewelry Finding | Ming series |
| 131567 | 3/10/1942 | Alfred Philippe | Brooch | Ming house |
| 131746 | 3/24/1942 | Alfred Philippe | Brooch | Lamb |
| 131782 | 3/24/1942 | Alfred Philippe | Brooch | Ming dog |
| 131783 | 3/24/1942 | Alfred Philippe | Brooch | Bear |
| 131784 | 3/24/1942 | Alfred Philippe | Brooch | Floral |
| 131785 | 3/24/1942 | Alfred Philippe | Brooch | Jelly Belly dog |
| 131786 | 3/24/1942 | Alfred Philippe | Brooch | Floral |
| 131787 | 3/24/1942 | Alfred Philippe | Brooch | Pansy |
| 131824 | 3/31/1942 | Alfred Philippe | Brooch | Floral |
| 131836 | 3/31/1942 | Alfred Philippe | Brooch | Flag |
| 131863 | 3/31/1942 | Alfred Philippe | Brooch | Flowers in pot |
| 131864 | 3/31/1942 | Alfred Philippe | Brooch | Tree |
| 131865 | 3/31/1942 | Alfred Philippe | Brooch | Duck |
| 131866 | 3/31/1942 | Alfred Philippe | Brooch | Floral leaves |
| 131867 | 3/31/1942 | Alfred Philippe | Brooch | Frog on lily pad |
| 131868 | 3/31/1942 | Alfred Philippe | Brooch | Bow |
| 131869 | 3/31/1942 | Alfred Philippe | Brooch | Fishing woman |
| 131871 | 3/31/1942 | Alfred Philippe | Brooch | Jelly Belly dog |
| 131881 | 3/31/1942 | Alfred Philippe | Brooch | Floral |
| 131882 | 3/31/1942 | Alfred Philippe | Brooch | Floral |
| 131883 | 3/31/1942 | Alfred Philippe | Brooch | Birds on a branch |
| 131884 | 3/31/1942 | Alfred Philippe | Brooch | Bird on a branch |
| 131885 | 3/31/1942 | Alfred Philippe | Brooch | Floral |
| 131886 | 3/31/1942 | Alfred Philippe | Brooch | Bird on branch |
| 131887 | 3/31/1942 | Alfred Philippe | Brooch | Floral |
| 131888 | 3/31/1942 | Alfred Philippe | Brooch | Floral |
| 131889 | 3/31/1942 | Alfred Philippe | Brooch | Floral |

131426

131428

131458

131535

131537

131746

131564

131539

TRIFARI JEWELRY

131867

131871

131882

131868

| 131961 | 4/7/1942 | Alfred Philippe | Brooch | Floral |
|---|---|---|---|---|
| 131962 | 4/7/1942 | Alfred Philippe | Brooch | Jelly Belly bird |
| 131963 | 4/7/1942 | Alfred Philippe | Brooch | Archer |
| 131964 | 4/7/1942 | Alfred Philippe | Brooch | Floral |
| 131966 | 4/7/1942 | Alfred Spaney | Brooch | Floral |
| 131975 | 4/7/1942 | Alfred Philippe | Brooch | Floral |
| 132001 | 4/7/1942 | Alfred Philippe | Brooch | Jelly Belly elephant |
| 134026 | 10/6/1942 | Alfred Philippe | Brooch | Bird |
| 134027 | 10/6/1942 | Alfred Philippe | Brooch | Bird |
| 134028 | 10/6/1942 | Alfred Philippe | Brooch | Bird |
| 134029 | 10/6/1942 | Alfred Philippe | Brooch | Leaf |
| 134030 | 10/6/1942 | Alfred Philippe | Brooch | Leaf |
| 134031 | 10/6/1942 | Alfred Philippe | Brooch | Bird |
| 134032 | 10/6/1942 | Alfred Philippe | Brooch | Leaf |
| 134033 | 10/6/1942 | Alfred Philippe | Brooch | Leaf |
| 134034 | 10/6/1942 | Alfred Philippe | Brooch | Leaf |
| 134035 | 10/6/1942 | Alfred Philippe | Brooch | Floral leaves |
| 134036 | 10/6/1942 | Alfred Philippe | Brooch | Floral |

**1942 Trifari red enamel bow brooch.** This magnificent 4" x 1" red enamel and pavé rhinestone bow brooch is design patent number 131868 issued March 31, 1942, to Alfred Philippe. Interestingly, this brooch was also produced with black enameling. (Note: Pavé rhinestones coupled with red or black enameling are commonly found features on jewelry from this era.) It is signed "Trifari Pat. Pend." $100.00 – 150.00. From the collection of Debi Reece.

TRIFARI JEWELRY

131961

134027

134033

# TRIFARI 1943

| Design Patent Number | Date Issued | Designer | Jewelry Type | Brief Description |
|---|---|---|---|---|
| 135169 | 3/2/1943 | Alfred Philippe | Brooch | Jelly Belly rabbit |
| 135170 | 3/2/1943 | Alfred Philippe | Brooch | Jelly Belly turtle |
| 135171 | 3/2/1943 | Alfred Philippe | Brooch | Jelly Belly bird |
| 135172 | 3/2/1943 | Alfred Philippe | Brooch | Jelly Belly frog |
| 135173 | 3/2/1943 | Alfred Philippe | Brooch | Jelly Belly pig |
| 135174 | 3/2/1943 | Alfred Philippe | Brooch | Jelly Belly sailboat |
| 135175 | 3/2/1943 | Alfred Philippe | Brooch | Jelly Belly heron |
| 135176 | 3/2/1943 | Alfred Philippe | Brooch | Jelly Belly chick-in-egg |
| 135177 | 3/2/1943 | Alfred Philippe | Brooch | Jelly Belly angel fish |
| 135188 | 3/9/1943 | Alfred Philippe | Brooch | Jelly Belly circus seal |
| 135189 | 3/9/1943 | Alfred Philippe | Brooch | Jelly Belly penguin |
| 135190 | 3/9/1943 | Alfred Philippe | Brooch | Jelly Belly spider |
| 135191 | 3/9/1943 | Alfred Philippe | Brooch | Jelly Belly owl |
| 136079 | 8/3/1943 | Alfred Philippe | Brooch | Female rag doll "Nenette" (See 136080 for "Rintintin.") |
| 136080 | 8/3/1943 | Alfred Philippe | Brooch | Male rag doll "Rintintin" (See 136079 for "Nenette.") |
| 136126 | 8/10/1943 | Alfred Philippe | Brooch | Abstract |

135177

135188

135172

**1943 Trifari Jelly Belly frog brooch.** In my opinion, this adorable Jelly Belly frog brooch is one of the best Trifari figural pins ever designed. The design is patent number 135172 issued March 2, 1943, to Alfred Philippe for Trifari. This sweetie measures approximately 2¾" x 1½". He is sterling silver with a gold wash. His belly is clear Lucite that is nicely shaped to give him a Lucite spine. Clear rhinestones outline his legs, arms, and mouth. He is marked "Trifari," "Des. Pat. No. 135172," and "Sterling." This example of the famous Trifari Jelly Belly frog is authentic; however, be aware that some Jelly Belly pieces have been reproduced. Jelly Belly recasts are well done, so it is important to buy only from a reputable dealer who guarantees the authenticity of the piece. $600.00 – 800.00.

136126

136079

1943 I. Magnin & Co. Christmas advertisement featuring Trifari jewelry. This I. Magnin & Co. store advertisement showcases the Trifari male and female rag doll pins in the lower left corner. I. Magnin was an upscale department store founded by Mary Ann Magnin in the late nineteenth century.

**TRIFARI JEWELRY**

137201

137543

137544

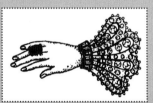

138203

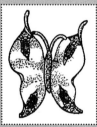

138520

139254

| Design Patent Number | Date Issued | Designer | Jewelry Type | Brief Description |
|---|---|---|---|---|
| 137200 | 2/8/1944 | Alfred Philippe | Brooch | Jelly Belly fly |
| 137201 | 2/8/1944 | Alfred Philippe | Brooch | Jelly Belly swan |
| 137322 | 2/22/1944 | Alfred Philippe | Brooch | Kiwi bird |
| 137323 | 2/22/1944 | Alfred Philippe | Brooch | Jelly Belly lizard |
| 137324 | 2/22/1944 | Alfred Philippe | Brooch | Jelly Belly rooster |
| 137541 | 3/28/1944 | Alfred Philippe | Brooch | Bow |
| 137542 | 3/28/1944 | Alfred Philippe | Brooch | Crown |
| 137543 | 3/28/1944 | Alfred Philippe | Brooch | Floral chrysanthemum |
| 137544 | 3/28/1944 | Alfred Philippe | Brooch | Bow |
| 137545 | 3/28/1944 | Alfred Philippe | Brooch | Abstract |
| 137546 | 3/28/1944 | Alfred Philippe | Brooch | Abstract |
| 137547 | 3/28/1944 | Alfred Philippe | Brooch | Abstract |
| 137548 | 3/28/1944 | Alfred Philippe | Brooch | Abstract |
| 137557 | 3/28/1944 | Alfred Philippe | Brooch | Fly |
| 137572 | 3/28/1944 | Alfred Philippe | Brooch | Jelly Belly eagle |
| 137573 | 3/28/1944 | Alfred Philippe | Brooch | Jelly Belly bird |
| 138202 | 7/4/1944 | Alfred Philippe | Brooch | Elephant |
| 138203 | 7/4/1944 | Alfred Philippe | Brooch | Hand |
| 138353 | 7/18/1944 | Alfred Philippe | Brooch | Jelly Belly horse |
| 138520 | 8/15/1944 | Alfred Philippe | Brooch | Butterfly |
| 138521 | 8/15/1944 | Alfred Philippe | Brooch | Bow |
| 138522 | 8/15/1944 | Alfred Philippe | Brooch | Sword |
| 138652 | 8/29/1944 | Alfred Philippe | Brooch | Jelly Belly orchid |
| 138695 | 9/5/1944 | Alfred Philippe | Brooch | Jelly Belly small turtle |
| 138696 | 9/5/1944 | Alfred Philippe | Brooch | Jelly Belly rose |
| 139254 | 10/24/1944 | Alfred Philippe | Brooch | Jelly Belly Lily of the Valley |
| 139255 | 10/24/1944 | Alfred Philippe | Brooch | Jelly Belly peony |
| 139256 | 10/24/1944 | Alfred Philippe | Brooch | Floral with Lucite |
| 139257 | 10/24/1944 | Alfred Philippe | Brooch | Starburst |
| 139696 | 12/12/1944 | Alfred Philippe | Brooch | Surry with fringe |

| Design Patent Number | Date Issued | Designer | Jewelry Type | Brief Description |
|---|---|---|---|---|
| 139913 | 1/2/1945 | Alfred Philippe | Brooch | Jelly Belly bird |
| 139954 | 1/2/1945 | Alfred Philippe | Brooch | Jelly Belly flower |
| 140778 | 4/10/1945 | Alfred Philippe | Brooch | Stylized floral |
| 140779 | 4/10/1945 | Alfred Philippe | Brooch | Crown |
| 140781 | 4/10/1945 | Alfred Philippe | Brooch | Floral |
| 140801 | 4/10/1945 | Alfred Philippe | Brooch | Rhinestone coat-of-arms style |
| 140843 | 4/10/1945 | Alfred Philippe | Brooch | Queen chess piece (See 140844 for king chess piece.) |
| 140844 | 4/10/1945 | Alfred Philippe | Brooch | King chess piece (See 140855 for knight chess piece.) |
| 140855 | 4/10/1945 | Alfred Philippe | Brooch | Knight chess piece (See 140843 for queen chess piece.) |
| 140856 | 4/10/1945 | Alfred Philippe | Brooch | Stylized shell shape |
| 140894 | 4/17/1945 | Alfred Philippe | Brooch | Circle |
| 140895 | 4/17/1945 | Alfred Philippe | Brooch | Circle with rhinestones |
| 140896 | 4/17/1945 | Alfred Philippe | Brooch | Bow with rhinestones |
| 140897 | 4/17/1945 | Alfred Philippe | Clip | Half-moon shape with bow and large dangling rhinestone |
| 140898 | 4/17/1945 | Alfred Philippe | Clip | Stylized floral |
| 141057 | 5/1/1945 | Alfred Philippe | Brooch | Floral |
| 141058 | 5/1/1945 | Alfred Philippe | Brooch | Abstract |
| 141435 | 6/5/1945 | George Bachner | Brooch | Heart |
| 141907 | 7/31/1945 | Alfred Philippe | Clip | Floral leaf |
| 142584 | 10/16/1945 | Alfred Philippe | Brooch | Dragonfly |
| 142585 | 10/16/1945 | Alfred Philippe | Brooch | Frog |
| 142586 | 10/16/1945 | Alfred Philippe | Clip | Beetle |
| 142587 | 10/16/1945 | Alfred Philippe | Clip | Turtle |
| 142658 | 10/23/1945 | Alfred Philippe | Brooch | India-style brooch |
| 142659 | 10/23/1945 | Alfred Philippe | Brooch | Bird, "Lyre" |
| 142660 | 10/23/1945 | Alfred Philippe | Brooch | Floral |
| 142661 | 10/23/1945 | Alfred Philippe | Brooch | Fish |
| 142662 | 10/23/1945 | Alfred Philippe | Brooch | Floral |
| 142663 | 10/23/1945 | Alfred Philippe | Brooch | Floral |
| 142664 | 10/23/1945 | Alfred Philippe | Clip | Female figural (See 142665 for matching male.) |
| 142665 | 10/23/1945 | Alfred Philippe | Clip | Male figural (See 142664 for matching female.) |
| 142666 | 10/23/1945 | Alfred Philippe | Clip | Abstract floral sunburst |
| 142905 | 11/13/1945 | Alfred Philippe | Brooch | Oval disk with stars |

140779

140843

140898

142658

142659

142661

142664

142666

# TRIFARI 1946

TRIFARI JEWELRY

145259

145272

| Design Patent Number | Date Issued | Designer | Jewelry Type | Brief Description |
|---|---|---|---|---|
| 143751 | 2/5/1946 | Alfred Philippe | Brooch | Abstract floral |
| 143752 | 2/5/1946 | Alfred Philippe | Bracelet | Rhinestones and half-moon shapes |
| 145258 | 7/23/1946 | Alfred Philippe | Brooch | Crescent moon |
| 145259 | 7/23/1946 | Alfred Philippe | Brooch | Abstract with dangles (See 145264 for matching earring.) |
| 145260 | 7/23/1946 | Alfred Philippe | Brooch | Abstract |
| 145261 | 7/23/1946 | Alfred Philippe | Brooch | Jelly Belly rooster head |
| 145264 | 7/23/1946 | Alfred Philippe | Earring | Abstract dangles (See 145259 for matching brooch.) |
| 145266 | 7/23/1946 | Alfred Philippe | Brooch | Bird |
| 145267 | 7/23/1946 | Alfred Philippe | Pin | Leaf |
| 145270 | 7/23/1946 | Alfred Philippe | pin | Abstract with dangles |
| 145271 | 7/23/1946 | Alfred Philippe | Pin | Jelly Belly bird head |
| 145272 | 7/23/1946 | Alfred Philippe | Brooch | Jelly Belly rooster head |
| 145273 | 7/23/1946 | Alfred Philippe | Pin | Heart |
| 145325 | 7/30/1946 | Alfred Philippe | Brooch | Floral |
| 145533 | 9/3/1946 | Alfred Philippe | Brooch | Ribbon |
| 145585 | 9/10/1946 | Alfred Philippe | Brooch | Floral |
| 145676 | 10/1/1946 | Alfred Philippe | Brooch | Floral |

# TRIFARI 1947

| Design Patent Number | Date Issued | Designer | Jewelry Type | Brief Description |
|---|---|---|---|---|
| 146381 | 2/18/1947 | Alfred Philippe | Brooch | Frog on lily pad |
| 146584 | 4/8/1947 | Alfred Philippe | Necklace | Lariat style |
| 147066 | 7/8/1947 | Alfred Philippe | Brooch | Abstract floral |
| 147067 | 7/8/1947 | Alfred Philippe | Brooch | Abstract ribbons |
| 147068 | 7/8/1947 | Alfred Philippe | Brooch | Abstract |
| 147069 | 7/8/1947 | Alfred Philippe | Brooch | Floral leaf |
| 147070 | 7/8/1947 | Alfred Philippe | Brooch | Twisted bow (See 147200 for matching earring.) |
| 147071 | 7/8/1947 | Alfred Philippe | Brooch | Abstract |
| 147072 | 7/8/1947 | Alfred Philippe | Brooch | Floral leaf |
| 147073 | 7/8/1947 | Alfred Philippe | Brooch | Floral |
| 147074 | 7/8/1947 | Alfred Philippe | Brooch | Semicircle starburst (See 147297 for matching earring.) |
| 147077 | 7/8/1947 | Alfred Philippe | Brooch | Abstract ribbon |
| 147078 | 7/8/1947 | Alfred Philippe | Brooch | Abstract floral |
| 147079 | 7/8/1947 | Alfred Philippe | Brooch | Key |
| 147080 | 7/8/1947 | Alfred Philippe | Brooch | Crescent |
| 147147 | 7/15/1947 | Alfred Philippe | Brooch | Crown |
| 147148 | 7/15/1947 | Alfred Philippe | Brooch | Jeweled hand |
| 147200 | 7/22/1947 | Alfred Philippe | Earring | Twisted bow (See 147070 for matching brooch.) |

147070

147072

147074

147079

147147

**1947 Trifari key brooch featured in 1946 Trifari "Day Evening" advertisement.** In the 1940s Trifari produced several versions of the key pin, including this spectacular 2½" sterling silver pin signed "Trifari Pat. Pend." It is design patent number 147079 issued July 8, 1947, to Alfred Philippe for Trifari. Trifari often produced and advertised jewelry before the patent was officially issued, which explains why this lovely pin is featured in a 1946 Trifari advertisement but was not patented until 1947. The 1946 "Day/Evening" advertisement (see page 168) shows a model wearing a pair of royal-looking gold-tone key pins for daytime wear and two silver-tone crown pins for evening wear. $95.00 – 135.00. From the collection of Debi Reece.

147148

147866

148087

148088

| 147201 | 7/22/1947 | Alfred Philippe | Brooch | Abstract dangles |
|---|---|---|---|---|
| 147202 | 7/22/1947 | Alfred Philippe | Brooch | Abstract |
| 147203 | 7/22/1947 | Alfred Philippe | Brooch | Abstract |
| 147204 | 7/22/1947 | Alfred Philippe | Brooch | Abstract floral |
| 147205 | 7/22/1947 | Alfred Philippe | Brooch | Abstract circle |
| 147206 | 7/22/1947 | Alfred Philippe | Brooch | Abstract |
| 147295 | 8/12/1947 | Alfred Philippe | Necklace | Three loops |
| 147296 | 8/12/1947 | Alfred Philippe | Brooch | Stickpin-style with tassel |
| 147297 | 8/12/1947 | Alfred Philippe | Earring | Semicircle starburst (See 147074 for matching brooch.) |
| 147299 | 8/12/1947 | Alfred Philippe | Brooch | Bow with dangles |
| 147376 | 8/26/1947 | Alfred Philippe | Brooch | Abstract floral |
| 147865 | 11/11/1947 | Alfred Philippe | Brooch | Female dancer "Tasha" (See 147866 for male "Sasha.") |
| 147866 | 11/11/1947 | Alfred Philippe | Brooch | Male dancer "Sasha" (See 147865 for female "Tasha.") |
| 148087 | 12/9/1947 | Alfred Philippe | Brooch | Woman with flowers |
| 148088 | 12/9/1947 | Alfred Philippe | Brooch | Ballerina |
| 148185 | 12/23/1947 | Alfred Philippe | Brooch | Abstract |

DAY

EVENING

Jewels by TRIFARI
Designs patented

Trifari 1946 "Day/Evening" advertisement. Interestingly, the key brooch shown in this advertisement was patented in 1947 as number 147079 issued July 8, 1947, to Alfred Philippe. The crown brooch was also patented in 1947 as number 147147 issued July 15, 1947. Clearly Trifari did not wait for the patents to be issued before advertising and producing a design.

TRIFARI JEWELRY

# TRIFARI 1948

| Design Patent Number | Date Issued | Designer | Jewelry Type | Brief Description |
|---|---|---|---|---|
| 148015 | 3/16/1948 | Alfred Philippe | Brooch | Royal-style abstract |
| 148387 | 1/13/1948 | Alfred Philippe | Brooch | Scarf style (See 149295 for another scarf-style pin.) |
| 148388 | 1/13/1948 | Alfred Philippe | Brooch | Flower in pot |
| 148389 | 1/13/1948 | Alfred Philippe | Brooch | Abstract shell shape |
| 148390 | 1/13/1948 | Alfred Philippe | Brooch | Flower center with leaves |
| 148435 | 1/20/1948 | Alfred Philippe | Brooch | Flower center, snowflake style (See 148437 for matching earring.) |
| 148436 | 1/20/1948 | Alfred Philippe | Brooch | Stylized floral |
| 148437 | 1/20/1948 | Alfred Philippe | Earring | Flower center, snowflake style (See 148435 for matching brooch.) |
| 148438 | 1/20/1948 | Alfred Philippe | Brooch | Cactus |
| 148439 | 1/20/1948 | Alfred Philippe | Brooch | Floral |
| 148562 | 2/3/1948 | Alfred Philippe | Brooch | Love birds on branch |
| 148563 | 2/3/1948 | Alfred Philippe | Brooch | Monkey hanging by tail and holding gem |
| 148564 | 2/3/1948 | Alfred Philippe | Brooch | Jewelry belly duck |
| 148565 | 2/3/1948 | Alfred Philippe | Brooch | Rabbit holding gem |
| 148566 | 2/3/1948 | Alfred Philippe | Brooch | Sea serpent |
| 148567 | 2/3/1948 | Alfred Philippe | Brooch | Flower center (See 148885 for matching earring.) |
| 148568 | 2/3/1948 | Alfred Philippe | Brooch | Bug |
| 148569 | 2/3/1948 | Alfred Philippe | Brooch | Key |
| 148570 | 2/3/1948 | Alfred Philippe | Brooch | Sword |
| 148571 | 2/3/1948 | Alfred Philippe | Brooch | Duck with top hat and cane |
| 148572 | 2/3/1948 | Alfred Philippe | Brooch | Bird |
| 148885 | 3/2/1948 | Alfred Philippe | Earring | Flower center (See 148567 for matching brooch.) |
| 148953 | 3/9/1948 | Alfred Philippe | Brooch | Floral |
| 149015 | 3/16/1948 | Alfred Philippe | Brooch | "Talisman" |
| 149016 | 3/16/1948 | Alfred Philippe | Brooch | Abstract |
| 149017 | 3/16/1948 | Alfred Philippe | Brooch | Floral |
| 149020 | 3/16/1948 | Alfred Philippe | Brooch | Double ribbon |

148438

148563

148566

TRIFARI JEWELRY

**1996 reissue of 1948 Trifari sea serpent brooch.** In mint condition, this 2¾" x 1¼" serpent brooch is signed "Trifari 1996" and is a reissue of design patent number 148566 issued February 3, 1948, to Alfred Philippe for Trifari. Wisely, Trifari dated this piece, which helps to avoid any confusion between this reissue and the original 1948 piece. The value of the original piece is $400.00 – 600.00. The value of this reissue is $85.00 – 100.00.

TRIFARI JEWELRY

149015

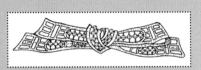

151179

150648

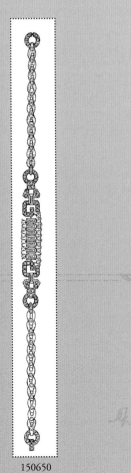

150650

| 149067 | 3/23/1948 | Alfred Philippe | Brooch | Flying insect |
|---|---|---|---|---|
| 149068 | 3/23/1948 | Alfred Philippe | Brooch | Sailboat |
| 149069 | 3/23/1948 | Alfred Philippe | Brooch Separable | Flying insects |
| 149087 | 3/23/1948 | Alfred Philippe | Brooch | Torch |
| 149209 | 4/6/1948 | Alfred Philippe | Necklace | Metal "Trifari" links with draping decoration |
| 149210 | 4/6/1948 | Alfred Philippe | Bracelet | Flat band with abstract center decoration |
| 149212 | 4/6/1948 | Alfred Philippe | Brooch | Floral |
| 149213 | 4/6/1948 | Alfred Philippe | Brooch | Pearls and rhinestones (See 149296 for matching necklace.) |
| 149214 | 4/6/1948 | Alfred Philippe | Brooch | Scarf-style pin (See 148387 for another scarf-style pin.) |
| 149295 | 4/13/1948 | Alfred Philippe | Brooch | Scarf-style pin (See 150648 for another scarf-style pin.) |
| 149296 | 4/13/1948 | Alfred Philippe | Necklace | Pearls and rhinestones (See 149213 for matching brooch.) |
| 149298 | 4/13/1948 | Alfred Philippe | Bracelet | Abstract floral |
| 149582 | 5/11/1948 | Alfred Philippe | Brooch | Fan |
| 149584 | 5/11/1948 | Alfred Philippe | Brooch | Abstract floral |
| 149585 | 5/11/1948 | Alfred Philippe | Brooch | Abstract floral |
| 149586 | 5/11/1948 | Alfred Philippe | Brooch | Floral |
| 149587 | 5/11/1948 | Alfred Philippe | Brooch | Snowflake style |
| 149673 | 5/18/1948 | Alfred Philippe | Brooch | Floral leaves with rhinestone drop |
| 149770 | 5/25/1948 | Alfred Philippe | Brooch | Floral |
| 149836 | 6/1/1948 | Alfred Philippe | Brooch | Floral |
| 149837 | 6/1/1948 | Alfred Philippe | Necklace | Fruit salad floral (See 149838 for matching necklace.) |
| 149838 | 6/1/1948 | Alfred Philippe | Necklace | Fruit salad floral (See 149837 for matching necklace.) |
| 149903 | 6/8/1948 | Alfred Philippe | Necklace | Floral |
| 150446 | 8/3/1948 | Alfred Philippe | Brooch | Abstract |
| 150447 | 8/3/1948 | Alfred Philippe | Brooch | Leaf |
| 150450 | 8/3/1948 | Alfred Philippe | Brooch | Abstract |
| 150451 | 8/3/1948 | Alfred Philippe | Brooch | Abstract floral |
| 150452 | 8/3/1948 | Alfred Philippe | Brooch | Four leaf clover |
| 150453 | 8/3/1948 | Alfred Philippe | Brooch | Floral |
| 150454 | 8/3/1948 | Alfred Philippe | Brooch | Floral |
| 150455 | 8/3/1948 | Alfred Philippe | Brooch | Abstract |
| 150515 | 8/10/1948 | Alfred Philippe | Brooch | Floral leaf |
| 150648 | 8/17/1948 | Alfred Philippe | Brooch | Scarf-style pin (See 149214 for another scarf-style pin.) |

**Late 1940s Trifari molded glass necklace.** This rare blue molded stone 15½" necklace is signed "Trifari Pat. Pend." It is also signed with "L." Unfortunately, I was unable to locate the patent for this necklace. Trifari jewelry utilizing similar molded glass stones was made in the early 1940s, again in 1948, and again after 1955. For several reasons, I believe this necklace dates to 1948. First, the blue stones in the necklace are similar to those used in the Trifari leaf brooch design patent number 150515 issued August 10, 1948, to Alfred Philippe. Next, it is not sterling. However, the metal has a patina consistent with Trifari jewelry from this era. Finally, the signature of the necklace indicates it was made before 1955. $125.00 – 150.00.

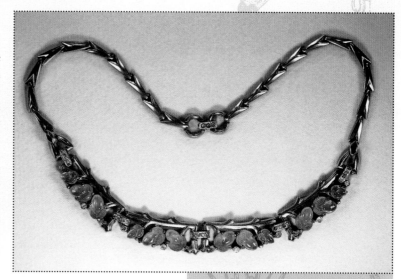

Close view of blue molded glass stones and clear pavé decorations on 1948 Trifari necklace.

## • TRIFARI 1948 •

| 150650 | 8/17/1948 | Alfred Philippe | Necklace | Advertised as "Winter Jewels" (Ad not shown; see 150651 for matching bracelet.) |
|---|---|---|---|---|
| 150651 | 8/17/1948 | Alfred Philippe | Bracelet | Advertised as "Winter Jewels" (Ad not shown; see 150650 for matching necklace.) |
| 150884 | 9/7/1948 | Alfred Philippe | Brooch | Bird and nest |
| 151068 | 9/21/1948 | Alfred Philippe | Necklace | "Trifari" link with draping ribbon center decoration |
| 151169 | 9/28/1948 | Alfred Philippe | Brooch | Abstract |
| 151170 | 9/28/1948 | Alfred Philippe | Brooch | Fly |
| 151171 | 9/28/1948 | Alfred Philippe | Brooch | Floral leaf |
| 151172 | 9/28/1948 | Alfred Philippe | Brooch | Floral bow |
| 151173 | 9/28/1948 | Alfred Philippe | Brooch | Crown |
| 151174 | 9/28/1948 | Alfred Philippe | Brooch | Bird |
| 151176 | 9/28/1948 | Alfred Philippe | Brooch | Abstract |
| 151177 | 9/28/1948 | Alfred Philippe | Brooch | Floral |
| 151178 | 9/28/1948 | Alfred Philippe | Brooch | Floral leaf |
| 151179 | 9/28/1948 | Alfred Philippe | Brooch | "Heavenly Angel" female (See 151180 for male.) |

150515

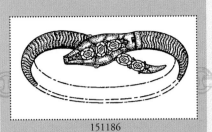

151186

151533

151535

TRIFARI JEWELRY

| 151180 | 9/28/1948 | Alfred Philippe | Brooch | "Heavenly Angel" male (See 151179 for female.) |
|--------|-----------|-----------------|--------|----------------|
| 151181 | 9/28/1948 | Alfred Philippe | Brooch | Oval-shaped abstract |
| 151184 | 9/28/1948 | Alfred Philippe | Earring | Snake or serpent (See 151185 for matching necklace.) |
| 151185 | 9/28/1948 | Alfred Philippe | Necklace | Snake or serpent (See 151186 for matching bracelet.) |
| 151186 | 9/28/1948 | Alfred Philippe | Bracelet | Snake or serpent (See 151184 for matching earrings.) |
| 151389 | 10/12/1948 | Alfred Philippe | Brooch | Floral with two drops |
| 151390 | 10/12/1948 | Alfred Philippe | Brooch | Small stylized bow |
| 151391 | 10/12/1948 | Alfred Philippe | Brooch | Large stylized bow |
| 151392 | 10/12/1948 | Alfred Philippe | Brooch | Floral leaves |
| 151393 | 10/12/1948 | Alfred Philippe | Brooch | Floral |
| 151394 | 10/12/1948 | Alfred Philippe | Brooch | Floral |
| 151395 | 10/12/1948 | Alfred Philippe | Brooch | Key |
| 151396 | 10/12/1948 | Alfred Philippe | Brooch | Rooster |
| 151397 | 10/12/1948 | Alfred Philippe | Brooch | Fly |
| 151399 | 10/12/1948 | Alfred Philippe | Brooch | Turtle |
| 151465 | 10/19/1948 | Alfred Philippe | Bracelet | Three rows of pearls |
| 151530 | 10/26/1948 | Alfred Philippe | Necklace | Abstract |
| 151533 | 10/26/1948 | Alfred Philippe | Earring | Four-stone floral earring (See 151537 for matching bracelet.) |
| 151535 | 10/26/1948 | Alfred Philippe | Necklace | Nine-stone floral (See 151533 for matching earring.) |
| 151537 | 10/26/1948 | Alfred Philippe | Bracelet | Nine-stone floral (See 151535 for matching necklace.) |
| 151538 | 10/26/1948 | Alfred Philippe | Brooch | Snowflake-style floral |

**1948 Trifari gold-tone and green rhinestone necklace and bracelet set.** Elegant emerald green rhinestones seem to be exploding from this attractive and wearable set patented by Alfred Philippe for Trifari on October 26, 1948. The 15½" choker is design patent number 151535, the 7¼" bracelet is design patent number 151537, and the earrings are design patent number 151533. All pieces are signed "Trifari Pat. Pend." $350.00 – 450.00.

| 151544 | 10/26/1948 | Alfred Philippe | Brooch | Floral with three drops |
|---|---|---|---|---|
| 151545 | 10/26/1948 | Alfred Philippe | Brooch | Leaf |
| 151548 | 10/26/1948 | Alfred Philippe | Brooch | Floral |
| 151549 | 10/26/1948 | Alfred Philippe | Brooch | Floral |
| 151551 | 10/26/1948 | Alfred Philippe | Brooch | Bow with rhinestones (See 151921 for matching necklace.) |
| 151552 | 10/26/1948 | Alfred Philippe | Brooch | Floral with drop |
| 151553 | 10/26/1948 | Alfred Philippe | Brooch | Floral |
| 151554 | 10/26/1948 | Alfred Philippe | Brooch | Abstract |
| 151555 | 10/26/1948 | Alfred Philippe | Brooch | Bug |
| 151706 | 11/9/1948 | Alfred Philippe | Necklace | Floral |
| 151708 | 11/9/1948 | Alfred Philippe | Necklace | Deco-style |
| 151709 | 11/9/1948 | Alfred Philippe | Necklace | Abstract center decoration |
| 151710 | 11/9/1948 | Alfred Philippe | Necklace | Abstract center decoration |
| 151915 | 11/30/1948 | Alfred Philippe | Brooch | Abstract floral |
| 151916 | 11/30/1948 | Alfred Philippe | Brooch | Abstract floral |
| 151917 | 11/30/1948 | Alfred Philippe | Brooch | Duette-like abstract |
| 151920 | 11/30/1948 | Alfred Philippe | Necklace | Chain with center decoration |
| 151921 | 11/30/1948 | Alfred Philippe | Necklace | Chain with bow and rhinestone center decoration (See 151551 for matching brooch.) |
| 151922 | 11/30/1948 | Alfred Philippe | Necklace | Chain with elaborate floral center decoration |
| 151923 | 11/30/1948 | Alfred Philippe | Necklace | Pearls with bow and two pearl drops |
| 151924 | 11/30/1948 | Alfred Philippe | Brooch | Cable car |
| 151926 | 11/30/1948 | Alfred Philippe | Brooch | Bow with pearl drops |
| 151927 | 11/30/1948 | Alfred Philippe | Brooch | Basket with pearls |
| 151928 | 11/30/1948 | Alfred Philippe | Brooch | Leaf |
| 151929 | 11/30/1948 | Alfred Philippe | Brooch | Bow with six pearl drops |
| 151930 | 11/30/1948 | Alfred Philippe | Brooch | Floral |
| 151931 | 11/30/1948 | Alfred Philippe | Brooch | Floral |
| 151932 | 11/30/1948 | Alfred Philippe | Brooch | Floral |
| 151933 | 11/30/1948 | Alfred Philippe | Brooch | Floral leaf |

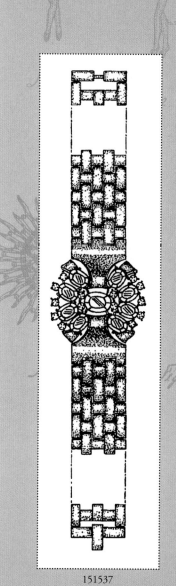

151537

TRIFARI JEWELRY

TRIFARI JEWELRY

153307

153309

153385

153391

| Design Patent Number | Date Issued | Designer | Jewelry Type | Brief Description |
|---|---|---|---|---|
| 152364 | 1/11/1949 | Alfred Philippe | Earring | Crescent shape with five-pointed rhinestone flower stones (See 152728 for another rhinestone flower piece.) |
| 152366 | 1/11/1949 | Alfred Philippe | Brooch | Floral with five-pointed rhinestone flower stones (See 152364 for another piece with rhinestone flower stones.) |
| 152367 | 1/11/1949 | Alfred Philippe | Brooch | Horse |
| 152728 | 2/15/1949 | Alfred Philippe | Necklace | Floral with five-pointed rhinestone flower stones (See 153026 for another rhinestone flower piece.) |
| 152730 | 2/15/1949 | Alfred Philippe | Necklace | Triple-strand pearls |
| 152735 | 2/15/1949 | Alfred Philippe | Necklace | Floral with five-pointed rhinestone flower stones (See 152366 for another piece with rhinestone flower stones.) |
| 153017 | 3/8/1949 | Alfred Philippe | Brooch | Floral with five-pointed rhinestone flower stones (See 153549 for another piece with rhinestone flower stones.) |
| 153018 | 3/8/1949 | Alfred Philippe | Brooch | Floral with five-pointed rhinestone flower stones (See 153017 for another piece with rhinestone flower stones.) |
| 153019 | 3/8/1949 | Alfred Philippe | Brooch | Floral with five-pointed rhinestone flower stones (See 153018 for another piece with rhinestone flower stones.) |
| 153024 | 3/8/1949 | Alfred Philippe | Necklace | Floral with five-pointed rhinestone flower stones (See 153389 for another piece with five-pointed rhinestone flower stones.) |
| 153026 | 3/8/1949 | Alfred Philippe | Earring | Heart shape with five-pointed rhinestone flower stones (See 153019 for another piece with rhinestone flower stones.) |
| 153028 | 3/8/1949 | Alfred Philippe | Necklace | Jelly Belly shell |
| 153029 | 3/8/1949 | Alfred Philippe | Necklace | Necklace with two crescent shaped jelly belly stones (See 153382 for another piece from this group.) |
| 153078 | 3/15/1949 | Alfred Philippe | Brooch | Crown |
| 153079 | 3/15/1949 | Alfred Philippe | Brooch | Abstract |
| 153080 | 3/15/1949 | Alfred Philippe | Brooch | Floral |
| 153081 | 3/15/1949 | Alfred Philippe | Brooch | Long-stemmed floral |

| 153082 | 3/15/1949 | Alfred Philippe | Brooch | Floral |
|---|---|---|---|---|
| 153083 | 3/15/1949 | Alfred Philippe | Brooch | Abstract fan-shape |
| 153307 | 4/5/1949 | Alfred Philippe | Brooch | Bird |
| 153308 | 4/5/1949 | Alfred Philippe | Brooch | Owl |
| 153309 | 4/5/1949 | Alfred Philippe | Brooch | Bird |
| 153310 | 4/5/1949 | Alfred Philippe | Brooch | Bird hatching from egg |
| 153311 | 4/5/1949 | Alfred Philippe | Brooch | Bird on branch |
| 153379 | 4/12/1949 | Alfred Philippe | Brooch | Butterfly |
| 153380 | 4/12/1949 | Alfred Philippe | Necklace | Abstract Floral |
| 153381 | 4/12/1949 | Alfred Philippe | Necklace | Abstract |
| 153382 | 4/12/1949 | Alfred Philippe | Necklace | Abstract crescent Jelly Belly (See 153453 for another piece from this group.) |
| 153383 | 4/12/1949 | Alfred Philippe | Necklace | Abstract floral |
| 153385 | 4/12/1949 | Alfred Philippe | Brooch | Male ballet dancer (See 153388 for female dancer.) |
| 153386 | 4/12/1949 | Alfred Philippe | Necklace | Abstract floral |
| 153387 | 4/12/1949 | Alfred Philippe | Necklace | Floral with five-pointed rhinestone flower stones (See 154063 for another piece with rhinestone flower stones.) |
| 153388 | 4/12/1949 | Alfred Philippe | Brooch | Female ballet dancer (See 153385 for male dancer.) |
| 153389 | 4/12/1949 | Alfred Philippe | Necklace | Floral with five-pointed rhinestone flower stones (See 153387 for another piece with five-pointed rhinestone flower stones.) |
| 153390 | 4/12/1949 | Alfred Philippe | Brooch | Bird |
| 153391 | 4/12/1949 | Alfred Philippe | Brooch | Poodle with faceted rhinestone belly (See 153393 for faceted-belly frog.) |
| 153392 | 4/12/1949 | Alfred Philippe | Brooch | Elephant with faceted rhinestone belly. (See patent 153391 for faceted-belly poodle.) |
| 153393 | 4/12/1949 | Alfred Philippe | Brooch | Frog with faceted rhinestone belly. (See 153392 for faceted-belly elephant.) |
| 153446 | 4/19/1949 | Alfred Philippe | Brooch | Rooster with crescent-shaped Jelly Belly (See 153630 for a brooch with the same crescent belly.) |
| 153447 | 4/19/1949 | Alfred Philippe | Brooch | Bird with molded stones (See 153448 for similar pin.) |
| 153448 | 4/19/1949 | Alfred Philippe | Brooch | Bird with molded stones (See 153449 for a similar pin.) |

**1949 Trifari ballet dancer pins.** These well-crafted miniature ballet dancer pins are design patent numbers 153388 (female) and 153385 (male) issued April 12, 1949, to Alfred Philippe for Trifari. Measuring 1½" x ¾", they are each signed "Trifari Pat. Pend." and are intended to be worn together. $85.00 – 135.00.

**Trifari 1949 miniature poodle pin.** Popular with collectors, this diminutive ¾" x ¾" poodle pin is signed "Trifari Pat. Pend." It is design patent number 153391 issued April 12, 1949, to Alfred Philippe for Trifari. In the same year, Trifari patented designs for a tiny elephant pin (design patent number 153392) and frog pin (design patent number 153393). $65.00 – 100.00.

TRIFARI JEWELRY

175

TRIFARI JEWELRY

153447

153453

153550

153551

| | | | | |
|---|---|---|---|---|
| 153449 | 4/19/1949 | Alfred Philippe | Brooch | Bird rooster with molded stones (See 153451 for a similar pin.) |
| 153450 | 4/19/1949 | Alfred Philippe | Brooch | Bug |
| 153451 | 4/19/1949 | Alfred Philippe | Brooch | Moth with molded stones (See 153452 for similar pin.) |
| 153452 | 4/19/1949 | Alfred Philippe | Brooch | Dragonfly with molded stones. (See 153447 for similar pin.) |
| 153453 | 4/19/1949 | Alfred Philippe | Brooch | Jelly Belly snail with crescent shaped belly (See 153446 for another piece from this group.) |
| 153454 | 4/19/1949 | Alfred Philippe | Brooch | Abstract |
| 153549 | 4/26/1949 | Alfred Philippe | Brooch | Wheelbarrow with five-pointed rhinestone flower stones (See 153024 for another piece with rhinestone flower stones.) |
| 153550 | 4/26/1949 | Alfred Philippe | Brooch | Hourglass |
| 153551 | 4/26/1949 | Alfred Philippe | Brooch | Female figure advertised as "Pom-pom" (Ad not shown; see 153552 for matching male pin.) |
| 153552 | 4/26/1949 | Alfred Philippe | Brooch | Male figure advertised as "Tom-tom" (Ad not shown; see 153551 for matching female pin.) |
| 153624 | 5/3/1949 | Alfred Philippe | Brooch | Abstract design with crescent-shaped Jelly Belly stone (See 153029 for another piece from this group.) |
| 153625 | 5/3/1949 | Alfred Philippe | Brooch | Triple circle |
| 153626 | 5/3/1949 | Alfred Philippe | Brooch | Long-stemmed floral with five-pointed rhinestone flower stones (See 152735 for another piece with rhinestone flower stones.) |
| 153627 | 5/3/1949 | Alfred Philippe | Brooch | Floral |
| 153629 | 5/3/1949 | Alfred Philippe | Brooch | Abstract |
| 153630 | 5/3/1949 | Alfred Philippe | Brooch | Crescent-shaped brooch with crescent-shaped Jelly Belly (See 153624 for another brooch from this group.) |
| 154063 | 6/7/1949 | Alfred Philippe | Necklace | Lariat-style floral with five-pointed rhinestone flower stones (See 154214 for another piece with rhinestone flower stones.) |

| | | | | |
|---|---|---|---|---|
| 154214 | 6/21/1949 | Alfred Philippe | Brooch | Floral scarf with five-pointed rhinestone flower stones (See 154629 for another piece with rhinestone flower stones.) |
| 154306 | 6/28/1949 | Alfred Philippe | Brooch | Floral |
| 154307 | 6/28/1949 | Alfred Philippe | Brooch | Long-stemmed floral |
| 154429 | 7/5/1949 | Alfred Philippe | Brooch | Basket with five-pointed rhinestone flower stones (See 153626 for another piece with rhinestone flower stones.) |
| 154628 | 7/26/1949 | Alfred Philippe | Brooch | Basket |
| 154629 | 7/26/1949 | Alfred Philippe | Brooch | Basket five-pointed rhinestone flower stones (See 154429 for another piece with rhinestone flower stones.) |
| 154630 | 7/26/1949 | Alfred Philippe | Necklace | Abstract dangles |
| 154631 | 7/26/1949 | Alfred Philippe | Necklace | Abstract dangles |
| 154633 | 7/26/1949 | Alfred Philippe | Necklace | Abstract dangles |
| 154634 | 7/26/1949 | Alfred Philippe | Necklace | Abstract |
| 154635 | 7/26/1949 | Alfred Philippe | Necklace | Abstract |
| 154636 | 7/26/1949 | Alfred Philippe | Necklace | Part of the Moghul series |
| 155181 | 9/13/1949 | Alfred Philippe | Brooch | Floral |
| 155182 | 9/13/1949 | Alfred Philippe | Brooch | Butterfly |
| 155184 | 9/13/1949 | Alfred Philippe | Earring | Floral with molded glass stones, Moghul series |
| 155185 | 9/13/1949 | Alfred Philippe | Brooch | Sword |
| 155186 | 9/13/1949 | Alfred Philippe | Brooch | Abstract bow |
| 155187 | 9/13/1949 | Alfred Philippe | Brooch | Key |
| 155188 | 9/13/1949 | Alfred Philippe | Brooch | Abstract tree |
| 155189 | 9/13/1949 | Alfred Philippe | Brooch | Floral leaf "Scheherazade" |
| 155190 | 9/13/1949 | Alfred Philippe | Brooch | Turtle, ribbed stone belly, often called "Moghul" jewelry |
| 155193 | 9/13/1949 | Alfred Philippe | Brooch | Abstract |
| 155194 | 9/13/1949 | Alfred Philippe | Brooch | Floral Moghul brooch with molded glass rhinestones |
| 155195 | 9/13/1949 | Alfred Philippe | Brooch | Elephant, ribbed stone belly, often called "Moghul" jewelry |
| 155196 | 9/13/1949 | Alfred Philippe | Brooch | Bird, ribbed stone belly, often called "Moghul" jewelry |
| 155197 | 9/13/1949 | Alfred Philippe | Brooch | Long-stemmed floral |
| 155198 | 9/13/1949 | Alfred Philippe | Brooch | Tree with molded glass stones, Moghul series |
| 155199 | 9/13/1949 | Alfred Philippe | Brooch | Fan |
| 155200 | 9/13/1949 | Alfred Philippe | Brooch | Long-stemmed floral |

154629

155198

TRIFARI JEWELRY

177

**1949 Trifari Snowflake brooch and earrings set.** Classically lovely, this Trifari 1¼" Snowflake brooch and matching ¾" earrings set is featured in the 1949 "this Christmas every woman can have the thrill of Jewels by Trifari" advertisement (see page 179). The brooch originally sold for $4.00 and the earrings for $5.00. (A larger version of this brooch sold for $7.50.) Signed "Trifari Pat. Pend.," the brooch is design patent number 155214 issued September 13, 1949, to Alfred Philippe for Trifari. $45.00 – 65.00.

155214

155218

155219

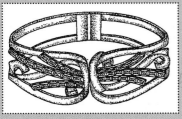

155230

## • TRIFARI 1949 •

| 155201 | 9/13/1949 | Alfred Philippe | Brooch | Staff with molded glass stones, "Moghul" |
|---|---|---|---|---|
| 155202 | 9/13/1949 | Alfred Philippe | Brooch | Called the "Wasps Nest Brooch," part of the Moghul series |
| 155204 | 9/13/1949 | Alfred Philippe | Necklace | Floral with molded glass stones, Moghul series |
| 155205 | 9/13/1949 | Alfred Philippe | Necklace | "Meteor" (See 155230 for matching bracelet.) |
| 155207 | 9/13/1949 | Alfred Philippe | Necklace | Floral |
| 155208 | 9/13/1949 | Alfred Philippe | Earring | "Meteor" (See 155205 for matching necklace.) |
| 155209 | 9/13/1949 | Alfred Philippe | Brooch | Cornucopia with molded glass stones, Moghul series |
| 155210 | 9/13/1949 | Alfred Philippe | Brooch | Cornucopia with molded glass stones, Moghul series |
| 155211 | 9/13/1949 | Alfred Philippe | Brooch | Long-stemmed floral |
| 155212 | 9/13/1949 | Alfred Philippe | Brooch | "Meteor" (See 155208 for matching earring.) |
| 155213 | 9/13/1949 | Alfred Philippe | Brooch | Butterfly with ribbed stone, often called "Moghul" |
| 155214 | 9/13/1949 | Alfred Philippe | Brooch | Floral |
| 155217 | 9/13/1949 | Alfred Philippe | Brooch | Floral |
| 155218 | 9/13/1949 | Alfred Philippe | Brooch | Floral, triple plumes |
| 155219 | 9/13/1949 | Alfred Philippe | Brooch | Horse with ribbed stone belly, often called "Moghul" jewelry |
| 155227 | 9/13/1949 | Alfred Philippe | Necklace | Floral with molded glass stones, "Moghul" series |
| 155228 | 9/13/1949 | Alfred Philippe | Necklace | Rhinestone dangles |
| 155230 | 9/13/1949 | Alfred Philippe | Bracelet | Advertised as "Meteor" in 1949. (See 155212 for matching brooch.) |
| 155317 | 9/20/1949 | Alfred Philippe | Brooch | Floral Pansy |

**1949 Trifari Meteor necklace, bracelet, and earrings.** Advertised in the Trifari 1949 "this Christmas every woman can have the thrill of Jewels by Trifari" advertisement as "Meteor," this popular set features fiery shooting strands of baguette rhinestones set in gold-tone Trifanium. The set is signed "Trifari Pat. Pend." The 15" choker originally sold for $10.00, the cuff bracelet for $12.50, and the 1½" clip earrings for $7.50. The choker necklace is design patent number 155205 issued September 13, 1949, to Alfred Philippe, the earrings are design patent number 155208, a brooch ( not shown in the photograph or the advertisement) is design patent number 155212, and the cuff bracelet is design patent number 155230. $80.00 – 120.00. From the collection of Debi Reece.

Across top: "Meteor" set — Earrings $7.50, Necklace $10, Bracelet $12.50. Second row: "Snowflake" pin $7.50, (smaller size $4), Earrings $5.— Rhinestone Leaf $20. Third row: Book Locket Bracelet $5, "Scheherazade" Pendant Necklace $20, "Scheherazade" Clip Pin $25, Pendant Earrings $15. Fourth Row: "Golden Twist" Necklace $10, Earrings $5, (matching bracelet $6). Tax extra.

Trifari 1949 "this Christmas every woman can have the thrill of Jewels by Trifari" advertisement. Original prices, top: Meteor earrings, $7.50, with necklace, $10.00, and bracelet, $12.50. Original prices, second row left: Snowflake pin, $7.50, and earrings, $5.00. Original price, second row right: Rhinestone Leaf, $20.00. Original price, third row left: Book Locket bracelet, $5.00. Original prices, third row middle and right: Scheherazade necklace, $20.00, with brooch, $25.00, and earrings, $15.00. Original prices, bottom row: Golden Twist necklace, $10.00, and earrings, $5.00.

### • TRIFARI 1949 •

| 155318 | 9/20/1949 | Alfred Philippe | Brooch | Long-stemmed floral |
|---|---|---|---|---|
| 155320 | 9/20/1949 | Alfred Philippe | Necklace | Abstract dangles |
| 156161 | 11/22/1949 | Alfred Philippe | Necklace | Ribbed stone center Moghul-style necklace |
| 156162 | 11/22/1949 | Alfred Philippe | Necklace | Ribbed stone Moghul necklace advertised in 1949 as "Scheherazade" |
| 156165 | 11/22/1949 | Alfred Philippe | Bracelet | Clamper with molded glass stones, Moghul series |
| 156166 | 11/22/1949 | Alfred Philippe | Bracelet | Clamper floral |
| 156167 | 11/22/1949 | Alfred Philippe | Bracelet | Clamper floral |
| 156270 | 11/29/1949 | Alfred Philippe | Pin Clip | Abstract |
| 156271 | 11/29/1949 | Alfred Philippe | Brooch | Branch with leaves |
| 156272 | 11/29/1949 | Alfred Philippe | Brooch | Abstract |
| 156274 | 11/29/1949 | Alfred Philippe | Brooch | Abstract no rhinestones |
| 156655 | 12/27/1949 | Alfred Philippe | Earring | Floral Moghul earrings (advertised as "Scheherazade" in 1949) with molded glass rhinestones |
| 156656 | 12/27/1949 | Alfred Philippe | Brooch | Long-stemmed floral |

156162
(Moghul necklace patent)

156655
(Moghul earring patent)

**1949 Trifari molded-glass bracelet and clip.** Attractive and highly collectible, this 2" x 1¼" clip and 7¼" bracelet are signed "Trifari" without the copyright symbol. The royal blue, deep red, and emerald green stones are molded glass. These molded stones resemble the molded glass stones used in the Scheherazade earrings featured in the 1949 "this Christmas every woman can have the thrill of Jewels by Trifari" advertisement. The Scheherazade earrings shown in the advertisement are design patent number 156655 issued December 27, 1949, to Alfred Philippe for Trifari. Sometimes jewelry with these molded glass stones is referred to by collectors as "Moghul" jewelry. (Note: In 1965 Trifari issued a similar jewelry set called the "Jewels of India." This set is signed "Trifari" with the copyright symbol, helping to distinguish it from the 1949 Moghul jewelry, which is signed "Trifari" without the copyright symbol.) Due to this similarity in stones, I believe the beautiful clip and bracelet in the above photograph also date from 1949. Highly sought after by collectors, today this set would sell for between $500.00 and $800.00. From the collection of Debi Reece.

# TRIFARI 1950

| Design Patent Number | Date Issued | Designer | Jewelry Type | Brief Description |
|---|---|---|---|---|
| 156761 | 1/3/1950 | Alfred Philippe | Brooch | Geometric, no rhinestones |
| 156762 | 1/3/1950 | Alfred Philippe | Brooch | Geometric, no rhinestones |
| 156763 | 1/3/1950 | Alfred Philippe | Brooch | Leaf |
| 156912 | 1/17/1950 | Alfred Philippe | Brooch | Abstract floral |
| 156913 | 1/17/1950 | Alfred Philippe | Brooch | Abstract floral |
| 156914 | 1/17/1950 | Alfred Philippe | Brooch | Abstract floral |
| 156995 | 1/24/1950 | Alfred Philippe | Brooch | Bow |
| 157190 | 2/7/1950 | Alfred Philippe | Brooch | Abstract |
| 157191 | 2/7/1950 | Alfred Philippe | Brooch | Wreath with Clair de Lune stones (See 157200 for another Clair de Lune piece.) |
| 157192 | 2/7/1950 | Alfred Philippe | Brooch | Abstract |
| 157193 | 2/7/1950 | Alfred Philippe | Brooch | Necklace with Clair de Lune stones (See 157518 for matching bracelet.) |
| 157194 | 2/7/1950 | Alfred Philippe | Brooch | Bird on branch |
| 157195 | 2/7/1950 | Alfred Philippe | Brooch | Abstract |
| 157196 | 2/7/1950 | Alfred Philippe | Brooch | Floral |
| 157197 | 2/7/1950 | Alfred Philippe | Brooch | Bird |
| 157198 | 2/7/1950 | Alfred Philippe | Brooch | Long-stemmed floral |
| 157199 | 2/7/1950 | Alfred Philippe | Brooch | Leaf |
| 157200 | 2/7/1950 | Alfred Philippe | Brooch | Tree, Clair de Lune stones (See 157526 for another Clair de Lune piece.) |
| 157201 | 2/7/1950 | Alfred Philippe | Brooch | Fish, Clair de Lune stones (See 157193 for another Clair de Lune piece.) |
| 157282 | 2/14/1950 | Alfred Philippe | Necklace | Abstract lines of baguettes on metal (See 157283 for matching bracelet.) |
| 157283 | 2/14/1950 | Alfred Philippe | Bracelet | Abstract lines of baguettes on metal (See 157282 for matching necklace.) |
| 157417 | 2/21/1950 | Alfred Philippe | Brooch | Bug |
| 157418 | 2/21/1950 | Alfred Philippe | Brooch | Duck with molded glass feathers (See 157419 for another molded glass figural piece.) |
| 157419 | 2/21/1950 | Alfred Philippe | Brooch | Frog with molded glass feet (See 157420 for another piece with molded glass details.) |
| 157420 | 2/21/1950 | Alfred Philippe | Brooch | Bug with molded glass wings (See 157421 for another piece with molded glass details.) |

157191

157200

**1950 Trifari Clair de Lune tree and wreath brooches.** The wonderful semicircle translucent stones prominently present in these two Trifari pieces are referred to in the 1950 Trifari "For a Jewel of a Mother" advertisement as "pseudo-moonstones." Both of these brooches are part of Trifari's "Clair de Lune" series featuring these interesting stones. (Translated into English, the phrase *Clair de Lune* means "moonlight" or "light of the moon." It is also a term used to describe a pale grayish blue glaze used for some Chinese porcelain.) Both pieces are signed "Trifari Pat. Pend." The design patent for a similar tree (larger than the one in the photograph, with 10 Clair de Lune stones instead of 6) is 157200 issued February 7, 1950, to Alfred Philippe for Trifari. The wreath is design patent number 157191 issued to Philippe on the same day. Right: 1½" x 1¼" Clair de Lune tree pin, $150.00 – 250.00. Left: 1½" diameter wreath Clair de Lune clip, $85.00 – 125.00.

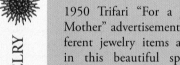

1950 Trifari "For a Jewel of a Mother" advertisement. Seven different jewelry items are featured in this beautiful spring 1950 Trifari advertisement, each beautifully packaged in "Luxurious Jeweler's Cases." Top left: Clair de Lune necklace with "pseudo-moonstones," originally selling for $12.50. Top right: Petalettes, originally selling for $5.00 a pair and available in white, rose quartz, or turquoise color. Second row: Golden Laurel, available in gold- or silver-tone Trifanium, originally selling for $10.50 per set. Third row: Petaltime necklace and earrings, originally selling for $10.50 a set and available in white, rose quartz, or turquoise color. Fourth row left: Forget-me-not, originally selling for $7.00 and available in rose quartz, turquoise, white, or chartreuse color. Fourth row right: Maple Leaf, originally selling for $7.50. Bottom row: Pearls by Trifari simulated pearls, in single strand, $10.00; double strand, $15.00; or triple strand (not shown), $20.00.

## • TRIFARI 1950 •

| 157421 | 2/21/1950 | Alfred Philippe | Brooch | Fish with molded glass fins (See158127 for another molded glass piece.) |
|---|---|---|---|---|
| 157422 | 2/21/1950 | Alfred Philippe | Brooch | Lizard |
| 157423 | 2/21/1950 | Alfred Philippe | Brooch | Frog |
| 157424 | 2/21/1950 | Alfred Philippe | Brooch | Bird on branch |
| 157516 | 5/28/1950 | Alfred Philippe | Necklace | Three drops, Clair de Lune stones |
| 157518 | 2/28/1950 | Alfred Philippe | Bracelet | Cuff, Clair de Lune stones (See 157200 for another Clair de Lune piece.) |
| 157522 | 2/28/1950 | Alfred Philippe | Brooch | Abstract |
| 157523 | 2/28/1950 | Alfred Philippe | Brooch | Female dancer with molded glass details advertised with male dancer as "Petalettes" and sold for $5.00 pair (See 157787 for another molded glass detail piece.) |
| 157524 | 2/28/1950 | Alfred Philippe | Brooch | Long-stemmed floral with molded glass petals (See 157418 for another molded glass figural piece.) |

| | | | | |
|---|---|---|---|---|
| 157525 | 2/28/1950 | Alfred Philippe | Brooch | Fan with molded glass (See 157524 for another molded glass piece.) |
| 157526 | 2/28/1950 | Alfred Philippe | Necklace | Necklace with Clair de Lune stones (See 157201 for another Clair de Lune piece.) |
| 157528 | 2/28/1950 | Alfred Philippe | Brooch | Abstract |
| 157529 | 2/28/1950 | Alfred Philippe | Brooch | Floral |
| 157530 | 2/28/1950 | Alfred Philippe | Brooch | Floral |
| 157531 | 2/28/1950 | Alfred Philippe | Brooch | Leaf |
| 157532 | 2/28/1950 | Alfred Philippe | Necklace | Abstract floral |
| 157785 | 3/21/1950 | Alfred Philippe | Brooch | Parrot on branch |
| 157786 | 3/21/1950 | Alfred Philippe | Brooch | Bird on birdbath |
| 157787 | 3/21/1950 | Alfred Philippe | Brooch | Parrot on branch with molded glass feathers (See 157525 for another figural with molded glass details.) |
| 158007 | 4/4/1950 | Alfred Philippe | Bracelet | Abstract cuff |
| 158124 | 4/11/1950 | Alfred Philippe | Brooch | Jelly Belly poodle |
| 158125 | 4/11/1950 | Alfred Philippe | Brooch | Abstract bow |
| 158126 | 4/11/1950 | Alfred Philippe | Brooch | Male dancer with molded glass arms advertised with female dancer as "Petalettes" and originally sold for $5.00 pair. (See 157523 for female dancer.) |
| 158127 | 4/11/1950 | Alfred Philippe | Brooch | Squirrel with molded glass tail (See 158126 for another molded glass figural piece.) |
| 158315 | 4/25/1950 | Alfred Philippe | Brooch | Abstract shell |
| 158317 | 4/25/1950 | Alfred Philippe | Brooch | Long-stemmed cactus-style floral (See 158324 for matching bracelet.) |
| 158318 | 4/25/1950 | Alfred Philippe | Brooch | Long-stemmed floral |
| 158319 | 4/25/1950 | Alfred Philippe | Brooch | Long-stemmed floral |
| 158320 | 4/25/1950 | Alfred Philippe | Necklace | Abstract nine dangles |

158124

158317

158126

**Trifari 1950 turquoise color Petalettes dancer pins.** Advertised in the 1950 "For a Jewel of a Mother" advertisement (see page 182) as "Petalettes," these wonderful 2" x 1" dancing figural pins originally came in turquoise, rose quartz, or white, and sold for $5.00 a pair. The male dancer is design patent number 158126 issued April 11, 1950, to Alfred Philippe. The female dancer is design patent number 157523 issued February 28, 1950. Note the interestingly shaped plastic inserts in each arm of the male dancer pin. Inserts of this shape are featured in many other Trifari figural designs from 1950, including the following design patents: 158127, 157418, 157419, 157420, 157421, 157524, 157525, and 157787. Interestingly, the Petalettes in the photograph are unmarked. $60.00 – 90.00 pair.

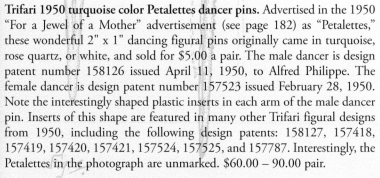

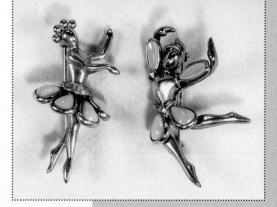

Pick
her
gift
from
the
TRIFARI
tree
of
dreams

*Jewelry by*

TRIFARI

*From the top of the tree down: "Lucky Clover" Pin and Earrings $5.00 each. "Forbidden Fruit" Bracelet $10.00, Necklace $7.50, Earrings (not shown) $7.50. "Diadem" Necklace $20.00, Matching Earrings (not shown) $15.00. "Coronet" Necklace $7.50, Matching Earrings $7.50, Cuff Bracelet $10.00. "Golden Maze" Necklace $5.00, Bracelet (not shown) $4.00, Earrings (under the tree) $4.00. "Jeweled Symphony" Bowknot Pin (under the tree) $25.00, Matching Earrings $15.00. Tax Extra.*

1950 "Pick her gift from the Trifari tree of dreams" advertisement. Original prices, tree: Lucky Clover, $5.00 each piece; Forbidden Fruit bracelet, $10.00, and necklace, $7.50; Diadem necklace, $20.00; Coronet necklace, $7.50, with earrings, $7.50, and bracelet, $10.00; Golden Maze necklace, $5.00. Original prices, under tree left: Jeweled Symphony brooch, $25.00, and earrings, $15.00. Original price, under tree right: Golden Maze earrings, $4.00.

159529

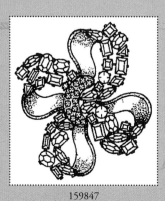

159847

## • TRIFARI 1950 •

| 158324 | 4/25/1950 | Alfred Philippe | Bracelet | Cactus-style floral clamper (See 158317 for matching brooch.) |
|---|---|---|---|---|
| 158402 | 5/2/1950 | Alfred Philippe | Brooch | Bow, no rhinestones |
| 158609 | 5/16/1950 | Alfred Philippe | Brooch | Floral |
| 158610 | 5/16/1950 | Alfred Philippe | Brooch | Wreath |
| 158786 | 5/30/1950 | Alfred Philippe | Necklace | Abstract floral |
| 158787 | 5/30/1950 | Alfred Philippe | Brooch | Tree branch |
| 158789 | 5/30/1950 | Alfred Philippe | Brooch | Grapes |
| 158790 | 5/30/1950 | Alfred Philippe | Brooch | Grapes |
| 158791 | 5/30/1950 | Alfred Philippe | Brooch | Grapes |
| 159436 | 7/25/1950 | Alfred Philippe | Brooch | Abstract pearl dangle |
| 159516 | 8/1/1950 | Alfred Philippe | Brooch | Abstract |
| 159517 | 8/1/1950 | Alfred Philippe | Brooch | Abstract |
| 159518 | 8/1/1950 | Alfred Philippe | Brooch | Crown |
| 159519 | 8/1/1950 | Alfred Philippe | Brooch | Abstract |
| 159520 | 8/1/1950 | Alfred Philippe | Brooch | Key |
| 159521 | 8/1/1950 | Alfred Philippe | Brooch | Three rows of baguettes advertised in 1950 as "Heiress" (Ad not shown; originally sold for $12.50.) |

| 159522 | 8/1/1950 | Alfred Philippe | Necklace | Abstract |
|---|---|---|---|---|
| 159523 | 8/1/1950 | Alfred Philippe | Necklace | Abstract bars of baguettes |
| 159524 | 8/1/1950 | Alfred Philippe | Necklace | Floral with six baguette sticks (See 159529 for matching brooch.) |
| 159525 | 8/1/1950 | Alfred Philippe | Brooch | Abstract |
| 159526 | 8/1/1950 | Alfred Philippe | Brooch | Abstract |
| 159527 | 8/1/1950 | Alfred Philippe | Brooch | Abstract |
| 159528 | 8/1/1950 | Alfred Philippe | Brooch | Heart |
| 159529 | 8/1/1950 | Alfred Philippe | Brooch | Floral with six baguette sticks (See 161050 for matching bracelet.) |
| 159530 | 8/1/1950 | Alfred Philippe | Brooch | Floral |
| 159838 | 8/22/1950 | Alfred Philippe | Brooch | Twisted stick with dangling rhinestone |
| 159839 | 8/22/1950 | Alfred Philippe | Brooch | Abstract crescent |
| 159840 | 8/22/1950 | Alfred Philippe | Brooch | Abstract floral |
| 159841 | 8/22/1950 | Alfred Philippe | Brooch | Abstract |
| 159842 | 8/22/1950 | Alfred Philippe | Brooch | Abstract circular design |
| 159843 | 8/22/1950 | Alfred Philippe | Brooch | Baton with two tassels |
| 159845 | 8/22/1950 | Alfred Philippe | Brooch | Leaf |
| 159846 | 8/22/1950 | Alfred Philippe | Brooch | Star |
| 159847 | 8/22/1950 | Alfred Philippe | Brooch | Advertised as "Jeweled Symphony" this bow-knot brooch originally sold for $25.00 |
| 159848 | 8/22/1950 | Alfred Philippe | Brooch | Leaves |
| 159849 | 8/22/1950 | Alfred Philippe | Brooch | Abstract floral |
| 159852 | 8/22/1950 | Alfred Philippe | Necklace | Floral leaves |
| 159853 | 8/22/1950 | Alfred Philippe | Necklace | Floral |
| 159855 | 8/22/1950 | Alfred Philippe | Necklace | Abstract |
| 159856 | 8/22/1950 | Alfred Philippe | Necklace | Abstract |
| 159857 | 8/22/1950 | Alfred Philippe | Bracelet | Floral clamper |
| 159922 | 8/28/1950 | Alfred Philippe | Brooch | Bug |
| 159923 | 8/29/1950 | Alfred Philippe | Brooch | Bird |
| 159924 | 8/29/1950 | Alfred Philippe | Brooch | Butterfly |
| 159925 | 8/29/1950 | Alfred Philippe | Brooch | Rooster |
| 160115 | 9/12/1950 | Alfred Philippe | Brooch | Long-stemmed floral |
| 160116 | 9/12/1950 | Alfred Philippe | Brooch | Floral leaf |
| 160117 | 9/12/1950 | Alfred Philippe | Brooch | Abstract |
| 160118 | 9/12/1950 | Alfred Philippe | Brooch | Abstract floral bell |
| 160119 | 9/12/1950 | Alfred Philippe | Brooch | Abstract |
| 160120 | 9/12/1950 | Alfred Philippe | Brooch | Floral grapes (See 160197 for matching necklace.) |
| 160197 | 9/19/1950 | Alfred Philippe | Necklace | Abstract floral with pearls (See 160120 for matching brooch.) |

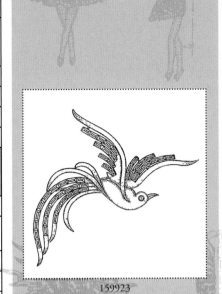

159923

**1950 Trifari gold-tone and baguette rhinestone bird pin.** Glistening clear baguettes simulate feathers on this 3" x 2" Trifari flying bird pin. This pin is design patent number 159923 issued August 29, 1950, to Alfred Philippe for Trifari. It is signed "Trifari Pat. Pend." $65.00 – 90.00.

TRIFARI JEWELRY

160202

**1950 Trifari amber and clear rhinestone brooch.** Pretty as a snowflake, this beautiful 1½" brooch is design patent number 160202 issued September 19, 1950, to Alfred Philippe for Trifari. Interestingly, this amber-colored brooch comes equipped with a hook so it can be worn as an enhancer on a chain or ribbon. It is signed "Trifari Pat. Pend." $40.00 – 55.00. From the collection of Debi Reece.

| | | | | |
|---|---|---|---|---|
| 160201 | 9/19/1950 | Alfred Philippe | Brooch | "Forbidden Fruit" (See 160429 for matching bracelet.) |
| 160202 | 9/19/1950 | Alfred Philippe | Brooch | Floral |
| 160203 | 9/19/1950 | Alfred Philippe | Brooch | Four leaf clover |
| 160206 | 9/19/1950 | Alfred Philippe | Necklace | Abstract floral |
| 160207 | 9/19/1950 | Alfred Philippe | Necklace | Abstract two dangles |
| 160208 | 9/19/1950 | Alfred Philippe | Bracelet | Advertised in 1950 as "Coronet," originally sold for $10.00 (See 160427 for matching necklace.) |
| 160271 | 9/26/1950 | Alfred Philippe | Bracelet | Clamper with baguette rhinestones |
| 160334 | 10/3/1950 | Alfred Philippe | Brooch | Leaf |
| 160424 | 10/10/1950 | Alfred Philippe | Brooch | Abstract |
| 160425 | 10/10/1950 | Alfred Philippe | Necklace | "Forbidden Fruit" necklace, originally sold for $7.50 (See 160201 for matching brooch.) |
| 160427 | 10/10/1950 | Alfred Philippe | Necklace | Advertised in 1950 as "Coronet," originally sold for $7.50 (See 160208 for matching bracelet.) |
| 160428 | 10/10/1950 | Alfred Philippe | Necklace | Abstract floral |

160427

**1950 Trifari Coronet or crown necklace.** Called "Coronet" in the 1950 "Pick her gift from the Trifari tree of dreams" advertisement, this regal 14½" royal crown necklace originally sold for $7.50. The necklace is signed "Trifari Pat. Pend." It was available in several colors, including emerald green, clear, and purple. The necklace is design patent number 160427 issued October 10, 1950, to Alfred Philippe for Trifari. $45.00 – 65.00.

TRIFARI JEWELRY

**1950 Coronet purple rhinestone bracelet.** Featured in the 1950 "Pick her gift from the Trifari tree of dreams" advertisement (see page 184), this noble cuff bracelet originally sold for $10.00 and was available in several colors, including clear, green, and purple. The bracelet is design patent number 160208 issued September 19, 1950, to Alfred Philippe for Trifari. It is signed "Trifari Pat. Pend." and fits an average-size wrist. $55.00 – 85.00.

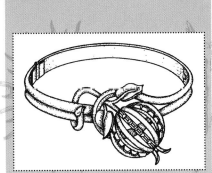

### • TRIFARI 1950 •

| | | | | |
|---|---|---|---|---|
| 160429 | 10/10/1950 | Alfred Philippe | Bracelet | "Forbidden Fruit" cuff bracelet originally sold for $10.00 (See 160425 for matching necklace.) |
| 160958 | 11/21/1950 | Alfred Philippe | Bracelet | Abstract |
| 160961 | 11/21/1950 | Alfred Philippe | Brooch | Leaves on curling branch |
| 160962 | 11/21/1950 | Alfred Philippe | Brooch | Leaf |
| 160963 | 11/21/1950 | Alfred Philippe | Brooch | Fan with four dangles |
| 160964 | 11/21/1950 | Alfred Philippe | Brooch | Abstract floral |
| 160965 | 11/21/1950 | Alfred Philippe | Necklace | Abstract floral two dangles |
| 160966 | 11/21/1950 | Alfred Philippe | Brooch | Twisted pin one dangle |
| 160967 | 11/21/1950 | Alfred Philippe | Brooch | Abstract floral, one dangle |
| 161038 | 11/28/1950 | Alfred Philippe | Necklace | Bow two dangling florals |
| 161039 | 11/28/1950 | Alfred Philippe | Necklace | Abstract three dangles |
| 161043 | 11/28/1950 | Alfred Philippe | Brooch Separable | Interesting long-stemmed floral separable brooch without the Trifari Clip-mate mechanism |
| 161044 | 11/28/1950 | Alfred Philippe | Necklace | Abstract with dangle |
| 161046 | 11/28/1950 | Alfred Philippe | Necklace | Rhinestone flexible wrap |
| 161047 | 11/28/1950 | Alfred Philippe | Necklace | Rhinestone flexible wrap |
| 161048 | 11/28/1950 | Alfred Philippe | Necklace | Rhinestone flexible wrap |
| 161049 | 11/28/1950 | Alfred Philippe | Bracelet | Abstract clamper |
| 161050 | 11/28/1950 | Alfred Philippe | Bracelet | Floral with six baguette sticks (See 159524 for matching necklace.) |
| 161204 | 12/12/1950 | Alfred Philippe | Necklace | Rhinestone flexible wrap |

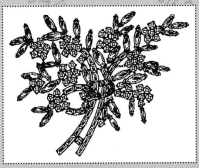

160429

161043

162446

162454

| Design Patent Number | Date Issued | Designer | Jewelry Type | Brief Description |
|---|---|---|---|---|
| 161961 | 2/13/1951 | Alfred Philippe | Necklace | Abstract |
| 162069 | 2/20/1951 | Alfred Philippe | Brooch | Feather |
| 162070 | 2/20/1951 | Alfred Philippe | Brooch | Basket |
| 162071 | 2/20/1951 | Alfred Philippe | Brooch | Long-stemmed floral |
| 162074 | 2/20/1951 | Alfred Philippe | Necklace | Loop inside loop floral plastic flowers with rhinestone center (See 162453 for matching brooch.) |
| 162077 | 2/20/1951 | Alfred Philippe | Brooch | Abstract floral |
| 162078 | 2/20/1951 | Alfred Philippe | Brooch | Abstract |
| 162137 | 5/1/1951 | Alfred Philippe | Necklace | Rope lariat style |
| 162446 | 3/13/1951 | Alfred Philippe | Brooch | Rhinestone cluster flowers (See 162447 for matching necklace.) |
| 162447 | 3/13/1951 | Alfred Philippe | Necklace | Rhinestone cluster flowers (See 162448 for matching bracelet.) |
| 162448 | 3/13/1951 | Alfred Philippe | Bracelet | Rhinestone cluster flowers (See 162446 for matching brooch.) |
| 162451 | 3/13/1951 | Alfred Philippe | Brooch | Abstract |
| 162452 | 3/13/1951 | Alfred Philippe | Brooch | Plastic flowers with rhinestone center (See162461 for matching brooch.) |
| 162453 | 3/13/1951 | Alfred Philippe | Brooch | Long-stemmed floral plastic flowers with rhinestone center (See 162452 for matching brooch.) |
| 162454 | 3/13/1951 | Alfred Philippe | Brooch | Basket of flowers |
| 162455 | 3/13/1951 | Alfred Philippe | Necklace | Floral leaves |
| 162456 | 3/13/1951 | Alfred Philippe | Brooch | Long-stemmed floral |
| 162457 | 3/13/1951 | Alfred Philippe | Necklace | Floral |

**1951 Trifari basket pin.** This lovely 2" x 2¾" Trifari gold-tone flower basket is overflowing with three white molded-glass flowers. It is design patent number 162454 issued March 13, 1951, to Alfred Philippe for Trifari. (Note: In the same year, Trifari produced many other designs utilizing these same molded glass flowers. See design patents 162074, 162452, 162453, and 162461.) This basket pin is signed "Trifari Pat. Pend." $45.00 – 65.00.

| 162458 | 3/13/1951 | Alfred Philippe | Bracelet | Floral clamper |
|---|---|---|---|---|
| 162460 | 3/13/1951 | Alfred Philippe | Brooch | Abstract |
| 162461 | 3/13/1951 | Alfred Philippe | Brooch | Plastic flowers with rhinestone center (See 162454 for matching brooch.) |
| 162462 | 3/13/1951 | Alfred Philippe | Necklace | Abstract |
| 162464 | 3/13/1951 | Alfred Philippe | Necklace | Floral grapes |
| 162466 | 3/13/1951 | Alfred Philippe | Brooch | Long-stemmed floral |
| 162466 | 3/13/1951 | Alfred Philippe | Brooch | Long-stemmed floral |
| 162467 | 3/13/1951 | Alfred Philippe | Brooch | Swan |
| 162477 | 3/13/1951 | Alfred Philippe | Necklace | Floral |
| 162488 | 3/13/1951 | Alfred Philippe | Bracelet | Floral clamper |
| 162576 | 3/20/1951 | Alfred Philippe | Necklace | Floral bow |
| 162577 | 3/20/1951 | Alfred Philippe | Necklace | Floral |
| 162747 | 4/3/1951 | Alfred Philippe | Necklace | Double Sunflower (See 162748 for matching bracelet.) |
| 162748 | 4/3/1951 | Alfred Philippe | Bracelet | Sunflower clamper (See 162747 for matching necklace.) |
| 163962 | 7/17/1951 | Alfred Philippe | Brooch | Safety pin with dangling rhinestone |
| 163963 | 7/17/1951 | Alfred Philippe | Necklace | Abstract weave |
| 163964 | 7/17/1951 | Alfred Philippe | Necklace | Abstract leaves |

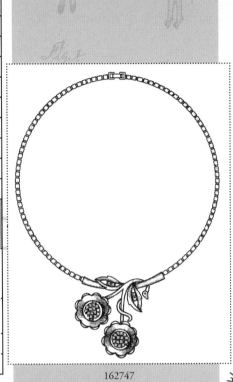

162747

164132

**1951 Trifari double Sunflower necklace.** Part of Trifari's Sunflower series, this sparkling double-flower 15" necklace is design patent number 162747 issued April 3, 1951, to Alfred Philippe for Trifari. (See design patent number 162748 for the matching bracelet.) It is signed "Trifari Pat. Pend." $50.00 – 65.00.

TRIFARI JEWELRY

189

| 164129 | 7/31/1951 | Alfred Philippe | Pin Clip | Abstract ribbon of baguettes |
| 164130 | 7/31/1951 | Alfred Philippe | Brooch | Long-stemmed floral with diamond-shaped rhinestones (See 164132 for matching brooch.) |
| 164131 | 7/31/1951 | Alfred Philippe | Brooch | Floral |
| 164132 | 7/31/1951 | Alfred Philippe | Brooch | Leaf with diamond-shaped rhinestones (See 164652 for matching necklace.) |
| 164652 | 9/25/1951 | Alfred Philippe | Necklace | Diamond-shaped rhinestones (See 164711 for matching bracelet.) |
| 164711 | 10/2/1951 | Alfred Philippe | Bracelet | Diamond-shaped rhinestones (See 163963 for matching necklace.) |
| 164714 | 10/2/1951 | Alfred Philippe | Necklace | Collar with baguette rhinestones |

164722

**1951 Trifari small Star Flower pin.** This dainty leaf pin is signed "Trifari Pat. Pend." and is design patent number 164722 issued October 2, 1951, to Alfred Philippe for Trifari. The larger version of this Star Flower pin, with matching earrings, is shown in the "it wouldn't be Christmas without Jewels by Trifari" 1951 advertisement (see the blue ornament). Notice the four-petal design of the three rhinestone flowers featured on this 2½" x 1¼" Trifari pin. Trifari produced several jewelry designs in 1951 utilizing this four-petal rhinestone motif, including design patent numbers 164715, 164718, 164721, 164725, and 164730. $45.00 – 60.00.

1951 "it wouldn't be Christmas without Jewels by Trifari" advertisement. Original prices, top left: Duchess necklace, $20.00, and earrings, $15.00. Original prices, top right (green ornament): Queen of Diamonds necklace, $15.00, with pin, $5.00, and earrings, $5.00. Original prices, second row: Gem of India bracelet (hanging), $15.00, with necklace (red ornament), $10.00, and pin (small silver ornament), $7.50, and earrings (small green ornament), $7.50. Original prices, third row: Starflower (blue ornament) pin, $10.00, and earrings, $7.50. Original prices, bottom: Golden Flame necklace, $7.50, with bracelet, $5.00, and earrings, $3.00.

| 164715 | 10/2/1951 | Alfred Philippe | Necklace | "Star Flower" (See164718 for another necklace with this flower.) |
|--------|-----------|-----------------|----------|---|
| 164716 | 10/2/1951 | Alfred Philippe | Necklace | "Gem of India" (See 164728 for matching earring.) |
| 164717 | 10/2/1951 | Alfred Philippe | Necklace | Abstract |
| 164718 | 10/2/1951 | Alfred Philippe | Necklace | "Star Flower" (See 164721 for matching brooch.) |
| 164720 | 10/2/1951 | Alfred Philippe | Brooch | Abstract |
| 164721 | 10/2/1951 | Alfred Philippe | Brooch | Flower in pot, "Star Flower" (See 164722 for another brooch.) |
| 164722 | 10/2/1951 | Alfred Philippe | Brooch | Branch with flowers, "Star Flower" (See 164730 for matching bracelet.) |
| 164723 | 10/2/1951 | Alfred Philippe | Brooch | "Gem of India." Can be found with or without top rhinestone. (See 164808 for matching bracelet.) |
| 164724 | 10/2/1951 | Alfred Philippe | Brooch | Mushrooms |

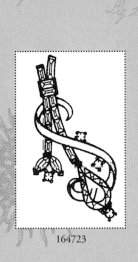

164723

**1951 Gem of India necklace and pin.** This pretty 14" choker necklace and 2" pin were advertised in the 1951 Trifari "it wouldn't be Christmas without Jewels by Trifari" advertisement as part of the Gem of India group. Both pieces are signed "Trifari Pat. Pend." Produced in both gold-tone and silver-tone metal, the necklace originally sold for $10.00 and the pin for $7.50. The pin, necklace, bracelet, and earrings are design patent numbers 164723, 164716, 164808, and 164728, respectively. All four patents were issued October 2, 1951, to Alfred Philippe for Trifari. $40.00 – 65.00 each.

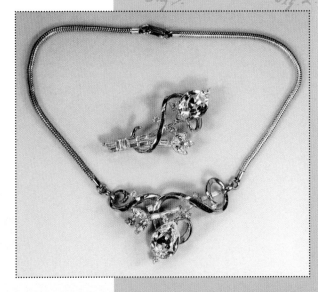

**1951 Trifari Dogwood bracelet, pin, and earrings set.** Trifari produced many jewelry items using white poured-glass petals, including this spectacular parure. This set was advertised in a 1951 advertisement (not shown) as "Dogwood." Each piece sold between $3.00 and $7.50. The ad states that this set is part of Trifari's "Fashion Blossoms from the Garden of Jewels." The bracelet measures 2½" in diameter, the clip earrings are 1½", and the pin is 1½". Each piece is signed "Trifari" without the copyright symbol. $75.00 – 100.00. From the collection of Debi Reece.

TRIFARI JEWELRY

| 164725 | 10/2/1951 | Alfred Philippe | Brooch | Long-stemmed floral "Star Flower" (See 164715 for matching necklace.) |
|---|---|---|---|---|
| 164726 | 10/2/1951 | Alfred Philippe | Brooch | Abstract three dangles |
| 164728 | 10/2/1951 | Alfred Philippe | Earring | "Gem of India" (See 164723 for matching brooch.) |
| 164729 | 10/2/1951 | Alfred Philippe | Earring | Abstract floral |
| 164730 | 10/2/1951 | Alfred Philippe | Bracelet | "Star Flower" clamper (See 164725 for matching brooch.) |
| 164808 | 10/9/1951 | Alfred Philippe | Bracelet | "Gem of India" (See 164716 for matching necklace.) |
| 164811 | 10/9/1951 | Alfred Philippe | Brooch | Floral |
| 164814 | 10/9/1951 | Alfred Philippe | Necklace | Abstract |
| 164815 | 10/9/1951 | Alfred Philippe | Necklace | Abstract triangle center (See 164816 for matching bracelet.) |
| 164816 | 10/9/1951 | Alfred Philippe | Bracelet | Abstract Triangle (See 164815 for matching necklace.) |
| 164817 | 10/9/1951 | Alfred Philippe | Necklace | Abstract |
| 164950 | 10/23/1951 | Alfred Philippe | Pin Clip | Swirling leaf |

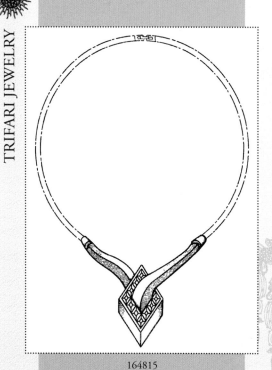

164815

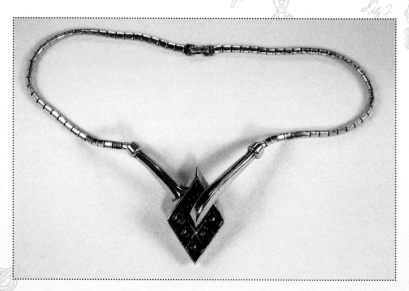

**1951 Deco-style Trifari necklace.** For several reasons, this interesting 15" Trifari necklace is a standout with collectors. First, the design for this necklace is design patent number 164815 issued October 9, 1951, to Alfred Philippe. Next, the retro Art-Deco design of the necklace is a classic style as wearable today as it was 50 years ago. Finally, the emerald diamond-shaped rhinestones decorating this terrific Trifari design are invisibly set. Collectors love jewelry with invisibly set rhinestones. Interestingly, the diamond-shaped rhinestones are a style trait found on other Trifari designs from 1951. (See design patent number 164816 for the matching bracelet and design patent number 164132 for a leaf brooch featuring these same diamond-shaped rhinestones.) This necklace is signed "Trifari Pat. Pend." $65.00 – 85.00.

| 164951 | 10/23/1951 | Alfred Philippe | Brooch | Long-stemmed floral |
| 164952 | 10/23/1951 | Alfred Philippe | Brooch | Snowflake |
| 164953 | 10/23/1951 | Alfred Philippe | Brooch | Abstract |
| 164954 | 10/23/1951 | Alfred Philippe | Brooch | Abstract |
| 165020 | 10/30/1951 | Alfred Philippe | Brooch | Long-stemmed floral |
| 165298 | 11/27/1951 | Alfred Philippe | Brooch | Abstract floral |
| 165299 | 11/27/1951 | Alfred Philippe | Necklace | Abstract |
| 165300 | 11/27/1951 | Alfred Philippe | Bracelet | Abstract floral |
| 165544 | 12/25/1951 | Alfred Philippe | Brooch | Rhinestone branches (See 165546 for another brooch.) |
| 165545 | 12/25/1951 | Alfred Philippe | Brooch | Rhinestone branches (See 165544 for another brooch.) |
| 165546 | 12/25/1951 | Alfred Philippe | Brooch | Rhinestone branches (See 165549 for matching bracelet.) |
| 165547 | 12/25/1951 | Alfred Philippe | Necklace | Rhinestone branches (See 165545 for matching brooch.) |
| 165548 | 12/25/1951 | Alfred Philippe | Necklace | Floral |
| 165549 | 12/25/1951 | Alfred Philippe | Bracelet | Rhinestone branches (See 165547 for matching necklace.) |

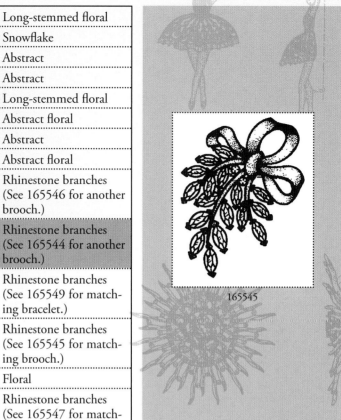

165545

**1951 Heart Throbs necklace and earrings set.** This lovely gold-tone 15½" heart necklace and earrings set is featured in the 1951 "In the foreground of Fashion…Jewels by Trifari" advertisement as "Heart Throbs." The necklace originally sold for $10.00 and the earrings for $7.50. Made of Trifanium, this set features beautiful baguette rhinestones "crisscrossed" lovingly across the hearts. The 1½" heart pendant and ¾" clip earrings are signed "Trifari Pat. Pend." Unfortunately, I was unable to locate the patent for this design. $55.00 – 75.00.

1951 "In the foreground of Fashion…Jewels by Trifari" Heart Throbs advertisement. This ad reads "Heart-to-heart expression of true design genius. Golden Trifanium hearts filled with criss-cross baguettes. Necklace $10, Bracelet $12.50, Earrings $7.50, Large Pin $12.50, Small Pin $7.50, Miniature Pin (not shown) $4."

TRIFARI JEWELRY

166215

**1952 Trifari white crab pin.**
Sweet and well made, this 1½" x
1¼" Trifari crab pin is design patent number 166215 issued March
18, 1952, to Alfred Philippe. The
white beads defining the eyes of
this little critter are a characteristic design element found in many
Trifari figural designs from 1952.
(See design patent numbers
166214, 166216, 166217, and
166218 for additional designs
featuring these white beads.) It is
signed "Trifari Pat. Pend." $55.00
– 85.00.

166220

| Design Patent Number | Date Issued | Designer | Jewelry Type | Brief Description |
|---|---|---|---|---|
| 165644 | 1/18/1952 | Alfred Philippe | Brooch | Three leaves, no rhine-stones |
| 166211 | 3/18/1952 | Alfred Philippe | Brooch | Abstract |
| 166214 | 3/18/1952 | Alfred Philippe | Brooch | Poodle with white bead accents (See 166216 for another white bead fig-ural pin.) |
| 166215 | 3/18/1952 | Alfred Philippe | Brooch | Crab with white bead accents (See 166217 for another white bead fig-ural pin.) |
| 166216 | 3/18/1952 | Alfred Philippe | Brooch | Frog with white bead accents (See 166215 for another white bead fig-ural pin.) |
| 166217 | 3/18/1952 | Alfred Philippe | Brooch | Owl on branch with white bead accents (See 166218 for another white bead figural pin.) |
| 166218 | 3/18/1952 | Alfred Philippe | Brooch | Bird on branch with white bead accents (See 166214 for another white bead figural pin.) |
| 166219 | 3/18/1952 | Alfred Philippe | Brooch | Abstract triple circle |
| 166220 | 3/18/1952 | Alfred Philippe | Brooch | "Park Avenue Zoo" charm pins elephant (See 166351 for duck.) |

1952 "Mothers of every
age…love Jewels by Trifari"
advertisement. Original prices, top left: Lorelei necklace,
$7.50, and earrings, $4.00.
Original prices, top right:
Spring Fantasy necklace,
$7.50, with bracelet, $10.00,
and earrings, $5.00, and
pin, $7.50. Original prices,
middle: Camellias bracelet,
$7.50, with necklace, $5.00,
and earrings, $3.00, and
pin $5.00. Original prices,
bottom middle: Enchanted
Garden pin, $6.00, and ear-
rings, $4.00. Original prices,
bottom right: Park Avenue
Zoo charm pins (Poodle,
Lady Bug, Frog, Elephant
(not shown are Horseshoe,
Elephant, Duck), $3.00
each.

| 166221 | 3/18/1952 | Alfred Philippe | Brooch | "Park Avenue Zoo" charm pins poodle (See166222 for frog.) |
|---|---|---|---|---|
| 166222 | 3/18/1952 | Alfred Philippe | Brooch | "Park Avenue Zoo" charm pins frog (See 166220 for elephant.) |
| 166339 | 4/1/1952 | Alfred Philippe | Brooch | Branch |
| 166340 | 4/1/1952 | Alfred Philippe | Brooch | Feather |
| 166341 | 4/1/1952 | Alfred Philippe | Brooch | Abstract |
| 166342 | 4/1/1952 | Alfred Philippe | Necklace | Abstract |
| 166343 | 4/1/1952 | Alfred Philippe | Necklace | Seven-loops abstract |
| 166344 | 4/1/1952 | Alfred Philippe | Necklace | Abstract |
| 166345 | 4/1/1952 | Alfred Philippe | Necklace | Six-point floral (See 166489 for matching brooch.) |
| 166346 | 4/1/1952 | Alfred Philippe | Brooch | Leaf |
| 166347 | 4/1/1952 | Alfred Philippe | Brooch | Leaf |
| 166348 | 4/1/1952 | Alfred Philippe | Brooch | Leaf |
| 166349 | 4/1/1952 | Alfred Philippe | Brooch | Bow |
| 166351 | 4/1/1952 | Alfred Philippe | Brooch | "Park Avenue Zoo" charm pins (See 166352 for horseshoe.) |
| 166352 | 4/1/1952 | Alfred Philippe | Brooch | "Park Avenue Zoo" charm pins (See 166355 for ladybug.) |
| 166353 | 4/1/1952 | Alfred Philippe | Necklace | Collar, five sections |
| 166355 | 4/1/1952 | Alfred Philippe | Brooch | "Park Avenue Zoo" charm pins ladybug (See 166221 for poodle.) |
| 166489 | 4/15/1952 | Alfred Philippe | Bracelet | Six-point floral (See 166345 for matching necklace.) |
| 166491 | 4/15/1952 | Alfred Philippe | Brooch | Abstract |
| 166565 | 4/22/1952 | Alfred Philippe | Brooch | Circle |
| 166566 | 4/22/1952 | Alfred Philippe | Brooch | Circle |
| 166567 | 4/22/1952 | Alfred Philippe | Brooch | Abstract floral |
| 166568 | 4/22/1952 | Alfred Philippe | Brooch | Abstract floral |
| 166569 | 4/22/1952 | Alfred Philippe | Brooch | Snowflake style |
| 166570 | 4/22/1952 | Alfred Philippe | Brooch | Pinwheel style |
| 166571 | 4/22/1952 | Alfred Philippe | Brooch | Starburst |
| 166622 | 4/29/1952 | Alfred Philippe | Brooch | Pearls and tiny rhinestones (See 166624 for matching brooch.) |
| 166623 | 4/29/1952 | Alfred Philippe | Brooch | "Enchanted Garden" pearl and rhinestone wreath, originally sold for $6.00. |
| 166624 | 4/29/1952 | Alfred Philippe | Brooch | Branch pearls and tiny rhinestones (See 166708 for matching necklace.) |

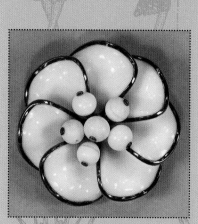

**1952 Trifari Camellia pin.** This creamy white 2" brooch is featured in the 1952 "Mothers of every age... love Jewels by Trifari" advertisement (see page 194) and originally sold for $5.00. It is signed "Trifari" without the copyright symbol. $35.00 – 55.00.

166622

166623

TRIFARI JEWELRY

167054

167227

**1952 Trifari Twinkle sapphire blue rhinestone pin.** This beautiful blue 2" x 1¼" rhinestone brooch is design patent number 167227 issued July 8, 1952, to Alfred Philippe for Trifari. It is signed "Trifari Pat. Pend.," is part of the Twinkle line advertised in the 1952 "The Most Enchanted Gift of All" Trifari advertisement (see page 197), and originally sold for $5.00. Twinkle jewelry was available in either silver-tone or gold-tone metal. (See design patent numbers 167226, 167229, 167369, 167370, 167421, 167584, and 167585 for additional Twinkle designs.) $45.00 – 60.00. From the collection of Debi Reece.

**TRIFARI JEWELRY**

| 166625 | 4/29/1952 | Alfred Philippe | Brooch | Tree |
|---|---|---|---|---|
| 166626 | 4/29/1952 | Alfred Philippe | Brooch | Abstract wreath |
| 166627 | 4/29/1952 | Alfred Philippe | Brooch | Heart |
| 166628 | 4/29/1952 | Alfred Philippe | Brooch | Leaf with butterfly |
| 166631 | 4/29/1952 | Alfred Philippe | Brooch | Bug |
| 166632 | 4/29/1952 | Alfred Philippe | Brooch | Floral |
| 166708 | 5/6/1952 | Alfred Philippe | Necklace | Pearls and tiny rhinestones (See 166622 for matching brooch.) |
| 166709 | 5/6/1952 | Alfred Philippe | Necklace | Abstract |
| 166710 | 5/6/1952 | Alfred Philippe | Necklace | Three leaves |
| 166711 | 5/6/1952 | Alfred Philippe | Brooch | Four-leaf floral |
| 167050 | 6/17/1952 | Alfred Philippe | Earring | Five-petal flowers, tiny white beads (See 167099 for matching necklace.) |
| 167051 | 6/17/1952 | Alfred Philippe | Brooch | Five-petal flowers, tiny white beads (See 167050 for matching earring.) |
| 167052 | 6/17/1952 | Alfred Philippe | Brooch | Five-petal flowers, tiny white beads (See 167051 for another brooch.) |
| 167053 | 6/17/1952 | Alfred Philippe | Brooch | Five-petal flowers, tiny white beads (See167052 for another brooch.) |
| 167054 | 6/17/1952 | Alfred Philippe | Brooch | Five-petal flowers, tiny white beads (See 167053 for another brooch.) |
| 167055 | 6/17/1952 | Alfred Philippe | Brooch | Abstract |
| 167056 | 6/17/1952 | Alfred Philippe | Brooch | Abstract |
| 167057 | 6/17/1952 | Alfred Philippe | Brooch | Floral wreath |
| 167098 | 6/24/1952 | Alfred Philippe | Necklace | Floral |
| 167099 | 6/24/1952 | Alfred Philippe | Necklace | Five-petal flowers, tiny white beads (See 167054 for matching brooch.) |
| 167224 | 7/8/1952 | Alfred Philippe | Brooch | Abstract |
| 167225 | 7/8/1952 | Alfred Philippe | Brooch | Abstract |
| 167226 | 7/8/1952 | Alfred Philippe | Brooch | "Twinkle" rhinestone star design (See 167227 for another brooch.) |
| 167227 | 7/8/1952 | Alfred Philippe | Brooch | "Twinkle" rhinestone star design (See 167228 for another brooch.) |
| 167228 | 7/8/1952 | Alfred Philippe | Brooch | "Twinkle" rhinestone star design (See 167229 for another brooch.) |

| 167229 | 7/8/1952 | Alfred Philippe | Brooch | "Twinkle" rhinestone star design (See 167274 for another brooch.) |
|--------|----------|-----------------|--------|---------------------------------|
| 167274 | 7/15/1952 | Alfred Philippe | Brooch | "Twinkle" rhinestone star design (See 167369 for matching necklace.) |
| 167364 | 7/29/1952 | Alfred Philippe | Earring | "Twinkle" rhinestone star design (See 167226 for matching brooch.) |
| 167367 | 7/29/1952 | Alfred Philippe | Brooch | Abstract floral |
| 167368 | 7/29/1952 | Alfred Philippe | Necklace | Abstract |
| 167369 | 7/29/1952 | Alfred Philippe | Necklace | "Twinkle" rhinestone star design (See 167370 for matching bracelet.) |
| 167370 | 7/29/1952 | Alfred Philippe | Bracelet | "Twinkle" rhinestone star design (See 167421 for matching necklace.) |

167228

"Twinkle"...upper left. Couture Earrings $5, Five-Star Necklace $12.50, Bracelet $10. "Twinkle"...upper right. Star Earrings $4, Pin $5, Two-Star Necklace $7.50. "Promenade"...center. Earrings $5, Pin $7.50, Necklace $10, Bracelet $10. "Golden Crest"... lower left. Earrings $3, Necklace $7.50, Bracelet $5. "Place Vendome"... lower right. Earrings $10, Pin $20, Necklace $20, Bracelet $20. All prices plus Federal tax.

1952 "The Most Enchanted Gift of All/Jewels by Trifari" advertisement. Original prices, top left: Twinkle five-star necklace, $12.50, with bracelet, $10.00, and earrings, $5.00. Original prices, top right: Twinkle two-star necklace, $7.50, with pin, $5.00, and earrings, $4.00. Original prices, middle: Promenade earrings, $5.00, with pin, $7.50, and necklace, $10.00, and bracelet $10.00. Original prices, bottom left: Golden Crest earrings, $3.00, with necklace, $7.50, and bracelet, $5.00. Original prices, bottom right: Place Vendome earrings, $10.00, with pin, $20.00, and bracelet, $20.00.

**1952 Twinkle amber-colored rhinestone pin.** This attractive 2½" x 1½" amber-colored brooch features four rhinestone star flowers. It is design patent number 167228 issued July 8, 1952, to Alfred Philippe for Trifari. The style is similar to the Twinkle jewelry advertised in the 1952 "The Most Enchanted Gift of All" Trifari advertisement. It is signed "Trifari Pat. Pend." $45.00 – 60.00. From the collection of Debi Reece.

TRIFARI JEWELRY

197

167652

**1952 Trifari bow brooch.** This large 2¾" x 2" classically beautiful bow brooch is signed "Trifari Pat. Pend." It is similar in style to the "Place Vendome" brooch advertised in the 1952 "The Most Enchanted Gift of All" Trifari advertisement (see page 197) and is likely a design variation of this brooch. (The brooch in the advertisement originally sold for $20.00.) $45.00 – 65.00.

**1952 Trifari Promenade necklace, bracelet, and earrings.** This mint condition, astoundingly lovely, Trifari parure was advertised in the 1952 "The Most Enchanted Gift of All" advertisement (see page 197) as "Promenade." The 15" necklace, 7" bracelet, and matching ¾" clip earrings are signed "Trifari Pat. Pend." In 1952, the necklace and bracelet sold for $10.00 each and the earrings for $5.00. The necklace is design patent number 167652 issued September 2, 1952, to Alfred Philippe for Trifari. The bracelet is design patent number 167654 issued on the same day. A few days later, on September 9, 1952, design patent number 167716 was issued for the earrings. $75.00 – 125.00.

| 167421 | 8/5/1952 | Alfred Philippe | Necklace | "Twinkle" rhinestone star design (See 167584 for matching necklace design.) |
| 167584 | 8/26/1952 | Alfred Philippe | Necklace | "Twinkle" rhinestone star design (See 167585 for matching bracelet.) |
| 167585 | 8/26/1952 | Alfred Philippe | Bracelet | "Twinkle" rhinestone star design (See 167364 for matching earring.) |
| 167649 | 9/2/1952 | Alfred Philippe | Necklace | Teardrop stones with halo (See 167711 for matching brooch.) |
| 167651 | 9/2/1952 | Alfred Philippe | Necklace | Abstract |
| 167652 | 9/2/1952 | Alfred Philippe | Necklace | "Promenade" baguette curl design (See 167654 for matching bracelet.) |
| 167653 | 9/2/1952 | Alfred Philippe | Bracelet | Abstract |
| 167654 | 9/2/1952 | Alfred Philippe | Bracelet | "Promenade" baguette curl design (See 167715 for matching brooch.) |
| 167711 | 9/9/1952 | Alfred Philippe | Brooch | Teardrop stones with halo (See 167712 for matching brooch.) |
| 167712 | 9/9/1952 | Alfred Philippe | Brooch | Teardrop stones with halo (See 167649 for matching necklace.) |
| 167713 | 9/9/1952 | Alfred Philippe | Brooch | Abstract |
| 167714 | 9/9/1952 | Alfred Philippe | Brooch | Abstract |
| 167715 | 9/9/1952 | Alfred Philippe | Brooch | Abstract |
| 167716 | 9/9/1952 | Alfred Philippe | Brooch | "Promenade" baguette curl design (See 167652 for matching necklace.) |
| 168067 | 10/28/1952 | Alfred Philippe | Brooch | Abstract |
| 168068 | 10/28/1952 | Alfred Philippe | Brooch | Abstract |
| 168069 | 10/28/1952 | Alfred Philippe | Brooch | Abstract fan shape (See 168184 for matching necklace.) |
| 168184 | 11/11/1952 | Alfred Philippe | Necklace | Abstract fan shape (See 168069 for matching brooch.) |

167711

169096

169171

**1953 Trifari elephant pin.** This engaging 1½" x 1" little elephant pin is designed to bring joy and good luck. He features an upturned trunk, round belly, red baguette rhinestone feet, a red rhinestone eye, and blue rhinestone ears. He is signed "Trifari Pat. Pend." This pin is design patent number 169171 issued March 31, 1953, to Alfred Philippe for Trifari. $75.00 – 90.00.

TRIFARI JEWELRY

| Design Patent Number | Date Issued | Designer | Jewelry Type | Brief Description |
|---|---|---|---|---|
| 168590 | 1/6/1953 | Alfred Philippe | Brooch | Abstract circle |
| 168591 | 1/6/1953 | Alfred Philippe | Brooch | Abstract triple loop (168635 matching necklace) |
| 168592 | 1/6/1953 | Alfred Philippe | Necklace | Rhinestone drops (168634 matching earring) |
| 168635 | 1/13/1953 | Alfred Philippe | Necklace | Abstract triple loop (168591 matching brooch) |
| 168636 | 1/13/1953 | Alfred Philippe | Bracelet | Abstract |
| 169096 | 3/24/1953 | Alfred Philippe | Earring | Four- and five-petal rhinestone flowers (See 169097 for another style earring.) |
| 169097 | 3/24/1953 | Alfred Philippe | Earring | Four- and five-petal rhinestone flowers (See 169098 for another style earring.) |
| 169098 | 3/24/1953 | Alfred Philippe | Earring | Four- and five-petal rhinestone flower (See 169105 for matching brooch.) |
| 169101 | 3/24/1953 | Alfred Philippe | Bracelet | Four- and five-petal rhinestone flower (See 169096 for matching earring.) |
| 169103 | 3/24/1953 | Alfred Philippe | Bracelet | "Enchanted Garden" (See ad page 202 and 169168 for matching brooch.) |
| 169104 | 3/24/1953 | Alfred Philippe | Brooch | Floral fruit (169099 matching earring) |
| 169105 | 3/24/1953 | Alfred Philippe | Brooch | Four- and five-petal rhinestone flower (See 169106 for another style brooch.) |
| 169106 | 3/24/1953 | Alfred Philippe | Brooch | Four- and five-petal rhinestone flower (See169186 for another style brooch.) |
| 169168 | 3/31/1953 | Alfred Philippe | Brooch | "Enchanted Garden" (See ad page 202 and 169189 for matching brooch.) |
| 169169 | 3/31/1953 | Alfred Philippe | Brooch | Poodle |
| 169170 | 3/31/1953 | Alfred Philippe | Brooch | Duck |
| 169171 | 3/31/1953 | Alfred Philippe | Brooch | Elephant |
| 169172 | 3/31/1953 | Alfred Philippe | Brooch | Fish |
| 169173 | 3/31/1953 | Alfred Philippe | Brooch | Cat |

| 169174 | 3/31/1953 | Alfred Philippe | Necklace | Plastic "Beau Belles" triple bloom necklace (See ad page 202 and 169211 for matching figural ballet dancer.) |
|--------|-----------|-----------------|----------|-------------------------------------------------|
| 169175 | 3/31/1953 | Alfred Philippe | Necklace | Four- and five-petal rhinestone flower (See169201 for matching bracelet.) |
| 169176 | 3/31/1953 | Alfred Philippe | Necklace | Four- and five-petal rhinestone flower (See 169175 for matching necklace.) |
| 169177 | 3/31/1953 | Alfred Philippe | Necklace | Four- and five-petal rhinestone flower (See 169176 for matching necklace.) |
| 169180 | 3/31/1953 | Alfred Philippe | Necklace | "Enchanted Garden" (See ad page 202 and 169103 for matching bracelet.) |
| 169183 | 3/31/1953 | Alfred Philippe | Brooch | Plastic "Beau Belles" triple bloom flower (See ad page 202 and 169174 for matching necklace.) |
| 169184 | 3/31/1953 | Alfred Philippe | Brooch | Plastic "Beau Belles" single bloom flower (See ad page 202 and 169183 for matching brooch.) |
| 169185 | 3/31/1953 | Alfred Philippe | Brooch | Plastic "Beau Belles" set (See ad page 202, photo of this piece, and 169184 for matching brooch.) |
| 169186 | 3/31/1953 | Alfred Philippe | Brooch | Four- and five-petal rhinestone flower (See169187 for another style brooch.) |
| 169187 | 3/31/1953 | Alfred Philippe | Brooch | Four- and five-petal rhinestone flower (See169188 for another style brooch.) |
| 169188 | 3/31/1953 | Alfred Philippe | Brooch | Four- and five-petal rhinestone flower (See 169190 for another style brooch.) |
| 169189 | 3/31/1953 | Alfred Philippe | Brooch | Floral "Enchanted Garden" (See ad page 202 and 169180 for matching necklace.) |
| 169190 | 3/31/1953 | Alfred Philippe | Brooch | Four- and five-petal rhinestone flower (See 169197 for another style brooch.) |

169172

**1953 Trifari fish pin.** This fabulous 2½" x 1¾" Trifari fish figural is design patent number 169172 issued March 31, 1953, to Alfred Philippe for Trifari. The deep sapphire blue belly is flanked by emerald green rhinestones. The tail sparkles with three teardrop-shaped rhinestones. It is signed "Trifari Pat. Pend." $65.00 – 85.00.

TRIFARI JEWELRY

169185

**1953 Trifari Beau Belles double-flower pin.** This wonderful white double-flower 2½" x 1¾" pin is signed "Trifari Pat. Pend." It is design patent number 169185 issued March 31, 1953, to Alfred Philippe for Trifari. This pin was advertised in the 1953 "She will think it's Christmas!" advertisement as part of the Beau Belles jewelry group, which also included a matching necklace and earrings. The pin originally sold for $4.00. $25.00 – 40.00.

169189

169199

1953 "She will think it's Christmas!" Trifari advertisement. Original prices, top right: Spring Melodies necklace, $7.50, with earrings, $5.00, and pin, $7.50, and bracelet, $7.50. Original prices, middle row left: Magnolia necklace, $5.00, and earrings, $3.00. Original prices, middle row right: Enchanted Garden pin, $7.50, and earrings, $5.00. Original prices, bottom row left: Sea Spray necklace, $7.50, and earrings, $5.00. Original price, bottom row center: Crown Pin, $7.50. Original prices, bottom row right: Beaux Belles necklace, $5.00, with earrings, $4.00, and pin, $4.00.

## • TRIFARI 1953 •

| 169191 | 3/31/1953 | Alfred Philippe | Brooch | Bird |
|---|---|---|---|---|
| 169192 | 3/31/1953 | Alfred Philippe | Brooch | Abstract |
| 169193 | 3/31/1953 | Alfred Philippe | Brooch | Heart, called "Captive Heart" in 1953 ad (not shown) |
| 169195 | 3/31/1953 | Alfred Philippe | Brooch | Queen |
| 169195 | 3/31/1953 | Alfred Philippe | Brooch | King |
| 169197 | 3/31/1953 | Alfred Philippe | Brooch | Four- and five-petal rhinestone flower (See 169177 for matching necklace.) |
| 169198 | 3/31/1953 | Alfred Philippe | Brooch | Floral |
| 169199 | 3/31/1953 | Alfred Philippe | Brooch | Floral fruit (See 169204 for matching necklace.) |
| 169201 | 3/31/1953 | Alfred Philippe | Bracelet | Four and five petal rhinestone flower (See 169101 for matching bracelet.) |
| 169203 | 3/31/1953 | Alfred Philippe | Necklace | Abstract |
| 169204 | 3/31/1953 | Alfred Philippe | Necklace | Floral fruit (See 169335 for matching brooch.) |
| 169206 | 3/31/1953 | Alfred Philippe | Brooch | Abstract |
| 169207 | 3/31/1953 | Alfred Philippe | Brooch | "Spring Melodies" (See ad this chapter and 169214 for matching necklace.) |

| 169208 | 3/31/1953 | Alfred Philippe | Brooch | Abstract |
|---|---|---|---|---|
| 169209 | 3/31/1953 | Alfred Philippe | Brooch | Heart |
| 169210 | 3/31/1953 | Alfred Philippe | Brooch | Wreath |
| 169211 | 3/31/1953 | Alfred Philippe | Brooch | Female dancer, "Beau Belles" series  (See ad page 202 and 169212 for male dancer.) |
| 169212 | 3/31/1953 | Alfred Philippe | Brooch | Male dancer, "Beau Belles" series (See ad page 202 and 169185 matching double bloom flower.) |
| 169213 | 3/31/1953 | Alfred Philippe | Necklace | Abstract |
| 169214 | 3/31/1953 | Alfred Philippe | Necklace | "Spring Melodies" (See ad page 202 and 169207 for matching brooch.) |
| 169215 | 3/31/1953 | Alfred Philippe | Necklace | Abstract, "Spring Melodies" series |
| 169216 | 3/31/1953 | Alfred Philippe | Necklace | Abstract,"Sea Spray" series |
| 169331 | 4/14/1953 | Alfred Philippe | Brooch | Heart |
| 169332 | 4/14/1953 | Alfred Philippe | Brooch | Abstract |
| 169333 | 4/14/1953 | Alfred Philippe | Brooch | Abstract |
| 169334 | 4/14/1953 | Alfred Philippe | Brooch | Abstract |
| 169335 | 4/14/1953 | Alfred Philippe | Brooch | Floral fruit (See 169199 for another style brooch.) |
| 169690 | 5/26/1953 | Alfred Philippe | Bracelet | Abstract |
| 169692 | 5/26/1953 | Alfred Philippe | Necklace | Abstract |
| 169693 | 5/26/1953 | Alfred Philippe | Necklace | Abstract |
| 170208 | 8/18/1953 | Alfred Philippe | Brooch | Three rhinestones with halos in pot (See 170209 for another style brooch.) |
| 170209 | 8/18/1953 | Alfred Philippe | Brooch | Three rhinestone halo flowers (See 170211 for matching necklace.) |
| 170211 | 8/18/1953 | Alfred Philippe | Necklace | Rhinestone halo drop (See 170214 for matching brooch.) |

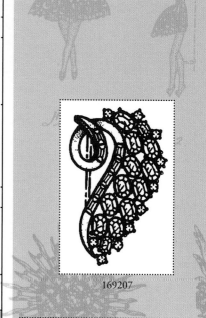

169207

169216

170208

**1953 Trifari flower basket pin.** Notice the design of the three flowers in this 2" x 1¾" stylized pot. Each flower has a center rhinestone surrounded by a halo of smaller rhinestones. In 1953, Trifari manufactured several designs featuring the same "rhinestone halo" motif. (For additional jewelry featuring the rhinestone halo motif, see the following patent numbers: 170209, 170211, 170214, 170227, 170368, and 170369.) This piece is design patent number 170208 issued August 18, 1953, to Alfred Philippe. It is signed "Trifari Pat. Pend." $35.00 – 45.00.

TRIFARI JEWELRY

| 170213 | 8/18/1953 | Alfred Philippe | Brooch | Abstract "Comet," originally sold for $10.00 (See photograph, ad, and 170215 for matching necklace.) |
| 170214 | 8/18/1953 | Alfred Philippe | Brooch | Five rhinestone halo flowers (See 170368 for matching necklace.) |
| 170215 | 8/18/1953 | Alfred Philippe | Necklace | Abstract "Comet," originally sold for $10.00 (See photograph, ad this chapter and 170367 for matching bracelet.) |
| 170221 | 8/18/1953 | Alfred Philippe | Brooch | Abstract |
| 170222 | 8/18/1953 | Alfred Philippe | Brooch | Abstract |
| 170223 | 8/18/1953 | Alfred Philippe | Brooch | Abstract |
| 170224 | 8/18/1953 | Alfred Philippe | Brooch | "Promenade" (See photo, ad, and 170375 for matching necklace.) |
| 170227 | 8/18/1953 | Alfred Philippe | Earring | Rhinestone halo (See 170208 for matching brooch.) |

Trifari 1953 lady in red dress Comet jewelry advertisement. This beautiful advertisement features the popular Trifari Comet jewelry group. The necklace originally sold for $10.00, the pin for $7.50, the earrings for $5.00, and the bracelet for $15.00. (Note that in this advertisement and in the 1953 "She will think it's Christmas!" Trifari advertisement, all of the featured necklaces are adjustable. Before this year, the Trifari advertisements feature a combination of both fixed length and adjustable necklaces, suggesting that beginning in 1953 most Trifari necklaces produced were

170367

**1953 Trifari Comet jewelry set.** This beautiful set is featured in the above 1953 Trifari advertisement showing a picture of a lovely lady in a red dress wearing the jewelry. The jewelry group is advertised as "Comet…Trifari's brilliant new star of golden fire, designed to be the most beautiful blaze in the fashion heavens!" The 6½" bracelet is design patent number 170367 issued September 8, 1953, to Alfred Philippe for Trifari. The 1½" clip earrings are design patent number 170213 and the necklace (not shown) is design patent number 170215. I was unable to locate the patent number for the 2¾" x 1½" brooch. The bracelet originally sold for $15.00, the brooch for $7.50, and the earrings for $5.00. All pieces are signed "Trifari Pat. Pend." $85.00 – 100.00. From the collection of Debi Reece.

| 170228 | 8/18/1953 | Alfred Philippe | Brooch | "Promenade" (See 170224 for matching brooch.) |
|---|---|---|---|---|
| 170271 | 8/25/1953 | Alfred Philippe | Brooch | Abstract |
| 170272 | 8/25/1953 | Alfred Philippe | Brooch | Abstract floral |
| 170276 | 8/25/1953 | Alfred Philippe | Brooch | Tornado shape (170273 matching earring) |
| 170277 | 8/25/1953 | Alfred Philippe | Brooch | Abstract one dangle |
| 170278 | 8/25/1953 | Alfred Philippe | Brooch | Abstract |
| 170279 | 8/25/1953 | Alfred Philippe | Brooch | Abstract |
| 170280 | 8/25/1953 | Alfred Philippe | Brooch | Abstract |
| 170281 | 8/25/1953 | Alfred Philippe | Brooch | Abstract |
| 170282 | 8/25/1953 | Alfred Philippe | Brooch | Abstract |
| 170283 | 8/25/1953 | Alfred Philippe | Brooch | Abstract |
| 170284 | 8/25/1953 | Alfred Philippe | Brooch | Similar to "Comet" (See "Comet" ad page 204 and 170608 for matching bracelet.) |
| 170367 | 9/8/1953 | Alfred Philippe | Bracelet | Abstract "Comet," originally sold for $10.00 (See 170213 for matching brooch.) |
| 170368 | 9/8/1953 | Alfred Philippe | Necklace | Three rhinestone halo flowers (See 170369 for another style necklace.) |
| 170369 | 9/8/1953 | Alfred Philippe | Necklace | Four rhinestone halo flowers (See170227 for matching earring.) |
| 170373 | 9/8/1953 | Alfred Philippe | Bracelet | "Promenade" originally selling for $10.00 (See 170228 for matching brooch.) |
| 170374 | 9/8/1953 | Alfred Philippe | Bracelet | Abstract |
| 170375 | 9/8/1953 | Alfred Philippe | Necklace | "Promenade" originally selling for $10.00 (See 170373 for matching bracelet.) |
| 170377 | 9/8/1953 | Alfred Philippe | Necklace | Abstract |
| 170378 | 9/8/1953 | Alfred Philippe | Necklace | Interlocking loops (170476 matching bracelet) |
| 170379 | 9/8/1953 | Alfred Philippe | Necklace | Abstract |
| 170476 | 9/22/1953 | Alfred Philippe | Bracelet | Abstract |
| 170607 | 10/13/1953 | Alfred Philippe | Necklace | Abstract |
| 170608 | 10/13/1953 | Alfred Philippe | Bracelet | Abstract similar to "Comet" (See "Comet" ad page 204 and 170609 for matching necklace.) |

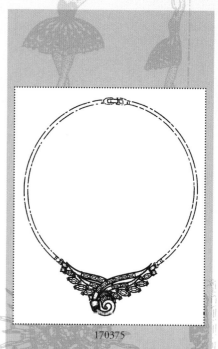

170375

170608

TRIFARI JEWELRY

171728

**1954 Trifari White Apple pin.** This creamy white 2" x 1¼" molded plastic pin is design patent number 171728 issued March 16, 1954, to Alfred Philippe for Trifari. It is signed "Trifari Pat. Pend." A matching necklace and earrings are featured in the 1954 "She will love you more for remembering her…" Trifari advertisement (see page 207) as part of the White Apple group. The White Apple jewelry group included various necklaces, brooches, and earrings. One of the rarest pieces today is the White Apple bracelet design patent number 171815. The pin is valued today at $30.00 – 45.00.

| Design Patent Number | Date Issued | Designer | Jewelry Type | Brief Description |
|---|---|---|---|---|
| 170609 | 10/13/1953 | Alfred Philippe | Necklace | Abstract similar to "Comet" (See "Comet" ad page 204 and 170284 for matching brooch.) |
| 171518 | 2/16/1954 | Alfred Philippe | Brooch | S-shape baguette rhinestones (See 171519 for similar style brooch.) |
| 171519 | 2/16/1954 | Alfred Philippe | Brooch | Circle-shape baguette rhinestones (See 171518 for similar brooch.) |
| 171660 | 3/9/1954 | Alfred Philippe | Necklace | Adjustable apple |
| 171661 | 3/9/1954 | Alfred Philippe | Necklace | Similar to "Comet" (See "Comet" ad page 204 and 171730 for matching brooch.) |
| 171722 | 3/16/1954 | Alfred Philippe | Earring | "White Apple" (See ad page 207 and 171723 for matching earring.) |
| 171723 | 3/16/1954 | Alfred Philippe | Earring | "White Apple" (See ad page 207 and 171815 for matching bracelet.) |
| 171724 | 3/16/1954 | Alfred Philippe | Earring | "White Apple" (See ad page 207 and 171660 for matching necklace.) |
| 171728 | 3/16/1954 | Alfred Philippe | Brooch | "White Apple" single drop (See 171729 for matching brooch.) |
| 171729 | 3/16/1954 | Alfred Philippe | Brooch | Double "White Apple" (See 171724 for matching earring.) |
| 171730 | 3/16/1954 | Alfred Philippe | Brooch | Similar to "Comet" (See "Comet" ad page 204 171661 for matching necklace.) |
| 171815 | 3/23/1954 | Alfred Philippe | Bracelet | "White Apple" (See ad page 207 and 171817 for matching necklace.) |
| 171817 | 3/23/1954 | Alfred Philippe | Necklace | "White Apple" (See page 207 and 171818 for matching necklace.) |
| 171818 | 3/23/1954 | Alfred Philippe | Necklace | Adjustable "White Apple" |
| 171819 | 3/23/1954 | Alfred Philippe | Necklace | "White Apple" (See page 207 171728 for matching brooch.) |
| 171820 | 3/23/1954 | Alfred Philippe | Earring | Pear (See 171821 for matching brooch.) |
| 171821 | 3/23/1954 | Alfred Philippe | Brooch | Pear on branch (See 171822 for matching brooch.) |

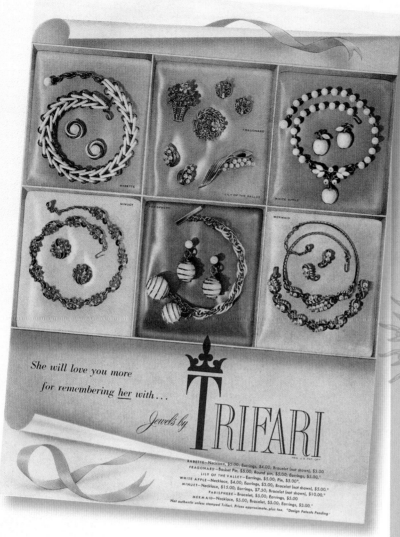

1954 "She will love you more for remembering her with…Jewels by Trifari" advertisement. Seven beautiful jewelry sets are featured in this pretty advertisement. Original prices, top left: Babette necklace, $5.00, and earrings, $4.00. Original prices, top middle (above): Fragonard basket pin, $5.00, with round pin, $5.00, and earrings, $5.00. Original prices, top middle (below): Lily of the Valley earrings, $5.00, and pin, $5.00. Original prices, top right: White Apple necklace, $4.00, and earrings, $3.00. Original prices, second row left: Minuet necklace, $15.00, and earrings, $7.50. Original prices, second row middle: Parisphere bracelet, $5.00, and earrings, $5.00. Original prices, second row right: Mermaid necklace, $5.00, with bracelet, $5.00, and earrings, $3.00.

## • Trifari 1954 •

| 171822 | 3/23/1954 | Alfred Philippe | Brooch | Two pears on branch (See 172172 for matching bracelet.) |
|---|---|---|---|---|
| 172107 | 5/4/1954 | Alfred Philippe | Brooch | Abstract |
| 172172 | 5/11/1954 | Alfred Philippe | Bracelet | Pears (See 172358 for matching necklace.) |
| 172184 | 5/11/1954 | Alfred Philippe | Earring | Leaf with pearls (See 172192 for matching brooch.) |
| 172185 | 5/11/1954 | Alfred Philippe | Brooch | Cornucopia |
| 172186 | 5/11/1954 | Alfred Philippe | Brooch | Abstract |
| 172187 | 5/11/1954 | Alfred Philippe | Brooch | Abstract |
| 172188 | 5/11/1954 | Alfred Philippe | Brooch | Abstract |
| 172192 | 5/11/1954 | Alfred Philippe | Brooch | Leaf with pearls (See 172184 for matching earrings.) |
| 172193 | 5/11/1954 | Alfred Philippe | Brooch | Abstract |
| 172304 | 5/25/1954 | Alfred Philippe | Brooch | Abstract |
| 172305 | 5/25/1954 | Alfred Philippe | Brooch | Floral |
| 172306 | 5/25/1954 | Alfred Philippe | Brooch | Abstract |
| 172307 | 5/25/1954 | Alfred Philippe | Brooch | Abstract floral |

| 172358 | 6/1/1954 | Alfred Philippe | Necklace | Adjustable pear (See 172359 for matching necklace.) |
|---|---|---|---|---|
| 172359 | 6/1/1954 | Alfred Philippe | Necklace | Triple pear (See 171820 for matching earring.) |
| 172539 | 6/1/1954 | Alfred Philippe | Necklace | Adjustable three pears |
| 172553 | 7/6/1954 | Alfred Philippe | Necklace | Floral leaves |
| 172554 | 7/6/1954 | Alfred Philippe | Necklace | Floral rhinestone flowers |
| 172556 | 7/6/1954 | Alfred Philippe | Brooch | Floral rhinestone flowers |
| 172557 | 7/6/1954 | Alfred Philippe | Brooch | Flowers in pot, "Fragonard" |
| 172558 | 7/6/1954 | Alfred Philippe | Brooch | Floral rhinestone flowers, "Fragonard" (See photograph page 209.) |
| 172559 | 7/6/1954 | Alfred Philippe | Brooch | Floral |
| 172560 | 7/6/1954 | Alfred Philippe | Brooch | "Lily of the Valley" (See advertisement page 207.) |
| 172634 | 7/13/1954 | Alfred Philippe | Necklace | Abstract |
| 172635 | 7/13/1954 | Alfred Philippe | Necklace | Abstract |
| 172639 | 7/13/1954 | Alfred Philippe | Brooch | Abstract |
| 172640 | 7/13/1954 | Alfred Philippe | Brooch | Abstract |
| 172641 | 7/13/1954 | Alfred Philippe | Brooch | Abstract |
| 172678 | 7/20/1954 | Alfred Philippe | Necklace | Abstract |
| 172679 | 7/20/1954 | Alfred Philippe | Necklace | Abstract |
| 172680 | 7/20/1954 | Alfred Philippe | Necklace | Abstract |
| 172681 | 7/20/1954 | Alfred Philippe | Brooch | Broken circle, no rhinestones |
| 172682 | 7/20/1954 | Alfred Philippe | Brooch | Abstract |

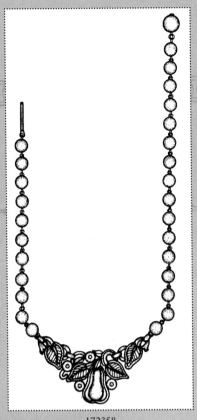

172358

**1954 Trifari White Pear necklace and bracelet set.** Similar in materials, construction, and style to the Trifari White Apple jewelry (see pages 206, 207), this White Pear set was patented in the same year. All pieces are signed "Trifari Pat. Pend." The 16" necklace is design patent number 172358 issued June 1, 1954, to Alfred Philippe. I was unable to locate the exact patent for the matching 1¼" x 1" clip earrings; however, design patent number 171820 features a similar pair of White Pear earrings. Other patent numbers for White Pear jewelry include 171821, 171822, 172172, and 172359. The value of the set today is $60.00 – 90.00.

| 173081 | 9/21/1954 | Alfred Philippe | Brooch | Abstract fruit |
|--------|-----------|-----------------|--------|----------------|
| 173082 | 9/21/1954 | Alfred Philippe | Brooch | Abstract pinwheel with pearls |
| 173085 | 9/21/1954 | Alfred Philippe | Brooch | Abstract |
| 173086 | 9/21/1954 | Alfred Philippe | Brooch | Abstract floral circle |
| 173087 | 9/21/1954 | Alfred Philippe | Brooch | Double broken circle advertised as "Carousel" (Ad not shown; see 173379 for matching bracelet.) |
| 173379 | 11/2/1954 | Alfred Philippe | Bracelet | Broken circle advertised as "Carousel" (Ad not shown; see 173382 for matching necklace.) |
| 173380 | 11/2/1954 | Alfred Philippe | Necklace | Floral leaf |
| 173382 | 11/2/1954 | Alfred Philippe | Necklace | Broken circle advertised as "Carousel" (Ad not shown; see 173087 for matching brooch.) |
| 173384 | 11/2/1954 | Alfred Philippe | Brooch | Abstract |
| 173508 | 11/16/1954 | Alfred Philippe | Earring | Abstract no rhinestones |

172558

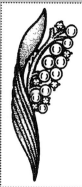

172560

173087

**1954 Trifari Fragonard brooch and earrings.** Pretty pastel yellow, pink, and blue flowers decorate this tiny 1¼" Trifari pin and matching ¾" clip earrings. Signed "Trifari Pat. Pend.," this set is called "Fragonard" after the French painter Jean Fragonard. It is featured in the 1954 "She will love you more for remembering her with … Jewels by Trifari" advertisement (see page 210). Each piece originally sold for $5.00. This set is design patent number 172558 issued July 6, 1954, to Alfred Philippe. $35.00 – 60.00.

**1954 Trifari Gemini Zodiac charm bracelet.** In 1954, Trifari advertised 12 large 1¼" dimensional Zodiac charms to be worn on a Trifarium chain bracelet (see page 210). This example represents Gemini, May 21 – June 21. Each charm originally sold for $5.00, and the bracelet for $4.00. This bracelet is marked "Trifari" with the copyright symbol. $20.00 – 30.00.

209

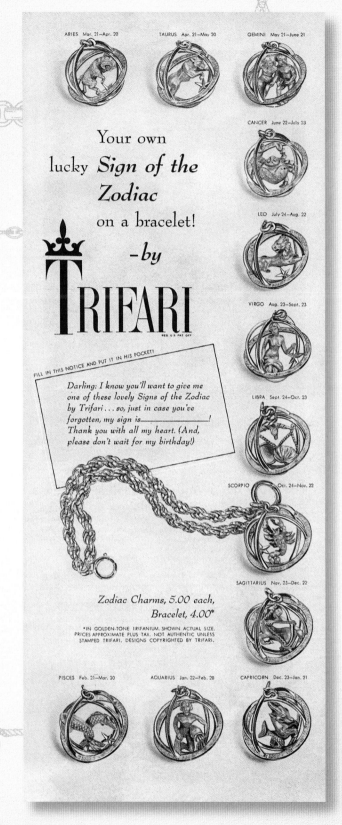

1954 "Your own lucky Sign of the Zodiac on a bracelet!" Trifari advertisement. Each Zodiaz charm sold for $5.00. The bracelet was available in golden-tone Trifanium and sold for $4.00.

**Early 1940s Trifari pavé link bracelet.** The heavy use of pavé rhinestones and the buckle design suggest that this elegant 7" Trifari bracelet was produced in the early 1940s. It is signed "Trifari" without the copyright symbol. $95.00 – 125.00.

**Early 1940s Trifari pavé rhinestone, red cabochon, and red enamel bracelet.** Trifari produced some of the most elegant and beautiful bracelets ever sold in the early 1940s, including this 7" beauty signed "Trifari" without the copyright symbol. Unfortunately, many early Trifari pavé link bracelets are not patented. $150.00 – 300.00. From the collection of Debi Reece.

**Early 1940s Trifari pavé rhinestone bow pin.** This lovely 1½" x 2" bow pin is marked "Trifari" without the copyright symbol. Trifari made many versions of bow pins in the 1940s. The design of the pin and the use of pavé rhinestones indicate this beautiful bow dates to the early 1940s. $50.00 – 70.00. From the collection of Debi Reece.

**Two early 1950s Trifari flower brooches.** These pretty poured-glass Trifari flower pins originally were produced in two sizes and may have been intended to be worn in pairs. The larger pin measures 2½" x 1½" and the smaller is 1½" x 1". The white glass leaves are similar to the poured-glass necklace shown in the "For a Jewel of a Mother" 1950 advertisement (see page 182), suggesting that these twin pins date from that time. They are signed "Trifari" without the copyright symbol. $50.00 – 65.00 pair. From the collection of Debi Reece.

TRIFARI JEWELRY

**1948 – early 1950s Trifari Mother Goose pin.** This darling 2" x 1" Mother Goose figural pin is signed "Trifari" without the copyright symbol. The signature and nonuse of sterling help to date this sweet pin to 1948 – early 1950s. $30.00 – 50.00.

**1948 – early 1950s Trifari gold-tone choker necklace and earrings.** This classically styled set is signed "Trifari Pat. Pend." Unfortunately, I was unable to locate the patent for this creamy gold-tone 15½" choker and matching 1" clip earrings. The style, signature, and non-use of sterling date this set to 1948 – early 1950s. $50.00 – 65.00. From the collection of Debi Reece.

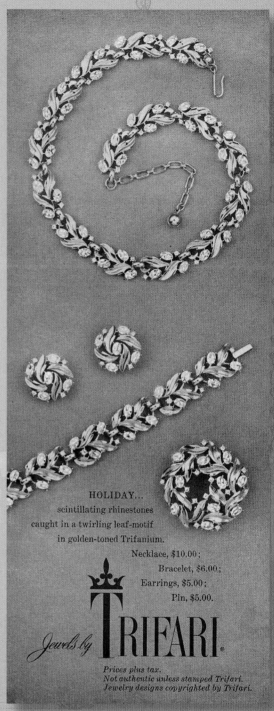

HOLIDAY...
scintillating rhinestones
caught in a twirling leaf-motif
in golden-toned Trifanium.

Necklace, $10.00;
Bracelet, $6.00;
Earrings, $5.00;
Pin, $5.00.

*Jewels by* TRIFARI®

Prices plus tax.
Not authentic unless stamped Trifari.
Jewelry designs copyrighted by Trifari.

**1955 "Holiday…" Trifari advertisement.** This black and white advertisement showcases a Trifari rhinestone and gold-tone leaf-design necklace, bracelet, pin, and earrings set. The advertisement reads, "Holiday…scintillating rhinestones caught in a twirling leaf-motif in golden-toned Trifanium. Necklace, $10.00; Bracelet, $6.00; Earrings, $5.00; Pin, $5.00."

**1948 – early 1950s Trifari blue art-glass necklace.** This unusual 17" necklace features clear, highly faceted, fan-shaped beads with vibrant blue centers. These rare beads graduate in size with the smallest beads near the clasp. This beauty is signed "Trifari" without the copyright symbol. $75.00 – 125.00. From the collection of Debi Reece.

**Mid-to-late 1950s Trifari baguette flower set.** The silver-tone flowers in this otherwise gold-tone parure by Trifari are each composed of five baguette rhinestones standing on end like rays of sunshine. All of the pieces are signed "Trifari" with the copyright symbol. The adjustable choker measures 15½", the clip-back earrings are 1". The top flower pin is 1½" in diameter, and the bottom flower pin is 2" long. The signature and the design of this set date it to the second half of the 1950s. $120.00 – 150.00. From the collection of Debi Reece.

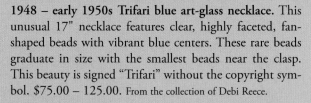

**Mid-to-late 1950s Trifari baguette flower 15½" necklace with green rhinestones.** This pretty necklace is signed "Trifari" with the copyright symbol. $35.00 – 55.00.

TRIFARI JEWELRY

213

**Mid-to-late 1950s Trifari white wildflower bracelet and brooch.** Flowing leaves of textured gold-tone metal and white plastic inserts gracefully convey the image of wildflowers swaying in the wind. A tiny gold bead is set in the center of each four-petal white plastic flower. Clear rhinestones are randomly set around the pretty floral display to add a bit of sparkle to this lovely set. The lovely 2½" brooch and the matching 7½" bracelet are signed "Trifari" with the copyright symbol. $75.00 – 95.00.

**Mid-to-late 1950s Trifari brown plastic necklace and earrings.** The creamy brown plastic 16" necklace and the 1" clip earrings are signed "Trifari" with the copyright symbol. The Caravan advertisement (unfortunately, the advertisement is not dated) describes this set as "Caravan…Trifari's own portrayal of the exotic in fashion. Here in two versions: Sumatra, square stones. Kashmir, oval stones. In colors fired with the glow of a Maharajah's gems: Bombay Brown (you see it here!), Bengal Blue, Ganges Green, Rajah Red, and a most unusual Burmese Black." Originally the necklace sold for $7.50 and the earrings for $5.00. $45.00 – 65.00.

Late 1950s Caravan Trifari advertisement. Unfortunately, I do not know the correct date for this wonderful Trifari advertisement; however, it likely dates to the late 1950s. This advertisement features Trifari's Caravan jewelry available in "Sumatra," or square stones, and "Kashmir," or oval stones. Both stone styles were also available in the following colors: Bombay Brown (shown in the ad), Bengal Blue, Ganges Green, Rajah Red, and Burmese Black. The jewelry sold for between $3.00 and $7.50 each piece.

TRIFARI JEWELRY

**Mid-to-late 1950s Trifari jewel-tone lariat-style necklace, bracelet, and earrings set.** The lovely Trifari 16" gold-tone lariat-style necklace, matching 7¼" bracelet, and ¾" x ½" clip earrings feature teardrop-shaped, open-backed cabochons in realistic purple, green, and blue jewel tones. The necklace and bracelet are signed "Trifari" with the copyright symbol. However, the earrings do not have a copyright symbol. Therefore, I believe this set was produced at the time when Trifari was in the process of adding the copyright symbol to the Trifari signature and that it most likely dates from 1954 to 1956. $65.00 – 85.00.

1955 "Fleurette" Trifari advertisement. This colorful advertisement features enameled posies in light blue, white, pink, and yellow. The necklace originally sold for $7.50, the bracelet for $6.00, the pin for $5.00, and the earrings for $6.00. The advertisement reads, "Fleurette [French for "little flower"]/Spring flowering in the Trifari manner! Enameled pastel posies in white, yellow or pink blossoming on a trellis of golden-toned Trifanium; or blue on platinum-toned."

1955 Trifari Fleurette necklace, bracelet, and earrings. The 1955 Trifari "Fleurette" advertisement shows this beautiful jewelry in pretty pastel colors. Originally the 16" choker sold for $7.50, the 7½" bracelet for $6.00, and the 1" clip earrings for $4.00. Each piece is signed "Trifari" with the copyright symbol. $65.00 – 100.00.

TRIFARI JEWELRY

215

The rhythm of fashion!
The short and the long of it!
The colour of fashion!
The smart and the chic of it!
That's BOLERO!
*Jewels by* TRIFARI
REG U S PAT OFF.

Make-believe stones in turquoise (as illustrated), coral, or alabaster white set off by a crescendo of golden-toned Trifanium! To be mixed, matched or mated: rope, $12.50; matinee length, $7.50; adjustable throat-line necklace, $7.50*; earrings, $4.00*; bracelet, $5.00* Plus tax. Not authentic unless stamped Trifari. *Design Copyrighted. Dress by Talmack.

TRIFARI JEWELRY

1955 Trifari "The rhythm of fashion!" advertisement. The advertisement reads, "The rhythm of fashion! The short and the long of it! The colour of fashion! The smart and the chic of it! That's BOLERO!" The long rope necklace originally sold for $12.50, the shorter necklace for $7.50, the bracelet for $5.00, and the earrings for $4.00. This set was available in turquoise, coral, white, or green.

**1955 Trifari Bolero turquoise necklace, bracelet, and earrings set.** The 1955 advertisement featuring this beautiful turquoise jewelry reads, "The rhythm of fashion! The short and the long of it! The colour of fashion! The smart and the chic of it! That's BOLERO!" The metal is gold-tone Trifanium a plating process patented by Trifari in the 1940s that simulates the look of gold or silver and, fortunately for collectors, preserves the look of the metal over time. The necklace is 16", the bracelet 7", and the earrings 1¼". All pieces are signed "Trifari" with the copyright symbol. $45.00 – 65.00.
From the collection of Debi Reece.

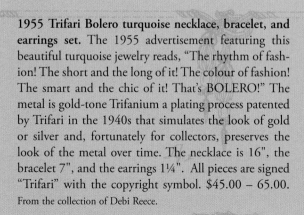

**1955 Trifari Betty Crocker homemaker award brooch.** This interesting 2¼" x 1¼" brooch features a gold-tone heart suspended from three floral branches. The front of the heart depicts a three-dimensional image of a home, complete with landscaping details. The back of the heart is inscribed, "Betty Crocker State Homemaker of Tomorrow 1955." This is a heavy, well-made pin. It is difficult to place a value on a specialty item like this award brooch. Best guess: $65.00 – 85.00.

1955 Trifari "Make it a Wonderful Christmas with Jewels by Trifari" advertisement. Seven beautiful Trifari sets are shown in this advertisement. Original prices, top left: Caprice necklace, $7.50, with bracelet, $5.00, and earrings, $5.00. Original prices, top right: Golden Gate necklace, $5.00, with expansion bracelet, $5.00, and earrings, $3.00. Original prices, second row: Princess necklace, $7.50, with bracelet, $6.00, and earrings, $5.00. Original prices, third row left: Rendezvous pin, $7.50, and earrings, $5.00. Original prices, third row right: Wreath pin, $5.00, and earrings, $5.00. Original prices, bottom row left: Royal Plume pin, $15.00, and earrings, $12.50. Original prices, bottom row right: Rhapsody necklace, $25.00, with bracelet, $15.00, and earrings, $10.00.

1. CAPRICE*

2. GOLDEN GATE*

3. PRINCESS*

Make it a
WONDERFUL CHRISTMAS
with *Jewels by* TRIFARI.®

1. Necklace, $7.50; Bracelet, $5.00; Earrings, $5.00.
2. Necklace, $5.00; (Matching Bracelet—not shown—$5.00);
   Expansion Bracelet, $5.00; Earrings, $3.00.
   (Also in Platinum-toned Trifanium)
3. Necklace, $7.50; Bracelet, $6.00; Earrings, $5.00.
   (Also in Platinum-toned Trifanium)
4. Pin, $7.50; Earrings, $5.00.
   (Also in Golden-toned Trifanium)
5. Pin, $15.00; Earrings, $12.50.
6. Necklace, $25.00; Bracelet, $15.00;
   (Two-Row Bracelet—not shown—$25.00);
   Earrings, $10.00.
7. Pin, $5.00; Earrings, $5.00.

PRICES PLUS TAX. NOT AUTHENTIC UNLESS STAMPED TRIFARI
*JEWELRY DESIGNS COPYRIGHTED BY TRIFARI.

4. RENDEZVOUS*

7. WREATH*

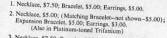

5. ROYAL PLUME*

6. RHAPSODY*

TRIFARI JEWELRY

217

**1956 Trifari Cordon D'or bracelet and earrings set.** Amazingly beautiful and in mint condition, this 7¼" Trifari bracelet and matching ¾" clip earrings still have the original gold and black Trifari hangtags. All pieces are signed "Trifari" with the copyright symbol. This set is called "Cordon D'or" ("ribbon of gold") in the 1956 "Merry Christmas Jewels by Trifari" advertisement. The bracelet originally sold for $10.00 and the earrings for $7.50. The matching choker (not shown in the photograph) sold for $15.00. $50.00 – 65.00. From the collection of Debi Reece.

**1956 Trifari Plume pin.** Easy to find today, this 2" Trifari Plume pin is shown in the "Merry Christmas Jewels by Trifari" 1956 advertisement and originally sold for $3.00. It is signed "Trifari" with the copyright symbol. Today's value isn't much higher. $15.00 – 20.00.

1956 Trifari "Merry Christmas Jewels by Trifari" advertisement. With the jewelry pieces arranged in the shape of a pinwheel, this beautiful advertisement features 11 different jewelry groups. The spectacular center collar necklace called "Egret" originally sold for $35.00. The matching earrings sold for $10.00. The four pins shown and their original prices are Wreath, $7.50; Plume, $3.00; Autumn Leaves, $6.00; and Leaf, $15.00. The sets shown clockwise from the top left, and their original prices, are Cordon D'or collar, $15.00, with bracelet, $10.00, and earrings, $7.50; Queen Anne collar, $15.00, and bracelet, $15.00; Stonybrook collar, $7.50, and bracelet, $7.50; Rivulette collar, $7.50, and bracelet, $7.50; Wellesley collar, $5.00, and bracelet, $5.00; and Seaweave collar, $5.00, and bracelet, $4.00.

**1956 Trifari Pebble Beach necklace and brooch.** Even though the jewelry produced in the middle of the 1950s was mass produced, Trifari continued to market lovely jewelry. This set, called "Pebble Beach" in the 1956 "For Her…Jewels by Trifari" advertisement, is an example Trifari's expertise at combining lightweight and inexpensive plastic inserts with rhinestones to create lovely and wearable jewelry. The 16½" collar necklace originally sold for $5.00. There is no original price known for the matching 2" diameter pin. Both pieces are marked "Trifari" with the copyright symbol. $35.00 – 55.00.

1956 "For Her…Jewels by Trifari" advertisement. Seven summer sets are showcased in this lovely blue and white advertisement. Original prices, top left: Valencia collar, $7.50, with bracelet, $5.00, and earrings, $4.00. Original prices, top middle: Colleen collar, $7.50, with bracelet, $5.00, and earrings, $5.00, and basket pin, $7.50. Original prices, top right: Pebble Beach collar, $5.00, with bracelet, $4.00, and earrings, $4.00. Original prices, center: Fluerettes pin, $5.00, and button earrings, $6.00. Original prices, bottom left: Brazil collar, $7.50, with bracelet, $5.00, and earrings, $3.00. Original prices, bottom middle: Fleurettes collar, $7.50, with bracelet, $6.00, and earrings, $4.00. Original prices, bottom right: Trinidad collar, $6.00, with bracelet, $5.00, and earrings, $4.00.

For Her… *Jewels by* TRIFARI

219

**1957 Trifari Whirlwind necklace and bracelet set.** Called "Whirlwind" in the 1957 "she can't see a thing but jewels by Trifari" advertisement, this interesting Trifari set was originally available in white, turquoise, or coral. The 16" necklace and 7½" x 1⅛" bracelet are marked "Trifari" with the copyright symbol and originally sold for $7.50 each. Notice that the tiny seed pearls covering the necklace and earrings vary in size and, amazingly, are all still present almost fifty years later! $65.00 – 90.00.

TRIFARI JEWELRY

1957 Trifari "she can't see a thing but jewels by Trifari" advertisement. This intriguing advertisement shows a woman with a blind fold happily wearing Whirlwind jewelry by Trifari. Available in turquoise, coral or white the necklace and bracelet originally sold for $7.50 each. The pin and bracelet sold for $5.00 each.

© 1957 TRIFARI

she can't see a thing but *jewels by* TRIFARI.

WHIRLWIND...Necklace and Bracelet, 7.50 each; Pin, 5.00. Earrings, 5.00 a pair. The colors: Turquoise, Coral or White. *Prices plus tax. Jewelry designs copyrighted. Not authentic unless stamped TRIFARI.*

COIFFURE BY GUILLAUME OF MANCEL.

1958 "She can't see a thing but jewels by Trifari" advertisement. Ten beautiful sets are featured in this summery Trifari advertisement. Original prices, top left: South Seas necklace, $5.00, with bracelet, $5.00, and earrings, $3.00. Original prices, top middle: Allure necklace, $10.00, with bracelet, $10.00, and earrings, $3.00. Original prices, top right: Santa Anita necklace, $6.00, with bracelet, $5.00, and earrings, $3.00. Original prices, bottom left: Ebbtide pin, $5.00, and earrings, $4.00. Original prices, bottom middle: Spring Frost (blue set) pin, $7.50, and earrings, $7.50; Garden Party white flower earrings, $6.00; White Garland plain white earrings, $4.00. Original prices, bottom right: Garden Party necklace, $7.50, with bracelet, $7.50, and earrings, $4.00. Original prices, on model: Syncopation necklace, $6.00, with bracelet, $5.00, and earrings, $4.00. White button earrings below model's hand: Doubloon, $3.00.

1959 "Sorrento..." Trifari advertisement. The pearls featured in these four brooches are described in this advertisement as "Baroque pseudo-pearls in textured golden-tone settings, tipped with fake black diamonds." The pins ranged in value from $5.00 to $10.00.

1959 "The Freshest Fashion of Spring!" Trifari advertisement. This advertisement features jewelry called "Southampton" and described as "... pseudo-pearls tipped with turquoise, coral, or pearl tones; in a golden-tone setting. Necklace, 7.50; Bracelet, 5.00; Earrings, 4.00..."

**1959 Trifari Sorrento brooch.** The 1959 Trifari "Sorrento..." advertisement describes the pearls in this 1½" diameter brooch as "Baroque pseudo-pearls in textured golden-tone settings, tipped with fake black diamonds." Today collectors sometimes refer to the petite baroque pearls as baby's teeth. This brooch is marked "Trifari" with the copyright symbol. $50.00 – 75.00.

**Late 1950s Trifari pearl "hugs and kisses" necklace, bracelet, and earrings set.** This lovely 16" brushed gold-tone hugs and kisses necklace features creamy white pearls. The bracelet is 7" and the clip earrings are 1". All pieces are signed "Trifari" with the copyright symbol and date to the late 1950s or early 1960s. $45.00 – 65.00.

TRIFARI JEWELRY

**Late 1950s or 1960s Trifari pearl and crystal necklace and earrings set.** Signed "Trifari" with the copyright symbol, this set features white pearls, sparkling clear rhinestones and dangling blue and green crystals. The necklace measures 15" and each clip earring is ½" x 1¼". $65.00 – 85.00.

1960 Trifari Andante advertisement. This elegant Trifari advertisement features "Andante" jewelry, described as "…a gift of shining beauty. Rhinestones exquisitely cut and mounted in platinum-toned Trifanium. The necklace 25.00, bracelet and pin 15.00 each, earrings 7.50."

TRIFARI JEWELRY

*Fig. 1.*

**Late 1950s Trifari sapphire blue rhinestone brooch.** Sapphire blue teardrop-shaped rhinestones decorate both layers of this delicate yet well-made Trifari pin. Measuring 2" x 1½", this dainty pin is signed "Trifari" with the copyright symbol, dating it to the late 1950s or early 1960s. Amazingly, it still has its original tag! $40.00 – 55.00. From the collection of Debi Reece.

*Fig. 2.*

TRIFARI JEWELRY

1960 "Punctuation White" Trifari advertisement. This interesting advertisement shows white Trifari jewelry designs resting in the model's long red hair. The ad reads, "Striking accents from Trifari's full-range collection of fashion-white jewelry. Illustrated, necklaces and bracelet, $5 each; earrings $4."

*"Punctuation White"*

Striking accents from Trifari's full-range collection of fashion-white jewelry. Illustrated, necklaces and bracelets, $5 each; earrings $4. Other styles up to $20. Prices plus tax.
JEWELRY DESIGNS COPYRIGHTED

*Jewels by* TRIFARI

**1960 Trifari Fantasies bird pin.** This sweet 1¾" blue moonstone bird pin is part of a Trifari series called Fantasies (ad not shown). It is signed "Trifari" with the copyright symbol. Produced in three sizes (2¾", 2¼", 1¾") and with coordinating earrings, these birds were also available with red bellies. Popular at the time, these pretty birds were produced for several years. $30.00 – 55.00.

**1961 Trifari golden rhinestone brooch.** Originally selling for $7.50, this lovely 2" x 1¾" golden rhinestone, crescent-shaped brooch is advertised (shown in green) in the "Memo to a smart woman…" 1961 Trifari advertisement (see page 226). It is signed "Trifari" with the copyright symbol. $60.00 – 80.00.

**1961 Trifari purple rhinestone wreath brooch and matching earrings.** Featured in the 1961 Trifari "Memo to a smart woman…" advertisement (see page 226), this 2" in diameter brooch and matching 1" clip earrings sparkle with pretty purple rhinestones and reflective silver-tone metal. All pieces are signed "Trifari" with the copyright symbol. The brooch originally sold for $7.50 and the earrings for $6.00 a pair. $75.00 – 90.00.

TRIFARI JEWELRY

225

Memo to a smart woman: Circle your choice and slip this page into his pocket.

1961 Trifari "Memo to a smart woman" advertisement. This advertisement features some of the most beautiful Trifari jewelry produced in the 1960s. The advertisement reads, "Memo to a smart woman: Circle your choice and slip this page into his pocket." The jewelry originally ranged in price from $5.00 to $15.00.

TRIFARI JEWELRY

**1961 Trifari golden nuggets Etoile key brooch and matching earrings.** The fabulous glowing yellow nuggets decorating this 2½" x 1" Trifari key pin and matching ¾" clip earrings are advertised in the 1961 Etoile advertisement as "…nuggets of pure light caught amidst the rainbowing facets of fabulous fake gems!" These nuggets are spectacularly beautiful in person. All pieces are signed "Trifari" with the copyright symbol. $85.00 – 125.00.

**1961 "…obviously by Trifari" advertisement.** Hugely popular with collectors today, this 1961 Trifari advertisement features five glowing brooches. The advertisement reads "Etoile… breath-taking magnificence in a startlingly beautiful jewel series by Trifari! Nuggets of pure light caught amidst the rainbowing facets of fabulous fake gems! Sheer wizardry for fashion's elegant simplicity." The brooches ranged in price from $7.50 to $25.00 each.

**1961 Trifari golden nuggets Etoile brooch.** This beautiful 2¼" x 2" brooch is featured in the 1961 "…obviously by Trifari" advertisement promoting the Etoile ("star") collection. Originally selling for $7.50 – 25.00, the Etoile jewelry features beautiful, irregularly shaped stones that Trifari referred to as "nuggets of pure light." These spectacular stones glow as if lit from within. The brooch is signed "Trifari" with the copyright symbol. $75.00 – 100.00.

**1962 turquoise Trifari tassel necklace.** The pretty model in the 1962 "Suspended Animation" advertisement is wearing this beautiful turquoise plastic beaded tassel necklace. Measuring 24", with a 3" tassel, this necklace is signed "Trifari" with the copyright symbol and originally sold for between $7.50 and $15.00. It is a bargain today at $20.00 – 25.00.

TRIFARI JEWELRY

1962 "Suspended Animation" Trifari advertisement. This advertisement features five variations of Trifari's long beaded tassel necklaces originally selling for $7.50 to $15.00 each. The advertisement reads "Suspended Animation: The richly tasseled sautoir, an exciting daytime fashion…from Trifari's long-look collection."

*Jewels by* TRIFARI®

*Suspended Animation: The richly tasseled sautoir, an exciting daytime fashion…from Trifari's long-look collection. 7.50 to 15.00, plus tax.*

1962 "The fashion spotlight…" Trifari advertisement. This advertisement showcases five beautiful gold-tone brooches made of textured Trifanium: wheat, acorn, drape, palm tree, and shell. Each pin originally sold for $5.00.

The fashion spotlight is on the fascinating pin. Glowing examples…these extraordinarily beautiful ones, elegantly designed and crafted by Trifari in richly textured, golden-toned Trifanium. Counterclockwise: Wheat, Acorn, Drape, Palm Tree, Shell, 5.00 each, plus tax. Matching earrings available.

**Eight of these pins are $15 or under. One costs $2900. Which?**

Eight pins are costume jewelry by Trifari. The other pin has 92 full-cut diamonds set in 18 karat gold. Quite frankly, a jeweler may have no trouble guessing which is which. But your friends will not find it quite so easy. The point is, Trifari's rhinestone pins set in golden-toned Trifanium are so exquisite in design and craftsmanship, they look almost real!

A tip to a wise woman: Circle your favorites (choose two to play it safe) and slip this page into his pocket or his shoe. If your heart is set on diamonds, the $2900.00 (tax included) pin is the lovely leaf, second from left, available at the famous Fifth Avenue jewelers, Black Starr & Frost. Trifari's pins are $7.50* to $15.00*, available at fine stores throughout the country.

*Jewels by* TRIFARI.

1962 Trifari "Eight of these pins are $15 or under" advertisement. Eight gold-tone Trifanium and clear rhinestone brooches are displayed on elegant pedestals. A ninth brooch, displayed in the same manner, is real, costing $2,900.00. The advertisement challenges the customer to identify the "real" brooch. (The "real" brooch is the leaf pin second from the left.)

**1962 Trifari wheat pin and earrings set.** Measuring a long 3½", this shiny golden wheat pin, along with the 1" earrings, is featured in the 1962 Trifari "The fashion spotlight…" advertisement and originally sold for $5.00. All pieces are signed "Trifari" with the copyright symbol. $25.00 – 35.00 set.

**1963 Trifari blue rhinestone choker necklace and earrings set.** Rich, beautiful blue channel-set rhinestones give this lovely Trifari necklace and earrings set a plus quality. The set was called "Cavalcade" in the 1963 "…a wise man gives his wife Trifari, too" advertisement (see page 231). All pieces are signed "Trifari" with the copyright symbol. Originally, the 15½" necklace sold for $7.50, and the 1" clip earrings for $5.00. Today's value for the set is $55.00 – 85.00.

**Early 1960s Trifari pearl and rhinestone bracelet and earrings set.** Clear rhinestones and creamy pearls decorate this rich-looking Trifari 7¼" bracelet and 1¾" dangling earrings. Signed "Trifari" with the copyright symbol, this lovely set is a creative variation of the Trifari Cavalcade jewelry featured in the 1963 "…and a wise man gives his wife Trifari, too" advertisement (see page 231) and date from the same era. $45.00 – 70.00.

1963 Trifari "…and a wise man gives his wife Trifari, too." advertisement. This advertisement features jewelry called "Cavalcade" available in gold-tone or platinum-tone Trifanium and originally selling for between $5.00 and $10.00 each piece.

**1964 Trifari pearl and rhinestone floral brooch.** This beautiful 2½" x 2" brooch holds center place in Trifari's 1964 "For every frantic…" advertisement. Originally selling for between $5.00 and $12.50, these brooches exhibit beautiful designs and high-quality workmanship. Note the use of both silver-tone and gold-tone metal. This example is signed "Trifari" with the copyright symbol. $45.00 – 65.00.

TRIFARI JEWELRY

1964 "For every frantic…" Trifari Christmas Collection advertisement. This lovely advertisement features eight beautiful pearl and rhinestone brooches and one pair of earrings, in either gold-tone or platinum-tone Trifanium, originally selling for between $5.00 and $12.50 each.

1966 "Trifari sees mosaics in a whole new light" advertisement. The beautiful mosaic jewelry in this advertisement is described as "…beautifully translucent simulated jewels in peacock tones of blue and green set in golden-toned Trifanium. Any one — or two or three — of these could be the light of your fashion life. From a collection of pins, necklace, bracelets and earrings — including enormous pendulum earrings. Also available in multi-color, jet or simulated topaz. $5 to $25."

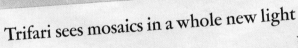

Trifari sees mosaics in a whole new light

If you thought mosaics belonged to the Dark Ages, it's time you discovered the Modern Mosaics: beautifully translucent simulated jewels in peacock tones of blue and green set in golden-toned Trifanium. Any one — or two or three — of these could be the light of your fashion life. From a collection of pins, necklaces, bracelets and earrings — including enormous pendulum earrings. Also available in multi-color, jet or simulated topaz. $5 to $25   *Jewels by* TRIFARI   JEWELRY DESIGNS COPYRIGHTED–TRIFARI, KRUSSMAN AND FISHEL, INC.

**1966 Trifari Modern Mosaics maple leaf pin and earrings set.** In 1966 Trifari advertised a line of jewelry called "Modern Mosaics," described in the "Trifari sees mosaics in a whole new light" advertisement as "beautifully translucent simulated jewels in peacock tones of blue and green set in golden-toned Trifanium." Modern Mosaics jewelry sold for $5.00 – 25.00. Today collectors love these translucent jewels, and the values continue to rise. The 3" x 2¼" maple leaf brooch and matching 1" clip earrings illustrate the glowing peacock colors of the Modern Mosaics line. All pieces are signed "Trifari" with the copyright symbol. $95.00 – 135.00.

233

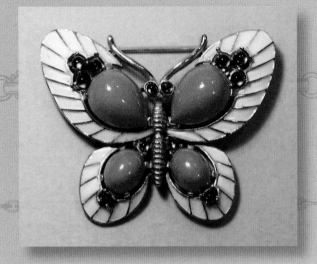

**1968 Trifari faux coral and white enamel butterfly pin.** Similar in design to coral and white jewelry featured in a 1968 Trifari advertisement (not shown in this volume), this colorful 2" coral and emerald green cabochon Trifari butterfly pin illustrates Trifari's ceaseless dedication to quality in design and materials. It is signed "Trifari" with the copyright symbol. $35.00 – 50.00.

**1968 Trifari brightly enameled strawberry and parrot pins.** The 1968 Trifari "Pardon me, but there's a ladybug on your collar…" advertisement (see page 235) features these sweet little pins. The strawberry pin measures 1" x ¾" and the parrot is 1½" x ¾". Both are signed "Trifari" with the copyright symbol. $45.00 – 65.00 each.

**1960s Trifari sapphire blue and clear rhinestone brooch.** Magnificent and large, this 2½" brooch is signed "Trifari" with the copyright symbol. The design of the brooch is reminiscent of 1960s Maltese cross jewelry. The high-quality brooch features nine starburst-style rays encrusted with clear pavé rhinestones surrounding a deep blue rhinestone center. $65.00 – 85.00. From the collection of Debi Reece.

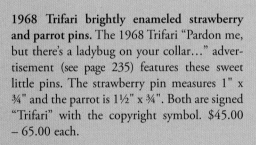

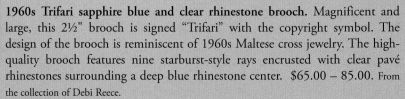

*Pardon me, but there's a ladybug on your collar*

*a Penguin on your scarf*

*a parrot on your shoulder*

*and a flock of birds on your lapel*

*a strawberry on your belt*

*row of flowers on your sleeve*

*a starfish on your pocket*

*d your flair for fashion is showing.*

Jewels by TRIFARI

EACH PIN ABOUT $5   JEWELRY DESIGNS COPYRIGHTED: TRIFARI, KRUSSMAN AND FISHEL, INC.

1968 Trifari "Pardon me, but there's a ladybug on your collar…" advertisement. Twelve tiny enameled figural pins are featured in this colorful advertisement originally selling for $5.00 each.

1968 Trifari "You're beautiful by Trifari-light" advertisement. Five rhinestone pins and one pair of rhinestone earrings all set in silver-tone metal are advertised as evening wear in this elegant advertisement. The ad reads "Moonlight, candlelight, Trifari-light. Beautiful light for him to see you by: rhinestones of pure brilliance. Pins and earrings, about $10 to $15."

You're beautiful by Trifari-light

Moonlight, candlelight, Trifari-light. Beautiful light for him to see you by: rhinestones of pure brilliance. Pins and earrings, about $10 to $15.

Jewels by TRIFARI

TRIFARI JEWELRY

**1960s Trifari red rhinestone apple pin and earrings set.** Dating from the 1960s, when fruit pins were made popular by Weiss, Har and Warner, this 1¼" red-violet apple pin and matching ¾" clip earrings are signed "Trifari" with the copyright symbol. $55.00 – 75.00. From the collection of Debi Reece.

**1960s Trifari pearl and gold-tone branch pin.** In the 1960s, and in later years, Trifari produced many versions of pearl and gold-tone pins, including this huge 4¼" x 2¾" tree branch brooch signed "Trifari" with the copyright symbol. $25.00 – 35.00. Courtesy of Esta Pratt.

**After 1960 Trifari rabbit-in-a-hat pin.** Marked "Trifari" with the copyright symbol, this sweet 1½" rabbit pin is a later piece produced after 1960. $20.00 – 30.00.

**After 1960 Trifari faux-stained-glass necklace and earrings set.** This lovely faux-stained-glass set is signed "Trifari" with the copyright symbol. The pendant measures 5" x 1½" and is suspended from a 22" double-strand gold-tone chain. The clip earrings measure 1" in diameter. $40.00 – 50.00.

TRIFARI JEWELRY

**1970s Trifari Egyptian-style enameled pendant.** This beautiful 3" x 3¼" tri-color enameled pendant is suspended from a 16" snake chain and signed "Trifari" with the copyright symbol. This Egyptian-style jewelry was produced in the mid-1970s to commemorate the first U.S. tour of artifacts from King Tut's tomb (1976 – 1979). $65.00 – 95.00.

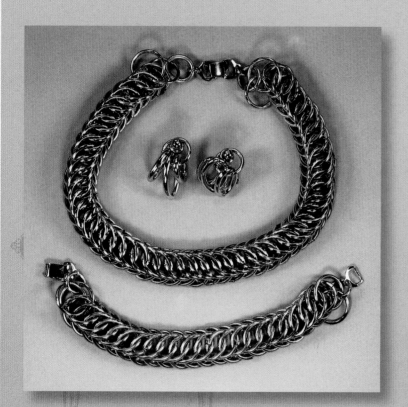

Close view of the "Made in France for Trifari" signature.

**Trifari gold-tone necklace, bracelet, and earrings set with unusual "Made in France" signature.** All of the pieces in this lightweight gold-tone set are signed "Made in France for Trifari" with a crown over the "T." The 15" necklace, 7¼" bracelet, and 1" clip earrings lack vintage Trifari's normal high quality. I can find no information on when Trifari jewelry was produced in France, so I am unable to date this set. $20.00 – 30.00 set.

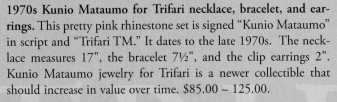

**1970s Kunio Mataumo for Trifari necklace, bracelet, and earrings.** This pretty pink rhinestone set is signed "Kunio Mataumo" in script and "Trifari TM." It dates to the late 1970s. The necklace measures 17", the bracelet 7½", and the clip earrings 2". Kunio Mataumo jewelry for Trifari is a newer collectible that should increase in value over time. $85.00 – 125.00.

**1970s Kunio Mataumo for Trifari faux-marble cuff bracelet.** This fascinating 1970s bracelet is signed "Kunio Mataumo" in script and "Trifari" with the copyright symbol. The front half of the cuff bracelet is made of a silver gray porcelain-like material that simulates the look of marble. The back half is gold-tone metal. This unusual bracelet is large enough for an average wrist. $65.00 – 95.00.

**1970s Diane Love for Trifari necklace.** Although it is a newer collectible, Diane Love for Trifari jewelry is skyrocketing in value. The 1970 "The Diane Love collection for Trifari" advertisement (see page 239) describes the Diane Love jewelry as "Authentic replicas of ancient art objects…" This necklace still has the original Diane Love hangtag, which reads, "Replica of a Byzantine reliquary crucifix 5th century…." The heavy pendant measures 3½" in diameter. The necklace, with the pendant, measures almost 20". Unfortunately, some and perhaps all of these designs are only signed on a removable paper tag identifying the piece as a Diane Love for Trifari design. $300.00+.

SCULPTURESQUE

Premiere! Designer Jonathan Bailey's first and exclusive Trifari creations. Dramatic. Provocative. Important. From a collection. About $7.50 to $30.

1970 Trifari Jonathan Bailey "Sculpturesque" advertisement. This advertisement showcases unique jewelry designed especially for Trifari by designer Jonathan Bailey. The advertisement reads, "Premiere! Designer Jonathan Bailey's first and exclusive Trifari creations. Dramatic. Provocative. Important. From a collection. About $7.50 to $30."

1970 "The Diane Love collection for Trifari" advertisement. This advertisement features a portrait of jewelry designer Diane Love wearing a collar, earrings, and rings from her Diane Love for Trifari collection. The designs are described as "authentic replicas of ancient art objects, embellished with exquisite contemporary design."

THE DIANE LOVE COLLECTION FOR TRIFARI

A NEW ART CONCEPT IN JEWELRY.
Authentic replicas of ancient art objects, embellished with exquisite contemporary design. Diane Love photographed at home, wears a collar, earrings, and rings from this magnificent collection by Trifari.

TRIFARI JEWELRY

239

# CHAPTER 4

# OTHER *Jewelry Makers*

• • • • • • • • • • • • • • • • • • •

(LISTED ALPHABETICALLY)

## • ACCESSOCRAFT •

### APPROXIMATELY 1930 – 1998

| Design Patent Number | Date Issued | Designer | Jewelry Type | Brief Description |
|---|---|---|---|---|
| 124279 | 12/24/1940 | Theodore Steinman | Brooch | Eagle |
| 128833 | 8/12/1941 | Theodore Steinman | Brooch | Scroll |
| 128834 | 8/12/1941 | Theodore Steinman | Brooch | Patriotic |

**1948 – 1955 Accessocraft Art Nouveau pendant.** This fascinating 2¼" Art Nouveau face pendant (no chain) is signed "Accessocraft" without the copyright symbol. This signature and the nonuse of sterling date this piece to 1948 – 1955. $45.00 – 60.00. From the collection of Debi Reece.

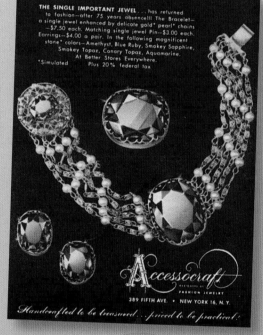

124279

1952 Accessocraft "The Single Important Jewel" advertisement. The advertising slogan for Accessocraft was "Handcrafted to be treasured…priced to be practical!" The advertisement reads, "THE SINGLE IMPORTANT JEWEL…has returned to fashion — after 75 years absence!!! The bracelet — a single jewel enhanced by delicate gold* pearl* chains — $7.50 each. Matching single jewel Pin — $3.00 each. Earrings — $4.00 pair. In the following magnificent stone* colors — Amethyst, Blue Ruby, Smokey Sapphire, Smokey Topaz, Canary Topaz, Aquamarine… *Simulated."

1946 – Unknown

by *Am Lee*
*Sterling Silver*

**1954 Am Lee necklace and earrings set in original box.** This 15½" choker necklace and 1" clip earrings feature a filigree design set in sterling silver. All three pieces in this set are signed only "Sterling," so it is fortunate they are sill in the original Am Lee presentation box. This beautiful Am Lee jewelry set is similar to the Am Lee "Florentine Fantasy" jewelry advertised in the 1954 *Jewelers' Buyers Guide*. The 1954 advertisement reads, "The ancient art of hand made filigree jewelry is reborn under the skilled perfection of the Am-Lee craftsmen." $25.00 – 35.00.

Fig.2

Fig.3

1954 Am Lee "Florentine Fantasy" advertisement. This advertisement features sterling silver filigree jewelry resting in a 1954 Am Lee presentation box. The advertisement reads, "The ancient art of hand made filigree jewelry is reborn under the skilled perfection of the Am-Lee craftsmen. A complete line of outstanding styles designed by Am-Lee awaits your inspection. Our sterling silver jewelry has been imitated but never equaled."

*Florentine Fantasy*

HAND MADE BY *Am Lee*

by *Am Lee*
*Sterling Silver*

The ancient art of hand made filigree jewelry is reborn under the skilled perfection of the Am-Lee craftsmen.

A complete line of outstanding styles designed by Am-Lee awaits your inspection.

Our sterling silver jewelry has been imitated but never equaled.

Sold through wholesalers only.

*Am Lee* JEWELRY COMPANY, INC.
80-82 CLIFFORD STREET
PROVIDENCE 3, R. I.

OTHER JEWELRY MAKERS

241

## UNKNOWN, APPROXIMATELY 1955 – 1970s

Art jewelry often reflects classic styles, so narrowing the range when one piece of Art jewelry could have been produced is difficult. I have never seen a piece of signed Art jewelry without a copyright symbol, so it is likely Art jewelry was produced after 1955. For the jewelry featured in this book, any narrowing of the 1955 – 1970s range is a subjective change based on the style of the piece.

**1955 – early 1960s green Bakelite comma bracelet.** It is difficult to assign an accurate date to jewelry marked "ART" because very little is known about the maker. Yet, many Art designs are high-quality and well worth collecting. For dating purposes, each piece must be evaluated by the style of the design, the condition of the jewelry, and the use of materials. The comma-shaped stones in this magnificent and rare 7½" Art bracelet are made of green swirl Bakelite. The bracelet is signed "ART" with the copyright symbol. The presence of the copyright symbol, the design of the bracelet, and the use of materials helps to date this piece to 1955 – early 1960s. Note the exceptional design of this bracelet, including the way the lavender rhinestones compliment the olive green Bakelite swirls. $100.00 – 125.00. From the collection of Debi Reece.

**1955 – 1960s expressive red-belly parrot brooch by Art.** This colorful 3¼" x 1" Art parrot pin is signed "ART" with the copyright symbol and dates to 1955 – 1970. Note the interesting red cabochon belly and golden topaz-colored rhinestone eyes. This open-mouthed parrot pin is a splendid example of the exceptionally fine figural jewelry produced by Art. $45.00 – 60.00.

**1955 – 1960s Art deep red rhinestone neck-lace, bracelet, and earrings set.** Each piece of this beautiful parure is signed "ART" with the copyright symbol. The set features intensely red navette rhinestones set in brushed gold-tone metal. The choker necklace measures 15½", the bracelet is 7", and the clip earrings are 1¼". $45.00 – 70.00.

**1955 – 1970s Art snake bracelet, ear-rings, and brooch.** There are several ver-sions of signed "ART" snake motif jew-elry. Some of it is gold-tone like the 1" coiled snake pin in the photograph (said to be a symbol of everlasting love). Other designs, like the 7½" bracelet and 1" earrings in the photograph, are done in antique white enamel. Art jewelry was produced from 1955 through the 1970s, dating this Art snake jewelry to that time. $55.00 – 75.00.

**1960s unusual beaded brooch and earrings set by Art.** This large 3" x 2" brooch signed "ART" and matching 1¼" clip earrings feature irregularly shaped plastic beads slipped over metal wires. The beads vary in color from bright green to brown and vary in size from ¼" to ¾". This set is signed "ART" with the copyright symbol and dates to the 1960s, when unusual beads were popular. $25.00 – 35.00.

OTHER JEWELRY MAKERS

**Mid 1960s Art fleur-de-lis brooch and earrings set.** This delicate 2" x 1½" fleur-de-lis brooch and the matching ¾" clip earrings are coated with tiny seed pearls. The set is signed "ART" with the copyright symbol. The fleur-de-lis (at one time the coat of arms for the French royal family) is the trademark of Trifari jewelry, so it is interesting that Art decided to produce jewelry in this shape. In the 1964 "Trifari Christmas Collection" advertisement (shown on page 232), Trifari advertises a similar pearl-covered fleur-de-lis brooch. This Art set also dates from that era. $25.00 – 35.00.

**1976 – 1979 Art Egyptian-style necklace and earrings set.** The above Egyptian-style 15" collar necklace is spectacular looking when worn. The 1½" fan-shaped earrings are clips. All pieces are signed "ART" with the copyright symbol. Egyptian styles have inspired jewelry designers since the 1930s, with the 1934 release of the movie *Cleopatra*. Additional Egyptian-style jewelry was produced in 1963 to coincide with the release of Elizabeth Taylor's *Cleopatra*. However, much of the Egyptian-motif jewelry in the collectibles market today, particularly a new-looking set like the one above, was produced from 1976 to 1979 to commemorate the King Tut exhibit that was touring the U.S. at that time. $65.00 – 95.00.

## 1971 – PRESENT

**1986 – 1995 Kenneth J. Lane for Avon necklace and bracelet set.** Massive and heavy, this huge 17" necklace is signed "K.J.L. for Avon" and features red, blue, green, and purple stones set in heavy gold-tone metal. Interestingly, the 9" toggle bracelet is only signed "Avon." Kenneth J. Lane created designs for Avon from 1986 to 1995. $35.00 – 50.00.

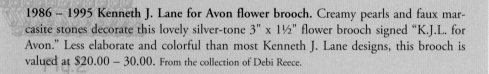

**1986 – 1995 Kenneth J. Lane for Avon flower brooch.** Creamy pearls and faux marcasite stones decorate this lovely silver-tone 3" x 1½" flower brooch signed "K.J.L. for Avon." Less elaborate and colorful than most Kenneth J. Lane designs, this brooch is valued at $20.00 – 30.00. From the collection of Debi Reece.

**1986 – 1995 Kenneth J. Lane for Avon pink flower earrings.** Kenneth J. Lane created many extraordinary designs for Avon from 1986 to 1995. These signed "KJL for Avon" earrings date from that era. The 1¼" pink flower earrings are a good example of high-quality Avon designs created by this master designer. $20.00 – 30.00.

OTHER JEWELRY MAKERS

**1987 Celia Sebiri–designed Avon pin.** This unusual 2" x 1½" egg-shaped pin features a creamy pink stone surrounded by two coordinating colors of enamel. It is signed "CS for Avon." "CS" represents Celia Sebiri, who designed for Avon in 1987. $15.00 – 25.00.

**1989 – 1996 Barerra for Avon brooch and earrings set.** This royal-looking huge 3" x 2¼" fleur-de-lis brooch and the matching 2½" x 1¼" clip earrings are signed "Barerra for Avon." José Maria Barrera designed for Avon from 1989 to 1996. $45.00 – 65.00.

**1989 – 1996 Barrera for Avon necklace and earrings set.** This lovely lavender and pink 20" triple-strand necklace and matching 2" clip earrings are signed "Barrera for Avon." José Maria Barrera created designs for Avon from 1989 – 1996, dating this lovely set to that era. $35.00 – 50.00.

**1989 – 1996 Barerra for Avon pearl drop earrings.** Signed "Barerra for Avon," these 2½" x 1¼" pearl and purple rhinestone earrings were designed by José Maria Barrera, who created jewelry designs for Avon from 1989 to 1996. $15.00 – 20.00.

**1993 Elizabeth Taylor for Avon Egyptian-theme ring.** Signed "Elizabeth Taylor for Avon," this beautiful Egyptian motif ring features a large amethyst teardrop-shaped rhinestone outlined by turquoise seed pearls. Elizabeth Taylor for Avon jewelry was produced from 1993 to 1997. This size six ring is part of Elizabeth Taylor's 1993 Egyptian Collection. $45.00 – 60.00.

**2000 Avon decorative Christmas tree pin.** It is easy to date this snowy 2" x 1¼" Avon Christmas tree pin, because it was found in its original presentation box. The bottom of the box is marked "@2000 Avon." The pin is signed "Avon" with the copyright symbol. $25.00 – 35.00.

OTHER JEWELRY MAKERS

# • B. DAVID •

## 1945 – 1993

**1948 – 1955 B. David brooch and earrings set.** B. David produced jewelry like this lovely 1½" brooch and ¾" clip earrings from 1945 through 1993. These pieces are signed "B. David" without the copyright symbol. B. David jewelry is usually pretty, delicate, and well crafted. This wonderful set is in mint condition and, amazingly, is still attached to its original pink velveteen display card. The signature and use of materials indicate this set dates to 1948 – 1955. $45.00 – 65.00. From the collection of Debi Reece.

# • BARCLAY •

## 1946 – 1957

**Early 1950s Barclay pseudo-moonstone bird and earrings set.** Jewelry signed "Barclay" (not McClelland Barclay) was produced from 1946 to 1957 for the Rice-Weiner Co. This adorable 1½" x ¾" bird pin and matching ¾" clip earrings feature pseudo-moonstones set in gold-tone metal. The set is signed "Barclay" without the copyright symbol. The Trifari 1950 "For a Jewel of a Mother" advertisement shown on page 182 features pseudo-moonstone jewelry, dating this Barclay set to the same era. $65.00 – 85.00.

Fig.1

Fig.2

**Early 1950s Barclay heart-shaped poured-glass necklace and earrings set.** Signed "Barclay" without the copyright symbol, this rare and lovely poured-glass necklace features heart-shaped translucent green glass that seems to glow with an inner fire. The necklace measures 16", and each screw-back earring is 1". Note the poured-glass decoration at the end of the adjustable extension chain. This detail is an indication of a quality piece. Trifari produced poured glass jewelry in 1952 (see the 1952 Trifari "Mothers of Every Age" advertisement on page 194), dating this poured-glass Barclay set to the same era. $100.00 – 125.00. From the collection of Debi Reece.

**1948 – 1955 Barclay rectangular brooch and earrings set.** This 2" x ¾" brooch and the 1" clip earrings are signed "Barclay" without the copyright symbol. This signature and the nonuse of sterling date this set to 1948 – 1955. Note the varying sizes and shapes of light blue rhinestones artistically arranged in the "antiqued" silver-tone settings. $45.00 – 55.00. From the collection of Debi Reece.

OTHER JEWELRY MAKERS

## 1935 – 1943

**Early 1940s McClelland Barclay brooch.** This interesting 2" brooch is a classic McClelland Barclay design. It is signed "McClelland Barclay" in script. (Note: Jewelry signed "Barclay" in script is not McClelland Barclay jewelry and does not have the same high value as McClelland Barclay designs.) McClelland Barclay was a famous graphic artist in the 1930s and 1940s until his death in 1943. The Rice-Weiner company produced McClelland Barclay jewelry from 1938 to 1943. Unfortunately, McClelland Barclay was killed in World War II. His importance in the world of graphic art, the beauty and rarity of his jewelry, and his untimely death all contribute to the high value placed on McClelland Barclay jewelry today. $100.00 – 175.00.

## • BEAU JEWELS •

## 1950s – 1970s

**1955 – 1970s Beau Jewels blue rhinestones flower brooch and earrings.** The 1¾" clip earrings in this beautiful blue set are signed "Beau Jewels" without the copyright symbol. The 2½" x 2" triple-flower brooch is unsigned. (Note: In most cases, Beau Jewels signed only the earrings.) The rhinestone center stones have the aurora borealis coating, which indicates this lightweight set was produced after 1955. $65.00 – 85.00.

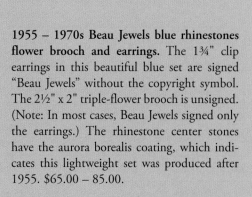

**1955 – 1970s Beau Jewels red art-glass brooch and earrings set.** The aurora borealis red rhinestones decorating this splendid 2¼" brooch and 1½" earrings set indicate this Beau Jewels set was produced after 1955. Only the earrings are signed "Beau Jewels." Note the interesting teardrop-shaped rhinestones with carved starburst centers. $65.00 – 85.00. From the collection of Debi Reece.

# • BEN REIG •

## 1950s – 1970s

**1950s – 1960s Ben Reig pearl and rhinestone earrings.** Ben Reig produced beautiful women's fashions for decades. The firm, founded in 1929, was still operating in the 1960s. Famous fashion designer Omar Kiam designed for Ben Reig in the early years. In the 1960s, Eva Rosencrans worked for Ben Reig. Jewelry signed "BENREIG" in caps, like these 1½" clip earrings, is extraordinarily rare. The design and style of these earrings indicate they date to the 1950s or 1960s. The earrings are marked "BENREIG" and "Pat. Pend.," but I was unable to locate a matching patent. It is difficult to place an accurate value on these rare earrings. Best guess: $100.00 – 150.00. From the collection of Debi Reece.

## 1946 – 1979

**1957 Bergère faux baroque pearl earrings.** These ¾"
Bergère earrings are similar in style to the earrings featured
in the 1957 "Freshwater Baroque" Bergère advertisement
shown on this page and likely date from the same time
period. They are signed "Bergère." $15.00 – 25.00.

1957 Bergère "Freshwater
Baroque" advertisement. This
advertisement features several dif-
ferent pieces of jewelry decorated
with faux baroque pearls. The
advertisement reads, "Freshwater
Baroque…rimmed with fake dia-
monds and old golden settings.
Single dangle bracelet, 4.00.
Four-baroque bracelet, 12.50.
Triple dangle bracelet, 7.50.
Button earrings, 6.00."

OTHER JEWELRY MAKERS

1958 Bergère "the News in Jewelry" advertisement. This advertisement features beautiful beads imported from France. The advertisement reads, "Sculptured Beads from France... Magnifique! Carved white perfection, some encased in golden cages, others pure and simple. Wonderful colors too, matrix blue, lush pink, china jade, sea coral. Beads in golden cages: necklace, 12.50; bracelet, 6.00; Earrings, 4.00. Pure and simple: necklace, 6.00; bracelet, 4.00. Button or drop earrings, 2.00; all plus tax."

**1970s multicolor Bergère rhinestone necklace, bracelet, and earrings set.** Only the earrings in this set are signed "Bergère" in script without a copyright symbol. Multicolor rhinestone-encrusted jewelry, like the above Bergère set, is similar in style to the 1970s Sarah Coventry Shangri-La set shown later in this chapter and dates to the same era. In this instance, the new look of the jewelry is more important for dating purposes than the lack of a copyright symbol in the signatures. The 3" pendant is suspended from a 26" chain. The oval cuff bracelet does not have a clasp. It is held to the wrist by the tightness of the hinge mechanism. The clip earrings measure ¾". $45.00 – 65.00.

## 1940 – UNKNOWN

**Early 1940s long-stemmed enamel Fred Block floral brooch.** More of an enameled corsage than a brooch, this Fred Block masterpiece measures 4½" x 3½". Each enameled flower is a separate piece; they are gathered together to form the bouquet. The gathered stems are wrapped with brass wire to secure the bouquet. Green, prong-set rhinestones are attached in clusters to wires and gathered with the enameled flowers to form the elaborate design. It is signed "Fred A. Block." Fred Block jewelry is highly collectible and rare. The style of the brooch, with the gathering of long stems into a bouquet, and the nonuse of sterling date this brooch to the early 1940s. $100.00 – 150.00.

**1943 – 1948 Fred Block sterling silver starburst brooch.** Marked "Sterling" and "Block," this dynamic sunburst brooch was produced by Fred A. Block Jewelry. The use of sterling dates this three-dimensional brooch to 1943 to 1948. Fred Block jewelry is extraordinarily rare, especially lovely examples like this 2½" diameter sterling brooch. $100.00 – 150.00. From the collection of Debi Reece.

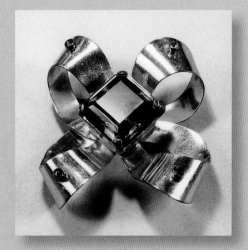

**Late 1940s Fred Block ribbon brooch.** Ribbon brooches like this 3" gold-tone and amethyst brooch were popular in the late 1940s. This rare piece is signed "Fred A. Block" and features a large ¾" square-cut amethyst rhinestone. $85.00 – 100.00. From the collection of Debi Reece.

1896 – 1943

**1948 – 1955 BN (Bugbee & Niles) brooch/pendant and earrings set.** This beautiful set is signed "BN" without the copyright symbol and rests in its original Bugbee & Niles presentation box. This lovely flower pin can be worn either as a brooch or as a pendant. Amazingly, the chain remains in the box. The 2¼" brooch and 1" screw-back earrings feature lavender rhinestones prong set in silver-tone metal. This set originally sold for $12.50. Bugbee & Niles Co. was located in North Attleboro, Mass. The warranty paper reads, "Established in 1859, Bugbee and Niles has maintained the highest standards in the true tradition of the Jewelers' craft. No paste or glue is used in our Jewelry and all stones are pronged in individual settings. This Warranty guarantees our Jewelry for a period of one year against any manufacturing defects." Bugbee & Niles is listed in the 1954 *Jewelers' Buyers Guide* so the company was still operating at that time. The signature without a copyright symbol and the nonuse of sterling date this jewelry to 1948 – 1955. $20.00 – 25.00.

OTHER JEWELRY MAKERS

## 1946 – ABOUT 1959

| Design Patent Number | Date Issued | Designer | Jewelry Type | Brief Description |
|---|---|---|---|---|
| 148277 | 1/6/1948 | Herman Bogoff | Brooch | Stylized bow |
| 148278 | 1/6/1948 | Herman Bogoff | Earring | Abstract |
| 148279 | 1/6/1948 | Herman Bogoff | Earring | Horseshoe shape |
| 148280 | 1/6/1948 | Herman Bogoff | Earring | Rhinestone heart |
| 148406 | 1/20/1948 | Herman Bogoff | Earring | crescent |
| 151868 | 11/30/1948 | Henry Bogoff | Brooch | Long-stemmed floral |
| 151958 | 12/7/1948 | Herman Bogoff | Necklace | Rhinestones with seven rhinestone drops |
| 152669 | 2/15/1949 | Henry Bogoff | Brooch | Long-stemmed floral |
| 153204 | 3/29/1949 | Herman Bogoff | Necklace | Three dangles |
| 155121 | 9/13/1949 | Henry Bogoff | Brooch | Floral |
| 155122 | 9/13/1949 | Henry Bogoff | Brooch | Floral |
| 156312 | 12/6/1949 | Herman Bogoff | Earring | Abstract |
| 159777 | 8/22/1950 | Herman Bogoff | Brooch | Abstract floral |
| 159778 | 8/22/1950 | Herman Bogoff | Brooch | Abstract floral |

148277

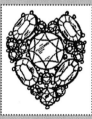

148280

**1940s Bogoff rhinestone heart-shaped necklace.** The patent for earrings to match this beautiful Bogoff heart-shaped rhinestone necklace is design patent number 148280 issued January 6, 1940, to Herman Bogoff for Bogoff. The patent number for the lovely 15" necklace was not found. Interestingly, this 1940s necklace features rhodium plating. Rhodium plating was available before the war, but not widely used for jewelry before 1948. Either this necklace is an exception to this dating jewelry guideline, or a later remake (post 1948) of the earlier design. It is signed "Bogoff" without the copyright symbol. $100.00 – 125.00.

OTHER JEWELRY MAKERS

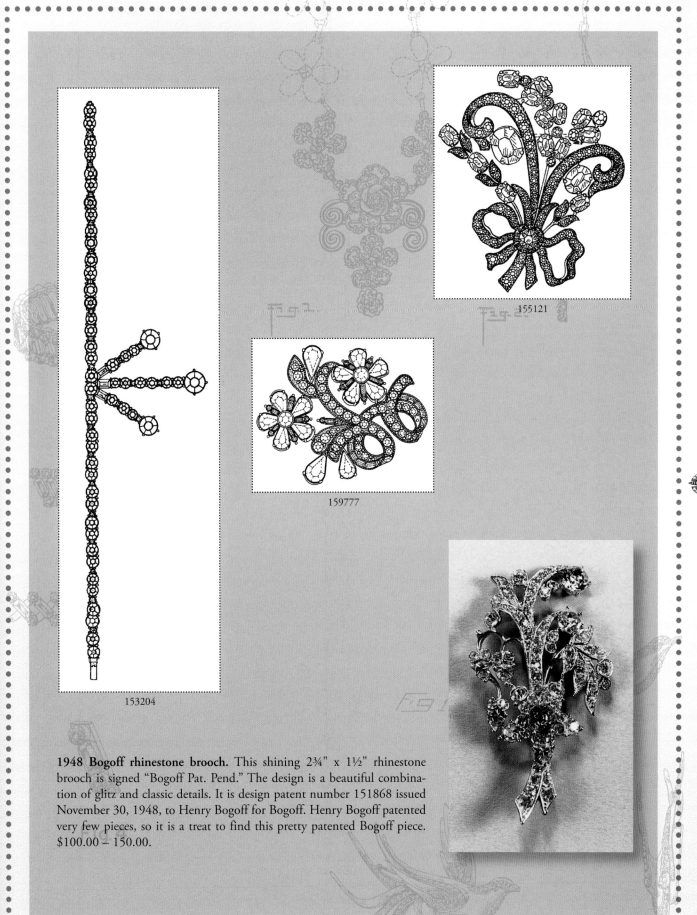

155121

159777

153204

**1948 Bogoff rhinestone brooch.** This shining 2¾" x 1½" rhinestone brooch is signed "Bogoff Pat. Pend." The design is a beautiful combination of glitz and classic details. It is design patent number 151868 issued November 30, 1948, to Henry Bogoff for Bogoff. Henry Bogoff patented very few pieces, so it is a treat to find this pretty patented Bogoff piece. $100.00 – 150.00.

**1948 – 1955 Bogoff sapphire blue rhinestone necklace and earrings.** The style of this sensational 15" Bogoff sapphire blue baguette rhinestones necklace and ¾" matching earrings is reminiscent of Marcel Boucher jewelry produced in the late 1940s or early 1950s and dates to that era. The necklace and earrings are signed "Bogoff" without the copyright symbol. Bogoff jewelry is renowned for its beautiful, well-executed designs. Note the exquisitely finished look of the clasp and the beautifully detailed design of the necklace. $125.00 – 175.00. From the collection of Debi Reece.

**1948 – 1955 Bogoff colorful pastel rhinestone basket pin.** This large and extraordinarily lovely pink Bogoff basket pin measures 2" x 2¼". Notice the attractive combination of differently shaped rhinestones, varying shades of pastel color, and the pretty pink basket-weave design. This brooch is signed "Bogoff Pat. Pend." No patent was found for this piece; however, the signature and use of materials dates this brooch to 1948 – 1955. $100.00 – 135.00.

**1953 Bogoff pearl and rhinestone necklace and earrings set.** Beautiful and delicate, this 15" pearl and aqua rhinestone necklace and ¾" clip earrings are signed "Bogoff" without the copyright symbol. The set is similar in style to the Sea Spray Bogoff design shown in the 1953 Bogoff "Sea spray" advertisement and dates from that era. In 1953 Bogoff necklaces sold for between $7.00 and $10.00. Earrings sold for $3.00 or $4.00 a pair. Today's value for this charming set is $95.00 – 125.00. From the collection of Debi Reece.

1953 Bogoff "Sea spray" advertisement. This black and white advertisement features beautiful Bogoff pearl and rhinestone jewelry. The advertisement reads "Sea spray Iridescence of pearls…radiance of diamonds…magnificence of original design… Sea Spray, so exquisitely beautiful in rhinestones and simulated pearls…so distinctively Bogoff." The advertising slogan for Bogoff was "Jewels by Bogoff." The necklace in the advertisement sold for $7.50 – 10.00, bracelet or pin for $7.50, earrings for $3.00 – 4.00.

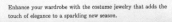

1956 Premiere Bogoff advertisement. I wonder if the man lighting a cigarette shown in the right hand corner of this advertisement is Henry Bogoff? The ad does not say. It reads, "A glittering new season ahead for you…A world of luxurious brilliance created in Premiere…the dramatic, new Jewels by BOGOFF." The necklaces sold for $7.50 and $16.00, the bracelets for $6.00 – 12.00, and the earrings for $3.00 – 7.00. Notice that in 1956, Bogoff was offering adjustable-length necklace designs.

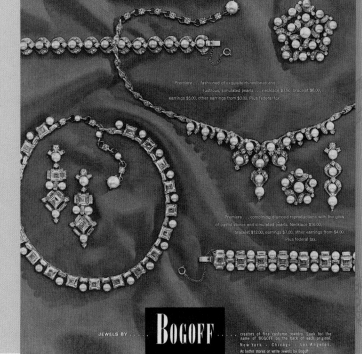

## 1937 – 1971

| Design Patent Number | Date Issued | Designer | Jewelry Type | Brief Description |
|---|---|---|---|---|
| 103385 | 3/2/1937 | Marcel Boucher | Brooch | Center flower with two carved leaves |
| 109292 | 4/19/1938 | Marcel Boucher | Brooch | Military signal man |
| 116472 | 9/5/1939 | Marcel Boucher | Brooch | Bow with pearl center |
| 116473 | 9/5/1939 | Marcel Boucher | Brooch | Bow, studded rhinestones |
| 119649 | 3/26/1940 | Marcel Boucher | Brooch | "Punchinello" moveable arms and legs |
| 120027 | 4/16/1940 | Marcel Boucher | Brooch | Dancing Oriental figure |
| 120539 | 5/14/1940 | Marcel Boucher | Pin | Bird |
| 120540 | 5/14/1940 | Marcel Boucher | Pin | Two birds |
| 120611 | 5/21/1940 | Marcel Boucher | Pin | Bow |
| 120612 | 5/21/1940 | Marcel Boucher | Pin | Bow |
| 126621 | 4/15/1941 | Marcel Boucher | Brooch | Stylized letter "B" |
| 126900 | 4/29/1941 | Marcel Boucher | Brooch | Praying mantis |
| 126901 | 4/29/1941 | Marcel Boucher | Brooch | Mexican man sleeping under cactus |
| 126902 | 4/29/1941 | Marcel Boucher | Brooch | Mexican man sleeping in donkey cart |
| 126903 | 4/29/1941 | Marcel Boucher | Brooch | Dragonfly |
| 126944 | 4/29/1941 | Marcel Boucher | Brooch | Oriental dragon |
| 127014 | 5/6/1941 | Marcel Boucher | Brooch | Floral |
| 127015 | 5/6/1941 | Marcel Boucher | Brooch | Grasshopper on branch |
| 128104 | 7/8/1941 | Marcel Boucher | Brooch | Corn |
| 128324 | 7/15/1941 | Marcel Boucher | Brooch | Pineapple |
| 129842 | 10/7/1941 | Marcel Boucher | Brooch | Bird |
| 129843 | 10/7/1941 | Marcel Boucher | Brooch | Bird |
| 131415 | 2/17/1942 | Marcel Boucher | Brooch | Male Russian dancer |
| 131416 | 2/17/1942 | Marcel Boucher | Brooch | Sailor |
| 131798 | 3/31/1942 | Marcel Boucher | Brooch | Hand holding torch |
| 139674 | 12/12/1944 | Marcel Boucher | Brooch | Fish |
| 139675 | 12/12/1944 | Marcel Boucher | Brooch | Ice skater |
| 139676 | 12/12/1944 | Marcel Boucher | Brooch | Ballerina |
| 139677 | 12/12/1944 | Marcel Boucher | Brooch | Ballerina |
| 139678 | 12/12/1944 | Marcel Boucher | Earring | Ice skater |

119649

120539

120611

126621

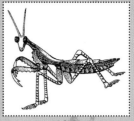

126900

128104

129842

131415

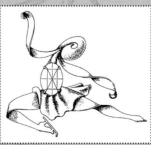

139675

**1940 Boucher blue enamel and rhinestone bird brooch.** Marcel Boucher is responsible for creating some of the most magnificent bird brooches ever produced. This beautiful blue bird of paradise 3¾" x 2" brooch is an excellent example of 1940s Boucher jewelry. The back is signed "MB" (the older Phrygian cap mark). It is not sterling. The letter "H" is also stamped into the metal, most likely the mark of the craftsperson who worked on the piece. The style of this spectacular and rare bird matches design patent number 120539 issued May 14, 1940, to Marcel Boucher for Boucher. $500.00 – 750.00.

OTHER JEWELRY MAKERS

261

| Design Patent Number | Date Issued | Designer | Jewelry Type | Brief Description |
|---|---|---|---|---|
| 145054 | 6/25/1946 | Marcel Boucher | Earring | Butterfly |
| 145055 | 6/25/1946 | Marcel Boucher | Brooch | Butterfly |
| 145056 | 6/25/1946 | Marcel Boucher | Brooch | Pinwheel |
| 145057 | 6/25/1946 | Marcel Boucher | Brooch | Ribbon with dangle |
| 145058 | 6/25/1946 | Marcel Boucher | Brooch | Stylized ribbon |
| 145151 | 7/9/1946 | Marcel Boucher | Brooch | Abstract |
| 145152 | 7/9/1946 | Marcel Boucher | Brooch | Abstract |
| 145561 | 9/10/1946 | Marcel Boucher | Brooch | Abstract |
| 146276 | 1/28/1947 | Marcel Boucher | Brooch | Bow |
| 147394 | 9/2/1947 | Marcel Boucher | Brooch | Shell |
| 147395 | 9/2/1947 | Marcel Boucher | Earring | Bow with dangles (See 147830 for matching brooch.) |
| 147396 | 9/2/1947 | Marcel Boucher | Brooch | Stylized floral leaf with arrow-shaped dangles |
| 147397 | 9/2/1947 | Marcel Boucher | Brooch | Abstract floral with arrow-shaped dangles |
| 147398 | 9/2/1947 | Marcel Boucher | Brooch | Abstract floral with arrow-shaped dangles |
| 147399 | 9/2/1947 | Marcel Boucher | Brooch | Figural man with turban |
| 147525 | 9/23/1947 | Marcel Boucher | Brooch | Bow |
| 147830 | 11/11/1947 | Marcel Boucher | Brooch | Bow with dangles (See 147395 for matching earring.) |
| 147887 | 11/18/1947 | Marcel Boucher | Brooch | Bow with dangles |
| 147951 | 11/25/1947 | Marcel Boucher | Brooch | Figural man |
| 147952 | 11/25/1947 | Marcel Boucher | Brooch | Figural woman |
| 147953 | 11/25/1947 | Marcel Boucher | Brooch | Antebellum woman |
| 147954 | 11/25/1947 | Marcel Boucher | Brooch | Mexican man |
| 148672 | 2/17/1948 | Marcel Boucher | Brooch | Ribbon with dangles |

145055

145151

147399

147830

| 148751 | 2/24/1948 | Marcel Boucher | Brooch | Elephant with wings |
| 150546 | 8/17/1948 | Marcel Boucher | Earring | Triple circle |
| 151029 | 9/21/1948 | Marcel Boucher | Brooch | Blooming brooch (See 151493 for similar brooch.) |
| 151490 | 10/26/1948 | Marcel Boucher | Brooch | Blooming long-stemmed flower (See 151029 for similar brooch.) |
| 151491 | 10/26/1948 | Marcel Boucher | Brooch | Blooming flower on bouquet (See 151490 for similar brooch.) |
| 151492 | 10/26/1948 | Marcel Boucher | Brooch | Blooming long-stemmed flower, plain leaves |

148751

151492

151500

**1948 Boucher Day and Night brooch.** This unique 2¾" x 2" gold-tone flower pin has petals that open and close. It is signed with the older Boucher (Phrygian cap) "MB" mark used by Boucher from 1937 to 1949, inventory number 2649, and "Pat. Pend." Design patent number 151492 was issued October 26, 1948, to Marcel Boucher for this piece, which dates this unique brooch to that year. $125.00 – 225.00.

Closed view of the 1948 Boucher Day and Night flower pin.

| | | | | |
|---|---|---|---|---|
| 151493 | 10/26/1948 | Marcel Boucher | Brooch | Blooming long-stemmed flower, no leaves (See 151492 for similar brooch.) |
| 151494 | 10/26/1948 | Marcel Boucher | Brooch | Stylized ribbon with two dangles |
| 151495 | 10/26/1948 | Marcel Boucher | Brooch | Abstract bow |
| 151496 | 10/26/1948 | Marcel Boucher | Brooch | Five-loop bow |
| 151497 | 10/26/1948 | Marcel Boucher | Brooch | Royal-looking bow |
| 151498 | 10/26/1948 | Marcel Boucher | Brooch | Stylized bow |
| 151499 | 10/26/1948 | Marcel Boucher | Necklace | Six lacy slides |
| 151500 | 10/26/1948 | Marcel Boucher | Brooch | Bird on branch |
| 151501 | 10/26/1948 | Marcel Boucher | Brooch | Abstract |
| 151502 | 10/26/1948 | Marcel Boucher | Brooch | Abstract |
| 151503 | 10/26/1948 | Marcel Boucher | Brooch | Squirrel with nut |
| 151504 | 10/26/1948 | Marcel Boucher | Brooch | Poodle |
| 151505 | 10/26/1948 | Marcel Boucher | Brooch | Abstract |
| 151734 | 11/16/1948 | Marcel Boucher | Brooch | Abstract with two dangles |
| 151735 | 11/16/1948 | Marcel Boucher | Brooch | Abstract |
| 151808 | 11/23/1948 | Marcel Boucher | Earring | Circular floral |
| 154095 | 6/14/1949 | Marcel Boucher | Brooch | Ballerina |
| 154096 | 6/14/1949 | Marcel Boucher | Brooch | Male ballet dancer |
| 155681 | 10/25/1949 | Marcel Boucher | Brooch | Ribbed disk with top decoration |
| 155682 | 10/25/1949 | Marcel Boucher | Brooch | Ribbed disk with top decoration |
| 158925 | 6/13/1950 | Marcel Boucher | Brooch | Safety pin (See 159588 for another safety pin design.) |
| 158926 | 6/13/1950 | Marcel Boucher | Earring | Abstract shell shape |
| 159582 | 8/8/1950 | Marcel Boucher | Brooch | Kneeling ballet dancer clown |
| 159583 | 8/8/1950 | Marcel Boucher | Brooch | Ballerina |
| 159584 | 8/8/1950 | Marcel Boucher | Brooch | Male ballet dancer |
| 159585 | 8/8/1950 | Marcel Boucher | Brooch | Male ballet dancer |
| 159586 | 8/8/1950 | Marcel Boucher | Brooch | Female ballet dancer |
| 159587 | 8/8/1950 | Marcel Boucher | Brooch Watchcase | Bow dangling round case |
| 159588 | 8/8/1950 | Marcel Boucher | Brooch Watchcase | Safety pin dangling round case (See 158925 for another safety pin style.) |
| 159589 | 8/8/1950 | Marcel Boucher | Brooch | Abstract twisted staff (See 159590 for a similar design.) |

151503

151504

154095

155681

**Two mid-1950s Boucher circle pins.** Both of these pins are similar in design to design patent number 155681 issued October 25, 1949, to Marcel Boucher. Boucher produced many variations of these circle pins over several years. Both pins measure 1¼" in diameter. The left pin is decorated with ruby red baguette rhinestones and clear rhinestones set in silver-tone leaves. It is signed "Boucher" with the copyright symbol and design number 5466, indicating this piece was made after 1955. The right pin features ribbed gold-tone vines enhanced by three clear rhinestone flowers. It is signed "Boucher" with the copyright symbol but without an item number. (Most Boucher jewelry produced after 1945 includes a four-digit item number. See page 11 for more about Boucher inventory numbers.) This pin has a loop so it can also be worn as a pendant. $45.00 – 65.00 each.

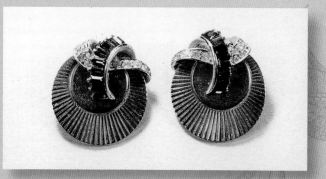

**Mid-1950s Boucher circle-motif earrings.** These 1" earrings are signed "Boucher" with the copyright symbol, indicating they were made after 1955. This classic Boucher circle motif, with variations, was produced from 1949, when the first patent was issued for this style of pin, until 1955, when the copyright was added to the signature, or after. $30.00 – 45.00.

OTHER JEWELRY MAKERS

OTHER JEWELRY MAKERS

| | | | | |
|---|---|---|---|---|
| 159590 | 8/8/1950 | Marcel Boucher | Brooch | Abstract twisted staff (See 159685 for a similar design.) |
| 159591 | 8/8/1950 | Marcel Boucher | Brooch | Long-stemmed floral (See 159594 for matching earrings.) |
| 159592 | 8/8/1950 | Marcel Boucher | Earring | Abstract twist |
| 159594 | 8/8/1950 | Marcel Boucher | Earring | Floral (See 159591 for matching brooch.) |
| 159685 | 8/8/1950 | Raymonde Semensohn | Brooch | Abstract staff (See 159589 for a similar design.) |
| 160361 | 10/10/1950 | Marcel Boucher | Earring | Star over-the-ear style |
| 161238 | 12/19/1950 | Marcel Boucher | Brooch | Abstract |
| 161239 | 12/19/1950 | Marccl Boucher | Earring | Over-the-ear Earrite style (See 160361 for another Earrite style.) |
| 161240 | 12/19/1950 | Marcel Boucher | Brooch | Lattice rose advertised as "Rose of Seville" and originally sold for $25.00 (See 161241 for matching earring.) |
| 161241 | 12/19/1950 | Marcel Boucher | Earring | Lattice rose advertised as "Rose of Seville" and originally sold for $15.00 (See 161240 for matching brooch.) |
| 161286 | 12/19/1950 | Raymonde Semensohn | Earring | Over-the-ear Earrite style (See 161239 for another Earrite style.) |
| 161287 | 12/19/1950 | Raymonde Semensohn | Brooch | Abstract |
| 161288 | 12/19/1950 | Raymonde Semensohn | Earring | Over-the-ear Earrite style (See 161286 for another Earrite style.) |
| 161289 | 12/19/1950 | Raymonde Semensohn | Earring | Over-the-ear Earrite style originally sold for $17.00 (See 161283 for another "Earrite" style.) |
| 161415 | 1/2/1951 | Marcel Boucher | Brooch | Curling ribbons of rhinestones |
| 161566 | 1/19/1951 | Marcel Boucher | Bracelet | Cuff with shooting stars |
| 161567 | 1/9/1951 | Marcel Boucher | Necklace | Faux collar with bow center |
| 169458 | 4/28/1953 | Raymonde Semensohn | Brooch | Abstract |
| 169459 | 4/28/1953 | Raymonde Semensohn | Brooch | Abstract |
| 169653 | 5/26/1953 | Marcel Boucher | Necklace | Abstract |
| 169828 | 6/9/1953 | Raymonde Semensohn | Necklace | Abstract |

159583

159585

**1950 Boucher Ballet of Jewels male and female ballet dancer pins.** Both of these outstanding Boucher ballet dancer pins are part of the Boucher Ballet of Jewels series launched in 1950. Three groups of ballet dancer pins were issued as part of this series: Peter and Sonia, Sleeping Beauty, and Carnival. A Prima Ballerina pin was also designed at this time. Left: Measuring 2" x 1½", this beautiful ballerina pin features a full skirt outlined in rhinestones, a rhinestone-studded bodice, and graceful outstretched arms and legs. Her head is elegantly turned downward and her hair is highlighted with one red rhinestones. She is signed "Boucher," "3047," and "Pat. Pend." This pin is design patent number 159583 issued August 8, 1950, to Marcel Boucher of Boucher. She is part of the Carnival group. Right: Measuring 1¾" x 1¼", this male ballet dancer pin is part of the Boucher Sleeping Beauty group. He is signed "Boucher" and "3051" and is design patent number 159585 issued August 8, 1950, to Marcel Boucher of Boucher. He is wearing a rhinestone-studded shirt with one red rhinestone at the center. His face is proudly turned upward. He has black enameled hair. $100.00 – 135.00 each. From the collection of Evelyn Hodgson.

159591

Fig. 3

159685

161240

ROSE OF SEVILLE

A rose in midnight black of lacey, dull finished metal… dramatically lighted with rhinestones and baguettes. Complete with a beautiful black velour jewel box. **$25.**
Matching earrings (not shown). **$15.** prices plus tax

*Styled by the master craftsman*

**Marcel Boucher**

*Boucher jewelry available at better stores in United States and Canada*
Marcel Boucher et Cie, 347 Fifth Ave., New York
Avon Jewelry Ltd., Belleville, Ontario, Canada
*Design patent pending. U. S. Pat. Off.

**1950 "Rose of Seville"** Boucher advertisement. This rare Boucher advertisement features a latticework rose with japanned metal and clear rhinestone decorations. It is called the "Rose of Seville." The advertisement reads, "A rose in midnight black of lacey, dull finished metal…dramatically lighted with rhinestones and baguettes. Complete with a beautiful black velour jewel box. $25. Matching earrings (not shown). $15." Design patent number 161240 was issued for this brooch on December 19, 1950, to Marcel Boucher.

OTHER JEWELRY MAKERS

| | | | | |
|---|---|---|---|---|
| 169891 | 6/23/1953 | Marcel Boucher | Bracelet | Abstract faux lace cuff |
| 170300 | 9/1/1953 | Marcel Boucher | Brooch | Abstract |
| 170661 | 10/20/1953 | Raymonde Semensohn | Brooch | Abstract |
| 170837 | 11/10/1953 | Raymonde Semensohn | Necklace | Abstract |
| 170847 | 11/17/1953 | Marcel Boucher | Necklace | Abstract floral leaves |
| 170907 | 11/24/1953 | Marcel Boucher | Brooch | Moveable hour and minute clock hands |
| 170950 | 11/24/1953 | Raymonde Semensohn | Brooch | Abstract |
| 171058 | 12/8/1953 | Raymonde Semensohn | Brooch | Abstract |
| 171059 | 12/8/1953 | Raymonde Semensohn | Earring | Abstract |
| 171060 | 12/8/1953 | Raymonde Semensohn | Brooch | Abstract single leaf |
| 171061 | 12/8/1953 | Raymonde Semensohn | Brooch | Abstract double leaf |
| 171077 | 12/15/1953 | Marcel Boucher | Brooch | Adjustable abstract wings or leaves |
| 171233 | 12/29/1953 | Raymonde Semensohn | Necklace | Abstract faux collar |
| 171273 | 1/12/1954 | Marcel Boucher | Necklace | Gold-tone collar-style necklace with jewel-tone cabochon stones, Boucher item number 5529. |
| 171321 | 1/26/1954 | Marcel Boucher | Necklace Brooch | Combination abstract necklace and brooch |
| 171425 | 2/2/1954 | Raymonde Semensohn | Brooch | Abstract |
| 171467 | 2/9/1954 | Raymonde Semensohn | Brooch | Abstract |
| 171622 | 3/2/1954 | Raymonde Semensohn | Brooch | Abstract |

161287

**1949 Boucher comma earrings.** These earrings are marked "MB" with item number 2804. The markings date these earrings to 1949. Interestingly, Raymonde Semensohn, Marcel Boucher's second wife, patented several designs around this time. Design patent number 161287 issued December 19, 1950, to Raymonde Semensohn for Boucher is stylistically similar to the style of these beautiful 1" x ¾" Boucher earrings, indicating that these earrings may have been designed by Semensohn. $45.00 – 65.00.

169653

161566

169458

171273

**1954 Boucher jeweled collar necklace.** Rare and royal looking, this jeweled collar necklace is a match for design patent number 171273 issued January 12, 1954, to Marcel Boucher. This magnificent Byzantine style necklace is constructed in three sections and studded with jewel-tone red, green, and blue cabochons. It measures slightly over 15" and is signed "Boucher" and "Pat. Pend.," with item number 5529. $100.00 – 200.00.

**1937 – 1945 Boucher triple-flower brooch.** Much prettier in person (the camera darkens clear rhinestone pieces), this large 3½" x 2" brooch sparkles from every angle. It is signed "MB" with the Phrygian cap, indicating it could have been produced between 1937 and 1949. Since this piece does not have an inventory number (Boucher began marking the jewelry designs with inventory numbers in 1945), it is reasonable to conclude that this beautiful brooch dates from between 1937, when the "MB" and Phrygian cap signature was in use, and 1945, when inventory numbers were added to the signature. $150.00 – 250.00. From the collection of Debi Reece.

**1943 – 1948 Boucher sterling silver bow brooch with rare "Parisina" mark.** During the war years, some Marcel Boucher jewelry designs were made in Mexico. These designs are signed "Sterling" and "Parisina." Parisina jewelry is hard to find on the collectibles market today. Many dealers do not recognize that jewelry marked "Parisina" was designed by Marcel Boucher, so it is possible to find this wonderful World War II–era Boucher jewelry at bargain prices. Measuring 2½" x 2¼", this lovely brooch features swirling loops of sterling silver gracefully framing one large pear-shaped blue rhinestone. $100.00 – 175.00.

**1943 – 1948 Boucher sterling silver matador and bull pin with rare "Parisina" mark.** This exceptionally well-sculpted figural pin is signed "Parisina Sterling" which is a rare mark used for Boucher Mexican-made pieces produced during the war years. This three-dimensional 2¼" x 1½" brooch depicts the action of a proud matador swishing his cape in the face of a charging bull. The subject and astounding detail in this brooch testify to the genius of Marcel Boucher's designs. $200.00 – 350.00.

**1943 – 1948 Boucher bow brooch with large moonstone center.** As part of writing this book, I re-examined jewelry that I had stored away. This outstandingly beautiful 2½" x 1¾" signed "Sterling" bow brooch held a special surprise for me. Hiding beneath the loops of sterling silver was a partially visible symbol that resembles the top of the Marcel Boucher Phrygian cap signature. Boucher used this mark from 1937 to 1949. Could this brooch be Boucher? Possibly. $150.00 – 250.00.

**1950 Boucher bow brooch.** This pretty silvertone, rhodium-plated bow brooch is signed "Boucher" without the copyright symbol and has the inventory number 3370. This inventory number indicates this lovely 2½" x 1" brooch was produced in 1950. $70.00 – 100.00.

**1951 – 1955 Boucher sapphire baguette rhinestone brooch and earrings.** This triangular pin and earrings set features characteristically Boucher blue baguette rhinestones set in rhodium-plated silver-tone metal. The pin measures 1¼" on each side of the triangle and is signed with the Phrygian cap mark and inventory number 5421. The 1" clip earrings are also signed with the Phrygian cap mark, but the item number on the earrings is unreadable. The Phrygian cap mark (often referred to by collectors as the chicken mark) was used from 1937 through 1949. It is a small mark, so it might also appear on jewelry produced after 1949 when there was no room for the larger Boucher signature. The inventory number indicates this brooch was produced after 1950. (See chapter 1 for a list of inventory numbers and dates used.) Since there is no copyright symbol, this set dates to 1951 – 1955. $65.00 – 85.00. From the collection of Debi Reece.

1951 "Croix de Malte" Boucher advertisement. Maltese cross jewelry was popular in the 1960s. This advertisement indicates this style of jewelry was also produced in the 1950s. The advertisement reads, "Distinctive gold plated brooch and necklace combination set with simulated light amethyst quartz and sapphires or with simulated chrysoprase and rubies. $20."

**1954 Boucher mother-of-pearl angelfish brooch and earrings set.** This splendid 2" double angelfish pin is signed "Boucher" with the inventory number 5693. The matching 1" angelfish clip earrings are signed "Boucher" with the inventory number 5692. The round mother-of-pearl disc bodies of these darling fish are similar to the mother-of-pearl discs decorating the sea-motif jewelry featured in the 1954 Boucher "Nautic" advertisement. The advertisement reads, "Crustacean fantasies in Mother-of-Pearl discs on gold plated jewelry...the leeward fashion for Spring." The sea-motif design and use of materials dates the angelfish set to the same era. $100.00 – 125.00.

**1954 Boucher mother-of-pearl leaf brooch and matching earrings.** This 2½" x 1" brooch and the ¾" clip earrings feature the same round mother-of-pearl discs as the Nautic set shown in the 1954 Boucher "Nautic" advertisement and date to the same time. This three-disc floral Boucher brooch is signed "Boucher" with item number 5605. The earrings are unsigned. $60.00 – 75.00.

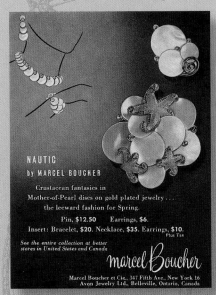

1954 Boucher "Nautic" advertisement. This interesting advertisement features sea-motif jewelry decorated with mother-of-pearl. The ad reads, "Crustacean fantasies in Mother-of-Pearl discs on gold plated jewelry... the leeward fashion for Spring." Original prices: pin, $12.50; earrings, $6.00; bracelet, $20.00; necklace, $35.00; dangle earrings, $10.00.

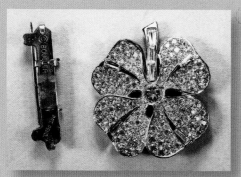

**Boucher reversible four-leaf clover brooch made after 1955.** This interesting 1½" brooch is reversible, so the gold-tone metal and pearl decoration can be worn during the day and then reversed to the sparkling rhinestone side for night. The bar clasp expands to clip firmly over the edge of the brooch. This mechanism is signed "Boucher" with the copyright symbol and "Pat. Pend." No patent has been found for this piece. There is no inventory number. The presence of the copyright symbol dates this unique brooch to after 1955. $75.00 – 110.00.

Another view of the Boucher four-leaf clover reversible brooch.

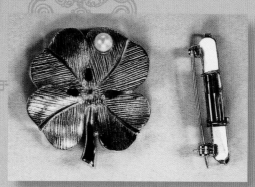

**1956 Marboux Palette baby blue plastic bracelet, brooch, and earrings set.** This beautiful light blue plastic parure is signed "Marboux," which is a Boucher mark used for lower-priced jewelry. Marboux jewelry is signed with a three-digit inventory number. (Jewelry with the Boucher signature has a four-digit inventory number.) The earrings in this set are signed "558" and the pin "571." It was advertised in the 1956 "Marboux Jewelry" advertisement (see page 274) as "Palette." The 6¾" x 1¼" bracelet originally sold for $5.00, the 2" brooch for $3.00, and the 1½" earrings for $3.00. $70.00 – 95.00.

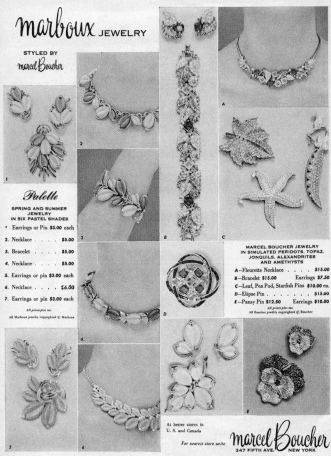

1956 "Marboux Jewelry Styled by Marcel Boucher" advertisement. Several different examples of Marboux jewelry are featured in this advertisement. All of the jewelry on the left hand side of this advertisement is called "Palette" and was originally available in six different pastel colors. The necklaces and bracelets sold for $5.00 or $6.00. The earrings were $3.00. Top right: Fleurette necklace, originally priced $15.00 (bracelet shown to the left). Middle right: Leaf, Pea Pod, and Starfish pins, originally priced $10.00 each; Elipse pin, originally priced $15.00. Bottom right: Pansy pin, originally priced $12.50.

OTHER JEWELRY MAKERS

1956 Boucher "Bangkok" and "Vendôme" jewelry advertisement. Note: All of the jewelry in this advertisement was designed by Boucher. "Vendôme" refers to a place in France, not the Vendôme jewelry by Coro. Top left: Bangkok jewelry described as "An Eastern Opulence of Simulated Oriental Gems. Necklace, $30; Bracelet, $20; Pin, $10; Earrings, Pair, $7.50." Middle and bottom: Vendôme simulated turquoise jewelry in green and blue, described as "The Subtle Glow of Simulated Turquoise, Jade, or Lapis Lazuli Cabochons in a Gold-plated Setting. Necklace, $30; Bracelet, Not Shown, $25; Pin, $7.50; Earrings, Pair, $7.50."

**Late 1950s Boucher plastic-leaf brooch.** This 1¾" turquoise and purple brooch is signed "Boucher" with the copyright symbol and inventory number 5978. The turquoise and purple plastic leaves slip under graceful gold-tone metal centers. Interestingly, this design is similar to an early Boucher 1937 patent shown on page 25. The inventory number and the copyright symbol date this piece to the late 1950s. $50.00 – 70.00.

**1960s Marboux sunburst brooch.** This beautiful 2¼" brooch is signed "Marboux" with the copyright symbol and inventory number 915. The art-glass center stone resembles a beautiful green paperweight. The style of this brooch and the inventory number date it to the 1960s. $45.00 – 75.00.

**1960s Boucher Skye terrier pin.** This sweet 1½" pin is part of a series of dog pins produced by Boucher in the 1960s. Each dog pin is labeled with the breed name. Most are gold-tone with some enamel (note the red enameled tongue on this pin) and an occasional rhinestone. This pin is signed "Boucher" with the copyright symbol, inventory number 8170 P, and "Skye Terrier." Cast in two pieces, the head of this cutie is attached to the body with a rivet. Pins from this series are gaining in popularity as collectors discover these whimsical designs. $45.00 – 60.00.

**1960s Boucher Pekinese pin.** Signed "Pekinese," this exceptionally well-crafted 1¼" dog pin is similar to signed Boucher Pekinese pins. However, without the signature it is difficult to be certain this pin is Boucher. $45.00 – 65.00.

OTHER JEWELRY MAKERS

**1960s Boucher red plastic Griffin pin.** This 2" x 1½" pin depicts a mythological griffin. It is signed "Boucher" with inventory number 1098P. In mythology, a griffin is a monster with the body of a lion and the head and wings of an eagle. Griffins are thought to know the locations of buried treasures and to guard those treasures. In addition, mythological griffins build nests and lay agate stones instead of eggs. Since mythological griffins do not lay eggs, we must assume that the fierce griffin pin created by Boucher is guarding a precious pearl treasure. Interestingly, this piece is composed of a gold-tone metal frame. The smooth plastic body was slipped over the frame, and the eagle head was attached to the frame. The style and the materials date this brooch to the 1960s. $75.00 – 125.00.

# • BROOKS, NATACHA •

## 1944 – UNKNOWN

**1944 – 1948 Natacha Brooks sterling silver brooch.** Jewelry with the Natacha Brooks mark is extremely rare. Natacha Brooks was a freelance designer who, in 1944, began a line of jewelry of her own. The 2½" x 1" brooch shown here is marked "Natacha Brooks" and "Sterling." The use of sterling dates this piece to 1944 – 1948. $100.00 – 200.00.

OTHER JEWELRY MAKERS

## 1948 – About 1983

**Late 1950s or early 1960s B.S.K. enamel and rhinestone bracelet and earrings set.** The little enameled flowers on the bracelet alternate in color between light lavender and gray. Surrounding these enameled flowers are clear, pink, and amber-colored rhinestones. The little leaves have white enamel. The bracelet measures 7½" and the earrings are 1½" long. All pieces are signed "B.S.K." with the copyright symbol, dating this set to the late 1950s or early 1960s. $25.00 – 35.00.

**Late 1950s B.S.K. My Fair Lady jewelry.** The B.S.K. My Fair Lady series of pins, bracelets, cuff links, etc., were originally produced to celebrate the 1956 Broadway play. B.S.K. My Fair Lady jewelry is well made. All pieces are signed "BSK My Fair Lady" with the copyright symbol. Top row: ¾" cuff links, 2" x 1" hat. Middle row left to right: 1½" x 1½" basket, 7¼" bracelet, 2¼" x 2" flower bouquet, 1½" round hat. Bottom row left to right: 2½" x 1" top hat and cane, 1½" hat. Brooches sell for $30.00 – 40.00, bracelets (rarer) $45.00 – 70.00, and cuff links (top center) $25.00 – 35.00.

Another example of late 1950s B.S.K. My Fair Lady jewelry. This pretty pin measures 2" x 1¼" and is signed "BSK My Fair Lady" with the copyright symbol.

**OTHER JEWELRY MAKERS**

1955 – 1960s B.S.K. yellow and green enameled fish pin. This fabulous fish pin measures 2" x ¾". It is signed "B.S.K." with the copyright symbol, dating it to after 1955. The high-quality design and the use of materials date this brooch to the late 1950s or 1960s. $45.00 – 65.00.

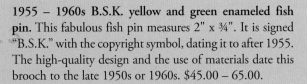

1960s B.S.K. pearl flower pin. This pretty B.S.K. 2½" pearl and gold-tone flower pin is similar to Trifari pins advertised in the 1964 "For every frantic..." Trifari Christmas Collection advertisement shown on page 232 and dates to the same era. It is signed "BSK" with the copyright symbol. $20.00 – 35.00. Courtesy of Esta Pratt.

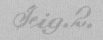

## 1945 – 1980s

**1955 – 1980s Cadoro "heart on a string" brooch.** Cadoro styles are often bold and interesting. This diminutive, 1¾" x ½" "heart on a string" hand pin is a sweet exception. This piece is signed "Cadoro" with the copyright symbol, indicating it was produced after 1955. Cadoro ceased operation in the 1980s, dating this pin to 1955 – 1980s. $35.00 – 50.00.

**1955 – 1980s Cadoro antique white cuff bracelet.** This interesting antique white cuff bracelet fits up to a size eight wrist. It is signed "Cadoro" with the copyright symbol, indicating this bracelet dates to 1955 – 1980s. $35.00 – 50.00. From the collection of Debi Reece.

# • CALVAIRE •

## 1920s – 1960s

**1940s Calvaire faux golden topaz brooch.** The style of this golden 2½" x 1½" brooch is similar to Hobé designs from the 1940s and dates from that era. The three large citrine-colored stones are each surrounded by a frame of tiny gold-tone flowers. This fancy but feminine brooch is signed "Calvaire" without the copyright symbol. $100.00 – 150.00.

1952 – 1977

**1952 – 1955 Capri pink rhinestone brooch.** This lovely Capri brooch measures a large 2½" x 2". It is domed (1¼" high) and features coordinating shades of purple, red, pink, and green rhinestones. The stones are pasted-in; however, this is a high-quality brooch with open-backed rhinestones. Capri jewelry was produced from 1952 to 1977. This beauty is signed "Capri" without the copyright symbol, dating it to 1952 – 1955. $60.00 – 80.00.

1958 Capri "spring carousel" advertisement. The slogan for Capri jewelry was "looks costly…costs little." This interesting advertisement showcases two necklaces, a bracelet, and two pair of earrings, all in a style called "Spring Carousel." The advertisement reads, "Fashion-jewels in the newest Spring colors combine pearls, beads and brilliants in thrilling floral arrangements. Feminine as perfume — in ombré-tones [shadow tones] of yellow, green, blue, pink, beige, melon, white, or coral and turquoise with white." Each piece originally sold for $3.00.

**Late 1950s Capri mother-of-pearl pin.** This 2¼" x 1½" pretty bouquet of flowers pin is signed "Capri" with the copyright symbol. The mother-of-pearl discs incorporated in this interesting design are similar to those shown in the 1954 Boucher "Nautic" advertisement (see page 272), dating this piece to the same era. $35.00 – 45.00.

## JEWELRY FROM 1939 – 1970s

| Design Patent Number | Date Issued | Designer | Jewelry Type | Brief Description |
|---|---|---|---|---|
| 139539 | 11/28/1944 | Hugo De Alteriis | Brooch | Aquarius (See 139540 for another Carnegie zodiac patent.) |
| 139540 | 11/28/1944 | Hugo De Alteriis | Brooch | Pisces (See 139541 for another Carnegie zodiac patent.) |
| 139541 | 11/28/1944 | Hugo De Alteriis | Brooch | Cancer (See 139542 for another Carnegie zodiac patent.) |
| 139542 | 11/28/1944 | Hugo De Alteriis | Brooch | Scorpio (See 140526 for another Carnegie zodiac patent.) |
| 140526 | 3/6/1945 | Hugo De Alteriis | Brooch | Zodiac Taurus (See 139539 for another Carnegie Zodiac patent.) |

139539

139542

139540

140526

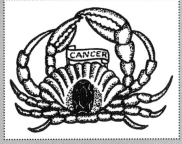

139541

OTHER JEWELRY MAKERS

**1948 – 1955 Hattie Carnegie faux turquoise bracelet and earrings set.** This classically styled faux turquoise 7½" bracelet and matching 1" clip earrings are signed "Hattie Carnegie" without the copyright symbol. Each turquoise stone is surrounded by tiny gold-tone flowers. Then each of these tiny flowers is decorated with a clear rhinestone center. The signature and the nonuse of sterling date this set to 1948 – 1955. $75.00 – 95.00.

1955 Hattie Carnegie "Dancing Jewels À La Carnegie" advertisement. This rare Hattie Carnegie advertisement features a pearl and rhinestone pin and earrings set with moving, or "trembling," elements. The pin originally sold for $8.00 and the earrings for $4.75. The advertisement reads, "Golden leaves tipped with rhinestones, blossoming with pretend pearl buds on tiny golden springs to move when you do."

**1948 – 1955 Hattie Carnegie enameled flower brooch.** This yummy yellow 1¾" x 1½" flower brooch is signed "Hattie Carnegie" without the copyright symbol. Notice the beautiful, high-quality enameling. The nonuse of sterling and the signature indicate this pretty bloom dates to 1948 – 1955. $65.00 – 95.00. From the collection of Debi Reece.

**1948 – 1955 Hattie Carnegie fancy rhinestone and pearl brooch.** This especially rich-looking 3" x 2¾" brooch is signed "Hattie Carnegie" without the copyright symbol. Imagine this magnificent brooch as the centerpiece of a hat or turban. The signature and nonuse of sterling date this brooch to 1948 – 1955. $125.00 – 175.00. From the collection of Debi Reece.

Fig.1

**1948 – 1955 Hattie Carnegie genie on a flying carpet brooch.** This fabulous 2½" x 1¾" figural brooch is signed "Hattie Carnegie" without the copyright symbol and dates to 1948 – 1955. The design is well sculpted and amazingly well defined. The genie is beautifully decorated with blue rhinestones and turquoise seed pearls. $250.00 – 350.00. From the collection of Debi Reece.

**1955 – 1960s Hattie Carnegie donkey pin.** This cute creature measures 2½" x 1¾" and is signed "Hattie Carnegie" with the copyright symbol. Creamy champagne pearls, orange beads, and light green rhinestones pop with color on the donkey's basket-weave body. The signature and japanned metal body date this piece to the late 1950s or early 1960s. $90.00 – 130.00.

OTHER JEWELRY MAKERS

283

**1955 – 1970s Hattie Carnegie Lucite figural pins.** Both of these cute figural pins feature off-white Lucite bodies, silver-tone metal, and clear rhinestones. They are signed "Hattie Carnegie" with the copyright symbol dating them to after 1955. Lucite Carnegie figural pins are popular with collectors. The 1¾" x 1" turtle and the 2¼" x 1½" rooster are each valued at $95.00 – 175.00. From the collection of Debi Reece.

**1970s Hattie Carnegie Christmas holly and berry set.** This delightful holly and berry Christmas set is new looking and dates from the end of Carnegie jewelry production in the 1970s. All three pieces are signed "Hattie Carnegie" with the copyright symbol on an oval cartouche. The brooch measures 3¼" x 1¾". Each clip earring is 1¼" x ¾". $45.00 – 65.00.

OTHER JEWELRY MAKERS

## 1918 – 1977

| Design Patent Number | Date Issued | Designer | Jewelry Type | Brief Description |
| --- | --- | --- | --- | --- |
| 122218 | 8/27/1940 | Willard Markle | Brooch | Clock with bow |
| 124039 | 12/17/1940 | Willard Markle | Brooch | Crocodile with top hat and cane |
| 124390 | 12/31/1940 | Willard Markle | Brooch | Mushroom |
| 125693 | 3/4/1941 | Willard Markle | Brooch | Grasshopper playing the violin |
| 138141 | 6/27/1944 | Clifford Furst | Brooch | Giraffe with knot in neck |
| 142553 | 10/16/1945 | Clifford Furst | Brooch | Floral |
| 142554 | 10/16/1945 | Clifford Furst | Brooch | Balancing scales with angel and coins |
| 142555 | 10/16/1945 | Clifford Furst | Brooch | Abstract snowflake style |
| 142556 | 10/16/1945 | Clifford Furst | Brooch | Abstract snowflake style |
| 156981 | 1/24/1950 | Williard G. Markle | Brooch | Cards in basket |

The Castlecliff signature was first used to sign jewelry in 1941.

124039

142555

1946 Castlecliff "The Talked-About Jewelry…" advertisement. This fabulous advertisement features a pair of green opera glasses and a fancy Castlecliff pearl and rhinestone necklace and earrings set. The advertisement implies that the Castlecliff jewelry is beautiful enough to wear to the opera or a Broadway show.

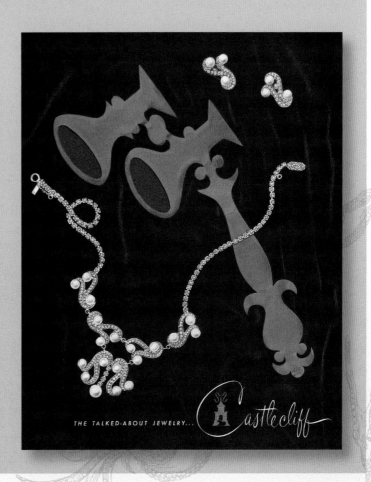

THE TALKED-ABOUT JEWELRY… Castlecliff

156981

1955 Castlecliff "Rue de la Paix" advertisement. Translated into English, *Rue de la Paix* means "street of peace." It is unclear why these colorful crystal bracelets merit this name; however, they are lovely. Each bracelet originally sold for $7.50. The ad reads, "Bracelets To Be Worn by the Wristful/Fashion Favors Jewel Tones and/Simulated Pearls for Perfect Blending/ Handsomely Clasped…/Triple Strands with Flashing Rhinestones/ and Baguettes or Four Strands/with Textured Gold Plate."

**1948 – 1955 Castlecliff rhinestone leaf brooch and earrings.** This glitzy Castlecliff 2" x 1½" brooch and 1" clip earrings set is signed "Castlecliff." Notice the creamy gold-tone stems surrounded by clear pavé rhinestones in this well-made, three-dimensional set. The nonuse of sterling and the lack of a copyright symbol indicate this set dates to 1948 – 1955. (Castlecliff jewelry was produced from 1937 to 1977; however, the Castlecliff signature was first used in 1941.) $45.00 – 65.00. From the collection of Debi Reece.

**1948 – 1955 Castlecliff bracelet.** Measuring 7" x ½", this heavy gold-tone Castlecliff bracelet features ribbed white plastic inserts set in textured metal. It is signed "Castlecliff" without the copyright symbol. This signature and the 1950s plastic inserts indicate this classic Xs and Os design brooch dates to 1948 – 1955. $20.00 – 30.00.

**1970s Egyptian style blue and red enamel Castlecliff pendant.** This pretty pendant is signed "Castlecliff" without the copyright symbol. The lack of a copyright symbol often indicates a piece was produced before 1955. However, the style of this 2¼" Egyptian-design pendant (without the chain) suggests it was produced in the 1970s when the King Tut exhibit toured the U.S. and Egyptian-style jewelry, especially finely enameled pieces like this example, were popular. As shown: $75.00 – 95.00.

# • CATHÉ •

## 1961 – UNKNOWN

**1960s – 1970s Cathé pink pearl brooch and earrings set.** Found in its original Cathé box (not shown), this creamy light pink pearl and rhinestone set is in mint condition. The 2" brooch and 1½" clip earrings are lightweight and comfortable to wear. Cathé jewelry was first produced in 1961. It is unknown when production ceased. The style of this set dates it to the 1960s or 1970s. $65.00 – 85.00 with box. From the collection of Debi Reece.

## 1945 – APPROXIMATELY 1997

**1948 – 1970 Alice Caviness multicolor rhinestone brooch.** This beauty is signed "Alice Caviness." It measures 2¼" x 2" and features a delightful mixture of elements including tiny yellow, pink, blue, and green flowers intermixed with rhinestones of several different shapes and shades of color. The style of this brooch indicates it dates to 1948 – 1970. $65.00 – 85.00. From the collection of Debi Reece.

**Mid-1960s Caviness green flower pin and earrings set.** This warm long-stemmed Alice Caviness flower set dates to the mid-1960s for two reasons. First, many companies produced jewelry with enameling and rhinestones at this time. Next, the olivine color of the flower petals was favored by designers in the 1960s. This amazing 3" flower features open-backed stones, a yellow carved plastic center, and enameled leaves. The attractive 1" wedge-shaped clip earrings are decorated with tiny yellow enamel and rhinestone flowers. All pieces are signed "Alice Caviness" without a copyright symbol. $80.00 – 100.00.

**1950s – 1960s Alice Caviness green glass necklace and earrings set.** The 24" light green art glass necklace is signed "Alice Caviness" without a copyright symbol. (Note: The lack of a copyright symbol is not useful in dating Caviness jewelry. Many examples of Caviness jewelry lack the copyright symbol.) The matching 2" earrings are unsigned. Alice Caviness jewelry was produced from 1945 through 1997. Some of the sterling silver pieces are delicate designs, but much of the other Caviness jewelry reflects large, bold designs often incorporating unusual art glass stones. Caviness jewelry is challenging to date because the date of manufacture must be determined by the style. Since long glass beads were popular in the 1950s and 1960s, this set dates to that era. $65.00 – 85.00.

**1970 – 1997 Alice Caviness colorful enameled bird pin.** This tiny 1¼" pin is signed "Alice Caviness" and features beautiful bright yellow, green, and blue enameling. The expressive, open-mouthed birds are decorated with tiny marcasite stones outlining each wing. The condition and style of this brooch indicate this pin is a newer Caviness design dating to 1970 – 1997. $40.00 – 55.00.

## 1914 – 1939, 1954 – Present

**1985 Chanel bar brooch.** It is especially fun for a collector to find a pin that is both signed and dated. Measuring 3" in length, this beautiful bar pin is signed "Chanel" with the copyright symbol and "1985." Interestingly, the clasp is a simple nonlocking clasp more typically found on some 1940s designs. $70.00 – 100.00. From the collection of Debi Reece.

Fig.1

## • Charel •

### 1945 – Unknown

Fig.2

**1955 Charel green Bakelite parure.** Amazingly, the swirled green inserts decorating this signed Charel parure are Bakelite! The 16" necklace is signed "Charel" without the copyright symbol. However, the 7¼" x 1½" bracelet and 1¼" x ½" clip earrings are signed "Charel" with the copyright symbol, indicating this is a transitional set made in 1955, when companies first began to routinely copyright designs. $100.00 – 150.00. From the collection of Debi Reece.

OTHER JEWELRY MAKERS

## JEWELRY, 1931 – PRESENT

**1955 – 1960s Ciner domed rhinestone bracelet.** This high-end 7¼" x ¾" bracelet is signed "Ciner" with the copyright symbol. The clasp is designed so that when it is closed, the mechanism is completely hidden from view. The elegant bracelet appears to be an unbroken ring of diamond-like stones surrounding the wrist. Ciner first produced costume jewelry in 1931. The company is still operating today. Ciner jewelry is known for its high-quality construction and design. The jewelry was expensive to purchase when new and has retained its beauty over time. The style of this bracelet dates it to 1955 – 1960s. $100.00 – 150.00. From the collection of Debi Reece.

## • CLAUDETTE •

### 1945 – UNKNOWN

**1955 – 1960s Claudette purple rhinestone brooch and earrings set.** Often Claudette jewelry consists of well-crafted sets with colorful plastic inserts; however, Claudette also produced beautiful rhinestone jewelry like this large 3" deep purple brooch and earrings set. The 1" earrings are signed "Claudette." The brooch is unsigned. Some of the purple stones have the aurora borealis coating invented by Swarovski in 1955. These stones and the style of the jewelry indicate this set dates to 1955 – 1960s. $75.00 – 90.00. From the collection of Debi Reece.

OTHER JEWELRY MAKERS

## 1949 – 1983, OPENED AGAIN 2002 – 2003

**1959 Sarah Coventry rhinestone bracelet and earrings set.** One of the best ways to date Sarah Coventry jewelry is to review vintage advertisements found in jewelry books. This especially well-made 7" triple-row rhinestone bracelet and the matching 1¾" earrings are shown on page 16 of *Fine Fashion Jewelry from Sarah Coventry* by Jennifer A. Lindbeck. Page 16 of that book also includes a picture from a promotional brochure for the 1959 Miss Ozone pageant held in Louisiana. The winner of the pageant is shown wearing this set, including a matching necklace. This beautiful bracelet and earrings set is extraordinarily rare. It is heavy, has a creamy rhodium back, and rivals the quality of the higher-end costume jewelry produced at the time. It is signed "SAC" in a diamond. $70.00 – 85.00.

**1962 Sarah Coventry leaf brooch.** This lovely 3" x 1½" gold-tone leaf brooch is signed "SarahCov" with the copyright symbol. It is featured in the 1962 "Designer's Choice" Sarah Coventry advertisement. The advertisement states that this brooch was featured on "QUEEN FOR A DAY-TV." This well-made piece features golden topaz rhinestones decorating the top of the brooch and tiny clear rhinestones highlighting the gold-tone leaf. $45.00 – 65.00.

**1962 "Designer's Choice" Sarah Coventry advertisement.** This advertisement features a rhinestone-decorated leaf and earrings set. The advertisement reads, "...shown only at Sarah Coventry Home Jewelry Shows."

OTHER JEWELRY MAKERS

Fig. 1

Fig. 2

Fig. 3

**1964 Sarah Coventry Blue Lagoon brooch.** This vibrant blue 2¼" x 2" rhinestone brooch is signed "Sarah Cov" with the copyright symbol. The blue rhinestones are all prong set in rhodium-plated metal. This brooch is part of the Blue Lagoon jewelry group produced by Sarah Coventry in 1964. $45.00 – 65.00. Courtesy of Esta Pratt.

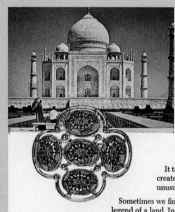

WHAT IN THE WORLD INSPIRES SARAH?

It takes inspiration to create Sarah Coventry's unusual jewelry.

Sometimes we find it in the lore and legend of a land. India's legendary tribute to love—the Taj Mahal—inspired the oriental splendor reflected in Sarah's "Light of the East" brooch.

Jewelry shown actual size

Sometimes a nation's traditions suggest an idea. In Spain, colorful pageantry is a tradition. Striking adornment is another, as symbolized here in Sarah's distinctive "Senorita" earrings.

The Earth itself often models for Sarah. The Austrian Alps provide the thought, an appropriate setting, and the sparkling crystals for this "Mountain Flower" pin.

Beauty is where you find it. And Sarah searches the world to bring you the most beautiful fashion jewelry. To see our latest collection, write: Sarah Coventry, Inc. Newark 90, New York State 14513

*Sarah Coventry*
FINE FASHION JEWELRY

Shown only at our Home Jewelry Shows

©1968 Sarah Coventry, Inc.

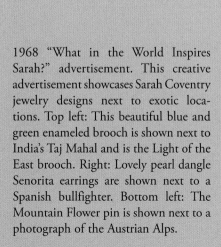

1968 "What in the World Inspires Sarah?" advertisement. This creative advertisement showcases Sarah Coventry jewelry designs next to exotic locations. Top left: This beautiful blue and green enameled brooch is shown next to India's Taj Mahal and is the Light of the East brooch. Right: Lovely pearl dangle Senorita earrings are shown next to a Spanish bullfighter. Bottom left: The Mountain Flower pin is shown next to a photograph of the Austrian Alps.

"Every Cinderella finds her Prince with Sarah Coventry!"

No fairy Godmother? No magic wand? Never fear. Sarah Coventry Jewelry gives any costume a fabulous touch that will win praise from *your* Prince! And Sarah's flattering styles are so modestly priced that you can own a royal wardrobe on a working-girl's budget.

Write today for full details about our famous Home Jewelry Shows —and how you may receive a valuable Hostess Gift of this fine fashion jewelry. Address Aileen Van Tyle, Fashion Coordinator, Sarah Coventry, Inc., Newark, New York State.

*Sarah Coventry*
FINE FASHION JEWELRY

AS FEATURED ON QUEEN FOR A DAY—TV

*Shown exclusively at Sarah Coventry Home Jewelry Shows*

1962 "Every Cinderella finds her Prince with Sarah Coventry!" advertisement. The intent of this advertisement is two fold. First, it beautifully showcases high-quality Sarah Coventry jewelry. Next, it is intended to recruit women to hold Sarah Coventry parties by offering "fine fashion jewelry" as hostess gifts.

OTHER JEWELRY MAKERS

**1970 Sarah Coventry owl pin.** Some of my favorite Sarah Coventry pieces are figural pins like this golden 1½" x 1" owl pin with unusual glass eyes! When I shine a black light on them, they glow! This outstanding owl pin is called "Hooter" in the 1970 "Sarah fashions magic from a walk in the wild" advertisement. It is signed "SarahCov" with the copyright symbol. $30.00 – 50.00.

**Sarah fashions magic from a walk in the wild.**
From nature's awesome beauty which surrounds us, Sarah Coventry finds inspiration in a tiny flower, a dew-capped bud, a wispy cloud, a brilliant bird, a colorful butterfly. ❦ Our designers interpret each wonder in the artistry of still another exclusive fashion jewelry creation. Nature's grand design will always inspire us in our business of the beautiful. To see Sarah's latest and loveliest jewelry collection write: Sarah Coventry, Inc., Newark 160, New York State 14513. ❦ Also Canada, Australia and Scotland.
*Photos by Gene Howard*

*Sarah Coventry*
FINE FASHION JEWELRY
Shown only at our Home Jewelry Shows

1970 "Sarah fashions magic from a walk in the wild" advertisement. This advertisement features five different nature-inspired jewelry designs. Top left: Wild Honey bracelet and pendant. Bottom left: Allusion flower pin. Top right: Moon-lites bracelet. Bottom right: Fashion Splendor flower brooch and Hooter owl brooch.

**Two 1970 Sarah Coventry large flower pins.** Both of these beautiful and large Sarah Coventry brooches are featured in the 1970 "Sarah fashions magic from a walk in the wild" advertisement. Left: This 3½" x 2" gold-tone and clear aurora borealis rhinestone flower pin was originally called "Allusion" in the 1970 advertisement. Right: This round pink, green, and pearl flower measures a large 2¾" in diameter and was named Fashion Splendor. $20.00 – 30.00 each.

1970s Shangri-La Sarah Coventry pendant, pin, and ring. Called "Shangri-La" in the 1970s, this exceptionally fine Arabian-style Sarah Coventry jewelry set features silver-tone metal decorated with turquoise seed pearls, amethyst-colored rhinestones, and clear rhinestones. There is a matching cuff bracelet (not shown). The flying carpet brooch measures 2" x 1¼", the 2¼" pendant is suspended from a 24" chain, and the ring is adjustable up to a size 9. All pieces are signed "Sarah Cov" with the copyright symbol. $50.00 – 70.00.

1971 "Sarah means lovely in every language" advertisement. This advertisement features Sarah Coventry jewelry designs and postcards from different parts of the world. The advertisement reads, "Sarah's world-famed designers find inspiration in every nation, on every continent."

## LATE 1930s – AT LEAST 1978

Fig. 1

Fig. 2

Fig. 3

1956 Dalsheim "first sign of spring" advertisement. This advertisement reads, "first sign of spring and its…the slim look in chalk white wafers by Dalsheim." Each piece originally sold for $2.00.

1955 – 1970s Dalsheim clock brooch. This magnificent 3" x 1½" brooch is signed "Dalsheim" with the copyright symbol. The brooch is exquisitely designed and so well balanced that it can stand upright on a table like a real clock. Dalsheim produced jewelry from the 1930s until the late 1970s. Much of the jewelry is unsigned. Due to the style of the brooch and the presence of the copyright symbol, this terrific timepiece brooch dates to 1955 – 1970s. $30.00 – 40.00.

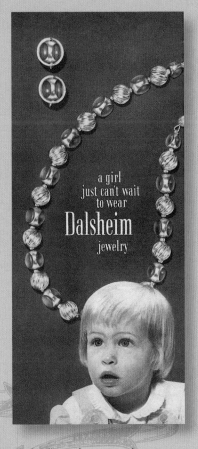

1962 "a girl just can't wait to wear Dalsheim jewelry" advertisement. The advertisement reads, "Patience, Cherie. Soon you'll be old enough to wear fascinating jewels by Dalsheim. Like these light in weight 'Golden Jewels'… spiraled golden globes with imported lantern shaped beads between. In shades of topaz, ruby, sapphire, emerald, jet, gold, and silver…to delightfully complement any new autumn outfit you may want to accent." The single strand necklace originally sold for $6.00, and the earrings for $3.00.

1948 Dalsheim "Daisy chain" advertisement. This interesting advertisement features a necklace and earrings set. The five-row necklace and button earrings originally sold for $2.00 each.

# • DAVID-ANDERSEN •

## 1876 – PRESENT

Fig.1

**1940 – present sterling silver necklaces.** These two sterling silver necklaces are especially beautiful examples of David Andersen sterling jewelry. The family-owned-and-operated company has been in constant production since 1876. Left: This heart necklace measures 1⅛" and is suspended from a 16½" sterling chain. It is signed "David-Andersen Sterling 925S." Right: This octagonal-shaped necklace features a rare figural decoration. It measures ¾" and has a 16" chain. This piece is signed "David-Andersen Norway Sterling." It is difficult to establish an accurate date of manufacture for David Andersen sterling pieces. However, most of the David Andersen jewelry found today was produced between 1940 and the present. $100.00 – 200.00 each. From the collection of Debi Reece.

## • DEAUVILLE •

Fig.2

Fig.3

Jewelry signed "Deauville" was produced by J.R. Wood & Sons, established in 1850. It is unknown when the Deauville name was first used to mark jewelry, but the styles of the jewelry shown here indicate that these pieces were probably made in the 1950s or 1960s.

**Late 1950s Deauville black beaded necklace.** This wonderful double-strand 16" necklace, signed "Deauville," has a surprising feature. Nestled beneath each gold-tone cap is a bright turquoise bead. Deauville jewelry was produced by the J.R. Wood & Sons Co., which is today called ArtCarved, Inc. Today ArtCarved, Inc., specializes in class and college rings, commemorative family jewelry, and bridal jewelry designs. Jewelry signed "Deauville" is no longer produced. The dates of operation when Deauville jewelry could have been produced is not known. The style of this necklace indicates it was produced in the late 1950s. $25.00 – 35.00.

# • DeLizza & Elster, Inc. •

## 1947 – 1990s

DeLizza and Elster, Inc., was a manufacturer that made jewelry designs for other companies, including Weiss, Kramer, Hobé, and Eisenberg. For two years, in 1967 and 1968, DeLizza and Elster, Inc., designed, produced, and marketed jewelry under the name "Juliana." This jewelry was unsigned except for removable hangtags. The jewelry shown in this section is unmarked "Juliana style/D & E style" jewelry. The following designs are included under the heading of DeLizza and Elster (D & E jewelry) because that is the way most collectors think about this style of unmarked jewelry.

The following is a partial list of "Juliana" or "D & E" style traits accepted by many collectors:

- Rhinestones: heavy use of aurora borealis stones, navette-shaped stones, stones set in open-backed settings, art glass, or molded glass stones
- Construction: bracelets often have five oval or rectangular links, safety chains, layers of rhinestones, dangling crystals or pearls, and decorated clasps

D & E jewelry is difficult to date. This style of glitzy jewelry was produced for a long time. All of the examples in this book include some aurora borealis rhinestones, indicating the jewelry was produced after 1955. The style indicates the jewelry dates to 1955 – 1970, so that range is assigned to the D & E style jewelry in this book.

**1955 – 1970 D & E style bracelet and earrings set.** Large and showy aurora borealis rhinestones cover this 7¼" D & E style five link bracelet and 1¼" earring. Notice the different sizes and shapes of rhinestones in this incredibly sparkly set. $90.00 – 130.00.

1954 DeLizza and Elster, Inc., advertisement. This advertisement appeared in the 1954 *Jewelers' Buyers Guide*. This advertisement lists the different types of jewelry manufactured by DeLizza and Elster, including button earrings, drop earrings, pierced earrings, pins, Duettes, barettes, necklaces, chignon earrings, and clips. Note the interesting "Jewelry by DeLizza" logo.

Fig.2

1955 – 1970 **blue navette D & E style rhinestone brooch and earrings set.** This large 2½" blue brooch and 1½" clip earrings set features open-backed, navette-shaped rhinestones. Layers of these rhinestones are expertly connected to form this well-made, beautiful brooch. $100.00 – 150.00.

**1955 – 1970 blue rhinestone D & E style butterfly pin and earrings set.** This attractive butterfly pin measures 2½". Each earring is 1½" long. Thick navette-shaped rhinestones were placed in open-backed settings to form the shape. Then blue and clear aurora borealis rhinestones were used to outline the charming butterfly design. $100.00 – 150.00.

**1955 – 1970 D & E style long-stemmed flower pin and earrings set.** This uniquely styled 3¼" x 1½" flower brooch and matching 1" earrings feature an unusual color palate. Included in the open-backed design are thick navette-shaped orange and citrine rhinestones coupled with red aurora borealis rhinestones. Art-glass beads enhance the interest and appeal of this beautiful set. $75.00 – 100.00. From the collection of Debi Reece.

**1955 – 1970 D & E style blue rivoli stone brooch and earrings set.** This unmarked but spectacular 2¾" blue rivoli-stone brooch and matching 1" clip earrings feature navette-shaped rhinestones in open-backed settings. These are arranged in layers to produce an astoundingly bright and beautiful set. $100.00 – 125.00. From the collection of Debi Reece.

**1955 – 1970 D & E style green rhinestone brooch and earrings set.** This gorgeous 2½" green rhinestone brooch and matching 1¼" clip earrings feature thick navette-shaped rhinestones in open-backed settings surrounded by clear aurora borealis rhinestones. Look closely at the earrings. A thin gold-tone wire with a clear aurora borealis rhinestone on top extends above the design. This type of three-dimensional construction is often found on D & E style jewelry. $70.00 – 90.00. From the collection of Debi Reece.

OTHER JEWELRY MAKERS

**1955 – 1970 D & E style duck pin.** This sweet 2¼" x 1½" duck pin features thick navette-shaped rhinestones in open-backed settings. Note the cluster of clear aurora borealis rhinestones attached to a gold-tone wire and bent over the center green rhinestone body. These wire overlays add dimension to the design and are a trait found on many D & E style pieces. $65.00 – 85.00. From the collection of Debi Reece.

**1955 – 1970 D & E style necklace.** This pretty 15½" necklace features navette-shaped amber rhinestones surrounded by blue aurora borealis stones. The intriguing arrangement of these navette-shaped rhinestones and the unusual color combination indicate this is a D & E style piece. $90.00 – 120.00. Courtesy of Esta Pratt.

**1955 – 1970 D & E style bracelet and earrings with belt-buckle clasp.** This sparkling 7" x 1" bracelet and matching 1" clip earrings are unmarked. The bracelet features five oval links decorated with golden topaz rhinestones and clear rhinestones. Notice the rare clasp. Each horseshoe-shaped end is covered with tiny golden topaz rhinestones so that when the clasp is closed, it resembles a decorative belt buckle. Tiny clusters of rhinestones set on gold-tone wires overlay the larger golden topaz stones on both the bracelet and earrings. These design elements indicate this is DeLizza and Elster style jewelry dating to 1955 – 1970. $90.00 – 130.00.

(THE DELTAH NAME WAS FIRST USED IN 1934.
TODAY DELTAH IS PART OF THE IMPERIAL-DELTAH GROUP.)

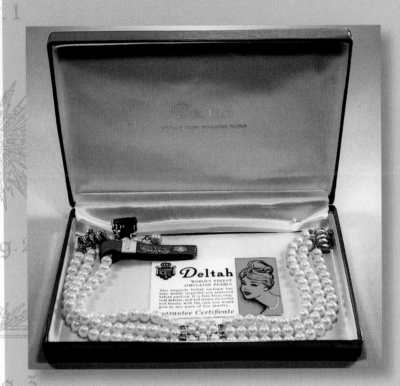

*Fig. 1.*

**1960s Deltah triple-strand pearl necklace in original box.** This triple strand Deltah pearl necklace measures 14" in length. It is unmarked. The original sale price for the necklace was $15.75. It comes with the Deltah blue ribbon tag and the Deltah guarantee certificate. The Deltah sales slogan, "WORLD'S FINEST SIMULATED PEARLS," appears on the box, on the guarantee, and on the blue ribbon. The guarantee included with this necklace reads, "Your Deltah Necklace is a product of the leading maker of simulated pearls! Over sixty years experience in manufacture and styling are good reasons why your Deltah Simulated Pearl Necklace is the finest you can own." First established in 1892, the name Deltah was not used for pearls until 1934. The low original price, and the style of the necklace, indicates these pearls date to the 1960s. $25.00 – 35.00.

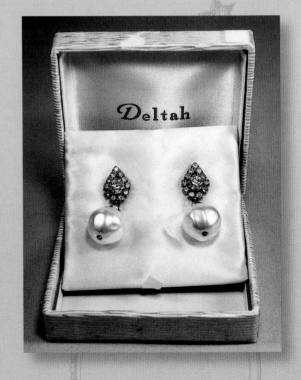

**1950s – 1960s Deltah baroque pearl drop earrings.** Deltah produced many simulated pearl designs. Some designs, like these 1½" baroque pearl dangle earrings, are enhanced by the sparkle of rhinestones. Prized by their owners, Deltah pearl jewelry pieces can sometimes be found carefully stored in original boxes, which in this case is fortuitous, because these Deltah earrings are unmarked. Baroque-style clip earrings were popular in the 1950s and 1960s, dating these earrings to that era. $25.00 – 35.00 in box. From the collection of Debi Reece.

Fig.1

Fig.2

Fig.4

1955 Deltah "Lizabeth Scott" advertisement. This advertisement is a good example of a Deltah celebrity advertisement (see many more vintage Deltah advertisements at www.imperial-deltah.com). Lizabeth Scott, star of *You Came Along*, is shown wearing a single strand of Deltah pearls. The ad reads, "Glamour for lovely necklines/It's so easy to glamorize your neckline, add allure to your fleshtones. Let your jeweler show you an exquisite necklace of DELTAH simulated pearls, so like precious Orientals in luster and iridescence. Wear it as the perfect finishing touch with every daytime or evening costume."

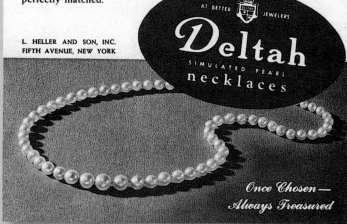

Lizabeth Scott
starring in
"YOU CAME ALONG"
A Hal Wallis Production
released through Paramount

### Glamor for lovely necklines

It's so easy to glamorize your neckline, add allure to your fleshtones. Let your jeweler show you an exquisite necklace of DELTAH simulated pearls, so like precious Orientals in lustre and iridescence. Wear it as the perfect finishing touch with every daytime or evening costume. Necklaces and earrings, perfectly matched.

L. HELLER AND SON, INC.
FIFTH AVENUE, NEW YORK

AT BETTER JEWELERS

**Deltah**
SIMULATED PEARL
necklaces

*Once Chosen —
Always Treasured*

OTHER JEWELRY MAKERS

## 1950s – 1960s

**1950s – 1960s Denbé faux turquoise bracelet and earrings.** Only the 7" x 1" bracelet in this fabulous faux turquoise and rhinestones bracelet and earrings set is signed "Denbé." Little is know about Denbé jewelry. One source indicates Denbé jewelry was produced by J. J. Denberg, N.Y. J. J. Denberg is listed in the 1954 *Jewelers' Buyers Guide*, so the company was operating at that time. Denbé jewelry is rare and well crafted. Note the interesting design of these 1" earrings. They clip to the front and the back of the ear lobe so that the turquoise design hangs in a loop below the ear. The design is visible both from the front and the back. The style and the reference in the *Jewelers' Buyers Guide* date this Denbé set to 1950s – 1960s. $50.00 – 70.00.

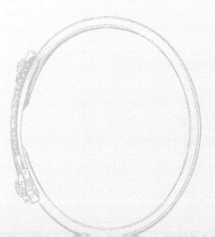

OTHER JEWELRY MAKERS

1957 – 1970

**1960s DeNicola Aquarius pin.** This 1¾" x 1½" imaginative rendition of Aquarius is signed "DeNicola" with the copyright symbol and is part of the DeNicola zodiac series. This creative design features faux jade, rhinestones, and colorful enameling. DeNicola jewelry was produced from 1957 to 1970. Zodiac style jewelry was popular in the 1960s, indicating this piece dates to that era. $100.00 – 200.00.

**Two 1957 – 1970 DeNicola figural pins.** DeNicola figural pins are amazingly imaginative. In my opinion, quality designs, like these two DeNicola pins, are going to increase in value over time. Both pins date from between 1957 and 1970 and are signed "DeNicola" with the copyright symbol. Left: Amazingly, this tiny 1¾" x 1" pin depicts two unrestrained satyr creatures dancing wildly around a tree decorated with red beads and topped by prong-set rhinestones. In Greek mythology, a satyr is a woodland deity with horns, pointed ears, the head and body of a man, and the hind legs of a goat. Satyr beings are known for wild merriment and unrestrained sexuality. $65.00 – 95.00. Right: This peaceful ocean-motif collage measures 1¾" x 1½". It is a complete contradiction to the wild satyr pin, illustrating the versatility of DeNicola's creative genius. $65.00 – 85.00 each.

OTHER JEWELRY MAKERS

## 1934 – 1970

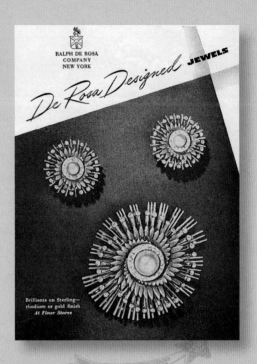

**1943 – 1948 De Rosa sterling brooch.** Signed De Rosa jewelry is exceedingly rare. This excellent 2¾" x 2¼" four-leaf flower clip is signed "De Rosa Sterling." The design and the use of sterling date this rare and charming piece to 1943 – 1948. Notice the beautiful flowing design and the latticework detail on each petal. The creamy pearl center is encircled by a sunburst of clear rhinestones. $150.00 – 250.00. From the collection of Debi Reece.

1946 "De Rosa Designed Jewels" advertisement. This rare advertisement features an asymmetrical starburst design brooch and matching clip earrings. The advertisement reads, "Brilliants on Sterling – rhodium or gold finish." At this time the jewelry was still produced in sterling and then coated with rhodium or gold finish. Note the interesting De Rosa logo at the top of this advertisement.

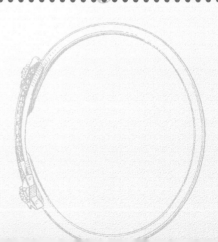

## 1948 – PRESENT

**1950s Christian Dior by Kramer cascade of rhinestones flower pin.** In the 1950s, Kramer produced Christian Dior jewelry. This beautiful example is signed "Christian Dior by Kramer" and dates to that time. Collectors look for this mark, because it usually indicates well-crafted jewelry with an especially lovely or interesting design. This graceful pin, with its cascade of yellow and clear rhinestone flowers, is an excellent example of quality Christian Dior by Kramer jewelry. Measuring 3" x 1½", this lightweight pin features open-backed rhinestones and creamy rhodium plating. The center portion of the pin is articulated so that it gently moves when worn. $100.00 – 150.00. Courtesy of Carol Dike.

**1950s Christian Dior by Kramer pearl and rhinestone bracelet.** This amazingly rare bracelet is a Christian Dior design manufactured in the 1950s by Kramer. It is signed "Christian Dior by Kramer." The well-made 7¼" x 1" bracelet features four segments joined together with rhinestone-studded links. This type of construction is both beautiful and comfortable to wear. $85.00 – 125.00. From the collection of Debi Reece.

**1950s Christian Dior by Kramer dangle earrings.** These well-made 1½" x ¾" earrings are signed "Christian Dior by Kramer" and feature an unusual combination of colors and textures. The central stone is a speckled orange cabochon topped by a peridot-colored rhinestone. The bottom three dangles are decorated with light pink rhinestones. Jewelry with this signature dates to the 1950s. $45.00 – 75.00.

**1950s Christian Dior by Kramer baguette rhinestone earrings.** These spectacular 1¼" x 1¼" earrings are signed "Christian Dior by Kramer" and date to the 1950s. The design is creative and unique. First, Dior designed a classic rhodium-plated clip earring decorated with channel-set baguette rhinestones. Then, to add pizzazz to the design, Dior wrapped a string of dark blue, translucent glass beads through the base of the earring. $55.00 – 85.00. From the collection of Debi Reece.

**1990s Christian Dior choker necklace.** This classically beautiful 17" necklace is signed "Chr. Dior" with the copyright symbol. The design of this necklace is a modern version of the 1948 Coro slide necklace shown in chapter 2, but the slide decoration on this contemporary necklace is stationary. The construction and condition of this necklace indicate it dates to the 1990s or later. $35.00 – 45.00.

# • Doddz •

## 1952 – 1997

**Mid-1960s Doddz green and pink rhinestone bug pin and earrings set.** Aside from extreme cuteness, this signed "Doddz" 1¼" fly pin and matching 1" clip earrings have a hidden quality. Amazingly, the light green wings glow under a black light! Doddz jewelry was produced from 1952 to 1997. This sweet set dates to the mid-1960s, when bug-style jewelry was popular. Due to the interesting glowing wings, this set is valued at $35.00 – 55.00.

## 1950s – 1960s

Fig.2

Fig.3

Early 1950s green and clear rhinestone Duane necklace and earrings set. This elegant rhinestone necklace features baguette-shaped emerald rhinestones set in gold-tone metal. The Duane signature is rare but not widely collected, which keeps the values modest. Interestingly, only the earrings in this set are signed, indicating that not all Duane jewelry was marked. The necklace in this set measures 15", and each earring is ½". The dates of operation are unknown for Duane; however, the similarity in style to the jewelry featured in the 1954 Duane "Fashion Line of the Stars" advertisement suggest that this set dates to the early 1950s. $40.00 – 60.00. From the collection of Debi Reece.

1954 Duane Jewels "Fashion Line of the Stars" advertisement. This interesting advertisement for Duane Jewels appeared in the 1954 *Jewelers' Buyers Guide* and features three rhinestone necklace and earrings sets. The actress in the righthand corner is Patrice Munsel. The advertisement reads, "Patrice Munsel, star of United Artists' Technicolor Production *Melba* is shown wearing Duane's Melba Necklace. Write to us for free window counter display cards to tie in with the motion picture when it is shown in your city."

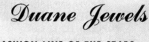

Duane Jewels

**FASHION LINE OF THE STARS**

Patrice Munsel, star of United Artists' Technicolor Production Melba is shown wearing Duane's Melba Necklace. Write to us for free window counter display cards to tie in with the motion picture when it is shown in your city.

Lovely heart-shaped centered with a cluster of fancy shaped stones, baguette and Rhinestone chain with safety clasp. Matching cluster ear-rings, aqua or all crystal. Rhodium finish.

The new midnight ice blue series. Unusual combination of pear shaped and baguette stones. Pears in midnight and ice blue. Baguettes, also in all crystal, with blending earrings.

Tailored and stone motif. Shimmering clusters of Rhinestones set as precious jewelry. Rhodium and crystal only.

Sold through
the wholesaler

**DUANE JEWELS**

861 Broad Street
Providence, R. I.

## 1950s – UNKNOWN

*Fig. 1*

*Fig. 2*

**Late 1950s Edlee green art-glass brooch.** Amazingly vibrant, this rare 2½" x 2¼" brooch is signed "Edlee" in caps with the copyright symbol. Little is known about this rare maker. The company is listed in the 1954 *Jewelers' Buyers Guide,* so it was in business at that time. This exceptional brooch features several different shades of green, with both faceted and cabochon navette-shaped rhinestones. Round, green aurora borealis stones are strategically placed to add sparkle to this interesting design. Note the two crescent-shaped pavé icing decorations and the rare fluted floral shape art-glass stone featured in this piece. The signature, style, and use of aurora borealis rhinestones date this scarce brooch to the late 1950s. $150.00 – 225.00.

## • EISENBERG •

*Fig. 3*

*Fig. 1*

OTHER JEWELRY MAKERS

## 1914 – PRESENT

| Design Patent Number | Date Issued | Designer | Jewelry Type | Brief Description |
|---|---|---|---|---|
| 131479 | 3/3/1942 | Florence Nathan | Brooch | Stylized floral |
| 131530 | 3/10/1942 | Florence Nathan | Brooch | Floral |
| 131531 | 3/10/1942 | Florence Nathan | Brooch | Floral |
| 131688 | 3/24/1942 | Florence Nathan | Brooch | Bow |
| 132434 | 5/19/1942 | Florence Nathan | Brooch | Floral |
| 132435 | 5/19/1942 | Florence Nathan | Brooch | Floral |
| 132436 | 5/19/1942 | Florence Nathan | Brooch | Bow |
| 132437 | 5/19/1942 | Florence Nathan | Brooch | Abstract |
| 132438 | 5/19/1942 | Florence Nathan | Brooch | Abstract floral |
| 132439 | 5/19/1942 | Florence Nathan | Brooch | Abstract |
| 132440 | 5/19/1942 | Florence Nathan | Brooch | Floral |
| 132443 | 5/19/1942 | Florence Nathan | Brooch | Swan |
| 132444 | 5/19/1942 | Florence Nathan | Brooch | Floral |
| 132445 | 5/19/1942 | Florence Nathan | Brooch | Abstract |
| 132446 | 5/19/1942 | Florence Nathan | Brooch | Bow |
| 132447 | 5/19/1942 | Florence Nathan | Brooch | Abstract |

| 132448 | 5/19/1942 | Florence Nathan | Brooch | Abstract |
|---|---|---|---|---|
| 132449 | 5/19/1942 | Florence Nathan | Brooch | Abstract |
| 132450 | 5/19/1942 | Florence Nathan | Brooch | Abstract |
| 132451 | 5/19/1942 | Florence Nathan | Brooch | Abstract |
| 132452 | 5/19/1942 | Florence Nathan | Brooch | Circular |
| 132453 | 5/19/1942 | Florence Nathan | Brooch | Floral |
| 132454 | 5/19/1942 | Florence Nathan | Brooch | Abstract |
| 132455 | 5/19/1942 | Florence Nathan | Brooch | Circular abstract |
| 132456 | 5/19/1942 | Florence Nathan | Brooch | Abstract |
| 132457 | 5/19/1942 | Florence Nathan | Brooch | Abstract |

131688

132434

132436

132437

132443

132449

132454

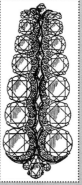

132457

OTHER JEWELRY MAKERS

**Late 1930s – early 1940s Eisenberg ribbon-style clip.** This 2¾" x 2" clip is signed "Eisenberg Original" with the number 9. The mark and the design indicate that this clip dates from the late 1930s or early 1940s. Interestingly, the sweet young ladies at the photo shop where I have my film developed believe this pin resembles the pink ribbons worn today to promote breast cancer awareness. I agree. $150.00 – 250.00. From the collection of Debi Reece.

**Late 1930s – early 1940s Eisenberg rhinestone clip.** This huge, magnificent clip measures 2¾" x 2½" and is signed "Eisenberg Original" with the stone setter's mark, "N." These marks, coupled with the early white metal and Deco design indicate this clip is an early example of Eisenberg jewelry dating from the late 1930s to the early 1940s. Interestingly, this brooch closely resembles design patent number 132437 issued May 19, 1942, to Florence Nathan for Eisenberg. $200.00 – 300.00. From the collection of Debi Reece.

**1943 – 1948 Eisenberg Original sterling multicolored rhinestone clip.** Marked "Eisenberg Original" and "Sterling," this astonishingly beautiful clip dates to 1943 – 1948. Measuring a whopping 3" x 2½", this clip features an array of colorful stones and channel-set square rhinestones. This substantial, rare clip is sterling silver with a gold wash. $400.00 – 600.00. From the collection of Debi Reece.

**1943 – 1948 Eisenberg sterling clear rhinestone clip.** Well made, heavy, and sparkling, this signed "Eisenberg Sterling" clip dates to 1943 – 1948. It measures 2" x 1¾". $95.00 – 150.00.

**1948 – 1955 red and lavender rhinestone Eisenberg brooch.** Signed "Eisenberg" in block letters, this magnificent red and lavender brooch measures 2" x 1¾". The block-letter signature, nonuse of sterling, and lack of copyright symbol indicate this red beauty dates to 1948 – 1955. Notice the combination of colors used for this brooch. Subtle shading of colors and nonuse of aurora borealis rhinestones are typical design traits for Eisenberg jewelry. $90.00 – 125.00.

*Eisenberg Ice*

The lavish look that's made to be *worn*... not banished to the dark safety of vaults. That's Eisenberg Ice—an idea as welcome today as when the first precious piece was created. Richly designed, brilliant with icy fire, crafted and hand-set like precious gems...it fulfills your love of luxury but is never a burden or care. Have it in bright abundance. Wear it. *Enjoy* it.

New spring motifs in crystal or jewel tones: Pins $11.50 to $22.00; earrings $7.50 and $14.00. Plus tax.

EISENBERG JEWELRY, INC., 22 West Madison, Chicago • 151 West 46, New York

**1952 Eisenberg Ice** "The lavish look that's made to be *worn...*" advertisement. The beautiful brooches and earrings featured in this advertisement originally came in clear crystal rhinestones or jewel tones. The pins sold for $11.50 – 22.00, the earrings for $7.50 – 14.00.

OTHER JEWELRY MAKERS

1948 – 1954 Eisenberg brilliant blue rhinestone brooch and earrings set. This splendid set features beautiful blue-faceted prong-set rhinestones with pavé icing details. The silver-tone metal is rhodium plated. The 1¾" brooch and ½" clip earrings are signed "Eisenberg" in block letters without the copyright symbol. This signature dates this brilliant brooch and earrings set to 1945 – 1958. The nonuse of sterling narrows this range to 1948 – 1958. The lack of a copyright symbol further narrows this range, to 1948 – 1954. This set is similar to the jewelry featured in the 1953 Eisenberg Ice "Ribbon Ice" advertisement shown in this book. $125.00 – 200.00. From the collection of Debi Reece.

OTHER JEWELRY MAKERS

1953 Eisenberg Ice "Ribbon Ice" advertisement. The ad reads, "Ribbon Ice melting into frozen fire…big, bold, beautiful blaze of brilliance for a season of glittering elegance. Pins, Earrings, Necklaces, Bracelets: from $7.50 to $25.00."

### Ribbon Ice

melting into frozen fire
…big, bold, beautiful blaze
of brilliance for a season
of glittering elegance.
Pins, Earrings, Necklaces,
Bracelets: from $7.50
to $25.00 (plus tax).

Eisenberg Ice

Eisenberg Jewelry, Inc., 22 West Madison Street, Chicago 2, Illinois

**1955 Eisenberg double-row rhinestone necklace.** This breathtakingly beautiful 15½" clear rhinestone choker necklace is signed "Eisenberg" in block letters without the copyright symbol. The exact necklace is featured in the 1955 Eisenberg Ice "matchless magnificence…" advertisement, accurately dating this piece to that year. The high level of sparkle still gleaming from this piece is testimony to the high-quality stones found in Eisenberg jewelry of the era. $200.00 – 250.00.

Fig.1

Fig.2

1955 Eisenberg Ice "matchless magnificence…" advertisement. Obviously a Christmas promotion, this beautiful advertisement features three elegant Eisenberg rhinestone necklaces and one brooch. The ad reads, "matchless magnificence, startlingly opulent, gem-set like the world's finest jewels. From $21 to $35. Also Bracelets and Earrings to match."

Fig.4

matchless
magnificence,
startlingly opulent,
gem-set
like the world's
finest jewels.
From $21 to $35.
Also Bracelets and
Earrings to match.
Eisenberg Jewelry, Inc.
14 East 38th Street, New York
22 West Madison, Chicago, Ill.

*Eisenberg Ice*

the little black dress...
and the **GLITTERING** company it keeps

*This year's most significant new fashion alliance: the stark simplicity of black, illuminated by a spotlight of ice-pure brilliance... gem set like the world's great jewels.*
*Priced from $10 to $40 plus tax.*
*Eisenberg Jewelry, 22 W. Madison, Chicago, Ill.*
*14 E. 38 Street, New York*

OTHER JEWELRY MAKERS

1956 Eisenberg Ice "the little black dress..." advertisement. The ad reads, "the little black dress...and the GLITTERING company it keeps/ This year's most significant new fashion alliance: the stark simplicity of black, illuminated by a spotlight of ice-pure brilliance...gem set like the world's great jewels. Priced from $10 to $40 plus tax."

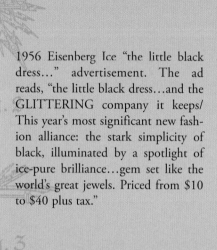

**1950s Eisenberg brooch and earrings set.** This dimensional 1¾" brooch and 1" clip earrings set features rare triangular rhinestones sometimes referred to by collectors as "kite-shaped stones." The set is signed "Eisenberg" in block letters. This signature was used from 1945 to 1958. The 1955 "matchless magnificence..." Eisenberg Ice advertisement features a necklace with similar kite-shaped stones. The style of the signature and the 1955 advertisement establish that this splendid set dates to the 1950s. $100.00 – 150.00. From the collection of Debi Reece.

AUTUMN— arriving in a blaze of brilliance. Reflecting in mood, in motif, the Empire opulence of incoming fashion, and gem-set like the world's most fabled jewels. Jewelry shown priced from $9 to $33 plus tax.

1956 Eisenberg Ice "AUTUMN" advertisement. This advertisement reads, "AUTUMN — arriving in a blaze of brilliance. Reflecting in mood, in motif, the Empire opulence of incoming fashion, and gem-set like the world's most fabled jewels. Jewelry shown priced from $9 to $33 plus tax."

1960 Eisenberg Ice "Basic necessity for Basic Black" advertisement. The ad reads, "Subtle splendor…ablaze with dramatic brilliance against starkest black — and gem-set like the world's finest jewels. Pins $10 to $25, Earrings $15, Necklace $25, Bracelet $45."

Basic necessity for Basic Black

Subtle splendor…ablaze with dramatic brilliance against starkest black—and gem-set like the world's finest jewels. Pins $10 to $25, Earrings $15, Necklace $25, Bracelet $45. Prices plus tax.

Eisenberg Jewelry, 22 West Madison Street, Chicago
14 East 38th Street, New York

Authentic only when trademarked Eisenberg. Eisenberg designs copyrighted

**1948 – 1950s Eisenberg bracelet and 1970 – present Eisenberg Ice earrings.** The sensational shine of the clear rhinestones in this 7½" x ¾" Eisenberg bracelet and 1¼" clip earrings is lost in the photograph. In real life, the sparkle of this set is so vibrant it draws attention from across a large, crowded party. Note the comma-shaped swirls of rhinestones (pavé icing), a characteristic trait of many Eisenberg designs. The bracelet is signed "Eisenberg" in small print without the copyright symbol. This signature was used in the mid-1940s; however, the Eisenberg signatures are inconsistently applied. The rhodium plating and nonuse of sterling dates this bracelet to after 1948. The earrings are signed "Eisenberg Ice" in block letters, indicating the earrings date 1970 – present. Bracelet: $175.00 – 250.00. Earrings: $45.00 – 60.00.

PINK GLACÉ

*blazed to brilliance, and cooled
by subtle tints of spring's most
exhilarating hue . . . gem-cut like
the finest jewels. Pins from $7.50 to $12.50.
Earrings from $6.00. Prices plus tax.*

*Eisenberg Ice*

*Eisenberg Jewelry, 22 West Madison Street, Chicago
14 East 38th Street, New York*

*Authentic only when trademarked Eisenberg • Eisenberg designs copyrighted*

1961 Eisenberg Ice "Pink Glacé" advertisement. This charming colorful advertisement features an array of colorful Eisenberg designs. Pins sold from $7.50 to $12.50, earrings from $6.00.

The Sparkle of Elegance...

in precious-looking accent notes
richly glowing in the magnificent light
of Eisenberg Ice. All are gem-set,
naturally, like the world's finest jewels.
Pins shown, from 7.50 to 20.00.
Earring, 7.50; Ring,** 10.00. Prices plus tax.

*Eisenberg Ice*

Eisenberg Jewelry, 22 West Madison Street, Chicago
14 East 38th Street, New York

**Eisenberg Adjustable Rings U.S. Patent Pending    All Eisenberg designs are copyrighted

Fig.3

1962 Eisenberg Ice "The Sparkle of Elegance…" advertisement. Note the pearl and rhinestone brooch featured in this advertisement. The pins sold for $7.50 to $20.00, the earrings for $7.50, and the ring for $10.00. Interestingly, there is a footnote at the bottom of the advertisement stating, "Eisenberg Adjustable Rings U.S. Patent Pending," indicating that adjustable Eisenberg rings were introduced at this time.

**1970s Eisenberg enameled bracelet and earrings set.** Beautiful shades of purple, pink, and gray enamel cover this Eisenberg hinged bracelet and 1" clip earrings. The set is signed with "E" and the copyright symbol. In the 1970s, Carl Eisenberg commissioned famous artists of the time to design enameled jewelry like this rich-looking set. $60.00 – 85.00. From the collection of Debi Reece.

OTHER JEWELRY MAKERS

319

**1970s Eisenberg enameled owl pin.** Eisenberg enameled jewelry, like this colorful 2" owl pin, was produced in the 1970s under the direction of Carl Eisenberg and designed by leading artists of the time, including Braque, Calder, Chagall, Miro, and Picasso. It is signed "Eisenberg" in block letters with the copyright symbol. Note: Sometimes jewelry from this line is signed with "E" and the copyright symbol. $55.00 – 75.00.

**1970s Eisenberg enameled bird pendant.** This colorful 24" soaring bird necklace is signed "Eisenberg" in block letters with the copyright symbol. It is an example of the fine enameled jewelry designed by leading artists of the 1970s for Eisenberg jewelry. $55.00 – 75.00.

**1970 – present Eisenberg Ice rhinestone brooch.** Signed "Eisenberg Ice" in block letters, this pretty 1¾" x 1½" clear rhinestone brooch dates from 1970 to the present. $60.00 – 75.00.

**1976 – 1978 Eisenberg enameled King Tut Egyptian-design pendant.** Mint, with its original "Eisenberg Enamels" hangtag, this majestic King Tut necklace was produced in the mid-1970s to coincide with the 1976 – 1978 King Tut exhibit touring the United States at the time. Notice the magnificently detailed sculpting of the figure. The pendant measures 2½" x 1¾" and is suspended from a 24" snake chain. In addition to the Eisenberg Enamels hangtag, this necklace is signed "Eisenberg" in block letters with the copyright symbol. $100.00 – 150.00.

OTHER JEWELRY MAKERS

## 1941 – AT LEAST 1946

| Design Patent Number | Date Issued | Designer | Jewelry Type | Brief Description |
|---|---|---|---|---|
| 135096 | 2/23/1943 | Elliot Handler | Brooch | Ceramic woman's head |
| 135100 | 2/23/1943 | Elliot Handler | Brooch | Ceramic woman's face |
| 135101 | 2/23/1943 | Elliot Handler | Brooch | Ceramic woman's face with bonnet |
| 135102 | 2/23/1943 | Elliot Handler | Brooch | Ceramic woman's face |
| 135103 | 2/23/1943 | Elliot Handler | Brooch | Ceramic woman's face |
| 135519 | 4/20/1943 | Elliot Handler | Brooch | Ceramic squirrel |
| 135520 | 4/20/1943 | Elliot Handler | Brooch | Ceramic mule |
| 135521 | 4/20/1943 | Elliot Handler | Brooch | Ceramic pony |
| 135522 | 4/20/1943 | Elliot Handler | Brooch | Ceramic dog |
| 135523 | 4/20/1943 | Elliot Handler | Brooch | Ceramic braying donkey |
| 135595 | 4/27/1943 | Elliot Handler | Brooch | Ceramic Pegasus |
| 135596 | 4/27/1943 | Elliot Handler | Brooch | Ceramic baby ducks |
| 136221 | 8/24/1943 | Elliot Handler | Brooch | Ceramic woman with long braids |
| 136222 | 8/24/1943 | Elliot Handler | Brooch | Ceramic boy |
| 136223 | 8/24/1943 | Elliot Handler | Brooch | Ceramic girl |
| 136447 | 10/5/1943 | Elliot Handler | Brooch | Ceramic bird |
| 136750 | 11/30/1943 | Elliot Handler | Brooch | Ceramic rabbit |

135102

135101

**1943 Elzac ceramic face pin.** Zachary Zemby founded Elzac, Inc., in 1941. The company produced jewelry using Lucite, wood, and ceramics. Many of the Elzac designs, including the ceramic face pin in the photograph, were patented by free-lance designer Elliot Handler. Originally selling for $1.00 – 8.00, the plain ceramic face above measures 2⅛" x 1¼". It is design patent number 135102 issued February 23, 1943, to Elliot Handler for Elzac. $45.00 – 80.00.

OTHER JEWELRY MAKERS

135520

136221

**1943 Elzac Missouri Mule and Hobby horse ceramic and Lucite pins.** Right: Titled the "Missouri Mule," this 3¼" x 3" sleepy-looking ceramic mule features light yellow and black enameling. The ears and tail are clear, carved Lucite. Unsigned, this piece matches design patent number 135520 issued April 20, 1943, to Elliot Handler for Elzac, Inc. Left: Called "Hobby," this 3" x 1¼" unmarked horse is clearly an Elzac creation. Note the flowing amber-colored Lucite mane! Interestingly, these Elzac Lucite and ceramic pieces were designed at the same time Trifari was producing its famous Lucite Jelly Belly designs. In 1943, Lucite-enhanced designs were a creative way to manufacture jewelry during the war years when the harder metals were unavailable. Increasingly popular with collectors, the value today of these creatively designed creatures is $85.00 – 125.00 each. From the collection of Debi Reece.

**1945 Elzac Bonnet Head ceramic and Lucite face pin.** This large 3" x 2½" ceramic and Lucite pin is called "Bonnet Head" in a 1945 advertisement (not shown). The design of the face matches design patent number 135101 issued February 23, 1943, to Elliot Handler for Elzac, illustrating that these ceramic faces were made for several years. $85.00 – 125.00.

**1940s Elzac ceramic and Lucite mule figurine.** Sweet as he can be, this 5" x 2" yellow ceramic mule figurine is signed "Gift Art by Elzac Made in California" on a paper tag. Elzac produced this type of Lucite-adorned figurine in the 1940s. These figurines are highly collectible today due to the appealing design, but also because of the connection to the popular Elzac jewelry designs. $75.00 – 100.00. From the collection of Debi Reece.

1949 – 1981

**1955 – 1960s Emmons green art-glass necklace, earrings, and bracelet set.** The beautiful glowing green Emmons set in the above photograph is signed "Emmons" with the copyright symbol, indicating it was produced after 1955. The interesting green glass inserts are composed of clusters of molded flowers decorated with rhinestones. The 16½" choker, 7¼" bracelet, and 1¼" clip earrings resemble jewelry styles produced in great quantities during the 1950s and 1960s. $60.00 – 75.00.

Fig.2

Fig.3

Fig.4

**1960s Her Majesty Emmons hostess set including a bracelet, brooch, and clip earrings.** This highly collectible Emmons parure originally came in a deluxe presentation box that included a snake chain so the brooch could also be worn as a necklace. The amber-colored carved glass stones are similar to the finely carved glass found in Whiting & Davis jewelry of the same era. The brooch measures 2½" x 2", the bracelet 7½" x 1½", and the clip earrings 1½". The bracelet and earrings are signed "Emmons" with the copyright symbol. The earrings are also signed "Pat. Pend.," likely referring to a utility patent for the clip mechanism. $80.00 – 100.00. From the collection of Debi Reece.

OTHER JEWELRY MAKERS

323

Fig. 1

Fig. 2

Fig. 3

OTHER JEWELRY MAKERS

**1960s Emmons pearl necklace and bracelet in original box.** Resting comfortably in its original "Jewels by Emmons" box, this creamy double-strand pearl necklace and bracelet set testifies to the lasting beauty of Emmons jewelry designs. Called the "Queen of Fashion," this jewelry set dates to the 1960s. It was a hostess set available as a gift to a lady who successfully hosted an Emmons jewelry party. The necklace measures 16½" and the bracelet is 7¼". $65.00 – 90.00. From the collection of Debi Reece.

**1976 Emmons Cleopatra necklace, bracelet, and earrings set in original boxes.** In 1976 Emmons titled this set "Cleopatra." The 7½" bracelet, 26" necklace, and 1¾" clip earrings all feature Egyptian-style pyramid shapes set in gold-tone metal and decorated with green, purple, and topaz-colored rhinestones. All of the pieces are signed "Emmons" with the copyright symbol and are still nestled in signed Caroline Emmons boxes. $70.00 – 90.00.

## 1952 – APPROXIMATELY 1962

Fig 1

**1952 – 1955 Eugene triple-strand beige necklace and earrings set.** Eugene jewelry is the creation of Eugene Schultz. Signed pieces are rare. This classically designed necklace features three strands of beige glass beads graduating in size, with a brown faux-agate clasp. The 17" necklace is signed "Eugene" in script without the copyright symbol. The ¾" clips are unsigned. $85.00 – 100.00. From the collection of Debi Reece.

## • EVANS •

Fig.2

Fig.3

## 1920s – APPROXIMATELY 1965

**1958 Evans green enameled necklace.** This rare 18" necklace is signed "Evans" in script on oval hangtag. It was produced by the Evans Case Company of Attleboro, Massachusetts. The Evans Case Company specialized in compacts, cigarette cases, and decorative lipstick cases. It is unclear when, or how much, jewelry was produced. This design, called "the Pastel Look," is featured in a 1958 Evans advertisement (not shown) and originally sold for $16.00. $50.00 – 70.00.

## 1950s – UNKNOWN

**1950s molded plastic Featherweights earrings.** Signed "Featherweights" on the silver-tone clips, these lovely lime green ¾" molded plastic earrings are decorated with light green rhinestones. An advertisement for Featherweights in the 1954 *Jewelers' Buyers Guide* (not shown) advertises this type of jewelry as "Washable, Unbreakable, No Adhesive." It was made by the Greenbaum Novelty Co. $10.00 – 20.00.

## • FLORENZA •

### 1940s – 1981

The Florenza name was first used to mark jewelry in 1949 or 1950. The styles of the jewelry featured in this section are consistent with jewelry produced in the 1950s and 1960s. Some companies copyrighted designs before 1955, including Florenza; therefore, the presence of the copyright symbol in the Florenza mark is not useful in dating the jewelry.

| Design Patent Number | Date Issued | Designer | Jewelry Type | Brief Description |
|---|---|---|---|---|
| 152268 | 1/4/1949 | Daniel Kasoff | Pin | Fob style |
| 152269 | 1/4/1949 | Daniel Kasoff | Pin | Double-sided locket |
| 152420 | 1/18/1949 | Daniel Kasoff | Pin | Fob style |
| 152421 | 1/18/1949 | Daniel Kasoff | Pin | Fob style |
| 152422 | 1/18/1949 | Daniel Kasoff | Pin | Fob style |
| 152423 | 1/18/1949 | Daniel Kasoff | Pin | Fob style |
| 152424 | 1/18/1949 | Daniel Kasoff | Pin | Fob style |
| 152425 | 1/18/1949 | Daniel Kasoff | Pin | Fob style |

152268

152269

**1950s – 1960s Florenza moonstone bracelet and brooch.** Especially attractive, this 7½" bracelet and matching 2" brooch set features triangular pseudo-moonstones surrounded by tiny blue, green, and yellow rhinestones. Both pieces are signed "Florenza" with the copyright symbol. $125.00 – 175.00.

**1950s – 1960s Florenza amber-colored rhinestone brooch and earrings set.** This heraldic 2" brooch and matching 1¼" clip earrings are signed "Florenza" with a copyright symbol. Notice how the large central stone and surrounding aurora borealis rhinestones sparkle with a rainbow of golden color. $75.00 – 100.00.

**1950s – 1960s Florenza green cameo brooch and earrings set.** This 2" x 2" pretty cameo brooch and matching 1" clip earrings are surprisingly lightweight for Florenza jewelry. All pieces are signed "Florenza" with the copyright symbol. $65.00 – 85.00.

OTHER JEWELRY MAKERS

**1950s – 1960s Florenza Maltese cross brooch and earrings set.** This unique fob-style brooch measures 3½" x 1½". Each clip earring is 1" in diameter. All three pieces are signed "Florenza" with the copyright symbol. Notice the interesting six-sided rhinestones. A checkerboard pattern glows from inside these unique rhinestones. Maltese cross jewelry, like this set, was popular in the mid-1950s through the 1960s. $65.00 – 85.00.

**1950s – 1960s Florenza oversized rhinestone stickpin.** This 5" x 1½" stickpin looks like a stylized serpent or dragon coiling around an antique gold-tone trunk. It is signed "Florenza" with the copyright symbol. $65.00 – 85.00.

**1950s – 1960s Florenza moonstone necklace, bracelet, and earrings set.** This lovely set features creamy blue cabochon moonstones, blue enameled leaves, and light blue fluted ribbed beads capped with clear rhinestones. The necklace measures 16", the bracelet 7", and the clip earrings 1¼". All pieces are signed "Florenza" with the copyright symbol. $90.00 – 120.00. From the collection of Debi Reece.

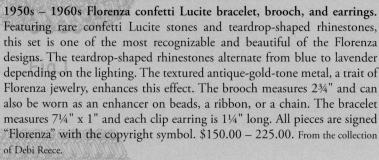

**1950s – 1960s Florenza confetti Lucite bracelet, brooch, and earrings.** Featuring rare confetti Lucite stones and teardrop-shaped rhinestones, this set is one of the most recognizable and beautiful of the Florenza designs. The teardrop-shaped rhinestones alternate from blue to lavender depending on the lighting. The textured antique-gold-tone metal, a trait of Florenza jewelry, enhances this effect. The brooch measures 2¾" and can also be worn as an enhancer on beads, a ribbon, or a chain. The bracelet measures 7¼" x 1" and each clip earring is 1¼" long. All pieces are signed "Florenza" with the copyright symbol. $150.00 – 225.00. From the collection of Debi Reece.

**1950s – 1960s Florenza leaf brooch.** The paisley design of this 3" x 1¾" brooch was popular in the 1960s. Notice how the small turquoise seed pearls, purple and blue rhinestones, and blue aurora borealis rhinestones add texture to this inspired design. Interestingly, this brooch is not only signed "Florenza" with the copyright symbol, it is also inexplicably signed "Lori." $65.00 – 85.00.

**1950s – 1960s Florenza floating opal style bracelet.** Florenza jewelry often exhibits unusual stones like the eight-sided smoky gray stones decorating this rare 7½" bracelet. It is signed "Florenza" with the copyright symbol. Inside each gray stone are tiny bits or chips of white material that form a kaleidoscope-style design in the bottom of the gray stones. The white chips inside these stones remind me of the floating opal jewelry popular in the mid-1950s (see chapter 1). Floating opal jewelry consists of bits of real opal stones floating in oil. The stones in this Florenza bracelet appear to be simulating this floating opal style. $95.00 – 145.00.

OTHER JEWELRY MAKERS

**1950s – 1960s Florenza Oriental motif chunky charm bracelet.** This magnificent Florenza charm bracelet features Oriental-motif plastic inserts popularized by Hobé in the late 1940s (see examples of Hobé Oriental-motif jewelry late in this chapter). The bracelet measures 7" and has six Orient-inspired charms. It is signed "Florenza" with the copyright symbol. $60.00 – 80.00.

**1950s – 1960s Florenza bracelet with rare S-shaped rhinestones.** Light green glowing S-shaped rhinestones swirl across this magnificent 7½" x 1" Florenza bracelet. This exceptional bracelet is signed "Florenza" with the copyright symbol. $85.00 – 125.00. From the collection of Debi Reece.

**1950s – 1960s Florenza necklace with dangling pearls.** This fabulous necklace is signed "Florenza" with the copyright symbol. Note the rare six-sided diamond-shaped rhinestones decorating this 16" necklace. They change color from amber to olive green depending on the light. In addition, tiny champagne faux pearls dangle freely from each section of this magnificent necklace. $75.00 – 90.00.

# • FREIRICH •

## 1900 – 1990
### (THE "FREIRICH" MARK WAS FIRST USED IN THE 1960S.)

**1960s – 1990 Freirich faux baroque pearl brooch.** This handmade 2¼" Freirich brooch features faux baroque pearls fastened to a gold-tone filigree frame. It is signed "Freirich" without the copyright symbol. Freirich first began signing jewelry in the 1960s, so all "Freirich" signed jewelry dates from the 1960s to 1990, when the company ceased operations. $15.00 – 25.00.

Fig.1

# • GELL, WENDY •

Fig.2

## 1975 – PRESENT

Fig.3

**1980s Wendy Gell Disney-design brooch.** This amazing 2½" x 3" hand-crafted pin is signed "Wendy Gell Disney Co." with the copyright symbol. Wendy Gell began designing jewelry in 1975 and continues today. In the 1980s, she produced designs such as this one for Disney. Most of Wendy Gell's designs are one-of-a-kind. All of them are wonderful. Some of the enamel is chipped away on this example; however, the magical arrangement remains intact. $100.00 – 125.00.

OTHER JEWELRY MAKERS

# • GIVENCHY •

## 1952 – PRESENT

**1977 Givenchy necklace with removable slides.** This unique 17" necklace is signed "Givenchy Paris New York 1977." Wonderfully versatile, this necklace features three removable tubes (faux ivory, faux onyx, and faux jade) that can be worn alone or together. $35.00 – 55.00. *Courtesy of Carol Dike.*

# • GOLDETTE •

## 1958 – APPROXIMATELY 1977

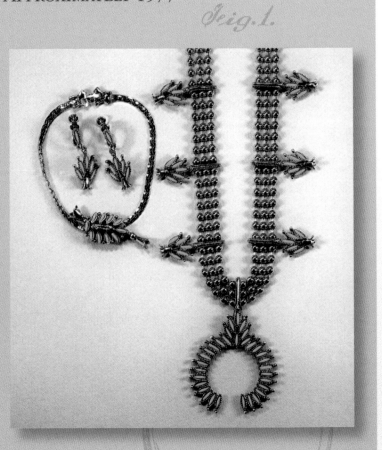

**1958 – 1970s Goldette squash blossom necklace, bracelet, and earrings set.** This squash blossom necklace measures 27½". The bracelet is an extra long 8¾", and the screw-back earrings are 1¼". The necklace and bracelet are signed "Goldette" with the copyright symbol. The earrings, however, are unsigned except for utility patent number 3,176,475. This utility patent was issued April 6, 1965, to Nazareno J. Saccoccio for an enhancement to the design of adjustable clip earrings. $50.00 – 70.00.

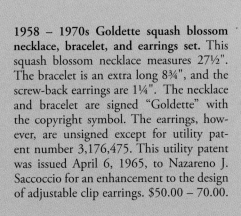

OTHER JEWELRY MAKERS

1958 – 1970s Goldette slide charm bracelet. This well-crafted charm bracelet measures 7¼". It is signed "Goldette" with the copyright symbol. The four charms slide along two strands of antique-gold-tone chain. Goldette utilized decorated charms like these to make many different jewelry creations. $25.00 – 35.00. From the collection of Debi Reece.

Fig.1

Fig.2

# • GRAY, FRED •

## 1940s – 1950s

Jewelry signed "S" inside a star is attributed to Fred Gray; however, this information is unconfirmed.

1940s – 1950s Fred Gray sapphire and clear rhinestone flower brooch. Little is known about jewelry from the Fred Gray Corp. The jewelry appears to have been produced in the 1940s and early 1950s. It is sometimes crudely enameled and often average to below average in quality. This large 2¾" x 2½" example is better than most due to the interesting rhinestone petals. It is signed "Fred. Gray Corp." $20.00 – 30.00.

## UNKNOWN, APPEARS TO DATE FROM THE EARLY 1950s.

**Early 1950s Halbe ribbon brooch and earrings set.** This well-crafted looping ribbon pin and matching earrings attest to the quality of hard-to-find Halbe jewelry. Dating to the early 1950s, this pin features both gold- and silver-tone metal and clear baguette rhinestones. All three pieces are signed "Halbe" in block letters. The pin measures 2" x 1¼". The clip earrings are 1". $75.00 – 95.00.

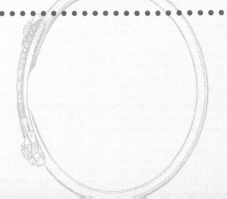

**Early 1950s Halbe five-petal flower brooch.** There is little reliable information on Halbe jewelry. Most collectors believe Halbe jewelry was produced in the 1950s and 1960s, but exact dates are unknown. Jewelry with the Halbe mark is rare. The jewelry is usually high quality. This well-crafted 2¼" flower brooch features black enameled stripes and clear rhinestones in the style of classic early 1940s Trifari jewelry. It is signed "Halbe" in capital letters. $65.00 – 85.00. From the collection of Debi Reece.

OTHER JEWELRY MAKERS

## Mid-1950s – 1960s

**1955 – 1960s HAR enameled songbird pin.** Signed "HAR" with the copyright symbol, this sweet songbird measures 1½". It features a large pearl belly and beautiful enameling. There is little information on the dates of operation for the Hargo Jewelry Company except that the designs appear to have been produced in the late 1950s and 1960s. $30.00 – 45.00.

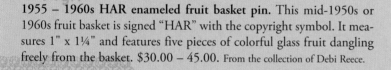

**1955 – 1960s HAR enameled fruit basket pin.** This mid-1950s or 1960s fruit basket is signed "HAR" with the copyright symbol. It measures 1" x 1¼" and features five pieces of colorful glass fruit dangling freely from the basket. $30.00 – 45.00. From the collection of Debi Reece.

**1955 – 1960s HAR cobra brooch.** Astonishing, extraordinary, exceptional — there are not enough adjectives to describe this famous HAR cobra brooch! It is signed "HAR" with the copyright symbol. The design of this large 2¾" x 1¾" brooch is interesting and unique. It is recognized by collectors as one of the best and rarest figural pieces produced. Note the sculptured three-dimensional cobra's head and the rare molded glass stones decorating the cobra's body. Originally HAR produced a matching cobra necklace, bracelet, and earrings. This brooch alone is valued at $600.00 – 800.00. From the collection of Debi Reece.

OTHER JEWELRY MAKERS

## 1937 – UNKNOWN

Fig. 1

Fig. 2

Fig. 3

**Two 1940s – 1950s Harwood expansion bracelets.** Left: This lovely gold-tone expansion bracelet features a classic Roman column design decorated with light blue rhinestones. The bracelet is signed "Harwood" in script. The Harwood mark was first used in 1937 by the W. & H. Jewelry Co. Right: Ruby red and clear pavé rhinestones embellish the beauty of this heavy and well-crafted Harwood expansion bracelet. This example of Harwood jewelry is signed "Leading Lady." The "Leading Lady" mark was first used in 1940. $55.00 – 75.00 each. From the collection of Debi Reece.

1954 Harwood "New Jack 'n Jill Sets" advertisement. The Jack 'n Jill sets shown in this advertisement are intended for children. The purpose of this advertisement is to encourage retailers to sell Harwood jewelry. Notice the interesting six-bracelet display box for the Jack 'n Jill sets.

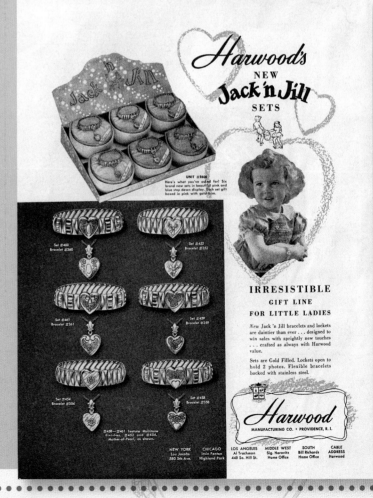

## 1924 – PRESENT

**1940s unsigned Miriam Haskell clip.** This interesting 2" x 1½" clip is unsigned. However, the design and the use of materials suggest it is an early Miriam Haskell clip dating to the early to mid-1940s. Red, green, and frosted white beads (with clear bead caps) are hand strung to a plastic mesh back. As an unsigned early Haskell, the value is $65.00 – 100.00. If it could be positively identified as Haskell, the value would be higher. (Not all clips with plastic backs are early Haskell designs. I consulted the book *Miriam Haskell Jewelry* by Cathy Gordon and Sheila Pamfiloff for examples of unmarked Haskell clips to determine that this clip is possibly an unmarked Haskell piece. This book is an excellent resource for clues on how to identify unmarked Haskell Jewelry. It is important to consult a reliable resource like this book, or a Haskell expert, before purchasing an unsigned Haskell.)

**1950s Miriam Haskell pink necklace and earrings set.** This spectacular 15" necklace and 1" x 1" clip earrings are signed "Miriam Haskell." The necklace features two rows of pink opaque glass beads connected to an elaborate 2½" x 1½" center decoration. This center piece is covered with light pink beads in a technique called tapestry beading. The fabulous marble-like green glass leaves add color, interest, and texture to this delightful design. Notice the beaded flower clasp, which is a typical Haskell design feature. In excellent condition, this set is valued at $1,500.00 – 2,500.00.

JEWELS *Miriam Haskell*

AT SAKS FIFTH AVENUE, NEW YORK AND SMART STORES THROUGHOUT THE COUNTRY — MIRIAM HASKELL, 392 FIFTH AVENUE, NEW YORK, N. Y.

1950 Harper's Bazaar Jewels by Miriam Haskell advertisement featuring an elaborate baroque pearl necklace and earrings set.

Fig.1

Fig.2

Fig.3

**1950s – 1960s Miriam Haskell triple-strand blue beaded necklace and earrings set.** This spectacular 15½" shades-of-blue triple-fan necklace and matching crescent earrings set is signed "Miriam Haskell" on the hook and again on an oval cartouche attached to the back of the center decoration. The 1" clip earrings are also signed "Miriam Haskell." Amazingly, the beautiful blue beads in this *mint* condition set are strung on matching blue cord. $1,500.00 – 2,500.00.

1954 Harper's Bazaar Miriam Haskell advertisement featuring a colorful red, green, and white hand-beaded necklace.

OTHER JEWELRY MAKERS

Fig.1

Fig.2

Fig.3

OTHER JEWELRY MAKERS

1950s – 1970s Miriam Haskell pink double-strand beads with pink rhinestone clasp and matching pink rhinestone earrings. This lovely 15" pink necklace and 1" clip earrings set is signed "Miriam Haskell" and features two rows of light, translucent pink glass beads. Notice the sparkling hot-pink baguette rhinestone clasp that matches the sparkling earrings. $400.00 – 600.00.

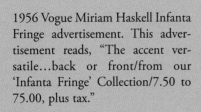

1956 Vogue Miriam Haskell Infanta Fringe advertisement. This advertisement reads, "The accent versatile...back or front/from our 'Infanta Fringe' Collection/7.50 to 75.00, plus tax."

1957 Vogue Miriam Haskell Queen Blue advertisement. This advertisement reads, "Enchanting 'Queen Blue' — simulated moonstones and sapphires. $7.50 to $65.00 plus tax."

**1950s – 1970s Miriam Haskell crystal and rhinestone brooch and dangle earrings.** This wonderfully elaborate 2¾" brooch and 2¾" dangle earrings set features varying shapes of clear faceted crystal beads and sparkling clear rhinestones set in antique-gold-tone metal. All pieces are signed "Miriam Haskell." $400.00 – 550.00. From the collection of Debi Reece.

OTHER JEWELRY MAKERS

**1950s – 1970s Miriam Haskell red brooch and earrings set.** This great brooch measures 2½" x 1" and is made of three gold-tone half spheres fully covered with tiny red beads, rhinestones, and larger, deep red beads. Typical of Haskell quality, the brooch is "finished" with a clear rhinestone set at the top of the design and another set at the bottom. Each earring measures ¾" and has the same tapestry beading. All pieces are signed "Miriam Haskell." $325.00 – 450.00 set. From the collection of Debi Reece.

**1950s – 1970s Miriam Haskell blue-green beaded necklace.** This beautiful 15½" blue-green beaded necklace is signed "Miriam Haskell." Notice the attractive and colorful baroque pearl drop and the artistic arrangement of the different shapes and sizes of beads. $150.00 – 250.00. From the collection of Debi Reece.

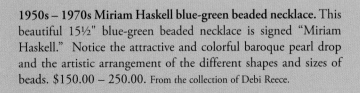

OTHER JEWELRY MAKERS

Fig. 1

Fig. 2

Fig. 3

**1950s – 1970s Miriam Haskell yellow and orange necklace.** This glowing 17½" necklace features yellow tapestry beading, white baroque pearls, faux amber beads, yellow crackle beads, and tiny orange beads. Notice the especially elaborate center decoration composed of three floral arrangements all decorated with tapestry beading, hand-set rhinestones, and baroque pearls. This necklace truly glows with golden color. $1,000.00 – 2,000.00.

Fig. 4

1960 Harper's Bazaar Miriam Haskell Evening Flower advertisement. This advertisement reads, "From our collection of Treasured Fashion Jewelry: 'Evening Flower'...simulated baroque and smooth pearls, brilliants, antiqued golden settings."

OTHER JEWELRY MAKERS

343

**1950s – 1970s Miriam Haskell pink choker necklace.** This 16" pretty pink Miriam Haskell necklace features three strands of yummy pink glass beads. Each bead is separated by two clear spacers. The typical Haskell-style hook is made of silver-tone metal and decorated with a characteristic Haskell hand-wired flower. The choker is signed "Miriam Haskell" on the hook. $150.00 – 250.00.

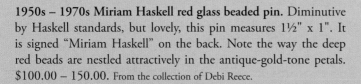

**1950s – 1970s Miriam Haskell red glass beaded pin.** Diminutive by Haskell standards, but lovely, this pin measures 1½" x 1". It is signed "Miriam Haskell" on the back. Note the way the deep red beads are nestled attractively in the antique-gold-tone petals. $100.00 – 150.00. From the collection of Debi Reece.

**1950s – 1970s Miriam Haskell pearl and rhinestone brooch.** This pretty 2¼" x 1¼" brooch features a smooth champagne center pearl surrounded by amber-colored aurora borealis rhinestones. The brooch is signed "Miriam Haskell" on an oval plaque. $75.00 – 95.00.

OTHER JEWELRY MAKERS

Fig.2

**1979 – present Miriam Haskell raspberry glass beaded necklaces.** These two raspberry glass necklaces are both signed "Miriam Haskell" on a single-sided oval hangtag. (The name can only be read from one side of the tag. The other side is blank.) The shorter necklace measures 15" and the longer strand is 23". Both necklaces have identical shades of red and pink art-glass beads, so they can be worn separately or clasped together to form one long 38" strand. The slide clasp (see close view below) is marked with utility patent number 3,427,691 issued February 18, 1969, to James R. Johnson. $100.00 – 200.00 each.

Fig.4

Close view of the sliding clasp and the smooth back of the oval cartouche.

# • HOBÉ •

## IN U.S., 1927 – SOLD IN 1995

| Design Patent Number | Date Issued | Designer | Jewelry Type | Brief Description |
|---|---|---|---|---|
| 108543 | 2/22/1938 | William Hobé | Brooch | Floral |
| 108544 | 2/22/1938 | William Hobé | Brooch | Floral |
| 109804 | 5/24/1938 | William Hobé | Bracelet | Hand heart key |
| 123164 | 10/22/1940 | William Hobé | Brooch | Floral in rectangular frame |
| 123200 | 10/22/1940 | William Hobé | Brooch | Floral with round cabochon stones (See 123166 for matching brooch.) |
| 123265 | 10/29/1940 | William Hobé | Brooch | Floral in rectangular frame |
| 123266 | 10/29/1940 | William Hobé | Brooch | Floral in oval frame |
| 126475 | 4/8/1941 | William Hobé | Brooch | Box with large central metal flower |
| 126476 | 4/8/1941 | William Hobé | Brooch | Bow with six small blooms |
| 126786 | 4/22/1941 | William Hobé | Brooch | Floral |
| 126787 | 4/22/1941 | William Hobé | Brooch | Floral in oval |
| 126811 | 4/22/1941 | William Hobé | Brooch | Floral |
| 128423 | 7/22/1941 | William Hobé | Brooch | Two flowers in rectangular frame |
| 130247 | 11/4/1941 | William Hobé | Brooch | Oval with two flowers |
| 130869 | 12/23/1941 | William Hobé | Brooch | Triple flower simple design |
| 130871 | 12/23/1941 | William Hobé | Brooch | Floral in oval |
| 130872 | 12/23/1941 | William Hobé | Brooch | Floral in circle |
| 130873 | 12/23/1941 | William Hobé | Brooch | Floral in oval |
| 131086 | 1/13/1942 | William Hobé | Brooch | Two flowers in circular frame |
| 131854 | 3/31/1942 | William Hobé | Brooch | Three flowers in oval frame |
| 131855 | 3/31/1942 | William Hobé | Brooch | Bouquet of flowers inside bow |
| 131856 | 3/31/1942 | William Hobé | Brooch | Flowers and bow |
| 131857 | 3/31/1942 | William Hobé | Brooch | Oval shaped flowers and bow |
| 131858 | 3/31/1942 | William Hobé | Brooch | Flower and bow |
| 131874 | 3/31/1942 | William Hobé | Brooch | Ribbon floral |
| 131930 | 4/7/1942 | William Hobé | Brooch | Bow with center flower |
| 131931 | 4/7/1942 | William Hobé | Brooch | Floral |
| 131967 | 4/7/1942 | William Hobé | Brooch | Floral in heart-shaped frame |
| 131968 | 4/7/1942 | William Hobé | Brooch | Floral |
| 132323 | 5/5/1942 | William Hobé | Brooch | Floral |
| 132324 | 5/5/1942 | William Hobé | Brooch | Floral |
| 132325 | 5/5/1942 | William Hobé | Brooch | Floral |
| 132326 | 5/5/1942 | William Hobé | Brooch | Floral |
| 132327 | 5/5/1942 | William Hobé | Brooch | Floral |
| 132328 | 5/5/1942 | William Hobé | Brooch | Floral |
| 132329 | 5/5/1942 | William Hobé | Brooch | Floral |
| 132330 | 5/5/1942 | William Hobé | Brooch | Floral |

OTHER JEWELRY MAKERS

123164

126476

**1941 – 1948 Hobé sterling silver triple-tassel brooch.** Interestingly, this 2¼" x 2¾" Hobé triple tassel brooch is signed "Hobé 1/20th 14K on Sterling Des. Pat'd." on a six-sided shield. I was unable to locate the design patent for this piece. However, the style of the signature and the use of sterling indicate this brooch dates to 1941 – 1948. $175.00 – 250.00.

Fig.1

130869

130871

**1948 – 1955 Hobé lariat necklace and earrings with hand-strung beaded decoration.** This vintage set is signed "Hobé" in a rectangle without the copyright symbol. This mark and the nonuse of sterling indicate this lovely set dates to 1948 – 1955. Note the hand-strung beads, which are reminiscent of Miriam Haskell designs of the era. The olive green, white, and pink lariat-style necklace measures 32". Amazingly, the heavy gold-tone chain is ¼" in diameter! Each 1½" clip earring mirrors the delightful, detailed design of the necklace. $85.00 – 125.00. From the collection of Debi Reece.

| 133027 | 7/7/1942 | William Hobé | Brooch | Floral in oval frame |
|---|---|---|---|---|
| 133028 | 7/7/1942 | William Hobé | Brooch | Floral in oval frame |
| 137644 | 4/11/1944 | William Hobé | Brooch | Floral |
| 138929 | 9/26/1944 | William Hobé | Brooch | Floral |
| 138930 | 9/26/1944 | William Hobé | Brooch | Floral |
| 138932 | 9/26/1944 | William Hobé | Brooch | Floral |
| 138933 | 9/26/1944 | William Hobé | Brooch | Floral |
| 138934 | 9/26/1944 | William Hobé | Brooch | Floral |
| 138935 | 9/26/1944 | William Hobé | Brooch | Floral |
| 138936 | 9/26/1944 | William Hobé | Brooch | Floral |
| 138937 | 9/26/1944 | William Hobé | Brooch | Floral |
| 138938 | 9/26/1944 | William Hobé | Brooch | Floral |
| 138939 | 9/26/1944 | William Hobé | Brooch | Asian man |
| 138954 | 10/3/1944 | William Hobé | Brooch | Floral |
| 138957 | 10/3/1944 | William Hobé | Brooch | Jelly belly bird |
| 138977 | 10/3/1944 | William Hobé | Brooch | Floral |
| 138978 | 10/3/1944 | William Hobé | Brooch | Floral |
| 138979 | 10/3/1944 | William Hobé | Brooch | Three graduating in size birds |
| 138980 | 10/3/1944 | William Hobé | Brooch | Floral in rectangular frame |
| 138981 | 10/3/1944 | William Hobé | Brooch | Basket |
| 138982 | 10/3/1944 | William Hobé | Brooch | Floral |
| 139169 | 10/17/1944 | William Hobé | Bracelet | Cinderella-style coach and star chatelaine charms |
| 139170 | 10/17/1944 | William Hobé | Brooch | Floral |
| 139171 | 10/17/1944 | William Hobé | Brooch | Floral |
| 139261 | 10/24/1944 | William Hobé | Brooch | Floral |
| 139263 | 10/24/1944 | William Hobé | Brooch | Floral |
| 139339 | 11/7/1944 | William Hobé | Brooch | Floral with rhinestone and metal flowers |
| 141285 | 5/22/1945 | William Hobé | Brooch | Floral |
| 141301 | 5/22/1945 | William Hobé | Earring | Floral |
| 141302 | 5/22/1945 | William Hobé | Brooch | Long-stemmed floral with heart |
| 141303 | 5/22/1945 | William Hobé | Brooch | Rectangular floral with large center stone |
| 141304 | 5/22/1945 | William Hobé | Brooch | Floral with heart center and tassels |
| 141343 | 5/22/1945 | William Hobé | Brooch | Floral |
| 141344 | 5/22/1945 | William Hobé | Brooch | Double heart |
| 141367 | 5/29/1945 | William Hobé | Brooch | Heart on heart |
| 141368 | 5/28/1945 | William Hobé | Brooch | Hanging heart |
| 141440 | 6/5/1945 | William Hobé | Brooch | Double heart inside heart |
| 141441 | 6/5/1945 | William Hobé | Brooch | Flower basket |
| 141443 | 6/5/1945 | William Hobé | Bracelet | Floral |
| 141845 | 7/10/1945 | William Hobé | Brooch | Flower basket |

130873

131967

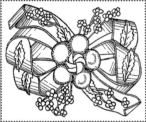

132327

138933

138980

*Sculptured 'Fleur'*
*A harmony of graceful petals, shimmering rhinestones and pearls.® Matching earrings.*

*"Mélange Bouquet"*
*A sunburst of faceted stones®, in warm, muted colors. Matching earrings.*

*"Blossom d' Elegance"*
*A beautiful blending of frosted leaves, stones® and iridescent beads. Matching earrings.*

*Interesting brochure free on request*

SIMULATED **Hobé** 1961
*jewels of legendary splendor*
9 East 37th St., New York 16, N. Y.

1961 Hobé advertisement. Three elaborate flower brooches and matching earrings are featured in this black and white 1961 Hobé advertisement. Top: Sculptured "Fleur." Middle: "Mélange Bouquet." Bottom: "Blossom d' Elegance."

1962 Hobé "Nofretete Inspiration" advertisement. This tiny advertisement features a bib necklace and matching earrings. The ad reads, "Golden-hued links with sparkling tinted beads of the Nile (in Topaz, Blue or Green) that capture the romance and beauty of ancient Egypt."

*Nofretete Inspiration*

Golden-hued links with sparkling tinted beads of the Nile (in Topaz, Blue or Green) that capture the romance and beauty of ancient Egypt.

*at fine stores everywhere*

Matching
Pin
Bracelet
Shower Earring

FREE BROCHURE ON REQUEST

© 1962

**Hobé**
*jewels of legendary splendor*
9 East 37th St., New York 16, N. Y.

| 143318 | 12/25/1945 | William Hobé | Brooch | Large, lacy abstract with heart-shaped rhinestone center |
| 143487 | 1/8/1946 | William Hobé | Brooch | Crown |
| 143488 | 1/8/1946 | William Hobé | Brooch | Crown with dangling heart |
| 143489 | 1/8/1946 | William Hobé | Brooch | Bow with dangling heart |
| 145213 | 7/16/1946 | William Hobé | Brooch | Double heart |
| 145214 | 7/16/1946 | William Hobé | Brooch | Heart |
| 149490 | 5/4/1948 | Sylvia Hobé | Brooch | Asian man with floral, left arm raised |
| 149491 | 5/4/1948 | Sylvia Hobé | Brooch | Sitting Asian man with arm raised, holding cup |
| 149492 | 5/4/1948 | Sylvia Hobé | Brooch | Sitting Asian man with arm raised, holding cup |
| 149493 | 5/4/1948 | Sylvia Hobé | Brooch | Sitting Asian man with arm lowered |
| 149494 | 5/4/1948 | Sylvia Hobé | Earring | Asian head with hat |
| 149495 | 5/4/1948 | Sylvia Hobé | Brooch | Asian face |
| 149496 | 5/4/1948 | Sylvia Hobé | Brooch | Standing Asian figure |
| 149497 | 5/4/1948 | Sylvia Hobé | Brooch | Asian face in elaborate floral with ribbon |
| 149746 | 5/25/1948 | Sylvia Hobé | Brooch | Standing Asian man with beard |
| 149747 | 5/25/1948 | Sylvia Hobé | Brooch | Asian face with floral and a tassel |
| 149748 | 5/25/1948 | Sylvia Hobé | Brooch | Sitting asian with fingers together |
| 149749 | 5/25/1948 | Sylvia Hobé | Brooch | Asian face, floral, and five tassels |
| 149750 | 5/25/1948 | Sylvia Hobé | Brooch | Man on horse under floral arch |
| 149751 | 5/25/1948 | Sylvia Hobé | Brooch | Asian face surrounded by floral with three tassels |
| 149752 | 5/25/1948 | Sylvia Hobé | Brooch | Asian face with heart-shaped floral and bow |
| 149753 | 5/25/1948 | Sylvia Hobé | Brooch | Asian figure with fan |
| 150844 | 9/7/1948 | Sylvia Hobé | Brooch | Woman's portrait |
| 150856 | 9/7/1948 | Sylvia Hobé | Brooch | Asian mask, rhinestone headdress |
| 150857 | 9/7/1948 | Sylvia Hobé | Brooch | Asian figure standing surrounded by dripping rhinestones |
| 150858 | 9/7/1948 | Sylvia Hobé | Brooch | Asian figure with fan, walking |
| 150859 | 9/7/1948 | Sylvia Hobé | Brooch | Asian mask |
| 151990 | 12/7/1948 | William Hobé | Brooch | Large bow |
| 151991 | 12/7/1948 | William Hobé | Brooch | Double flower |
| 152071 | 12/14/1948 | William Hobé | Brooch | Long-stemmed floral |
| 152072 | 12/14/1948 | William Hobé | Brooch | Intricate fan-shaped floral |
| 152073 | 12/14/1948 | William Hobé | Brooch | Floral |
| 152075 | 12/14/1948 | William Hobé | Brooch | Flower basket with long-stemmed flowers |

139339

141304

145214

**1948 – 1955 Hobé pink wrap bracelet and earrings set.** Sparkling hot pink crystals and rare art-glass beads give this 7½" Hobé triple-strand wire bracelet and matching 1" Hobé earrings a plus quality. The bracelet is unsigned. Each clip earring is signed "Hobé" without the copyright symbol. This signature and the nonuse of sterling date this set to 1948 – 1955. $100.00 – 150.00. From the collection of Debi Reece.

1962 Hobé "Tari-Ballerina" advertisement. Notice the Egyptian-motif background for this interesting jewelry set. The ad reads, "Refreshing as a cool desert breeze. Delightfully different as only Hobé can be. A variety of matching accessories in three summery pastel shades of Sungold Yellow, Wedgewood Blue, and Wisteria Rose."

149493

**1948 Hobé Asian-man-in-a-garden brooch.** All Hobé sterling silver jewelry is collectible, but Hobé brooches featuring carved Asian figures are especially hard to find. This 2" x 1½" man sitting in a garden brooch is signed "Hobé 1/20th 14K on Sterling Des. Pat'd." on a six-sided shield. This signature indicates this brooch dates to 1941 – 1948. However, the design is similar to design patent number 149493 issued to Sylvia Hobé on May 4, 1948, dating this piece to that year. The interesting, rare figure is made of resin or hard plastic. $500.00 – 800.00.

OTHER JEWELRY MAKERS

351

| | | | | |
|---|---|---|---|---|
| 152076 | 12/14/1948 | William Hobé | Brooch | Circular floral |
| 152077 | 12/14/1948 | William Hobé | Brooch | Circular floral with stem |
| 152080 | 12/14/1948 | William Hobé | Brooch | Wedding-style bouquet |
| 152082 | 12/14/1948 | William Hobé | Brooch | Floral |
| 152083 | 12/14/1948 | William Hobé | Necklace | Floral |
| 152084 | 12/14/1948 | William Hobé | Necklace | Floral |
| 152086 | 12/14/1948 | William Hobé | Necklace | Floral |
| 152337 | 1/11/1949 | William Hobé | Necklace | Floral |
| 152541 | 2/1/1949 | William Hobé | Brooch | Floral with female portrait |
| 164927 | 10/23/1951 | William Hobé | Display | Hands as a display for perfume bottle |

149746

149751

151990

152337

152075

152082

152541

Fig. 1

Fig. 2

Fig. 3

OTHER JEWELRY MAKERS

Fig.1

Fig.2

**Early 1960s Hobé brightly enameled Egyptian-motif parure.** This extraordinary parure including a 17" necklace, 8" x 1½" bracelet, and 1¼" clip earrings is unmarked. However, the set can be attributed to Hobé because a signed necklace, exactly matching this set, has been found online. The exquisitely executed enameled Egyptian motif dates this set to the early 1960s to coincide with the release of the movie *Cleopatra*. Tiny green enamel snakes surround each Egyptian figure. Pie-shaped green/brown Bakelite wedges further frame the figures. Notice the highly detailed sarcophagi with black, red, yellow, green, and brown enameling. It is difficult to accurately place a value on this rare set. Best guess: $400.00 – 650.00. From the collection of Debi Reece.

**1965 Hobé green enamel flower pin and earrings set.** This beautiful 2" x 1½" green enamel and rhinestones pin is signed "Hobé 1965." The 1¼" clip earrings are signed "Hobé" with the copyright symbol. From 1957 to 1966 Hobé occasionally signed jewelry with the date, which is lovely for collectors wanting to accurately date jewelry designs. $55.00 – 75.00.

OTHER JEWELRY MAKERS

Saffron

Jet

*Mayorka Petals*

Blue/Golden Quartz,

Delicate Mayorka petal stones in a variety of individual ensembles — each set in it's own distinctive color; Jet, Blue/Golden Quartz, Saffron. All with sparkling rhinestones.

at fine stores everywhere

**Hobé** ®

INTERESTING BROCHURE FREE ON REQUEST

© 1962

*jewels of legendary splendor*

9 E. 37 St., New York 16, N.Y.

**1962 Hobé Mayorka Petal Stone necklace.** Notice the amazingly rare and unusually shaped stones in this necklace. The heart-shaped speckled white and faux amber stones are called "Mayorka petal stones" in the 1962 Hobé "Mayorka Petals" advertisement. Jewelry with these interesting stones is highly collectible today. The above necklace measures 17". It is signed "Hobé" with the copyright symbol over the "o." Interestingly, the stones in this necklace closely resemble the jewelry finding shown in design patent 178000 issued June 12, 1956, to Julio J. Marsella. (See illustration from this patent below.) $100.00 – 150.00. From the collection of Debi Reece.

1962 Hobé "Mayorka Petals" advertisement. Note the interesting heart-shaped stones featured in this highly collectible Hobé jewelry. The ad reads, "Delicate Mayorka petal stones in a variety of individual ensembles — each set in it's [sic] own distinctive color; Jet, Blue/Golden Quartz, Saffron. All with sparkling rhinestones."

178000

1966 Hobé lavender rhinestone flower pin and earrings set. Dark and light amethyst-colored rhinestones set in toothy gold-tone prongs gleam from this 3¼" x 2" triple-flower brooch and the matching 1" clip earrings. This well-made set is signed "Hobé 1966." $75.00 – 100.00.

1966 Hobé crescent rose and pink rhinestone brooch. This beautiful 2½" x 2" shades-of-pink and gold-tone rose brooch is signed "Hobé 1966." As an added element of quality, in the center of each rose is a small, prong-set green rhinestone. $55.00 – 70.00. From the collection of Debi Reece.

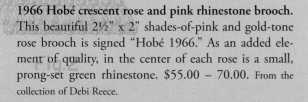

1958 – 1983 Hobé stylized green rhinestone flower brooch. Notice the blue and green rainbow rhinestones composing the colorful flower center in this grand 3¾" x 1¼" brooch. Rows of prong-set olive green and aurora borealis rhinestones curve gracefully around this fabulous floral centerpiece. The brooch is signed "Hobé" with the copyright symbol on an oval cartouche, which indicates this brooch dates to 1958 – 1983. $80.00 – 100.00.

OTHER JEWELRY MAKERS

**1958 – 1983 blue, green, and white hand-beaded Hobé brooch.** Hand-strung blue, white, and green beads form the design of this unusual 2½" x 2" floral brooch signed "Hobé" with the copyright symbol. The signature indicates this brooch dates to 1958 – 1983. Notice the tiny clear rhinestones set at the ends of the wire-strung blue beads. The addition of these tiny enhancements testifies to the careful workmanship present in vintage Hobé designs. $55.00 – 85.00. From the collection of Debi Reece.

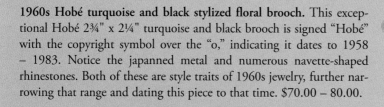

**1960s Hobé turquoise and black stylized floral brooch.** This exceptional Hobé 2¾" x 2¼" turquoise and black brooch is signed "Hobé" with the copyright symbol over the "o," indicating it dates to 1958 – 1983. Notice the japanned metal and numerous navette-shaped rhinestones. Both of these are style traits of 1960s jewelry, further narrowing that range and dating this piece to that time. $70.00 – 80.00.

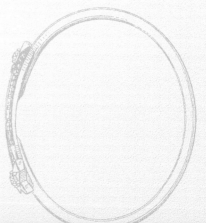

## 1930s – 1971

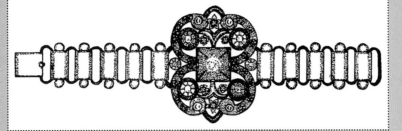

Design patent number 144562 issued April 30, 1956, to John H. Hazard for the Hollywood Jewelry Mfg. Co. (Hollycraft). Early jewelry is unmarked. Hangtags appeared in 1948. Jewelry marked "Hollycraft" with the date was produced in the 1950s. Jewelry with the Hollycraft name and the copyright symbol dates to 1960s – 1971.

Fig. 2

**1954 Hollycraft golden topaz rhinestone cuff bracelet.** This astoundingly lovely Hollycraft cuff bracelet is signed "Hollycraft Corp. 1954." It fits up to a size eight wrist. The center clasp is decorated with golden topaz rhinestones in a circle pattern. Then eight decorated egg-shaped pieces are placed evenly around the cuff to complete the exquisite design. $150.00 – 250.00. From the collection of Debi Reece.

Fig. 3

**1960s Hollycraft red cabochon brooch and earrings set.** Deep red oval-shaped cabochons give this Hollycraft 2½" x 2" brooch and matching 1" x ¾" clip earrings a vibrant inner glow. Note the interesting rounded and etched antique-gold-tone prongs holding these magnificent stones in place. The earrings are signed "Hollycraft" with the copyright symbol, but the brooch is unmarked. It is fortunate the set has remained together all of these years or we might never know that this dynamic brooch is by Hollycraft. This set dates to the 1960s. $135.00 – 165.00. From the collection of Debi Reece.

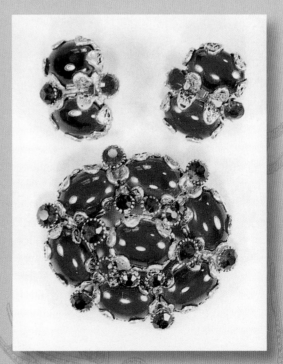

**1960s Hollycraft japanned pear pin and earrings set.** This splendid 2" x 1¾" white-beaded pear brooch and the matching 1" earrings feature green enameled leaves, white enameled flowers, and white beads all set in japanned (black enamel) metal. Only the brooch is signed "Hollycraft" with the copyright symbol. Jewelry with japanned metal was popular in the early 1960s (see the Weiss "Art Nouveau" 1961 advertisement later in this chapter). $75.00 – 90.00. From the collection of Debi Reece.

**1960s multicolored Hollycraft brooch.** This outstandingly vibrant 2¼" x 2" brooch features an array of colorful rhinestones including orange, brown, and dark and light green. Interestingly, the light green rhinestones glow under a black light. This eye-catching brooch is signed "Hollycraft" with the copyright symbol and dates to the 1960s. $70.00 – 95.00.

**1960s Hollycraft five-candle Christmas tree brooch.** Hollycraft jewelry was produced from the 1930s to 1971. The founder of Hollycraft, Joseph Chorbajian, was responsible for the production of outstandingly beautiful Hollycraft Christmas tree pins like this 2¼" x 2" five-candle tree. Signed "Hollycraft" with the copyright symbol, this highly collectible tree dates to the 1960s. $60.00 – 90.00.

**1960s Hollycraft enameled butterfly pin.** This 2¼" x 1¾" orange and yellow butterfly pin is signed "Hollycraft" with the copyright symbol and dates to the 1960s. $35.00 – 45.00.

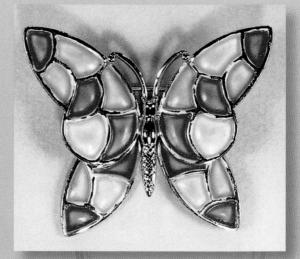

OTHER JEWELRY MAKERS

## UNKNOWN, APPEARS TO DATE LATE 1950s – 1960s

**Late 1950s – 1960s Jeanne figural pins.** All four of these fabulous figural pins are signed "Jeanne" with the copyright symbol. Left: This artistic Jeanne peacock pin measures 2 ½" x ½" and features red, white, green, and turquoise seed pearls. Top center: Measuring 2" x 1½", this Jeanne gold leaf pin is also a trembler. A tiny rhinestone frog attached to a spring hops up and down in the center of the leaf. Bottom center: This expressive Jeanne frog sitting under a mushroom pin measures 1¾" x 1". He has great green rhinestone eyes. Right: Trunk up for good luck, this 2½" x 1½" prancing circus elephant brooch by Jeanne is wearing a red rhinestone necklace and clear rhinestone leg bracelets. $50.00 – 75.00 each. From the collection of Debi Reece.

Fig. 1

Fig. 2

Fig. 3

Fig. 4

OTHER JEWELRY MAKERS

## 1946 – UNKNOWN

Jeray jewelry was produced by Rice-Weiner. Rice-Weiner was still operating in 1954. It is unknown how long the Jeray name was used for jewelry.

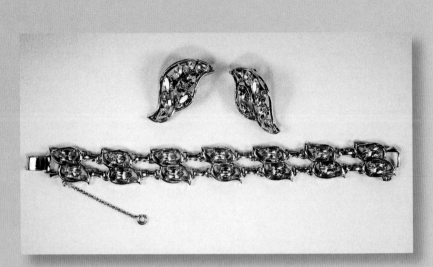

**1948 – 1950s Jeray golden citrine color rhinestone bracelet and earrings set.** This double-row bracelet measures 7½". It is signed "Design by Bel Geddes." Each 1½" clip earring is signed "Jeray" in script. Bel Geddes was a well-respected jewelry designer from the 1940s who created jewelry for the Rice-Weiner Co. and for Trifari. The nonuse of sterling indicates this fascinating set was produced 1948 – 1950s. $50.00 – 70.00 set. From the collection of Debi Reece.

**1946 – 1948 Jeray sterling silver chatelaine and earrings set.** This rare chatelaine is signed "Jeray Sterling" and features large faux aquamarine blue rectangular rhinestones enhanced by deep red rhinestones. The matching 1" clip earrings are also sterling silver. The Jeray mark was first used in 1946 when the Rice-Weiner Co. split into two separate companies. One half, led by Alvin and Robert Rice working with designer Louis Mark, produced jewelry marked "Barclay." The other half produced jewelry signed "Jeray" and "American Beauty Pearls." Rice-Weiner was still operating in 1954. It is unknown how long the Jeray name was used to mark jewelry; however, the use of sterling silver dates this set to 1946 – 1948. $65.00 – 85.00. From the collection of Debi Reece.

## 1943 – 1950s

| Design Patent Number | Date Issued | Designer | Jewelry Type | Brief Description |
|---|---|---|---|---|
| 136741 | 11/30/1943 | Lester Hess | Brooch | Dancing woman |
| 138056 | 6/6/1944 | Lester Hess | Brooch | Russian dancer |
| 146467 | 3/18/1947 | George Fearn | Brooch | Male playing card figure |
| 146468 | 3/18/1947 | George Fearn | Brooch | Female playing card figure |
| 152783 | 2/22/1949 | Lester Hess | Brooch | Seal |

138056

146468

**1943 – 1948 Jolle sterling silver crown brooch.** This regal Jolle 2" x 1¾" vermeil crown pin is heavy, lovely, and well made. It features open-backed faux amber cabochon stones and is signed "Jolle Sterling." Sterling silver was routinely used for costume jewelry from 1943 to 1948, helping to date this piece to that era. Jolle jewelry was produced by Hess-Appel from 1943 through the 1950s. $70.00 – 100.00.

(JONNÉ WAS PRODUCED BY H.M. SCHRAGER & CO., WHICH OPERATED FROM 1925 TO 1962.
IT IS BELIEVED THE JONNÉ NAME WAS USED IN THE 1950S AND 1960S.)

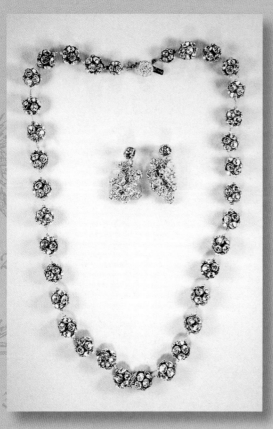

**1950s – 1960s Jonné rhinestone necklace and earrings set.** Top-quality in design and materials this spectacular 24" Jonné necklace features 34 prong-set rhinestone beads strung on chain rather than string. Silver-tone spacers are placed at the top and bottom of each rhinestone bead. The necklace is signed "Jonné" on a rectangular hangtag. Small rhinestone beads and crystal beads dangle in a soft cluster from the matching 1½" clip earrings. The earrings are unsigned. Most Jonné jewelry dates to the 1950s – 1960s. $100.00 – 120.00. Courtesy of Carol Dike.

**1950s – 1960s Jonné double-strand black and golden beaded necklace.** This classically styled 22" black and antique-gold-tone necklace is signed "Jonné" on the clasp. Jonné jewelry was produced by H. M. Schrager & Co., which was in operation from 1925 through 1962. Jonné jewelry was most likely produced in the 1950s or early 1960s. $55.00 – 75.00.

## 1938 – PRESENT

The design of the Joseff signature is important to collectors, because some of the older Joseff designs are being reproduced. Older Joseff pieces are signed either "Joseff Hollywood" in block letters or "Joseff" in script. The reproduced pieces are also signed "Joseff" in script, which can be confusing. Occasionally a reproduction will be signed with the older signature. It is important to carefully inspect jewelry to be sure the metal has the patina expected on older Joseff jewelry.

**1948 – 1950s Joseff of Hollywood necklace and bracelet set.** This rare antique-gold-tone 15" necklace is signed "Joseff Hollywood" in block letters without the copyright symbol. The matching 7¼" bracelet features the same pretty floral design accented by radiant red cabochon stones. It is also signed "Joseff Hollywood" in block letters. Joseff jewelry is still produced today; however, the block signature indicates this is a vintage set. The nonuse of sterling and the design date this set to 1948 – 1950s. $450.00 – 600.00.
From the collection of Debi Reece.

1948 B. Altman & Co. Joseff of Hollywood advertisement. Three wonderful necklaces are shown in this rare Joseff of Hollywood advertisement. The model is wearing a coil necklace called "Juliet." The necklace with interlocking rings is called "Ali Baba," and the last necklace is called "temple bells." The advertisement reads, "Necklaces by Joseff of Hollywood with his high flair for drama, this young man from the coast twists great coils and baubles about your throat this season. Drawing the eye like a magnet, his new 'Juliet' triple coil lies wide on the shoulders, low on the back…from an exclusive Altman collection at 2.00 to 50.00."

**B. ALTMAN & CO.**
FIFTH AVENUE    NEW YORK

*"Juliet", above, and "Ali Baba" and "temple bells", all in the famous Joseff finish    each at 7.50*

*from an exclusive Altman collection at 2.00 to 50.00*

**NECKLACES BY JOSEFF OF HOLLYWOOD**

*with his high flair for drama, this young man from the coast twists great coils and baubles about your throat this season. Drawing the eye like a magnet, his new "Juliet" triple coil lies wide on the shoulders, low on the back.  Altman jewelry . . . main floor*

**1950s Joseff green rhinestone brooch.** Joseff of Hollywood jewelry is rare, including this 2¼" x 2" emerald green rhinestone brooch signed "Joseff" in script. Unfortunately for collectors, the script signature appears on both vintage and modern-day Joseff pieces. To date Joseff jewelry with this script signature, the collector must examine the piece for age-related elements. For example, the metal on this brooch is dull compared to new brooches, the pin back is bent from frequent use, and the rhinestones are beginning to show some clouding from age. All of these elements indicate this is a vintage Joseff brooch dating to the 1950s. $85.00 – 125.00.

# • KAFIN, N.Y. •

## 1950s – 1960s

**1950s – 1960s Kafin blue art-glass necklace and bracelet set.** This remarkable set is signed "Kafin New York" in block letters. It is an astonishingly beautiful set! Both pieces are decorated with Montana blue rhinestones and rare art-glass stones that seem to glow from within. The 7½" bracelet has three rows of stones. The 14½" choker also has a "hidden" row of stones tucked under the gold-tone filigree. Little is known about Kafin jewelry, including the dates the company was in operation. Most collectors agree that Kafin designs date from the 1950s and 1960s. $250.00 – 350.00.

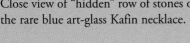

Close view of "hidden" row of stones on the rare blue art-glass Kafin necklace.

1950s – 1960s Kafin emerald green rhinestone necklace. This extraordinary 16" Kafin necklace and matching 1" clip earrings set is signed "Kafin N.Y." and dates to the 1950s or 1960s. Notice the depth to the design and the large, emerald green rhinestones. $85.00 – 100.00.

1950s – 1960s Kafin pink floral bracelet and earrings set. This pretty 7½" x 1¼" bracelet and the 1¼" earrings are signed "Kafin, N.Y." Large pink cabochon stones glow from a bed of tiny pink enameled flowers all set in gold-tone metal. $85.00 – 100.00. From the collection of Debi Reece.

OTHER JEWELRY MAKERS

365

## UNKNOWN, APPEARS TO DATE 1940S

**1940s Kandell & Marcus rhinestone waterfall brooch.** Pretty prong-set clear rhinestones in round and tear drop shapes decorate this 2" x 5¼" waterfall-style brooch signed "Kandell & Marcus N.Y." I can find no reliable information on the dates of operation for Kandell & Marcus; however, the jewelry appears to be from the 1940s. $45.00 – 60.00. From the collection of Debi Reece.

**1940s Kandell & Marcus brushed-gold-tone floral brooch.** This large 3" x 2¼" brooch is signed "Kandell & Marcus N.Y." It features antique-gold-tone metal flowers with purple rhinestone centers. The style of this brooch is reminiscent of late 1940s Joseff of Hollywood jewelry. $35.00 – 45.00. From the collection of Debi Reece.

**1940s Kandell & Marcus bracelet.** Black cabochon stones and creamy pearls decorate this elaborate 7¼" x 1¼" bracelet signed "Kandell & Marcus N.Y." This interesting piece dates to the 1940s. $55.00 – 75.00. From the collection of Debi Reece.

## THIEF OF BAGDAD, 1941 – UNKNOWN

Jewelry signed "Korda Thief of Bagdad" ("Baghdad" is spelled "Bagdad" on the jewelry) was manufactured by Rice-Weiner.

Fig. 1

**1940s Korda Thief of Bagdad Arabian woman brooch.** This interesting 2" x 1½" brooch is signed "Thief of Bagdad" and "Korda." $85.00 – 125.00. From the collection of Debi Reece.

Fig. 2

Fig. 3

Fig. 4

## 1943 – 1980

Some Kramer jewelry produced after 1955 is signed "Kramer" without the copyright symbol, indicating that the presence or absence of the copyright symbol is not necessarily useful when dating Kramer designs.

| Design Patent Number | Date Issued | Designer | Jewelry Type | Brief Description |
|---|---|---|---|---|
| 152271 | 1/4/1949 | Louis Kramer | Brooch | Abstract |
| 159646 | 8/8/1950 | Louis Kramer | Brooch | Sword |
| 162666 | 3/27/1951 | Morris Kramer | Brooch | Couple in buggy |
| 172541 | 7/6/1954 | Louis Kramer | Brooch | Floral leaves (See 172753 for matching earrings.) |
| 172542 | 7/6/1954 | Louis Kramer | Brooch | Cluster of tiny flowers (See 172543 for matching earrings.) |
| 172543 | 7/6/1954 | Louis Kramer | Earring | Cluster of tiny flowers (See 172890 for matching cluster of flowers necklace.) |
| 172544 | 7/6/1954 | Louis Kramer | Brooch | Cluster of tiny flowers in basket (See 172542 for another cluster-design brooch.) |
| 172753 | 8/3/1954 | Louis Kramer | Earring | Floral leaves (See 172541 for matching brooch.) |
| 172890 | 8/24/1954 | Louis Kramer | Necklace | Cluster of tiny flowers necklace (See 172891 for matching cluster of flowers bracelet.) |
| 172891 | 8/24/1954 | Louis Kramer | Bracelet | Floral |

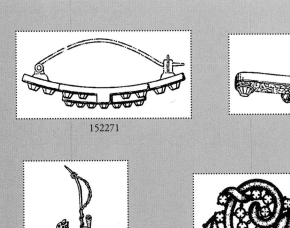

152271

159646

162666

172541

172544

**Early 1950s Kramer green rhinestone necklace and earrings set.** This lovely 15½" Kramer necklace features rich-looking, open-backed green rhinestones set in silver-tone metal. It is signed "Kramer N.Y." without the copyright symbol. The matching 1½" earrings are unsigned. $100.00 – 130.00.

1954 Kramer "Empress Collection" advertisement. The advertisement reads, "Collection in flawed-emerald, ruby, or sapphire. From $7.50 to $40.00."

1950 "Golden Twist by Kramer" advertisement. The ad reads, "A brilliant strand of pseudo jewels weaves its charms about a golden snake chain…and you! In precious-jewel colors or crystal. Bracelet, about $5; Necklace (not illustrated), about $10; Earrings, about $5."

OTHER JEWELRY MAKERS

1956 "beauty, beauty, burning bright…" Kramer advertisement. The beautiful jewelry featured in this advertisement originally sold for $7.50 to $20.00.

1958 Kramer "Heirloom" advertisement. The jewelry featured in this sweet advertisement originally sold for $6.00 – 25.00.

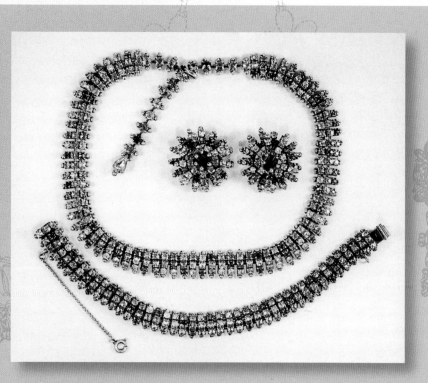

Fig.1

Fig.2

**Early 1950s Kramer multicolored rhinestone necklace, bracelet, and earrings set.** This stunning Kramer set features light blue, pink, green, dark blue, and golden topaz-colored rhinestones. The slinky 16" adjustable necklace and 7½" x ½" bracelet are flexible and comfortable to wear. Each 1" clip earring features the same array of colorful rhinestones in a starburst design. The earrings are signed "Kramer of N. Y." with utility patent number 2583988 issued to F. A. Ballou, Jr., on January 29, 1952, for the clip mechanism. This patent establishes that the set could not be earlier than 1952 but could have been manufactured any time after that. The necklace and bracelet are signed "Kramer of N.Y." without the copyright symbol. The signature and the use of multicolored pastel rhinestones indicate this set dates to the early 1950s. $100.00 – 150.00. From the collection of Debi Reece.

Fig.3

Fig.4

**Early 1950s Kramer blue and green rhinestone bracelet and earrings set.** The large green rhinestones in this spectacular Kramer 7" x ¾" bracelet and 1" clip earrings seem to change from blue to green depending on how the light reflects off the stones. All of the rhinestones are prong set in rhodium-plated metal. The earrings are signed "Kramer" without the copyright symbol. The bracelet is unsigned. $75.00 – 100.00. From the collection of Debi Reece.

OTHER JEWELRY MAKERS

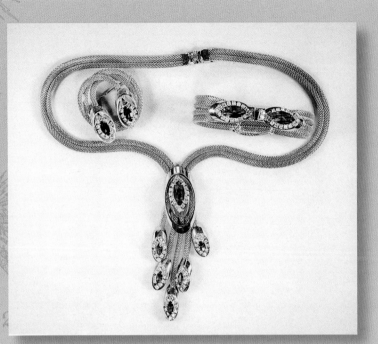

**Early 1950s Kramer golden mesh and green rhinestone parure.** Interestingly, the 7" mesh bracelet is signed "Kramer of N.Y." and the 1½" matching brooch is signed "Kramer." The 24" lariat-style necklace is unsigned. This wonderful set combines the elegance of emerald green navette-shaped rhinestones with the casual comfort of the soft mesh chains. $100.00 – 150.00. From the collection of Debi Reece.

**Early 1950s Kramer "fruit salad" style necklace.** Black, red, and green irregularly shaped plastic nuggets, clear rhinestones, and pearls all beautifully come together in this extraordinary 20" Kramer fruit salad-style necklace. The plastic nuggets glow with color as if they were made of glass. The silver-tone metal is coated with a creamy rhodium finish. The necklace is signed "Kramer" without the copyright symbol. This necklace is an excellent example of how a designer can creatively combine different colors and textures to create beauty. $85.00 – 100.00.

1959 Kramer "Golden Goddess…" advertisement. The advertisement reads, "Golden Goddess…a fugue of glow and sparkle. The flame of crystals, or crystals and pretend-pearls, played against a muted golden look. Another great idea, crystals against silver. For Christmas? From $5 to $20…"

Fig.1

1959 Kramer "Fleur Mist" advertisement. The advertisement reads, "Twinkling dew with a spray of golden filigree leaves — catching all the secret fire and light of a thousand shimmering auroras. In shades of mauve, white, blue, and yellow — from $3 to $10 plus tax."

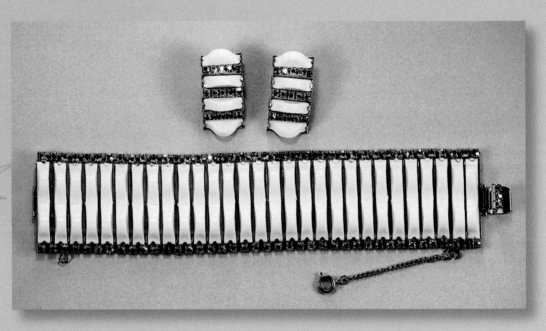

**1955 – 1960s Kramer elegant white bracelet and earrings set.** This gleaming white 7½" x 1" plastic bracelet is signed "Kramer" with the copyright symbol. The matching 1¼" clip earrings are unsigned. Even though the white inserts are plastic instead of glass, this set is elegant enough to be worn at night. It is also lightweight and comfortable for all-day wear. $75.00 – 95.00.

**1955 – 1956 Kramer black netting bracelet and earrings set.** This rare Kramer 7½" x 1" bracelet and the matching 1" clip earrings feature black netting covering glowing golden topaz-colored rhinestones. Surrounding the large golden rhinestones are small smoky quartz rhinestones all set in gold-tone metal. Netted Kramer jewelry is hard to find. The bracelet is signed "Kramer of New York." One earring is signed "Kramer" without the copyright symbol, and the other is signed "Kramer" with the copyright symbol. This suggests the set was produced in 1955 or 1956, when Kramer first started copyrighting designs. Nothing was wasted. Kramer continued to use earring backs with the older signature until the supply was exhausted. $90.00 – 125.00. From the collection of Debi Reece.

Fig. 1

**1959 Kramer lavender rhinestone full parure.** The 1959 "Kramer, from the word glow!" advertisement features this set called "Waltz Time." The advertisement describes this luscious lavender set as "Alexandrite in gold finish." The 15½" necklace, 7¼" bracelet, and 1½" earrings originally sold for between $7.50 and $15.00. The 2¼" brooch is not shown in the advertisement. Interestingly, all pieces are signed "Kramer of N.Y." without the copyright symbol. The earrings are also signed with utility patent number 2583988 issued January 29, 1952, to Frederick Ballou for the clip mechanism. $150.00 – 225.00.

1959 "Kramer, from the word glow!" advertisement. This advertisement features seven exquisite Kramer sets. Top right, dark blue ornament: "Waltz Time…Alexandrite in gold finish. Necklace, bracelet, earrings, pins. 7.50 – 15.00." Left and middle, red and yellow ornaments: "Regal… rhinestones in platinum finish. Necklace, bracelet, earrings. 5.00 to 20.00." Right middle, green ornament: "Holiday…emerald, ruby or sapphire-colored stones with rhinestones or all rhinestone. Set in gold finish. Necklace, bracelet, earrings, pins. 2.00 to 5.00." Bottom left, light blue ornament: "Royalty…sapphire, emerald, or ruby-colored stones with rhinestones, set in platinum finish. Pins and earrings. 5.00 and 10.00." Bottom center, small red ornament: "Versailles…blue enamel with rhinestones on gold finish. Bracelets and earrings. 4.00 and 7.50." Bottom right, pink ornament: "Snow Daisy…simulated pearls with rhinestones in platinum finish. Necklaces, bracelets, earrings, pins. 3.00 to 12.50."

THE DIAMOND LOOK® BY
# KRAMER
New York, Los Angeles, Dallas, Paris

**1963 Kramer Amourelle white beaded necklace and earrings set.** The ¾" clip earrings in this set are signed "Amourelle," which is a rare signature used to mark Kramer jewelry designed in 1963 by Frank Hess, formerly of Haskell jewelry. The 15" double-strand white bead necklace is unsigned. Note the hand-strung yellow beads in the center of each flower, reminiscent of fine handmade Haskell jewelry designs. $85.00 – 100.00.

**1963 Kramer Amourelle blue enamel and rhinestone pin.** This 1½" pin is small in size but it is packed full of style. Signed "Amourelle," this little beauty is the creation of Frank Hess, former head designer for Haskell jewelry, and encompasses much of the handmade quality found on expensive Haskell designs. Each element in the brooch is carefully hand wired to a gold-tone filigree back. The decoration almost completely covers the filigree frame and the style is slightly asymmetrical, both Hess design traits. Amourelle jewelry dates to 1963. $65.00 – 80.00.

1963 Kramer Amourelle red necklace, earrings, and ring. This radiant red necklace is signed "Amourelle" on a heart-shaped cartouche. It was designed for Kramer in 1963 by Frank Hess, formerly of Haskell. The glorious pendant necklace features 24" of translucent red glass beads and an amazing 3" hand-wired red rhinestone centerpiece. In the style of fine Haskell jewelry, the red rhinestones are hand wired to the japanned filigree frame. The matching size nine ring is unmarked. Unfortunately, the ¾" earrings have been converted to pierced earrings, and are therefore also unsigned. All Amourelle jewelry is rare, but Amourelle jewelry of this quality and beauty is extraordinarily rare. $500.00 – 750.00.

Close view of the heart-shaped Amourelle signature plaque.

Close view of the intricate red rhinestone and black enameled Amourelle pendant.

OTHER JEWELRY MAKERS

## 1913 – 1977

### (THIS JEWELRY WAS FIRST PRODUCED IN THE MID-1940s.)

| Design Patent Number | Date Issued | Designer | Jewelry Type | Brief Description |
|---|---|---|---|---|
| 143130 | 12/11/1945 | Helen D. Cole and William Diehl | Brooch | Simulates the look of a military war decoration or ribbon. |
| 143131 | 12/11/1945 | Helen D. Cole and William Diehl | Brooch | Simulates the look of a military war decoration or ribbon. |
| 143559 | 1/15/1946 | Kurt Speck | Brooch | Abstract floral |
| 143560 | 1/15/1946 | Kurt Speck | Brooch | Abstract floral |
| 143561 | 1/15/1946 | Kurt Speck | Brooch | Abstract floral |
| 143562 | 1/15/1946 | Kurt Speck | Brooch | Floral |
| 143956 | 2/26/1946 | William Diehl | Brooch | Jelly belly frog |
| 143957 | 2/26/1946 | William Diehl | Brooch | Squirrel |
| 143958 | 2/26/1946 | William Diehl | Brooch | Clown |
| 143959 | 2/26/1946 | William Diehl | Brooch | Angel with hearts |
| 143999 | 2/26/1946 | Kurt Speck | Brooch | Viking ship |
| 144000 | 2/26/1946 | Kurt Speck | Brooch | Stylized bird |
| 144001 | 2/26/1946 | Kurt Speck | Brooch | Tree branches with bow |
| 144002 | 2/26/1946 | Kurt Speck | Brooch | Dancing girl |
| 144239 | 3/26/1946 | William Diehl | Brooch | Spanish man |
| 144240 | 3/26/1946 | William Diehl | Brooch | Spanish woman |
| 144242 | 3/26/1946 | William Diehl | Brooch | Rooster |
| 144243 | 3/26/1946 | William Diehl | Brooch | Rooster |
| 144265 | 3/26/1946 | Kurt Speck | Brooch | Dancing man (See 144266 for woman.) |
| 144266 | 3/26/1946 | Kurt Speck | Brooch | Dancing woman (See 144265 for man.) |
| 144267 | 3/26/1946 | Kurt Speck | Brooch | Hawaiian musician (See 144268 for another Hawaiian brooch.) |
| 144268 | 3/26/1946 | Kurt Speck | Brooch | Hula dancer (See 144267 for another Hawaiian brooch.) |
| 144424 | 4/9/1946 | Kurt Speck | Brooch | King of Hearts (See 144425 for queen.) |
| 144425 | 4/9/1946 | Kurt Speck | Brooch | Queen of Hearts (See 14426 for king.) |
| 144426 | 4/9/1946 | Kurt Speck | Brooch | King of Hearts (See 144424 for another king.) |
| 144875 | 5/28/1946 | Kurt Speck | Brooch | Starburst |
| 145591 | 9/10/1946 | Kurt Speck | Brooch | Abstract |

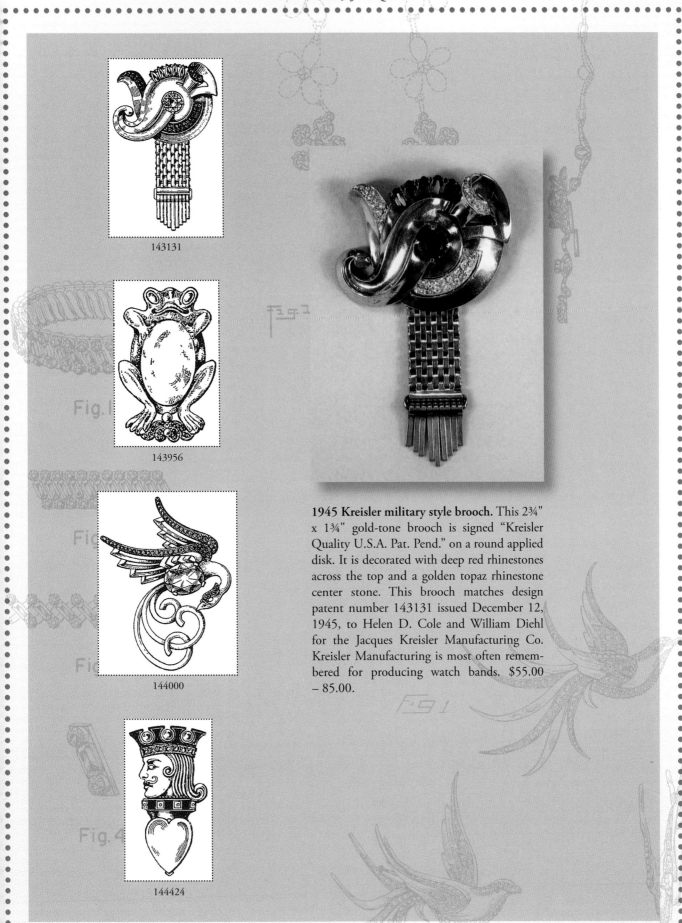

143131

143956

144000

144424

**1945 Kreisler military style brooch.** This 2¾" x 1¾" gold-tone brooch is signed "Kreisler Quality U.S.A. Pat. Pend." on a round applied disk. It is decorated with deep red rhinestones across the top and a golden topaz rhinestone center stone. This brooch matches design patent number 143131 issued December 12, 1945, to Helen D. Cole and William Diehl for the Jacques Kreisler Manufacturing Co. Kreisler Manufacturing is most often remembered for producing watch bands. $55.00 – 85.00.

## 1866 – SOLD IN 1997

Krementz designs are often not copyrighted. The lack of a copyright symbol does not necessarily indicate the jewelry was produced before 1955.

**1950s Krementz necklace, pin, and earrings in original Krementz box.** This white gold overlay Krementz set includes a 15½" necklace, a 2¼" x 1" floral pin, and ¾" screw-back earrings. All pieces are signed "Krementz." Krementz jewelry was first produced in 1866. Expensive at the time (in 1965 Krementz costume jewelry sold for between $7.50 for earrings and as much as $35.00 for a bracelet), collectible Krementz jewelry today sells in much the same price range. Finding the jewelry in its original box is a plus that adds value. $65.00 – 95.00. From the collection of Debi Reece.

For Her Christmas

Bangle Bracelet
$19.00 plus tax
Beautifully boxed in leatherette

Diamond-cut Austrian crystals, set in a bangle with fashionable leaf design. Fine quality jewelry, superbly made with an overlay of 14 Karat white gold.

*Krementz*
FINE QUALITY JEWELRY
*since 1866*
Bracelets • Earrings • Necklaces • Brooches
Evening Jewelry • Cuff Links • Tie Bars • Belt Buckles
*Available wherever fine jewelry is sold*

**1951 Krementz "For Her Christmas" advertisement.** This ad reads, "Diamond-cut Austrian crystals, set in a bangle with fashionable leaf design. Fine quality jewelry, superbly made with an overlay of 14 Karat white gold." The bracelet sold for $19.00 in 1951.

OTHER JEWELRY MAKERS

1950s – 1960s Krementz white gold overlay bracelet. Delicate and pretty, this classically styled 7½" x ¼" Krementz clear rhinestone bracelet dates from the 1950s or 1960s and remains sparkly and wearable today. It is signed "Krementz." $45.00 – 65.00. From the collection of Debi Reece.

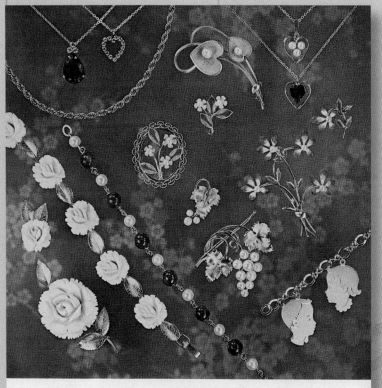

1965 Krementz "In the Tradition of Precious Jewelry" advertisement. The 14 kt. gold overlay jewelry in this advertisement ranged in value from $3.50 to $35.00. The bracelet is cultured pearl and jade.

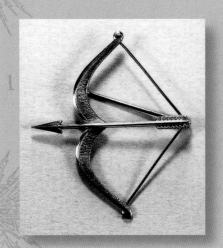

**1950s – 1970s Krementz bow and arrow pin.** This unique bow and arrow pin is signed "Krementz" along the pin stem. Krementz jewelry is usually found in good condition, because it was initially well made. Some designs were marketed for many years. It is difficult to assign a date of manufacture to Krementz jewelry even if the piece is featured in an advertisement. Krementz produced popular designs for several years. When buying Krementz jewelry, look for appealing, interesting designs like this 1½" x 1½" bow and arrow pin. $25.00 – 35.00.

**1950s – 1970s classic Krementz gold overlay double-rose pin.** This golden beauty measures 2¼" x 1" and is signed "Krementz" along the pin. $20.00 – 30.00.

1970 Krementz "Imaginative design and superb craftsmanship…" advertisement. The 14K gold overlay jewelry in this advertisement ranges in value from $13.00 to $30.00. This ad reads, "Cultured pearls…genuine opal, jade, coral and ivory."

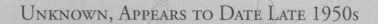

UNKNOWN, APPEARS TO DATE LATE 1950s

**Late 1950s Lady Ellen Magnetic Interchangeable earrings.** Little is known about Lady Ellen jewelry, and it is not widely collected. However, this set of Lady Ellen Magnetic Interchangeable earrings is interesting for several reasons. First, the set is mint in its original box. Next, the box contains an advertising insert providing the buyer with important information about these earrings. The insert reads, "The secret of this remarkable new idea in earrings lies in the use of Alnico Permanent Magnets attached to the base of the earrings. These magnets and Ritium finish are guaranteed for the life of the earrings." Finally, the insert gives us a clue to the age of these earrings by including utility patent number 2,752,764 in the text. This utility patent was issued to H. B. Lederer on July 3, 1956, for the use of magnets in designing interchangeable earrings. Therefore, the earliest these earrings could have been made is 1956. The Lady Ellen advertising insert states that magnetic earrings are a "new" idea. This information helps to date the first use of magnets for interchangeable jewelry to this era. $20.00 – 30.00.

OTHER JEWELRY MAKERS

1944 – 1980s

**1962 Laguna Crown Jewels Collection necklace, bracelet, and earrings set.** In mint condition, this lovely Laguna 7½" bracelet with original tag, the 15½" necklace, and the 1½" clip earrings are similar to the jewelry shown in the 1962 Laguna "Glad You're Not Mad about the Haircut, Samson" advertisement. Amazingly, every piece in this set is unmarked. However, the style of the jewelry, the original tags, and the 1962 advertisement all attest to its authenticity. $85.00 – 100.00.

OTHER JEWELRY MAKERS

1962 Laguna "Glad You're Not Mad About the Haircut, Samson" advertisement. The caption in this 1962 advertisement reads, "…from Laguna's Crown Jewels Collection — Necklaces, Bracelets, Earrings, Pins — to $50."

"GLAD YOU'RE NOT MAD ABOUT THE HAIRCUT, SAMSON"

"Delilah, baby—you're a sight for sore eyes. Cuddle up to this Look-of-Queens—gem-cut Aurora Borealis Crystals* lavished with fluted gold-like baubles, gathered with a star-crossed clasp." "You're cute…but are they Laguna?" "Natch!" From Laguna's Crown Jewel Collection—Necklaces, Bracelets, Earrings, Pins—to $50. Write Dept. VC for your free illustrated booklet "How To Change One Outfit Into Many." Laguna-Royal Craftsmen, Inc., 389 Fifth Ave., New York 16, N.Y.

*Laguna* CROWN JEWEL COLLECTION

1945 Laguna "Oriental Pearl Replicas at Their Lovliest" advertisement. This interesting vintage advertisement features movie star Ann Rutherford. The necklace is a single strand of faux Oriental pearls. Depending on the length, faux pearl necklaces sold for between $10.00 and $30.00. Interestingly, for an additional charge of $50.00, a diamond-mounted clasp could be added.

**Early 1950s Laguna pink and white beads and matching clip earrings.** This lovely Laguna double-strand beaded necklace measures 15½". The clip earrings are 1". All pieces are signed "Laguna" without the copyright symbol, dating this set to the early 1950s. $45.00 – 55.00.

OTHER JEWELRY MAKERS

1921 – 1959

| Design Patent Number | Date Issued | Designer | Jewelry Type | Brief Description |
|---|---|---|---|---|
| 107523 | 11/23/1937 | Walter Lampl | Charm | Church Stanhope |
| 114541 | 5/2/1939 | Walter Lampl | Charm | Building Stanhope |
| 114542 | 5/2/1939 | Walter Lampl | Charm | Movie camera |
| 116324 | 8/22/1939 | Walter Lampl | Charm | Abstract |
| 120436 | 5/7/1940 | Walter Lampl | Brooch | Palm trees with thermometer |
| 120446 | 5/7/1940 | Walter Lampl | Clip | Asian man with flower |
| 120462 | 5/7/1940 | Walter Lampl | Brooch | Asian woman |
| 135050 | 2/16/1943 | Walter Lampl | Charm | Heart |
| 135051 | 2/16/1943 | Walter Lampl | Charm | Heart |
| 135052 | 2/16/1943 | Walter Lampl | Charm | Heart |
| 135053 | 2/16/1943 | Walter Lampl | Charm | Heart |
| 135054 | 2/16/1943 | Walter Lampl | Charm | Heart |
| 135055 | 2/16/1943 | Walter Lampl | Charm | Heart |
| 135056 | 2/16/1943 | Walter Lampl | Charm | Heart |
| 135057 | 2/16/1943 | Walter Lampl | Charm | Heart |
| 135058 | 2/16/1943 | Walter Lampl | Charm | Heart |
| 135059 | 2/16/1943 | Walter Lampl | Charm | Heart |
| 135060 | 2/16/1943 | Walter Lampl | Charm | Heart |
| 135061 | 2/16/1943 | Walter Lampl | Charm | Heart |
| 159491 | 8/1/1950 | Walter Lampl, Jr. | Brooch | Abstract |

**Late 1930s – early 1940s unmarked Stanhope church charm resembling patented Walter Lampl design.** This rare ½" x ¼" Stanhope church charm is marked "Sterling" and "Washington D.C." It closely resembles design patent number 114541 issued May 2, 1939, to Walter Lampl. The charm in the photograph matches the patent illustration except that the roof line is slightly different. "Stanhope" refers to Lord Stanhope, who is credited with inventing the glass lens (the round glass window above the church door) through which a person can see a tiny, microscopic image. In this case, when a person peeks through the Stanhope lens, a tiny copy of the Lord's Prayer is visible. Stanhope lenses have been used since the mid-nineteenth century to enhance many objects, including pens and jewelry. As an unmarked sterling Stanhope church charm, today's value is $40.00 – 65.00. As a sterling Walter Lampl Stanhope church charm from 1939, the value is much higher: $200.00 – 350.00.

107523

130141

120462

135050

135054

**Early 1940s Walter Lampl sterling silver flower pin.** This 2½" silver beauty is signed "WL Sterling." Notice the design of the sterling silver flower finding used on this brooch. This finding is design patent number 130141 issued October 28, 1941, to Carl Schraysshuen. Walter Lampl utilized this flower finding in many early 1940s jewelry designs. Jewelry makers purchased pre-made findings, like this flower, and incorporated them into original designs. The presence of this finding dates this pin to the early 1940s. Walter Lampl designed many sterling silver and gold-fill jewelry items, but is especially renowned for his delightful and highly collectible charms. Walter Lampl, Sr., died in late 1945. His son, Walter Lampl, Jr., headed the company until its closing in 1959. $75.00 – 90.00.

**Mid-1940s – 1959 Walter Lampl heart with key charm.** This amazingly detailed tiny ½" Walter Lampl sterling heart charm is signed "WL" in a shield. This style of signature dates this charm to the mid-1940s through 1959 when the company closed. Interestingly, at the top of the heart is a sliding C-clasp, making it easy to attach the lovely charm to a bracelet. The sterling key is decorative and does not fit or work in the lock. Lampl charms, especially the heart charms, are highly collectible today. $125.00 – 200.00.

**Mid-1940s – 1959 heart charm bracelet with signed Walter Lampl charm.** Notice the center padlock-style heart charm on this 7" puffed heart charm bracelet. It is signed "WL" and dates to the mid-1940s – 1959. The other four ½" charms are unsigned. Vintage puffed heart charm bracelets featuring even one signed Lampl charm are rising rapidly in value. $225.00 – 350.00. Courtesy of Julia Tingle.

OTHER JEWELRY MAKERS

Mid-1940s – 1959 Walter Lampl sterling bird brooch with zipper-pull attachment. This stunning 2½" x 2½" sterling silver brooch is signed "WL" in a shield, dating this beauty to the mid-1940s – 1959. Interestingly, this piece is also signed "Tabby Pat. Apl. For." This signature refers to a patented zipper-pull attachment that is attached to the back of the brooch. Using this attachment, the brooch can be connected to a zipper pull. $175.00 – 225.00. Courtesy of Barbara Magee.

Back view of the Walter Lampl bird brooch, showing the unique "Tabby" zipper pull attachment.

# • LANE, KENNETH J. •

## 1963 – PRESENT

The dates of manufacture for Kenneth J. Lane jewelry are approximate, based on the style of the signature and the style of the jewelry. In my experience, dating Kenneth J. Lane jewelry by the signature style alone is speculative at best. One signature is not necessarily retired when a new one is issued. New, Kenneth J. Lane jewelry sold on QVC is usually signed "KJL" (no periods) and with the copyright symbol, or "Kenneth Lane" on a cartouche and with the copyright symbol.

1960s – 1970s Kenneth J. Lane coral and white brooch. Creamy coral and white cabochon beads decorate this highly dimensional 2" brooch signed "K.J.L." without the copyright symbol, which dates to the 1960s and 1970s. (This date is based on the signature style. The brooch is in mint condition and may be a later piece with an earlier signature.) $50.00 – 65.00. From the collection of Debi Reece.

OTHER JEWELRY MAKERS

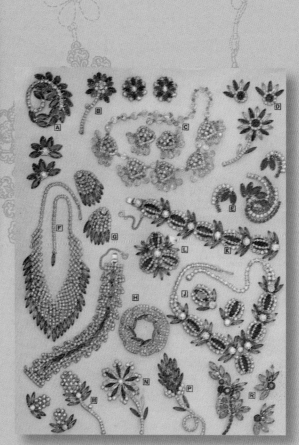

**1960s Kenneth J. Lane blue navette rhinestone brooch.** This beautiful shades-of-blue 3" brooch is signed "KJL" without the copyright symbol and dates to the 1960s. Note: The 1962 Mayers catalog page shows similar unmarked jewelry featuring long navette-shaped rhinestones. $75.00 – 100.00. From the collection of Marty Morganstern.

1962 Mayers catalog page showing an array of unmarked jewelry. Notice the frequent use of long navette-shaped rhinestones in the jewelry designs featured in this advertisement. All of the jewelry is unmarked and ranged in price from $7.00 – 21.00.

**1960s – 1970s Kenneth J. Lane coral bracelet and earrings set.** This bright 8" coral bracelet and the 1" clip earrings are signed "K.J.L." without the copyright symbol and date to the 1960s and 1970s. (This date is based on the signature style. The bracelet and earrings are in mint condition and may be later pieces with an earlier signature.) The large bracelet features 16 strands of coral-colored plastic beads separated by gold-tone spacers and bright white pearls. $45.00 – 65.00. From the collection of Debi Reece.

## 1939 – At Least into the 1950s

**1950s unmarked LaTausca triple-strand plastic beaded necklace in original box.** This interesting 15½" LaTausca triple-strand necklace is unmarked, so it is fortunate the necklace remains in its original signed box. This necklace is a mixture of real-looking plastic beads and glass beads. LaTausca jewelry was first marketed in 1939; however, this set is much newer, dating to the 1950s. $20.00 – 25.00.

1948 LaTausca "The Green Goddess" advertisement. This ad reads, "Lovely new simulated pearl necklace by La Tausca with that precious look. Exquisite, rhinestone-set sterling silver clasp. Presentation case in beautiful jade color. $5.00 plus tax, at better stores."

*The Green Goddess*

Lovely new simulated pearl necklace by La Tausca with that precious look. Exquisite, rhinestone-set sterling silver clasp. Presentation case in beautiful jade color. $5.00 plus tax, at better stores.

La Tausca
SIMULATED PEARLS
WORLD'S FINEST

UNKNOWN

137747

**1944 Sterling silver brooch and earrings set by Leary.** One of the joys of researching the jewelry patents is uncovering sleeping beauties like this interesting compass brooch. The brooch is signed "Pat. Pend. Sterling" and each 1" earring is signed "Sterling." The 3½" brooch is an exact match to design patent number 137747 issued April 25, 1944, to Arthur Gerald Leary. Interestingly, the compass arm, decorated with a heart-shaped arrow, spins in a circle so that the heart can be facing any direction. The manufacturer of this set is unknown. $50.00 – 70.00.

Fig.1

Fig.2

Fig.3

Fig.4

OTHER JEWELRY MAKERS

# • LEDO •

## 1911 – 1980s
### (THE LEDO MARK WAS USED FROM 1948 to 1962,
### WHEN THE COMPANY WAS RENAMED POLICINI.)

**1950 Ledo rhinestone brooch.** This beautiful 2" x 1½" oval pin is featured in the 1950 Ledo "Rondelet" advertisement. The original selling price was $15.00. Well made, this lovely pin features baguette rhinestones and clear round rhinestones set in a creamy rhodium-plated finish. It is signed "Ledo." $50.00 – 70.00.

1950 Ledo "Rondelet" advertisement. This artistic advertisement features six Ledo pins all featuring baguette-shaped rhinestones that originally sold for $4.00 – 20.00.

1951 Ledo "Grand Jewels" advertisement. This ad reads, "This Fall…the dazzling gloriously big jewel is yours in Ledo's magnificent rhinestone pins. Clever you to wear the costly new 3-dimensional look at Ledo's delightfully sane prices. On Lapel, $16/On Hat, $6/On Purse, $5."

1948 – 1962 Ledo pavé link bracelet. The photograph does not capture the beauty of this 7" x ½" well-constructed, heavy bracelet signed "Ledo." When fastened, the clasp becomes part of the design and virtually disappears. This high-quality bracelet has a thick rhodium back and is encrusted with clear rhinestones, giving it the look of fine jewelry. $65.00 – 95.00.

**1948 – 1962 Ledo brushed-gold-tone and pearl necklace, bracelet, and earrings in original Ledo presentation box.** The 1½" clip earrings are signed "Ledo." All of the other pieces are unmarked. The choker-style necklace measures approximately 16" and is constructed in six sections. Each section looks like a tiny royal crown decorated with five pearls. The Ledo signature dates this lovely set to 1948 – 1962. In 1960 the company name changed, and shortly thereafter the jewelry was marked "Polcini." $75.00 – 125.00. Courtesy of Marian Dietrich.

**1948 – 1962 Ledo green rhinestone earrings.** In the 1950s, Ledo earrings sold for about $5.00 a pair. Today these beautiful 1950s emerald green rhinestone 1" clip earrings, signed "Ledo," are valued at $20.00 – 30.00.

**Mid-1960s – 1984 Polcini decorative profile brooch.** Due to the style, the use of pavé rhinestones, and the black enamel highlights, this extraordinarily well-designed 2½" x 1½" Polcini brooch appears at first glance to be a late 1930s or early 1940s piece. However, it is much newer than that. The Polcini mark was first used in the mid-1960s. Polcini jewelry was no longer produced by the time of Damon Polcini's death in 1984, limiting the time when this beauty could have been made to mid-1960s – 1984. This wonderful brooch is signed "Polcini" with the copyright symbol. $45.00 – 60.00. From the collection of Debi Reece.

OTHER JEWELRY MAKERS

## 1958 – 1980s

Fig.1

Fig.2

**Early 1960s Judy Lee pink rhinestone brooch and earrings set.** All three pieces in this pretty pink and faux smoky quartz rhinestone 2" pin and matching 1¼" clip earrings set are signed "Judy Lee" in script. This signature was first used in 1958. This set features long navette-shaped rhinestones popular in the early 1960s and dates from that era. (See the 1962 Mayers catalog advertisement shown with Kenneth J. Lane jewelry on page 389 for examples of 1960s jewelry featuring long navette-shaped rhinestones.) $55.00 – 70.00. From the collection of Debi Reece.

**1958 – 1980s Judy Lee pink cabochon brooch and earrings set.** This beautiful 2" brooch is signed "Judy Lee" in script. This signature was first used in 1958. Each lovely light pink cabochon stone is surrounded by prong-set pink rhinestones. The clip earrings measure 1" in diameter. Set in gold-tone metal, this set is a brilliant showstopper. $50.00 – 70.00. From the collection of Debi Reece.

**1958 – 1980s Judy Lee golden topaz-colored rhinestone brooch and earrings set.** Note the interesting stripes of color in the large marble-like brown stones in this amazing brooch and earrings set signed "Judy Lee." Each irregularly shaped stone is striated with streaks of color like fine marble. Navette-shaped faux golden topaz rhinestones topped with clear aurora borealis rhinestones are nestled on top of these interesting marble-like stones, adding sparkle and dimension to the brooch. The brooch measures 2¼". Each clip earring is 1¼". $55.00 – 70.00. From the collection of Debi Reece.

OTHER JEWELRY MAKERS

## 1956 – 1960s

**1957 Leru "Pearled Nuggets" necklace and earrings set.** Shown in a 1957 advertisement for Leru jewelry, this antique-white plastic necklace and earrings set was called "Pearled Nuggets" in the 1957 "Jewelry by Leru" advertisement and originally sold for $2.00 each piece. The adjustable 15½" necklace and 1½" clip earrings are lightweight and comfortable to wear. The necklace is unsigned. The earrings are signed "Leru" with the copyright symbol. $25.00 – 35.00.

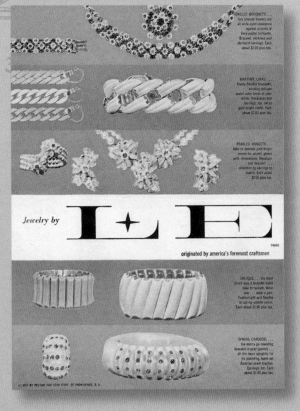

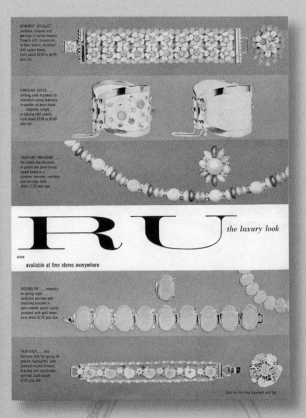

1957 "Jewelry by Leru" advertisement. This colorful advertisement features 10 different Leru designs. Page one top to bottom: Jeweled Bouquets, $2.00 each; Maytime Links, $2.00 each; Pearled Nuggets, $2.00 each; Oblique, $2.00 each bracelet; Spring Carousel, $2.00 each. Second page top to bottom: Dewdrop Bouquet, $3.00 – 8.95 each; Parisian Cuffs, $2.00 – 3.00 each; Tahitian Treasure, $2.00 each; Moonglow, $2.00 each; Fair Lady, $2.00 each.

**1957 Leru Dewdrop Bouquet blue and white enameled necklace, earrings, and bracelet set.**
The pink version of this magnificent enamel, pearl, and rhinestone set is shown in the 1957
"Jewelry by Leru" advertisement as "Dewdrop Bouquet." The advertisement reads, "…dainty
enamel flowers with rhinestones at their hearts. Accented with pastel beads. Each about $3.00
to $8.95." The blue bracelet measures 7¼" x 1¼", the necklace 15½", and the clip earrings
1¼". The beads in the necklace and bracelet are strung on tiny, but strong, silver chains. All
pieces are signed "Leru" with the copyright symbol. $65.00 – 85.00.

**1957 Leru Moonglow pink plastic bracelet.** This pretty pink 7½" plastic bracelet is signed "Leru" with
the copyright symbol. It is featured in the 1957 "Jewelry by Leru" advertisement as "Moonglow." The
advertisement reads, "MOONGLOW…romantic as spring night…necklace, earrings and matching
bracelet in satin-smooth pastel Lucite, accented with gold tones. Each about $2.00 plus tax." $20.00
– 30.00.

OTHER JEWELRY MAKERS

397

## 1963 – 1996

**1963 – 1996 Les Bernard scarecrow pin.** Les Bernard jewelry was produced from 1963 to 1996, making it a newer collectible. The cute scarecrow pin above measures 2" x 1" and is signed "Les Bernard Sterling." $35.00 – 45.00.

**1963 – 1996 Les Bernard fish and bull figural pins.** Simply signed "Les Bernard, Inc." these two adorable figural pins illustrate the fine quality of Les Bernard jewelry. Both pins were produced between 1963 and 1996 and are newer collectibles. The 2¼" fish pin features many jeweled scales and a delightfully expressive face. The proud 2¼" bull pin is decorated with bright orange enamel. His head is richly jeweled. $35.00 – 45.00.

## 1904 – APPROXIMATELY 1985

The Lisner mark was first used in 1938.

Fig.1

Fig.2

Fig.3

**Late 1950s Lisner Melody ribbed glass stone necklace.** Pretty pastel ribbed molded glass stones give this 16" choker-style necklace a plus quality. It is signed "Lisner" with the copyright symbol. Each pink, yellow, blue, or green ribbed stone is surrounded by sparkling clear aurora borealis rhinestones. The design of this necklace matches the Lisner necklace shown in the 1959 Lisner "Melody..." advertisement and dates from the same era. $70.00 – 100.00. From the collection of Debi Reece.

1959 Lisner "Melody..." advertisement. This ad reads, "Melody... bright with the aurora-iridescence of stones in imported glass. Crystal, rose, ice-blue, green, multi-color... all set in fake silver. Necklace, bracelet, pin, earrings: each $2 plus tax."

OTHER JEWELRY MAKERS

**1950s Lisner mother-of-pearl bracelet.** This delicate 7½" bracelet glows with iridescent mother-of-pearl disks and sparkling rhinestones. It is signed "Lisner" with the copyright symbol. The 1954 Boucher "Nautic" advertisement (see page 272) features Boucher designs utilizing these same mother-of-pearl disks, helping to date this bracelet to the 1950s. $45.00 – 55.00. Courtesy of Esta Pratt.

**1955 – 1960s Lisner ribbed plastic necklace, bracelet, and earrings set.** This amber-colored glowing hearts plastic 16" choker necklace, the 7" bracelet, and 1" clip earrings are signed "Lisner" with the copyright symbol, indicating the set was produced after 1955. Choker necklaces with plastic inserts were popular in the 1950s and 1960s, dating this set to that time. $90.00 – 125.00.

**1955 – 1960s Lisner ribbed green plastic necklace and earrings set.** This 16" green glowing hearts plastic necklace and 1" clip earrings set is identical in size and age to the amber-colored set shown on this page. All pieces are signed "Lisner" with the copyright symbol. $70.00 – 90.00.

OTHER JEWELRY MAKERS

**1955 – 1960s Lisner enamel and rhinestone bracelet, brooch, and clip earrings.** This lovely set is signed "Lisner" with the copyright symbol and features white enamel leaves surrounded by pretty pastel pink, blue, and clear rhinestones flowers. These tiny flowers were popular motifs in jewelry produced in the mid-1950s and the 1960s, dating this set to that time. The bracelet measures 7", the clip earrings are 1", and the pin is 1½". $55.00 – 75.00.

**1955 – 1960s Lisner blue rhinestone necklace, bracelet, and brooch.** This beautiful blue parure is signed "Lisner" with the copyright symbol and dates to 1955 – 1960s. The 16" necklace, 7" bracelet, and 1½" brooch sparkle with light blue aurora borealis flowers alternating with deep blue rectangular rhinestones all set in silver-tone metal. $60.00 – 80.00. From the collection of Debi Reece.

**1955 – 1960s Lisner rabbit brooch.** This fantastic 2¼" x 1" rabbit brooch by Lisner features a large egg-shaped head made of glowing plastic, green rhinestone eyes, a black cabochon nose, and silver-tone metal whiskers. There is a stripe of clear rhinestones leading from the nose to the floppy gold-tone rabbit ears. This brooch is signed "Lisner" with the copyright symbol and dates to 1955 – 1960s. $45.00 – 70.00.

**1955 – 1960s Lisner extraordinarily fine blue and white necklace and brace-let set.** This blue and white 17" necklace and 6¾" bracelet rival top designers like Schreiner in terms of the quality of the workmanship and the variety of materials used to complete the design. It is signed "Lisner" with the copyright symbol. This magnificent set is heavy. Each oval blue faceted rhinestone is set with dogtooth-style prongs. Between each blue rhinestone rests an elaborate white enameled flower arrangement, which includes a white enameled rose with a rhinestone center, two branches decorated with white enameled leaves, a round prong-set blue rhinestone, and three white beads. It is difficult to place an accurate value on such a rare, high-end Lisner set. Best guess: $100.00 – 150.00. From the collection of Debi Reece.

**1955 – 1960s Lisner molded plastic leaf necklace.** This 16" molded leaf necklace features off-white molded plastic leaves sur-rounded by clear aurora borealis rhinestones. The metal is silver-tone. It is signed "Lisner" with the copyright symbol and dates to 1955 – 1960s. $50.00 – 70.00.

OTHER JEWELRY MAKERS

**1955 – 1980s Lisner rhinestone flower pin.** This classically pretty 2" clear rhinestone flower pin is signed "Lisner" with the copyright symbol. This type of Lisner brooch is commonly found and difficult to date. It could have been made anytime after 1955. $20.00 – 25.00.

Fig.1

**1955 – 1980s Lisner japanned metal rhinestone pins.** Both of these lovely Lisner pins measure 2" and feature japanned metal. They are signed "Lisner" with the copyright symbol. $20.00 – 25.00 each.

Fig.2

Fig.3

Fig.4

OTHER JEWELRY MAKERS

## 1913 – 1978

**Early 1940s LN/25 flower brooch decorated with sapphire blue rhinestones.** This huge 2¾" faux-pewter brooch with dark blue rhinestones is signed "LN/25," which is one of the signatures used by the Little Nemo Manufacturing Company founded in 1913. It is difficult to date Little Nemo jewelry. $45.00 – 60.00.

**Two early 1940s Little Nemo brooches.** Left: Measuring a stately 3½" x 2¼" and featuring rare orange rhinestones, this faux-pewter flower brooch is signed "LN/25." Right: This colorful brooch measures 2¼" x 2" and features multi-colored rhinestones encircling pink and blue enameled flowers. The metal is dark-colored faux pewter. This brooch is signed "L/N." Both of these pieces have the look of early 1940s jewelry. $45.00 – 60.00 each. From the collection of Debi Reece.

**Early 1940s LN/25 amethyst rhinestone clip.** This large 2½" x 2¼" clip features faux pewter decorated with light amethyst rhinestones. It is signed "LN/25." $45.00 – 60.00.

OTHER JEWELRY MAKERS

## UNKNOWN, PROBABLY LATE 1950s – 1960s

**Late 1950s – 1960s Karen Lynne sterling cameo brooch and earrings.** In its original Karen Lynne presentation box, this 2" x 1¼" cameo is signed "KL Sterling." The matching ½" screw-back earrings are signed "CRC Sterling." CRC is the mark of the Reiss Company, Inc., of Indianapolis, Indiana. Interestingly, the logo on the Karen Lynn box has a key with the letter "R" as part of the design, which may relate to the Reiss Company. It is unknown what the connection was between Karen Lynne jewelry and the Reiss Company. A similar Karen Lynn cameo set named "Heirloom," done in 12 kt. gold-filled metal and originally sold for $31.50 a set, is featured in a 1962 Mayers catalog page. This catalog advertisement helps to date the cameo set in the photograph to the early 1960s. $35.00 – 45.00.

Fig. 2

Fig. 3

1962 Karen Lynne jewelry Mayers catalog page. The Karen Lynne jewelry featured in this advertisement includes genuine onyx, carnelian, and hand-carved ivory set in gold-filled metal. Karen Lynne jewelry straddles the line between fine jewelry made in precious metals with precious and semi-precious stones and costume jewelry. The jewelry featured on this page ranged in price from $7.50 to $36.00.

OTHER JEWELRY MAKERS

## 1938 – CLOSING IN 1940s

Jewelry marked "R. Mandle" was made by the R. Mandle Co., founded in 1956 by Urie Mandle's son. Urie Mandle jewelry is older and is often unmarked.

| Design Patent Number | Date Issued | Designer | Jewelry Type | Brief Description |
|---|---|---|---|---|
| 140737 | 4/3/1945 | Urie Mandle | Necklace | "Peace Everlasting" |
| 145460 | 8/20/1946 | Murray Slater | Brooch | Crown with heart, spade, diamond, club |
| 145461 | 8/20/1946 | Murray Slater | Brooch | Horn of plenty |
| 145462 | 8/20/1946 | Murray Slater | Brooch | King |
| 145463 | 8/20/1946 | Murray Slater | Brooch | Queen |
| 145464 | 8/20/1946 | Murray Slater | Brooch | King |
| 146751 | 5/6/1947 | Murray Slater | Brooch | Female figural |
| 146752 | 5/6/1947 | Murray Slater | Brooch | Male playing instrument |
| 146753 | 5/6/1947 | Murray Slater | Brooch | Starburst |
| 146754 | 5/6/1947 | Murray Slater | Brooch | Abstract |
| 146950 | 6/17/1947 | Murray Slater | Brooch | Sword and holder |
| 149095 | 3/23/1948 | Murray Slater | Brooch | Dragon head |

145462

146752

146950

**1947 Urie Mandle sterling silver Harlequin figure.** The design of the brooch matches design patent 146752 issued March 6, 1947, to Murray Slater. At the time, Slater designed jewelry for Urie F. Mandle. Measuring 2½" x 2", this interesting Harlequin figure is playing a mandolin. He has a moonstone face, a green rhinestone collar, and a red rhinestone decorated hat. The mandolin is decorated with clear rhinestones and an oval moonstone center. The pin is signed "Sterling." $80.00 – 95.00.

## UNKNOWN, APPEARS TO DATE 1950s – 1960s

Marhill jewelry is listed in the 1954 *Jewelers' Buyers Guide* and the company was operating at that time.

**1950s – 1960s Marhill necklace and earrings set.** Classic gray mother-of-pearl disks decorate this silver-tone 14½" Marhill necklace and matching 1" clip earrings. Interestingly, only the earrings are signed "Marhill." Marhill is known for producing beautiful compacts and cigarette cases; however, little is known about Marhill jewelry. The designs suggest the jewelry dates to the 1950s or 1960s. $40.00 – 50.00.

OTHER JEWELRY MAKERS

## UNKNOWN, DATES TO THE 1940s

| Design Patent Number | Date Issued | Designer | Jewelry Type | Brief Description |
|---|---|---|---|---|
| 144575 | 4/30/1946 | Frederick Pearsall | Brooch | Pirate ship |
| 144576 | 4/30/1946 | Frederick Pearsall | Brooch | Pirate hat and sword |
| 144577 | 4/30/1946 | Frederick Pearsall | Brooch | Pirate |
| 144578 | 4/30/1946 | Frederick Pearsall | Brooch | Pistol |
| 144579 | 4/30/1946 | Frederick Pearsall | Brooch | Pirate's head |
| 146678 | 4/22/1947 | Frederick Pearsall | Brooch | Bird |
| 146679 | 4/22/1947 | Frederick Pearsall | Brooch | Shell |
| 146775 | 5/13/1947 | Frederick Pearsall | Brooch | Owl |
| 146776 | 5/13/1947 | Frederick Pearsall | Brooch | Frog |
| 147679 | 10/14/1947 | Frederick Pearsall | Brooch | Clown carrying pearl |
| 147680 | 10/14/1947 | Frederick Pearsall | Brooch | Dancing woman |
| 147681 | 10/14/1947 | Frederick Pearsall | Brooch | Dancing woman |
| 147682 | 10/14/1947 | Frederick Pearsall | Brooch | Arrow |
| 147683 | 10/14/1947 | Frederick Pearsall | Brooch | African woman's head |
| 149140 | 3/30/1948 | Frederick Pearsall | Brooch | Head of woman wearing pearl headdress |

144577

146775

144579

1946 "Marleen" sterling silver pirate brooch. Guaranteed to start a conversation, this 2" x 1¾" large-nosed pirate pin is a showstopper. It is design patent number 144579 issued to Frederick J. Pearsall on April 30, 1946, for the Marleen Costume Jewelry Co. The brooch is signed "Marleen Sterling Pat. Pend. D121544." Interestingly, D121544 is not the design patent number for this piece. $75.00 – 95.00.

146776

OTHER JEWELRY MAKERS

## 1911 — PRESENT

Fig.1

Fig.2

Fig.3

Late 1950s – 1960s Marvella red molded plastic necklace and earrings set. This especially pretty 15½" choker necklace and the matching 1½" clip earrings are signed "Marvella" with the copyright symbol. This signature and the style date this set to the late 1950s – 1960s. A departure from traditional Marvella beads, this set features glowing ruby red ribbed plastic flowers surrounded by gold-tone ribbed leaves. $50.00 – 80.00.

PINK CHAMPAGNE...effervescent crystals in a fizz of color...great new aperitif for the season's clothes. Showing the Hi-Rise® look...a 3-strand choker with a 3-strand dog collar worn together, $15.00 each. Pin, $10.00. Earrings, $6.00. Other "Spirit" colors: Campari, Pernod, Sherry, Blue Curaçao. Prices plus fed. tax.
At stores listed and other fine stores everywhere. Write: Marvella, Inc., 385 Fifth Avenue, New York 16, N.Y.
BLOOMINGDALE'S NEW YORK; T. A. CHAPMAN CO. MILWAUKEE; CITY OF PARIS SAN FRANCISCO; M. M. COHN CO. LITTLE ROCK; B. FORMAN CO. ROCHESTER; F. & R. LAZARUS CO. COLUMBUS; MABLEY & CAREW CO. CINCINNATI; MILLER & RHOADS, INC. RICHMOND; THE PEERLESS CO. PROVIDENCE; SAGE, ALLEN & CO. HARTFORD; STIX, BAER & FULLER ST. LOUIS

MARVELLA®

1960 Marvella "Pink Champagne..." jewelry advertisement. The model in this advertisement is wearing two Marvella crystal three-strand necklaces called "Pink Champagne" originally sold for $15.00 each. The pin sold for $10.00 and the earrings for $6.00.

**Late 1950s – 1960s Marvella Siamese dancer pin.** Siamese-style jewelry was popular from the mid-1950s through the 1960s, partly due to the 1956 release of the movie *The King and I* staring Yule Brenner and Deborah Kerr. This marvelously well-crafted 2¼" x 1¼" Siamese dancer is decorated with faux jade stones. It is signed "Marvella" with the copyright symbol. $35.00 – 50.00.

OTHER JEWELRY MAKERS

Speak low if you speak love. Say it with sighs and soft whispers that echo the muted glow of your Marvella 95 simulated pearls. Yes, this is your beloved...emblazoned with a dome-shaped Mabé pearl, deep-set in a clasp woven of gold-washed braided strands. Flaunt it front, side or back as the mood moves you. The uniform three-row choker $17.50. The earrings $5. Prices plus Federal tax. At the finest shops or write Marvella, Inc., 385 Fifth Avenue, New York 16, N.Y.

.marvella
could it be the real thing?

1962 Marvella pearl necklace advertisement. This advertisement features a triple-strand Marvella simulated pearl necklace that originally sold for $17.50 and matching earrings that sold for $5.00.

410

## 1923 – 1981

The "Mazer Bros." mark was used from 1926 to 1951. The mark "Mazer" was used from 1946 to 1981. The "Jomaz" mark was used from 1946 to 1981.

| Design Patent Number | Date Issued | Designer | Jewelry Type | Brief Description |
|---|---|---|---|---|
| 109875 | 5/31/1938 | Louis Mazer | Brooch | Floral bouquet molded leaves |
| 109876 | 5/31/1938 | Louis Mazer | Brooch | Floral spray molded leaves |
| 109877 | 5/31/1938 | Louis Mazer | Brooch | Basket molded leaves |
| 109878 | 5/31/1938 | Louis Mazer | Brooch | Floral molded leaves |
| 109898 | 5/31/1938 | Louis Mazer | Brooch | Basket molded leaves |
| 114801 | 5/16/1939 | Joseph Wuyts | Brooch | Male with turban |
| 123910 | 12/10/1940 | Louis Mazer | Brooch | Mask with headdress (See 123911 for another mask brooch.) |
| 123911 | 12/10/1940 | Louis Mazer | Brooch | Mask without headdress (See 123910 for another mask brooch.) |
| 124521 | 1/7/1941 | Joseph Wuyts | Brooch | "Whispering Good" (See 124522 for "Whispering Evil.") |
| 124522 | 1/7/1941 | Joseph Wuyts | Brooch | "Whispering Evil" (See 124521 for "Whispering Good.") |
| 126417 | 4/8/1941 | Louis Mazer | Brooch | Mask decorated with floral vines |
| 126418 | 4/8/1941 | Louis Mazer | Brooch | Mask with rhinestone headdress |
| 130951 | 12/30/1941 | Louis Mazer | Brooch | Man in turban |
| 156085 | 11/22/1949 | André Fleuridas | Earring | Decorated back, double drop |
| 157360 | 2/21/1950 | André Fleuridas | Earring | Decorated back, two navette rhinestone drops |
| 159968 | 9/5/1950 | André Fleuridas | Earring | Decorated back, two rhinestone drops |
| 159969 | 9/5/1950 | André Fleuridas | Earring | Decorated back, one rhinestone drop |
| 159970 | 9/5/1950 | André Fleuridas | Earring | Decorated back, one large rhinestone drop |
| 159971 | 9/5/1950 | André Fleuridas | Earring | Decorated back, one rhinestone drop in front and one in back |
| 159972 | 9/5/1950 | André Fleuridas | Earring | Decorated back, baguettes and two drops |

109877

114801

123910

124521

**1948 – early 1950s.** This magnificent 3" x 1¾" bow brooch is signed "Mazer" without the copyright symbol and features a single golden topaz rhinestone center stone accented by ribbons of pavé icing. Mazer jewelry was produced by the Joseph Mazer Company from 1946 to 1981. The nonuse of sterling and 1940s style of this brooch date this piece to 1948 – early 1950s. $80.00 – 100.00.

126417

130951

**1955 – 1981 Jomaz blue cabochon brooch.** This dimensional 2¼" x 1¼" brooch is signed "Jomaz" with the copyright symbol and features a jumbo-sized blue cabochon stone nestled between gold-tone leaves. Interestingly, the back of the large light blue stone is painted blue on the back. The "Jomaz" signature was in use from 1946 to 1981. The copyright symbol narrows the time period when this piece could have been made to between 1955 and 1981. $65.00 – 85.00. From the collection of Debi Reece.

156085

**1955 – 1981 Jomaz butterfly pin.** Petite and pretty, this 1¾" x ¾" butterfly pin is signed "Jomaz" with the copyright symbol. The metal is gold-tone, and the wings are decorated with colorful rhinestones and turquoise seed pearls. This classic design could have been produced anytime between 1955 and 1981. $45.00 – 60.00. From the collection of Debi Reece.

157360

Fig. 1

**1950s Mazer André Fleuridas design pearl and rhinestone clip earrings.** The design of these 1" pearl and rhinestone clip earrings is similar to design patent number 157360 issued February 21, 1950, to André Fleuridas for Mazer. At this time, Fleuridas created several different variations of a unique clip earring design. The backs of ordinary clip earrings are plain, with all of the decorations attached to the front of the earrings. The unique Fleuridas earrings are different. Half of the design is attached to the front of the earring and half of the design is attached to the back of the earring. These earrings are signed "Mazer" without the copyright symbol. $35.00 – 45.00.

Opened view of the 1950s Mazer Fleuridas design earrings.

OTHER JEWELRY MAKERS

413

### 1955 – 1975

**1959 Judith McCann turquoise-colored glass beads with unique clasp.** This beautiful and uniquely styled 26" glass bead necklace is signed "J. McCann 1959" with the copyright symbol. The clasp on this necklace is called a "shuvon" clasp and was invented by Judith McCann to add versatility to necklaces. Each end of the necklace has a hook decorated with rhinestones. These hooks enable the wearer to adjust the length and style of the necklace. The photographs in this book illustrate two methods of wearing this unique necklace. $50.00 – 75.00.

Another view of the versatile "shuvon" clasp.

Back view of blue and white Wingback earrings.

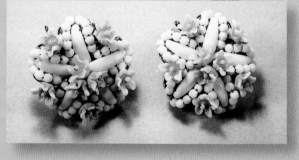

**1950s – 1960s blue and white wingback earrings.** "Wingback" refers to earrings with the characteristic V-shaped "wing" portion of the earring that sits inside the ear. A long wire then rests on the back of the ear to balance the earring and hold it comfortably in place. Utility patent number 2414382 was issued January 14, 1947, to Judith McCann for the design of the unique earring back. Wingback earrings were produced through the 1950s and into the 1960s by many makers. The beautiful 1½" wingback earrings above feature hand-strung blue and white beads in the style of Miriam Haskell jewelry. They are signed "Wingback" with the patent number along the long wire. $40.00 – 50.00.

## 1962 – 1970s

**1960s Mimi di N gold-tone and rhinestone brooch.** Bold in design, this gold-tone and clear rhinestone brooch is also bold in size, measuring 3" x 2¼". It is signed "Mimi di N" with the copyright symbol. Mimi di N began producing jewelry in 1962 and continued through the 1970s. This brooch could have been made anytime during those years. (Some Mimi di N jewelry from the 1970s is both signed and dated.) $35.00 – 45.00. From the collection of Debi Reece.

Fig. 1

# • Miracle •

## 1946 – Present

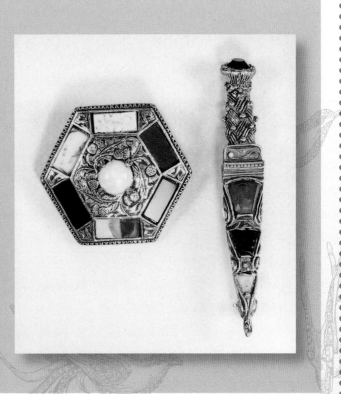

**1946 – present Miracle brooches.** Both of these colorful brooches are signed "Miracle" and were produced by A. Hill and Company Ltd., England, between 1946 and the present day. These pieces are reproductions of Victorian-era Scottish jewelry. The six-sided brooch on the left measures 2 x 1¾". The Scottish dirk kilt pin on the right measures 3" x ½". Both pieces feature polished agate stones in vibrant, earthy colors. $35.00 – 45.00 each. From the collection of Debi Reece.

## 1937 – Present

| Design Patent Number | Date Issued | Designer | Jewelry Type | Brief Description |
| --- | --- | --- | --- | --- |
| 101105 | 9/8/1936 | Michael Chernow | Pendant | Initials |
| 132531 | 5/26/1942 | Michael Chernow | Brooch | Vase or urn |
| 146461 | 3/18/1947 | Michael Chernow | Brooch | Stylized circle (See 146762 for matching earring.) |
| 146762 | 3/18/1947 | Michael Chernow | Earring | Stylized circle (See 146461 for matching brooch.) |
| 148143 | 12/23/1947 | Michael Chernow | Brooch | Abstract |
| 158555 | 5/16/1950 | Michael Chernow | Necklace | Lariat style with tassels |
| 161905 | 2/13/1951 | Michael Chernow | Necklace | Collar with dangles, no rhinestones |
| 163934 | 7/17/1951 | Michael Chernow | Necklace | Lariat style, no rhinestones |
| 163989 | 7/24/1951 | Michael Chernow | Bracelet | Faux-lariat style, four dangles (See 163990 for matching necklace.) |
| 163990 | 7/24/1951 | Michael Chernow | Necklace | Lariat style, four dangles (See 163989 for matching bracelet.) |
| 163991 | 7/24/1951 | Michael Chernow | Necklace | Lariat style, four dangles |
| 173145 | 10/5/1954 | Michael Chernow | Earring | Basket-weave style |

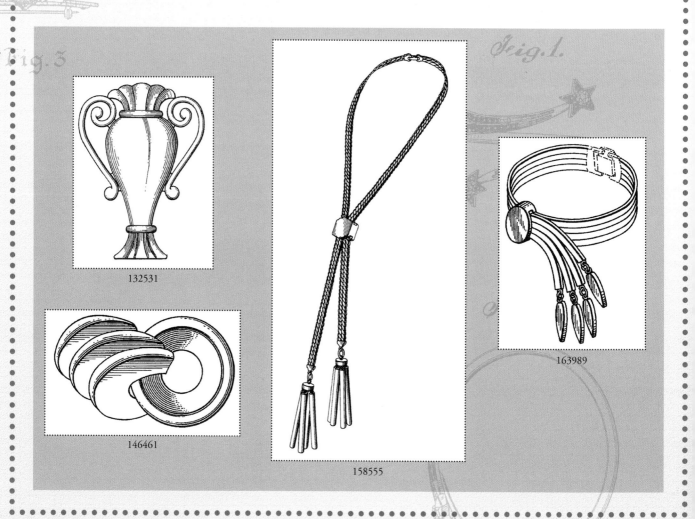

132531

146461

158555

163989

**1950s Monet slide bracelet.** Monet produced many versions of gold-tone decorated slide bracelets. For example, design patent number 163989 issued to Michael Chernow of Monet on July 24, 1951, shows a 1950s version of the Monet slide bracelet. Page 49 of the 1963 Monet catalog features another, similar slide bracelet advertised as "Priscilla" and selling for $10.00. This Monet slide bracelet is signed "Monet" without a copyright symbol and dates to the early 1950s. It fits an average-size wrist. While lovely, plain gold-tone jewelry is not widely collected, so the values remain low. $25.00 – 35.00.

1963 Monet Priscilla slide necklace, bracelet, and matching earrings advertisement. This is page 49 of the *1963 Monet Catalog and Mat Book* featuring a gold tone slide set called "Priscilla." The caption reads, "Heirloom quality — beautifully simple in design and finely crafted — Priscilla has a special appeal to the woman who appreciates perfection. Supple snake chain is caught with a handsome clasp to adjust the necklace so that it may be worn high or low. The adjustable slide necklace $12.50, adjustable slide bracelet $10.00, drop earrings $7.50." From the collection of David Mayer.

OTHER JEWELRY MAKERS

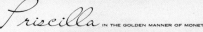

1949 Monet "Girandole Earrings" advertisement. This beautiful vintage advertisement reads, "Fascinating earrings inspired by the Crystal Girandole [pendant earring] of the pre-Victorian Era…Finely wrought pendantry that twinkles with every movement to lend enchantment to your ear. Each is a superb bit of craftsmanship, a finished work of art in famous MONET plate for enduring wear. Each bears the signature of MONET. Rubens $5…daVinci 15…Durer 7.50…Watteau 10…Degas 3…Rembrandt 15…At finer shops everywhere."

**1963 Monet gold-tone brooch.** This 2¾" Monet fringe pin is shown on page 28 of the 1963 Monet catalog with a selling price of $10.00. It is signed "Monet" with the copyright symbol. This style of plain gold jewelry is not widely collected, so that the value of this pin today remains at $10.00.

*Pins* MAKE FASHION NEWS... PR

Suggest them . . . to feminize a tailored suit . . . to hold a scarf or stole . . . to accent belts . . . to wear sm

MASQUERADE · PN 1855 $5 · ER 9856 $5  NANETTE · PN 1585 $3 · ER 9586 $4  CRESTMAR · PN 1564 $4 · ER 9564 $4  FLEUR · PN 1536 $7.50 · ER 9536 $4

WHIRLWIND · PN 1905 $10 · ER 6905 $7.50  ARCADIA · PN 1899 $5 · ER 9899 $5  PN 1874 $5 · ER 9898 $4  CORDELIA · PN 1070 $10 · ER 9645 $5

LISETTE · PN 1818 $4 · ER 9817 $3  BOWKNOT · PN 1521 $6 · ER 9609 $4  FROND · PN 1460 $5 · ER 9461 $5  FLORES · PN 1985 $5 · ER 9982 $5

PRIMROSE · PN 1520 $7.50  RONDELAY · PN 1857 $6 · ER 9858 $5  PN 1858 $5 · ER 9859 $5  ANDALUSIA · PN 1526 $7.50 · ER 6525 $7.50

FEATHER · PN 1465 $5 · ER 9467 $5  KARANI · PN 1836 $6 · ER 9876 $6  SHASTA · PN 1531 $6  STARFIRE · PN 1540 $7.50 · ER 9540 $7.50

1963 Monet "Pins Make Fashion News" catalog page. This is page 28 of the 1963 *Monet Catalog and Mat Book* and features an array of Monet pins that originally ranged in price from $5.00 to $10.00. From the collection of David Mayer.

**1963 – 1968 Monet Milano chunky charm bracelet with moveable charms.** The 7¼" Monet charm bracelet to the left is adorned with 12 chunky charms, 8 of which are moveable. It is signed "Monet" with the copyright symbol. The moveable charms in the bracelet include a carriage with four rotating wheels, a Santa charm with a mouth that opens to reveal the Christmas message "Have a happy," a little man charm that opens to reveal the message "Have a nice day," a cat charm with a winking eye, a Happy Birthday charm with an adjustable date, a clown that sticks out his tongue, a duck that opens to reveal a hidden compartment, and a dog who sticks out his tongue. Each charm measures 1" – 1½" long. Page 53 of the 1963 *Monet Catalog and Mat Book* features an array of chunky charms for sale ranging in value from $2.00 to $5.00 each. In addition, the 1968 Monet "charms in the golden manner of Monet" advertisement features similar chunky charms, indicating that these charms were big sellers for Monet and remained in production for at least five years. $70.00 – 100.00.

1963 Monet "Beautiful…and so easy to attach" catalog page. This is page 53 of the 1963 *Monet Catalog and Mat Book* featuring an array of Monet chunky charms ranging in price from $2.00 to $5.00 each. From the collection of David Mayer.

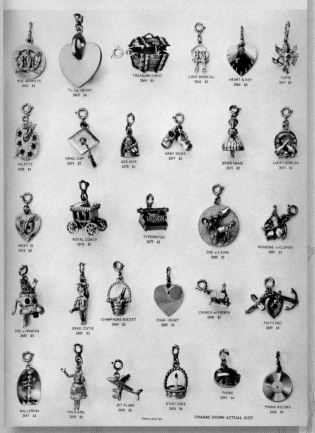

1968 "charms in the golden manner of Monet" advertisement. This creative advertisement features a Monet chunky charm bracelet. The bracelet and charms ranged in value from $3.00 to $7.50.

OTHER JEWELRY MAKERS

419

**1960s Monet slide necklace.** This Monet slide necklace measures 17" and is comfortable on most necklines. It is signed "Monet" with the copyright symbol and dates to the 1960s. $20.00 – 30.00.

jewelry in the golden manner of **Monet**

OTHER JEWELRY MAKERS

1962 "jewelry in the golden manner of Monet" advertisement. This colorful advertisement features Monet's Minaret necklace (originally $18.50) and matching earrings (originally $7.50).

Fig.1

Fig.2

**1980s Monet rhinestone parure.** In the 1980s, Monet manufactured jewelry for Yves Saint Laurent. At the same time, Monet produced beautiful jewelry sets like the one in the photograph. This set has the same look as the beautiful Yves Saint Laurent jewelry of that time. The 3½" x 2" pendant is suspended from a 15" silver-tone snake chain. The cuff bracelet is comfortable on an average 7½" wrist. Each clip earring measures 1¾". All pieces are signed "Monet" with the copyright symbol. The teardrop-shaped rhinestones are an amber or copper color. The pentagon-shaped stones are frosted white rhinestones. The baguettes appear blue in the photograph, but they are clear with an aurora borealis finish, so the color changes depending upon the lighting. This set is bold and wonderful. The prices for first-rate 1980s Monet sets are increasing rapidly. $150.00 – 200.00.

**Late 1980s – 1990s Monet red, white, and black geometric design parure.** This modern Monet set exhibits a bold well-executed design. The necklace measures 16" and is enhanced by four geometric charms that slide along the chain. The 1¾" x 1" pierced earrings exhibit the same geometric design. The large-sized cuff bracelet fits up to an 8" wrist. All pieces are signed "Monet" with the copyright symbol. $35.00 – 45.00.

OTHER JEWELRY MAKERS

# • MORTON, JOSEF •

## LATE 1950s, EARLY 1960s – UNKNOWN

**Early 1960s Josef Morton hand-strung pearl floral brooch.** Hand made in the style of Miriam Haskell jewelry, this creamy pearl and rhinestone 2" brooch is signed "Josef Morton." There are two good reasons Josef Morton jewelry resembles Haskell designs. First, Josef Morton was Miriam Haskell's nephew. Next, Morton jewelry produced in the early 1960s was designed by Frank Hess, formerly head designer for Miriam Haskell. This spectacular brooch features hand-strung pearls and rhinestones set in an antique-gold-tone metal. In the style of Haskell, nearly every surface is artistically coated with these pretty pearls. $95.00 – 130.00.

# • MOSELL, FREDERICK •

## 1941 – UNKNOWN BUT LIKELY 1960s

| Design Patent Number | Date Issued | Designer | Jewelry Type | Brief Description |
|---|---|---|---|---|
| 123912 | 12/10/1940 | Frederic Mosell | Brooch | Patriotic |
| 126403 | 4/8/1941 | Frederic Mosell | Brooch | Maltese dog |
| 127708 | 6/10/1941 | Frederic Mosell | Brooch | Ram |

126403

**1955 – 1960s Frederick Mosell blue rhinestone bracelet.** This 7" x ¾" brushed-gold-tone bracelet is another version of the beautiful baroque pearl parure shown in this book. It is signed "Mosell" with the copyright symbol and dates to 1955 – 1960s. $65.00 – 85.00.

OTHER JEWELRY MAKERS

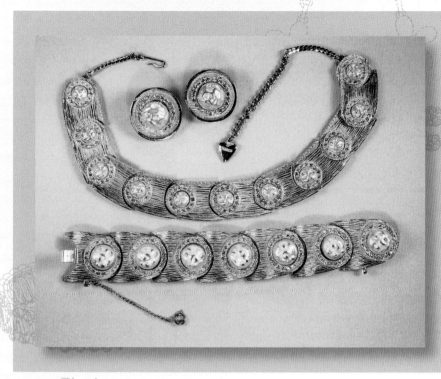

1955 – 1960s Frederick Mosell baroque pearl necklace, bracelet, and earrings set. Signed Mosell jewelry is rare. This golden baroque pearl and rhinestone necklace measures 14", the bracelet is 7" x ¾", and the clip earrings measure 1" in diameter. Mosell produced jewelry from 1941 through the 1960s. The bracelet is signed "Mosell" in capital letters with the copyright symbol, dating this set to 1955 – 1960s. $135.00 – 225.00. From the collection of Debi Reece.

Fig.1

# • NAPIER •

## 1915 – PRESENT

Fig.2

Fig.3

1948 – 1955 Napier necklace and earrings with large blue stones. Notice the glow radiating from the beautiful blue beads decorating this early Napier 30" necklace and 1" x ¾" earrings set. This set is signed "Napier" without the copyright symbol. This signature and the nonuse of sterling indicate this set dates to 1948 – 1955. $50.00 – 65.00 set. From the collection of Debi Reece.

OTHER JEWELRY MAKERS

**1948 – 1955 Napier red and gold-tone necklace.** Resting in its original presentation box, this 17" gold filigree and deep red beaded necklace reflects the fine quality of design and materials sometimes found in early Napier jewelry. Strung on a chain instead of string, this first-class necklace features large gold-tone "cages" containing glowing red glass beads. It is signed "Napier" without the copyright symbol and dates to 1948 – 1955. $45.00 – 55.00. From the collection of Debi Reece.

**1955 – 1960s Napier poodle pin.** This great gray poodle pin is signed "Napier" with the copyright symbol and could have been produced anytime after 1955. Poodle pins were especially popular in the 1950s and 1960s. Interestingly, the 1" gray enameled poodle features a rotating head (it spins all the way around). $25.00 – 35.00.

## 1910 – 1978

**1948 – 1955 Nemo red rhinestone necklace and screw-back earrings.** This lightweight red and clear 15½" rhinestone necklace is unmarked. Fortunately, the ½" screw-back ear rings are signed "Nemo." Jewelry signed "Nemo" was produced by Brier Manufacturing Company. However, jewelry marked "LN" was produced by Little Nemo Manufacturing Company. (See "Little Nemo" for an example of "LN" jewelry.) There is some speculation that there was a connection between these companies. However, the jewelry signed "Nemo" and the jewelry signed "LN" are vastly different in style. $40.00 – 50.00.

# • NORMA •

## UNKNOWN, APPEARS TO DATE 1940s –1950s

**1940s – early 1950s Norma sterling songbird pin.** This sweet 2" x 1½" singing lovebird pin is signed "Norma" in print and "Sterling Pat. Pend." Interestingly, no patents were found for the Norma Jewelry Company. It is unclear when "Norma" jewelry was first produced. In the 1954 *Jewelers' Buyers Guide,* the Norma Jewelry Company advertised 14 karat gold and cultured pearl jewelry. The advertisement (not shown) suggests that the company specialized in fine jewelry and sterling silver designs rather than costume jewelry. The company was not listed in the 1957 *Jewelers' Buyers Guide* and may have been out of business by that time. Based on this information, and on the style of the piece, this pin dates from the 1940s to the early 1950s. $50.00 – 80.00.

## 1921 – PRESENT

Ora jewelry was not signed until 1940. The lack of a copyright symbol in the signature is not useful when dating Ora jewelry. Even new Ora jewelry is signed "ORA" without the copyright symbol.

| Design Patent Number | Date Issued | Designer | Jewelry Type | Brief Description |
|---|---|---|---|---|
| 110532 | 7/19/1938 | Oreste Agnini and Mary Granville | Brooch | Trumpet with arms and legs (See 110533 for saxophone.) |
| 110533 | 7/19/1938 | Oreste Agnini and Mary Granville | Brooch | Saxophone with arms and legs (See 110534 for bass fiddle.) |
| 110534 | 7/19/1938 | Oreste Agnini and Mary Granville | Brooch | Base fiddle with arms and legs (See 110535 for banjo.) |
| 110535 | 7/19/1938 | Oreste Agnini and Mary Granville | Brooch | Banjo with arms and legs (See 110558 for piano.) |
| 110557 | 7/19/1938 | Oreste Agnini and Mary Granville | Brooch | Base drum with arms and legs (See 110532 for trumpet.) |
| 110558 | 7/19/1938 | Oreste Agnini and Mary Granville | Brooch | Grand piano with arms and legs (See 110557 for base drum.) |

110533

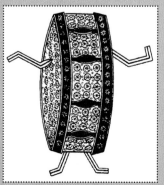

110557

**1938 unmarked but patented Ora base drum pin.** When researching jewelry design patents from 1938, I found six patents for whimsical musical instrument pins, all with dancing arms and legs. These six patents were issued to Oreste Agnini and Mary Granville. Oreste Agnini was one of the founders of Ora jewelry. Intrigued, I began searching eBay for instrument pins with arms and legs. Amazingly, on the very first search, I located this rare 1½" x 1¼" base drum pin identical to design patent number 110551 issued July 19, 1938, to Oreste J. Agnini and Mary C. Granville for Ora. Although unsigned (Ora did not sign jewelry until 1940), I am certain this amazing base drum pin with pavé rhinestones and black enamel is by Ora. $65.00 – 90.00.

**1953 Ora New Dimension rhinestone necklace.** It is easy to assign a date to this high-quality Ora necklace because it is an exact match to the necklace shown in the 1953 Ora "New Dimension" advertisement. Amazingly, this 14½" necklace has survived in beautiful condition for over 50 years. Originally selling for $9.00, this necklace was made in both clear and lavender rhinestones. It is signed "ORA" without the copyright symbol. $65.00 – 85.00.

**1953 Ora "New Dimension" adver-tisement.** This rare Ora advertisement features a lovely necklace called "New Dimension." The advertisement reads, "Terraced clusters of scintillating stones suggest the tri-dimensional effect so popular this fall. Each brilliant stone, each sparkling surface, guaranteed to last a lifetime. Tri-D earrings to match. At fine stores everywhere. Necklace about $9.00, plus tax. Earrings about $7.00 plus tax."

**1940 – present Ora rhinestone deer pin and earrings set.** The Ora mark was first used in 1940 and it is still in use today, so dating this interesting 1" x ¾" deer head brooch and matching 1" x ¾" clip earrings set is difficult. The set is signed "ORA" without the copyright symbol. The selling prices for the new jewelry range from $28.00 for a pin to $96.00 for a larger, more elaborately decorated brooch. Today Ora jewelry specializes in fraternal jewelry styles as well as newly produced vintage designs. This creative deer head set could have been produced anytime from 1940 to the present. $30.00 – 45.00. From the collection of Debi Reece.

OTHER JEWELRY MAKERS

**Early 1950s Ora choker-style necklace.** Bright blue rhinestones decorate this rare, vintage Ora 15½" necklace. It is signed "ORA" without the copyright symbol. Ora jewelry is still produced today; however, this necklace dates to the early 1950s when choker-style necklaces were popular. $65.00 – 85.00. From the collection of Debi Reece.

1957 "Occasion by Ora Creations" advertisement. This colorful advertisement features several 1957 Ora designs. The beautiful pearl and gold-tone necklace, bracelet, and earrings set is called "Occasion" and was designed by Anne Geyer. The necklace originally sold for $11.00, the bracelet for $7.00, and the earrings for $3.00. Featured in the left-hand corner are blue earrings called "Caprice" for $5.00 and a golden topaz rhinestone brooch called "Epic" for $7.00.

1954 "only Ora Creations offer so much…" advertisement. This advertisement appeared in the 1954 *Jewelers' Buyers Guide*. The focus of the advertisement is to encourage retailers to carry Ora jewelry. The advertisement states that Ora offers "beauty guaranteed for life," "fashion awareness: 32 years of timely creative designs," and "honest shipments — no substitutions." The Ora slogan at the time was "Jewels of the Hour…a product of Ralph Singer Company."

**1940 – present Ora rhinestone sword pin.** This magnificent 2" x 2" pin is signed "ORA" and features clear rhinestones set in silver-tone metal. A gold-tone sword is riveted to the bottom of the pin. Well crafted, this crown pin is fraternal jewelry, likely a Shriners piece, and could have been produced anytime between 1940, when Ora began signing jewelry, and the present. $45.00 – 55.00. From the collection of Debi Reece.

# • ORIGINAL BY ROBERT •

## 1942 – 1979

Fig.1

**1943 – 1948 colorful Original by Robert sterling bow brooch and earrings set.** This amazing set is signed "Sterling Original by Robert" and dates from 1943 to 1948. The style of this 2" in diameter bow brooch and the matching 1" clip earrings is reminiscent of Hobé designs of the time. Notice the swirling ropelike decorations on the edges of the bow. Original by Robert jewelry from this era is scarce, especially sterling silver sets. $125.00 – 175.00. From the collection of Debi Reece.

**1948 – 1950s Original by Robert baroque pearl flower pin.** Most signed Original by Robert jewelry consists of well-made enameled jewelry. However, Robert also produced amazing designs that reflect the handmade style of Miriam Haskell jewelry. Measuring 3" long, this delightful signed Original by Robert pin could easily be mistaken for Miriam Haskell jewelry because of the irregularly shaped pearls in the design and the hand-strung tiny clusters of pearl and rhinestone flowers. However, the gold-tone metal in this example is bright, unlike Haskell pieces, which normally have an antique-gold-tone appearance. Original by Robert jewelry was produced from 1942 to 1979. This is an early example likely dating from 1948 to 1950s. $70.00 – 90.00. From the collection of Debi Reece.

1945 – 1980s

**1970 – 1980s Panetta pearl necklace and matching dangling pearl earrings.** This creamy pearl, clear rhinestone, and faux opal set is signed "Panetta" with the copyright symbol. The locking clasp on the necklace is frequently found on newer jewelry, suggesting this set dates to the 1970s – 1980s. The creamy pearls in this 14" choker are knotted like "real" pearls, so that should one pearl come loose, the others will stay in place. This type of construction is one indication of a high-quality faux pearl necklace. The 1" long clip earrings reflect the same quality in design and workmanship. $45.00 – 65.00. From the collection of Debi Reece.

**1970s – 1980s Panetta rabbit pin.** This well-crafted 2½" rabbit pin is signed "Panetta" with the copyright symbol. He is reminiscent of Thumper from Walt Disney's *Bambi*. This sweetie is a newer Panetta design dating to the 1970s – 1980s. Note the playful expression and the rhinestone bow tie on this high-quality piece. $30.00 – 40.00.

## UNKNOWN, APPEARS TO DATE LATE 1940s – 1950s

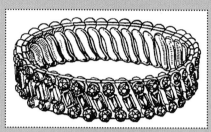

160008

**1950 Pargo rhinestone expansion bracelet.** Expansion bracelets, like this clear rhinestone Pargo bracelet, were popular in the 1950s. This example is signed "Pargo Des. Pat. 160008," and the patent was issued September 5, 1950, to Charles T. Parisi of Pargo. Today, most of these expansion bracelets can be purchased for under $30.00; however, the patent information accompanying this one adds value to the piece. $45.00 – 65.00.

# • PENNINO •

## 1926 – 1966

| Design Patent Number | Date Issued | Designer | Jewelry Type | Brief Description |
|---|---|---|---|---|
| 114905 | 5/23/1939 | Oreste Pennino | Brooch | Pinocchio |
| 119091 | 2/20/1940 | Oreste Pennino | Brooch | Tree |
| 121372 | 7/9/1940 | Victor Primavera | Brooch | Floral in square frame |
| 121373 | 7/9/1940 | Victor Primavera | Brooch | Floral in oval frame |
| 121374 | 7/9/1940 | Victor Primavera | Brooch | Floral in circular frame |
| 143877 | 2/12/1946 | Oreste Pennino | Brooch | Stylized floral |
| 143878 | 2/12/1946 | Oreste Pennino | Brooch | Stylized floral |
| 147762 | 10/28/1947 | Oreste Pennino | Brooch | Starburst with lightening and arrows |
| 149832 | 6/1/1948 | Oreste Pennino | Brooch | Tree with rhinestones |
| 149833 | 6/1/1948 | Oreste Pennino | Brooch | Tree with pearls |
| 151163 | 9/28/1948 | Oreste Pennino | Brooch | Double hearts with crown |

Fig. 1

119091

Fig. 2

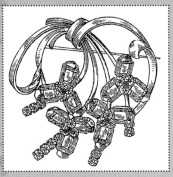

143877

Fig. 3

147762

149832

143878

**1946 Pennino sterling silver rhinestone flower brooch.** This spectacular brooch is design patent number 143878 issued February 12, 1946, to Oreste Pennino for Pennino. This sensational 2¾" x 3" brooch is signed "Pennino" and "Sterling." $175.00 – 250.00.

**1948 – 1955 Pennino rhinestone bracelet.** Not only is this 7½" x 1" Pennino cactus and flower bracelet beautiful and rare, it is also amazingly flexible and comfortable. Each little cactus is a separate section, giving this magnificent bracelet fabulous fluidity. It is signed "Pennino" without the copyright symbol. The nonuse of sterling dates this breathtaking bracelet to 1948 – 1955. $150.00 – 225.00. From the collection of Debi Reece.

Fig. 1

Fig. 2

Fig. 3

1949 Pennino "These exciting New Fashion Jewelry Creations" advertisement. This interesting Pennino advertisement features costume jewelry and Pennino watches. Notice that at this time, the necklace is a fixed length. Also, one of the watches is designed with a covered face. This advertisement invites readers to the ANRJA (American National Retail Jewelers Association) Convention at the Waldorf-Astoria hotel.

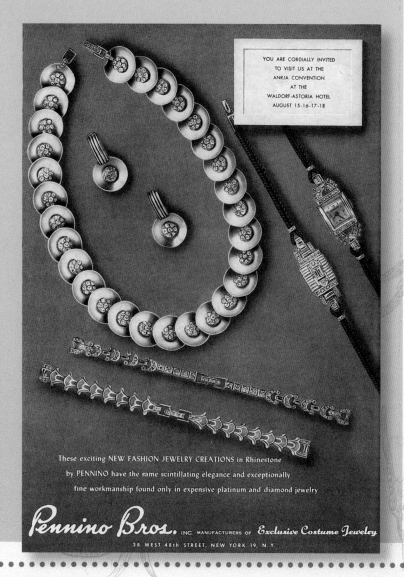

YOU ARE CORDIALLY INVITED
TO VISIT US AT THE
ANRJA CONVENTION
AT THE
WALDORF-ASTORIA HOTEL
AUGUST 15-16-17-18

These exciting NEW FASHION JEWELRY CREATIONS in Rhinestone by PENNINO have the same scintillating elegance and exceptionally fine workmanship found only in expensive platinum and diamond jewelry

*Pennino Bros.* INC. MANUFACTURERS OF *Exclusive Costume Jewelry*
38 WEST 48th STREET, NEW YORK 19, N.Y.

**1948 – 1955 Pennino rhinestone necklace.** Pennino jewelry is consistently high quality, including this elegant 16" Pennino choker necklace. The rare channel-set baguette rhinestones and creamy rhodium plating give this necklace a plus quality. It is signed "Pennino" without the copyright symbol. The signature and the rhodium finish date this piece to 1948 – 1955. $85.00 – 100.00.

**1948 – 1955 Pennino gold-tone leaf necklace and earrings set.** This classically styled 15" choker necklace and matching 1½" leaf design clip earrings feature brushed-gold-tone metal highlighted with tiny clear rhinestones. It is one of the most popular and easy-to-find Pennino sets. Interestingly, the necklace is unmarked. Each earring is marked "Pennino" without the copyright symbol. Pennino jewelry was produced from 1927 to 1961. Adjustable necklaces were fashionable in the 1950s. The lack of a copyright in the signature and the adjustable style of the necklace indicate this set dates to 1948 – 1955. $85.00 – 100.00.

**1948 – 1955 Pennino gold-tone leaf bracelet and earrings set.** This pretty gold-tone 7¼" leaf bracelet and matching 1½" earrings are signed "Pennino" without the copyright symbol. Leaf motif jewelry was a popular subject for Pennino jewelry. $65.00 – 90.00.

OTHER JEWELRY MAKERS

# • POMERANTZ, H. & CO. N.Y. •

## UNKNOWN, APPEARS TO DATE 1930s – 1960s

| Design Patent Number | Date Issued | Designer | Jewelry Type | Brief Description |
|---|---|---|---|---|
| 106058 | 9/14/1937 | Herman Pomerantz | Belt | Figural, Siamese |
| 106148 | 9/21/1937 | Herman Pomerantz | Brooch Belt | Insects |
| 137958 | 5/23/1944 | Herman Pomerantz | Chatelaine | Dagger and sheath |

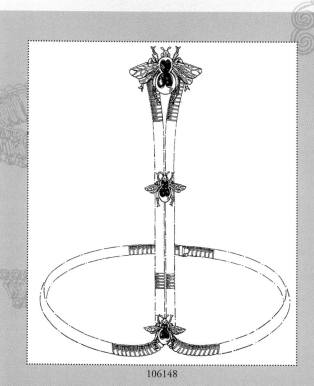

106148

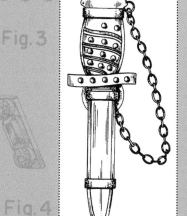

Fig. 3

Fig. 4

137958

**1954 – 1955 Pomerantz light blue art-glass brooch.** This sparkling 2" brooch features shimmering textured blue art-glass stones surrounded by blue aurora borealis rhinestones. It also features creamy rhodium metal. This heavy, well-made brooch is signed "H. Pomerantz & Co. N.Y." and dates to the mid-1950s. $65.00 – 80.00. From the collection of Debi Reece.

## 1953 – UNKNOWN

**1950s Princess Pride blue rhinestone necklace and bracelet set in original box.** Sapphire blue and deep emerald green rhinestones decorate this lovely 16" necklace and 7" bracelet by Princess Pride. "Princess Pride Creations" is the trademark (first issued in 1953) of the Donald Bruce Company of Chicago, Illinois. Fortunately, this otherwise unmarked set is still in its original Princess Pride presentation box and has its original Princess Pride Creations paper tag. In the 1950s, many companies produced similar rhinestone jewelry sets. Good condition sets by different, somewhat obscure makers are fun to find and collect. $35.00 – 55.00 set. From the collection of Debi Reece.

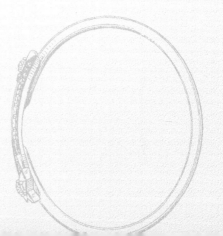

## 1963 – LATE 1980s

**1960s Pauline Rader bug pins with trembling wings.** The wings on this pair of bug pins by Pauline Rader are suspended on tiny springs so that they tremble when the wearer moves. Each pin measures 1½" long and features green rhinestone eyes and gold-tone bodies. Both are signed "Pauline Rader" without the copyright symbol. Early Pauline Rader jewelry was unsigned. However, by 1968, when Pauline and her husband Benton Rader opened a showroom in Forest Hills, New York, Pauline Rader jewelry was marked with an oval cartouche or rectangular hantag. $30.00 – 45.00.

# • REGENCY •

## 1950s – 1970s

The lack of a copyright symbol in the signature is not useful when dating Regency jewelry. Most designs, regardless of the date of manufacture, are signed "Regency" without the copyright symbol.

**1955 – 1960s Regency pink rhinestone brooch.** This sparkling 2" wide triple-drop pink brooch is signed "Regency." Some of the stones are aurora borealis, indicating the brooch was produced after 1955. $65.00 – 85.00.

**1955 – 1960s Regency blue rhinestone brooch.** This pretty 1¾" brooch is signed "Regency" and features two large art-glass beads. The aurora borealis rhinestones date this interesting piece to after 1955. $60.00 – 80.00. From the collection of Debi Reece.

**1955 – 1960s Regency red and pink rhinestone brooch.** This pretty 1¾" x 1¾" red and pink Regency brooch features both faceted and cabochon stones. The faceted rhinestones have the aurora borealis coating, dating this brooch to after 1955. It is signed "Regency" without the copyright symbol. $60.00 – 80.00. From the collection of Debi Reece.

**1960s Regency blue rhinestone brooch and earrings set.** This 2" x 1½" vibrant blue Regency rhinestone brooch and the matching 1" clip earrings are set in japanned metal, indicating the set dates to the 1960s. Each piece is signed "Regency" without the copyright symbol. The larger, highly faceted rhinestones are open backed, which is one indication of high-quality costume jewelry. $90.00 – 125.00.

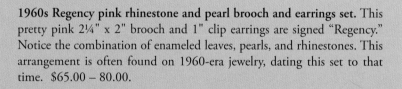

**1960s Regency pink rhinestone and pearl brooch and earrings set.** This pretty pink 2¼" x 2" brooch and 1" clip earrings are signed "Regency." Notice the combination of enameled leaves, pearls, and rhinestones. This arrangement is often found on 1960-era jewelry, dating this set to that time. $65.00 – 80.00.

**1960s Regency blue rhinestone brooch.** This 2½" dark blue navette-shaped rhinestone brooch is signed "Regency." In the 1960s, many makers produced large sparkling brooches featuring navette-shaped rhinestones as the main design element. $60.00 – 80.00.

## 1922 – 1950s

The "Sceptron" signature was first used in 1944.

**1944 – 1948 Reinad "Sceptron" sterling silver bow brooch.** This interesting sterling silver bow brooch is signed "Sceptron Sterling." "Sceptron" is a mark that was registered in 1944 to the Reinad Jewelry Company, which produced jewelry from 1922 through the 1950s. This post-1944 signature and the use of sterling dates this 2½" x 1½" brooch to 1944 – 1948. $100.00 – 150.00.

Fig. I

**1948 – early 1950s Reinad red rhinestone long-stemmed flower brooch.** This rare 3¾" x 3" brooch is signed "Reinad." Note the interesting triangular radiant red rhinestone flowers. The style of this brooch and the nonuse of sterling date this piece to 1948 – early 1950s. $90.00 – 125.00.

Design patent number 155326 issued September 20, 1949, to William Wrenner for Reinad.

Fig. 3

**1948 – early 1950s Reinad rhinestone brooch.** As is sometimes the way with Reinad jewelry, the signature on this 1¾" x 1½" brooch is difficult to read. Only the last three letters ("nad") are visible. This pyramid-shaped brooch features an assortment of clear rhinestones geometrically arranged to form a sparkling tower of glitz. $65.00 – 85.00.

## 1939 – 1953

| Design Patent Number | Date Issued | Designer | Jewelry Type | Brief Description |
|---|---|---|---|---|
| 144772 | 5/21/1946 | Solomon Finkelstein | Brooch | African woman |
| 144773 | 5/21/1946 | Solomon Finkelstein | Brooch | African woman |
| 144774 | 5/21/1946 | Solomon Finkelstein | Brooch | Woman in turban |
| 146764 | 5/13/1947 | Solomon Finkelstein | Brooch | Jack-in-the-box |

144772

146764

**1939 – 1941 Déja flower brooch.** This brightly enameled 3" yellow flower pin is signed "Déja Original," which is an early mark of Réja, Inc., used from 1939 to 1941. After that date, the signature changed to "Réja." The original name of the company founded in 1939 by Sol Finkelstein was Déja. Another company, DuJay, accused Déja of trademark infringement, so in 1941, just two years after opening for business, the name of the company was changed to Réja. $95.00 – 125.00.

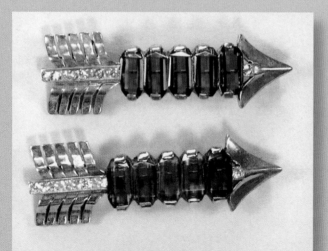

**1943 Réja sterling arrow pins.** These exceptional, emerald green 2½" arrow pins are signed "Réja-Sterling." A 1943 Réja jewelry advertisement (not shown) features these pins. Note the interesting way the green rhinestones are set, with just a tab of metal at the top and bottom of each emerald rhinestone. Tiny clear rhinestones decorate the shafts of each arrow. $200.00 – 400.00 pair. From the collection of Debi Reece.

OTHER JEWELRY MAKERS

Fig. 1

**1939 – 1941 Déja pearl and rhinestone flower brooch.** This vintage 3" x 1¾" brooch is signed "Déja" and dates to 1939 – 1941. It was made by Réja and is typical of pre-war 1940s-style pot metal jewelry that was coated with a gold wash. Most of the rhinestones have darkened with age, but amazingly, the creamy pearls decorating the center of the flower are in good condition. $95.00 – 125.00.

**1943 – 1948 Réja sterling flower brooch with faceted faux golden topaz stones.** This spectacular 3¼" x 2" brooch is signed "Réja Sterling" and dates to 1943 – 1948. Notice the flowing, graceful lines in this spectacular design. The tips of the leaves are encrusted with tiny rhinestones, as are the tops of the teardrop-shaped golden topaz rhinestones. $200.00 – 300.00. From the collection of Debi Reece.

Fig. 3

Fig. 4

OTHER JEWELRY MAKERS

441

## RENIOR, 1946 – 1964
## MATISSE LTD. 1952 – 1964

**1946 – 1955 Renoir "Shadow Box" necklace, bracelet, and earrings set.** Collectors refer to this set as the "Renoir Shadow Box Set" because the copper links resemble shadow boxes. The 15½" necklace is unmarked, the 7½" bracelet is marked "Renoir" in script and "Pat. Pend.," and the ¾" clip earrings are marked "Renoir" in script. Unfortunately, I could not locate the patent for this classic Renoir set. The lack of a copyright symbol indicates this set was produced before 1955. $95.00 – 125.00.

**1952 – 1955 Matisse red enameled copper necklace and earrings set.** Matisse Ltd. was founded in 1952 by Jerry Fells, who also founded Renoir of California, Inc. Matisse jewelry designs differ from Renoir jewelry because Matisse jewelry is often brightly enameled. This beautiful red and white enameled Matisse 17" necklace and ¾" clip earrings set is a good example of the fine quality enameling found on Matisse jewelry. All three pieces are signed "Matisse" without the copyright symbol, indicating they date to before 1955. $135.00 – 165.00.

Fig.1

Fig.2

Fig.3

Fig.4

**1952 – 1955 Matisse copper necklace and earrings set with white, snowflake stone decoration.** This unique 17" Matisse copper necklace and the matching ¾" square earrings are decorated with raised white enameled squares. The center of each square is coated with crushed tiny white stones resembling snowflakes. Each earring is signed "Matisse" in script, without the copyright symbol, dating this set to before 1955. The matching necklace is unmarked. $135.00 – 165.00. From the collection of Debi Reece.

**1955 – 1964 Matisse Renoir enameled bangle bracelet.** This copper bracelet is signed "Matisse Renoir" with the copyright symbol, indicating it was produced after 1955. It features gray, white, and orange enamel and fits an average-size wrist. $65.00 – 85.00.

OTHER JEWELRY MAKERS

## 1911 – 2003

**1950s Richelieu eight-strand beaded bracelet and earrings set.** This colorful eight-strand pearl and autumn-colored glass beaded Richelieu bracelet measures an unusually large 8½". The matching 1" clip earrings are signed "Richelieu" without the copyright symbol and feature an adjustable tightening screw. The style of the jewelry and this signature date this set to the early 1950s. $45.00 – 55.00. From the collection of Debi Reece.

1962 Richelieu "Cascade" advertisement. This lovely advertisement features a six-strand Richelieu pearl and crystal necklace and earrings set called "Cascade." The necklace originally sold for $30.00, the earrings for $3.00.

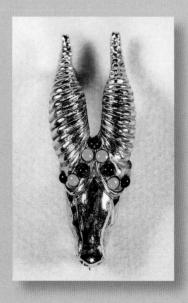

**1950s Richelieu antelope-head brooch.** This 2½" x 1" antelope-head brooch is signed "Richelieu" without the copyright symbol. It is part of a series of figural fantasy jewelry produced by Richelieu that includes a double ram head bangle bracelet and a ram head brooch. The lack of a copyright symbol and the style indicates this set dates to the early 1950s. $55.00 – 75.00. From the collection of Debi Reece.

1935 – 1975

Late 1940s Nettie Rosenstein sterling silver necklace and earrings set. Nettie Rosenstein jewelry is scarce on the collectibles market, because it was originally produced in small quantities. Beginning her career in the fashion industry, Rosenstein designed jewelry from 1935 until approximately 1975. This 17" pendant is signed "Sterling Nettie Rosenstein." Interestingly, the matching 1" clip earrings are unsigned. The use of sterling and the "royal" style indicate this set dates to the late 1940s. $200.00 – 250.00.

Fig. 3

1943 – 1948 Nettie Rosenstein sterling birdcage brooch. This outstanding 4½" x 2" birdcage brooch is signed "Sterling Nettie Rosenstein." It features red rhinestones, turquoise and white seed pearls, and a dangling tassel. The use of sterling and the tassel design date this piece to 1943 – 1948. All Rosenstein jewelry is hard to find, but the sterling examples are especially rare. $200.00 – 350.00.

1938 – 1972

**Early 1940s Sandor red rhinestone flower brooch.** This 1¾" well-crafted brooch is an example of early 1940s Sandor jewelry. It is signed "Sandor" without the copyright symbol and features both gold- and silver-tone metal enhanced by ruby red rhinestones. Notice the use of black enamel to add dimension to the curling petals. This use of enameling is typical of late 1930s and early 1940s jewelry. $70.00 – 100.00. From the collection of Debi Reece.

**1948 – 1955 Sandor pink multistrand necklace, brooch, and earrings set.** Eight strands of light pink glass beads dangle from the pink enameled flower clasp of this rare 16" necklace signed "Sandor" without the copyright symbol. The matching 1" bell-shaped brooch is identical in design to the necklace clasp. However, the 1" bell-shaped clip earrings are differently styled. Instead of three rhinestone center flowers, the earrings are decorated with light green leaves. The lack of a copyright symbol indicates this set dates to 1948 – 1955. $65.00 – 85.00 set. From the collection of Debi Reece.

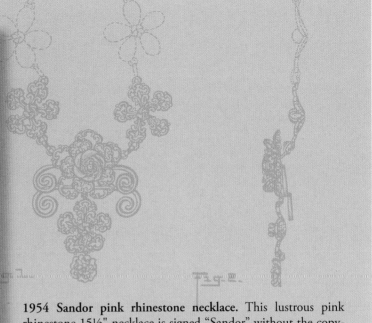

**1954 Sandor pink rhinestone necklace.** This lustrous pink rhinestone 15½" necklace is signed "Sandor" without the copyright symbol. All of the stones, including the iridescent teardrop center stone, are coated with the aurora borealis finish. This finish indicates this shimmering necklaces dates to 1954, when this coating was first applied to rhinestones but before the copyright symbol was added to the signature in 1955. $65.00 – 85.00.

**Late 1950s – 1960s Sandor fancy pearl necklace.** This spectacular multistrand pearl and crystal bead necklace is signed "Sandor" with the copyright symbol, indicating it was made after 1955. Measuring 21" in length, this masterpiece features an elaborate gold-tone clasp with a cluster of dangling white pearls and clear crystals. Nestled on top of the clasp are pretty filigree leaves capped by three rhinestone flowers. The style and construction of this necklace is similar to expensive Miriam Haskell jewelry. The signature and style of this necklace indicate it dates to the late 1950s – 1960s. Sandor jewelry of this quality is rare, so it is difficult to place a value on this necklace. Best guess: $100.00 – 200.00. From the collection of Debi Reece.

## 1931 – 1973

The Schiaparelli script signature was first used in
1949, before that jewelry was signed in lowercase print.

**1949 – 1955 Schiaparelli rhinestone earrings.** These dark amber-colored 1½" x 1" rhinestone earrings are signed "Schiaparelli" in script without the copyright symbol. This mark and the lack of a copyright symbol date these beauties to 1949 – 1955. $45.00 – 75.00.

**1949 – 1955 Schiaparelli black and white rhinestone bracelet.** Bold yet classic, this 7¾" x 1½" bracelet coordinates nicely with many different outfits. Each of the black and white stones is faceted and set in silver-tone metal. The bracelet is signed "Schiaparelli" in script without the copyright symbol, dating this piece to 1949 – 1955. $400.00 – 600.00. From the collection of Debi Reece.

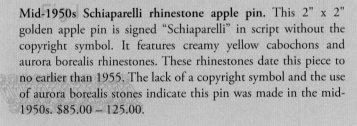

**Mid-1950s Schiaparelli clamper bracelet.** The picture cannot capture the bold size of this clamper bracelet or the glowing aurora borealis shine of the unique flat-surfaced rhinestones. The bracelet is 1½" tall and fits up to an 8" wrist! Each rhinestone is capped with a smaller aurora borealis rhinestone set in a decorative gold-tone crown-shaped setting. This rare beauty is signed "Schiaparelli" in script without the copyright symbol. The aurora borealis rhinestones indicate this magnificent bracelet was produced after 1955. These stones and the lack of a copyright symbol date this rare piece to the mid-1950s. $500.00 – 700.00.

**Mid-1950s Schiaparelli rhinestone apple pin.** This 2" x 2" golden apple pin is signed "Schiaparelli" in script without the copyright symbol. It features creamy yellow cabochons and aurora borealis rhinestones. These rhinestones date this piece to no earlier than 1955. The lack of a copyright symbol and the use of aurora borealis stones indicate this pin was made in the mid-1950s. $85.00 – 125.00.

OTHER JEWELRY MAKERS

## 1939 – 1977

Even post-1955 Schreiner jewelry is not signed with the copyright symbol. Most Schreiner jewelry is well made and reflects classic styles, so dating Schreiner jewelry by style difficult. Based on the style, the Schreiner jewelry featured in this book dates from 1948 to 1977. For some of the jewelry, when style trends can be identified, this range is narrowed.

**1960s Schreiner pineapple pin.** This yummy 2" x 1" pineapple pin is signed "Schreiner of New York" and dates to the 1960s, when olive green navette-shaped rhinestones were popular. $65.00 – 85.00. From the collection of Debi Reece.

**1960s – 1970s Schreiner faux amber and green cabochon locket and earrings set.** Rich dark green cabochon stones and golden faux amber rhinestones wrap the top of this 2½" locket. Nestled between the green and amber cabochon stones are smaller yellow and green rhinestones set point side up. This unique setting is a recognizable trait of many Schreiner designs. The locket is suspended from a 15" chain, so it sits close to the neck. Interestingly, the locket is unsigned but the matching 1" clip earrings are both signed "Schreiner." The use of natural-looking materials dates this set to the 1960s – 1970s, when jewelry designs temporarily moved away from glitzy rhinestones to earth tones and jewelry made of natural materials. $100.00 – 175.00.

**Large 1970s Schreiner turtle pin.** This Schreiner 2½" x 1½" turtle pin features a clear Lucite shell. The feet and tail are copper-colored rhinestones and the head is a brown marblelike stone. The metal is dark but not japanned. This pin is signed "Schreiner." Modern jewelry often has the same metal, indicating that this turtle pin dates to the 1970s, toward the end of Schreiner jewelry production. $50.00 – 75.00.

**1970s Schreiner lobster pin.** All decked out in patriotic red, white, and blue, this 2" x 1½" lobster pin dates to the 1976 bicentennial. It is signed "Schreiner New York." $65.00 – 85.00. From the collection of Debi Reece.

*Fig.1*

# • SEGAL, LEWIS •

## 1950s – UNKNOWN

*Fig.2*

*Fig.*

**1950s – 1960s Segal gold-tone rose jewelry.** All of the jewelry in the above photograph appears to be from the same series; however, only the 1" earrings are marked "Lewis Segal California" without a copyright symbol. In my experience, Segal only marked the earrings, which explains why there are so many Lewis Segal earrings for sale online and no sets. The bracelets fit an average-size wrist. The brooch measures 2" x 1½". $35.00 – 45.00.

## 1950s – 1960s

Jewelry signed "Selro" and signed "Selini"
were both produced by the Paul Selenger Co.

OTHER JEWELRY MAKERS

**1955 – 1960s blue rhinestone brooch and earrings set.** This beautiful 2¼" antique-silver-tone brooch and matching 1" clip earrings are signed "Selini" with the copyright symbol. The brooch features three different styles of blue rhinestones: thin navette-shaped blue rhinestones, round dark blue rhinestones, and small blue aurora borealis rhinestones. $65.00 – 95.00. From the collection of Debi Reece.

**1960s Egyptian-motif Selro charm bracelet.** This 7¼" charm bracelet is signed "Selro" with the copyright symbol. It is adorned with nine charms including Siamese dancers, Siamese musicians, vases (three), and the image of Nefertari. This Egyptian theme indicates this bracelet dates to the early 1960s. $90.00 – 120.00. From the collection of Debi Reece.

Early 1950s Selro pink cabochon cuff bracelet and earrings set. This elaborately decorated flexible cuff bracelet fits a 7" wrist. The matching 1" pink and pearl clip earrings are uniquely designed so that when worn, the pearls dangle from both the fronts and the backs of the ears. All pieces are signed "Selro" without the copyright symbol, indicating they date to before 1955. $150.00 – 200.00. From the collection of Debi Reece.

1955 – 1960s Selro silver-tone charm bracelet. This well-made 7¼" chunky charm bracelet is signed "Selro" with the copyright symbol, indicating it dates to after 1955. It features 15 charms in two styles. Some of the charms are double-sided moonstones set with dogtooth prongs. The others are faceted blue beads capped with filigree silver-tone caps. $100.00 – 120.00. From the collection of Debi Reece.

Fig.2

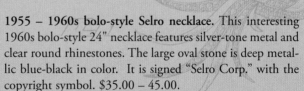

1955 – 1960s bolo-style Selro necklace. This interesting 1960s bolo-style 24" necklace features silver-tone metal and clear round rhinestones. The large oval stone is deep metallic blue-black in color. It is signed "Selro Corp." with the copyright symbol. $35.00 – 45.00.

OTHER JEWELRY MAKERS

| Design Patent Number | Date Issued | Designer | Jewelry Type | Brief Description |
|---|---|---|---|---|
| 108902 | 3/22/1938 | Vally Wieselthier | Brooch | Unicorn |
| 120174 | 4/23/1940 | Victor Silson | Brooch | Questions mark with locket |
| 120967 | 6/4/1940 | Victor Silson | Brooch | "Liberté Egalité Fraternité" |
| 121341 | 7/2/1940 | Victor Silson | Earring | Ribbon |
| 121352 | 7/2/1940 | Victor Silson | Brooch | Patriotic ribbon |
| 121402 | 7/9/1940 | Victor Silson | Brooch | Patriotic ribbon |
| 121403 | 7/9/1940 | Victor Silson | Brooch | Eagle |
| 121482 | 7/16/1940 | Victor Silson | Brooch | Brooch and flower holder in shape of human hand |
| 121640 | 7/23/1940 | Victor Silson | Brooch | Lion holding Belgian flag |
| 121734 | 7/30/1940 | Victor Silson | Brooch | Patriotic ribbon |
| 122211 | 8/17/1940 | Victor Silson | Brooch | Shield with British symbols |
| 123216 | 10/22/1940 | Samuel Rubin | Brooch | Tiger with champagne |
| 123659 | 11/19/1940 | Victor Silson | Brooch | Geometric, possibly a bug |
| 123823 | 12/3/1940 | Victor Silson | Brooch | Locket in shape of man in tuxedo |
| 123824 | 12/3/1940 | Victor Silson | Brooch | Owl |
| 123846 | 12/3/1940 | Victor Silson | Brooch | Bug |
| 123847 | 12/3/1940 | Victor Silson | Brooch | Geometric |
| 123848 | 12/3/1940 | Victor Silson | Brooch | Serpent |
| 123849 | 12/3/1940 | Victor Silson | Brooch | Stylized creature |
| 123850 | 12/3/1940 | Victor Silson | Brooch | Stylized bird |
| 123920 | 12/10/1940 | Victor Silson | Brooch | Stylized creature |
| 123921 | 12/10/1940 | Victor Silson | Brooch | Stylized creature |
| 123922 | 12/10/1940 | Victor Silson | Brooch | Stylized bird |
| 123923 | 12/10/1940 | Victor Silson | Necklace | Stylized birds |
| 124114 | 12/17/1940 | Victor Silson | Brooch | Anchor and port hole |
| 124115 | 12/17/1940 | Victor Silson | Brooch | Propeller and locket |
| 124116 | 12/17/1940 | Victor Silson | Brooch | Rifle, sword, port hole |
| 124276 | 12/24/1940 | Victor Silson | Brooch | Tri-cornered hat and rifle (See 124277 for another American Revolution piece.) |
| 124277 | 12/24/1940 | Victor Silson | Brooch | Boston Tea Party Indian (See 124416 for another American Revolution piece.) |
| 124395 | 12/31/1940 | Victor Silson | Brooch | Three diamonds representing "Body, Mind and Spirit" for YWCA |
| 124398 | 12/31/1940 | Victor Silson | Brooch | Clown |
| 124399 | 12/31/1940 | Victor Silson | Brooch | Male monkey with hat (See 124400 for female.) |
| 124400 | 12/31/1940 | Victor Silson | Brooch | Female monkey with hat (See 124399 for male.) |
| 124401 | 12/31/1940 | Victor Silson | Brooch | Greek figure with flags |

| | | | | |
|---|---|---|---|---|
| 124402 | 12/31/1940 | Paul Plato | Brooch | Leaf |
| 124415 | 12/31/1940 | Victor Silson | Brooch | Geometric |
| 124416 | 12/31/1940 | Victor Silson | Brooch | Declaration of Independence (See 124417 for another American Revolution piece.) |
| 124417 | 12/31/1940 | Victor Silson | Brooch | Town crier (See 124276 for another American Revolution piece.) |
| 124984 | 2/4/1941 | Victor Silson | Brooch | Cannon |
| 125041 | 2/4/1941 | Victor Silson | Brooch | Woman with head wrap |
| 125042 | 2/4/1941 | Victor Silson | Brooch | Masked ballerina |
| 125043 | 2/4/1941 | Victor Silson | Brooch | Masked male ballet dancer |
| 125044 | 2/4/1941 | Victor Silson | Brooch | Masked figural in costume with horns |
| 125293 | 2/18/1941 | Victor Silson | Brooch | RAF patriotic design |
| 125294 | 2/18/1941 | Victor Silson | Brooch | RAF emblem |
| 126489 | 4/8/1941 | Victor Silson | Brooch | Male bust |
| 128427 | 7/22/1941 | Victor Silson | Brooch | Four-leaf clover in five-pointed star |
| 128831 | 8/12/1941 | Victor Silson | Brooch | Exclamation point locket |
| 130159 | 10/28/1941 | Jack Silson | Brooch | Eagle sitting on "V" |
| 130574 | 12/2/1941 | Victor Silson | Brooch | Rose with bow |
| 130575 | 12/2/1941 | Victor Silson | Brooch | Cupid |
| 139353 | 11/7/1944 | Jack Silson | Brooch | Heart |
| 152031 | 12/7/1948 | Victor Silson | Brooch | Abstract |
| 159232 | 7/4/1950 | Victor Silson | Gloves/Umbrella Holder | Hands |

Fig.2

120174

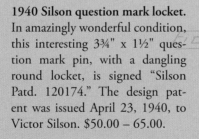

**1940 Silson question mark locket.**
In amazingly wonderful condition, this interesting 3¾" x 1½" question mark pin, with a dangling round locket, is signed "Silson Patd. 120174." The design patent was issued April 23, 1940, to Victor Silson. $50.00 – 65.00.

120967

**1940 Silson French cockade patriotic ribbon clip.** This patriotic clip is design patent number 120967 issued June 4, 1940, to Victor Silson. It is called the "French cockade" or "French ribbon clip." This 2¾" x 2" red, white and blue enameled clip was issued to help raise funds for the Americas Friends of France. The three enameled ribbons read "Liberté," "Egaleté," and "Fraternité" (or "Liberty," "Equality," and "Fraternity."). It is signed "Silson" without the copyright symbol. $55.00 – 65.00.

123824

126489

124416

**1941 Silson male profile clip.** This interesting and well-crafted 1¾" clip is signed "Silson Pat. Pend." It matches design patent number 126489 issued April 8, 1941, to Victor Silson. $65.00 – 95.00. From the collection of Debi Reece.

125043

OTHER JEWELRY MAKERS

## 1940s – 1950s

**1950s Adele Simpson clear rhinestone brooch.** This classic 2" round rhinestone brooch is signed "Adele Simpson" and dates to the 1950s. Interestingly, all of the settings are open in the back, simulating the construction of fine jewelry. $50.00 – 65.00. From the collection of Debi Reece.

**1950s Adele Simpson rhinestone earrings.** These pretty 1¼" blue and yellow rhinestone clip earrings are signed "Adele Simpson." The nonuse of sterling and the style indicate these lovely earrings date to the 1950s. $35.00 – 45.00. From the collection of Debi Reece.

Fig.1

Fig.2

## • STAR-ART •

### UNKNOWN, APPEARS TO DATE 1950s – 1960s

Fig.3

**1950s – 1960s Star-Art sterling filigree pocket watch–style brooch.** This delicate 1¾" x 1½" brooch is signed "Star-Art Sterling." The 1954 Star-Art advertisement from the *Jewelers' Buyers Guide* showcases two sets of jewelry called "Jewels by Helene" and manufactured by Star-Art. (See chapter 1 to view this advertisement.) In the mid-1950s, Star-Art offered "Popular Two-Tone Gold Filled Jewelry" and "Lovely Sterling Ice Blue and Crystal Creations." $20.00 – 30.00.

## 1940s – 1960s

There is no reliable information on the maker of this jewelry.

**1962 Star gold-tone flower pin.** Although unmarked, this 2" pin is identical to the Star brooch shown in the 1962 "It's the Real McCoy" Star advertisement. Originally selling for $2.00, this pin has a genuine cultured pearl. $10.00 – 20.00.

1962 "It's the Real McCoy" Star advertisement. This advertisement features a gold-tone pin with a real cultured pearl. The ad reads, "It has a genuine cultured pearl. It's bathed in gold. You'll see its precious design in some of the most expensive jewelry stores. Is it worth cracking a safe for? Confidentially — why bother? You can buy it for the unbelievable price of just $2."

It has a genuine cultured pearl. It's bathed in gold. You'll see its precious design in some of the most expensive jewelry stores. Is it worth cracking a safe for? Confidentially – why bother? You can buy it for the unbelievable price of just $2. The petal pin shown and matching earrings (not shown) are $2 each piece. Plus tax. Just one from a varied and unique collection at $2...at fine stores everywhere. **STAR JEWELRY** Co.,Inc.,411 Fifth Ave.,N.Y.

## 1940s – UNKNOWN

**Early 1940s Staret rhinestone clip.** This grand 2½" x 2¼" clip is signed "Staret." It is not sterling. Many collectors believe Staret jewelry strongly resembles early Eisenberg pieces. $100.00 – 200.00. From the collection of Debi Reece.

# • STEINER, ERNEST •

## 1940s – UNKNOWN

It is unknown when jewelry marked "Ernest Steiner Original" was produced. The jewelry shown in the Steiner patent chart may or may not be marked in this way. It is possible Steiner was a freelance designer who designed for others and, in the mid-1940s, created jewelry with the "Ernest Steiner Original Sterling" mark.

| Design Patent Number | Date Issued | Designer | Jewelry Type | Brief Description |
|---|---|---|---|---|
| 105034 | 5/22/1937 | Ernest Steiner | Brooch | Grapes spray with bow |
| 112036 | 11/8/1938 | Bernhard Bauer and Ernest Steiner | Brooch | Deer with leaves in frame |
| 137647 | 4/11/1944 | Ernest Steiner | Brooch | Bow |
| 137649 | 4/11/1944 | Ernest Steiner | Brooch | Floral |
| 137670 | 4/11/1944 | Ernest Steiner | Brooch | Floral |
| 147621 | 10/7/1947 | Paul Marino and Ernest Steiner | Brooch | Abstract |

**1944 Ernest Steiner sterling and blue rhinestone bow brooch.** This 2¾" bow pin studded with light blue rhinestones is signed "Ernest Steiner Original Sterling." The style is similar to design patent number 137647 issued to Ernest Steiner April 11, 1944, and dates from that era. $40.00 – 75.00.

137647

# • VOGUE •

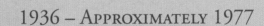
1936 – APPROXIMATELY 1977

**Mid-1950s Vogue iridescent glass bead necklace and bracelet set.** Light reflects off this 20" bead necklace, revealing several colors including deep purple, copper, green, and black. The bracelet measures 7" and is made of the same wonderful beads. The clasps on both pieces are hand wired in the style of Miriam Haskell jewelry. They are signed "Vogue" without the copyright symbol. This signature and the style of the beads indicate this set dates to the mid-1950s. $50.00 – 80.00.

OTHER JEWELRY MAKERS

## 1950s – 1970s

Most of the Warner jewelry is signed "Warner" without the copyright symbol, so the lack of a copyright symbol is not useful when dating Warner designs.

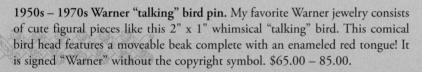

**1950s – 1970s gold-tone Warner flower brooch and matching earrings.** This amazingly lightweight 2½" x 1½" Warner brooch looks like a golden snowball composed of many tiny golden blooms. Each tiny golden bloom is suspended on a lightweight stem and enhanced by a prong-set red rhinestone center. The brooch and the 1" clip earrings are signed "Warner" without the copyright symbol. $65.00 – 85.00. From the collection of Debi Reece.

**1950s – 1970s Warner "talking" bird pin.** My favorite Warner jewelry consists of cute figural pieces like this 2" x 1" whimsical "talking" bird. This comical bird head features a moveable beak complete with an enameled red tongue! It is signed "Warner" without the copyright symbol. $65.00 – 85.00.

**1955 – 1970s Warner bug brooch.** This sweet 1" bug brooch is signed "Warner" without the copyright symbol. It features aurora borealis rhinestones. These stones help to date this piece to after 1954, when the aurora borealis finish was first applied to rhinestones. $40.00 – 50.00.

OTHER JEWELRY MAKERS

461

**1950s – 1970s Warner double-sided key chain with original Warner hangtag.** The original tag attached to this sparkling key chain states that it was made by Joseph Warner, owner of Warner jewelry. This lovely half-dollar size accessory is a fun addition to any costume jewelry collection. $25.00 – 35.00. From the collection of Debi Reece.

# • WEISS •

## 1942 – 1971

Weiss did not design or manufacture the jewelry carrying the Weiss name. Albert Weiss contracted with makers to produced selected designs with the Weiss name. The lack of a copyright symbol in the Weiss signature is not a reliable indication that the piece was produced before 1955. Jewelry featured in 1960s advertisements is sometimes signed "Weiss" without the copyright symbol. For Weiss, the rule is: If there is a copyright symbol in the signature, then the piece dates to after 1955; however, the lack of a copyright symbol does not necessarily indicate the piece was produced before 1955.

OTHER JEWELRY MAKERS

**1950s – 1960s Weiss white rhinestone brooch and earrings set.** This summery 2" white Weiss brooch and the matching 1" clip earrings date to the 1950s – 1960s. The brooch is unsigned, but the earrings are marked "Weiss" without a copyright symbol. All of the white and clear faceted rhinestones are prong set. The silver-tone metal is coated with highly reflective rhodium plating. $50.00 – 70.00.

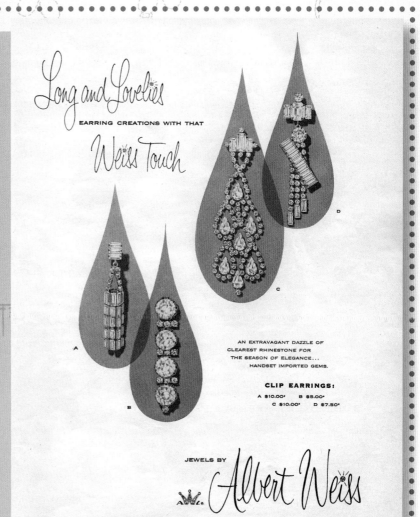

1955 "Long and Lovelies" Weiss earring advertisement. Four long rhinestone earring designs are featured in this advertisement, originally selling for between $5.00 and $10.00 each.

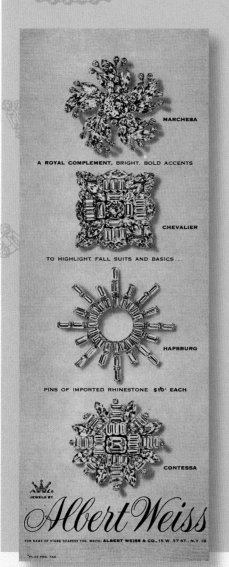

1955 "A Royal Complement..." Weiss advertisement. This advertisement features four Weiss rhinestone brooches selling for $10.00 each. Top down, they are Marchesa, Chevalier, Hapsburg, and Contessa.

**1950s – 1960s Weiss multicolored rhinestone bracelet.** This wonderful 7¼" x ¾" Weiss bracelet seems to have everything but the kitchen sink included in the design. There are navette-shaped deep blue rhinestones and round blue rhinestones. Raspberry rhinestones and raspberry beads are clustered with the deep blue stones. Peeking from underneath blue enameled leaves are creamy white pearls. All of these elements are artistically arranged and set in gold-tone metal. This beauty is signed "Weiss" without the copyright symbol and dates to the 1950s or 1960s. $60.00 – 75.00. From the collection of Debi Reece.

**1950s – 1960s Weiss green rhinestone necklace and bracelet set.** Glowing green rhinestones decorate this 16" Weiss gold-tone necklace and 7" bracelet. The simple design of this set is elevated to a top-quality Weiss set due to the radiant fire of these spectacular rhinestones. Both pieces are signed "Weiss" without the copyright symbol. $100.00 – 150.00.

cuff clingers
expansible evening bracelets

JEWELS BY
*Albert Weiss*

1955 Weiss "cuff clingers" advertisement. Three beautiful rhinestone cuff bracelets called "Cuff Clingers" are featured in this interesting advertisement. They originally sold for between $10.00 and $15.00. (See page 75 of *Collecting Costume Jewelry 101: The Basics of Starting, Building, and Upgrading* for a photograph of the bottom bracelet in blue.)

OTHER JEWELRY MAKERS

Fig. 1

**1950s – 1960s Weiss green rhinestone flower brooch and earrings set.** The gorgeous green "rivoli" rhinestones decorating this 3" x 1½" Weiss brooch and matching 1" x ¾" clip earrings glow with an inner fire. Each stone is highly faceted. These prismlike stones reflect a rainbow of colors including green, red, and yellow. Set in antiqued gold-tone metal, this is a high-quality, well-made Weiss set. Signed "Weiss" without the copyright symbol, this set dates to the 1950s – 1960s. $70.00 – 95.00. From the collection of Debi Reece.

**1950s – 1960s Weiss pyramid-style rhinestone brooch and earrings.** Designed in the shape of a pyramid, this especially well-made 2" square Weiss brooch has the same hook-and-eye construction found on Schreiner brooches. The brooch and the ¾" clip earrings are signed "Weiss" without the copyright symbol and date to the 1950s – 1960s. $100.00 – 125.00.

Fig. 3

**1955 – 1960s Weiss multicolored butterfly pin.** The royal red, green, blue, purple, and golden topaz-colored rhinestones decorating this 2½" x 1½" Weiss butterfly pin give it a plus quality. Colorful examples of Weiss butterfly pins are popular with collectors. It is signed "Weiss" with the copyright symbol and dates 1955 – 1960s. $80.00 – 100.00.

Fig. 1

Fig. 2

Fig. 3

**1950s – 1960s deep red Weiss rhinestone necklace.** Ruby red prong-set rhinestones are the only design element on this simple but elegant 15½" Weiss necklace. Perfect for any holiday occasion, this pretty piece is as wearable today as it was in the 1950s or 1960s when it was made. It is signed "Weiss" without the copyright symbol. $50.00 – 65.00.

1959 Weiss "Bourbon on Ice" advertisement. This ad reads, "...a dazzling new look in jewelry by Albert Weiss. Hand-set Austrian stones alive with the bourbon topaz, amber and brown tones... and shimmering irissé. Accenting the glitter, a golden Florentine finish. Necklace, $15. Bracelet, $12.50. Pin, $7.50. Contour earrings, $5 pair."

## Bourbon on Ice

...a dazzling new look in jewelry by Albert Weiss. Hand-set Austrian stones alive with the bourbon topaz, amber and brown tones . . . and shimmering irissé. Accenting the glitter, a golden Florentine finish. Necklace, $15. Bracelet, $12.50. Pin, $7.50. Contour earrings, $5 pair. Prices plus tax.

Jerry Parnis silk linen dress and jacket, about $100.

*Jewelry on opposite page:* glittering rhinestone baguettes. Necklace, about $40. Bracelet, about $7.50. Earrings, about $10. Available in leading stores across the country.

JEWELS BY
*Albert Weiss*
15 West 37th Street, New York 18

**1950s – 1960s Weiss lovebirds brooch.** These colorful 2" x 1½" lovebirds are happily perched on a gold-tone branch. One bird sports a green rhinestone belly and the other blue. Both birds have red rhinestone eyes and clear pavé rhinestone wings. The pin is signed "Weiss" without the copyright symbol. $40.00 – 55.00.

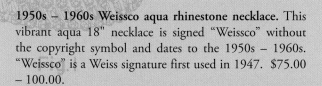

**1950s – 1960s Weissco aqua rhinestone necklace.** This vibrant aqua 18" necklace is signed "Weissco" without the copyright symbol and dates to the 1950s – 1960s. "Weissco" is a Weiss signature first used in 1947. $75.00 – 100.00.

**1950s – 1960s A W Co. (Weiss) rhinestone necklace.** This beautiful 16" Weiss choker necklace is especially interesting, because it is signed "Weiss" without a copyright symbol and also signed "A W Co.," which is a rare Weiss signature. This pretty piece dates to the 1950s – 1960s. $65.00 – 85.00.

OTHER JEWELRY MAKERS

1950s – 1960s Weiss elegant blue rhinestone necklace and earrings set. Beautiful blue and green aurora borealis rhinestones sparkle from this 17" fully jeweled necklace and matching 1" clip earrings. This spectacular set is signed "Weiss" without the copyright symbol. $150.00 – 175.00. From the collection of Debi Reece.

Here, there, everywear . . . Paris calls for the jewelled-look of rhinestone to add elegance to your fall and winter wardrobe.

*Big, bold and beautiful*

Pins by *Albert Weiss*

AVAILABLE AT LEADING STORES. FOR THE ONE NEAREST YOU WRITE: ALBERT WEISS & CO., INC., 15 WEST 37TH STREET, NEW YORK 18

1961 Weiss "Big, bold and beautiful" advertisement. This advertisement features four Weiss rhinestone brooches. Top left: Dahlia, originally priced $15.00. Top right: Leaf pin, originally priced $12.50. Middle right: Snowflake, originally priced $10.00. Bottom: Starfish, originally priced $5.00.

**1955 – 1960s Weiss pink rhinestone brooch and earrings set.** This interesting Weiss set features pink aurora borealis rhinestones set in gold-tone square settings. The brooch measures 1". Each clip earring measures 1¼". All pieces are signed "Weiss" with the copyright symbol and date to 1955 – 1960s. $30.00 – 40.00.

Fig.1

**1960s Weiss lavender long-stemmed flower pin.** Open-backed lavender rhinestones and gorgeous green rhinestone leaves decorate this 3" long-stemmed flower pin signed "Weiss" without the copyright symbol. Similar long-stemmed beauties are shown in the 1961 advertisement (see page 470), helping to date this pin to the 1960s. $50.00 – 75.00.

Fig.2

**1960s Weiss white apple brooch.** This wonderful 2¾" apple brooch by Weiss shares two style traits with the flower jewelry advertised as "Art Nouveau" in the 1961 advertisement (see page 471), indicating that this pin was also produced in the 1960s. First, the apple brooch and the "Art Nouveau" flowers have open-work bodies to help lighten the weight of the large brooches. Next, all of the pieces feature black enameled metal. This delicious white apple brooch is signed "Weiss" with the copyright symbol. The value of the delicious white apple pin today is $45.00 – 60.00.

OTHER JEWELRY MAKERS

**1961 Weiss "Long-stemmed beauty" blue rhinestone flower brooch.** The 1961 Weiss "Long-stemmed beauties" advertisement features eight long-stemmed rhinestone flowers similar in style to this 4" beauty. The ad reads, "Inspired by the famous gardens of the Tuileries [central park in Paris], these Albert Weiss pins will bring a fashion distinction to your Spring wardrobe." This brooch features two layers of teardrop-shaped light blue aurora borealis rhinestones, each surrounded by tiny blue rhinestones. The center is a sapphire blue rhinestone. Amazingly, like some of the flowers in the advertisement, the stem of the above beauty is completely wrapped with prong-set green rhinestones. In 1961, these high-end flower brooches sold for between $7.50 and $15.00 each. Interestingly, this brooch is signed "Weiss" without the copyright symbol. However, the 1961 style of this pin and the aurora borealis rhinestones indicate this beauty dates to 1961. $100.00 – 175.00.

1961 Weiss "Long-stemmed beauties" advertisement. Eight colorful rhinestone long-stemmed flower brooches are advertised, originally selling for between $7.50 and $15.00 each.

OTHER JEWELRY MAKERS

**1961 Art Nouveau Weiss black enamel flower brooch.** This magnificent 2¾" x 3½" flower pin is similar to the pins featured in the 1961 Weiss "Art Nouveau" advertisement. It is signed "Weiss" without the copyright symbol and features a baroque pearl center and black metal. Originally selling for $17.50 in 1961, this flower brooch is valued today at $60.00 – 90.00.

1961 "Art Nouveau" Weiss advertisement. This rare advertisement features four large, black enameled flower pins. The ad reads, "Add to your understated fall elegance one of these dramatic Weiss pavé stone pins...delicately edged with the new French ebony finish...bold in size, gossamer light." The pins sold for between $10.00 and $17.50. Matching earrings were available for $5.00.

ART NOUVEAU

prices plus tax

Add to your understated fall elegance one of these dramatic Weiss pavé stone pins... delicately edged with the new French ebony finish... bold in size, gossamer light.

UPPER: Left $10, Right $15
LOWER: Left $12.50, Center $17.50, Right $15
Matching Earrings Available, $5

designs copyrighted

JEWELS BY *Albert Weiss*

**1960s Weiss black crown brooch.** This interesting Weiss crown pin features black enameled metal and black cabochon stones. In 1961 and 1962 Weiss advertised several different black or jet designs, suggesting this pin dates from this time. (See Weiss ads in this section and the Weiss black rhinestone ad in chapter 1.) Measuring 2" x 1¾", this brooch is signed "Weiss" without the copyright symbol. $45.00 – 55.00.

**1950s – 1960s Weiss art-glass bracelet.** This amazing 7¼" Weiss bracelet is chock-full of spectacular stones, including two art-glass stones that look like paperweights, several navette-shaped stones that gradate in color from green to blue, and many deep emerald- and sapphire-colored rhinestones. The bracelet is signed "Weiss" without the copyright symbol and dates to the 1950s – 1960s. $60.00 – 80.00.

**1955 – 1970s Weiss Christmas tree pin and earrings set.** This 2¼" Christmas tree pin and the matching 1" clip earrings feature colorful aurora borealis rhinestones set in antique-gold-tone metal. Notice the interesting slanted tree design. All pieces are signed "Weiss" with the copyright symbol. $50.00 – 65.00.

OTHER JEWELRY MAKERS

**1950s – 1970s Weiss leaping frog pin.** Well crafted, this gold-tone leaping frog pin is signed "Weiss" with the copyright symbol and dates to the 1950s – 1970s. The frog measures 2" long and features a faux-amber body, green rhinestone eyes, and clear rhinestones covering his expressive head. $45.00 – 65.00.

Fig.1

Fig.2

Fig.3

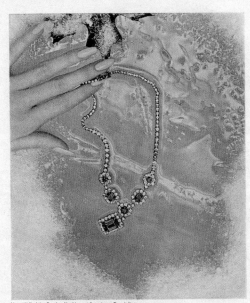

You will find the Czarina Necklace at fine stores. Ten dollars.

Did you ever find
something so beautiful that you didn't care
what it cost?

Albert Weiss
Four hundred four Fifth Avenue, New York

1967 Weiss "Did you ever find something so beautiful that you didn't care what it cost?" advertisement. The caption reads, "You will find the Czarina Necklace at fine stores. Ten dollars."

OTHER JEWELRY MAKERS

473

## 1949 – 1990

**1949 – 1990 US Zone Germany brooch and earrings set.** This unusually shaped 2" x 1½" brooch and matching 1¼" clip earrings have an equally unusual mark. All three pieces are signed "US Zone Germany." Although interesting, for dating purposes this signature is the same as if the piece were signed "Western Germany," indicating the brooch set could have been produced anytime from 1949 to 1990, when Germany was reunified. $30.00 – 50.00.

**1949 – 1990 Western Germany cuckoo clock pin.** Signed "Western Germany," this black forest style cuckoo clock measures 2" x ¾". Jewelry signed "Western Germany" was produced from 1949 to 1990. This cute piece could have been made in any of those years. $15.00 – 20.00.

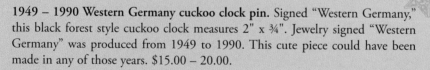
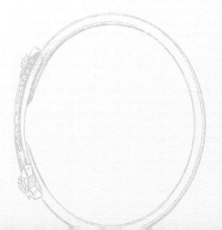

OTHER JEWELRY MAKERS

## 1926 – 1980 FOR NONMESH JEWELRY
## AND 1991 FOR MESH-TYPE JEWELRY

**1962 Whiting and Davis Limoges portrait bracelet and earrings set.** This gold-tone 7½" bracelet and the matching ¾" clip earrings feature a Limoges porcelain portrait of a lovely woman. The portrait is a transfer image with tiny drops of white enamel added by hand to form the necklace and hair ornamentation. The bracelet is signed "Whiting and Davis Co. Mesh Bags," and the earrings are signed "Whiting & Davis Co." This set is advertised in the 1962 Whiting and Davis "Limoges Jewels From France" advertisement. The ad reads, "Delicate little portraits on porcelain, set in golden or silvery traceries by Whiting & Davis artisans, and reminiscent of a Watteau painting." (This refers to French painter Antoine Watteau.) Limoges is a region in France renowned for producing fine porcelain. However, the name Limoges in the advertisement does not guarantee a hand-painted piece, only that the porcelain originated in Limoges, France. $75.00 – 100.00.

1962 Whiting & Davis "Limoges Jewels From France" advertisement. The ad features a pendant, earrings, and a bracelet, all decorated with the portrait of a woman on Limoges porcelain.

OTHER JEWELRY MAKERS

**1960s Whiting and Davis bracelet watch.** This wonderful Whiting and Davis bracelet opens to reveal a Swiss-made, "Norman" shock-resistant watch. The heavy gold-tone bracelet is textured like golden snakeskin and decorated with rows of red, blue, and turquoise flowers. Amazingly, the wind-up watch still works. The cuff bracelet is oval and measures 3" at it widest point. It is signed "Whiting and Davis Co. Mesh Bags." Bracelet watches like this were popular in the 1960s. $85.00 – 125.00.

**1950s – 1960s Whiting and Davis swan-motif necklace and earrings set.** This romantic Whiting and Davis necklace and earrings set features the image of two swans swimming happily together, carved from the backs of two frosted glass ovals. The gold-tone necklace measures 15½", and each clip earring is 1" x ¾". The necklace is signed "Whiting Davis" on an oval hangtag. Both earrings are signed "Whiting & Davis Co." $65.00 – 75.00.

**1976 – 1978 Egyptian-style Whiting and Davis bracelet.** The profile of young King Tut cast in vibrant turquoise resin takes center stage on this Egyptian-motif cuff bracelet signed "Whiting and Davis Co. Mesh Bags." This bracelet fits an average-size wrist and was probably produced to commemorate the 1976 – 1978 U.S. tour of King Tut artifacts. $65.00 – 85.00.

OTHER JEWELRY MAKERS

## UNKNOWN, APPEARS TO DATE EARLY 1950s

Fig.1

Fig.2

**Early 1950s Wiesner rhinestone basket pin.** Absolutely lovely, this 2½" x 2½" floral basket pin dates to the 1950s. It is signed "Joseph Wiesner N.Y." Notice the flowing flower design and the lovely aqua and pink rhinestone flowers. In mint condition, this beauty is as bright today as it was 50 years ago when it was first made. $70.00 – 100.00. From the collection of Debi Reece.

**Early 1950s Wiesner rhinestone arrow pin.** This beautiful 3" x 1" arrow-shaped pin features rare square-cut rhinestones. It is signed "Joseph Wiesner N.Y." and dates to the 1950s. $50.00 – 65.00. From the collection of Debi Reece.

Fig.4

OTHER JEWELRY MAKERS

## JEWELRY FROM 1959 – PRESENT

**1970s – 1980s Yves Saint Laurent earrings.** Highly collectible, these interesting 1970s – 1980s Yves Saint Laurent clip earrings measure 2" x 1¼". The design of these earrings is an artistic arrangement of enameled shapes, triangles and circles, coupled with navette-shaped, open-backed rhinestones. They are signed "YSL." YSL commands high prices in the collectibles market today partly because the jewelry was originally expensive to purchase. $55.00 – 85.00. Courtesy of Esta Pratt.

**1970s – 1980s Yves Saint Laurent red rhinestone necklace.** Some newer jewelry like this lovely Yves Saint Laurent necklace produced in the 1970s and 1980s is already collectible. This 22" necklace is both comfortable and attractive to wear. It is signed "YSL." YSL jewelry signed "Yves Saint Laurent Rive Gauche Made in France" commands much high prices in the collectibles market today than jewelry signed "YSL." $60.00 – 95.00.

*Découvrez les trésors d'Yves Saint Laurent.*

1982 "Découvrez les trésors d'Yves Saint Laurent" advertisement. The ad reads, "Uncover the treasures of Yves Saint Laurent. Stunningly bold. And crafted to endure both time and trend. A limited edition series, chosen by the artist, is numbered and bears his signature. To own one is to own an original Yves Saint Laurent. Yves Saint Laurent Jewelry, from $250 to $25."

# APPENDIX A: *Manufacturer and Marks Chart*

| Maker and/or Designer | Dates of Operation | Marks | Approximate Date Mark is First Used |
|---|---|---|---|
| 1928 | 1968 – present | Swirling design etched into the back of each piece | 1968 |
| 11 W. 30th Street | Mid-1950s – 1960s | "11 W. 30th St." | 1950s – 1960s |
| Accessocraft | 1935 – 1998 | "ACCESSOCRAFT" with or without "N.Y.C." | 1935 – 1998 |
| Am – Lee | 1946 – unknown | "Am Lee Sterling" | Unknown |
| Art | 1950s – 1970s | "ART" without copyright symbol | before 1955 |
| Art | | "ART" or "MODEART" with copyright symbol | after 1955 |
| Athennic Arts | Unknown | "Athennic Arts" on oval plaque | Unknown |
| Austria | 1900 – present | "Austria" | Unknown |
| Austria | | "Made in Austria" | Unknown |
| Avon | 1971 – present | "AVON" | 1971 |
| Avon | | "K.J.L. for Avon" | 1986 – 1995 |
| Avon | | "Barrera for Avon" | 1989 – 1996 |
| Avon | | "Elizabeth Taylor for Avon" | 1993 – 1997 |
| Avon | | "Louis Feraud for Avon" | 1984 |
| Avon | | "Centennial Jewelry for Trifari" | 1986 |
| Avon | | "Celia Sebiri" | 1987 |
| Avon | | "Shaill Jhevari" | 1993 – 1994 |
| Avon | | "Coreen Simpson" | 1994 |
| Avon | | "Seymour M. Kent" | 1976 – 1980 |
| B. David | 1945 – 1993 | "B. David" in an oval | Unknown |
| B. David | | "b. David" in a divided square | Unknown |
| B. David | | "bd" printed diagonally | Unknown |
| B.S.K. | 1948 – approximately 1983 | "B.S.K." | Usually found with copyright, so most likely after 1955. |
| B.S.K. | | "B.S.K. My Fair Lady" | Usually found with copyright, so most likely after 1955. |
| Ballou | Late 19th century – at least 1976 | "BALLOU" in arc shape | Unknown |
| Ballou | | "B.A.B." | 1908 |
| Ballou | | "B.A.B. & Co." | Unknown |
| Ballou | | Star with "B" inside | 1947 |
| Ballou | | Star with "B" inside and "Trade Mark" above star | Unknown |
| Barclay | 1946 – 1957 | "Barclay" in script | Unknown |
| Barclay | | "Barclay" Art in Jewelry | 1948 |
| Barclay | | "Peltanium" | 1953 |
| Barclay, McClelland | 1935 – 1943 | "McClelland Barclay" | Unknown |
| Beatrix (BJ) | 1946 – 1983 | "BEATRIX" | Unknown |
| Beatrix (BJ) | | "BJ" | Unknown |
| Beau Jewels | 1950s – 1970s | "Beau Jewels" | Unknown |
| Beau Sterling | 1944 – present | "Beausterling" | Unknown |
| Beau Sterling | | "Beaucraft" | Unknown |
| Beau Sterling | | "Beau B Sterling" | Unknown |
| Beau Sterling | | "B" followed by the word "sterling" or "ster." | Unknown |
| Ben Reig | 1929 – 1960 | "BENREIG" | Unknown |
| Bergère | 1946 – 1979 | "Bergère" | Unknown |
| BJ (See Beatrix) | | | |
| Block, Fred | 1940s – 1950s | "FRED A. BLOCK JEWELRY" | Unknown |

| | | | |
|---|---|---|---|
| BN (Bugbee & Niles) | 1859 – unknown | "BN" | Unknown |
| Bogoff | 1946 – late 1950s early 1960s | "Bogoff" | Unknown |
| Bogoff | | "Jewels by Bogoff" | Unknown |
| Boucher | 1937 – 1971 | "MB" | 1937 – 1949 |
| Boucher | | "Marcel Boucher" | 1938 |
| Boucher | | "BOUCHER" | 1950 – 1955 |
| Boucher | | "BOUCHER" with copyright symbol | After 1955 |
| Boucher | | "Marboux" | Registered in 1937, but not widely used until 1955. |
| Boucher | | "Earrite" | 1950 |
| Boucher | | "Parisina" | 1940s |
| Brania | 1950s – 1960s | "BRANIA" | Unknown |
| Brooks, Natacha | 1944 – unknown | "NATACHA STERLING BROOKS" | Probably 1940s |
| Cadoro | 1945 – 1980s | "Cadoro" | 1955 |
| Cadoro | | "Nina Ricci for Cadoro" | 1964 |
| Calvaire | 1920s – 1960s | "Calvaire" | Unknown |
| Capri | 1952 – 1977 | "Capri" | Usually found with copyright symbol, indicating probably after 1955. |
| Carnegie, Hattie | 1919 – late 1970s Jewelry production began in 1939. | "Carnegie" in script | No earlier than 1930, but most likely late 1940s – 1955, when the copyright was added. |
| Carnegie, Hattie | | "HC" in a diamond with oval frame | Early mark believed to be from 1939 – early 1940s. |
| Carnegie, Hattie | | "Hattie Carnegie" in script on oval cartouche without copyright symbol | Before 1955 |
| Carnegie, Hattie | | "Hattie Carnegie" in script with the copyright symbol | 1955 – late 1970s |
| Castlecliff | 1918 – 1977 | "Castlecliff" | After 1941 |
| Castlecliff | | "Sterling Castlecliff" | After 1941 |
| Castlecliff | | "Castlemark" | Possibly only a trademark. |
| Castlecliff | | "Cassandra" | 1957, possibly only a trademark. |
| Cathé | 1961 – unknown | "Cathé" | Unknown |
| Caviness, Alice | 1945 – 1997 | "Alice Caviness" | Unknown |
| Caviness, Alice | | "Alice Caviness Sterling Germany" | Unknown |
| Celebrity | 1950s – 1970s | "Celebrity" | Unknown |
| Celebrity | | "Celebrity, NY" with copyright symbol | After 1955 |
| Celebrity | | "Celebrity" with copyright symbol | After 1955 |
| Celebrity | | "Celebrity" in script with copyright symbol | After 1955 |
| Chanel | 1914 – present | "CHANEL" | Unknown |
| Charel | 1945 – unknown | "CHAREL" | Unknown |
| Ciner | Jewelry production began in 1931 | "Ciner" | Unknown |
| Ciner | | "MC" inside a rectangle | Unknown |
| Ciner | | "Ciner" with a copyright symbol | After 1955 |
| Ciner | | "Ciner" with "R" | Unknown |
| Cini | 1922 – present | "Cini" | Unknown |
| Cini | | "G. Cini" | Unknown |
| Cini | | "Cini for Gumps" | Unknown |
| Cini | | "Guglielmo Cini" in script | Unknown |
| Claudette | 1945 – unknown | "CLAUDETTE" with copyright symbol | Probably after 1955 |

| | | | |
|---|---|---|---|
| Claudette | | "C. CLAUDETTE" with copyright symbol | Probably after 1955 |
| Coro | 1901 – 1998 | "Coro" in script at an angle | 1919 |
| Coro | | "Coro" in script, no angle | 1919 |
| Coro | | "Coro Duette" or "Duette" | 1931 |
| Coro | | "Coro Craft" (two words, in script) | 1935 |
| Coro | | "Coro [in script] Craft [printed]" with Pegasus | 1938 |
| Coro | | "Corocraft" (one word in script at an angle, with the Pegasus) | 1933 – 1979 |
| Coro | | Glamour | 1940 |
| Coro | | "Coro Teens" | 1940 |
| Coro | | "Coro" (thick script) | 1940 |
| Coro | | "Corocraft Sterling" | Before 1950 |
| Coro | | "Coro" (in script at an angle, with the Pegasus) | 1945 |
| Coro | | Pegasus with empty rectangle | 1945 |
| Coro | | "Coro" (Made in Mexico in a small circle), "Coro" and "Silver" | 1943 – 1950 |
| Coro | | "Coro Magic" | 1960 |
| Coro | | "Vendôme" with a large "V" on an oval cartouche | 1944 – 1979 |
| Coro | | "Vendôme" impressed into the metal (Most Vendôme jewelry was produced after 1953.) | 1944 – 1979 |
| Coventry, Sarah | 1949 – 1983, 2002 – 2003 | "SarahCov" with a copyright symbol | Unknown |
| Coventry, Sarah | | "SARAH" with the copyright symbol | Unknown |
| Coventry, Sarah | | "Coventry" | Unknown |
| Coventry, Sarah | | "Sarah" in a diamond with the copyright symbol | Unknown |
| Coventry, Sarah | | "SaC" | Unknown |
| Coventry, Sarah | | "SaC" | Unknown |
| Coventry, Sarah | | "SC" | After 1953 |
| Coventry, Sarah | | "SARAH" with copyright symbol | Unknown |
| Coventry, Sarah | | "SARAH COVENTRY" with copyright symbol | Unknown |
| Dalsheim | 1930s – about 1978 | "DALSHEIM" | Unknown |
| Danecraft | 1934 – present | "DANECRAFT" in a circle, oval, or straight line with the word "STERLING" | Unknown |
| David Andersen | 1976 – present | "D – A Norway Sterling 925S" | Unknown |
| David Andersen | | "DAVID – ANDERSEN – 925S" | Unknown |
| Deauville (J. R. Wood & Sons Co. now Art – Carved) | 1850 – present | "Deauville" in script | Art – Carved is still operating, but jewelry marked "Deauville" is not longer produced. |
| Déja (See Réja) | | | |
| DeLizza & Elster (Juliana) | 1947 – 1990s | Unmarked (Juliana jewelry was made and marketed by DeLizza & Elster for two years, 1967 – 1969, with paper hangtags.) | Unmarked |
| Deltah | 1892 – present | "Deltah," script "D" and small "eltah," usually on removeable hangtag | 1934 |
| DeMario, Robert | 1945 – 1965 | "DeMARIO N.Y." | |
| DeMario, Robert | | "Hagler for DeMario" | 1966 |
| DeMario, Robert | | "DeMario" in script with copyright | After 1955 |
| Denbé | 1950s – 1960s | "Denbé" | Unknown |
| DeNicola | 1957 – early 1970s | "DeNicola" | Unknown |
| DeRosa | 1934 – 1970 | "DeRosa" in block or script imprinted into the metal | Unknown |
| DeRosa | | "RdeRosa" | Unknown |
| DeRosa | | "DeRosa Sterling" | 1942 – 1949 |

| | | | |
|---|---|---|---|
| Dior, Christian | 1948 – present | "Christian Dior by Kramer" | 1950s |
| Dior, Christian | | "Dior West Germany" | Before 1990, when Germany was reunited. |
| Dior, Christian | | "Christian Dior" followed by a date | Unknown |
| Dior, Christian | | "Made in Germany for Christian Dior" followed by a date | Unknown |
| Dior, Christian | | "Chr. Dior" with copyright symbol | After 1955 |
| Dior, Christian | | "Germany for Dior" with the date | Unknown |
| Dior, Christian | | "Mitchel Maer for Dior" | 1952 – 1956 |
| Doddz | 1952 – 1997 | "DODDZ" with copyright symbol | After 1955 |
| Doddz | | "DODDZ" | Unknown |
| Duane | 1950s – 1960s | "Duane" in print | Unknown |
| DuJay | 1934 – 1972 | "DU – JAY" | Unknown (rare mark) |
| Eisenberg | 1914 – present | Unmarked | Early 1930s, made of white metal. |
| Eisenberg | | "Eisenberg Original" | 1935 – 1945 |
| Eisenberg | | "Eisenberg" in lowercase with a two-digit number | 1935 – 1945 |
| Eisenberg | | "E" either in script or block — this is a rare mark. | 1942 – 1945 |
| Eisenberg | | "Eisenberg Sterling" | 1941 – 1945 |
| Eisenberg | | "Eisenberg Original Sterling" | 1941 – 1945 |
| Eisenberg | | "EISENBERG ICE" in block letters | 1945 – 1958 (Many pieces from this time period are unmarked.) |
| Eisenberg | | "EISENBERG" in block letters | 1945 – 1958 |
| Eisenberg | | Unmarked with only a paper tag or marked "EISENBERG ICE" | 1958 – 1970s |
| Eisenberg | | "EISENBERG" in block letters with earrings marked E in block letters | 1972 enamels |
| Eisenberg | | "EISENBERG ICE" impressed into metal in block letters with the copyright symbol | 1970s – 1985 (Many pieces from this era are unmarked.) |
| Eisenberg | | "Eisenberg Ice" in script with the copyright symbol on an applied oval cartouche | 1985 – present |
| Eisenberg | | "Eisenberg Ice" in script, the date (1994 or 2000) and the words "Classic Series" | 1994, 2000 |
| Elzac | 1941 – 1946 | Unmarked | Unmarked |
| Emmons | 1949 – 1981 | "Emmons" without copyright symbol | 1949 – 1955 |
| Emmons | | "Emmons" with copyright symbol | 1955 – 1981 |
| Emmons | | Capital "C" encasing a small "e" with a crown over the "C" | Unknown |
| Eugene | 1950s – 1960s | "Eugene" in script | Unknown |
| Evans | 1920s – 1965 | Unusually unmarked except for paper tag. If marked, "Evans" in script on oval hangtag. | Unknown |
| Featherweight | 1950s – ? | "Featherweight" in print | |
| Florenza | 1930s – 1981 | "Florenza" in print with the copyright symbol | After 1948 |
| Freirich | 1900 – 1990 | "Freirich" | 1964 |
| Gale | 1955 – unknown | "By Gale" | Unknown |
| Gale | | "Gale" in script with a crown over the "al" | Unknown |
| Garné | 1945 – 1960s | "GARNE" | Unknown |
| Gell, Wendy | 1975 – present | "WENDY GELL" on a cartouche | 1975 |
| Gell, Wendy | | "Wendy Gell" signed in a handwritten signature | Unknown |
| Gell, Wendy | | "WENDY GELL" plus the license holder's name. For example, "WENDY GELL DISNEY CO." | 1980s |
| Gerry's | 1950s – 2001 | "GERRY'S" with copyright symbol | Probably after 1955 |
| Givenchy | 1952 – present | "GIVENCHY" on a raised rectangle | Unknown |

| | | | |
|---|---|---|---|
| Givenchy | | "GIVENCHY Paris New York" on oval plaque (sometimes with the date) | Unknown |
| Givenchy | | "GIVENCHY" on a round plaque | Unknown |
| Glass, Leo | 1928 – 1957 | "Leo Glass" in script | Unknown |
| Glass, Leo | | "Leo Glass sterling" on an oval cartouche | Unknown |
| Glass, Leo | | "Leo Glass" in script on a five – sided cartouche | Unknown |
| Glass, Leo | | "LG sterling" | Unknown |
| Goldette | 1958 – 1977 | "Goldette" with copyright symbol | 1958 |
| Goldette | | "Goldette N.Y." with copyright symbol | 1958 |
| Gray, Fred | 1940s – 1950s | "S" in a star | Unknown |
| Gray, Fred | | "FRED GRAY CORP." | Unknown |
| Green, Sadie | 1981 – present | Sadie Green | 1981 (Many examples are un-marked.) |
| Halbe | 1950s – 1960s | "HALBE" | Unknown |
| Har | 1950s – 1960s | "HAR" with copyright symbol | Unknown |
| Harwood | 1937 – unknown | "Harwood" in script | Unknown |
| Haskell, Miriam | 1924 – present | Unsigned | 1924 – 1947 |
| Haskell, Miriam | | "MIRIAM HASKELL" in a horseshoe-shaped mark | Early signature, 1948 – 1950 |
| Haskell, Miriam | | "MIRIAM HASKELL" on an oval hangtag (The signature can be read from both sides of the hangtag.) | 1950 |
| Haskell, Miriam | | "MIRIAM HASKELL" on oval cartouche | 1950 |
| Haskell, Miriam | | "MIRIAM HASKELL" in oval, stamped into metal | 1950 |
| Haskell, Miriam | | "MIRIAM HASKELL" with number for limited edition series | Modern mark |
| Haskell, Miriam | | "MIRIAM HASKELL" on flat-backed oval hangtag (The signature can only be read on one side.) | 1979 |
| Hedy | 1909 – 1985 | "Hedy" with copyright symbol | After 1955 |
| Hedy | | "H" in a heart with the copyright symbol | After 1955 |
| Hedy | | "H" in a heart followed by "edy" | Unknown |
| Hobé | 1927 – present | "Hobé" with printed capital "H" and script "obe" | 1926 |
| Hobé | | "Hobé" in print | 1926 |
| Hobé | | "Hobé" in a six-sided shield | 1918 – 1932 |
| Hobé | | "Hobé" in an oval (The oval has straight lines for the top and bottom.) | 1903 – 1917 |
| Hobé | | "Hobé" in a triangle | 1933 – 1957 |
| Hobé | | "Hobé" in an oval with the copyright symbol over the "é" | 1958 – 1983 |
| Hobé | | "Hobé" in an oval with the copyright symbol over the "o" | Unknown |
| Hobé | | "Hobé" with copyright symbol and date | 1957 – 1966 |
| Hobé | | "Hobé Sterling" | 1941 – 1947 |
| Hobé | | "Hobé sterling 1/20 14K" | Unknown |
| Hobé | | "Hobé" under crossed swords | 1883 – 1902 |
| Hobé | | "Hobé" in a crown | Early, before 1927 |
| Hollycraft | 1938 – 1971 | "Hollycraft," no copyright | First used in 1948, then again after 1965. |
| Hollycraft | | "Hollycraft Corp." with date | 1950s |
| Hollycraft | | "Hollycraft" with the copyright symbol | After 1955 |
| Iskin | 1920s – 1940s | Initials "I" and "H" written together with the "I" covering the "H," on a circular cartouche with or without the word "sterling" | Unknown |
| Iskin | | "H" over "I" with "Iskin Jewelry" | Unknown |

| | | | |
|---|---|---|---|
| Japan | Most imported jewelry was after World War II | "Made in Japan" | After 1952 |
| Japan | | "Occupied Japan" | 1945 – 1952 |
| Jeanne | 1950s – 1960s | "Jeanne" on oval cartouche with copyright symbol | Unknown |
| Jeray | 1946 – unknown | "Jeray Sterling" in script | Unknown |
| Jeray | | "Jeray" in script | Unknown |
| JJ | 1937 – present | "JJ" | 1970 |
| JJ | | "Artifacts" | Trademark registered in 1985. |
| Jolle | 1943 – 1950s | "JOLLE STERLING" | Unknown |
| Jomaz (See Mazer) | | | |
| Jonné | 1925 – 1962 | "Jonné" | 1950s |
| Joseff of Hollywood | 1938 – present | "JOSEFF HOLLYWOOD" | Unknown; however, this is an early signature. |
| Joseff of Hollywood | | "JOSEFF" in script | This signature was in use as late as the 1990s. |
| Juliana (See DeLizza & Elster) | | | |
| Kafin, N.Y. | 1950s – 1960s | "KAFIN N.Y." | Unknown |
| Kafin, N.Y. | | "KAFIN NEW YORK" | Unknown |
| Kandell & Marcus | Unknown. Jewelry appears to date to the 1940s. | "KANDELL & MARCUS N.Y." | Unknown |
| Karu | 1940 – 1970s | "Karu" | 1940 |
| Karu | | "Karu Arke, Inc." | Unknown |
| Karu | | "Karu Arke, Inc." | Unknown |
| Karu | | "KARU of Fifth Avenue" | Unknown |
| Kenneth J. Lane (See Lane, Kenneth) | | | |
| Kirks Folly | 1979 – present | "Kirks Folly" with copyright symbol | 1979 |
| Kirks Folly | | "Kirks Folly," "Limited Edition" and edition number | Unknown |
| KJL (See Lane, Kenneth) | | | |
| Korda Thief of Bagdad | 1941 – ? | "THIEF OF BAGDAD KORDA" | Unknown |
| Kramer | 1943 – 1979 | "Kramer" | 1943 |
| Kramer | | "Christian Dior by Kramer" | 1950s – 1960s |
| Kramer | | "Amourelle" | 1963 |
| Kramer | | "Kramer sterling" | Unknown |
| Kramer | | "Kramer of New York" or "New York City" | Unknown |
| Kreisler | 1913 – 1977 | "Kreisler" (in script) "QUALITY USA PAT PEND" | Jewelry produced in the 1940s. |
| Kreisler | | "KREISLER" | Unknown |
| Krementz | Costume jewelry production began in the 1950s and ended in 1997. Krementz continues to produce fine jewelry today. | "KREMENTZ" | Unknown |
| Krementz | | "Krementz" | After 1997 |
| Krementz | | "DIANA" | Unknown |
| Krementz | | "KREMENTZ PLATE" | Early 1900s, rare mark |
| Lady Ellen | 1950s | Unmarked | Unmarked |
| Laguna | 1944 – 1980s | "LAGUNA" | 1944 |
| Laguna | | "KJL Laguna" | 1960s |

| | | | |
|---|---|---|---|
| Lampl, Walter | 1921 – 1959 | "LAMPL STERLING" | Unknown |
| Lampl, Walter | | "WL" in script on a shield | Mid-1940s – ? |
| Lampl, Walter | | "By Lampl" in script | Unknown |
| Lampl, Walter | | "STERLING WL" | Unknown |
| Lampl, Walter | | "WL" | Early mark |
| Lampl, Walter | | "WALBURT" | Unknown |
| Lampl, Walter | | "WALTER LAMPL" | Early mark |
| Lane, Kenneth | 1962 – present | "KJL" | Unknown |
| Lane, Kenneth | | "K.J.L." | Unknown, currently used for new items sold on QVC. |
| Lane, Kenneth | | "Kenneth Lane" | Unknown |
| Lane, Kenneth | | "Kenneth J. Lane" | Unknown |
| Lane, Kenneth | | "KJL for Avon" | 1986 – 1995 |
| Lane, Kenneth | | "KJL Laguna" | 1970s |
| LaRoco | 1918 – unknown | "La Roco" | Unknown |
| LaTausca | 1939 – 1950s | Often unmarked | Often unmarked |
| Ledo (Polcini) | 1911 – 1980s | "Ledo" | 1948 – 1962 |
| Ledo (Polcini) | | "Lee Menlcchi for Polcini" | 1971 |
| Ledo (Polcini) | | "Polcini" with copyright symbol | After 1960 |
| Lee, Judy | 1958 – 1980s | "Judy Lee" | Unknown |
| Lee, Judy | | "Judy Lee Jewels" | Unknown, may have been used only for advertising. |
| Leru | 1956 – 1960s | "LERU" with copyright symbol | 1956 |
| Les Bernard | 1963 – 1996 | "LES BERNARD" | Unknown |
| Les Bernard | | "LES BERNARD STERLING" | Unknown |
| Les Bernard | | "LES BERNARD" on a metal hangtag | Unknown |
| Les Bernard | | "LES BERNARD INC." | Unknown |
| Lisner | 1904 – 1979 | "Lisner" written with an elongated "L" and the "isner" in small print | 1959 |
| Lisner | | "Lisner," in script in an oval logo | 1956 |
| Lisner | | "LISNER" in block print | 1938 |
| Lisner | | "LISNER" in block print with copyright symbol | After 1955 |
| Little Nemo | 1913 – 1978 | "LN/25" | Unknown |
| Little Nemo | | "LN/50" | Unknown |
| Little Nemo | | "LN" in a diamond | Unknown |
| Little Nemo | | "Nemo" | Unknown |
| Little Nemo | | "LN" or "L/N" | Unknown |
| LN/25, LN/50 (See Little Nemo) | | | |
| Lynne, Karen | 1950s – 1960s | "KL Sterling" | Unknown |
| Mandle, R. | 1956 – 1990s | "R. Mandle" with copyright symbol | 1956 |
| Mandle, R. | | "MANDLE" with copyright symbol | Unknown |
| Mandle, R. | | "R. Mandle" with a crown over the "n" and the copyright symbol. | Unknown |
| Mandle, R. | | "Mandle" with a crown over the "n" and the copyright symbol. | Unknown |
| Mandle, Urie | 1938 – 1940s | Often only marked "Sterling" or unmarked. | Unmarked |
| Marboux (See Boucher) | | | |
| Marhill | Unknown, jewelry appears to date to the 1950s – 1960s. | "MARHILL" | Unknown |

| | | | |
|---|---|---|---|
| Marleen | Unknown. The jewelry appears to date to the 1940s. | "MARLEEN STERLING PAT. PEND," sometimes with the patent number. | Unknown |
| Marvella | 1911 – present | "MARVELLA" imprinted onto the metal | Unknown |
| Marvella | | "MARVELLA" with copyright symbol | Unknown |
| Marvella | | "marvella" | Believed to be the earliest Marvella mark. |
| Matisse (See Renoir) | | | |
| Mazer | 1920s – 1981 | "MAZER BROS." | 1926 – 1951 |
| Mazer | | "JOMAZ" | 1946 – 1981 |
| Mazer | | "MAZER" | 1946 – 1981 |
| Mazer | | "MAZER STERLING" | Unknown |
| Mazer | | "ADOLFO FOR MAZER" | Probably 1950s |
| Mazer | | "SANDI MILLER FOR MAZER" | Unknown |
| Mazer | | "THIERRY FOR MAZER" | 1978 |
| McCann, Judith | 1955 – 1975 | "J. MCCANN NYC" with the date and copyright symbol | Unknown |
| McCann, Judith | | "JUDITH MCCANN DESIGNS" | Unknown |
| Mimi d N | 1962 – unknown | "Mimi d N" | Unknown |
| Mimi d N | | "Mimi d N" with date | Probably 1970s |
| Miracle | 1946 – present | "Miracle" | Unknown |
| Miracle | | "A Miracle Creation" | Unknown |
| Miracle | | "Miracle Britain" | Unknown |
| Miracle | | A paper tag "Authentic Reproductions by Hills of Britain" | Unknown |
| Miracle | | "Miracle" followed by one of the following: "A," "AB," "AS," "Anglo – Saxon," "R," "V," "Viking," a number. | Unknown |
| Miracle | | "Celtic Jewelry" | Unknown |
| Miracle | | "Mirac Brin" | Unknown |
| Miracle | | "AH" with castle and thistle and the date letter code (Sterling Pieces) | Unknown |
| Monet | 1937 – present | "MONET" | 1927 |
| Monet | | "Monet" | Unknown |
| Monet | | "Monet" with upward slant that crosses over the letter "t." | Unknown |
| Monet | | "Monet 2" | Modern mark |
| Monet | | "MONOCRAFT" | Unknown |
| Monet | | "Monet Sterling" | Unknown |
| Monet | | "MONET Jewelers" | Unknown |
| Monet | | "MONET" with copyright | After 1955 |
| Morton, Joseph | 1950s – 1960s | "JOSEPH MORTON" | Unknown |
| Mosell | 1941 – 1960s | "MOSELL" with copyright symbol | Unknown |
| Mylu | 1960s – 1970s | "MYLU" with copyright | Unknown |
| Napier | 1875 (jewelry 1922) – present | "NAPIER" | 1922 |
| Napier | | "NAPIER STERLING" | Unknown |
| Napier | | "NAPIER" with copyright | After 1955 |
| Napier | | "Napier" with copyright | After 1955 |
| Nemo (Not Little Nemo) | 1910 – 1978 | "Nemo" | Unknown |
| Norma | 1940s – 1950s | "Norma" in print with "Sterling" and often "Pat. Pend.," even though no patents have been found to match Norma designs. | Unknown |
| Ora | 1921 – present | "ORA" | 1940 |
| Original by Robért | 1942 – 1979 | "Original by Robert" | 1942 |

| | | | |
|---|---|---|---|
| Original by Robért | | "Robért" | Unknown |
| Original by Robért | | "FASHIONCRAFT by ROBERT" | Unknown |
| Original by Robért | | "FASHIONCRAFT" | Unknown |
| Pam | Late 1950s – 1960s | "PAM" with copyright symbol | Unknown |
| Panetta | 1945 – 1995 | "PANETTA" | Unknown |
| Panetta | | "PANETTA" with copyright symbol | After 1955 |
| Panetta | | "PANETTA STERLING" | Unknown |
| Pargo | 1940s – 1950s | "Pargo" sometimes "Des. Pat. Pend." | Unknown |
| Pastelli | 1950s – 1980s | "Pastelli" on oval cartouche | Unknown |
| Pastelli | | "Pastelli Siam 925 Sterling" | Unknown |
| Pell | 1941 – present | "PELL" | Unknown |
| Pell | | "PELL" with copyright symbol | After 1955 |
| Pennino | 1927 – 1961 | "PENNINO" | Unknown |
| Pennino | | "PENNINO STERLING" | Unknown |
| Pennino | | "PENNINO Pat. Pend." | Before 1955 |
| Phyllis | 1950s – 1960s | "Phyllis Originals" | Unknown |
| Phyllis | | "Phyllis" unslanted script | 1946 |
| Phyllis | | "Phyllis STERLING" | Unknown |
| Phyllis | | "Scitarelli" | Unknown |
| Phyllis | | "Phyllis 12KGF" | Unknown |
| Polcini (See Ledo) | | | |
| Pomerantz N.Y. | Unknown | "POMERANTZ & Co. N.Y." | Unknown |
| Pomerantz N.Y. | | "H. POMERANTZ N.Y." | Unknown |
| Rader, Pauline | 1963 – late 1980s | "PAULINE RADER" | Approximately 1968 |
| Regency | 1950s – 1970s | "REGENCY" | Unknown |
| Regency | | "REGENCY JEWELS" on an oval plaque | Unknown |
| Regina Fashions | 1950s – 1960s | "REGINA FASHIONS" | Unknown |
| Reinad | 1920s – 1950s | "REINAD" | 1941 |
| Reinad | | "Reinad" | Unknown |
| Reinad | | "Chanel" in script | Only used in 1941 |
| Reinad | | "Septron" | 1944 |
| Réja | 1939 – 1953 | "RÉGA" | After 1941 |
| Réja | | "DEJA" | 1939 – 1941 |
| Réja | | "RÉGA REG." | After 1941 |
| Réja | | "DEJA REG." | 1939, 1940 |
| Réja | | "DEJA ORIGINAL" | Before 1941 |
| Réja | | "RÉJA, INC." | After 1941 |
| Renoir | 1946 – 1964 | "RENOIR" | Unknown |
| Renoir | | "Renoir" | 1946 |
| Renoir | | "Matisse" | 1952 – 1964 |
| Renoir | | "MATISSE RENOIR" | Unknown |
| Renoir | | "Matisse" with 4 "Ms" placed north, south, east, and west | 1956 |
| Renoir | | "Sauteur STERLING" | 1958 – 1963 |
| Renoir | | "STERLING SAUTEUR RENOIR" | 1958 – 1963 |
| Richelieu | 1911 – 2003 | "RICHELIEU" | Unknown |
| Richelieu | | "RICHELIEU" | After 1959 |
| Richelieu | | "Bill Smith of Richelieu" | 1970s |
| Richelieu | | "Mark Traynor of Richelieu" | Unknown |
| Richelieu | | "RICHELIEU STERLING" | Unknown |

| | | | |
|---|---|---|---|
| Richelieu | | "Ingeborg – Sant Angelo for Richelieu" | Unknown |
| Richelieu | | "Richelieu Iridelle." | Unknown |
| Richelieu | | "Cézanne by Richelieu" | Unknown |
| Rosenstein, Nettie | 1935 – 1975 | "STERLING Nettie Rosenstein" on a raised rectangle | Unknown |
| Rosenstein, Nettie | | "Nettie Rosenstein" | Unknown |
| Sandor | 1938 – 1972 | "SANDOR" | Unknown |
| Sandor | | "SANDOR GOLDBERGER" | 1939 – 1940 |
| Sandor | | "SANDOR" with copyright symbol | After 1955 |
| Sandor | | "Regimental Crests" | 1939 |
| Sandor | | "Antonio for Sandor Goldberger" | 1960s |
| Sandor | | "SANDOR CO." with copyright symbol | After 1955 |
| Schiaparelli | 1930s – 1973 | Unmarked or marked "Schiaparelli" in lowercase print | 1931 – 1949 (very rare) |
| Schiaparelli | | "Schiaparelli" in script | After 1949 |
| Schiaparelli | | "Schiaparelli" in script on an oval cartouche | Unknown |
| Schiaparelli | | "SCHIAPARELLI" with copyright symbol | Unknown |
| Schreiner | 1939 – 1977 | "SCHREINER" | Unknown |
| Schreiner | | "SCHREINER N.Y." | Unknown |
| Schreiner | | "SCHREINER NEW YORK" | Unknown |
| Segal, Lewis | 1950s – ? | "LEWIS SEGAL" | Unknown |
| Segal, Lewis | | "LEWIS SEGAL CALIFORNIA" | Unknown |
| Selini (See Selro) | | | |
| Selro (Selini) | 1950s – 1960s | "SELINI" with copyright symbol | Unknown |
| Selro (Selini) | | "SELRO CORP." with copyright symbol | Unknown |
| Selro (Selini) | | Some jewelry marked both "SELINI" and "SELRO CORP." Many examples are unmarked. | Unknown |
| Sherman | 1947 – 1981 | "SHERMAN" | Unknown |
| Sherman | | "Sherman" | Unknown |
| Sherman | | "SHERMAN STERLING" | Unknown |
| Silson | 1937 – 1945 | "SILSON" | Unknown |
| Silson | | "SILSON PAT. PEND." | Unknown |
| Simpson, Adele | 1940s – 1950s | "Adele Simpson" in script | 1940s – 1950s |
| Star | 1940s – 1960s | "STAR" | Unknown |
| Star – Art | 1940s – 1960s | "STAR – ART 1/20 K.G.G." | Unknown |
| Star – Art | | "STAR – ART STERLING" | Unknown |
| Staret | 1941 – 1947 | "STARET" | Unknown |
| Steiner, Ernest | 1940s – unknown | "Ernest Steiner Original" | Unknown |
| Tancer II | 1971 – unknown | "TANCER II" with the copyright symbol | Unknown |
| Tortolani | After World War II – present | "Tortolani" with copyright symbol above or next to the name | Unknown |
| Tortolani | | "Tortolani" with copyright symbol below the name | Modern mark |
| Tortolani | | Raised pimple next to "Tortolani" | Modern mark |
| Trifari | 1918 – present | Letter "T" with large Crown | 1920 |
| Trifari | | "Jewels by" above "Trifari" with a large crown over the "T" | 1920 |
| Trifari | | "KTF" | 1935 |
| Trifari | | "KTF" with crown over T | 1954 |
| Trifari | | "Trifari" in normal print, no crown | 1937 |
| Trifari | | "Trifari" in normal print with a thin crown | 1937 |
| Trifari | | "Trifari" written in tall, long letters with crown above T | 1930 – 1940 |
| Trifari | | "Trifari" in normal print with crown | 1940 – 1950 |
| Trifari | | "Trifari Pat. Pend." | Most likely 1940 – 1954 |

| | | | |
|---|---|---|---|
| Trifari | | "Trifari Sterling" | 1942 – 1947 |
| Trifari | | "Jewels by Trifari" (hangtag) "Trifari" in regular print with crown | 1940s – 1950s |
| Trifari | | Hanging stylized metal "T" tag | 1954 |
| Trifari | | "Trifari" with solid crown and copyright symbol | 1954 |
| Trifari | | "Trifari" in script enclosed in circle | 1970s – 1980s |
| Trifari | | "Trifari" with crown and copyright symbol in rectangle | Modern mark |
| Trifari | | "Trifari" in circle with copyright symbol | 1980 |
| Trifari | | "Trifari TM" | Modern mark |
| Uncas | 1911 – present | "U" with two arrows pointing to the letter | 1919 – 1988 |
| Uncas | | "Uncas" | 1959 |
| Uncas | | "Stylecraft Gems" in script | 1938 |
| Uncas | | "U" with an arrow going through | 1920 – 1988 |
| Uncas (Sorrento) | | "SORRENTO" and "SORRENTO STERLING" | 1955 |
| Van Dell | 1938 – present | "Van Dell 1/20 12K G.F." | Unknown |
| Van Dell | | "Van Dell Sterling" | Unknown |
| Vendôme (See Coro) | | | |
| Vogue | 1936 – 1975 | "Vogue Jlry" | Unknown |
| Vogue | | "VOGUE STERLING" (sometimes with a patent number) | Unknown |
| Vogue | | "VOGUE" with copyright | Probably after 1955 |
| Vogue | | "VOGUE" without copyright | Unknown |
| Volupté | 1926 – unknown | "VOLUPTÉ" ("V" larger than other letters) | Unknown |
| Volupté | | "VOLUPTÉ" (with pat. pend.) | Unknown |
| Volupté | | "VOLUPTÉ U.S.A." | Unknown |
| Warner | 1953 – 1971 | "WARNER" | Unknown |
| Warner | | "WARNER OF NEW YORK" | Unknown |
| Weiss | 1942 – 1971 | "WEISS" printed in caps | 1942 |
| Weiss | | "A W Co." with a crown over the "W" | 1950 |
| Weiss | | "Albert Weiss" in script | 1951 |
| Weiss | | "WEISS" in script | 1951 |
| Weiss | | "Weissco" | 1951 |
| Weiss | | "WEISS" with copyright symbol | Most likely after 1955 |
| Western Germany | 1949 – present | "WESTERN GERMANY" | Unknown |
| Western Germany | | "WEST GERMANY" | Unknown |
| Western Germany | | "W. GERMANY" | Unknown |
| Western Germany | | "GERMANY" | Before 1949 or after 1990 |
| Western Germany | | "WESTERN GERMANY US ZONE" | Unknown |
| Whiting and Davis | 1926 – present Non-mesh jewelry production ceased in 1980; all jewelry production stopped in 1991. | "WHITING & DAVIS" on oval metal hangtag | Unknown |
| Whiting and Davis | | "WHITING DAVIS" with "WHITING" printed above "DAVIS" | Unknown |
| Whiting and Davis | | "WHITING & DAVID CO." impressed into the metal on a stylized logo, with the word "MESH" above and "BAGS" below. | Unknown |
| Wingback (designed by Judith McCann) | 1946 – unknown | "WINGBACK" impressed onto the thin-back wire with patent number 2414382. (Sometimes designers such as Boucher and Danecraft utilized the Wingback style. These pieces are marked "WINGBACK" with the patent number and the name of the designer. | Unknown |

| | | | |
|---|---|---|---|
| Yves Saint Laurent (YSL) | For jewelry, 1970s – present | "YSL" with all three letters stacked together | Unknown |
| Yves Saint Laurent (YSL) | Unknown | "Yves Saint Laurent Rive Gauche Made in France" | Unknown |

APPENDIX A: MANUFACTURER AND MARKS CHART

# APPENDIX B: *Designers Chart*

| Maker | Designer(s) |
|---|---|
| Accessocraft | Theodore Steinman (patents from 1940, 1941) |
| Accessocraft | Philippe Israel |
| Accessocraft | Edgar Roedelheimer (also worked for Coro) |
| Accessocraft | Robert Appleby |
| Accessocraft | Albert Freedman |
| Albert Manufacturing Company | Albert Weiner |
| Albert Manufacturing Company | Ernest Steiner |
| Albert Manufacturing Company | Lester Gaba 1938 – 1939 |
| Albert Manufacturing Company | Natasha Brooks 1941 |
| Bogoff | Herman Bogoff |
| Bogoff | Henry Bogoff |
| Boucher | Marcel Boucher |
| Boucher | Raymonde Semensohn, "Sandra," Marcel Boucher's second wife |
| Carl-Art (Manufactured Walter Lampl jewelry) | Carl Schraysshuen |
| Carl-Art (Manufactured Walter Lampl jewelry) | Eugene Demmler 1948 |
| Carnegie, Hattie | Michael Paul |
| Carnegie, Hattie | Hugo de Alteriis 1944, 1945; Astrology patents |
| Carnegie, Hattie | Jack Libuono |
| Carnegie, Hattie | Many jewelry designs were created by wholesale companies for Carnegie, including Dan Kasoff, which designed and marketed Florenza jewelry. |
| Castlecliff | Willard Markle |
| Castlecliff | Elizabeth Hawes |
| Castlecliff | Clifford Furst |
| Castlecliff | Joanne Moonan; also Authentics, Inc. |
| Castlecliff | Anne Dogarthy |
| Coro | Adolph Katz 1937 – 1960s |
| Coro | Gene Verrecchio 1938 – 1942, again 1945, 1946 |
| Coro | Charles E. Pauzat 1939 – 1941 |
| Coro | Oscar Placco 1938 – 1945 |
| Coro | Henry Rosenblatt 1939 |
| Coro | Robert Geissman 1938 |
| Coro | Sidney Pearl 1941 |
| Coro | Carol McDonald 1940 |
| Coro | Lester Gaba 1941 |
| Coro | Marion Weeber 1940 – 1941 |
| Coro | Victor di Mezza 1950 |
| DuJay | J.H. Leff |
| DuJay | J. Hirsch |
| Eisenberg | Florence Nathan |
| Eisenberg | Ruth Kamke |
| Elzac | Elliot Handler |
| Elzac | Zachary Zemby |
| Elzac | H. Weiss |
| Elzac | Z. Taube |
| Elzac | A. Oben |
| Florenza | Dan Kasoff |
| Fred A. Block | Fred Block, possibly a connection to Sandor Goldberger of Sandor |
| Hobé | William Hobé |
| Hobé | Sylvia Hobé |
| Hollycraft | John Hazard 1946 |
| Jolle | George Fearn |
| Jolle | Lester Hess |
| Julio Marsella in 1955 (Perhaps freelance before that or unmarked.) | J. J. Marsella |
| Korda | Louis C. Mark of Rice-Weiner (Korda was a filmmaker, not a designer.) |
| Kramer | Louis Kramer |

| | | | | |
|---|---|---|---|---|
| Kramer | Morris Kramer | | Réja, which was called Déja (1939 – 1941) | Sol Finkelstein |
| Kreisler | Jacques Kreisler | | Rice-Weiner | Louis C. Mark 1938 – 1946 |
| Kreisler | William Diehl 1945 – 1947 | | Rice-Weiner | McClelland Barclay 1938 – 1943 |
| Kreisler | Kurt Speck | | Rice-Weiner | Natacha Brooks 1947 |
| Kreisler | Helen Cole | | Rice-Weiner | Norman Bel Geddes 1950 |
| Lampl | Walter Lampl | | Rice-Weiner | Betty Betz 1950 |
| Lampl | Walter Lampl, Jr. | | Sandor | Sandor Goldberger |
| Leo Glass | Leo Glass | | Silson | Victor Silson |
| Leo Glass | Ann Glass | | Silson | Jack Silson |
| Leo Glass | Beatrice Glass | | Silson | Samuel Ruben |
| Leo Glass | David Mir 1941 | | Silson | George Stangl |
| Mandle, Urie | Murray Slater | | Silson | Sue Harrison |
| Mandle, Urie | Urie Mandle | | Silson | Sally Stark |
| Marleen | Frederick Pearsall | | Steiner, Ernest | Steiner, Ernest |
| Mazer | Louis Mazer | | Steiner, Ernest | Bernhard Bauer and Ernest Steiner |
| Mazer | Marcel Boucher 1930 – 1937 | | Steiner, Ernest | Paul Marino and Ernest Steiner |
| Mazer | Joseph Wuyts 1939 – 1941 (also designed for Trifari) | | Trifari | Alfred Philippe 1930 – 1968 |
| Mazer | André Fleuridas | | Trifari | Joseph Wuyts 1940 – 1941 |
| Monet | Michael Chernow | | Trifari | David Mir 1941 – 1942 |
| Mosell | Frederic Mosell | | Trifari | Alfred Spaney 1941 – 1942 |
| Natasha Brooks | Natacha Brooks 1944, Napier 1944, Jeray in 1947 | | Trifari | Norman Bel Geddes 1941 |
| Ora | Oreste J. Angnini, Mary G. Granville 1938, Anne Geyer 1950s | | Trifari | George Bachner 1945 |
| | | | Trifari | Jean Paris 1958 – 1965 |
| Pargo | Charles T. Parisi | | Trifari | André Boeuf 1967 – 1979 |
| Pennino | Oreste Pennino | | Trifari | Jacques Philippe (Alfred's son) 1971 – 1974 |
| Pennino | Victor Primavera | | Trifari | Diane Love 1970 |
| Reinad | William Wienner | | Uncas | Nicholas Barbieri |

# APPENDIX C: *View Patents Online*

Using a computer and the internet to view design patents online is fun and interesting. It is also necessary to fully utilize the wealth of design and utility patent information in this book. There are over 4,000 design patent numbers listed in this volume, spanning the years 1935 – 1954. Even though over 500 illustrations from these patents are shown in the book, it is necessary for a serious collector to have the ability to view additional patents online. The following instructions provide step-by-step guidance on how to do this.

To begin, a collector must have a computer and access to the Internet. Access to the Internet requires a modem and an Internet provider. There are many Internet providers who will be happy to help with this step. If you do not have one, talk to your family, friends, and neighbors for advice on which is the best value for your area. There is a fee for Internet service, and this fee varies from one provider to another.

After your computer is connected to the Internet, follow the following steps to view patents online.

From your home page:

1. Go to www.uspto.gov.
2. On the left-hand side, under the heading Patents, click on Search.
3. The next screen appears. Again on the left-hand side, click on Patent Number Search.
4. The next screen appears. Carefully review this screen.

   • There is a space under Query to type the patent number.
   • Under this box are six examples of different types of patent numbers.
   • The first two, Utility and Design, are important for costume jewelry collectors.
   • Notice that the sample Utility patent number is seven digits long. Any seven-digit utility patent number can be entered in the Query box.
   • The sample Design patent number is six digits, but it is preceded by the letter "D." In the Query Box, the letter "D" must always be typed before the design patent number.
   • There is no need to type in the commas.

5. For example, type in design patent number D110142 in the box under the heading Query.
6. Click on the Search button.
7. The USPTO Patent Full-text and Image Database screen appears. To view the patent on the computer screen, click on the Images button. The full view of this patent will appear. (See Troubleshooting below if the image does not appear after executing this step.)
8. To view the other pages in the patent document, use the arrow keys or one of the selection buttons. The front page reveals that this patent is assigned to Coro. Geissman is the designer, but Coro is the maker.
9. Printing the patent is easy. Click on the printer icon and select how many pages you wish to print.
10. To view another patent, use the Back button on your Windows screen as many times as needed to return to the USPTO Patent Full-text and Image Database page.
11. From the USPTO Patent Full-text and Image Database screen, click on the Pat Num button. Enter a new patent number in the Query box.
12. Repeat steps 6 – 11.

TROUBLESHOOTING

If the wrong image appears, click on the Pat Num button at the top of the screen and try entering the number again. Be sure to put the letter "D" before the design patent numbers.

If the computer cannot display the image, a message will appear directing you to install a browser "plug-in." TIFF plug-ins are free for anyone using a PC with the Windows operating system. There are two choices: AlternaTIFF: http://www.alternatiff.com/, or interneTIFF: http://www.internetiff.com/. (Note: Apple's Quicktime 4.1 or later will also work. However, the images cannot be printed.)

If after installing one of the two plug-ins the images still do not appear, it may be necessary to disable any other viewer plug-ins you may have set as a default in your system. At this point it is a good idea to contact your friendly computer expert for help. Once the software is properly installed, viewing the images is easy. Taking the trouble to do this installation is amply rewarded by the vast library of information made available online to collectors by the United States Patent Office.

# BIBLIOGRAPHY

BOOKS:

*1954 Jewelers' Buyers Guide.* New York, NY: Sherry Publishing Company, Inc., 1953.

*1957 Jewelers' Buyers Guide.* New York, NY: Sherry Publishing Company, Inc., 1956.

Bell, Jeanenne. *Answers to Questions about Old Jewelry 1840 – 1950*, 3rd ed. Florence, AL: Books Americana, Inc., 1992.

_____. *How to be a Jewelry Detective.* Shawnee, KS: A.D. Publishing, 2000.

Brown, Marcia. *Signed Beauties of Costume Jewelry*, vol. 1. Paducah, KY: Collector Books, 2002.

_____. *Signed Beauties of Costume Jewelry*, vol. 2. Paducah, KY: Collector Books, 2003.

Brunialti, Carla Ginelli and Roberto. *American Costume Jewelry 1935 – 1950.* Edizioni Gabriele Mazzotta, Foro Buonaparte 52-201121. Milano, Italy: 1997.

_____. *A Tribute to American Costume Jewelry 1935 – 1950.* Milan, Italy: Publishing project by EDITA, 2002.

Carroll, Julia. *Collecting Costume Jewelry 101: The Basics of Starting, Building & Upgrading.* Paducah, KY: Collector Books, 2004.

Clements, Monica Lynn and Patricia Rosser. *Avon Collectible Fashion Jewelry and Awards.* Atglen, PA: Schiffer Publishing, Ltd., 1998.

Dolan, Marianne. *Collecting Rhinestone & Colored Jewelry*, 3rd ed. Florence, AL. Books Americana, Inc., 1993.

Ettinger, Roseann. *Forties & Fifties Popular Jewelry.* Atglen, PA: Schiffer Publishing, Ltd., 1992.

_____. *Popular Jewelry 1840 – 1940.* Atglen, PA: Schiffer Publishing, Ltd., 1997.

_____. *Popular Jewelry of the '60s, '70s & '80s.* Atglen, PA: Schiffer Publishing, Ltd., 1997.

Gordon, Cathy, and Sheila Pamfiloff. *Miriam Haskell Jewelry.* Atglen, PA: Schiffer Publishing, Ltd., 2004.

Klein, Susan Maxine and Jori. *Mid-Century Plastic Jewelry.* Atglen, PA: Schiffer Publishing, Ltd., 2005.

Lane, Kenneth Jay, and Harrice Simmons Miller. *Faking It.* New York, NY: Harry N. Abrams, Inc., 1996.

Lindbeck, Jennifer. *Sarah Coventry.* Atglen, PA: Schiffer Publishing, Ltd., 2000.

McCall, Georgiana. *Hattie Carnegie Jewelry.* Atglen, PA: Schiffer Publishing, Ltd., 2005.

Miller, Judith, and Dorothy Kindersley Limited. *Costume Jewelry.* New York, NY: DK Publishing, Inc., 2003.

Oshel, Kay. *Jewelry From Sarah Coventry and Emmons.* Atglen, PA: Schiffer Publishing, Ltd., 2005.

Pitman, Ann Mitchell. *Inside the Jewelry Box.* Paducah, KY: Collector Books, 2004.

Rainwater, Dorothy T. *American Jewelry Manufacturers.* Atglen, PA: Schiffer Publishing, Ltd., 1988.

Rezazadeh, Fred. *Collectible Silver Jewelry.* Paducah, KY: Collector Books, 1998.

Romero, Christie. *Warman's Jewelry*, 2nd ed. Iola, WI: Krause Publications, 1998.

Tolkien, Tracy, and Henrietta Wilkinson. *A Collector's Guide to Costume Jewelry.* Willowdale, Ontario: Firefly Books Ltd., 1997.


INTERNET SITE:

www.researchingcostumejewelry.com


MAGAZINE ARTICLES:

Flood, Kathy. "Finding Elzac." *Vintage Fashion and Costume Jewelry* 14, no. 2, 2004.

Gostick, Patricia. "McClelland Barclay, a Signature Style." *Vintage Fashion and Costume Jewelry* 15, no. 4, 2005.

Tempesta, Lucille. "The House of Juiliana." *Vintage Fashion and Costume Jewelry* 13, no. 2, 2003.

Van Hoover, Cheri. "Walter Lampl: Creator of the Unusual…As Usual." *Vintage Fashion and Costume Jewelry* 14, no. 1, 2004.

_____. "He Put the 'Carl' in Carl-Art." *Vintage Fashion and Costume Jewelry* 15, no. 3, 2005.

BIBLIOGRAPHY

# INDEX

INDEX